The Rough Guide to

Vietnam

written and researched by

Jan Dodd, Ron Emmons, Mark Lewis and Martin Zatko

roughguides.com

Contents

Introduction to
Vietnam

Few countries have changed so much over such a short time as Vietnam. Less than forty years since the savagery and slaughter of the American War, this resilient nation is buoyant with hope. It is a country on the move: access is now easier than ever, roads are being upgraded, hotels are springing up and Vietnam's raucous entrepreneurial spirit is once again alive and well as the old-style Communist system gives way to a socialist market economy. As the number of tourists visiting the country soars, their talk is not of bomb craters and army ordnance but of shimmering paddy fields and sugar-white beaches, full-tilt cities and venerable pagodas; Vietnam is a veritable phoenix arisen from the ashes.

The speed with which Vietnam's population has been able to put the bitter events of its recent past behind it, and focus its gaze so steadfastly on the future, often surprises visitors expecting to encounter shell-shocked resentment of the West. It wasn't always like this, however. The reunification of North and South Vietnam in 1975, ending twenty years of bloody civil war, was followed by a decade or so of hardline centralist economic rule from which only the shake-up of **doi moi** – Vietnam's equivalent of *perestroika* – beginning in 1986, could awaken the country. This signalled a renaissance for Vietnam, and today a high fever of commerce grips the nation: from the flash new shopping malls and designer boutiques to the hustle and bustle of street markets and the booming cross-border trade with China. From a tourist's point of view, this is a great time to visit – not only to soak up the intoxicating sense of vitality and optimism, but also the chance to witness a country in profound flux. Inevitably, that's not the whole story. *Doi moi* is an economic policy, not a magic spell, and life, for much of the population, remains hard. Indeed, the move towards a market economy has predictably polarized the gap between rich and poor. Average monthly incomes for city-dwellers are around US$100, while in the poorest provinces workers may scrape by on as little as US$30 a month – a difference that amply illustrates the growing gulf between urban and rural Vietnam.

TOP HANOI (P.347); **RIGHT** THE CENTRAL HIGHLANDS (P.174)

There is an equally marked difference between **north and south**, a deep psychological divide that was around long before the American War, and is engrained in Vietnamese culture. Northerners are considered reticent, thrifty, law-abiding and lacking the dynamism and entrepreneurial know-how of their more worldly wise southern compatriots. Not surprisingly, this is mirrored in the broader economy: the south is Vietnam's growth engine, it boasts lower unemployment and higher average wages, and the increasingly glitzy Ho Chi Minh City looks more to Bangkok and Singapore than Hanoi.

Many visitors find more than enough to intrigue and excite them in Hanoi, Ho Chi Minh City and the other major centres; but despite the cities' allure, it's the country's striking **landscape** that most impresses. Vietnam occupies a narrow strip of land that hugs the eastern borders of Cambodia and Laos, hemmed in by rugged mountains to the west, and by the South China Sea – or the East Sea, as the Vietnamese call it. To the north and south of its narrow waist, it fantails out into the splendid deltas of the Red River and the Mekong, and it's in these regions that you'll encounter the paddy fields, dragonflies, buffaloes and conical-hatted farmers that constitute the classic image of Vietnam.

In stark contrast to the pancake-flat rice land of the deltas, Ha Long Bay's labyrinthine network of **limestone outcrops** loom dramatically out of the Gulf of Tonkin – a magical spectacle in the early morning mist. Any trip to the remote upland regions of central and northern Vietnam is likely to focus upon the **ethnic minorities** who reside there. Elaborate tribal costumes, age-old customs and communal longhouses await those

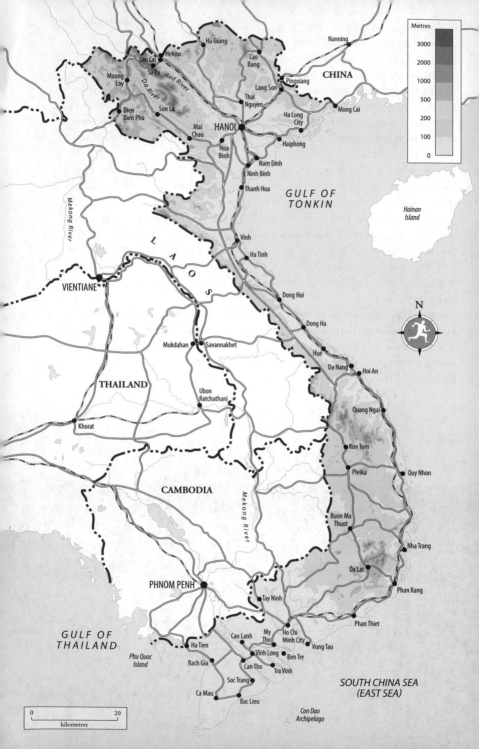

visitors game enough to trek into the sticks. As for **wildlife**, the discovery in recent years of several previously unknown species of plants, birds and animals speaks volumes for the wealth of Vietnam's biodiversity and makes the improving access to the country's **national parks** all the more gratifying.

Where to go

The "Hanoi or bust" attitude, prompting new arrivals to doggedly labour between the country's two major cities, no matter how limited their time, blights many a trip to Vietnam. If you want to travel the length of the country at some leisure, see something of the highlands and the deltas and allow for a few rest days, you'll really need a month. With only two weeks at your disposal, the choice is either to hopscotch up the coast calling at only the most mainstream destinations or, perhaps better, to concentrate on one region and enjoy it at your own pace. However, if you do want to see both north and south in a fortnight, internal flights can speed up an itinerary substantially, and aren't too expensive.

For the majority of visitors, **Ho Chi Minh City** provides a head-spinning introduction to Vietnam. Set beside the broad swell of the Saigon River, the southern capital is rapidly being transformed into a Southeast Asian mover and shaker to compete with the best of them. The city's breakneck pace of life translates into a stew of bizarre characters and unlikely sights and sounds, and ensures that almost all who come here quickly fall for its singular charm. Furious commerce carries on cheek-by-jowl with age-old traditions; grandly indulgent colonial edifices peek out from under the shadows of looming office blocks and hotels; and cyclo drivers battle it out with late-model Japanese taxis in the chaotic boulevards.

Few tourists pass up the opportunity to take a day-trip out of the city to **Tay Ninh**, the nerve centre of the indigenous Cao Dai religion. The jury is still out on whether the Cao Dai Holy See constitutes high art or dog's dinner, but either way it's one of Vietnam's most arresting sights, and is normally twinned with a stop-off at the Cu Chi tunnels,

TET

The biggest bash in Vietnam's festive calendar is the lunar New Year holiday known as **Tet Nguyen Dan**, or simply Tet. The date of the festival, which lasts for several days, varies from one year to the next, but falls somewhere between late January and the middle of February. Tet is the Vietnamese equivalent of Thanksgiving, New Year and a nationwide birthday celebration rolled into one – everyone becomes a year older at New Year. It is a time of forgiveness and fresh starts, when the trials and tribulations of the old year are left behind, to be replaced by renewed optimism for the year ahead. As the festival approaches, the streets fill with people buying new clothes, having their hair cut and stocking up on seasonal delicacies such as candied lotus seeds and sweetmeats made of sticky rice. Flower markets add to the colour with the first shy blossoms of peach, plum or apricot alongside miniature kumquat trees laden with their brash, golden fruit – the traditional symbols of Tet. The excitement culminates with municipal **fireworks displays** on New Year's Eve, after which the first few days of the year are traditionally devoted to renewing family ties – both with the living and with the ancestral spirits who come back to share in the feasting.

where Vietnamese villagers dug themselves a warren stretching over two hundred kilometres, out of reach of US bombing.

Another destination easily reached from Ho Chi Minh City is the **Mekong Delta**, where one of the world's truly mighty rivers finally offloads into the South China Sea; its skein of brim-full tributaries and waterways has endowed the delta with a lush quilt of rice paddies and abundant orchards. You won't want to depart the delta without spending a day or more messing about on the water and visiting a floating market, which is easily arranged at **Cai Be** and **Can Tho**.

Da Lat, the gateway to the central highlands, is chalk to Ho Chi Minh City's cheese. Life passes by at a rather more dignified pace at an altitude of 1500m, and the fresh breezes that fan this oddly quaint hillside settlement provide the best air conditioning in Vietnam. **Minority peoples** inhabit the countryside around Da Lat, but to visit some really full-on montagnard villages you'll need to push north to the modest towns of **Buon Ma Thuot**, **Pleiku** and **Kon Tum**, which are surrounded by E De, Jarai and Bahnar communities. Opt for Kon Tum, and you'll be able to visit minority villages independently or join treks that include river-rafting.

Northeast of Ho Chi Minh City, Highway 1, the country's jugular, carries the lion's share of traffic up to Hanoi and the north, though the recently completed Ho Chi Minh Highway offers drivers a tempting alternative route. For many people, the first stop along Highway 1 is at the delightful beach and sand dunes of **Mui Ne**, fast becoming one of the country's top coastal resorts. Further north, **Nha Trang** is another beach resort that also boasts a lively nightlife, and the tirelessly touted boat trips around the city's outlying islands are a must. North of Nha Trang, near Quang Ngai, **Son My** village attained global notoriety when a company of American soldiers massacred some five hundred Vietnamese, including many women

FACT FILE

• The Socialist Republic of Vietnam, the **Capital** of which is Hanoi, is one of the world's last surviving one-party **Communist states**. It shares land borders with China, Laos and Cambodia. Vietnam comprises over 330,000 square kilometres, with more than 3400km of coastline.

• Vietnam has a **population** of ninety million, of which around seventy percent live in the countryside, giving Vietnam some of the highest rural population densities in Southeast Asia. Over half the people are under 25 years old and thirteen percent belong to one of the many **ethnic minority groups**.

• Over half of the Vietnamese population earn their living from **agriculture**. The average per capita **income** hovers around $1000 a year, though many people survive on less than $2 a day.

• During the last decade the Vietnamese **economy** has grown at over seven percent a year. Vietnam has transformed itself from being a rice-importer before 1986 to become the world's second largest rice-exporter after Thailand. The percentage of households living in poverty has fallen from seventy percent in the 1980s to around ten percent today.

• Vietnam is home to a tremendous diversity of **plant and animal life**, including some of the world's rarest species, a number of which have only been discovered in the last few years. The Asiatic black bear, Sarus crane and Golden-headed langur are just some of the endangered species maintaining a toehold in the forests and wetlands of Vietnam.

and children; unspeakable horrors continue to haunt the village's unnervingly idyllic rural setting.

Once a bustling seaport, the diminutive town of **Hoi An** perches beside an indolent backwater, its narrow streets of wooden-fronted shophouses and weathered roofs making it an enticing destination. Inland, the war-battered ruins of **My Son**, the greatest of the Cham temple sites, lie mouldering in a steamy, forest-filled valley. **Da Nang**, just up the coast, lacks Hoi An's charm, but good transport links make it a convenient base for the area. From Da Nang a corkscrew ride over clifftop Hai Van Pass, or a straight run through the new 6km-long tunnel, brings you to the aristocratic city of **Hué**, where the Nguyen emperors established their capital in the nineteenth century on the banks of the languid Perfume River. The temples and palaces of this highly cultured city still testify to past splendours, while its Imperial mausoleums are masterpieces of architectural refinement, slumbering among pine-shrouded hills.

Only a hundred kilometres north of Hué, the tone changes as war-sites litter the Demilitarized Zone (**DMZ**), which cleaved the country in two from 1954 to 1975. More than three decades of peace have done much to heal the scars, but the monuments that pepper these windswept hills bear eloquent witness to a generation that lost their lives in the tragic struggle. The DMZ is most easily tackled as a day-trip from Hué, after which most people hop straight up to Hanoi. And there's little to detain you on the northward trek, save the glittering limestone caverns of **Phong Nha**, the entrance to a

massive underground river system tunnelling under the Truong Son Mountains, which includes Son Doong, discovered in 2009 and now thought to be the largest cave in the world. Then, on the very fringes of the northern Red River Delta, lie the ancient incense-steeped temples of **Hoa Lu** and, nearby, the mystical landscapes of **Tam Coc** and **Van Long**, where paddy fields lap at the feet of limestone hummocks.

Anchored firmly in the Red River Delta, **Hanoi** has served as Vietnam's capital for over a thousand years. It's a rapidly-growing, decidedly proud city, a place of pagodas and dynastic temples, tamarisk-edged lakes and elegant boulevards of

ABOVE VIETNAMESE CUISINE

TWILIGHT, HA LONG BAY

Author picks

From the breathtaking remoteness of the mountain communities in the north to the bustling floating markets of the Mekong, our authors trekked by bike, bus, boat and on foot to cover every corner of Vietnam for this new edition. Aside from the major sights, here are their personal picks...

Best night-time walk Travellers pay good money to overnight on a Ha Long Bay junk, but you can see the same spectacular scenery for free on Cat Ba Island – a cliffside path links two beaches, affording gorgeous views of umpteen limestone silhouettes and twinkling ship lights.

Most far-flung accommodation A rare example of decent accommodation off the main tourist trail, *Phong Nha Farmstay* is situated close to the eponymous cave in a dreamy, field-filled setting. Their bike tours of the area are a delight, as are the delectable dishes (and cocktails) served up in the evening.

Finest tearoom with a difference The three stunning Bahnar villages surrounding central Kon Tum can easily eat up a day of your time – how convenient that *Eva Café* happens to be

on the way back into town. This ramshackle affair has been designed with a level of attention rare in these parts, and is a fine place to sample the coffee of the central highlands.

Tradition with a twist Little Hoi An has an almost bewildering selection of mouthwateringly good restaurants, but *Morning Glory* just about takes the biscuit. For a reasonable price you can eat your fill of superbly prepared Hoi An specialities – only this time in an elegant restaurant, rather than a kindergarten-style plastic chair.

Most haunting musical performance You will be mesmerized by Ca Tru, an ancient form of chamber music that is inscribed by UNESCO as an intangible heritage, at weekly performances in Hanoi.

Our author recommendations don't end here. We've flagged up our favourite places – a perfectly sited hotel, an atmospheric café, a special restaurant – throughout the guide, highlighted with the ★ symbol.

WATER-PUPPETS

Vietnam's unique contribution to the world of marionettes, **water-puppetry** is a delightfully quirky form of theatre in which the action takes place on a stage of water. The tradition was spawned in the rice paddies of the northern Red River Delta where performances still take place after the spring planting. Obscured by a split-bamboo screen, puppeteers standing waist-deep in water manipulate the wooden puppets, some weighing over 10kg, which are attached to the end of long poles concealed beneath the surface. Dragons, ducks, lions, unicorns, phoenixes and frogs spout smoke, throw balls and generally cavort on the watery stage – miraculously avoiding tangled poles. Brief scenes of rural life, such as water-buffalo fights, fishing or rice planting, take place alongside the legendary exploits of Vietnam's military heroes or perhaps a promenade of fairy-like immortals. In the more sophisticated productions staged for tourists in Hanoi and Ho Chi Minh City, even fireworks emerge to dance upon the water, which itself takes on different characters, from calm and placid to seething and furious during naval battles.

French-era villas, of national monuments and stately government edifices. But Hanoi is also being swept along on a tide of change as Vietnam forges its own shiny, high-rise capital, throwing up new office blocks, hotels and restaurants.

From Hanoi most visitors strike out east to where northern Vietnam's premier natural attraction, **Ha Long Bay**, provides the perfect antidote to such urban exuberance, rewarding the traveller with a leisurely day or two drifting among the thousands of whimsically sculpted islands anchored in its aquamarine waters. Ha Long City, on the northern coast, is the most popular embarkation point for Ha Long Bay, but a more appealing gateway is mountainous **Cat Ba Island**, which defines the bay's southwestern limits. The route to Cat Ba passes via the north's major port city, **Hai Phong**, an unspectacular but genial place with an attractive core of faded colonial facades.

To the north and west of Hanoi mountain ranges rear up out of the Red River Delta. Vietnam's northern provinces aren't the easiest to get around, but these wild uplands are home to a patchwork of ethnic minorities and the country's most dramatic mountain landscapes. The bustling market town of **Sa Pa**, set in a spectacular location close to the Chinese border in the far northwest, makes a good base for exploring nearby minority villages, though a building boom has taken some of the shine off its laidback vibe. Southwest of Hanoi, the stilthouse-filled valley of **Mai Chau** offers an opportunity to stay in a minority village. Though few people venture further inland, backroads heading upcountry link isolated outposts and give access to the northwest's only specific sight, where the French colonial dream expired in the dead-end valley of **Dien Bien Phu**. East of the Red River Valley lies an even less-frequented region, whose prime attraction is its varied scenery, from the vertigo-inducing valleys of the **Dong Van Karst Plateau Geopark** to the limestone crags and multi-layered rainforest of **Ba Be National Park**, and the remote valleys around **Cao Bang**, farmed by communities still practising their traditional ways of life.

When to go

Vietnam has a tropical monsoon **climate**, dominated by the south or southwesterly monsoon from May to September and the northeast monsoon from October to April. The southern summer monsoon brings rain to the two deltas and west-facing slopes,

while the cold winter monsoon picks up moisture over the Gulf of Tonkin and dumps it along the central coast and the eastern edge of the central highlands. Within this basic pattern there are marked differences according to altitude and latitude; temperatures in the south remain equable all year round, while the north experiences distinct seasonal variations.

In **southern Vietnam** the dry season lasts from December to late April or May, and the rains from May through to November. Since most rain falls in brief afternoon downpours, this need not be off-putting, though flooding at this time of year can cause problems in the Mekong Delta. Daytime temperatures in the region rarely drop below 20°C, occasionally hitting 40°C during the hottest months (March, April and May). The climate of the central highlands generally follows the same pattern, though temperatures are cooler, especially at night. Again, the monsoon rains of May to October can make transport more complicated, sometimes washing out roads and cutting off remoter villages.

Along the **central coast** the rainfall pattern reverses under the influence of the northeast monsoon. Around Nha Trang the wet season starts with a flourish in November and continues through December. Further north, around Hué and Da Nang, the rains last a bit longer, from September to February, so it pays to visit these two cities in the spring (Feb–May). Temperatures reach their maximum (often in the upper 30s) from June to August, when it's pleasant to escape into the hills. The northern stretches of this coastal region experience a more extreme climate, with a shorter rainy season (peaking in Sept and Oct) and a hot dry summer. The coast of central Vietnam is the zone most likely to be hit by **typhoons**, bringing torrential rain and hurricane-force winds. Though notoriously difficult to predict, in general the typhoon season lasts from August to November.

Northern Vietnam is generally warm and sunny from October to December, after which cold winter weather sets in, accompanied by fine persistent mists which can last for several days. Temperatures begin to rise again in March, building to summer maximums that occasionally reach 40°C between May and August, though average temperatures in Hanoi hover around a more reasonable 30°C. However, summer is also the rainy season, when heavy downpours render the low-lying delta area almost unbearably hot and sticky, and flooding is a regular hazard. The northern mountains share the same basic regime, though temperatures are considerably cooler and higher regions see ground frosts, or even a rare snowfall, during the winter (Dec–Feb).

With such a complicated weather picture, there's no one particular season to recommend as the **best time** for visiting Vietnam. Overall, autumn (Sept–Dec) and spring (March and April) are probably the most favourable seasons if you're covering the whole country.

FROM TOP LAK LAKE (P.191); FACE MASKS FOR THE TET CELEBRATIONS (SEE BOX, P.7)

27

things not to miss

It's not possible to see everything that Vietnam has to offer in one trip – and we don't suggest you try. What follows, in no particular order, is a selective taste of the country's highlights: outstanding scenery, lively festivals, ancient sites and colonial architecture. Each one has a page reference to take you straight into the guide, where you can find out more.

2

3

1 ETHNIC MARKETS
Pages 408 & 409
Spectacular traditional dress and a lively atmosphere make the ethnic minority markets a must – especially those in Bac Ha and Can Cau.

2 TEMPLES AND PAGODAS
Page 229
Vietnamese temples and pagodas reflect the country's diverse range of religions: Long Son Pagoda in Nha Trang is a good example.

3 TET
Page 7
The most important festival in the Vietnamese calendar, Tet sees the New Year ushered in with colourful flower markets, spectacular fireworks and exuberant dragon dances.

4 CU CHI TUNNELS
Page 109

Look out for the spiked booby traps that Vietnamese guides reveal for visitors to the Cu Chi tunnels.

5 BIA HOI
Page 44

Bia hoi bars are fun, friendly, cheap and a great way to mingle with the locals. Order a bia hoi (lager-like draught) in any of the back lanes in the Old Quarter of Hanoi.

6 THE CITADEL, HUÉ
Page 281

The former capital's historic citadel, mausoleums and gardens are idiosyncratic enough to impress even the most jaded traveller.

7 WATER-PUPPETS
Page 12

Enjoy a performance of *mua roi nuoc*, an art form developed in the Red River Delta around Hanoi.

8 EXPRESS SILK TAILORING
Page 262

Visit one of the many Hoi An tailors who can rustle up a made-to-measure silk dress or suit in just a few hours.

9 TREKKING AROUND SA PA
Page 401

Trek in the northern mountains around Sa Pa – a small market town perched on a plateau facing Fan Si Pan, Vietnam's highest peak.

10 LAK LAKE
Page 191

Paddle the serene waters of Lak Lake in a dug-out canoe, ride on an elephant or take a guided trek into the surrounding forests before a sunset feast overlooking the water.

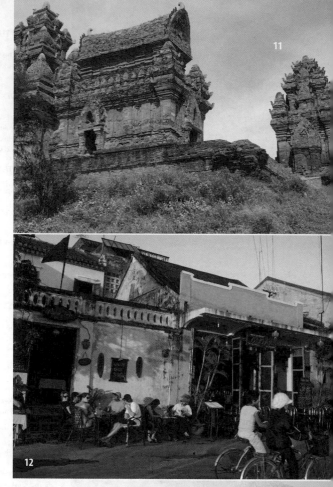

11 MY SON CHAM TOWERS

Page 264

These battered but beautiful towers near Hoi An are all that remain of the once-powerful Champa kingdom.

12 HOI AN

Pages 251–262

With its rich cultural heritage, beautifully preserved merchants' houses and slow pace of life, Hoi An is a captivating place to spend a few days.

13 THE RED RIVER DELTA

Pages 396–430

Slow the pace down with a trip to the countryside and experience a lifestyle little changed in centuries.

14 THE MEKONG DELTA

Pages 116–171

Putter through this fertile farming region, surrounded by classic Vietnamese scenery.

15 TAKE A CYCLO RIDE

Page 38

The quintessential Vietnamese mode of transport gives you an up-close view of street life.

19

20

16 A BOAT TRIP IN HA LONG BAY
Page 334

The thousands of limestone islands jutting out of these silent waters have been dubbed the eighth natural wonder of the world.

17 CHILL OUT ON PHU QUOC
Pages 164–171

Unspoilt beaches lined with coconut trees circle the island. You can also sail south to the unspoilt An Thoi islands for fine snorkelling.

18 RIDE THE REUNIFICATION EXPRESS
Page 33

Load your bike on, then sit back and relax as the train slowly chugs its way between Ho Chi Minh City and Hanoi.

19 COLONIAL ARCHITECTURE
Page 358

The legacy of French rule can be found in the impressive examples of colonial architecture, such as Hanoi's Opera House.

20 TRADITIONAL MUSIC
Page 480

Music is the most important of all Vietnam's performing arts and a traditional performance should feature on every itinerary.

21 BROWSE THE MARKETS
Page 84

Markets such as Binh Tay are good grazing grounds for snacks. Have a soup, spring roll, sticky rice cake – or even a baguette filled with pâte –to keep you going while you shop.

21

26

22 ADVENTURE SPORTS
Page 51

Rock-climbing, kitesurfing, kayaking and mountain biking are just a few of the heart-pumping activities awaiting thrill-seekers.

23 CAO DAI CATHEDRAL
Page 112

Vietnam's most charismatic indigenous religion goes in for exuberant architecture and ceremonies.

24 BAHNAR VILLAGES
Page 199

Spend the night in a communal house (*rong*) where timeless ceremonies are performed and village decisions made.

25 DONG VAN KARST PLATEAU GEOPARK
Page 424

Vietnam's most impressive mountainscapes are located in remote Ha Giang Province near the Chinese border.

26 STREET FOOD
Pages 41 & 380

Soak up the atmosphere at a street kitchen and have your plate piled high with a selection of fresh food for next to nothing.

27 NHA TRANG
Pages 228–238

Take a snorkelling trip in the emerald waters of the outlying islands around Nha Trang, or simply chill out on the beach.

27

Itineraries

THE GRAND TOUR

The classic tour for visitors to Vietnam, and with good reason – following this route gives you easy access to superb historical sights, high-octane nightlife, pristine beaches, mountain-dwelling minority groups and much more. It can easily eat up the full month of your visa.

❶ Ho Chi Minh City Although it's not the capital, most would agree that this buzzing, cosmopolitan city is the true hub of Vietnam – its range of bars, restaurants, shops and hotels is unsurpassed.

❷ Da Lat This mile-high mountain city is highly popular with travellers, and not just for its fresh air or cooler temperatures. Its relaxed atmosphere lends itself to a leisurely exploration of nearby sights, which include some wonderful minority villages.

❸ Mui Ne It's all about the beach at Mui Ne, a curl of sand now fringed with top-drawer resorts. However, there are still a few cheap places to stay and a couple of bars maintaining that old-fashioned backpacker vibe.

❹ Nha Trang Another place famed for its beach life, but with a totally different character to Mui Ne. This is one of Vietnam's party capitals, with bars galore attracting revellers with astonishingly long happy hours. Those who wake up before nightfall can hit the nearby Cham ruins, then sink into a mud bath.

❺ Hoi An This small city draws almost universally positive reactions from visitors: its food is the best in the country; its lantern-lit buildings are truly spellbinding at night; the nearby sea is great for diving; and the majestic Cham ruins of My Son are close by.

❻ Hué Notably relaxed for its size, Hué was capital of Vietnam's last dynasty, the Nguyen empire. Cross the Perfume River to the old Imperial City, a maze of opulent buildings that were home to emperors as recently as 1945.

❼ Hanoi The Vietnamese capital provides a truly startling contrast to Ho Chi Minh city – it has a far more traditional air and is home to some superb examples of colonial-era architecture. That said, its bars and restaurants are excellent too.

❽ Ha Long Bay There are few better ways to round off a Vietnamese tour than a trip to Ha Long Bay, a dizzying mass of limestone peaks jutting from the sea. Most visitors spend a night at sea on a wooden junk, after a feast of seafood and cocktails.

UNSEEN MEKONG DELTA

Eager to leave the tourist hordes behind? Our authors have never spotted another foreigner at the following locations.

❶ Sa Dec flower nurseries Apart from being the former home of French novelist Marguerite Dumas, Sa Dec is the base of over a hundred flower nurseries – a horticulturalist's dream.

❷ Hang Pagoda near Tra Vinh This Khmer-style pagoda painted in subtle pastel shades is home to many monks eager to practise their English, and also to hundreds of storks that roost in the treetops.

❸ Cape Ca Mau Take a speedboat from Ca Mau to Dat Mui, then hop on a xe om to country's end at Cape Ca Mau, where an observation tower offers views over mangrove swamps and the endless ocean.

❹ Route 63 This narrow road from Ca Mau to Rach Gia passes classic delta scenes of commerce being conducted on canals and locals crossing precarious monkey bridges.

ABOVE KHAI DINH MAUSOLEUM (P.299); **RIGHT** THE RIVERFRONT, HOI AN (P.251)

❺ Tra Su bird sanctuary Located near Chau Doc, this bird sanctuary is a wonderland of cajuput trees and waterways covered with lily pads that attract swarms of birds like egrets, cormorants and water cocks.

❻ Hon Chong Peninsula The beach doesn't compare with those on Phu Quoc, but it's extremely relaxing, especially on weekdays when you might be the only one swinging in a hammock beneath the casuarina trees.

ETHNIC CULTURE TOUR

Most of Vietnam's 54 ethnic minority groups live in the rugged hills of the north, and a circular journey from Hanoi passes several of the most interesting groups.

❶ White Thai in Mai Chau Girls with waist-length hair don traditional costumes and perform lively song and dance routines, then invite guests to share a huge jar of rice wine.

❷ Black Thai in Son La The most remarkable aspect of Black Thai clothing is the headdress, which features delicately embroidered panels.

❸ Red Dao near Sa Pa Easily spotted by their bright red headgear, the Red Dao are one of the most colourful tribes in the north and cling fiercely to their traditional ways.

❹ Flower Hmong around Bac Ha These are hands down the north's most flamboyant dressers, and the women are constantly looking for new accoutrements at local markets.

❺ White Hmong near Dong Van Satins and sequins are highly favoured by this group who live in one of the north's most inhospitable, yet also stunningly scenic, settings.

❻ Tay near Ba Be Lake The Tay are the most numerous of all ethnic groups in Vietnam, and have a rich tradition of song and dance, which they occasionally perform for tourists.

CYCLO IN HO CHI MINH CITY

Basics

Getting there

The number of direct flights to Vietnam's three main international airports – Ho Chi Minh City, Hanoi and Da Nang, in order of importance – have increased steadily in recent years. However, the majority of visitors take the cheaper option of an indirect flight routed through Bangkok, Singapore or Hong Kong; a stay in one of these cities can be factored into your schedule, often at no extra cost. You may well save even more by taking a bargain–basement flight to Bangkok, Kuala Lumpur or Singapore, and a separate ticket through one of the region's low–cost carriers, such as Jetstar, Tiger Airways and Air Asia, for the Vietnam leg.

Airlines that fly in and out of both Hanoi and Ho Chi Minh City normally sell you an open-jaw ticket, which allows you to fly into one city and out of the other, leaving you to travel up or down the country under your own steam.

Airfares always depend on the **season**, with the highest generally being July to August, during the Christmas and New Year holidays and around Tet, the Vietnamese New Year; fares drop during the "shoulder" season – September to mid-December – and you'll get the best prices during the low season, January to June.

You can often cut costs by going through a **specialist flight agent** – either a consolidator, who buys up blocks of tickets from the airlines and sells them at a discount, or a **discount agent**, who in addition to dealing with discounted flights may also offer special student and youth fares and a range of other travel-related services such as travel insurance, rail passes, car rentals, tours and the like.

Combining Vietnam with other **Southeast Asian countries** is becoming increasingly popular – and a lot cheaper and easier – thanks to some good-value regional air deals. Jetstar (W jetstar.com), for example, flies from Singapore to Ho Chi Minh City (from $50 one-way), while Tiger Airways (W tiger airways.com) flies from Singapore to Hanoi (from $70 one-way) and Ho Chi Minh City (from $50 one-way). Air Asia (W airasia.com) offers daily services from Bangkok and Kuala Lumpur to both Hanoi and Ho Chi Minh City, with fares starting at $50 one-way to Ho Chi Minh City, and a little more to Hanoi. As with all discount airlines, prices depend on availability, so the earlier you book the better,

though you may also find last-minute promotional fares, seat giveaways and so forth at less busy times of the year.

From the UK and Ireland

There are as yet no non-stop flights to Vietnam from the UK or Ireland (believed to be starting with Vietnam Airlines in December 2011). Instead, most people fly with a Southeast Asian carrier such as Singapore Airlines (W singaporeair.com), Thai Airways (W thaiairways.com), Malaysia Airlines (W malaysiaairlines.com) or Cathay Pacific (W cathay pacific.com) from London via the airline's home city. In recent years the big Middle Eastern airlines, Qatar (W qatarairways.com) and Emirates (W emirates .com), have also offered very competitive prices. Scheduled low-season **fares** from London start at around £450, rising to £600 or more at peak periods.

A good place to look for the best deals is the travel sections of the weekend newspapers and in regional listings magazines. **Students** and **under-26s** can often get discounts through specialist agents such as STA (W sta.com) or USIT in Ireland (W usit.ie). Whoever you buy your ticket through, check that the agency belongs to the travel industry bodies ABTA or IATA, so that you'll be covered if the agent goes bust before you get your ticket.

From the US and Canada

In 2004 United Airlines (W united.com) became the first American carrier to resume direct flights to Vietnam since 1975. The airline operates a daily service **from San Francisco** to Ho Chi Minh City via Hong Kong; standard return fares start at around $1100. As yet, no other American or Canadian carriers offer direct services, which means you'll either have to get a flight to San Francisco or catch one of the many flights to a regional hub, such as Bangkok, Singapore or Hong Kong, and continue on from there. Scheduled flights start at around $1400 **from New York**, $1200 **from Los Angeles**, CAN$2000 **from Vancouver** and CAN$2500 **from Toronto**.

Note that some routings require an **overnight stay** in another city such as Bangkok, Taipei, Hong Kong or Seoul, and often a hotel room will be included in your fare – ask the airline and shop around since travel agents' policies on this vary. Even when an overnight stay is not required, going to Vietnam can be a great excuse for a stopover: most airlines will allow you one free stopover in either direction.

From Australia and New Zealand

A reasonable range of flights connects Australia and New Zealand with Vietnam, with Qantas (Ⓦ qantas .com), Vietnam Airlines (Ⓦ vietnamairlines.com) and Jetstar offering direct services from Australia. The alternative is to fly to another Asian gateway, such as Bangkok, Kuala Lumpur, Singapore or Hong Kong, and then either get connecting flights or travel overland to Hanoi or Ho Chi Minh City.

By far the cheapest flight **from Australia** is the daily Jetstar service to Ho Chi Minh City from Sydney (AUS$390 one-way) via Darwin (AUS$250 one-way). Both Vietnam Airlines and Qantas operate direct flights to Ho Chi Minh City from Melbourne and Sydney; low-season scheduled fares start at around AUS$1100 with Vietnam Airlines, with Qantas often a little cheaper. If you want to stop off on the way, there are good deals to Hanoi and Ho Chi Minh City with Malaysia Airlines via Kuala Lumpur, Singapore Airlines via Singapore, and Thai Airways via Bangkok, all costing around AUS$1100 to AUS$1500. Cheaper still are the fares offered by Tiger Airways, a discount airline operating daily flights **between Perth and Singapore**: one-way fares sometimes dip below AUS$200. From Singapore you can get an onward flight to Hanoi (from around AUS$100 one-way) or Ho Chi Minh City (from around AUS$55 one-way).

From New Zealand, low-season fares with Malaysia Airlines, Thai, Qantas and Singapore Airlines are all around NZ$1500 to NZ$2200, with a change of plane in the carrier's home airport.

From neighbouring countries

It's increasingly popular to enter Vietnam overland from China, Laos or Cambodia, an option that means you can see more of the region than you would if you simply jetted in. However, it must be said that regional air connections are becoming better and better – you can fly from many cities in Southern China, from Phnom Penh or Siem Reap with Cambodia Angkor Air (bookable through codeshare partner Vietnam Airlines), or from Vientiane with Vietnam Airlines or Lao Airlines (Ⓦ laoairlines.com).

From China there are three overland possibilities. The Beijing–Hanoi train enters Vietnam at Dong Dang, north of Lang Son, where there's also a road crossing known as Huu Nghi Quan (see p.430). The border is also open to foot traffic at Lao Cai (see p.403) in the northwest and Mong Cai in the far northeast (see p.417).

From Laos, six border crossings are currently open to foreigners: Lao Bao (see p.306), the easiest and most popular, some 80km west of Dong Ha; Cau Treo and Nam Can, to the north and northwest of Vinh (see p.318); Na Meo, northwest of Thanh Hoa; Bo Y, northwest of Kon Tum (see p.203); and Tay Trang, just west of Dien Bien Phu (see p.414). While it's perfectly possible – and cheaper – to use local buses to and from the borders, international bus services also run from Savannakhet and Vientiane to Hanoi, Dong Ha, Vinh, Da Nang and other destinations in Vietnam: these direct services are recommended, as regular reports of extortion continue to come in from those crossing independently.

From Cambodia you can travel by air-conditioned bus ($9–14) from Phnom Penh straight through to Ho Chi Minh City, via the Moc Bai crossing. Cheaper operators charge half these prices, but use old buses and usually get you to switch at the border. Many tour companies in Phnom Penh will be able to organize boat-plus-bus services, which are a fun way to cross the border. There are two crossings in the Mekong Delta area – Vinh Xuong and Tinh Bien, which are respectively 30km north and 25km west of Chau Doc. There are also border crossings at Xa Xia, on the coast west of the delta, which is useful if you are coming from Kep or Sihanoukville on the Cambodian coast; and at Le Thanh in the central highlands, making it possible to go from Banlung in northeast Cambodia straight through to Pleiku.

As long as you have a **valid visa**, crossing these borders is generally not a problem, though you may

---

A BETTER KIND OF TRAVEL

At Rough Guides we are passionately committed to travel. We feel that travelling is the best way to understand the world we live in and the people we share it with – plus tourism has brought a great deal of benefit to developing economies around the world over the last few decades. But the growth in tourism has also damaged some places irreparably, and climate change is exacerbated by most forms of transport, especially flying. All Rough Guides' trips are carbon-offset, and every year we donate money to a variety of charities devoted to combating the effects of climate change.

still find the odd Vietnamese immigration official who tries to charge a "processing fee", typically one dollar. Most border gates are open from around 7am to 5pm and may close for an hour over lunch.

Organized tours

If you want to cover a lot of ground in a short time in Vietnam or have a specific interest, an organized tour might be worth considering. **Specialist tour operators** offer packages that typically include flights, accommodation, day excursions and internal travel by plane, train or road. These are expensive compared to what you'd pay if you arranged everything independently, but the more intrepid tours often feature activities that would be difficult to set up yourself. There's a wide variety of all-inclusive **packages** available, as well as **organized tours** that cover everything from hill-tribe visits to trekking and biking. Tours range in length from a few days to several weeks, and you can choose to explore Vietnam only, or combine a tour with Laos and Cambodia.

Alternatively, you can make arrangements through **local tour operators** in Ho Chi Minh City, Hanoi and other tourist centres either before you arrive or on the ground; they'll arrange your entire trip or just the first few days to get you started. Fixing it up before you arrive saves time, though all local operators will also arrange an itinerary for you on the spot.

Prices will be generally cheaper with a local operator and they should have more in-depth local knowledge. However, you'll need to check carefully that they're financially sound, reliable and can deliver what they promise – *never* deal with a company that demands cash upfront or refuses to accept payment by credit card, and get references if you can. Also check carefully before booking to make sure you know exactly what's included in the price.

We've listed some of the bigger and better-established agents outside Vietnam; all have a solid reputation for organizing small-group and custom-ized tours. However, there also exist a fair number of excellent Vietnam-based operators; most are based in Ho Chi Minh City (see box, p.90) and Hanoi (see box, p.373).

Specialist tour operators abroad
Multinational

Abercrombie & Kent UK ☎ 0845 618 2200, US ☎ 1 800 554 7016, Australia ☎ 1300 851 800; ⓦ abercrombiekent.co.uk, ⓦ abercrombiekent.com, ⓦ abercrombiekent.com.au. Luxury tour specialist; trips featuring Vietnam come as part of a greater trip through Indochina.

Intrepid Travel UK ☎ 020 3147 7777, Australia ☎ 1300 364 512, New Zealand ☎ 0800 600 610; ⓦ intrepidtravel.com. Affordable small-group trips, usually focusing on low-impact, cross-cultural contact. Tours can cover bits of Vietnam, the whole country or wider Indochina.

Peregrine Adventures UK ☎ 0845 004 0673, Australia ☎ 1300 854 444; ⓦ peregrineadventures.com. Good local knowledge for an outfit that goes everywhere. Most tours are small-group and adventure-based, often with a focus on trekking, cycling or even food.

World Expeditions UK ☎ 020 8545 9030, US & Canada ☎ 1 800 567 2216, Australia ☎ 1300 720 000, New Zealand ☎ 0800 350 354; ⓦ worldexpeditions.com. Adventure company with a wide variety of programmes, including cycle tours and kayaking in Ha Long Bay. Also offers community project trips, where participants help renovate a local school, for example, and arrange charity challenges.

Australia & NZ

Active Travel Australia ☎ 02 9264 1231, ⓦ activetravel.com.au. Renowned outfit with a wide range of culture and adventure tours, plus customized itineraries.

Griswalds Vietnamese Vacations Australia ☎ 02 9430 6426, ⓦ vietnamvacations.com.au. Long-running Vietnam specialists offering small-group, tailor-made itineraries.

US & Canada

Artisans of Leisure ☎ 1 800 214 8144, ⓦ artisansofleisure.com Luxury private and individually tailored tours, which often include cooking classes and spa therapy sessions.

Asian Pacific Adventures ☎ 1 800 825 1680, ⓦ asianpacificadventures.com. Regional specialists offering tailor-made and small-group tours, including trekking and hill-tribe markets.

Backroads ☎ 1 800 462 2848, ⓦ backroads.com. Cycling, hiking and multi-sport tours, with the emphasis on going at your own pace.

Global Exchange ☎ 415 255 7296, ⓦ globalexchange.org. A not-for-profit human rights organization that leads educational tours of Vietnam.

Journeys International ☎ 1 800 255 8735, ⓦ journeys.travel. Prestigious, award-winning operator focusing on eco-tourism and small-group trips.

VeloAsia ☎ 1 888 681 0808, ⓦ veloasia.com. Indochina specialist with a range of organized and tailor-made cycling adventure tours. Their famed Highlights of Vietnam tour connects Hanoi and Ho Chi Minh City, and lasts twelve days.

UK & Ireland

Exodus UK ☎ 0845 287 7690, ⓦ exodus.co.uk. Adventure-tour operator taking small groups on specialist programmes that take in trekking, biking, kayaking and cultural trips.

Imaginative Traveller UK ☎ 0845 287 7053, ⓦ imaginative-traveller.com. Affordable, small-group adventure tours from a responsible travel operator. The nine-day "Northern Vietnam Escape" tour is particularly popular.

Regent Holidays UK ☎ 0845 277 3317, ⓦ regent-holidays.co.uk. Any operators that can organize good tours to North Korea will surely find Vietnam a piece of cake. Good-value, tailor-made tours available, as well as off-the-shelf itineraries a twelve-day "Highlights of Vietnam" trip.

responsibletravel.com UK ☎ 01273 600030, Ⓦ responsibletravel.com. UK-based online travel agent listing pre-screened holidays from responsible tourism operators.

Airlines, agents and operators

Many **airlines** and **discount travel websites** offer you the chance to book your tickets online, cutting out the costs of agents and middlemen. The websites listed below offer good deals and useful price comparisons.

Online booking

Ⓦ expedia.co.uk (in UK)
Ⓦ expedia.com (in US)
Ⓦ expedia.ca (in Canada)
Ⓦ lastminute.com (in UK)
Ⓦ opodo.co.uk (in UK)
Ⓦ orbitz.com (in US)
Ⓦ travelocity.co.uk (in UK)
Ⓦ travelocity.com (in US)
Ⓦ travelocity.ca (in Canada)
Ⓦ travelocity.co.nz (in New Zealand)
Ⓦ zuji.com.au (in Australia)

Flight agents and tour operators

ebookers UK ☎ 020 3320 3320, Republic of Ireland ☎ 01 431 1311; Ⓦ ebookers.com, Ⓦ ebookers.ie. Low fares on an extensive selection of scheduled flights and package deals.

North South Travel UK ☎ 01245 608291, Ⓦ northsouthtravel .co.uk. Friendly, competitive travel agency, offering discounted fares worldwide. Profits are used to support projects in the developing world, especially the promotion of sustainable tourism.

STA Travel UK ☎ 0800 819 9339, US ☎ 1 800 781 4040, Australia ☎ 134 782, New Zealand ☎ 0800 474 400, South Africa ☎ 0861 781 781; Ⓦ statravel.com. Worldwide specialists in independent travel; also student IDs, travel insurance, car rental, rail passes and more. Good discounts for students and under-26s.

Trailfinders UK ☎ 0845 054 6060, Republic of Ireland ☎ 01 677 7888; Ⓦ trailfinders.com, Ⓦ trailfinders.ie. One of the best informed and most efficient agents for independent travellers.

Getting around

Though still a little rough around the edges, Vietnam's transport network is continuing to improve. Most travel takes place on the roads, which are largely of decent quality surface-wise. The vehicles themselves are also pretty good, with air-conditioned coaches ferrying tourists

(and an increasing number of locals) up and down Highway 1, a desperately narrow and shockingly busy thoroughfare that runs from Hanoi to Ho Chi Minh City, passing through Hué, Da Nang and Nha Trang en route. Off the main routes the vehicles are less salubrious. Trains run alongside Highway 1, and their sleeper berths are far more comfortable than buses for longer journeys. Lastly, the domestic flight network continues to evolve, and the cheap, comfortable services may save you days' worth of travel by road or rail. That said, there's plenty of room for improvement, particularly as regards road transport.

On the roads

Vietnam's busy, narrow roads were simply not built for overtaking, yet almost each and every vehicle is either overtaking or being overtaken at any given point – accidents are common.

Vietnam was once famed for bus drivers ripping off foreigners and cramming as many bodies as possible into their vehicles, but this is dying down; most routes now have tickets with fixed prices, and the advent of luxury "open-tour" buses on the main tourist trail saw comfort levels rocket. On the longer stretches, many buses are sleeper-berth for their whole length, though getting forty winks can be tough – the nature of local roads means that emergency stops are common, and Vietnamese drivers use their horn liberally, which can become grating very quickly on a long journey.

Security remains an important consideration. Never fall asleep with your bag by your side, and never leave belongings unattended.

By plane

Flying comes into its own on longer hauls, and can save precious hours or even days off journeys – the two-hour journey **between Hanoi and Ho Chi Minh City**, for instance, compares favourably with the thirty to forty hours you would spend on the train. Prices are reasonable at around 950,000đ with Jetstar, and a little more with Vietnam Airlines. Other **useful services** from Hanoi and Ho Chi Minh City fly to Hué, Da Nang, Nha Trang, and Phu Quoc Island. Note that you'll need your passport with you when taking internal flights.

The Vietnamese national carrier, Vietnam Airlines, operates a reasonably cheap, efficient and comprehensive network of **domestic flights**. The company maintains booking offices in all towns and cities with an airport; addresses and phone numbers are listed throughout the Guide.

Competition is keeping prices low on domestic flights; the aforementioned Jetstar now rival Vietnam Airlnes for local coverage, while 2009 startup Air Mekong (Ⓦairmekong.com.vn) fly from Hanoi and Ho Chi Minh City to all major airports in the south of the country. Vasco (Ⓦvasco.com.vn) also fly from Ho Chi Minh City to Con Dao and Ca Mau, but it's better to book through their codeshare partner Vietnam Airlines (and actually far better to go with Air Mekong's superior planes on the Con Dao route).

By rail

Given the amazing prices and regular services of the open-tour buses, few travellers opt for the train. However, **rail journeys** are well worth considering, for several reasons. Firstly, major roads tend to be lined in their entirety with ramshackle cafés, petrol pumps, snack stands and mobile phone shops; from the train, you'll actually see a bit of the countryside. Secondly, you'll be involved in far fewer near-collisions with trucks, motorbikes or dogs. Thirdly, you're almost guaranteed to get talking to a bunch of friendly locals – and perhaps get to join in on the feasts that some of them bring on board.

Vietnam Railways (Ⓦvr.com.vn) runs a single-track **train network** comprising more than 2500km of line, stretching from Ho Chi Minh City to the Chinese border. Much of it dates back to the colonial period, though it's gradually being upgraded. Most of the services are still relatively slow, but travelling by train can be far more pleasant than going by road – though prices on the coastal route can't compare with buses, you're away from the busy (and often dangerous) Highway 1, and get to see far more of the countryside. Keep a particularly close eye on your belongings on the trains, and be especially vigilant when the train stops at stations, ensure your money belt is safely tucked under your clothes before going to sleep and that your luggage is safely stowed.

The most **popular routes** with tourists are the shuttle from Da Nang to Hué (2–3hr), a picturesque sampler of Vietnamese rail travel and the overnighters from Hué to Hanoi (11–16hr) and from Hanoi up to Lao Cai, for Sa Pa (8–9hr).

Services

The country's **main line** shadows Highway 1 on its way from Ho Chi Minh City to Hanoi, passing through Nha Trang, Da Nang and Hué en route. From Hanoi, three branch lines strike out towards the northern coast and Chinese border. One line traces the Red River northwest to **Lao Cai**, just an hour by bus from Sa Pa and also the site of a border crossing into **China**'s Yunnan Province; unfortunately, the rail on the Chinese side is not in use. Another runs north to **Dong Dang**; this is the route taken by trains linking Hanoi and **Beijing**. The third branch, a shorter spur, links the capital with **Hai Phong**.

Five **Reunification Express** services depart daily from Hanoi to Ho Chi Minh City and vice versa, a journey that takes somewhere between thirty and forty hours. Most services arrive between 3am and 5am in both Hanoi and Ho Chi Minh City.

On the **northern lines**, four trains per day make the run from Hanoi to Hai Phong (2hr 30min) and two to Dong Dang (6hr). There are also four night trains (7–8hr) and a day service (9hr) to Lao Cai.

Trains usually leave on schedule from their departure points, and though delays can stack up further down the line, they're rarely too severe. Note that the only truly reliable way to learn the schedule is by checking those printed on the station wall.

Classes

When it comes to choosing which **class** to travel in, it's essential to aim high. At the bottom of the scale is a **hard seat**, which is just as it sounds, though bearable for shorter journeys; the carriages, however, tend to be filthy and since the windows are caged, views are poor and one can actually feel like an animal. **Soft seats** offer more comfort, especially in the new air-conditioned carriages, some of which are double-decker; the newer berths, unfortunately, tend to have flatscreen TVs operating at an ear-splitting volume. On overnight journeys, you'd be well advised to invest in a **berth** of some description, though since the country's rolling stock is being upgraded it's not always possible to know exactly what you're getting. The new **hard-berth** compartments are now quite comfortable and have six bunks, three either side – the cramped top ones are the cheapest, and the bottom ones the priciest – though some of the old hard-as-nails relics remain in service. Roomier **soft-berth** compartments, containing only four bunks, are always comfortable.

Note that luxury carriages are attached to regular services on a couple of routes from Hanoi. Those on trains to Hué and Da Nang are operated by Livitrans (Ⓦlivitrans.com), and to Lao Cai by an assortment of companies (see p.403).

Facilities

All Reunification Express trains now have **air-conditioning**, as do the overnight Lao Cai trains which have been upgraded with luxury soft-sleeper carriages. All trains are theoretically **non-smoking**; the rules are obeyed, by and large, in the sleeper rooms, though in hard-seat class, even the guards will be puffing away.

All train carriages have toilets, though again, it's hard to know what to expect. Most are fine, if a little grubby, though many are squat in nature; the latter are far more likely to be dirty, and to be devoid of paper or running water. Those in the soft sleeper carriages are proper sit-down toilets, and are comparatively clean.

Simple **meals** are often included in the price of the ticket, but you might want to stock up with goodies of your own. You'll also have plenty of opportunities to buy snacks when the train pulls into stations – and from carts that ply the aisles.

Tickets

Booking ahead is wise, and the further ahead the better, especially if you intend travelling at the weekend or a holiday period (when the lower sleeper berths are often sold as six seats, resulting in chaos). Sleeping compartments should be booked at least a day or two before departure, and even further ahead for soft-sleeper berths on the Hanoi–Hué and Hanoi–Lao Cai routes. It's not possible to buy through tickets and break your journey en route; each journey requires you to buy a separate ticket from the point of departure. Getting tickets is usually pretty painless at the station, though hotels and travel agencies will be able to book for a fee – sometimes as low as 50,000đ, though often much more.

Fares vary according to the class of travel and the train you take; as a rule of thumb, the faster the train, the more expensive it is. Prices (which are always quoted in dong) change regularly, but as an indication of the fare range, on the most expensive services from Hanoi to Ho Chi Minh City you'll pay around 1,500,000đ for a soft-sleeper berth, and around 1,250,000đ for a hard sleeper in the slowest trains; the equivalent fares for Hanoi to Hué are 750,000đ and 650,000đ respectively. Prices to Lao Cai vary from 80,000đ for a hard seat on the day train to over 300,000đ for a soft sleeper.

By bus

Most travellers use buses to get around Vietnam but never actually see a bus station. This is because the lion's share of tourist journeys are made on **privately operated** services, usually referred to as "open-tour" buses, which usually operate not from stations but the offices of the companies in question. The term comes from the fact that such companies typically sell through-tickets between Ho Chi Minh City and Hanoi, with customers free to stop off for as long as they like at the main points en route – Da Lat, Mui Ne, Nha Trang, Hoi An, Da Nang, Hué and Ninh Binh. There are, however, drawbacks to doing this (see box opposite).

Away from these private affairs, **national bus service**s link all major cities in Vietnam, and most minor towns too, though travellers only tend to use them off the open-tour route – open-tour buses have air-conditioning, limited seating and fixed timetables, which instantly gives them the edge over national services. In addition, the fact that they don't pick up on route makes them faster too, and competition is so fierce that prices are almost as low as the national bus network.

Open-tour buses

On the whole, open-tour buses are a reasonably comfortable way to get around Vietnam; these buses also call at the occasional tourist sight, such as the Marble Mountains and Lang Co, which can save considerable time and money when compared to doing the same thing independently. Buses are usually quite decent, but don't expect too much leg-room, or any on-board toilets; some of the more expensive services have them, but the vast majority will pull in every few hours for a combined loo-and-snack break. This tends to be at mediocre and overpriced restaurants; it's a good idea to arm yourself with snacks before your journey. Another downside to open-tour buses is that you'll be encouraged to book into the company's own or affiliated hotels (usually right next to the drop-off point), though there's nothing to stop you staying elsewhere.

Services tend to run on time, and on longer trips, some take place overnight. Most of the overnight buses are filled with sleeper berths, which sounds nice and comfortable, but these are Vietnamese roads, and Vietnamese drivers – don't expect to get too much sleep. Also note that some **operators** are more reliable than others; Mai Linh and Hoang Long have good reputations, though some other operators have very poor standards of service.

Ticket prices vary widely depending upon which company you choose, and (if you're booking a through-ticket) how many stops you'd like to make en route; sample prices are $35 and up from Ho Chi

Minh City to Hanoi, $25 from Ho Chi Minh City to Hué, and $5 from Hué to Hoi An. You can either make firm bookings at the outset or opt for an open-dated ticket for greater flexibility, in which case you may need to book your onward travel one or two days in advance to be sure of a seat. Alternatively, you can buy separate tickets as you go along, which is recommended (see box below). Each main town on the itinerary has an agent (one for each operator) where you can buy tickets and make onward reservations. To avoid being sold a **fake ticket** or paying over the odds, it's best to buy direct from the relevant agent rather than from hotels, restaurants or unrelated tour companies.

Other buses

On the national bus network, the government is slowly upgrading **state buses**, replacing the rickety old vehicles with air-conditioned models, particularly on the more popular routes. It's not uncommon to find yourself crammed in amongst the luggage, which could be anything from live pigs in baskets to scores of sacks of rice. Progress can be agonizingly slow as buses stop frequently to pick up passengers or for meal breaks. Among older vehicles, breakdowns are fairly common and can sometimes necessitate a roadside wait of several hours while driver, fare collector and mechanic roll up their sleeves and improvise a repair.

Tickets are best bought at bus stations, where **fares** are clearly indicated above the ticket windows. Prices are usually also marked on the tickets themselves, though there are still occasional cases of tourists being charged over the odds, particularly in more rural destinations – especially those from the Lao border. For long journeys, buy your ticket a day in advance since many routes are heavily oversubscribed.

Privately owned **minibuses** compete with public buses on most routes; they sometimes share the local bus station, or simply congregate on the roadside in the centre of a town. You can also flag them down on the road. If anything, they squeeze in even more people per square foot than ordinary buses, and often drive interminably around town,

touting for passengers. On the other hand, they do at least run throughout the day, and serve some routes not covered by public services. Such services are ticketless, so try to find what the correct fare should be and agree a price before boarding – having the right change will also come in handy. You may also find yourself dumped at the side of the road before reaching your destination, and having to cram onto the next passing service.

Most major cities have their own local bus networks, though prices and standards vary. Try to ascertain the correct price and have the exact money ready before boarding as fare collectors will often take advantage of your captive position.

By ferry and boat

A boat-tour around Ha Long Bay is one of Vietnam's most enjoyable trips, while scheduled **ferries** sail year-round – weather permitting – to the major islands off Vietnam's coastline, including Phu Quoc, Cat Ba and Con Dao. In addition, ferry and hydrofoil services run from Hai Phong to Cat Ba, and hydrofoils from Ho Chi Minh City to Vung Tau, and from Ha Long City to Mong Cai and Bai Tu Long. Though they are gradually being replaced by bridges, a few river ferries still haul themselves from bank to bank of the various strands of the Mekong from morning until night.

By car and jeep

Self-drive in Vietnam is not yet an option for tourists and other short-term visitors. However, it's easy to rent a **car**, **jeep** or **minibus** with driver from the same companies, agencies and tourist offices that arrange tours. This can be quite an economical means of transport if you are travelling in a group. Moreover, it means you can plan a trip to your own tastes, rather than having to follow a tour company's itinerary.

Prices vary wildly so it pays to shop around, but expect to pay in the region of $50 per day for a car, and $90 per day for a jeep or other 4WD, depending on the vehicle's size, age and level of comfort. When

---

THE DOWNSIDE OF OPEN-TOUR THROUGH TICKETS

The majority of travellers opt for one-way through tickets with one of the open-tour companies, which enable you to traverse the whole country with just one ticket. However, this course of action is not without its drawbacks: if you lose your ticket, there's no refund, and if you have the misfortune to choose a bad company, you'll be saddled with them the whole way. In addition, you'll be obliged to stick to your company's daily schedule; buying separate tickets en route will only cost a little more (if anything at all), yet give you far more freedom.

negotiating the price, it's important to clarify exactly who is liable for what. Things to check include who pays for the driver's accommodation and meals, fuel, road and ferry tolls, parking fees and repairs and what happens in the case of a major breakdown. There should then be some sort of contract to sign showing all the details, including an agreed itinerary, especially if you are renting for more than a day; make sure the driver is given a copy in Vietnamese. In some cases you'll have to settle up in advance, though, if possible, it's best if you can arrange to pay roughly half before and the balance at the end.

By motorbike

Motorbike rental is possible in most towns and cities regularly frequented by tourists, and pottering around on one can be an enjoyable and time-efficient method of sightseeing. Lured by the prospect of independent travel at relatively low cost, some tourists cruise the countryside on motorbikes, but inexperienced bikers would do well to think very hard before undertaking any **long-distance biking** since Vietnam's roads can be distinctly dangerous (see box below).

The appalling road discipline of most Vietnamese drivers means that the risk of an accident is very real, with potentially dire conse-quences should it happen in a remote area. Well-equipped hospitals are few and far between outside the major centres, and there'll probably be no ambulance service.

On the other hand, many people ride around with no problems and thoroughly recommend it

for both day-trips and touring. The best biking is to be found in the northern mountains, the central highlands and around the Mekong Delta, while the Ho Chi Minh Highway offers pristine tarmac plus wonderful scenery. Some also do the long haul up Highway 1 from Ho Chi Minh City to Hanoi (or vice versa), a journey of around two weeks, averaging a leisurely 150km per day.

There's no shortage of motorbikes **for rent** in Vietnam's major tourist centres; the average rate is around $7 per day, with discounts for longer periods. You'll sometimes be asked to pay in advance, sign a rental contract and/or leave some form of ID (a photocopy of your passport should suffice). If you're renting for a week or so, you may be asked to leave a deposit, often the bike's value in dollars though it might also be your air ticket or departure card. In the vast majority of cases, this shouldn't be a problem.

Although it's technically illegal for non-residents to own a vehicle, there's a small trade in **second-hand motorbikes** in the two main cities – look at the noticeboards in hotels, travellers' cafés and tour agents for adverts. So far the police have ignored the practice, but check the latest situation before committing yourself. The bike of choice is usually a **Minsk 125cc**, particularly for the mountains; it's sturdy, not too expensive, and the easiest to get repaired outside the main cities.

Whether you're renting or buying, remember to check everything over carefully, especially brakes, lights and horn. Wearing a **helmet** is now a legal requirement, and most rental outlets have helmets you can borrow, sometimes for a small charge, though they may not be top-quality.

RULES OF THE ROAD

There's no discernible method to the madness that passes as a **traffic** system in Vietnam so it's extremely important that you don't stray out onto the roads unless you feel a hundred percent confident about doing so. The theory is that you **drive on the right**, though in practice motorists and cyclists swoop, swerve and dodge wherever they want, using their **horn** as a surrogate indicator and brake. Unless otherwise stated, the **speed limit** is 60kph on highways and 40kph or less in towns.

Right of way invariably goes to the biggest vehicle on the road, which means that motorbikes and bicycles are regularly forced off the highway by thundering trucks or buses; note that overtaking vehicles assume you'll pull over onto the hard shoulder to avoid them. It's wise to use your horn to its maximum and also to avoid being on the road after dark, since many vehicles either don't have functioning headlights or simply don't bother to turn them on.

On the whole the **police** seem to leave foreign riders well alone, and the best policy at roadside checkpoints is just to drive by slowly. However, if you are involved in an **accident** and it was deemed to be your fault, the penalties can involve fairly major fines.

When **parking** your bike, it's advisable to leave it in a parking compound (*gui xe*) – the going rate is from 5000đ for a motorbike and 2000đ for a bicycle – or paying someone to keep an eye on it. If not, you run the risk of it being tampered with.

Note that international driving licences are not valid in Vietnam, but you will need your home **driving licence** and bike registration papers. You also need at least third-party **insurance**, which is available (with the aforementioned documentation) at Bao Viet insurance offices.

Though **road conditions** have improved remarkably in recent years, off the main highways they can still be highly erratic, with pristine asphalt followed by stretches of spine-jarring potholes, and plenty of loose gravel on the sides of the road. **Repair shops** are fairly ubiquitous – ask for *sua chua xe may* (motorbike repairs) – but you should still carry at least a puncture-repair kit, pump and spare spark plug. **Fuel** (*xang*) is cheap and widely available at the roadsides, often from bottles. Finally, try to travel in the company of one or more other bikes in case one of you gets into trouble. And if you want to get off the main highways, it really pays to take a guide.

By bicycle

Cycling is an excellent way of sightseeing around towns, and you shouldn't have to pay more than 50,000đ per day for the privilege, even outside the main tourist centres.

While you can now buy decent Japanese-made bikes in Vietnam, if you decide on a **long-distance cycling** holiday, you should really bring your own bike with you, not forgetting all the necessary spares and tools. Hardy **mountain bikes** cope best with the country's variable surfaces, though tourers and hybrids are fine on the main roads. Bring your own helmet and a good loud bell; a rear-view mirror also comes in handy.

When it all gets too much, or you want to skip between towns, you can always put your bike on the train (though not on all services; check when buying your ticket) for a small fee; take it to the station well ahead of time, where it will be packed and placed in the luggage van. Some open-tour buses will also take bikes – free if it goes in the luggage hold (packed up), otherwise you'll have to pay for an extra seat.

If you want to see Vietnam from the saddle, there are several companies that offer specialist **cycling tours**. In addition to a few of the international tour operators (see p.31), there are local outfits such as Phat Tire (⊕phattireventures.com).

Organized tours

Ever-increasing numbers of tourists are seeing Vietnam through the window of a minibus, on **organized tours**. Ranging from one-day jaunts to two- or three-week trawls upcountry, tours are ideal if you want to acquaint yourself speedily with the highlights of Vietnam; they can also work out much cheaper than car rental. On the other hand, by relying upon tours you'll have little chance to really get to grips with the country and its people, or to enjoy things at your leisure.

Hordes of state-owned and private **tour companies** compete for business – see our lists of well-established agents in Ho Chi Minh City (p.90) and Hanoi (p.373). While a few companies now put together more innovative itineraries, the vast majority offer similar tours. However, it pays to shop around since **prices** vary wildly depending, for example, on how many people there are in a group, the standard of transport, meals and accommodation, whether entry fees are included and so forth.

It's important to check exactly what is included in the price before handing over any cash. It's also a good idea to ask about the maximum number of people on the trip and whether your group will be amalgamated with others if you don't want to be travelling round in a great horde. Bear in mind, as well, that you're far better off dealing directly with the company organizing the tour, rather than going through a hotel or other intermediary. Not only are you more likely to get accurate information about the details of the tour, but you'll also be in a much stronger position should you have cause for complaint.

The other alternative is to set up your own **custom-made tour** by gathering together a group and renting a car, jeep or minibus plus driver (see p.35).

Local transport

In a country with a population so adept at making do with limited resources, it isn't surprising to see the diverse types of **local transport**. While taxis are increasingly common and a number of cities now boast reasonable **bus services**, elsewhere you'll be reliant on a host of two- and three-wheeled vehicles for getting around.

Most common by far are motorbike taxis known as **xe om**. In the cities you'll rarely be able to walk twenty yards without being offered a ride; prices tend to start at around 10,000đ for very short runs, though this goes up after dark (as does the possibility of extortion). At all times the rules of bargaining apply: when haggling, ensure you know which currency you are dealing in (five fingers held up, for instance, could mean 5000đ, 50,000đ or $5), and whether you're negotiating for a single or return trip, and for one passenger or two; it's always best to write the figures down. Should a difference of opinion emerge at the end of a ride, having the exact fare ready to press into an argumentative driver's hand can sometimes resolve matters.

Xe om have almost entirely replaced that quintessential Vietnamese mode of transport, the **cyclo**. These three-wheeled rickshaws comprising a "bucket" seat attached to the front of a bicycle can carry one person, or two people at a push, and are now only really found in tourist areas (though locals use them just as much as foreigners). Prices vary by area, and there are continuous stories of cyclo drivers charging outrageous sums for their services, so to avoid getting badly ripped off, find out first what a reasonable fare might be from your hotel; if the first driver won't agree to your offer, simply walk on and try another.

Taxis are now a common sight on the streets of all major cities. The vast majority are metered (with prices in dong) and fares are not expensive; a short ride within central Hanoi, for example, should cost around 30,000đ. Though standards have been improving with greater competition, some drivers need persuading to use their meters, while others dawdle along as the meter spins suspiciously fast, or take you on an unnecessarily long route. When arriving in a town, beware of drivers who insist the hotel you ask for is closed and want to take you elsewhere; this is usually a commission scam – be firm with your directions. In general, smarterlooking taxis and those waiting outside big hotels tend to be more reliable; the Mai Linh network has by far the best reputation, and you'll see their green cabs all across the land.

Accommodation

The standard of accommodation in Vietnam is, by and large, excellent. In the main tourist areas the range caters to all budgets, and though prices are a little expensive by Southeast Asian standards, the quality is generally quite high. Competition is fierce and with the construction boom still ongoing rooms are being added all the time – great for the traveller, as it keeps prices low and service standards high. There has been a massive increase in the number of luxury resorts along the coast (mainly aimed at the Asian package tour market), while budget travellers and those travelling off the tourist trail will find good budget accommodation throughout the country. Another consequence of the number of new hotels springing up in recent years is that getting **a reservation** is no longer the nightmare it once was, and even among international-class hotels there are some bargains to be had, particularly at weekends; however, booking in advance is a must around the **Tet** festival in early spring (see p.7).

Tourist booth staff at the airports in Ho Chi Minh City and Hanoi will phone to reserve a room for you, and it's increasingly simple to book online. Be wary of asking advice from **cyclo or taxi drivers**, as travellers are often told that their hotel of choice is full or closed. It's also important to note that Vietnam is full of copycat establishments – to avoid being taken to a similarly named hotel, write down the street name and show it to your driver.

Once you've found a hotel, look at a range of rooms before opting for one, as standards can vary hugely within the same establishment. You'll also need to check the bed arrangement, since there are many permutations in Vietnam. A "**single**" room could have a single or twin beds in it, while a "**double**" room could have two, three or four single beds, a double, a single and a double, and so on.

When you **check in** at a Vietnamese hotel or guesthouse, you'll be asked for your **passport**, which is needed for registration with the local authorities. Depending on the establishment, these will be either returned to you the same night, or kept as security until you check out. If you're going to lose sleep over being separated from your passport, say you need it for the bank; many places will accept photocopies of your picture and visa pages. It's normally possible to pay your bill when you leave, although a few budget places ask for payment in advance.

Room **rates** fluctuate according to demand, so it's always worth bargaining – making sure, of course, that it's clear whether both parties are talking per person or per room. Your case will be that much stronger if you are staying several nights.

All hotels charge 10 percent **government tax**, while top-class establishments also add a **service charge** (typically 5 percent). These taxes may or may not be included in the room rate, so check to be sure. Increasingly, **breakfast** is included in the price of all but the cheapest rooms; in budget places it will consist of little more than bread with jam or cheese and a cup of tea or coffee, while those splashing out a little more may be greeted by a gigantic morning buffet. Prices given in the guide are based on those found at the time of writing for the **cheapest double room**. Prices are often quoted in dong, which have been converted to dollars at the rate as it was at the time of going to press. However, because of the extreme volatility of the exchange rate (which can change by hundreds or thousands of dong each week), these prices are subject to constant change.

Although the situation is improving, hotel **security** can be a problem. Never leave valuables lying about in your room and keep documents, travellers' cheques and so forth with you at all times, in a money pouch. While top-end and many mid-range hotels provide safety deposit boxes, elsewhere you can sometimes leave things in a safe or locked drawer at reception; put everything in a sealed envelope and ask for a receipt. In the real cheapies, where the door may only be secured with a padlock, you can increase security by using your own lock.

In some older budget hotels, rooms are cleaned irregularly and badly, and **hygiene** can be a problem, with cockroaches and even rats roaming free; you can at least minimize health risks by not bringing foodstuffs or sugary drinks into your room.

Pretty much any guesthouse or hotel will offer a **laundry** service, and Western-style laundry and dry-cleaning services are widely available in Hanoi, Ho Chi Minh City and other major cities. Washing is often given a rigorous scrubbing by hand, so don't submit anything delicate.

Finally, **prostitution** is rife in Vietnam, and in less reputable hotels it's not unknown for Western men to be called upon, or even phoned from other rooms, during the night.

Types of accommodation

Grading accommodation isn't a simple matter in Vietnam. The names used (guesthouse, mini-hotel, hotel and so on) can rarely be relied upon to indicate what's on offer, and there are broad overlaps in standards. Vietnam's older hotels tend to be austere, state-owned edifices styled upon unlovely Eastern European models, while many private mini-hotels make a real effort. Some hotels cover all bases by having a range of rooms, from simple fan-cooled rooms with cold water, right up to cheerful air-conditioned accommodation with satellite TV, fridge and mini-bar. As a rule of thumb, the newer a place is, the better value it's likely to represent in terms of comfort, hygiene and all-round appeal.

There are a burgeoning number of **"resorts"** appearing across the country. In contrast to the Western image of an all-inclusive complex, in Vietnam these are simply hotels, usually with pretty landscaped gardens, located on the beach or in the countryside. All that's included in the rate is breakfast, though it is possible to eat all your meals here.

Budget accommodation

The very cheapest form of accommodation in Vietnam is a bed in a **dormitory**, though as yet, very few cities have such facilities – there are dedicated hostels in Hanoi, Ho Chi Minh City and Hué, where you can expect to pay from about $6 for a bed, sharing common facilities. Do note that though most of these have private rooms, you'll pay less elsewhere. In the two main cities there are also a fair few budget guesthouses equipped with "backpacker" dorms – you'll generally find these around the De Tham enclave in Ho Chi Minh City, and the Old Quarter in Hanoi (see the respective chapters for more). In Hanoi there is also a small network of **youth hostels** fully accredited by Hostelling International (Ⓦhihostels.com); you'll need a current Youth Hostel card, which you can buy when checking in.

If you prefer your own privacy, you'll find simple fan rooms in either a guesthouse or **hotel** (*khach san*), with prices starting at around $10; these are likely to be en suite, although you might not get hot water at this price level in the warmer south. Add air-conditioning, satellite TV and slightly better furnishings, maybe even a window, and you'll be paying up to $20. Upgrading to $20–30 will get you a larger room with better-standard fittings, usually including a fridge and bathtub, and possibly a balcony. Note that while many hotels advertise satellite TV, which channels you actually get varies wildly, let alone the quality of reception, so check first if it matters to you.

Mid- and upper-range accommodation

For upwards of $30 per room per night, accommodation can begin to get quite rosy. Rooms at this level will be comfortable, reasonably spacious and well appointed with decent furniture, air-conditioning, hot water, fridge, phone and satellite TV in all but the most remote areas.

Paying $30–75 will get you a room in a **mid-range hotel** of some repute, with in-house restaurant and bar, booking office, room service and so on. At the **top of the range** the sky's the limit. Most of the international-class hotels are located in the two major cities, which also have some reasonably charismatic places to stay, such as the *Metropole* in Hanoi and Ho Chi Minh's *Continental*. However, in recent years developers have targeted Nha Trang, Hoi An, Da Nang and Ha Long City, all of which now boast upmarket resort hotels. Off the main trail, there's usually one or two upper-range hotels in each main city, though very few exist in the countryside.

Village accommodation and camping

As Vietnam's minority communities have become more exposed to tourism, staying in stilthouses or other **village accommodation** has become more feasible.

In the north of the country, notably around Sa Pa and in the Mai Chau Valley, you can either take one of the tours out of Hanoi which includes a home-stay in one of the **minority villages**, or make your own arrangements when you get there (see p.400). In the central highlands, the Pleiku and Kon Tum tourist offices can also arrange a stilthouse home-stay for you.

Accommodation usually consists of a mattress on the floor in a communal room. Those villages more used to tourists normally provide a blanket and mosquito net, but it's advisable to take your own net and sleeping bag to be on the safe side, particularly as nights get pretty cold in the mountains. Prices in the villages vary from $5–15 per person per night, depending on the area and whether meals are included.

Where boat trips operate in the Mekong Delta, notably around Vinh Long, tour operators in Ho Chi Minh City or the local tourist board can arrange for visitors to stay with owners of **fruit orchards**, allowing a close-up view of rural life (see box, p.132).

Virtually no provisions exist in Vietnam for **camping** at the present time. The exceptions are at Nha Trang and Mui Ne, where some guesthouses offer tents for a few dollars a night when all rooms are full. Some tour companies also offer camping as an option when visiting Ha Long Bay (see pp.334–335).

Food and drink

Internationally speaking, Thai food may be the most heralded of all the Southeast Asian cuisines, but true connoisseurs would go for Vietnamese every time. Light, subtle in flavour and astonishing in their variety, Vietnamese dishes are boiled or steamed rather than stir-fried, and a huge emphasis is placed on herbs and seasoning – no great surprise in this land of diverse climates.

In the south, **Indian** and **Thai** influences add curries and spices to the menu, while other regions have evolved their own array of specialities, most notably the foods of Hué and Hoi An. Buddhism introduced a **vegetarian** tradition to Vietnam, while much later the **French** brought with them bread, dairy products, pastries and the whole café culture (see p.95). Hanoi, Ho Chi Minh City and the major tourist centres are now well provided with everything from street hawkers to hotel and Western-style restaurants, and even ice-cream parlours; in such places, you'll also find a few restaurants putting on **cooking classes**.

The quality and variety of food is generally better in the main towns than off the beaten track, where restaurants of any sort are few and far between. That said, you'll never go hungry; even in the back of beyond, there's always some stall selling a noodle soup or rice platter and plenty of fruit to fill up on.

Vietnam's national **drink** is green tea, which is the accompaniment to every social gathering or business meeting and is frequently drunk after meals. At the harder end of the spectrum, there's also **rice wine**, though some local **beer** is also excellent, and an increasingly wide range of imported **wines** and **spirits**. This guide includes a glossary of **food and drink terms** (see p.500).

Where to eat

Broadly speaking, there are two types of eating establishment to choose from. One step up from **hawkers** peddling their dish of the day from shoulder poles or handcarts are **street kitchens** – inexpensive joints aimed at locals. More formal, **Western-style restaurants** come in many shapes and sizes, from simple places serving unpretentious Vietnamese meals to top-class establishments offering high quality Vietnamese specialities and international cuisine.

Throughout the Guide we've given phone numbers for those restaurants where it's advisable to make **reservations**. While most eating establishments stay open throughout the year, some close over Tet (see p.50). The Vietnamese **eat early**: outside the major cities and tourist areas; food stalls and street kitchens rarely stay open beyond 8pm and may close even earlier, though they do stay open later in the south, especially in Ho Chi Minh

City. You'll need to brush up your **chopstick-handling** skills, too, although other utensils are always available in places frequented by tourists – in Western-style restaurants you won't be expected to tackle your *steak-frites* with chopsticks.

When it comes to **paying**, the normal sign language will be readily understood in most restaurants. In street kitchens you pay as you leave – either proffer a few thousand dong to signal your intentions, or ask *bao nhieu tien?* ("how much is it?"). As with accommodation, **prices** are listed in dollars throughout the guide but exchange rates may be wildly different by the time you travel and the smaller, local establishments often prefer to be paid in dong.

Street kitchens

Eating on the street may not be to every visitor's taste, but those willing to take the plunge usually put it up among their favourite experiences in the country – the food is often better in quality to that found at restaurants, it's much cheaper, and a whole lot more fun. **Street kitchens** range from makeshift food stalls, set up on the street round a cluster of pint-size stools, to eating houses where, as often as not, the cooking is still done on the street but you either sit in an open-fronted dining area or join the overspill outside. Both tend to have fixed locations, though only the eating houses will have an address – which usually doubles as their name. Some places stay open all day (7am–8pm), while many close once they've run out of ingredients and others only open at lunchtime (10.30am–2pm). To be sure of the widest choice and freshest food, it pays to get there early (as early as 11.30am at lunchtime, and by 7pm in the evening), and note that the best places will be packed around noon.

Most specialize in one type of food, generally indicated (in Vietnamese only) on a signboard outside, or offer the ubiquitous com (rice dishes) and pho (noodle soups). Com binh dan, "people's meals", are also popular. Here you select from an array of prepared dishes displayed in a glass cabinet or on a buffet table, piling your plate with such things as stuffed tomatoes, fried fish, tofu, pickles or eggs, plus a helping of rice; expect to pay from around 25,000đ for a good plateful. Though it's not a major problem at these prices, some street kitchens overcharge, so double-check when ordering.

Though eating street food is highly recommended, it's worth using a bit of judicious selection – look for places with a fast turnover, where the ingredients are obviously fresh. A bit of basic vocabulary will certainly help (see p.500).

In a similar vein to street kitchens are **bia hoi outlets** (see box, p.44). Though these are primarily drinking establishments, many provide good-value snacks or even main meals.

Restaurants

If you're after more relaxed dining, where people aren't queuing for your seat, then head for a Western-style **Vietnamese restaurant** (*nha hang*), which will have chairs rather than stools, a name, a menu and will often be closed to the street. In general these places serve a more varied selection of Vietnamese dishes than the street kitchens, plus a smattering of international – generally European – dishes.

Menus at this level usually show prices, particularly in areas popular with tourists. If there are no prices on your menu, confirm them with staff before you start eating to avoid any potential overcharging issues. Prices vary considerably depending upon what you order, but you'll get a modest meal for less than $5 per head. **Opening hours** at such places are usually from 10.30am to 2pm for lunch, and in the evening from 5pm to no later than 9pm, or 8pm in the north.

In the main tourist haunts, you'll find cheap and cheerful **cafés** aimed at the backpacker market and serving often mediocre Western and Vietnamese dishes – from burgers and banana pancakes to spring rolls, noodles and other Vietnamese standards. They have the advantage, however, of **all-day opening**, usually from 7am to 11pm or midnight. And, should you crave a reasonably priced Western-style breakfast, fresh fruit salad or a mango shake, these are the places to go.

As you move up the price scale, the decor and the cuisine become more sophisticated and the menu more varied. The more **expensive restaurants** (including the smarter hotel dining rooms) tend to stay open later in the evening, perhaps until 9.30pm or 10.30pm. Some have menus priced in dollars, and more and more accept credit cards. Usually menus indicate if there's a service charge, but watch out for an additional 3–4 percent on credit card payments. These restaurants can be relatively fancy places, with at least a nod towards decor and ambience, and correspondingly higher prices (a meal for two is likely to cost at least $20 and often much more).

The most popular **foreign cuisine** on offer is French, though both Hanoi and Ho Chi Minh City boast some pretty good international restaurants, including Thai, Chinese, Tex Mex, Indian and Italian.

BREAKFAST

Vietnamese traditionally breakfast on pho or some other noodle soup, reasoning that these provide enough energy to get through the day; many an expat has come around to this way of thinking. You may also find early-morning hawkers peddling *xoi*, a wholesome mix of steamed **sticky rice** with soya bean, sweet corn or peanuts. Simple **Western breakfasts** (such as bread with jam, cheese or eggs and coffee) are usually available in backpacker cafés or hotels. More upmarket places increasingly stretch to cereals and fresh milk, while some top-class hotels (and a whole bunch of cheaper ones) lay on the full works in their breakfast buffets. In towns, you could always buy jam and bread or croissants for a **do-it-yourself** breakfast.

You'll find these international cuisines, and upper-class Vietnamese restaurants, in Hanoi, Ho Chi Minh City, Hué, Da Nang, Hoi An and Nha Trang, though they're scarce in the rest of the country.

Vietnamese food

The staple of Vietnamese meals is **rice**, with noodles a popular alternative at breakfast or as a snack. Typically, rice will be accompanied by a fish or meat dish, a vegetable dish and soup, followed by a green tea digestive. **Seafood and fish** – from rivers, lakes, canals and paddy fields as well as the sea – are favoured throughout the country, either fresh or dried. The most commonly used **flavourings** are shallots, coriander and lemon grass. Ginger, saffron, mint, anise and a basil-type herb also feature strongly, and coconut milk gives some southern dishes a distinctive richness.

Even in the south, Vietnamese food tends not to be over-spicy; instead chilli sauces or fresh chillies are served separately. Vietnam's most famous seasoning is the ubiquitous **nuoc mam**, a nutrient-packed sauce which either is added during cooking or forms the base for various dipping sauces. *Nuoc mam* is made by fermenting huge quantities of fish in vats of salt for between six months and a year, after which the dark brown liquid is strained and graded according to its age and flavour. Foreigners usually find the smell of the sauce pretty rank, but most soon acquire a taste for its distinctive salty-sweetness.

The use of **monosodium glutamate** (MSG) can be excessive, especially in northern cooking, and some people are known to react badly to the seasoning. A few restaurants in the main cities have cottoned on to the foibles of foreigners and advertise MSG-free food; elsewhere, try saying *khong co my chinh* (without MSG), and keep your fingers crossed. Note that what looks like salt on the table is sometimes MSG, so taste it first.

The most famous Vietnamese dish has to be **spring rolls**, variously known as *cha gio, cha nem, nem ran* or just plain *nem*. Various combinations of minced pork, shrimp or crab, rice vermicelli, onions, bean sprouts and an edible fungus are rolled in rice-paper wrappers, and then eaten fresh or deep-fried. In some places they're served with a bowl of lettuce and/or mint. In addition, a southern variation has barbecued strips of pork wrapped in semi-transparent rice wrappers, along with raw ingredients such as green banana and star fruit, and then dunked in a rich peanut sauce – every bit as tasty as it sounds.

Soups and noodles

Though it originated in the north, another dish you'll find throughout Vietnam is pho (pronounced as the British say "fur"), a noodle **soup** eaten at any time of day but primarily at breakfast. The basic bowl of pho consists of a light beef broth, flavoured with ginger, coriander and sometimes cinnamon, to which are added broad, flat rice-noodles, spring onions and slivers of chicken, pork or beef. At the table you add a squeeze of lime and a sprinkling of chilli flakes or a spoonful of chilli sauce.

Countless other types of soup are dished up at street restaurants. *Bun bo* is another substantial beef and noodle soup eaten countrywide, though most famous in Hué; in the south, *hu tieu*, a soup of vermicelli, pork and seafood noodles, is best taken in My Tho. *Chao* (or *xhao*), on the other hand, is a thick rice gruel served piping hot, usually with shredded chicken or filleted fish, flavoured with dill and with perhaps a raw egg cooking at the bottom; it's often served with fried breadsticks (*quay*). Sour soups are a popular accompaniment for fish, while *lau*, a standard in local restaurants, is more of a main meal than a soup, where the vegetable broth arrives at the table in a steamboat (a ring-shaped metal dish on live coals or, nowadays, often electrically heated). You cook slivers of beef, prawns or similar in the simmering soup, and then drink the flavourful liquid that's left in the cooking pot.

Fish and meat

Among the highlights of Vietnamese cuisine are its succulent **seafood** and freshwater **fish**. *Cha ca* is the most famous of these dishes: white fish sauteed in butter at the table with dill and spring onions, then served with rice noodles and a sprinkling of peanuts; invented in Hanoi, it's now found in most upmarket restaurants. Another dish found in more expensive restaurants is *chao tom* (or *tom bao mia*), consisting of savoury shrimp pate wrapped round sweet sugar cane and fried. *Ca kho to*, fish stew cooked in a clay pot, is a southern speciality.

Every conceivable type of meat and part of the animal anatomy finds itself on the Vietnamese dining table, though the staples are straightforward beef, chicken and pork. **Ground meat**, especially pork, is a common constituent of stuffings, for example in spring rolls or the similar *banh cuon*, a steamed, rice-flour "ravioli" filled with minced pork, black mushrooms and bean sprouts; a popular variation uses prawns instead of meat. Pork is also used, with plenty of herbs, to make Hanoi's *bun cha*, small **hamburgers** barbecued on an open charcoal brazier and served on a bed of cold rice-noodles with greens and a slightly sweetish sauce. One famous southern dish is *bo bay mon* (often written *bo 7 mon*), meaning literally **beef** seven ways, consisting of a platter of beef cooked in different styles.

Roving gourmets may want to try some of the more unusual meats on offer. **Dog** meat (*thit cay* or *thit cho*) is a particular delicacy in the north, where "yellow" dogs (sandy-haired varieties) are considered the tastiest. Winter is the season to eat dog meat – it's said to give extra body heat, and is also supposed to remove bad luck if consumed at the end of the lunar month. **Snake** (*thit con ran*), like dog, is supposed to improve male virility. Dining on snake is surrounded by a ritual, which, if you're guest of honour, requires you to swallow the still-beating heart. Another one strictly for the strong of stomach is *trung vit lon*, embryo-containing **duck eggs** boiled and eaten only five days before hatching – bill, webbed feet, feathers and all.

Vegetables – and vegetarian food

If all this has put you off meat for ever, it is possible to eat **vegetarian** food in Vietnam, though not always easy. The widest selection of vegetables is to be found in Da Lat where a staggering variety of tropical and temperate crops thrive. Elsewhere, most restaurants offer a smattering of meat-free dishes, from stewed spinach or similar greens, to a more appetizing mix of onion, tomato, bean sprouts, various mushrooms, peppers and so on;

places used to foreigners may be able to oblige with vegetarian spring rolls (*nem an chay* or *nem khong co thit*). At street kitchens you're likely to find tofu and one or two dishes of pickled vegetables, such as cabbage or cucumber, while occasionally they may also have aubergine, bamboo shoots or avocado, depending on the season.

However, unless you go to a **specialist** vegetarian outlet – of which there are some excellent examples in Ho Chi Minh City, Hanoi and Hué – it can be a problem finding genuine veggie food: soups are usually made with beef stock, morsels of pork fat sneak into otherwise innocuous-looking dishes and animal fat tends to be used for frying.

The phrase to remember is *an chay* (vegetarian), or seek out a vegetarian rice shop (*tiem com chay*). Otherwise, make the most of the first and fifteenth days of the lunar month when many Vietnamese Buddhists spurn meat and you're more likely to find vegetarian dishes on offer.

Snacks

Vietnam has a wide range of snacks and nibbles to fill any yawning gaps, from huge rice-flour **crackers** sprinkled with sesame seeds to all sorts of dried fish, nuts and seeds. *Banh bao* are white, steamed **dumplings** filled with tasty titbits, such as pork, onions and tangy mushrooms or strands of sweet coconut. *Banh xeo*, meaning sizzling **pancake**, combines shrimp, pork, bean sprouts and egg, all fried and then wrapped in rice paper with a selection of greens before being dunked in a spicy sauce. A similar dish, originating from Hué – a city with a vast repertoire of snack foods (see box, p.290) – is *banh khoai*, in which the flat pancake is accompanied by a plate of star fruit, green banana and aromatic herbs, plus a rich peanut sauce.

Markets are often good snacking grounds, with stalls churning out soups and spring rolls or selling intriguing banana-leaf parcels of pate (a favourite accompaniment for bia hoi), pickled pork sausage or perhaps a cake of sticky rice.

A relative newcomer on the culinary scene is French **bread**, made with wheat flour in the north and rice flour in the south. Baguettes – sometimes sold warm from streetside stoves – are sliced open and stuffed with pate, soft cheese or ham and pickled vegetables.

Fruit

With its diverse climate, Vietnam is blessed with both tropical and temperate **fruits**, including dozens of banana species. The richest orchards are in the south, where pineapple, coconut, papaya,

BIA HOI KNOW-HOW

There are countless **bia hoi** (draught beer) outlets in most major cities in Vietnam, ranging from a few ankle-high stools gathered round a barrel on the pavement to beer gardens. Quality tends to be more consistent at the larger outlets supplied by major breweries such as Hanoi Beer and Halida (under the name Viet Ha), rather than the smaller places which usually buy their beer from microbreweries. On the whole, the more expensive – and colder – the beer, the better it is.

Bia hoi culture is about enjoying a few beers with a group of friends – usually all male, though in the cities you see a few women these days. People almost never drink alone and rarely drink without eating, so many places serve a range of snacks and more extensive dishes.

To help you order food in a bia hoi outlet, we've listed a few classic dishes below. Menus, if they exist, will be in Vietnamese. They normally give a price range for each dish (meat dishes typically range between 30,000đ and 50,000đ), so you order a small, medium or large amount, for example, depending on the size of your group. To maximize the variety, it makes sense to order small quantities of several dishes and share. If no prices are indicated on the menu, be sure to ask when ordering. Usually a note with the running total is left on the table, so you can keep track of how much you're spending.

bo luc lac	cubed spicy beef and green pepper stir-fry
ca bo lo	oven-cooked fish
dau chien ron	fried tofu
dau tu xuyen	tofu in a Chinese pork and tomato sauce
de tai chanh	lightly cooked goat with green banana, pineapple and lemon
dua chuot che	sliced cucumber
ech chien bo	deep-fried battered frogs' legs
ech xao mang	frogs' legs with bamboo shoots
ga xe phay	shredded chicken salad with bean peanuts and basil
khoai tay ran	chips/French fries
lac	peanuts
muc chien bo	squid fried in butter
muc kho	dried squid
muc tam bot	battered squid
nem chua	minced spicy cured pork wrapped in banana leaf
nom du du	papaya salad
nom hoa chuoi	banana-flower salad
nom ngo sen	lotus-stem salad
oc xao xa ot	stir-fried snail, lemongrass and chilli
rau bi xaoi	beef/pumpkin
bo/toi	leaf fried with garlic
tho quay	roast rabbit
tom hap bia	shrimps steamed in beer
tom nuong	grilled shrimps

mango, longan and mangosteen flourish. Da Lat is famous for its strawberries, while the region around Nha Trang produces the peculiar "dragon fruit" (*thanh long*). The size and shape of a small pineapple, the dragon fruit has skin of shocking pink, studded with small protuberances, and smooth, white flesh speckled with tiny black seeds. The slightly sweet, watery flesh is thirst-quenching, and so is often served as a drink, crushed with ice.

A fruit that is definitely an acquired taste is the durian, a spiky, yellow-green football-sized fruit with an unmistakably pungent odour reminiscent of mature cheese and caramel, but tasting like an onion-laced custard. Jackfruit looks worryingly similar to durian but is larger and has smaller spikes. Its yellow segments of flesh are deliciously sweet.

Sweet things

Vietnam is not strong on desserts – restaurants usually stick to ice cream and fruit, although fancier international places might venture into tiramisu territory. Those with a sweet tooth are better off hunting down a bakery – there'll be one within walking distance in any urban area – or browsing around street stalls where there are usually candied fruits and other Vietnamese **sweetmeats** on offer, as well as sugary displays of French-inspired cakes and pastries in the main tourist centres.

Green-coloured *banh com* is an eye-catching local delicacy made by wrapping pounded glutinous rice around sugary, green-bean paste. A similar confection, found only during the mid-autumn festival, is the "earth cake", *banh deo*, which melds the contrasting flavours of candied fruits, sesame and lotus seeds with a dice of savoury pork fat. **Fritters** are popular among children and you'll find opportunistic hawkers outside schools, selling *banh chuoi* (banana fritters) and *banh chuoi khoai* (mixed slices of banana and sweet potato).

Most cities now have **ice-cream** parlours selling tubs or sticks of the local, hard ices in chocolate, vanilla or green-tea flavours, though it's prudent to buy only from the larger, busier outlets and not from street hawkers. More exotic tastes can be satisfied at the European- and American-style ice-cream parlours of Hanoi and Ho Chi Minh City, while excellent yoghurts are also increasingly available at ice-cream parlours, and even some restaurants.

Drinks

Giai khat means "quench your thirst" and you'll see the signs everywhere, on stands selling fresh juices, bottled cold drinks or outside cafés and bia hoi (draught beer) outlets. Many drinks are served with ice: tempting though it may be, the only really safe policy is to avoid **ice** altogether – *dung bo da, cam on* ("no ice, thanks") should do the trick. That said, ice in the top hotels, bars and restaurants is generally reliable, and some people take the risk in less salubrious establishments with apparent impunity.

Water and soft drinks

Tap water is not safe to drink in Vietnam – since bottled **water** is both cheap and widely available, you shouldn't need to take the risk anyway. Avoid drinks with ice (see above) or those that may have been diluted with suspect water (see box, p.59).

Locally made **soft drinks** are tooth-numbingly sweet, but are cheap and safe – as long as the bottle or carton appears well sealed – and on sale just about everywhere. The Coke, Sprite and Fanta hegemony also means you can find fizzy drinks in surprisingly remote areas. Oddly, canned drinks are usually more expensive than the equivalent-sized bottle, whether it's a soft drink or beer – apparently it's less chic to drink from the old-fashioned bottle.

A more effective thirst-quencher is fresh coconut juice, though this is more difficult to find in the north. Fresh juices such as orange and lime are also delicious – just make sure they haven't been mixed with tap water. Sugar-cane juice (*mia da*) is safer, since it's pressed right in front of you. Pasteurized milk, produced by Vinamilk, is now sold in the main towns and cities.

Somewhere between a drink and a snack, **ché** is made from taro flour and green bean, and served over ice with chunks of fruit, coloured jellies and even sweet corn or potato. In hot weather it provides a refreshing sugar-fix.

A TRADITIONAL TIPPLE

While beer and imported spirits are drunk throughout Vietnam, the traditional tipple is **ruou can**, or rice-distilled liquor. Until recently, *ruou can* was regarded as decidedly downmarket, the preserve of labourers, farmers and ethnic minorities. Nowadays, however, it's becoming popular among the middle class and especially young urban sophisticates – including a growing number of women – as city-centre bars and restaurants begin to offer better quality *ruou can*.

Recipes for *ruou can* are a closely guarded secret, but its basic constituents are regular or glutinous rice, the latter of which is said to be more aromatic and have a fuller, smoother taste. Selected herbs and fruits are sometimes steeped in the liquor to enhance its flavour and, supposedly, to add all sorts of medicinal and health benefits. You'll also see jars containing snakes, geckos and even whole crows. Traditionally, the basic ingredients are heated together and buried in the ground for a month or more to ferment. Nowadays, more modern – and hygienic – techniques are used to produce *ruou can* for general consumption. Look out for the high-quality rice-distilled liquors marketed under the Son Tinh brand (Ⓦ sontinh.com).

The **ethnic minorities** of the northwest (Thai and Muong) concoct their own home-distilled *ruou can*, sometimes known as stem alcohol. Visitors are often invited to gather round the communal jar to drink the liquor through thin, bamboo straws. In more traditional villages it's regarded as a sacred ritual, which it would be an insult to refuse. You will hear the toast *Chuc suc khoe* (your health) and, for more serious drinking sessions, *Tram phan tram* (down in one)!

Tea and coffee

Tea drinking is part of the social ritual in Vietnam. Small cups of refreshing, strong, green tea are presented to all guests or visitors: water is well boiled and safe to drink, as long as the cup itself is clean, and it's considered rude not to take at least a sip. Although your cup will be continually replenished to show hospitality, you don't have to carry on drinking; the polite way to decline a refill is to place your hand over the cup when your host is about to replenish it. Green tea is also served at the end of every restaurant meal, particularly in the south, and usually provided free.

Coffee production has boomed in recent years, largely for export, with serious environmental and social consequences. The Vietnamese drink coffee very strong and in small quantities, with a large dollop of condensed milk at the bottom of the cup. Traditionally, coffee is filtered at the table by means of a small dripper balanced over the cup or glass, which sometimes sits in a bowl of hot water to keep it warm. However, places accustomed to tourists increasingly run to fresh (pasteurized) milk, while in the main cities you'll now find fancy Western-style cafés turning out decent lattes and cappuccinos. Highland Coffee has become Vietnam's very own Starbucks-style chain, while out in the sticks you're best off going for cafés with a Trung Nguyen sign.

Alcoholic drinks

In Vietnam, drinking alcohol is a social activity to be shared with friends. You'll rarely see the Vietnamese drinking alone and never without eating. Be prepared for lots of toasts to health, wealth and happiness, and no doubt to international understanding, too. It's the custom to fill the glasses of your fellow guests; someone else will fill yours.

Canned and **bottled beers** brewed under licence in Vietnam include Tiger, Heineken, Carlsberg and San Miguel, but there are also plenty of very drinkable – and cheaper – local beers around, such as Halida, 333 (Ba Ba Ba) and Bivina. Some connoisseurs rate Bière la Rue from Da Nang tops, though Saigon Export, Hanoi Beer and BGI are also fine brews. Many other towns boast their own local beers, such as Hué (where the main brand is Huda), Hai Phong and Thanh Hoa (where it's simply named after the town) – all worth a try.

Roughly forty years ago technology for making **bia hoi** (draught beer) was introduced from Czechoslovakia and it is now quaffed in vast quantities, particularly in the north. Bia hoi may taste fairly weak, but it measures in at up to four percent alcohol. It's also ridiculously cheap – between 2500đ and 5000đ a glass – and supposedly unadulterated with chemicals, so in theory you're less likely to get a hangover. Bia hoi has a 24-hour shelf life, which means the better places sell out by early evening, and that you're unlikely to be drinking it into the wee hours. In the south, you're more likely to be drinking **bia tuoi** ("fresh" beer), a close relation of bia hoi but served from pressurized barrels. Outlets are usually open at lunchtime, and then again in the evening from 5pm to 9pm.

Wine (the conventional kind) is becoming increasingly popular in Vietnam – even in small towns, you'll easily track some down, and imported bottles continue to crop up in the most unexpected places. Local production dates from the French era, and is centred around Da Lat – the main producer is Vang Da Lat, bottles of which will cost from 50,000đ in a shop, and 70,000đ at a restaurant. Only at top hotels, restaurants or specialist shops will you find decent imported bottles that have been properly stored; you'll be paying premium prices for these.

The media

Vietnam has several English–language newspapers and magazines, of which the daily *Viet Nam News* (⬦http://vietnam news.vnagency.com.vn) has the widest distribution. It provides a brief – and very select – run–down of local, regional and international news, as well as snippets on art and culture. Though short on general news, both the weekly *Vietnam Investment Review* (⬦vir.com.vn) and the monthly *Vietnam Economic Times* (⬦http://news.vneconomy.vn) cover issues in greater depth and are worth looking at for an insight into what makes the Vietnamese economy tick. Both also publish useful supplements (*Time Out* and *The Guide* respectively) with selective but up–to–date restaurant and nightlife listings mainly covering Hanoi and Ho Chi Minh City, plus feature articles on culture and tourist destinations. However, they have been superceded by the excellent free magazines The Word and AsiaLife, which both carry listings of bars and restaurants as well as articles on aspects of Vietnamese culture; look out for them in establishments that advertise in these publications.

All media in Vietnam are under tight government control. There is, however, a slight glimmer of less draconian censorship, with an increasing number of stories covering corruption at even quite senior levels and more criticism of government policies and ministers, albeit very mild by Western standards.

Foreign publications, such as the *International Herald Tribune, Time, Newsweek, The Financial Times* and the *Bangkok Post* are sold by street vendors and at some of the larger bookshops and in the newsstands of more upmarket hotels in Ho Chi Minh City (see pp.92–96) and Hanoi (see pp.375–378).

The government **radio** station, Voice of Vietnam (Ⓦhttp://english.vovnews.vn), began life in 1945 during the August Revolution. It became famous during the American War when "Hanoi Hannah" broadcast propaganda programmes to American GIs. Nowadays it maintains six channels, of which VOV5 broadcasts English-language programmes several times a day covering a whole range of subjects: news, weather, sport, entertainment and culture, even market prices. You can pick up the broadcasts on FM in and around Hanoi and Ho Chi Minh City.

To keep in touch with the full spectrum of international news, however, you'll need to go online or get a short wave radio to pick up one of the world service channels, such as **BBC** World Service (Ⓦbbc.co.uk/worldservice), **Radio Canada International** (Ⓦrcinet.ca) and **Voice of America** (Ⓦvoanews.com); local frequencies are listed on the relevant website.

Vietnamese **television** (VTV, Ⓦvtv.gov.vn) is also government-run and airs a mix of films, music shows, news programmes, soaps, sport and foreign (mostly American, Korean and Japanese) imports. VTV1, the main domestic channel, occasionally presents a news summary in English. However, most hotels provide satellite TV, offering BBC, CNN, MTV and HBO as standard.

Crime and personal safety

Vietnam is a relatively safe country for visitors, including women travelling alone. In fact, given the country's recent history, many tourists, particularly Americans, are pleasantly surprised at the warm reception that foreign travellers receive. That said, petty crime is on the rise – though it's still relatively small-scale and shouldn't be a problem if you

take common-sense precautions. Generally, the hassles you'll encounter will be the milder sort of coping with pushy vendors and over-enthusiastic touts and beggars.

Petty crime

As a tourist, you're an obvious target for thieves (who may include your fellow travellers): carry your passport, travellers' cheques and other valuables in a concealed **money belt**. Don't leave anything important lying about in your room: use a safe, if you have one. A cable lock, or **padlock** and chain, comes in handy for doors and windows in cheap hotels, and is useful for securing your pack on trains and buses. It's not a bad idea to keep $100 or so separate from the rest of your cash, along with insurance policy details and photocopies of important documents, such as the relevant pages of your passport including your visa stamp.

At street level it's best not to be ostentatious: forego eye-catching jewellery and flashy watches, try to be discreet when taking out your cash, and be particularly wary in **crowds** and on **public transport**. If your pack is on the top of the bus, make sure it's attached securely (usually everything is tied down with ropes) and keep an eye on it during the most vulnerable times – before departure, at meal stops and on arrival at your destination. On trains, either cable-lock your pack or put it under the bottom bench-seat, out of public view. The odd instance has been reported of travellers being drugged and then robbed, so it's best not to accept food or drink from anyone you don't know and trust. Bear in mind that when walking or riding in a cyclo you are vulnerable to moped-borne **snatch-thieves**; don't wear cameras or expensive sunglasses hanging round your neck and keep a firm grip on your bags. If you do become a target, however, it's best to let go rather than risk being pulled into the traffic and suffering serious injury.

The place you are most likely to encounter street crime is in Ho Chi Minh City, which has a fairly bad reputation for bag-snatchers, pickpockets and con artists. Be wary of innocent-looking kids and grannies who may be acting as decoys for thieves – especially in the bar districts and other popular tourist hangouts. It's best to avoid taking a cyclo at night, and you'd be unwise to walk alone at any time outside Districts One and Three.

Petty crime, much of it drug- and prostitution-related, is also a problem in Nha Trang, where you should watch your belongings at all times on the beach. Again, be wary of taking a cyclo after dark and women should avoid walking alone at night. Single males, on the other hand, are a particular target for "taxi girls", many of whom also double as thieves.

It's important not to get paranoid, however: crime levels in Vietnam are still a long way behind those of Western countries, and violent crime against tourists is extremely rare.

If you do have anything stolen, you'll need to go to the nearest **police** station to make a report in order to claim on your insurance. Try to recruit an English-speaker to come along with you – someone at your hotel should be able to help.

"Social evils" and serious crime

Since liberalization and *doi moi*, Vietnamese society has seen an increase in prostitution, drugs – including hard drugs – and more serious crimes. These so-called "**social evils**" are viewed as a direct consequence of reduced controls on society and ensuing Westernization. The police have imposed midnight closing on bars and clubs for several years now, mainly because of drugs, but also to curb general rowdiness, although you'll always find the occasional bar that somehow manages to keep serving, particularly around De Tham in Ho Chi Minh City. That apart, the campaign against social evils should have little effect on most foreign tourists.

Single Western males tend to get solicited by **prostitutes** in cheap provincial and seaside hotels, though more commonly by women cruising on motorbikes. Quite apart from any higher moral considerations, bear in mind that AIDS is a serious problem in Vietnam, though the epidemic has shown signs of stabilizing.

Finally, having anything to do with **drugs** in Vietnam is extremely unwise. At night there's a fair amount of drug selling on the streets of Ho Chi Minh City, Hanoi, Nha Trang and even Sa Pa, and it's not unknown for dealers to turn buyers in to the

EMERGENCY PHONE NUMBERS

The following numbers apply throughout Vietnam. If possible, get a Vietnamese-speaker to call on your behalf.
Police ☎ 113
Fire ☎ 114
Ambulance ☎ 115

police. Fines and jail sentences are imposed for lesser offences, while the death penalty is regularly imposed for possessing, trading or smuggling larger quantities.

Military and political hazards

Not surprisingly, the Vietnamese authorities are sensitive about **military installations** and strategic areas – including border regions, military camps (of which there are many), bridges, airports, naval dockyards and even train stations. Anyone taking photographs in the vicinity of such sites risks having the memory card removed from their camera or being fined.

Unexploded ordnance from past conflicts still poses a threat in some areas: the problem is most acute in the Demilitarized Zone, where each year a number of local farmers, scrap-metal scavengers or children are killed or injured. Wherever you are, stick to well-trodden paths and never touch any shells or half-buried chunks of metal.

Beggars, hassle and scams

Given the number of disabled, war-wounded and unemployed in Vietnam, there are surprisingly few **beggars** around. Most people are actually trying hard to earn a living somehow, and many day-tours include a visit to a factory that employs disabled workers to produce handicrafts or local products.

At many tourist spots, you may well be swamped by a gaggle of children or teenagers selling cold drinks, fruit and chewing gum. Although they can sometimes be a bit overwhelming, as often as not they're just out to practise their English and be entertained for a while. They may even turn out to be excellent guides, in which case it's only fair that you buy something from them in return.

A common **scam** among taxi drivers is to tell new arrivals in a town that the hotel they ask for is closed or has moved or changed its name. Instead, they head for a hotel that pays them commission. This may work out fine (new hotels often use this method to become known), but more often than not it's a substandard hotel and you will in any case pay over the odds since the room rate will include the driver's commission. To avoid being ripped off, always insist on being taken to the exact address of your chosen hotel, at least just to check the story.

Another common complaint is that organized tours don't live up to what was promised. There are more people on the tour than stated, for example, or the room doesn't have air-conditioning, or the guide's English is limited. If it's a group tour and you've paid up front, unfortunately there's very little you can do beyond complaining to the agent on your return; you may be lucky and get some form of compensation, but it's very unlikely. As always, you tend to get what you pay for, so avoid signing up for dirt-cheap tours.

Women travellers

Vietnam is generally a safe country for women to travel around alone. Most Vietnamese will simply be curious as to why you are on your own and the chances of encountering any threatening behaviour are extremely rare. That said, it pays to take the normal precautions, especially **late at night** when there are few people on the streets and you should avoid taking a cyclo by yourself; use a taxi instead – metered taxis are generally considered safest.

Most Vietnamese women **dress** modestly, keeping covered from top to toe, unless their profession requires them to show off their assets. It helps to dress modestly too and to avoid wearing skimpy shorts and vests, which are considered by some men an invitation to paid sex. Topless sunbathing, even beside a hotel pool, is a complete no-no.

Festivals and religious events

The Vietnamese year follows a rhythm of festivals and religious observances, ranging from solemn family gatherings at the ancestral altar to national celebrations culminating in Tet, the Vietnamese New Year. In between are countless local festivals, most notably in the Red River Delta, honouring the tutelary spirit of the village or community temple.

The majority of festivals take place in spring, with a second flurry in the autumn months. One festival you might want to make a note of, however, is **Tet**: not only does most of Vietnam close down for the week, but either side of the holiday local transport services are stretched to the limit and international flights are filled by returning overseas Vietnamese.

Many Vietnamese festivals are **Chinese** in origin, imbued with a distinctive flavour over the centuries, but minority groups also hold their own specific celebrations. The ethnic **minorities** continue to punctuate the year with rituals that govern sowing, harvest or hunting, as well as elaborate rites of passage surrounding birth and death. The **Cao Dai** religion has its own array of festivals, while **Christian** communities throughout Vietnam observe the major ceremonies. Christmas is marked as a religious ceremony only by the faithful, though it's becoming a major event for all Vietnamese as an excuse to shop and party, with sax-playing santas greeting shoppers in front of malls.

The ceremonies you're most likely to see are **weddings** and **funerals**. The tenth lunar month is the most auspicious time for weddings, though at other times you'll also encounter plenty of wedding cavalcades on the road, their lead vehicle draped in colourful ribbons. Funeral processions are recognizable from the white headbands worn by mourners, while close family members dress completely in white. Both weddings and funerals are characterized by streetside parties under makeshift marquees, and since both tend to be joyous occasions, it's often difficult to know what you're witnessing, unless you spot a bridal gown or portrait of the deceased on display.

Most festivals take place according to the **lunar calendar**, which is also closely linked to the Chinese system with a zodiac of twelve animal signs. The most important times during the lunar month (which lasts 29 or 30 days) are the full moon (day one) and the new moon (day fourteen or fifteen). Festivals are often held at these times, which also hold a special significance for Buddhists, who are supposed to pray at the pagoda and avoid eating meat during the two days. On the eve of each full moon, Hoi An now celebrates a **Full-Moon Festival**: traffic is barred from the town centre, where traditional games, dance and music performances take place under the light of silk lanterns.

All Vietnamese calendars show both the lunar and solar (Gregorian) months and dates, but to be sure of a festival date it's best to check locally.

> **PUBLIC HOLIDAYS**
> **January 1** New Year's Day
> **Late January/mid-February** (dates vary each year): Tet, Vietnamese New Year (four days, though increasingly offices tend to close down for a full week)
> **April 30** Liberation of Saigon, 1975
> **May 1** International Labour Day
> **September 2** National Day

VIETNAM'S MAJOR FESTIVALS

SPRING FESTIVALS (JAN–APRIL)

Tet The most important date in the Vietnamese festival calendar is New Year (*Tet Nguyen Dan*). After an initial jamboree, Tet is largely a family occasion when offices are shut, and many shops and restaurants may close for the seven-day festival. Officially only the first four days are public holidays, though many people take the whole week. First to seventh days of first lunar month; late January to mid-February.

Tay Son Festival Martial arts demonstrations in Tay Son District, plus garlanded elephants on parade. Fifth day of first lunar month; late January to mid-February.

Water-Puppet Festival As part of the Tet celebrations a festival of puppetry is held at Thay Pagoda, west of Hanoi. Fifth to seventh days of first lunar month; February.

Lim Singing Festival Two weeks after Tet, Lim village near Bac Ninh, in the Red River Delta, resounds to the harmonies of "alternate singing" (*quan ho*) as men and women fling improvised lyrics back and forth. Thirteenth to fifteenth days of the first lunar month; February–March.

Hai Ba Trung Festival The two Trung sisters are honoured with a parade and dancing at Hanoi's Hai Ba Trung temple. Sixth day of the second lunar month; March.

Perfume Pagoda Vietnam's most famous pilgrimage site is Chua Huong, west of Hanoi. Thousands of Buddhist pilgrims flock to the pagoda for the festival, which climaxes on the full moon (fourteenth or fifteenth day) of the second month, though the pilgrimage continues for a month either side; March–April.

Den Ba Chua Kho The full moon of the second month sees Hanoians congregating at this temple near Bac Ninh, to petition the goddess for success in business; March–April.

Thanh Minh Ancestral graves are cleaned and offerings of food, flowers and paper votive objects made at the beginning of the third lunar month; April.

SUMMER FESTIVALS (MAY–AUG)

Phat Dan Lanterns are hung outside the pagodas and Buddhist homes to commemorate Buddha's birth, enlightenment and the attainment of Nirvana. Eighth day of the fourth lunar month; May.

Tet: the Vietnamese New Year

"Tet", simply meaning festival, is the accepted name for Vietnam's most important annual event, properly known as **Tet Nguyen Dan**, or festival of the first day. Tet lasts for seven days and falls sometime between the last week of January and the third week of February, on the night of the new moon. This is a time when families get together to celebrate renewal and hope for the new year, when ancestral spirits are welcomed back to the household and when everyone in Vietnam becomes a year older – age is reckoned by the new year and not by individual birthdays.

There's an almost tangible sense of excitement leading up to midnight on the eve of Tet, though the welcoming of the new year is now a much more subdued – and less dangerous – affair since firecrackers were banned in 1995. Instead, all the major cities hold fireworks displays.

Tet kicks off seven days before the new moon with the **festival of Ong Tau**, the god of the hearth (23rd day of the twelfth month). Ong Tau keeps watch over the household throughout the year, wards off evil spirits and makes an annual report of family events, good or bad, to the Jade Emperor. In order to send Ong Tau off to heaven in a benevolent mood, the family cleans its house from top to bottom, and makes offerings to him, including pocket money and a new set of clothes. Ong Tau returns home at midnight on the first chime of the new year and it's this, together with welcoming the ancestral spirits back to share in the party, that warrants such a massive celebration.

Tet is all about **starting the year afresh**, with a clean slate and good intentions. Not only is the house scrubbed, but all debts are paid off and those who can afford it have a haircut and buy new clothes. To attract favourable spirits, good-luck charms are put in the house, most commonly cockerels or the trinity of male figures representing prosperity, happiness and longevity. The crucial moments are the first minutes and hours of the new year as these set the pattern for the whole of the following year. People strive to avoid arguments, swearing or breaking anything – at least during the

Chua Xu Festival The stone statue of Chua Xu at Sam Mountain, Chau Doc, is bathed, and thousands flock to honour her. Twenty-third to twenty-fifth day of fourth lunar month; May.

Tet Doan Ngo The summer solstice (fifth day of the fifth moon) is marked by festivities aimed at warding off epidemics brought on by the summer heat. This is also the time of dragon-boat races; late May to early June.

Trang Nguyen (or *Vu Lan*) The day of wandering souls is the second most important festival after Tet. Offerings of food and clothes are made to comfort and nourish the unfortunate souls without a home, and all graves are cleaned. This is also time for the forgiveness of faults, when the King of Hell judges everyone's spirits and metes out reward or punishment as appropriate. Until the fifteenth century prisoners were allowed to go home on this day. Fourteenth or fifteenth day of the seventh lunar month; August.

AUTUMN FESTIVALS (SEPT–DEC)

Do Son Buffalo-fighting Festival Held in Do Son village, near Hai Phong. Ninth and tenth days of the eighth lunar month; August

Kate Festival The Cham New Year is celebrated in high style at Po Klong Garai and Po Re Me, both near Phan Rang; September–October.

Trung Thu The mid-autumn festival, also known as Children's Day, is when dragon dances take place and children are given lanterns in the shape of stars, carp or dragons. Special cakes, *banh trung thu*, are eaten at this time of year. These are sticky rice cakes filled with lotus seeds, nuts and candied fruits and are either square like the earth (*banh deo*), or round like the moon (*banh nuong*) and containing the yolk of an egg. Fourteenth or fifteenth day of the eighth lunar month; September–October.

Whale Festival Lang Ca Ong, Vung Tau. Crowds gather to make offerings to the whales. Sixteenth day of the eighth lunar month; September–October.

Oc Bom Boc Festival Boat-racing festival in Soc Trang. Tenth day of tenth lunar month; November–December.

Da Lat Flower Festival An annual extravaganza in which the city shows off the abundance of blooms grown locally; December.

Christmas Midnight services at the cathedrals in Hanoi and Ho Chi Minh City and much revelry in the streets; December 24.

first three days when a single ill word could tempt bad luck into the house for the whole year ahead. The first visitor on the morning of Tet is also vitally significant: the ideal is someone respected, wealthy and happily married who will bring good fortune to the family; the bereaved, unemployed, accident-prone and even pregnant, on the other hand, are considered ill-favoured. This honour carries with it an onerous responsibility, however: if the family has a bad year, it will be the first-footer's fault.

The week-long festival is marked by **feasting**: special foods are eaten at Tet, such as pickled vegetables, candied lotus seeds and sugared fruits, all of which are first offered at the family altar. The most famous delicacy is *banh chung* (*banh tet* in the south), a thick square or cylinder of sweet, sticky rice that is prepared only for Tet. The rice is wrapped round a mixture of green-bean paste, pork fat and meat marinated in *nuoc mam*, and then boiled in banana leaves, which impart a pale green colour. According to legend, an impoverished prince of the Hung dynasty invented the cakes over two thousand years ago; his father was so impressed by the simplicity of his son's gift that he named the prince as his heir. Tet is an expensive time for Vietnamese families, many of whom save for months to get the new year off to a good start. Apart from special foods and new clothes, it's traditional to give children red envelopes containing *li xi*, or lucky money, and to decorate homes with spring blossoms. In the week before Tet, flower markets grace the larger cities: peach blossoms in the north, apricot in Hué and mandarin in the south. Plum and kumquat (symbolizing gold coins) are also popular, alongside the more showy, modern blooms of roses, dahlias or gladioli.

Sports and outdoor activities

Though Vietnam was slow to develop its huge potential as an outdoor adventure destination, things have really changed in the last few years. Apart from trekking

in the mountainous north, visitors can now also go rock–climbing, canyoning, sea kayaking or kitesurfing, among other activities. Da Lat has emerged as Vietnam's adventure sports capital and Mui Ne its surf city, though some sports like mountain biking can be done throughout the country.

Trekking

The easiest and most popular area for trekking is in the northwest mountains around Sa Pa and, to a lesser extent, Mai Chau. Sa Pa is also the starting point for ascents of the country's highest peak, Fan Si Pan, a challenge to be undertaken only by experienced hikers. Other options include hiking around Kon Tum or Da Lat in the central highlands or in one of Vietnam's many national parks, including Cat Ba, Cuc Phuong, Bach Ma, Cat Tien and Yok Don. In Yok Don you can even go elephant trekking, though prices are rather steep.

There's no problem about striking out on your own for a day's hiking. However, for anything more adventurous, particularly if you want to overnight in the villages, you'll need to make arrangements in advance. This is easily done either before you arrive in Vietnam or through local tour agents, most of which offer organized tours and tailor-made packages. In most cases you can also make arrangements through guesthouses and guides on the spot. Note that it's essential to take a guide if you are keen to get off the beaten track: many areas are still sensitive about the presence of foreigners.

Biking

Mountain biking is becoming increasingly popular in Vietnam. The classic ride is from Hanoi to Ho Chi Minh City, a journey of between two and three weeks. Previously, this would have taken you along Highway 1, battling with trucks and buses, but now the more switched-on tour companies are offering excursions down the Ho Chi Minh Highway which runs along the western Truong Son mountain chain, and is so far thankfully free of heavy traffic.

The area around **Sa Pa** is a focus for biking activity, with tour operators offering excursions to suit all levels of experience and fitness. You can choose from half-day excursions to multi-day outings including overnighting in minority villages. Other good areas for exploring by bike include Mai Chau, Bac Ha, Da Lat and the Mekong Delta.

North Vietnam is also popular among the **motor-biking** fraternity. Specialist outfits in Hanoi organize tailor-made itineraries taking you way off the beaten track.

Watersports

With its three-thousand-kilometre coastline, Vietnam should be a paradise for **watersports**, but the options remain fairly limited at present, for a variety of reasons. One is simply a matter of access: the infrastructure is not yet in place. More crucial is the presence of potentially dangerous **undercurrents** along much of the coast, accompanied by strong winds at certain times of year. Many of the big beach resorts have guards or put out flags in season indicating where it's safe to swim. Elsewhere, check carefully before taking the plunge.

Whilst many of the beaches along the coast are great for **swimming**, the best are those around Mui Ne and Nha Trang, with Hoi An and Da Nang close behind. Mui Ne is also the country's top venue for windsurfing and kitesurfing, both of which are now hugely popular. Phu Quoc Island, off Vietnam's southern coast, is also famed not only for its fabulous beaches but also as the country's top spot for **snorkelling** and **scuba-diving**. The Con Dao Islands and Nha Trang are other popular places to don a snorkel or wet suit, but wherever you dive, it's worth noting that standards of maintenance aren't always great, so check equipment carefully and only go out with a properly qualified and registered operator that you trust.

Heading inland, the rivers and waterfalls around Da Lat provide good possibilities for **canyoning** and **rock-climbing**, though Cat Ba Island is a good alternative if you'd like to combine rock-climbing with sightseeing in Ha Long Bay.

Mui Ne has a good reputation for **windsurfing and kitesurfing**, and even hosts an international competition in these sports each spring (usually Feb).

In north Vietnam Ha Long Bay is the watersports centre, while rock-climbing is becoming big as well, organized from Cat Ba. Most boat tours of the bay allow time for swimming – weather permitting – while there are decent beaches on Cat Ba and better still on remote Quan Lan Island. For those in search of more strenuous exercise, a number of tour agents offer **sea-kayaking** trips on the bay – not recommended in the heat of summer.

Other activities

Vietnam has over 850 species of birds, including several that have only been identified in the past few years. The best places for **birdwatching** are the national parks, including Cuc Phuong (famous also for its springtime butterfly displays), Bach Ma and Cat Tien. The rare Sarus crane, amongst many other species, spends the dry season in and around the Tram Chim National Park in the Mekong Delta. For more information check out ⓦ vietnambirding.com or birdwatchingvietnam.net.

Finally, there are now dozens of excellent **golf** courses in Vietnam – around Ho Chi Minh City, Hanoi, Phan Thiet and Da Lat amongst others – all with much cheaper green fees than in the West.

Shopping

Souvenir–hunters will find rich pickings in Vietnam, whose eye–catching handicrafts and mementos range from colonial currency and stamps to fabrics and basketware crafted by the country's ethnic minorities, and from limpet–like conical hats to fake US Army–issue Zippo lighters. Throughout the Guide, we've highlighted places to shop, but in general you'll find the best quality, choice and prices in Ho Chi Minh City, Hanoi and Hoi An. Though you'll find more shops now have fixed prices, particularly those catering to tourists, in markets and rural areas prices are almost always open to negotiation (see box above).

Clothing, arts and crafts

Few Western tourists leave Vietnam without the obligatory **conical hat**, or *non la*, sewn from rain- and sun-proof palm fronds; at around 25,000đ for a basic version, they're definitely an affordable keepsake. From the city of Hué comes a more elaborate version, the **poem hat**, or *non bai tho*, in whose brim are inlays which, when held up to the light, reveal lines of poetry or scenes from Vietnamese legend. Vietnamese women traditionally wear the **ao dai** – baggy silk trousers under a knee-length silk tunic slit up both sides. Extraordinarily elegant, *ao dai* can be bought off the peg anywhere in the country for around $30; or, if you can spare a few days for fitting, you can have one tailor-made for $40 or so, depending on the material.

THE ART OF BARGAINING

The Vietnamese, not unreasonably, see tourists as wildly rich – how else could they afford to stop working and travel the world – and a **first quoted price** is usually pitched accordingly. It makes sense, therefore, to be prepared.

First of all, do your homework. Find out the approximate going rate, either from your hotel or fellow travellers, or from one of the increasing number of fixed-price shops – remembering to take into account the difference in quality, for example, between mass-produced and hand-crafted goods.

The trick then is to remain **friendly** and amused, but also to be realistic: traders will quickly lose interest in a sale if they think you aren't playing the game fairly. Any show of aggression, and you've lost it in more ways than one. If you feel you're on the verge of agreement, **moving away** often pays dividends – it's amazing how often you'll be called back.

Keep a sense of **perspective**. If a session of bargaining is becoming very protracted, step back and remind yourself that you're often arguing the toss over mere pennies – nothing to you, but a lot to the average Vietnamese.

Local **silk** is sold by the metre in Vietnam's more sizeable markets and in countless outlets in Hoi An, along Dong Khoi in Ho Chi Minh City and on Hanoi's Hang Gai. These same shops also sell ready-made clothes and accessories, including embroidered silk handbags and shoes, and most also offer tailoring. In general, Hoi An's tailors have the best reputation, either working from a pattern book or copying an item you take along. Just make sure you allow plenty of time for fittings.

Embroidered **cotton**, in the form of tablecloths, sheets and pillowcases, also makes a popular souvenir. Meanwhile, the sartorial needs of backpackers are well catered for in major tourist destinations, where **T-shirt** sellers do brisk business. Predictably popular designs include a portrait of Uncle Ho, and the yellow Communist star on a red background.

Traditional handicrafts

Of the many types of traditional handicrafts on offer in Vietnam, **lacquerware** (*son mai*) is among the most beautiful. It is also incredibly light, so won't add significantly to your baggage weight. Made by applying multiple layers of resin onto an article and then polishing vigorously to achieve a deep, lustrous sheen, lacquer is used to decorate furniture, boxes, chopsticks and bangles and is sometimes embellished with eggshell or inlays of **mother-of-pearl** (which is also used in its own right, on screens and pictures) – common motifs are animals, fish and elaborate scrolling. More recently, the lacquerware tradition has been hijacked by more contemporary icons, and it's now possible to buy colourful lacquerware paintings of Mickey Mouse, Tin Tin and Batman. Imported synthetic lacquer has also made an appearance. These brightly coloured, almost metallic, finishes may not be for the purist, but they make for eye-catching bowls, vases and all sorts of household items.

Bronze, **brass** and **jade** are also put to good use, appearing in various forms such as carvings, figurines and jewellery. In Hué, brass and copper **teapots** are popular. Of the porcelain and ceramics available across the country, thigh-high **ceramic elephants** and other animal figurines are the quirkiest buys – though decidedly tricky to carry home. Look out, too, for boxes and other knick-knacks made from wonderfully aromatic **cinnamon** and **camphor wood**. For something a little more culturally elevated, you could invest in a **water-puppet** or a traditional **musical instrument** (see p.482).

Vietnam's **ethnic minorities** are producing increasingly sophisticated fare for the tourist market. Fabrics – sometimes shot through with shimmering gold braid – are their main asset, sold in lengths and also made into **purses**, **shoulder bags** and other accoutrements. The minorities of the central highlands are adept at **basketwork**, fashioning backpacks, baskets and mats, and **bamboo pipes**. Hanoi probably has the greatest variety of **minority handicrafts** on sale, though you'll also find plenty available in Ho Chi Minh City. In the far north, Sa Pa is a popular place to buy Hmong clothes, bags and **skull-caps**, and you'll find lengths of woven fabrics or embroidery in markets throughout the northern mountains.

Paintings

A healthy fine arts scene exists in Vietnam, and **painting** in particular is thriving. In the galleries of Hanoi, Ho Chi Minh City and Hoi An you'll find exquisite works in oil, watercolour, lacquer, charcoal and silk weaving by the country's leading artists. Hanoi is the best single place to look for contemporary art.

For the top names you can expect to pay hundreds or even thousands of dollars. Buyer beware, however: many artists find it lucrative to knock out multiple copies of their own or other people's work. You'll need to know what you're doing, or to buy from a reputable gallery.

A cheap alternative is to snap up a reproduction of a famous image by Dali or Van Gogh, while something essentially Vietnamese are the Communist **propaganda posters**, which are on sale everywhere.

Books, stamps and coins

You can buy photocopied editions of almost all the **books** ever published on Vietnam from strolling vendors in Hanoi and Ho Chi Minh City. There are also an increasing number of locally published coffee-table books, histories and guides available from bona-fide bookshops and the more upmarket hotels. However, if all you want is some general reading matter, both Hanoi and Ho Chi Minh City now have secondhand bookshops where you can exchange or buy used books.

Philatelists meanwhile will enjoy browsing through the old Indochinese **stamps** sold in the souvenir shops of Hanoi and Ho Chi Minh City. Similarly, old **notes** and **coins**, including French-issue piastres and US Army credits, are available.

Memorabilia, trinkets and food

Army surplus gear is still a money-spinner, though fatigues, belts, canteens and dog tags purportedly stolen from a dead or wounded GI aren't the most tasteful of souvenirs – and the vast majority are fakes anyway. The green **pith helmets** with a red star on the front, worn first by the NVA during the American War and now by the regular Vietnamese Army, find more takers. Other items that sell like hot cakes, especially in the south, are fake **Zippo lighters** bearing such pithy adages as "When I die bury me face down, so the whole damn army can kiss my ass" and "We are the unwilling, led by the unqualified, doin' the unnecessary for the ungrateful", though again they're very unlikely to be authentic GI issue. In Ho Chi Minh City, extravagant wooden **model ships** are sold in a string of shops on Hai Ba Trung, at the east side of Lam Son Square.

Finally, **foodstuffs** that may tempt you include coffee from the central highlands, candied strawberries and artichoke tea from Da Lat, coconut candies from the Mekong Delta, preserved miniature tangerines from Hoi An and packets of tea and dried herbs and spices from the northern highlands. As for **drinks**, most of the concoctions itemized on p.54 are securely bottled. The Soc Tinh range of rice-distilled liquor makes an attractively packaged souvenir.

Travel essentials

Addresses

Locating an **address** is rarely a problem in Vietnam, but there are a couple of conventions it helps to know about. Where two numbers are separated by a slash, such as 110/5, you simply make for no. 110, where an alley will lead off to a further batch of buildings – you want the fifth one. Where a number is followed by a letter, as in 117a, you're looking for a single block encompassing several addresses, of which one will be 117a. Vietnamese cite addresses without the words for street, avenue and so on; we've followed this practice throughout the Guide except where ambiguity would result.

Admission charges

Admission charges are usually levied at museums, historic sights, national parks and any place that attracts tourists – sometimes even beaches. Charges at some **major sights** range from a dollar or two up to around $4–5 for the Cham ruins at My Son or Hué's citadel and royal mausoleums. Elsewhere, however, the amount is usually just a few thousand dong. Note that there's often a hefty additional fee for **cameras** and **videos** at major sights.

Apart from those with some historical significance, **pagodas and temples** are usually free, though it's customary to leave a donation of a few thousand dong in the collecting box or on one of the altar plates.

Costs

With the average Vietnamese annual income hovering around $800–1000, daily expenses are low, and if you come prepared to do as the locals do, then food and drink can be incredibly cheap – and even accommodation needn't be too great an expense. However, constantly rising petrol prices mean that transport costs are creeping up all the time. **Bargaining** is very much a part of everyday life, and almost everything is negotiable, from fruit in the market to a room for the night (see box, p.53).

By eating at simple com (rice) and pho (noodle soup) stalls, picking up local buses and opting for the simplest accommodation there's no reason why you shouldn't be able to adhere to a **daily budget** in the region of $15–20. Upgrading to more salubrious lodgings with a few mod cons, eating good food followed by a couple of beers in a bar and signing up for the odd minibus tour and visiting a few sights could bounce your expenditure up to a more realistic $30–40. A fair mid-level budget, treating yourself to three-star hotels and more upmarket restaurants, would lie in the $50–100 range, depending on the number and type of tours you took. And if you stay at the ritziest city hotels, dine at the swankiest restaurants and rent cars with drivers wherever you go, then the sky's the limit.

AVERAGE DAILY MAXIMUM TEMPERATURES

HO CHI MINH CITY

	Jan	Feb	Mar	Apr	May	Jun	Jul	Aug	Sep	Oct	Nov	Dec
Temperature	27	28	29	30	29	29	28	28	27	27	27	27
Rainfall	15	3	13	43	221	330	315	269	335	269	114	56

DA NANG

	Jan	Feb	Mar	Apr	May	Jun	Jul	Aug	Sep	Oct	Nov	Dec
Temperature	22	23	24	27	29	30	30	30	28	26	25	23
Rainfall	102	31	12	18	47	42	99	117	447	530	221	209

HANOI

	Jan	Feb	Mar	Apr	May	Jun	Jul	Aug	Sep	Oct	Nov	Dec
Temperature	17	18	20	24	28	30	30	29	28	26	22	19
Rainfall	18	28	38	81	196	239	323	343	254	99	43	20

Electricity

The **electricity** supply in Vietnam is 220 volts. Plugs generally have two round pins, though you may come across sockets requiring two flat pins and even some requiring three pins. Adaptors can be found in any electrical shop. Power supplies can be erratic, so be prepared for cuts and surges.

Entry requirements

All foreign nationals need a visa to enter Vietnam, with certain exceptions: citizens of Sweden, Denmark, Norway, Finland, Japan and South Korea do not need a visa if they are travelling to Vietnam for less than fifteen days, have a passport valid for three months following the date of entry and hold a return air ticket. Citizens of certain ASEAN–member countries, including Thailand, Malaysia and Singapore are also exempt for stays of up to thirty days. Tourist visas are generally valid for thirty days and for a single entry, though three-month multiple–entry visas are also available. A standard thirty–day visa costs the local equivalent of $30–100, depending on how quickly you want it processed.

The majority of visitors apply for a visa in their country of residence, either from the embassy direct, or through a specialist visa agent or tour agent. Processing normally takes around a week, though many embassies also offer a more expensive "express" service.

If it's difficult to get to your nearest Vietnam Embassy, consider buying your visa online at Ⓦ vietnamvisa.com. Prices range from $22 plus $25 'stamping fee' (for a one-month, single-entry visa) to $34 plus $50 'stamping fee' (for a three-month, multiple-entry visa.) On receipt of your fee (usually within 24hr), you'll be sent a document to print out and show immigration on arrival. The process is very efficient and currently only requires a short wait upon arrival, though this wait could get longer if the system proves popular. If you follow this route, look out for the Visa on Arrival desk at the airport before you pass through immigration.

To apply for a tourist visa, you have to submit an **application form** with one or two passport-sized photographs (procedures vary) and the fee. The visa shows specific start and end **dates** indicating the period of validity within which you can enter and leave the country. The visa is valid for entry via Hanoi, Ho Chi Minh City and Da Nang international airports and any of Vietnam's land borders open to foreigners (see p.30).

Business visas are valid for one month upwards and can be issued for multiple entry, though you'll need a sponsoring office in Vietnam to underwrite your application.

One-year **student visas** are relatively easy to get hold of if you enrol, for example, on a Vietnamese language course at one of the universities; you'll be required to attend a minimum number of classes per week to qualify. It's easiest to arrange it in advance, but you can enter Vietnam on a tourist visa and apply for student status later – the only downside is that you may have to leave the country in order to get the visa stamp.

Special circumstances affect **overseas Vietnamese** holding a foreign passport: check with the Vietnamese embassy in your country of residence for details.

Visa extensions

Thirty-day extensions are issued in Hanoi, Ho Chi Minh City, Nha Trang, Da Nang, Hué and Hoi An. Some people have managed to obtain second and even third extensions, usually in Hanoi and Ho Chi Minh City. Applications have to be made via a tour agent. In general they take three to five days to process and cost $25 for the first one-month extension.

Holders of **business visas** can apply for an extension only through the office that sponsored their original visa, backed up with reasons as to why an extension is necessary.

Incidentally, **overstaying** your visa will result in fines of between $10 and $50, depending how long you overstay and the mood of the immigration official, and is not recommended.

Vietnamese embassies and consulates

A full list of Vietnamese embassies and consulates is available at Ⓦ vietnamtourism.com.

Australia Embassy: 6 Timbarra Crescent, O'Malley, Canberra, ACT 2606 ☎ 02 6286 6059, Ⓦ www.au.vnembassy.org. Consulate: 202–233 New South Head Rd, Edgcliff, NSW 2027 ☎ 02 9327 1912.

Cambodia Embassy: 436 Blvd Preach, Monivong, Phnom Penh ☎ 023 726 273, Ⓔ vnembpnh@online.com.kh. Consulates: Sihanoukville ☎ 034 933 669, Ⓔ tlsqsiha@camintel.com; Road No.3, Battambang ☎ 053 952 894, Ⓦ www.vietnamembassy-cambodia.org.

Canada 470 Wilbrod St, Ottawa K1N 6M8 ☎ 613 236 0772, Ⓦ vietnamembassy-canada.ca.

China Embassy: 32 Guang Hua Lu, Jian Guo Men Wai, PO Box 00600, Beijing ☎ 10 6532 1155, Ⓔ suquanbk@yahoo.com. Consulates: Jin Yanf Hotel, 92 Huanshi Western Rd, Guang Zhou ☎ 20 8652 7908; 15f Great Smart Tower, 230 Wanchai Rd, Hong Kong ☎ 852 2591 4510; 2f Kai Wah International Hotel, 157 Beijing Rd, Kunming 650011 ☎ 871 352 2669, Ⓔ tlsqcm@yahoo.com.

Ireland Contact UK office.
Lao PDR Embassy: 1 That Luang Rd, Vientiane ☎ 021 413 409,
Ⓦ mofa.gov.vn. Consulates: 31 Ban Pha Bat, Pakse ☎ 031 212 058;
118 Sisavang Rd, Savannakhet ☎ 041 212418.
Malaysia 4 Persiaran Stonor, 50450 Kuala Lumpur
☎ 03 2148 4534, Ⓦ mofa.gov.vn.
New Zealand Level 21, Grand Plimmer Tower, 2 Gilmer Terrace,
PO Box 8042, Wellington ☎ 04 473 5912, Ⓦ vietnamembassy
-newzealand.org.
Singapore 10 Leedon Park, Singapore 267887 ☎ 462 5938.
Thailand Embassy: 83 1 Wireless Rd, Bangkok 10330
☎ 02 267 9602, Ⓔ vnembassy@bkk.a-net.net.th. Consulate:
65 6 Chatapadung, Khonkaen 40000 ☎ 043 242190,
Ⓦ vietnamembassy-thailand.org.
UK 12–14 Victoria Rd, London W8 5RD ☎ 020 7937 1912,
Ⓦ vietnamembassy.org.uk/consular.html.
US Embassy: 1233 20th St NW, Suite 400, Washington DC 20036
☎ 202 861 0737, Ⓦ vietnamembassy-usa.org. Consulate: 1700
California St, Suite 430, San Francisco, CA 94109 ☎ 415 922 1577,
Ⓦ www.vietnamconsulate-sf.org.

Culture and etiquette

With its blend of Confucianism and Buddhism, Vietnamese society tends to be both conservative and, at the same time, fairly tolerant. This means you will rarely be remonstrated with for your dress or behaviour, even if your hosts do disapprove. By following a few simple rules, you can minimize the risk of causing offence. This is particularly important in rural areas and small towns where people are less used to the eccentric habits of foreigners.

As a visitor, it's recommended that you err on the side of caution. Shorts and sleeveless shirts are fine for the beach, but are not welcome in pagodas, temples and other religious sites. When dealing with officialdom, it also pays to look as neat and tidy as possible. Anything else may be taken as a mark of disrespect.

Women in particular should dress modestly, especially in the countryside and ethnic minority areas, where revealing too much flesh is regarded as offensive.

It's also worth noting that **nudity**, either male or female, on the beach is absolutely beyond the pale.

When entering a Cao Dai temple, the main building of a pagoda or a private home it's the custom to remove your **shoes**. In some pagodas nowadays this may only be required when stepping onto the prayer mats – ask or watch what other people do. In a pagoda or temple you are also expected to leave a small donation.

Officially, **homosexuality** is regarded as a "social evil", alongside drugs and prostitution. However, there

---

ETHICAL TOURISM AND THE ENVIRONMENT

The **expansion of tourism** in Vietnam has been spectacular, growing from just ten thousand foreign visitors in 1993 to more than five million in 2010. In addition, an estimated 25 million Vietnamese now take holidays within the country each year. While this has undoubtedly been a boon for the economy, tourism has brought with it serious and potentially disruptive effects environmentally, socially, culturally and economically. Some of the most distressing examples are to be found in Vietnam's ethnic minority areas. Sa Pa's famous "love market" attracted so much tourist attention it eventually relocated to a more remote location. Many families in the area have sold off their antique jewellery, while Hmong children beg for sweets, pens and money, and some even sell drugs.

---

is no law explicitly banning homosexual activity and, as long as it is not practised openly, it is largely ignored. Indeed, the number of openly gay men has increased noticeably in recent years, particularly in Ho Chi Minh City and Hanoi, and homosexuality is discussed more frequently in the media, although the lesbian scene remains very low-key. Although outward discrimination is rare, this is still a very traditional society and it pays to be discreet in Vietnam. For more information, consult the excellent Utopia Asia website, Ⓦ utopia-asia.com.

As in most Asian countries, it's not done to get angry, and it certainly won't get things moving any quicker. Passing round cigarettes (to men only) is always appreciated and is widely used as a social gambit aimed at progressing tricky negotiations, bargaining and so forth.

Tipping, while not expected, is always appreciated. In general, a few thousand dong should suffice. Smart restaurants and hotels normally add a service charge, but if not ten percent is the norm in a restaurant, while the amount in a hotel will depend on the grade of hotel and what services they've provided. If you're pleased with the service, you should also tip the guide, and the driver where appropriate, at the end of a tour.

Other social conventions worth noting are that you shouldn't touch **children** on the head and, unlike in the West, it's best to ignore a young baby rather than praise it, since it's believed that this attracts the attention of jealous spirits who will cause the baby to fall ill.

Health

Vietnam's health problems read like a dictionary of tropical medicine. Diseases that are under control elsewhere in Southeast Asia have been sustained here by poverty, dietary deficiencies, poor health-care and the disruption caused by half a century of war. The situation is improving, however, and by coming prepared and taking a few simple precautions while in the country, you're unlikely to come down with anything worse than a cold or a dose of travellers' diarrhoea.

Before you go

When planning your trip it's wise to visit a **doctor** as early as possible, preferably at least two months before you leave, to allow time to complete any recommended courses of **vaccinations**. It's also advisable to have a troubleshooting **dental check-up** – and remember that you generally need to start taking **anti-malarial tablets** at least one week before your departure.

For up-to-the-minute information, it may be worth visiting a specialized **travel clinic**; most clinics also sell travel-associated accessories, including mosquito nets and first-aid kits.

Vaccinations

No **vaccinations** are required for Vietnam (except yellow fever if you're coming directly from an area where the disease is endemic), but typhoid and hepatitis A jabs are recommended; it's also worth ensuring you're up to date with boosters such as tetanus and polio. Additional injections to consider, depending on the season and risk of exposure, are hepatitis B, Japanese encephalitis, meningitis and rabies. All these immunizations can be obtained at international clinics in Hanoi, Ho Chi Minh City and Da Nang, but it's less hassle and usually cheaper to get them done at home. Get all your shots recorded on an **International Certificate of Vaccination** and carry this with your passport when travelling abroad.

For protection against **hepatitis A**, which is spread by contaminated food and water, the vaccine is expensive but extremely effective – an initial injection followed by a booster after six to twelve months provides immunity for up to ten years. **Hepatitis B**, like the HIV virus, can be passed on through unprotected sexual contact, blood transfusions and dirty needles. The very effective vaccine (three injections over six months) is recommended for anyone in a high-risk category, including those travelling extensively in rural areas for prolonged periods, with access to only basic medical care. It's also now possible – and cheaper – to have a combined vaccination against both hepatitis A and B: the course comprises three injections over six months.

The risks of contracting **Japanese encephalitis** are extremely small, but, as the disease is untreatable, those travelling for a month or more in the countryside, especially in the north during and soon after the summer rainy season (June–Nov), should consider immunization. The course consists of two or three injections over a month with the last dose administered at least ten days before departure. Note that it is not recommended for those with liver, heart or kidney disorders, or for

AVIAN FLU

Avian flu or bird flu is a contagious disease normally limited to birds and, less commonly, pigs. However, the virus can spread to humans by direct contact with infected poultry or with contaminated surfaces. In the 2004–05 outbreak in Vietnam of the highly contagious H5N1 strain of the disease, there were around sixty confirmed cases involving humans, of which some forty were fatal, according to the World Health Organization. The vast majority of people infected had direct contact with diseased birds. Since the initial outbreak, a further sixty or so cases have been reported, the most recent in April 2010.

Evidence of human-to-human transmission has yet to be confirmed but the indications are that, if it is possible, it is extremely rare and has so far been limited to close family members. The main fear among health experts is that the virus will mutate into a form that is highly infectious to and easily spread among humans.

At present the risk to travellers visiting infected areas remains low. As a precaution, however, you are advised to avoid contact with live poultry and pigs, including live animal markets, and to eat only well-cooked poultry and eggs. Check the latest with your doctor or travel health specialist prior to travel. You'll also find up-to-date information on the following websites: Ⓦ avianinfluenza.org.vn, Ⓦ who.int/csr/disease/avian_influenza/en and Ⓦ cdc.gov/flu/avian.

WHAT ABOUT THE WATER?

The simple rule is don't drink tap **water** in Vietnam, with the exception of a few top hotels which now offer filtered water, and never drink river water. It's wise also to avoid **ice** in your drinks except, again, in top hotels and other trustworthy places. Contaminated water is a major cause of sickness due to the presence of pathogenic organisms: bacteria, viruses and cysts. These micro-organisms cause ailments and diseases such as diarrhoea, gastroenteritis, typhoid, cholera, dysentery, poliomyelitis, hepatitis A and giardia – and can be present even when water looks clean and safe to drink.

Fortunately there are plenty of alternative drinks around: hot tea is always on offer, while cheap, **bottled water** and carbonated drinks are widely available. When buying bottled water check the seal is unbroken and the water is clear, as bottles are occasionally refilled from the tap. Tap water in Hanoi and Ho Chi Minh City is chlorinated and most travellers use it for brushing their teeth without problem, but this is not recommended in rural areas, where water is often untreated. Particular care should be taken anywhere where there is flooding as raw sewage may be washed into the water system.

multiple-allergy sufferers. If your plans include long stays in remote areas your doctor may also recommend vaccination against **meningitis** (a single shot) and **rabies**.

Mosquito–borne diseases

Both the Red River and Mekong deltas (including Hanoi and Ho Chi Minh City) have few incidences of **malaria**. The coastal plain north of Nha Trang is also considered relatively safe. Malaria occurs frequently in the highlands and rural areas, notably the central highlands, as well as the southern provinces of Ca Mau, Bac Lieu and Tay Ninh. The majority of cases involve the most dangerous strain, *Plasmodium falciparum*, which can be fatal if not treated promptly.

The key preventive measure is to avoid getting bitten by mosquitoes (which carry the disease), but if you're travelling in high-risk areas it's advisable to take **preventive tablets**.

Mosquitoes are also responsible for transmitting dengue fever and Japanese encephalitis. **Dengue** is carried by a variety of mosquitoes active in the daytime (particularly two hours after sunrise and several hours before sunset) and occurs mostly in the Mekong Delta, including Ho Chi Minh City, though the chances of being infected remain small. There is a more dangerous version called dengue haemorrhage fever, which primarily affects children but is extremely rare among foreign visitors to Vietnam. If you notice an unusual tendency to bleed or bruise, seek medical advice immediately.

There are several things you can do to avoid getting bitten. Mosquitoes are most active at dawn and dusk, so at these times wear long sleeves, trousers and socks, avoid dark colours and perfumes, which attract mosquitoes, and put **repellent** on all exposed skin. Sprays and lotions containing around thirty to forty percent DEET (diethyltoluamide) are effective and can also be used to treat clothes, but the chemical is toxic: keep it away from eyes and open wounds.

Many hotels and guesthouses provide mosquito nets over beds or meshing on windows and doors. Air-conditioning and fans also help keep mosquitoes at bay, as do mosquito coils and knockdown insecticide sprays (available locally), though none of these measures is as effective as a decent net.

Bites and creepy–crawlies

Bed bugs, fleas, lice or scabies can be picked up from dirty bedclothes, though this is relatively unusual in Vietnam. Try not to scratch bites, which easily become septic. Ticks picked up walking through scrub may carry a strain of typhus; carry out regular body inspections and remove ticks promptly.

Rabies is contracted by being bitten, or even licked on broken skin or the eyes, by an infected animal. The best strategy is to give all animals, especially dogs, cats and monkeys, a wide berth.

Vietnam has several poisonous **snakes** but in general snakes steer clear of humans and it's very rare to get bitten. Avoid walking through long grass or undergrowth, and wear boots when walking off-road. If bitten, immobilize the limb (most snake bites occur on the lower leg) to slow down absorption of the venom and remove any tight-fitting socks or other clothing from around the wound. It's important to seek medical assistance as quickly as possible. It helps if you can take the (dead) snake to be identified, or at least remember what it looked like.

Leeches are more common and, though harmless, can be unpleasant. Long trousers, sleeves and socks help prevent them getting a grip. The best way to get rid of leeches is to burn them off with a lighted match or cigarette; alternatively rub alcohol or salt onto them.

Worms enter the body either via contaminated food, or through the skin, especially the soles of the feet. You may notice worms in your stools, or experience other indications such as mild abdominal pain leading, very rarely, to acute intestinal blockage (roundworm, the most common), an itchy anus (threadworm) or anaemia (hookworm). An infestation is easily treated with worming tablets from a pharmacy.

Heat trouble

Don't underestimate the strength of the tropical sun: **sunburn** can be avoided by restricting your exposure to the midday sun and liberal use of high-factor sunscreens. Drinking plenty of water will prevent **dehydration**, but if you do become dehydrated – signs are infrequent or irregular urination – drink a salt and sugar solution.

Heatstroke is more serious and may require hospital treatment. Indications are a high temperature, lack of sweating, a fast pulse and red skin. Reducing your body temperature with a lukewarm shower will provide initial relief.

High humidity often causes **heat rashes**, **prickly heat** and **fungal infections**. Prevention and cure are the same: wear loose clothes made of natural fibres, wash frequently and dry off thoroughly afterwards. Talcum powder helps, particularly zinc oxide-based products (prickly heat powder), as does the use of mild antiseptic soap.

Sexually transmitted diseases

Until recently Vietnam carried out very little screening for sex workers, injecting drug users and other high-risk groups. As a result, **sexually transmitted diseases** such as gonorrhoea, syphilis and AIDS had been flourishing, though fortunately awareness is growing and the number of AIDS victims, at least, is levelling out. It is, therefore, extremely unwise to contemplate casual unprotected sex, and bear in mind that Vietnamese condoms (*bao cao su*) are often poor-quality (more reliable imported varieties are available in major cities).

Getting medical help

Pharmacies can generally help with minor injuries or ailments and in major towns you will usually find a pharmacist who speaks English. The selection of reliable Asian and Western products on the market is improving rapidly, and both Ho Chi Minh City and Hanoi now have well-stocked pharmacies. That said, drugs past their shelf life and even counterfeit medicines are rife, so inspect packaging carefully, check use-by dates – and bring anything you know you're likely to need from home, including **oral contraceptives**. **Tampons** and reliable, imported brands of **condoms** (*bao cao su*) are sold in Hanoi and Ho Chi Minh City, but don't count on getting them easily elsewhere.

Local **hospitals** can also treat minor problems, but in a real emergency your best bet is to head for Hanoi or Ho Chi Minh City. Hospitals in both these cities can handle most eventualities and you also have the option of one of the excellent international medical centres. Addresses of clinics and hospitals can be found in our "Listings" sections for major towns throughout the book. Note that doctors and hospitals expect immediate cash payment for health services rendered; you will then have to seek reimbursement from your insurance

---

PRICING POLICY

Although Vietnamese law requires that all **prices** are quoted in dong, you'll find many hotels, the more upmarket restaurants, tour agents and so forth still use US dollars and, occasionally, euros. To reflect this and to avoid exchange-rate fluctuations, throughout the Guide we quote prices in the currency used on the spot.

Incidentally, don't be alarmed if you notice that Vietnamese pay less than you for plane tickets, at some hotels and at certain sights: Vietnam maintains a **two-tier pricing system**, with foreigners sometimes paying many times more than locals. The good news for tourists is that the system is being phased out, with prices for foreigners being adjusted downwards while those for Vietnamese rise to meet them. A single price system now applies on the trains, for example, while the gap has gradually been narrowing for air travel. It will take several more years before the practice disappears completely, however, and for the moment it remains something of a grey area, particularly as regards hotels and bus tickets, where the amount you pay may well depend on the person you happen to be dealing with.

company (make sure you get receipts for any payments you make).

Insurance

It is essential to have a good **travel insurance policy** to cover against theft, loss and illness or injury. It's also advisable to have medical cover that includes evacuation in the event of serious illness, as the local hospitals aren't that great. Most policies exclude so-called dangerous sports unless an extra premium is paid: in Vietnam this can include scuba diving, whitewater rafting, kitesurfing, rock-climbing and trekking. If you're doing any motorbike touring, you are strongly advised to take out full medical insurance including emergency evacuation; make sure the policy specifically covers you for biking in Vietnam, and ascertain whether benefits will be paid as treatment proceeds or only after you return home, and whether there is a 24-hour medical emergency number. If you need to make a claim, you should keep receipts for medicines and medical treatment, and in the event that you have anything stolen, you must obtain an official statement from the police.

Internet and email

Accessing the **internet** in Vietnam has become a great deal easier, though it is still monitored and controlled by a government fearful of this potentially subversive means of communication. Occasionally social networking sites like Facebook have been blocked.

There's no problem about logging on in the major cities and tourist centres in Vietnam, where you'll find dozens of **internet cafés,** while many hotels also offer internet access. Many upmarket and even some budget hotels offer wi-fi broadband access in your room – sometimes free to attract custom. Even remote regions are wired to the web these days, though the service may be slower and more expensive. Rates in the big cities currently stand at around 100đ per minute, with some places charging by the hour (about 6000đ).

Laundry

Most top- and mid-range hotels provide a **laundry service**, and many budget hotels too, but rates can vary wildly, so it's worth checking first. In the bigger cities, especially in tourist areas, you'll find laundry shops on the street, where the rate is usually around 10,000đ per kilo.

Mail

Mail can take anything from four days to four weeks in or out of Vietnam, depending largely where you are. Services are quickest and most reliable from the major towns, where eight to ten days is the norm. **Overseas postal rates** are reasonable: a postcard costs 7000–8000đ, while the price of a letter is in the region of 12,000đ for the minimum weight. **Express Mail Service** (EMS) operates to most countries and certain destinations within Vietnam; the service cuts down delivery times substantially and the letter or parcel is automatically registered. For a minimum-weight dispatch by EMS (under 250g), you'll pay around $30 to the UK, $32 to the US, $35 to Canada and $27 to Australia.

Poste restante services are available at all main post offices. You'll need to show your passport to collect mail and will be charged a small amount per item. Mail is held for two months before being returned. To avoid misfiling, your name should be printed clearly, with the surname in capitals and underlined, and it's still worth checking under all your names, just in case. Have letters addressed to you c/o Poste Restante, GPO, town or city, province.

When **sending parcels** out of Vietnam, take everything to the post office unwrapped since it will be inspected for any customs liability and wrapped for you, and the whole process, including wrapping and customs inspection, will cost you upwards of 30,000đ. Pirated CDs and DVDs and any other suspect items will be seized. Surface mail is the cheapest option, with parcels taking between one and four months.

Receiving parcels is not such a good idea. Some parcels simply go astray; those that do make it are subject to thorough customs inspections, import duty and even confiscation of suspicious items – particularly printed matter, videos or cassettes. However, if you do need to collect a parcel, remember to take your passport.

Maps

The most accurate and reliable map of Vietnam is the **Rough Guides** Map of Vietnam, Laos and Cambodia (1:1,200,000). Other decent maps are the International Travel Map of Vietnam (1:1,000,000) or Nelles (1:1,500,000) map of Vietnam, Laos and Cambodia: both feature plans of Ho Chi Minh City and Hanoi. Alternatively, the locally produced maps you'll find on sale in all the major towns and tourist destinations in Vietnam aren't bad.

If you need more detailed coverage, if you're cycling or motorbike touring for example, there's no beating the book of maps entitled Giao Thong Duong Bo Vietnam (1:500,000) published by Ban Do Cartographic Publishing House and available in bigger bookshops in Hanoi and Ho Chi Minh City. Trouble is, it weighs about a kilo. Another good option for cyclists and bikers is the Vietnam Administrative Atlas by the same publisher, with a map of each province per page. Look out, too, for Fauna and Flora International's Vietnam Ecotourism Map (1:1,000,000). Not only is it pretty accurate, but also includes information on visiting the national parks and other areas of environmental interest.

Money

Vietnam's unit of currency is the **dong**, which you'll see abbreviated as "đ", "d" or "VND" after an amount. Notes come in denominations of 500đ, 1000đ, 2000đ, 5000đ, 10,000đ, 20,000đ, 50,000đ, 100,000đ, 200,000đ and 500,000đ, coins in 200đ, 500đ, 1000đ, 2000đ and 5000đ (though coins are rarely seen). In addition to the dong, the **American dollar** operates as a parallel, unofficial currency and it's a good idea to carry some dollars as a back-up to pay large bills. On the whole, though, it's more convenient to operate in dong, and you'll often find dong prices are slightly lower than the equivalent in dollars.

At the time of writing, the **exchange rate** was around 33,000đ to £1; 20,000đ to US$1; 29,000đ to 1 Euro; 21,000đ to CA$1; 22,000đ to AUS$1; and 17,000đ to NZ$1. Recently the country has been plagued by high inflation rates, so these exchange rates are liable to fluctuate. For the latest exchange rates go to ⓦxe.com.

Dong are not available outside Vietnam at present, so take in some small-denomination American dollars to use until you reach a bank or ATM. Most **banks** and **exchange bureaux** don't charge for changing foreign currency into dong; banks in major cities will accept euros and other major currencies, but elsewhere may only accept dollars. Some tour agents and hotels will also change money, and most jewellery shops in Vietnam will exchange dollars at a slightly better rate than the banks, but watch out for scams. Wherever you change money, ask for a mix of denominations (in remote places, bigger bills can be hard to split), and refuse really tatty banknotes, as you'll have difficulty getting anyone else to accept them.

There's also a comprehensive network of **ATMs**, many open 24 hours: most accept Visa, MasterCard and American Express cards issued abroad. The maximum withdrawal is two million dong at a time, with a charge of 20,000–30,000đ per transaction (in addition to whatever surcharges your own bank levies). In Hanoi and Ho Chi Minh City you'll also find ATMs operated by ANZ and HSBC. These accept a wider range of cards, including those in the Cirrus and Plus networks.

Major **credit cards** – Visa, MasterCard and, to a lesser extent, American Express – are accepted in Vietnam's main cities and major tourist spots. All top-level and many mid-level hotels will accept them, as will a growing number of restaurants, though some places levy surcharges of three to four percent.

Travellers' cheques are less common now that ATMs are so widespread, but can be cashed at major banks (you need your passport as ID), for a commission of up to two percent. Vietinbank generally charges the lowest rates: at the time of writing these were 0.55 percent (minimum $1.1) when changing into dong and 1.1 percent (minimum $2.2) into dollars or other foreign currencies. Vietcombank waives commission on American Express travellers' cheques.

Having **money wired** from home via MoneyGram (UK ☎0800 8971 8971, US ☎1 800 ☎666 3947, ⓦmoneygram.com) or Western Union (US ☎1 800 325 6000, ⓦwesternunion.com) is never cheap, and should be considered a last resort. It's also possible to have money wired directly from a bank or post office in your home country to a bank in Vietnam, although this has the added complication of involving two separate institutions; money wired this way normally takes two working days to arrive, and charges vary according to the amount sent.

Opening hours

Basic **hours of business** are 7.30–11.30am and 1.30–4.30pm, though after lunch nothing really gets going again before 2pm. The standard closing day for offices is Sunday, and many now also close on Saturdays, including most state-run banks and government offices.

Most **banks** tend to work Monday to Friday 8–11.30am and 1–4pm, though some stay open later in the afternoon or may forego a lunch break. In tourist centres you'll even find branches open evenings and weekends. **Post offices** keep much longer hours, in general staying open from 6.30am through to 9pm with no closing day. Some sub-post offices work shorter hours and close at weekends.

Shops and **markets** open seven days a week and in theory keep going all day, though in practice most stallholders and many private shopkeepers will take a siesta. Shops mostly stay open late into the evenings, perhaps until 8pm or beyond in the big cities.

Museums tend to close one day a week, generally on Mondays, and their core opening hours are 8–11am and 2–4pm. **Temples** and **pagodas** occasionally close for lunch but are otherwise open all week and don't close until late evening.

Telephones

Rates for **international calls** are very reasonable, with international direct dialling (IDD) costing around 4,000đ per minute (depending where you are calling). Using the prefix 171 reduces rates by a further 10–20 percent. The 171 service can be used from any phone, except for operator-assisted calls, mobile phones, cardphones or faxes: post offices will charge a small fee for using it.

Nearly all post offices have IDD (international direct dialling) facilities, and most hotels offer IDD from your room, but you'll usually be charged at least ten percent above the norm and a minimum charge of one minute even if the call goes unanswered.

If you're running short of funds, you can almost always get a "**call-back**" at post offices. Ask to make a minimum (1min) call abroad and remember to get the phone number of the booth you're calling from. You can then be called back directly, at a total cost to you of a one-minute international call plus a small charge for the service. It's also possible to make **collect calls** to certain countries; ask at the post office or call the international operator on ☎110.

Local calls are easy to make and are often free, though you may be charged a small fee of a few thousand dong for the service. As in many countries, public phones are turning into battered monuments to outdated technology as mobile phones become ubiquitous (there's now more than one phone per user in Vietnam). However, transport centres like airports and bus stations still maintain a few functioning machines, which accept only pre-paid phone cards, not coins. All post offices also operate a public phone service, where the cost is displayed as you speak and you pay the cashier afterwards.

In late 2008, all phone numbers in Vietnam acquired an extra digit after the area code and before the actual number, so phone numbers in Hanoi and Ho Chi Minh City now have eight digits and other towns have seven digits after the area code. For subscribers to Vietnam Post and Telecommunications (VNPT), which is over 95 percent of the country, the extra digit is 3, though subscribers to smaller service providers have added a 2, 4, 5 or 6. We have included the new digits in this Guide, though you may still see some old numbers in Vietnam itself, and many businesses have yet to update their websites.

Mobile phones

If you want to use your own **mobile phone** in Vietnam, the simplest – and cheapest – thing to do is to buy a SIM card and a prepaid phone card locally. Both the big phone companies, Vinaphone (ⓦvinaphone.com.vn) and Mobiphone (ⓦmobiphone.com.vn), offer English-language support and similar prices, though Vinaphone perhaps has the edge for geographical coverage (which extends pretty much nationwide). At the time of writing, Vinaphone starter kits including a SIM card cost 120,000đ (with 100,000đ worth of calls credited to your account). Further prepaid cards are available in various sizes from 100,000đ to 500,000đ. Phone calls cost slightly more than from a land line, while sending an SMS message costs 100–300đ in Vietnam and about 2,500đ internationally. However, rates are falling rapidly as more competitors enter the increasingly deregulated market.

The other, far more expensive, option is to stick with your home service-provider – though you'll need to check beforehand whether they offer international roaming services.

DIALLING CODES

All phone numbers in Vietnam consist of nine to eleven digits, with the first two-four digits representing the area code and the remaining digits the specific number. The complete number must be dialled whether you are phoning locally or long distance.

To **call Vietnam from abroad**, dial your international access code, then ☎84 + number minus the first 0.

To **call abroad from Vietnam**, dial either ☎171 00 or just ☎00 followed by the country code (see below) + area code minus first 0 + number.

Australia ☎61	New Zealand ☎64
Canada ☎1	UK ☎44
Ireland ☎353	US ☎1

Time

Vietnam is seven hours ahead of London, twelve hours ahead of New York, fifteen hours ahead of Los Angeles, one hour behind Perth and three hours behind Sydney – give or take an hour or two when summer time is in operation.

Tourist information

Tourist information on Vietnam is at a premium. The Vietnamese government maintains a handful of **tourist promotion offices** and a smattering of accredited travel agencies around the globe, most of which can supply you with only the most general information. A better source of information, much of it based on firsthand experiences, is the internet, with numerous **websites** around to help you plan your visit. Some of the more useful and interesting sites are Ⓦ travelfish.org, a regularly updated online guide to Southeast Asia; Ⓦ worldtravelguide.net, a viewer-friendly source of information on Vietnam and other countries; Ⓦ activetravelvietnam.com, with helpful information about national parks and beaches; and Ⓦ thingsasian.com, which consists mostly of features on Asian destinations and culture.

In Vietnam itself there's a frustrating dearth of free and impartial advice. The **state-run tourist offices** – under the auspices of either the Vietnam National Administration of Tourism (Ⓦ vietnam tourism.com) or the local provincial organization – are thinly disguised tour agents, profit-making concerns which don't take kindly to being treated as information bureaux, though the official website has a lot of useful information about destinations and practicalities such as visas. In any case, Western concepts of information don't necessarily apply here – bus timetables, for example, simply don't exist. The most you're likely to get is a glossy brochure detailing their tours and affiliated hotels.

You'll generally have more luck approaching hotel staff or one of the many **private tour agencies** operating in all the major tourist spots (see "Listings" for individual cities in the Guide), where staff have become accustomed to Westerners' demands for advice.

Another useful source of information, including restaurant and hotel listings as well as feature articles, is the growing number of **English-language magazines**, such as Asialife, The Word and *The Guide* (see p.46). There's also a government-run **telephone information service** (☎ 1080) with some English-speaking staff who will answer all manner of questions – if you can get through, since the lines are often busy.

Travellers with special needs

Despite the fact that Vietnam is home to so many war-wounded, few provisions are made for the disabled. This means you'll have to be pretty self-reliant. It's important to contact airlines, hotels and tour companies as far in advance as possible to make sure they can accommodate your requirements.

Getting about can be made a little easier by taking internal flights, or by renting a private car or minibus with a driver. Taxis are widely available in Hanoi, Ho Chi Minh City and other major cities. Even so, trying to cross roads with speeding traffic and negotiating the cluttered and uneven pavements – where pavements exist – pose real problems. Furthermore, few buildings are equipped with ramps and lifts.

When it comes to **accommodation**, Vietnam's new luxury hotels usually offer one or two specially adapted rooms. Elsewhere, the best you can hope for is a ground-floor room, or a hotel with a lift.

One, albeit expensive, option is to ask a tour agent to arrange a **customized tour**. Saigontourist (Ⓦ saigontourist.com) has experience of running tours specifically for disabled visitors.

Travelling with children

Travelling through Vietnam with children can be challenging and fun. The Vietnamese adore kids and make a huge fuss of them, with fair-haired kids coming in for even more manhandling. The main concern will probably be **hygiene**: Vietnam can be distinctly unsanitary, and children's stomachs tend to be more sensitive to bacteria. Avoiding spicy foods will help while their stomachs adjust, but if children do become sick it's crucial to keep up their fluid intake, so as to avoid dehydration. Bear in mind, too, that **healthcare facilities** are fairly basic outside Hanoi and Ho Chi Minh City, so make sure your travel insurance includes full medical evacuation.

Long bus journeys are tough on young children, so wherever possible, take the train – at least the kids can get up and move about in safety. There are reduced fares for children on domestic flights, trains and open-tour buses. On trains, for example, it's free for under-fives (as long as they sit on your lap) and half-price for children aged 5 to 10. Open-tour buses follow roughly the same policy, though children paying a reduced fare are not entitled to a seat; if you don't want them on your lap you'll have to pay full fare. Tours are usually either free or half-price for children.

Many budget **hotels** have rooms with three or even four single beds in them. At more expensive hotels under-12s can normally stay free of charge in their parents' rooms and baby cots are becoming more widely available.

Working and studying in Vietnam

Without a prearranged job and work permit, don't bank on finding work in Vietnam. With specific skills to offer, you could try approaching some of the Western companies now operating in Hanoi and Ho Chi Minh City.

Otherwise, **English-language teaching** is probably the easiest job to land, especially if you have a TEFL (Teaching English as a Foreign Language), TESOL (Teacher of English to Speakers of Other Languages) or CELTA (Certificate in English Language Teaching to Adults) qualification. Universities are worth approaching, though pay is better at private schools, where qualified teachers earn upwards of $20 an hour. In either case, you'll need to apply for a work permit, sponsored by your employer, and then a working visa. Private tutoring is an unwieldy way of earning a crust, as you'll have to pop out of the country every few months to procure a new visa. Furthermore, the authorities are clamping down on people working without the proper authorizations.

The main English-language teaching operations recruiting in Vietnam include the British Council (ⓦbritishcouncil.org/Vietnam.htm), ILA Vietnam (ⓦilavietnam.com), Language Link Vietnam (ⓦlanguagelink.edu.vn) and RMIT International University (ⓦrmit.edu.vn). The TEFL website (ⓦtefl.com) and Dave's ESL Café (ⓦeslcafe.com) also have lists of English-teaching vacancies in addition to lots of other useful information.

There are also opportunities for **volunteer work.** Try contacting the organizations listed below, or look on the websites of the NGO Resource Centre Vietnam (ⓦngocentre.org.vn) and Volunteer Abroad (ⓦvolunteerabroad.com).

Study, work and volunteer programmes

Australian Volunteers International Australia ☎03 9279 1788, ⓦ australianvolunteers.com. Postings for up to two years, focusing on rural development, vocational education and capacity building.

British Council UK ☎0161 957 7755, ⓦbritishcouncil.org. TEFL vacancies are posted at ⓦ britishcouncil.org/teacherrecruitment, or call ☎020 7389 4931. Information on teacher exchange and development programmes abroad can be found at ⓦ britishcouncil.org/learning-ie-teaching-exchange.htm.

Brockport Vietnam Project US ☎1 800 298 7869, ⓦ brockportabroad.com. Opportunities for American undergraduates and graduates to study in Da Nang, and to participate in community service activities.

Council on International Educational Exchange (CIEE) US ☎1 800 407 8839, ⓦ ciee.org. The non-profit parent organization of Council Travel, CIEE runs semester and academic-year programmes in Vietnam.

Earthwatch Institute UK ☎01865 318838, US & Canada ☎1 978 461 0081, Australia ☎03 9682 6828; ⓦ earthwatch.org. Long-established international charity with environmental and archeological research projects worldwide, including Vietnam. Participation mainly as a paying volunteer but fellowships for teachers and students are available.

Global Volunteer Network UK ☎0800 032 5035, US ☎1 800 963 1198, Australia ☎1800 203 012, New Zealand ☎04 920 1451; ⓦ globalvolunteernetwork.org. Non-governmental organization that supports the work of local communities through the placement of international volunteers.

Voluntary Service Overseas (VSO) UK ☎020 8780 7500, ⓦvso.org.uk. A British government-funded organization that places volunteers in various projects around the world.

Volunteers for Peace US ☎802 540 3060, ⓦvfp.org. Non-profit organization with links to a huge international network of "workcamps", two- to four-week programmes that bring volunteers together from many countries to carry out needed community projects. Most workcamps are in summer, with registration by April/May.

Ho Chi Minh City and around

1

Ho Chi Minh City and around

Ho Chi Minh City – or Thanh Pho Ho Chi Minh, to give it its full Vietnamese title – is Vietnam's centre of commerce and the country's biggest city, though not its administrative capital – an honour that rests with Hanoi. As a result of the sweeping economic changes wrought by *doi moi* in 1986, this effervescent city, perched on the banks of the Saigon River and still known as Saigon to its eight million or so inhabitants, has changed its image from that of a war-torn city to one of a thriving metropolis, challenging Singapore, Bangkok and the other traditional Southeast Asian powerhouses. All the accoutrements of economic success – fine restaurants, flash hotels, glitzy bars and clubs, and shops selling imported luxury goods – are here, adding a glossy veneer to the city's hotchpotch landscape of French stones of empire, venerable pagodas and austere, Soviet-style housing blocks.

Sadly, however, Ho Chi Minh City (HCMC) is still full of people for whom economic progress has not yet translated into food, housing and jobs. Street children roam the tourist enclaves hawking books, postcards, lottery tickets and cigarette lighters; limbless mendicants haul themselves about on crude trolleys; and watchful pickpockets prowl crowded streets on the lookout for unguarded wallets. Though the number of beggars is gradually declining, tourists must quickly come to accept them as a hassle that goes with the territory. In addition, the arrival, en masse, of wealthy Westerners has lured many women into prostitution, for which the go-go bars of Dong Khoi became famous during the American War.

If Hanoi is a city of romance and mellow charms, then Ho Chi Minh City is its antithesis, a fury of sights and sounds, and the crucible in which Vietnam's rallying fortunes are boiling. Few corners of the city afford respite from the cacophony of **construction work** casting up new office blocks and hotels with logic-defying speed. An increasing number of cars and minibuses jostle with an organic mass of state-of-the-art Honda SUVs, choking the tree-lined streets and boulevards. Amid this melee, the local people go about their daily life: smartly dressed schoolkids wander past streetside baguette-sellers; women shoppers ride motorbikes clad in gangster-style bandanas to protect their skin from the sun and dust; while teenagers in designer jeans chirrup into mobile phones. Much of the fun of being in Ho Chi Minh City derives from the simple pleasure of absorbing its flurry of activity – something best done from the seat of a cyclo or a roadside café. To blink is to miss some new and singular sight, be it a motorbike stacked high with piglets bound for the market, or a boy on a bicycle rapping out a staccato tattoo on pieces of bamboo to advertise noodles for sale.

HCMC is divided into 24 districts, though tourists rarely travel beyond districts One, Three and Five. In addition, an increasing number of expats reside in **Phu My Hung**, aka South Saigon, in district Seven – a squeaky-clean suburb that wouldn't look out of place in Singapore, making quite a contrast to the rest of this seething metropolis. The city proper hugs the west bank of the **Saigon River**, and its central area, District One, nestles in the hinge formed by the confluence of the river with the **Ben Nghe Channel**; traditionally the French Quarter of the city, this area is still widely known as Saigon. **Dong Khoi** is its delicate backbone, and around the T-shape it forms with **Le Duan Boulevard** are located several of the city's museums and colonial remnants. However, many of the city's other sights are scattered further afield, so visitors have to effect a dot-to-dot of the sights that appeal most. These invariably

Highlights

1 **War Remnants Museum** The city's most moving museum, a stark reminder of man's inhumanity to man. **See p.80**

2 **Ben Thanh Market** Check the city's pulse here on an early-morning stroll. **See p.81**

3 **Jade Emperor Pagoda** Beautiful carved woodwork, an eclectic collection of deities and a constant fog of incense make this the city's most fascinating temple. **See p.83**

4 **Saigon's cafés** Linger over a latte and watch the world roll by at one of the city's hip cafés, such as Napoli Café or La Fenetre Soleil. **See pp.96–102**

5 **Cho Lon** Take an improvised wander around the streets of "big market" – Saigon's Chinatown. **See p.84**

6 **Saigon Skydeck** Enjoy the view from the 49th floor of the Bitexco Tower, the city's newest icon. **See p.77**

7 **Dong Khoi shops** The boutiques on and around this famous street specialize in silks and paintings. **See p.72**

8 **Live music** Check out the local talent at happening bars like *La Habana* and *Yoko's* **See pp.102–105**

HIGHLIGHTS ARE MARKED ON THE MAP ON PP.74–75

1

include one or more of the museums that pander to the West's fixation with the American War, the pick of the bunch being the **War Remnants Museum** and **Ho Chi Minh City Museum**.

For some visitors, the war is their primary frame of reference and such historical hot spots as the **Reunification Palace** rank highly on their itineraries. Yet the city pre-dates American involvement by several centuries, and not all of its sights revolve around planes, tanks and rusting ordnance. Ostentatious reminders of French rule abound, among them such memorable buildings as **Notre Dame Cathedral** and the grandiose **Hotel de Ville** – but even these look spanking-new when compared to gloriously musty edifices like **Quan Am Pagoda** and the **Jade Emperor Pagoda**, just a couple of the many captivating places of worship across the city. And if the chaos becomes too much, you can escape to the relative calm of the **Botanical Gardens** – also home to the city's **History Museum** and **zoo**.

It's one of Ho Chi Minh City's many charms that once you've exhausted, or been exhausted by, all it has to offer, paddy fields, beaches and wide-open countryside are not far away. The most popular trip **out of the city** is to the **Cu Chi tunnels**, where villagers dug themselves out of the range of American shelling. The tunnels are often

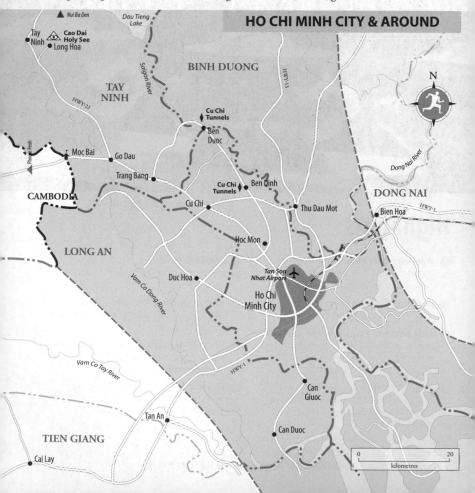

1

twinned with a tour around the fanciful Great Temple of the indigenous Cao Dai religion at **Tay Ninh**. A brief taster of the Mekong Delta at **My Tho** (see pp.120–123) or a dip in the South China Sea at **Ho Coc** (see p.218) are also eminently possible in a long day's excursion.

The **best time to visit** tropical Ho Chi Minh City is in the dry season, which runs from December through to April. During the wet season, May to November, there are frequent tropical storms, though these won't disrupt your travels too much. Average temperatures, year-round, hover between 26°C and 29°C; March, April and May are the hottest months.

Brief history

Knowledge of Ho Chi Minh City's early history is sketchy at best. Between the first and sixth centuries, the territory on which it lies fell under the nominal rule of the **Funan Empire** to the west. Funan was subsequently absorbed by the Kambuja peoples of the pre-Angkor **Chen La Empire**, but it is unlikely that these imperial machinations had much bearing upon the sleepy fishing backwater that would later develop into Ho Chi Minh City.

Khmer fishermen eked out a living here, building their huts on the stable ground just north of the delta wetlands, which made it ideal for human settlement. Originally named **Prei Nokor**, it flourished as an entrepô for Cambodian boats pushing down the Mekong River, and by the seventeenth century it boasted a garrison and a mercantile community that embraced Malay, Indian and Chinese traders.

Such a dynamic settlement was bound to draw attention from the north. By the eighteenth century, the **Viets** had subdued the kingdom of Champa, and this area was swallowed up by Hué's **Nguyen Dynasty**. With new ownership came a new name, **Saigon**, thought to be derived from the Vietnamese word for the kapok tree. Upon the outbreak of the **Tay Son Rebellion**, in 1772, Nguyen Anh bricked the whole settlement into a walled fortress, the eight-sided **Gia Dinh Citadel**. The army that put down the Tay Son brothers included an assisting **French** military force, who grappled for several decades to undermine Vietnamese control in the region and develop a trading post in Asia. Finally, in 1861, they seized Saigon, using Emperor Tu Duc's persecution of French missionaries as a pretext. The 1862 **Treaty of Saigon** declared the city the capital of French Cochinchina.

Colonial-era Saigon

Ho Chi Minh City owes much of its form and character to the French colonists: channels were filled in, marshlands drained and steam tramways set to work along its regimental grid of tamarind-shaded boulevards, which by the 1930s sported names like Boulevard de la Somme and Rue Rousseau. Flashy examples of European architecture were erected, cafés and boutiques sprang up to cater for its new, Vermouth-sipping, baguette-munching citizens and the city was imbued with such an all-round Gallic air that Somerset Maugham, visiting in the 1930s, found it reminiscent of "a little provincial town in the south of France, a blithe and smiling little place". The French *colons* (colonials) bankrolled improvements to Saigon with the vast profits they were able to cream from exporting Vietnam's **rubber** and **rice** out of the city's rapidly expanding seaport.

On a human level, however, French rule was invariably harsh; dissent crystallized in the form of strikes through the 1920s and 1930s, but the nationalist movement hadn't gathered any real head of steam before **World War II**'s tendrils spread to Southeast Asia. At its close, the **Potsdam Conference** of 1945 set the British Army the task of disarming Japanese troops in southern Vietnam. Arriving in Saigon two months later, they promptly returned power to the French and so began thirty years of war. Saigon saw little action during the anti-French war, which was fought mostly in the countryside and resulted in the French capitulation at Dien Bien Phu in 1954.

1

THE STREET OF MANY NAMES

Slender **Dong Khoi**, running for just over 1km from Le Duan to the Saigon River, has long mirrored Ho Chi Minh City's changing fortunes. The French knew the road as Rue Catinat, a tamarind-shaded thoroughfare that constituted the heart of French colonial life. Here the *colons* would promenade, stopping at chic boutiques and perfumeries, and gathering at noon and dusk at cafés such as the *Rotonde* and the *Taverne Alsacienne* for a Vermouth or Dubonnet, before hailing a *pousse-pousse* (a hand-pulled variation on the cyclo) to run them home. With the departure of the French in 1954, **President Diem** saw fit to change the street's name to Tu Do, "Freedom", and it was under this guise that a generation of young American GIs came to know it, as they toured the glut of bars – *Wild West, Uncle Sam's, Playboy* – that sprang up to pander to their more lascivious needs. After Saigon fell in 1975, the more politically correct moniker of Dong Khoi, or "Uprising", was adopted, but the street quickly went to seed in the dark, pre-*doi moi* years, and by the seventies had gone, in the words of Le Ly Hayslip, from "bejewelled, jaded dowager to shabby, grasping bag lady".

Saigon in the American War

Designated the capital of the **Republic of South Vietnam** by President Diem in 1955, Saigon was soon both the nerve centre of the American war effort, and its R&R capital, with a slough of sleazy bars along Dong Khoi (known then as Tu Do) catering to GIs on leave from duty. Despite the Communist bomb attacks and demonstrations by students and monks that periodically disturbed the peace, these were good times for Saigon, whose entrepreneurs prospered on the back of the tens of thousands of Americans posted here. The gravy train ran out of steam with the withdrawal of American troops in 1973, and two years later the **Ho Chi Minh Campaign** rolled into the city and through the gates of the presidential palace and the Communists were in control. Within a year, Saigon had been renamed **Ho Chi Minh City**.

Post-reunification Saigon

The **war years** extracted a heavy toll: American carpet-bombing of the Vietnamese countryside forced millions of refugees into the relative safety of the city, and ill-advised, post-reunification policies triggered a social and economic stagnation whose ramifications still echo like ripples on a lake. Persecution of southerners with links to the Americans saw many thousands sent to re-education camps. Millions more fled the country by boat.

Only in 1986, when the **economic liberalization**, *doi moi*, was established, and a market economy reintroduced, did the fortunes of the city show signs of taking an upturn. Today, more than two decades later, the city's resurgence is well advanced and its inhabitants are eyeing the future with unprecedented optimism.

Dong Khoi

Dong Khoi, the city's main street that runs through the centre of District one, is currently undergoing massive changes, with entire blocks being razed and towering monoliths such as "Times Square", half-way down the street, set to transform its image further still in the near future. Fortunately the street still has some character in the form of chic boutiques with eye-catching window displays and cute cafés in which to pause between shopping or sightseeing.

Notre Dame Cathedral

Han Thuyen • Sunrise to sunset • Free

The attractive redbrick bulk of the late nineteenth-century **Notre Dame Cathedral** straddles the northern reach of Dong Khoi. Aside from the few stained-glass windows above and behind its altar, and its marble relief *Stations of the Cross*, the interior boasts only scant decoration. There's plenty of scope for people-watching, however, as a steady trickle of Catholics pass through in their best silk tunics and black pants, fingering rosary beads, their whispered prayers merging with the insistent murmur of the traffic outside. A statue of the **Virgin Mary** provides the centrepiece to the small **park** fronting the cathedral, where cyclo drivers loiter and kids hawk postcards and maps. Take a close look at her face, as on occasion locals swear they have seen her shed tears.

The General Post Office and around

2 Cong Xa Paris

The Notre Dame Cathedral's twin compass-point spires were, for decades, one of Saigon's handiest landmarks, but they're now dwarfed by the glass facade of **Diamond Plaza**, a gleaming **shopping mall**, and by the telecom tower above the **General Post Office**. A classic colonial edifice unchanged since its completion in the 1880s, the GPO is worth a peek inside for its nave-like foyer, lent character by two huge map-murals, one charting Saigon and its environs in 1892, the other the telegraphic lines of southern Vietnam and Cambodia in 1936. Further in, a huge portrait of Uncle Ho sporting a healthy tan and warm smile gazes down at the aged wooden benches and tables of the cavernous main hall.

Municipal Theatre

Lam Son Square • ☎ 08 3829 9976 • Open during rare performances only

Standing grandly on the eastern side of Lam Son Square, its cyclopean, domed entrance peering southwestwards down Le Loi, is the century-old **Municipal Theatre**. The National Assembly was temporarily housed here in 1955, but today, lovingly restored to its former glory, it once again presents fashion shows, drama and dance, though only occasionally.

Caravelle Hotel

Just south of the Municipal Theatre, the 1958-built and now grandiosely revamped **Caravelle Hotel** (see p.92) gazes down across the square at the more diminutive *Continental*. In its former incarnation, the *Caravelle* found favour with those Western journalists assigned to cover the war and its terrace bar saw many a report drafted over a stiff drink.

LAM SON SQUARE – THE HUB OF HCMC

A couple of hundred metres south of the cathedral, Dong Khoi briefly widens where the smart, white walls of the *Hotel Continental* (see p.92) announce your arrival in **Lam Son Square**. Once a bastion of French high society, and still one of the city's premier addresses, the hotel front terrace was the place to see and be seen earlier last century. Little wonder, then, that **Somerset Maugham**'s nose for a story led him here in the mid-1920s: "Outside the hotels are terraces," he recounted, "and at the hour of the aperitif, they are crowded with bearded, gesticulating Frenchmen drinking the sweet and sickly beverages… which they drink in France and they talk nineteen to the dozen in the rolling accent of the Midi… It is very agreeable to sit under the awning on the terrace of the Hotel Continental, with an innocent drink before you, [and] read in the local newspaper heated controversies upon the affairs of the colony." Sadly the terrace no longer exists, and the block opposite has just been flattened, so if you want to tap into the history of the place, the best you can do is to ensconce yourself in the hotel's café.

1

Indian Jamia Mosque

66 Dong Du · Sunrise to sunset

Though glitzy boutiques predominate along Dong Khoi below the *Caravelle*, they haven't yet managed entirely to eradicate the past and it's still possible to winkle out relics of old Saigon. Wander south of Lam Son and you'll soon meet Dong Du, where a left turn reveals the white and blue-washed walls of the 1930s **Indian Jamia Mosque**,

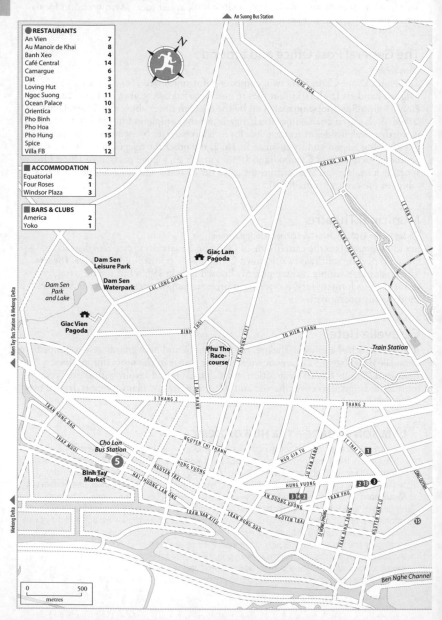

● RESTAURANTS	
An Vien	7
Au Manoir de Khai	8
Banh Xeo	4
Café Central	14
Camargue	6
Dat	3
Loving Hut	5
Ngoc Suong	11
Ocean Palace	10
Orientica	13
Pho Binh	1
Pho Hoa	2
Pho Hung	15
Spice	9
Villa FB	12

■ ACCOMMODATION	
Equatorial	2
Four Roses	1
Windsor Plaza	3

■ BARS & CLUBS	
America	2
Yoko	1

now towered over by the *Sheraton* (see p.94). The rounded curves of its arches and its slender minarets make a stark contrast to the utilitarian design of the hotel next door and there's a reassuring sense of peace that's enhanced by the slumbering worshippers lazing around the complex. If you're feeling peckish, check out the simple restaurant that is tucked round the back of the mosque, serving cheap and tasty dishes, many of which are vegetarian.

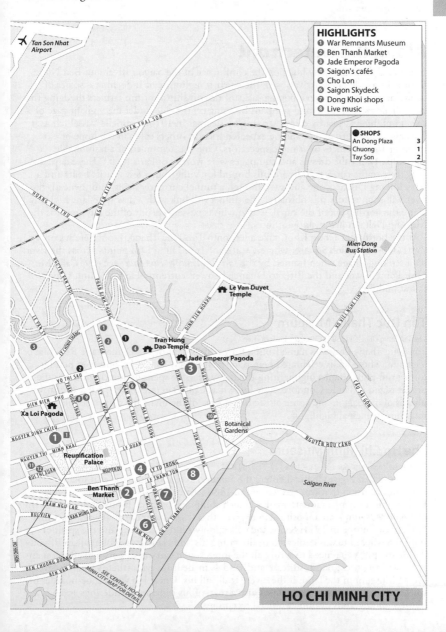

HIGHLIGHTS
1. War Remnants Museum
2. Ben Thanh Market
3. Jade Emperor Pagoda
4. Saigon's cafés
5. Cho Lon
6. Saigon Skydeck
7. Dong Khoi shops
8. Live music

● **SHOPS**
An Dong Plaza	3
Chuong	1
Tay Son	2

HO CHI MINH CITY

1

The Grand and Majestic hotels

A stroll to the river along Dong Khoi takes you past two of the city's more venerable hotels, the lovingly restored *Grand* (see p.94) on the left, followed thirty metres later on the right by the lavish, riverfront *Majestic* (see p.94). These two hotels have often vied for the title of best colonial-style hotel along Dong Khoi, but once the *Grand* opens a super-modern, two hundred-room extension in 2012, it seems the *Majestic* will be the only contender.

Along the waterfront

In colonial days, the **quay** hugging the confluence of the Saigon River and Ben Nghe Channel provided new arrivals with their first real glimpse of Indochina – scores of coolie-hatted dock-workers lugging sacks of rice off ships, shrimp farmers dredging the oozy shallows, and junks and sampans bobbing on the tide under the vigilant gaze of *colons* imbibing at nearby cafés. Arriving by steamer in 1910, Gabrielle Vassal felt as if "all Saigon had turned out". Some expected friends, others came in the hope of meeting acquaintances or as mere spectators. One was reminded of a fashionable garden party, for the dresses and equipages were worthy of Paris itself." These days the only river traffic consists of hydrofoils bound for Vung Tau, a few tourist boats and a ferry linking Districts one and two, though a tunnel currently being built beneath the river will soon render this obsolete. The tunnel will link with a new four-lane highway along the north bank of the canal, which whisks passengers out of the city towards the Mekong Delta in just twenty minutes.

At the bottom of Dong Khoi, take a left onto Ton Duc Thang. From here it's only a short skip to **Me Linh Square**, where a statue of Tran Hung Dao points across the river: it's a striking image when framed by the tall *Renaissance Riverside* (see p.94), the Me Linh Point Tower and the Bitexco Financial Tower, currently Ho Chi Minh City's tallest building.

Ton Duc Thang Museum

5 Ton Duc Thang • Tues–Sun 7.30–11.30am & 1.30–5pm • Free

Ton Duc Thang draws its name from a former president of the Democratic Republic of Vietnam, whose life is celebrated here. Don't expect any fireworks, however: besides some grim photographs highlighting the many years he spent de-husking rice on the prison island of Poulo Condore, now known as Con Dao (see p.209), a few evocative photos of old Saigon and some of the bric-a-brac of the man's life comprise the museum's principal highlights.

The Ho Chi Minh Museum

1 Nguyen Tat Thanh • Tues–Sun 7.30–11.30am & 1.30–5pm • 10,000đ

Where the Ben Nghe Channel enters the Saigon River, a bridge crosses it to an imposing mansion that was erected in the 1860s. Known as the *Nha Rong*, or Dragon House, this former headquarters of a French shipping company is now home to the **Ho Chi Minh Museum** – an apposite venue, given that it was from the abutting wharf that Ho left for Europe in 1911. Sadly, the collection within fails to capture the spirit of this man whose life was dedicated to liberating his homeland from colonialism. If you decide to visit, you'll need to wring all the interest you can out of personal effects such as his walking stick, rattan suitcase and sandals made from tyres (there's a pair in every HCM Museum in the land; if they were really all his, Uncle Ho was a shoe-hoarder of Imelda Marcos proportions). There's also a map of his itinerant wanderings and a few blurred photographs of him at official receptions.

Around Nguyen Hué

When Saigon's French administrators laid the 750m sweep of Charner Boulevard over a filled-in canal and down to the Saigon River, their brief was to replicate the elegance of a tree-lined Parisian boulevard, and in its day this broad avenue was known as the Champs Elysées of the East. These days, however, **Nguyen Hué**, as it is now known, is a mish-mash of architectural styles and has little character except on Sundays and at festival time. Each Sunday evening, the city's trendsetting youth converge here and on nearby Dong Khoi on their motorbikes, to circle round and round, girlfriends riding pillion, in a strange ritual that recreates the traffic jams that they suffer through on weekdays. During Tet the street also bursts into life, hosting a vast, riotously colourful flower market which draws Vietnamese belles in their thousands to pose in their best *ao dai* among the roses, sunflowers, chrysanthemums and conical orange trees.

Hotel de Ville

Le Thanh Ton

The stately edifice that stands at Nguyen Hué's northern extent is the former **Hotel de Ville**, the city's most photographed icon and an ostentatious reminder of colonial Europe's stubborn resolve to stamp its imprint on the countries it subjugated, no matter how incongruous. Built in 1902–08 as the city's administrative hub, this wedding cake of a building today houses the People's Committee behind its showy jumble of Corinthian columns, classical figures and shuttered windows, and thus is not open to the public. A **statue of Uncle Ho** cradling a small child watches over the tiny **park** fronting the building, where flowerbeds add a splash of colour.

The Rex Hotel

At the junction of Nguyen Hué and Le Loi

The **Rex Hotel** (see p.94) may give the impression of being venerable, but in fact has only operated as a hotel since 1976. Having started out as a garage for the Renaults and Peugeots of the city's French expat community, during the 1960s it billeted American officers, and hosted regular press briefing sessions that came to be known by jaded members of the press as the "Five O'Clock Follies". From its fifth-floor *Rooftop Garden* bar, the hotel yields a superb view of the whirl of life on the street below, best enjoyed over a fruit juice or cool glass of beer. At night, the hotel's emblem, a giant **crown**, lights up on the terrace, providing the city with one of its best-known landmarks.

Bitexco Financial Tower

Saigon skydeck (49th floor) • Sun–Thurs 9.30am–9.30pm, Fri–Sat 9.30am–10pm • 200,000đ • Last ticket 45min before closing

With its tapered shape and distinctive helipad protruding like a tongue near the top, this sleek, glass tower is destined to become one of Saigon's most memorable icons. It stands just to the east of the south end of Nguyen Hué and a stone's throw from the river. Visitors come not so much for its ground-floor car showrooms and offices of wheelers and dealers, but for the sweeping views from the Saigon Skydeck on the 49th floor, 178m above the ground. Look upwards and you'll see the lip of the helipad on the floor above; look down and you should spot a few familiar sights, such as Ben Thanh market, the Hotel de Ville, the Opera House and the tips of the spires of Notre Dame Cathedral far below you. From this vantage point, it's evident that Saigon's skyline is changing at a breakneck pace.

1

Sri Thendayyutthapani Temple ✈

66 Ton That Thiep • Sunrise to sunset

The southern face of the block south of the *Rex* hides peaceful **Sri Thendayyutthapani Temple**, whose colourful *gopuram* (sculpted gate tower) looks out of place on this trendy strip of boutiques and bars. The place manages a certain rag-tag charisma, the lavish murals normally associated with Hindu temples replaced by faded paintings of Jawaharlal Nehru, Mahatma Gandhi and various deities from the Hindu pantheon, plus a ceiling gaily studded with coloured baubles and lamps. Steps beyond the topiary to the right of the main sanctuary lead to a roof terrace that's dominated by a weather-beaten tower of deities, whose ranks have been infiltrated by two incongruous characters dressed like public schoolboys in braces, shorts and striped ties, and waving merrily.

The Ho Chi Minh City Museum

65 Ly Tu Trong • Daily 8am–5pm • 15,000đ

Of all the stones of empire thrown up in Vietnam by the French, few are more eye-catching than the former **Gia Long Palace**, built a block west of the Hotel de Ville in 1886 as a splendid residence for the governor of Cochinchina. Homeless after the air attack that smashed his own palace, Diem decamped here in 1962, and it was in the tunnels beneath the building that he spent his last hours of office, before fleeing to Cha Tam Church in Cho Lon where he finally surrendered (see p.85). Ironically, it now houses the **Ho Chi Minh City Museum**, which makes use of photographs, documents and artefacts to trace the struggle of the Vietnamese people against France and America. Even if you're not desperate to learn more about the country's war-torn past, you're likely to be enchanted by the grandeur of the building, and you might even witness couples posing for wedding photographs, as the regal structure and well-tended gardens are a favourite backdrop for photographers.

The collection

The downstairs area is a hotchpotch of ancient artefacts and antique collections, along with a section on nature and another featuring ethnic clothing and implements. The museum shifts into higher gear upstairs, where the focus turns to the war with America. The best exhibits are those showcasing the ingenuity of the Vietnamese – bicycle parts made into mortars, a Suzuki motorbike in whose inner tubes documents were smuggled into Saigon, a false-floored boat in which guns were secreted and so on. Look out, too, for sweaters knitted by female prisoners on Con Dao Island bearing the Vietnamese words for "peace" and "freedom". Elsewhere, there's a cross-sectional model of the Cu Chi tunnels, and a rewarding gallery of photographs of the Ho Chi Minh Campaign and the fall of Saigon.

As with many of Vietnam's museums, the hardware of war is on display in the **gardens**. Tucked away behind the frangipanis and well-groomed hedges out back are a Soviet tank, an American helicopter and an anti-aircraft gun, while out front are two sleek but idle jets.

The Reunification Palace

135 Nam Ky Khoi Nghia • Daily 7.30–11am & 1–4pm • 30,000đ including guided tour

Five minutes' stroll north up Nam Ky Khoi Nghia from the Ho Chi Minh City Museum, a red flag billows proudly above the **Reunification Palace**. A whitewashed concrete edifice with all the charm of a municipal library, the palace occupies the site of the former Norodom Palace, a colonial mansion erected in 1871 to house the governor-general of Indochina. After the French departure in 1954, Ngo Dinh Diem commandeered this extravagant monument as his presidential palace, but after

---

1

THE TAKING OF THE PRESIDENTIAL PALACE

The **Reunification Palace** is so significant to the Vietnamese because it was the storming of its gates by a tank belonging to the Northern Army, on April 30 1975, that became the defining moment of the fall of Saigon and the South. These days, two tanks stand in the grounds as a reminder of the incident.

Of the many Western journalists on hand to witness the spectacle, none was better placed than English journalist and poet **James Fenton**, who conspired to hitch a ride on the tank that first crashed through the gates: "The tank speeded up, and rammed the left side of the palace gate. Wrought iron flew into the air, but the whole structure refused to give. I nearly fell off. The tank backed again, and I observed a man with a nervous smile opening the centre portion of the gate. We drove into the grounds of the palace, and fired a salute. An NLF soldier took the flag and, waving it above his head, ran into the palace. A few moments later, he emerged on the terrace, waving the flag round and round. Later still, there he was on the roof. The red and yellow stripes of the Saigon regime were lowered at last."

Inside the palace, **Duong Van Minh** ("Big Minh"), sworn in as president only two days before, readied to perform his last presidential duty. "I have been waiting since early this morning to transfer power to you," he said to General Bui Tin, to which the general replied: "Your power has crumbled. You cannot give up what you do not have."

---

sustaining extensive damage in a February 1962 assassination attempt by two disaffected Southern pilots, the place was condemned and pulled down. The present building was named the Independence Palace upon completion in 1966, only to be retitled the Reunification Hall when the South fell in 1975 (see box above). The reversion to the label "Palace" was doubtless made for tourist appeal. All visitors are required to join a group tour in one of several languages.

The tour

Before the tour you enter a **movie room**, where a potted account of Vietnamese history and the American War is screened half-hourly. Guides then usher you through the hall's many chambers, proudly pointing out every piece of porcelain, lacquerwork, rosewood and silk on display. Spookily unchanged from its working days, much of the building's **interior** is a time capsule of sixties and seventies kitsch: pacing its airy banqueting rooms, conference halls and reception areas, it's hard not to think you've strayed into the arch-criminal's lair in a James Bond movie. Most interesting is the **third floor**, where, as well as the presidential library (with works by Laurens van der Post and Graham Greene alongside heavyweight political tomes), there's a curtained projection room, and an entertainment lounge complete with tacky circular sofa and barrel-shaped bar. Nearby, a set of sawn-off elephant's feet add an eerie touch to the decor. Perhaps the most atmospheric part of the building is the **basement** and former command centre, where wood-panelled combat staff quarters yield archaic radio equipment and vast wall maps.

Cong Vien Van Hoa Park

Adjoining the western edge of the Reunification Palace's grounds, **Cong Vien Van Hoa Park**, also known as Tau Dan Park, is a municipal park whose tree-shaded lawns are pleasant for a stroll and heave with life each Sunday. During the colonial era, the park's northernmost corner was home to one of the linchpins of French expat society, the **Cercle Sportif**, a Westerners-only sports club where the *colons* gathered to swim and play tennis before sinking an aperitif and discussing the day's events. Today it functions as the Workers' Sports Club and also houses the Golden Dragon Water Puppet Theatre.

1

The War Remnants Museum

28 Vo Van Tan • Daily 7.30am–noon & 1.30–5pm • 15,000đ

A block north of Cong Vien Van Hoa Park, the **War Remnants Museum** is the city's most popular attraction but not for the faint-hearted. Unlike at the Ho Chi Minh City Museum, you are unlikely to be distracted here by the building that houses the heart-rending exhibits – a distressing compendium of the horrors of modern warfare. Some of the instruments of destruction are on display in the courtyard outside, including a 28-tonne howitzer and a ghoulish collection of bomb parts. There's also a guillotine that harvested heads at the Central Prison on Ly Tu Trong, first for the French and later for Diem.

The collection

Inside, a series of halls present a grisly portfolio of **photographs** of mutilation, napalm burns and torture. Most shocking is the gallery detailing the effects of the 75 million litres of defoliant sprays dumped across the country: beside the expected images of bald terrain, hideously malformed foetuses are preserved in pickling jars. A gallery that looks at international opposition to the war as well as the American peace movement adds a sense of balance, and makes a change from the self-glorifying tone of most Vietnamese museums. Accounts of servicemen – such as veteran B52 pilot Michael Heck – who attempted to discharge themselves from the war on ethical grounds are also featured. Artefacts donated to the museum by returned US servicemen add to the reconciliatory tone.

At the back of the museum is a grisly mock-up of the **tiger cages**, the godless prison cells of Con Son Island (see p.209), which could have been borrowed from the movie set of *Papillon*.

Xa Loi Pagoda

89 Ba Huyen Thanh Quan • Daily 6–11.30am & 2–9pm

Vapid **Xa Loi Pagoda**, a short walk west of the War Remnants Museum, became a hotbed of Buddhist opposition to Diem in 1963. The austere, 1956-built complex is unspectacular, its most striking component a tall **tower** whose unlovely beige blocks lend it a drabness even six tiers of Oriental roofs can't quite dispel. The main **sanctuary**, accessed by a dual staircase (men scale the left-hand flight, women the right), is similarly dull: beyond a vast joss-stick urn inventively decorated with marbles and shards of broken china, it's a lofty hall featuring a huge gilt Buddha and fourteen murals that narrate his life. Turn left and around the back of the Buddha, and you'll come across a shrine commemorating Thich Quang Duc and the other monks who set fire to themselves in Saigon in 1963 (see box opposite). Quang Duc's is the ghostly figure holding a set of beads, to the left of the shrine.

GOLDEN DRAGON WATER PUPPET THEATRE

If you sink into the depths of depression on leaving the War Remnants' Museum (see above), the perfect antidote is just a block away at 55b Nguyen Thi Minh Khai. Water puppets are an ingenious concept and few people fail to be enchanted at their first encounter with these waterborne buffoons. The tradition of water puppetry is much stronger in the north, but it's such an appealing aspect of Vietnamese culture that there's plenty of demand for shows in the south as well. The early-evening timing of the shows (book tickets through ☎08 3840 4027, ⊛goldendragonwaterpuppet.com; shows 5pm, 6.30pm; 50min;120,000đ) make them a fun activity with the kids before bed or dinner and consist of a dozen or so sketches on themes like rearing ducks and catching foxes, boat racing and unicorns playing with a ball.

THE SELF-IMMOLATION OF THICH QUANG DUC

In the early morning of June 11, 1963, a column of Buddhist monks left the **Xa Loi Pagoda** and processed to the intersection of Cach Mang Thang Tam and Nguyen Dinh Chieu. There, **Thich Quang Duc**, a 66-year-old monk from Hué, sat down in the lotus position and meditated as fellow monks doused him in petrol, and then set light to him in protest at the repression of Buddhists by President Diem, who was a Catholic. As flames engulfed the impassive monk and passers-by prostrated themselves before him, the cameras of the Western press corps rolled, and by the next morning the grisly event had grabbed the world's headlines. More self-immolations followed, and Diem's heavy-handed responses at Xa Loi – some four hundred monks and nuns were arrested and others cast from the top of the tower – led to massed popular demonstrations against the government. Diem, it was clear, had become a liability. On November 2, he and his brother were assassinated after taking refuge in Cho Lon's Cha Tam Church (see p.85), the victims of a military coup.

Ben Thanh Market

Junction of Le Loi and Le Lai • Sunrist to sunset

There's much more beneath the pillbox-style clock tower of **Ben Thanh Market** than just the cattle and seafood pictured on its front wall. The city's busiest market for almost a century, and known to the French as the *Halles Centrales*, Ben Thanh's dense knot of trade has caused it to burst at the seams, disgorging stalls onto the surrounding pavements. Inside the main body of the market, a tight grid of aisles, demarcated according to produce, teems with shoppers, and, if it's souvenirs you're after, a reconnaissance here will reveal conical hats, basketware, bags, shoes, lacquerware, Da Lat coffee and Vietnam T-shirts. Sadly, all stalls are now designated 'fixed price', so there's no more good-natured bargaining, and prices are generally a bit higher than elsewhere. Walk through to the wet market along the back of the complex, and you'll find buckets of eels, clutches of live frogs tied together at the legs, heaps of pigs' ears and snouts and baskets wedged full of hens, among other gruesome sights. If you can countenance the thought of eating after seeing – and smelling – this patch of the market, com, pho and baguette stalls proliferate towards the back of the main hall. In the evenings, foodstalls specializing in seafood set up along the sides of the market, attracting a mixed crowd of locals and tourists.

Sri Mariamman Hindu Temple

45 Truong Dinh • Sunrise to sunset

A block northwest of Ben Thanh, the aroma of jasmine and incense replaces the stench of butchery at Truong Dinh's **Sri Mariamman Hindu Temple**. Less engaging than Sri Thendayyutthapani (see p.78), Sri Mariamman's imposing walls are sometimes lined with vendors selling oil, incense and jasmine petals. The walls are topped by a colourful *gopuram*, or bank of sculpted gods. Inside, the gods Mariamman, Maduraiveeran and Pechiamman reside in stone sanctuaries reminiscent of the Cham towers upcountry, and there are more deities set into the walls around the courtyard.

Fine Art Museum

97a Pho Duc Chinh • Tues–Sun 9am–5pm • 10,000đ

A short stroll from Ben Thanh Market down Pho Duc Chinh, in a grand colonial mansion, Ho Chi Minh City's **Fine Art Museum** is worth a visit to view some of the country's best Cham and Oc Eo relics on the third floor. The first floor hosts temporary exhibitions, while the courtyard out back is given over to commerce in the form of artworks on sale by various city galleries. If you're in the market for a piece of Vietnamese art, it's worth checking these places out as standards are high and some

1

prices are affordable. Revolutionary art dominates the second floor, relying heavily on hackneyed images of soldiers, war zones and Uncle Ho, though a few offerings capture the anguish and turmoil of the conflicts. Things get better on the third floor where there's an impressive collection of Oc Eo and Cham statues, gilt Buddhas and other antiquities.

Le Cong Kieu

Across the road from the Fine Art Museum, **Le Cong Kieu** is lined with "antique" shops selling Oriental and colonial bric-a-brac such as opium weights and vases, though your chances of finding genuine antiques are slim. Keep in mind when shopping here that the Vietnamese are very good at making new things look old.

Dan Sinh Market

Memorabilia reflecting Vietnam's more recent history are available at the army surplus stalls at the back of **Dan Sinh Market**, behind the Phung Son Tu Pagoda on Yersin; here you can pick up khaki gear, Viet Cong pith helmets, old compasses and Zippo lighters embossed with pearls of wisdom coined by GIs, such as "We are the unwilling, led by the unqualified, doing the unnecessary for the ungrateful." Keep in mind that none of this equipment is likely to be original, even if it looks a bit battered.

Le Duan Boulevard

North of Notre Dame Cathedral, **Le Duan Boulevard** runs between the Botanical Gardens and the grounds of the Reunification Palace. Known as Norodom Boulevard to the French, who lined it with tamarind trees to imitate a Gallic thoroughfare, it soon became a residential and diplomatic enclave with a crop of fine pastel-hued colonial villas to boot. Its present name doffs a cap to Le Duan, the secretary-general of the *Lao Dong*, or Workers Party, from 1959 until his death in 1986. Turn northeast from the

---

OPERATION FREQUENT WIND

Located at 4 Le Duan, the current nondescript building that houses the US Consulate was built right on top of the site of the infamous former American Embassy, where a commemorative plaque is now the only reminder of its existence and significance in the American War. Two events immortalized the former building on this site, in operation from 1967 to 1975 and left standing half-derelict until 1999 as a sobering legacy. The first came in the pre-dawn hours of January 31, 1968, when a small band of Viet Cong commandos breached the embassy compound during the nationwide Tet Offensive. That the North could mount such an effective attack on the hub of US power in Vietnam was shocking to the American public. In the six hours of close-range fire that followed, five US guards died, and with them the popular misconception that the US Army had the Vietnam conflict under control.

Worse followed seven years later, during "Operation Frequent Wind", the chaotic helicopter evacuation that marked the United States' final undignified withdrawal from Vietnam. The embassy building was one of thirteen designated landing zones where all foreigners were to gather upon hearing the words, "It is 112 degrees and rising" on the radio followed by Bing Crosby singing White Christmas. At noon on April 29, 1975, the signal was broadcast, and for the next eighteen hours scores of helicopters shuttled passengers out to the US Navy's Seventh Fleet off Vung Tau. Around two thousand evacuees were lifted from the roof of the embassy alone, before Ambassador Graham Martin finally left with the Stars and Stripes in the early hours of the following morning. In a tragic postscript to US involvement, as the last helicopter lifted off, many of the Vietnamese civilians who for hours had been clamouring at the gates were left to suffer the Communists' reprisals.

top of Dong Khoi and the sense of harmony created by Le Duan's graceful colonial piles ends abruptly with a number of brand-new edifices.

The Botanical Gardens and zoo

Junction of Le Duan and Nguyen Binh Khiem • Daily 7am–7pm • 12,000đ

The pace of life slows down considerably – and the odours of cut grass and frangipani blooms replace the smell of exhaust fumes – when you duck into the city's **Botanical Gardens**, accessed by a gate at the far eastern end of Le Duan, and bounded to the east by the Thi Nghe Channel. Established in 1864 by the Frenchmen Germain and Pierre (respectively a vet and a botanist), the gardens' social function has remained unchanged in decades, and their tree-shaded paths still attract as many courting couples and promenaders as when Norman Lewis followed the "clusters of Vietnamese beauties on bicycles" and headed there one Sunday morning in 1950 to find the gardens "full of these ethereal creatures, gliding in decorous groups, sometimes accompanied by gallants". In its day, the gardens harboured an impressive collection of tropical flora, including many species of orchid. Post-liberation, the place went to seed but nowadays a bevy of gardeners keep it reasonably well tended again, and portrait photographers are once again lurking to take snaps of you framed by flowers.

Stray right inside and you'll soon reach the **zoo**, home to camels, elephants, crocodiles and big cats, also komodo dragons – a gift from the government of Indonesia. Unfortunately, conditions are very poor and some animals look half-crazed, so it could be a harrowing experience if you're an animal lover. There's also an **amusement park** that is sometimes open, and you can get an ice cream or a coconut from one of the several **cafés** sprinkled around the grounds.

The History Museum

2 Nguyen Binh Khiem • Tues–Sun 8–11am & 1.30–4.30pm • 15,000đ • Water-puppetry shows on the hour from 10am to 4pm, except 1pm • $2

A pleasing, pagoda-style roof crowns the city's **History Museum**, next to the Botanical Gardens. It houses fifteen galleries illuminating Vietnam's past from primitive times to the end of French rule by means of a decent if unastonishing array of artefacts and pictures. Dioramas of defining moments in Vietnamese military history lend the collection some cohesion – included are Ngo Quyen's 938 AD victory at Bach Dang (see p.332), and the sinking of the *Esperance*. Should you tire of Vietnamese history, you might explore halls focusing on such disparate subjects as Buddha images from around Asia; seventh- and eighth-century Champa art; and the customs and crafts of the ethnic minorities of Vietnam. There's also a room jam-packed with exquisite ceramics from Japan, Thailand and Vietnam, and you could round off your visit at the **water-puppetry theatre**.

Jade Emperor Pagoda

73 Mai Thi Luu • Daily 5am–7pm • Free

A few blocks northwest of the Botanical Gardens, the **Jade Emperor Pagoda**, or Chua Phuoc Hai, was built by the city's Cantonese community at the beginning of the twentieth century. If you visit just one temple in town, make it this one, with its exquisite panels of carved gilt woodwork, and its panoply of weird and wonderful deities, both Taoist and Buddhist, beneath a roof that groans under the weight of dragons, birds and animals.

To the right of the tree-lined **courtyard** out front is a grubby pond whose occupants have earned the temple its alternative moniker of Tortoise Pagoda. Once over the threshold, look up and you'll see Chinese characters announcing: "the only enlightenment is in

1

Heaven" – though only after your eyes have adjusted to the fug of joss-stick smoke. A statue of the **Jade Emperor** lords it over the main hall's central altar, sporting an impressive moustache, and he's surrounded by a retinue of similarly moustached followers.

A rickety flight of steps in the chamber to the right of the main hall runs up to a **balcony** looking out over the pagoda's elaborate **roof**. Set behind the balcony, a neon-haloed statue of Quan Am (see p.86) stands on an altar. Left out of the main hall, meanwhile, you're confronted by Kim Hua, to whom women pray for fertility; judging by the number of babies weighing down the female statues around her, her success rate is high. The Chief of Hell resides in the larger chamber behind Kim Hua's niche. Given his job description, he doesn't look particularly demonic, though his attendants, in sinister black garb, are certainly equipped to administer the sorts of punishments depicted in the ten dark-wood reliefs on the walls before them.

Le Van Duyet Temple

Dinh Tien Hoang • Sunrise to sunset

A national hero is commemorated at the **Temple of Marshal Le Van Duyet**, known locally as Lang Ong and sited at the top of Dinh Tien Hoang, in the region of the city where the **Gia Dinh Citadel** once stood. A military mandarin and eunuch, Le Van Duyet (1764– 1832) succeeded in putting down the Tay Son Rebellion, and later became military governor of Gia Dinh. Strolling around the grounds reveals the tombs in which the marshal and his wife are buried. The temple itself, which underwent extensive renovations in 2008, stretches through three halls behind a facade decorated with unicorns assembled from shards of chinaware. Inside, a bronze statue of the marshal sits in front of an altar, flanked by an ancient pair of tusks. The temple receives a steady stream of visitors paying their respects with burning incense, and the ringing of a brass bell adds to the pious mood. On the first day of the eighth lunar month, to coincide with the marshal's birthday, a **theatre** troupe dramatizes his life; and there's more activity around Tet, when crowds of pilgrims gather to ask for safekeeping in the forthcoming year.

Cho Lon ⚔

The dense cluster of streets comprising the Chinese ghetto of **CHO LON** was once distinct from Saigon, though linked to it by the five-kilometre-long umbilical cord of Tran Hung Dao. The distinction was already somewhat blurred by 1950, when Norman Lewis found the city's Chinatown "swollen so enormously as to become its grotesque Siamese twin", and the steady influx of refugees into the city during the war years saw to it that the two districts eventually became joined by a swathe of urban development. Even so, a short stroll around Cho Lon (whose name, meaning "**big market**", couldn't be more apposite) will make clear that, even by this city's standards, the mercantile mania here is breathtaking. The largest of Cho Lon's many covered markets are Tran Phu's An Dong, built in 1991, and the more recent but equally vast An Dong II. If you're looking to sightsee rather than shop, then historic Binh Tay (see below) is of far more interest. You'll get most out of Cho Lon simply by losing yourself in its amorphous mass of life: amid the melee, streetside barbers clip away briskly, bird-sellers squat outside tumbledown **pagodas and temples**, heaving markets ring to fishwives' chatter and stores display mushrooms, dried shrimps and rice paper.

Binh Tay Market

Hau Giang • Sunrise to sunset

First impressions of **Binh Tay Market**, with its multi-tiered, mustard-coloured roofs stalked by serpentine dragons, are of a huge temple complex. Once inside, however, it

THE HISTORY OF CHO LON

The **ethnic Chinese**, or **Hoa**, first began to settle here around 1900; many came from existing enclaves in My Tho and Bien Hoa. The area soon became the largest Hoa community in the country, a title it still holds, with a population of over half a million. Residents gravitated towards others from their region of China, with each congregation commissioning its own places of worship and clawing out its own commercial niche – thus the Cantonese handled retailing and groceries, the Teochew dealt in tea and fish, the Fukien were in charge of rice, and so on.

The great wealth that Cho Lon generated had to be spent somewhere. By the early twentieth century, sassy restaurants, casinos and brothels existed to facilitate this. Also prevalent were **fumeries**, where nuggets of opium were quietly smoked from the cool comfort of a wooden opium bed. Among the expats and wealthy Asians who frequented them was Graham Greene, and he recorded his experiences in *Ways of Escape*. By the 1950s, Cho Lon was a potentially dangerous place to be, its vice industries controlled by the **Binh Xuyen** gang. First the French and then the Americans trod carefully here, while Viet Minh and Viet Cong **activists** hid out in its cramped backstreets – as Frank Palmos found to his cost, when the jeep he and four other correspondents were riding in was ambushed in 1968.

Post-reunification, Cho Lon saw hard times. As Hanoi aligned itself increasingly with the Soviet Union, Sino-Vietnamese tensions became strained. Economic **persecution** of the Hoa made matters worse, and, when Vietnam invaded Chinese-backed Cambodia, Beijing launched a punitive **border war**. Hundreds of thousands of ethnic Chinese, many of them from Cho Lon, fled the country in unseaworthy vessels, fearing recriminations. Today, the business acumen of the Chinese is valued by the local authorities, and the distemper that gripped Cho Lon for over a decade is a memory.

quickly becomes obvious that mammon is deified here. If any one place epitomizes Cho Lon's vibrant commercialism, it's Binh Tay, its well-regimented corridors abuzz with stalls offering products of all kinds, from dried fish, pickled vegetables and chilli paste to pottery piled up to the rafters, and the colourful bonnets that Vietnamese women so favour. Beyond Binh Tay's south side, stalls provide cheap snacks for shoppers and traders.

Tran Chanh Chieu

A few steps north of Binh Tay market, **Tran Chanh Chieu** is a street clogged by a **poultry market** full of chickens, geese and ducks tied together in bundles. **Cereals and pulses** are the speciality at the street's east end, with weighty sacks of rice, lentils and beans forming a sort of obstacle course for the cyclo that try to negotiate the narrow strip of roadway still visible.

Cha Tam Church

25 Hoc Lac • Sunrise to sunset

The slender spire of **Cha Tam Church** peers down from above the eastern end of cramped Tran Chanh Chieu, but you'll have to walk round to Tran Hung Dao to find the entrance. It was in this unprepossessing little church, with its Oriental outer gate and cheery yellow walls, that President Ngo Dinh Diem and his brother Ngo Dinh Nhu holed up on November 1, 1963, during the coup that saw them chased out of the Gia Long Palace (see p.78). Early the next morning, Diem phoned the leaders of the coup and surrendered. An M-113 armoured car duly picked them up, but they were shot dead by ARVN soldiers before the vehicle reached central Saigon.

With clearance from the janitor (who's usually somewhere around hoping for a tip) you can clamber up into the **belfry** and under the bells, Quasimodo-style, to join the statue of St Francis Xavier for the fine views he enjoys of Cho Lon. The janitor can also point out the pew where Diem and his brother sat praying as they awaited their fate.

THE SHOPS ON HAI THUONG LAN ONG

Five minutes' walk towards the river from the Cha Tam Church, along Tran Hung Dao, through the cloth market, brings you out at the eastern end of the street. **Shops** specializing in Chinese and Vietnamese traditional medicine have long proliferated here, identifiable by the sickly sweet aroma that hangs over them. Named after a famous herbalist who practised and studied in Hanoi two centuries ago, the street is lined by dingy shophouses banked with cabinets whose wooden drawers are crammed full of herbs. Step over the sliced roots laid out to dry along the pavement and peer inside any one of the shops, and you'll see rheumy men and women weighing out prescriptions on ancient balances. Steepled around them are boxes, jars and paper bags containing anything from dried bark to antler fur and tortoise glue. Predictably popular is **ginseng**, the Oriental cure-all said to combat everything from heart disease to acne. Also available are monkey-, tiger- and rhino-based medicines – despite a government ban on these products.

Quan Am Pagoda

12 Lao Tu • Sunrise to sunset

Cho Lon's greatest architectural treasures are its temples and pagodas, many of which stand on or around **Nguyen Trai**, whose four-kilometre sweep northeast to Pham Ngu Lao starts just north of Cha Tam Church. North of Nguyen Trai's junction with Chau Van Liem, on tiny Lao Tu, **Quan Am Pagoda** is the pick of the bunch in this part of town. Set back from the bustle of Cho Lon, it has an almost tangible air of antiquity, enhanced by the film of dust left by the incense spirals hanging from its rafters. Don't be too quick to dive inside, though: the pagoda's ridged roofs are impressive enough from the outside, their colourful crust of "glove-puppet" figurines, teetering houses and temples from a distance creating the illusion of a gingerbread house. Framing the two door gods and the pair of stone lions assigned to keeping out evil spirits are gilt panels depicting petrified scenes from traditional Chinese court life – dancers, musicians, noblemen in sedan chairs, a game of chequers being played.

When Cho Lon's Fukien congregation established this pagoda well over a century ago, they dedicated it to the Goddess of Mercy, but it's **A Pho**, the Queen of Heaven, who stands in the centre of the main hall, beyond an altar tiled like a mortuary slab. A pantheon of deities throngs the open courtyard behind her, decked out in sumptuous apparel and attracting a steady traffic of worshippers. Twin ovens, flanking the main chamber, burn a steady supply of fake money offerings and incense sticks.

Phuoc An Hoi Pagoda

Hung Vuong • Sunrise to sunset

Three minutes' walk north of the Quan Am Pagoda, **Phuoc An Hoi Quan Pagoda** (aka Minh Huong Pagoda) is a disarming place. Beyond the menacing dragons and sea monsters patrolling its roof, and the superb wood carving depicting a king being entertained by jousters and minstrels hanging over the entrance, is the temple's **sanctuary**, in which stately Quan Cong sits, instantly recognizable by his blood-red face, and fronted by two storks standing on top of turtles fashioned from countless plectrum-shaped ceramic shards.

Thien Hau Pagoda

Nguyen Trai • Sunrise to sunset

Local women come here in numbers to make offerings to Me Sanh, Goddess of Fertility, and to Long Mau, Goddess of Mothers and Newborn Babies. When Cantonese immigrants established the temple towards the middle of the nineteenth century, they named it after Thien Hau, Goddess of Seafarers. New arrivals from China would have hastened here to express their gratitude for a safe passage across the South China Sea. Three statues of her stand on the altar, one behind the other, while a large mural on the inside of the front wall depicts her guiding wildly pitching ships across a storm-tossed sea. The temple's most attractive aspect is its roof, bristling with so many figurines you wonder how those at the edge can keep their balance.

North of Cho Lon

Two of Ho Chi Minh City's oldest and most atmospheric places of worship, the **Giac Lam** and **Giac Vien Pagodas**, are tucked away in the hinterland to the north of Cho Lon – as is the thriving **Phu Tho Racecourse**, if you fancy a flutter. Also nearby is **Dam Sen leisure park**. The best way to get to these destinations is by xe om or cyclo, as they are hidden away in the backstreets.

Giac Lam Pagoda
118 Lac Long Quan • Sunrise to sunset

You'll see the gate leading up to **Giac Lam Pagoda** on Lac Long Quan, a couple of hundred metres northeast of its intersection with Le Dai Hanh. From the gate, a short track passes a newish tower (its seven levels are scaleable and afford good city views) and a cluster of monks' tombs on its way to the actual pagoda. Built in 1744, rambling Giac Lam is draped over 98 hardwood pillars, each inscribed with traditional *chu nom* characters (Vietnamese script, based on Chinese ideograms). From its terracotta floor-tiles and extravagant chandeliers to the antique tables at which monks sit to take tea, Giac Lam is characterized by a clutter that imbues it with an appealingly fusty feel, and a reassuring sense of age.

The funerary chamber
The entrance to the temple is at the back right of the building, which takes you through to the funerary chamber, flanked by row upon row of gilt tablets above photos of the deceased. The many-armed goddess that stands in the centre of the chamber is Chuan De, a manifestation of Quan Am. A right turn leads to a **courtyard-garden** around which runs a roof studded with blue and white porcelain saucers.

The classroom
Monks occasionally sit studying on the huge wooden benches in the peaceful old classroom at the back of the complex. The panels in this chamber depict the ten Buddhist hells; study them carefully, and you'll see sinners being variously minced, fed to dogs, dismembered and disembowelled by fanged demons.

The main sanctuary
To the left of the funerary chamber as you enter the pagoda is the main sanctuary, whose multi-tiered altar dais groans under the weight of the many Buddhist and Taoist statues it supports (remember to take off your shoes before entering). Elsewhere in this chamber you'll spot an ensemble of oil lamps balanced on a Christmas-tree-shaped wooden frame. Worshippers pen prayers on pieces of paper, which they affix to the tree and then feed the lamps with an offering of oil. A similar ritual is attached to the bell across the chamber, though in this case people believe that their prayers are hastened to the gods by the ringing of the bell.

1

Giac Vien Pagoda

Lac Long Quan • Sunrise to sunset

Hidden away in a maze of backstreets, **Giac Vien Pagoda** was founded in the late eighteenth century, and is said to have been frequented by Emperor Gia Long. Upon entering its red doors daubed with yellow *chu nom* characters, visitors are confronted by banks of old photos and funerary tablets flanking long refectory-style tables. The two rows of black pillars lend an arresting sense of depth to this first chamber, which is dominated by a panel depicting a ferocious-looking red lion. Continue around the stone walls (crafted, incongruously, in classical Greek style) and into the **main sanctuary**, and you'll find a sizeable congregation of deities, as well as a tree of lamps similar to the one at Giac Lam. The monks residing in Giac Vien are hospitable to a fault, and you'll probably be invited for a cup of tea before you leave.

Phu Tho Racecourse

2 Le Dai Hanh • Meets take place on Sat and Sun noon–5pm • 5,000đ; VIP room 50,000đ–100,000đ • ☎ 08 3855 1205

There's no more potent symbol of the Vietnamese love of gambling than **Phu Tho Racecourse**. Apart from a fourteen-year spell between 1975 and 1989, when gambling was seen as an example of bourgeois decadence and outlawed, the track resounds every weekend to the roar of the crowd urging on their favourite. Spending a few hours here is a great antidote to trudging round pagodas, though try not to get swept too deep into the crowd as pickpockets are rife. If you feel like a flutter, the minimum bet is 10,000đ and there's no upper limit. However, be warned that there are frequent allegations of horses being doped and races being fixed, so the form card is not to be relied on.

ARRIVAL AND DEPARTURE   **HCMC**

The lion's share of new **arrivals** to Vietnam fly into Ho Chi Minh City's Tan Son Nhat Airport, which is also the terminus for all internal flights. Arriving overland, you'll end up either at the train station, a short distance north of the downtown area, or at one of a handful of bus terminals scattered across the city.

BY PLANE

Tan Son Nhat Airport 7km northwest of the city centre. Facilities include duty-free; foreign exchange; taxi, limo and hotel booking desks; a post office (daily 9am–10pm); and left-luggage facilities (daily 7.30am–10pm; $3 per bag per day, $4 for larger items).

Taxi The journey downtown takes about 30–45min. The easiest way into the city centre is by metered taxi (about $7–8 to District One) from outside the terminal. Make sure the driver switches on the meter and knows exactly where you want to go; show him in writing if possible. Alternatively, many hotels offer a pick-up service for advance bookings.

Bus If you don't have much baggage, you can get the #152 a/c bus (every 15min; 3000đ) from the domestic terminal, 200m to the right of the international terminal, to Dong Khoi and Pham Ngu Lao. A xe om will run you into town for $4–5, but you'll have to bargain hard: to find one, walk outside the airport gates (only a hundred metres or so).

Domestic flights Vietnam's constantly growing network of domestic flights connects Ho Chi Minh City with every other major town in the country, which is good news for visitors with limited time. Fares are very reasonable, and

flying to places like Hanoi, Hué, Nha Trang and Da Lat can save both bags of time and a very sore bum. Apart from Vietnam Airlines (115 Nguyen Hué, ☎ 08 3832 0320, ⊕ vietnamairlines.com), Vasco (B114 Bach Dang, Tan Binh District ☎ 08 3842 2790, ⊕ vasco.com.vn) and Air Mekong (1st floor, Centre Point, 106 Nguyen Van Troi; ☎ 08 3846 3999, ⊕ airmekong.com.vn) also operate some routes.

Destinations: Buon Ma Thuot (5–6 daily; 1hr); Ca Mau (1–2 daily; 1hr); Can Tho (3 daily; 1hr); Con Dao (4–5 daily; 1hr); Da Lat (4 daily; 50min); Da Nang (10 daily; 1hr 10min); Hai Phong (4–5 daily; 2hr); Hanoi (16–18 daily; 2hr); Hué (4–5 daily; 1hr 20min); Nha Trang (8 daily; 1hr 10min); Phu Quoc (15–18 daily; 1hr); Pleiku (4 daily; 1hr 15min); Qui Nhon (3 daily; 1hr 10min).

Airlines Air France ☎ 08 3829 0981, ⊕ airfrance.com; British Airways ☎ 08 3930 2933, ⊕ britishairways.com; Cathay Pacific ☎ 08 3822 3203, ⊕ cathaypacific.com; China Airlines ☎ 08 3911 1591, ⊕ china-airlines.com; Emirates ☎ 08 3930 2939, ⊕ emirates.com; Japan Air Lines ☎ 08 3821 9098, ⊕ jal.com; Lufthansa ☎ 08 3829 8529; ⊕ lufthansa .com. Malaysia Airlines ☎ 08 3829 2529; ⊕ malaysiaairlines .com. Qantas ☎ 08 3823 8844; ⊕ qantas.com; Singapore

1

Airlines ☎ 08 3823 1588, 🌐 singaporeair.com; Thai Airways ☎ 08 3823 1588, 🌐 thaiair.com; United Airlines ☎ 08 3823 4755, 🌐 united.com.

BY TRAIN

Train station Trains from the north pull in at the Ga Saigon (☎ 08 3843 6528), 3km northwest of town, on Nguyen Thong. Since it's a few kilometres from the centre, it's best to take a taxi (about $3–4), though you might save a dollar if you bargain furiously with a cyclo or xe om driver.

Tickets Vietnamese trains are oversubscribed, so book as far ahead as possible – particularly for a sleeping berth (see p.34). Most tour operators, as well as some guesthouses and hotels can reserve tickets for a small fee. The official agent for the railways is Saigon Railways Tourist Service Company, 275c Pham Ngu Lao (☎ 08 3836 7640), which has computerized reservations and doesn't charge any extra commission.

Destinations: Da Nang (6 daily; 15–20hr); Dieu Tri (7 daily; 11–13hr); Hanoi (5 daily; 30–41hr); Hué (6 daily; 21–23hr); Muong Man (5 daily; 3–4hr); Nha Trang (8 daily; 6–7hr); Ninh Binh (3 daily; 34–37hr); Quang Ngai (5 daily; 13–16hr); Thap Cham (6 daily; 5–6hr); Vinh (5 daily; 29–33hr).

BY BUS

Regular **buses** stop at a clutch of different terminals, while open-tour buses and most arrivals from Phnom Penh in Cambodia terminate on De Tham in the heart of the budget accommodation area.

Mien Dong bus station Buses to and from the north arrive at this sprawling station 5km northeast of the city on Xo Viet Nghe Tinh; the #26 bus shuttles between here and Ben Thanh bus station.

Ben Thanh bus station Centrally located, the bus station is a five-minute walk from the budget hotel district.

Mien Tay bus station Buses to and from the southwest terminate here, 10km west of the city centre in An Lac District; take a taxi or a #2 bus to Ben Thanh bus station.

Shuttle buses Well-signposted shuttle buses between Mien Tay (#2) and Mien Dong (#26) terminals make it possible to bypass central Ho Chi Minh City altogether in

---

TOUR AGENTS

Tour agencies abound in Ho Chi Minh City and offer a range of itineraries, from one-day whistle-stop tours around the region to lengthy trips upcountry including accommodation. Most of the recommended tour operators can lay on **tailor-made itineraries**, **private cars** and personal **guides** for you. Provisos and tips on signing up for a tour in Vietnam are listed in Basics (see p.31). There are hundreds of tour agents in Ho Chi Minh City, but many of them are fly-by-night set-ups, and we receive numerous reports of inefficient and **unscrupulous companies**, so it's worth choosing your agent carefully. Those listed below have good reputations for consistent, reliable services.

Ann Tours 58 Ton That Tung ☎ 08 3925 3636, 🌐 anntours.com. Highly recommended, it offers good-value, tailor-made tours.

Buffalo Tours 81 Mac Thi Buoi ☎ 08 3827 9170, 🌐 buffalotours.com. This Western-managed set-up specializes in customized tours throughout Indochina.

Delta Adventure Tours 267 De Tham ☎ 08 3920 2112, 🌐 deltaadventure.info. Highly recommended for its boat tours to the Cu Chi tunnels, the Mekong Delta or all the way to Phnom Penh.

Exotissimo Travel 80–82 Phan Xich Long ☎ 08 3995 9898, 🌐 exotissimo.com. Has an extensive tour programme that includes special interests, Laos and Cambodia add-ons.

Grandeur Journeys 225 Hai Ba Trung ☎ 08 3820 0257, 🌐 grandeurjourneys.com. Organizes custom itineraries throughout Indochina and can deal with requests for specialized tours.

Innoviet 158 Bui Ven ☎ 08 6291 5406, 🌐 innoviet .com. This newish company runs eco-friendly, small-group bike and boat tours of the Delta as well as half-day city tours.

Kim Travel 189 De Tham ☎ 08 3920 5552, 🌐 kimtravel.com. A veteran of the independent travel scene, it offers open-tour buses, flight and rail bookings, car and minibus rental and guides.

The Sinh Tourist 246–248 De Tham ☎ 08 3838 9497, 🌐 thesinhtourist.com. Offers cut-price organized tours of Vietnam, open-bus tours, guides, visa services, buses and boats to Cambodia and vehicle rental. Beware of copycat operators.

Sinhbalo Adventure Travel 283/20 Pham Ngu Lao ☎ 08 3837 6766, 🌐 sinhbalo.com. A super-efficient set-up that specializes in customized tours such as bicycle expeditions along the Ho Chi Minh trail (see 🌐 cyclingvietnam.net), motorbike tours, long-distance boat cruises and kayaking in the Mekong Delta. They also have a wealth of reliable travel info.

TNK Travel 216 De Tham ☎ 08 3920 5847, 🌐 tnktravelvietnam.com. Cheap tours to destinations countrywide from this operator, which gets good feedback from those who sign up for them.

SAMPLE FARES AROUND TOWN

Costs of local transport are quite reasonable. For example, you can expect to pay about 15,000đ for a short **cyclo** or **xe om** ride within central Ho Chi Minh City, while the standard fare for **bus services** is 3000–5000đ. Fares for cyclo and xe om are negotiable, though the list below provides a guideline. Note that cyclo drivers charge more for extra passengers or luggage, and that by "centre" we mean Dong Khoi.

Pham Ngu Lao to GPO: 25,000đ
Train station to centre: 25,000–30,000đ
Pham Ngu Lao to Cho Lon: 45,000–50,000đ

Centre to Jade Emperor Pagoda: 30,000đ
Mien Dong bus station to centre: 50,000đ

the event that you want to travel direct from the Mekong Delta to the north, or vice versa.

Destinations: Buon Ma Thuot (7hr); Ca Mau (8hr 30min); Can Tho (4hr); Chau Doc (6hr); Da Lat (7hr); Da Nang (21hr); Hanoi (41hr); Ha Tien (9hr); Hué (25hr); My Tho (2hr); Nha Trang (10hr); Phan Thiet (4–5hr); Qui Nhon (13hr); Vung Tau (2hr).

Open-tour buses Many of the tour operators concentrated around De Tham sell tickets for open-tour buses that crisscross the country. Sample fares from Ho Chi Minh City are as follows: Hanoi $37, Hué $27, Nha Trang $9, Da Lat $8 and Hoi An $21, Phnom Penh in Cambodia $10. Tickets, information and departing buses, which leave daily in the early morning or evening, can be found at the various companies' offices around De Tham and Pham Ngu Lao.

BY BOAT

Boat trips One of the most popular boat trips from Ho Chi Minh City is to Phnom Penh, with a stopover in Chau Doc in the delta. Visas can be organized by tour agents, and if you book with a company like Delta Adventure Travel, you won't have to change boats halfway. Prices start at around $30 per person.

Hydrofoils to and from Vung Tau make approximately hourly departures from the Passenger Quay of Ho Chi Minh City (Bach Dang Wharf), opposite the end of Ham Nghi at 2 Ton Duc Thang. For tickets ($10) and further information, contact the Vina Express booth at the jetty (daily 6.30–11am & 1.30–4.30pm; ☎ 08 3829 7892).

Destinations: Vung Tau (about 8 daily; 1hr 15min).

GETTING AROUND

Faint-hearted visitors to Ho Chi Minh City will blanch upon first encountering the chaos that passes for its **traffic system**. Thousands of motorcycles, bicycles and cyclo fill the city's streets and boulevards in an insectile swarm that is now supplemented by a burgeoning number of cars and minibuses, most with their horns constantly blaring.

By cyclo Cyclo routes are sadly limited, being prohibited from several central streets, though for many visitors a leisurely ride around some of the city's main sights adds a uniquely Vietnamese touch to the experience. They are a dying breed in HCMC, since the local government plans to phase them out. Already they are forbidden to enter many key streets in the city centre, so if your rider seems to be taking a circuitous route, he is probably not doing so to bump up the fare. Despite these difficulties, a ride in a cyclo is usually a memorable experience, if only for the close encounter with the city's crazy traffic; about $3 an hour is the normal rate, though initially they will ask more than double this. Though it's feasible to ride two (very small) passengers to a cyclo, the corresponding rise in cost and lessening of comfort make this a false economy.

By Taxi Taxis are inexpensive and worth considering if only to avoid interminable haggling over fares. They're easy to flag down on the street, though it's just as easy to call for a pick-up wherever you are. The flag fare of 12,000đ goes up after dark but you can still traverse a decent chunk of the city for 40,000đ, so they are well worth considering, especially given the horrifying pollution levels of the city's

streets. Stick with reliable companies like Mai Linh (☎ 08 3838 3838) and Vinasun (☎ 08 3827 2727), as many drivers rig their meters to ratchet up the dong.

By xe om To get from A to B when you don't fancy walking, the xe om is the most prevalent and practical mode of transport. Translated, it means "motorbike embrace": passengers ride pillion on a motorbike, hanging on for dear life. Wearing helmets is compulsory for passengers as well as riders. Xe om are much more prevalent than cyclo, so you'll probably find yourself using them at some stage, but beware of riders who double up as pimps and drug dealers, of which there are many. If you find a reliable driver, take his phone number so you can call him again. One such driver is Tran Duc Thanh (☎ 0909 536457; ✉ tranducthanh128@yahoo.com), who knows the city well.

On foot Despite the city's massive sprawl, the majority of its attractions are conveniently clustered so that it is quite feasible to explore many of them on foot. But first you have to learn to cross the streets where the traffic never stops. There's an art to crossing the street in Vietnam: besides nerves of steel, a steady pace is required – motorbike riders

1

are used to dodging pedestrians, but you'll confuse them if you stop in your tracks.

By bus Few visitors ever take a public bus, though it's relatively easy to hop on one to Cho Lon from the backpacker district. When leaving the city, Ben Thanh bus station is a useful point of departure, linking other long-distance bus stations in Ho Chi Minh City, as well as offering direct services to Vung Tau and other places.

Motobike and bicycle rental This is the cheapest way to get around HCMC – just $6–7 and $2 per day

respectively, though you'll need bravery far beyond that necessary to cross the street to survive in the traffic. Most hotels and guesthouses can arrange a motorbike for you, though bicycles are a bit more difficult to track down. One place they have both is at 185b Pham Ngu Lao, a few steps east of the junction with De Tham. Budget (☎08 3930 1118; ⊛budget.com.vn).

By rental car Many tour operators offer car rental plus driver for $70–100 per day, depending on the vehicle and driver's proficiency in English.

INFORMATION

Tourist information For practical information with no strings attached, enquire at your guesthouse or hotel. Your hosts should also be able to provide you with a basic map of the city centre, while a more detailed map is available from bookshops and street hawkers.

Listings For information about what's on in Ho Chi Minh

City, you'll find in many hotels and restaurants the free magazines *The Word* or *Asia Life*, which are aimed at expats. Another useful source of info is *The Guide*, which covers the whole country and is available as a supplement to the *Vietnam Economic Times* in bookstores for 100,000đ. All are published monthly.

ACCOMMODATION

There are thousands of **hotel** rooms in Ho Chi Minh City, ranging from windowless cupboards to sumptuous suites, yet the city is so popular that rooms can be difficult to find, especially in December and January. **Advance bookings** will save you hauling your bags round the streets and you might even secure a pick-up from the airport or station. The best hotels in town are located around Dong Khoi in the city centre, and there are some smart mini-hotels on nearby Mac Thi Buoi. Ho Chi Minh City's budget enclave centres around Pham Ngu Lao, De Tham and Bui Vien, though it has gone noticeably upmarket in recent years. The area sits roughly 1km west of the city centre but is still convenient for visiting most city attractions, and restaurants, bars and shops are significantly cheaper out here. If the De Tham region is too crowded for you, there's a smaller clutch of budget hotels in an alley a few blocks south off Co Giang. Most places that charge more than $15 a night include breakfast in the price.

Incessant **traffic noise** is a big issue in Ho Chi Minh City and many hotels are fitting double glazing in an attempt to block it out; keep this in mind when choosing a room if you're a light sleeper.

DONG KHOI AND AROUND

Asian Ruby 26 Thi Sach ☎08 3827 2839, ⊛asianrubyhotel.com; map p.93. This centrally located mid-range hotel is the first of a growing chain with a winning combination of convenient locations, comfy rooms and helpful staff. Rooms are welcoming, with bedside control panels, thick mattresses and bright artwork. **$70**

★ **Caravelle** 19 Lam Son Square ☎08 3823 4999, ⊛caravellehotel.com; map p.93. The city's most prestigious hotel is steeped in history, and since its opening in 1959 its fortunes have echoed those of the country. A new 24-storey wing was opened in 1998, since when it has led the pack with its luxurious rooms and suites, impeccable service and fine dining options. Complimentary wi-fi in rooms is a real bonus (most five-star hotels provide this service at a hefty charge) and a sundowner at the *Saigon Saigon* bar on the rooftop of the old building is an essential experience. **$280**

Catina 109 Dong Khoi ☎08 3829 6296, ⊛hotelcatina .com.vn; map p.93. This is a newish upmarket hotel right at the heart of Dong Khoi. Superior rooms are rather

cramped, so it's worth paying a bit extra for a deluxe room. There's nothing special about the decor, but this place is all about location. **$112**

Continental 132–134 Dong Khoi ☎08 3829 9201, ⊛continentalvietnam.com; map p.93. The grandly carpeted staircases, marbled floors and dark-wood doors of this venerable address's halls and corridors convey a colonial splendour that doesn't quite extend to its rooms, though some do boast commanding views down Dong Khoi. **$120**

Deluxe 58 Mac Thi Buoi ☎08 3822 8558, ⊛deluxesaigon.com; map p.93. Formerly the *Kim Long*, this mini-hotel has had a makeover and change of name to give it another lease of life as a reasonable mid-range option. It's worth paying a bit more for a room with a window, and it's right in the heart of the action. **$30**

Dong Do 35 Mac Thi Buoi ☎08 3827 3637, ⊛dongdohotel.com; map p.93. Nicely furnished mini-hotel with all facilities and a restaurant with a view of the bustle around Dong Khoi on the sixth floor. Staff are friendly and helpful and rates are quoted in dong. Discounts available for long stay. **$32**

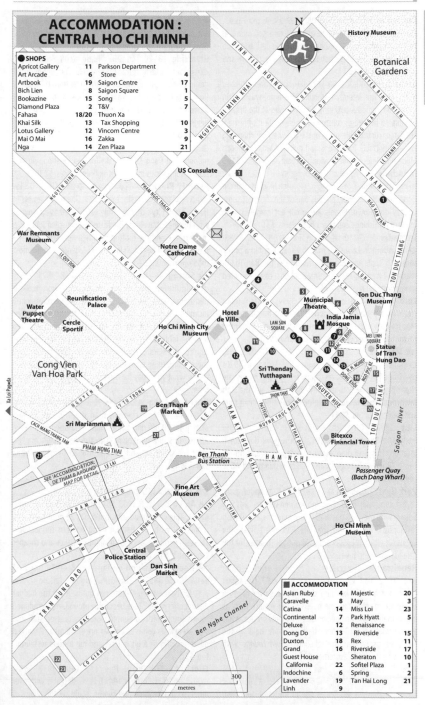

ACCOMMODATION : CENTRAL HO CHI MINH

● SHOPS

Apricot Gallery	11	Parkson Department	
Art Arcade	6	Store	4
Artbook	19	Saigon Centre	17
Bich Lien	8	Saigon Square	1
Bookazine	15	Song	5
Diamond Plaza	2	T&V	7
Fahasa	18/20	Thuon Xa	
Khai Silk	13	Tax Shopping	10
Lotus Gallery	12	Vincom Centre	3
Mai O Mai	16	Zakka	9
Nga	14	Zen Plaza	21

■ ACCOMMODATION

Asian Ruby	4	Majestic	20
Caravelle	8	May	3
Catina	14	Miss Loi	23
Continental	7	Park Hyatt	5
Deluxe	12	Renaissance	
Dong Do	13	Riverside	15
Duxton	18	Rex	11
Grand	16	Riverside	17
Guest House		Sheraton	10
California	22	Sofitel Plaza	1
Indochine	6	Spring	2
Lavender	19	Tan Hai Long	21
Linh	9		

History Museum

Botanical Gardens

US Consulate

War Remnants Museum

Notre Dame Cathedral

Reunification Palace

Water Puppet Theatre

Cercle Sportif

Ho Chi Minh City Museum

Hotel de Ville

Municipal Theatre

Ton Duc Thang Museum

India Jamia Mosque

LAM SON SQUARE

MEI LINH SQUARE

Statue of Tran Hung Dao

Cong Vien Van Hoa Park

Sri Thenday Yutthapani

Sri Mariamman

Ben Thanh Market

Bitexco Financial Tower

Ben Thanh Bus Station

Passenger Quay (Bach Dang Wharf)

Fine Art Museum

Ho Chi Minh Museum

Central Police Station

Dan Sinh Market

SEE 'ACCOMMODATION, DE THAM & AROUND' MAP FOR DETAIL

Saigon River

Ben Nghe Channel

Xa Loi Pagoda

0   300
metres

1

Duxton 63 Nguyen Huế ☎08 3822 2999; map p.93. There are nearly two hundred spacious, carpeted rooms in this classy hotel. Each is equipped with a big desk and a tub in the bathroom, and the hotel also boasts a restaurant and business centre. $160

Grand 8 Dong Khoi ☎08 3823 0163, ⊛grandhotel.vn; map p.93. This recently restored 1930s hotel was adding over two hundred rooms in two new towers at the time of writing, so beware of construction noise until it's finished. The large, comfortable suites in the old wing are charming with comfortable furnishings and polished wooden floors. Modern facilities include a swimming pool and jacuzzi. $125

Indochine 40–42 Hai Ba Trung ☎08 3822 0084, ⊛indochinehotel.com; map p.93. Just a block away from Dong Khoi, this friendly place is one of the cheapest spots to stay downtown. Rooms are small but carpeted with modern furnishings and smart bathrooms. $30

Lavender 208–210 Le Thanh Ton ☎08 2222 8888, ⊛lavenderhotel.com.vn; map p.93. Situated in a prime shopping spot, just along the road from the Ben Thanh market, *Lavender* features smallish but cosy, carpeted rooms with full facilities. $75

Linh 16 Mac Thi Buoi ☎08 3824 3954, ⊛linhhotelvn .com; map p.93. The most appealing of the mini-hotels on Mac Thi Buoi, this place has twenty bright, well-appointed rooms with attractive bamboo furnishings. $30

★ **Majestic** 1 Dong Khoi ☎08 3829 5517, ⊛majesticsaigon.com.vn; map p.93. A historic 1920s riverfront hotel that oozes character. All the rooms are charming (especially those with a river view) and the staff fall over themselves to be helpful. There's a first-floor pool and rooftop bar too. $251

May 28–30 Thi Sach ☎08 3823 4501, ⊛www .mayhotel.com.vn; map p.93. With a good downtown location, this new place features a pool, spa and fitness centre. Rooms are bright with solid furnishings and ADSL connections. $80

Park Hyatt 2 Lam Son ☎08 3824 1234, ⊛saigon.park .hyatt.com; map p.93. Enjoying a prime spot on Lam Son Square with over 250 classically elegant rooms, two stylish restaurants, a pool and spa, the *Park Hyatt* rivals the *Caravelle*, which it eyes over the Municipal Theatre, for the title of top spot in town. $272

Renaissance Riverside 8–15 Ton Duc Thang ☎08 3822 0033, ⊛marriott.com; map p.93. This smart hotel in a modern building down by the river offers a challenge to other top-line hotels in the vicinity with its immaculate rooms and personalized, friendly service. It has a neat rooftop pool where barbecues are held at the weekend, as well as the relaxing *Atrium Lounge* with refreshments and free internet. $155

Rex 141 Nguyen Huế ☎08 3829 2185, ⊛rexhotelvietnam.com; map p.93. A recent makeover has re-established the *Rex* as one of the most appealing options in Ho Chi Minh City, with plush, comfortable rooms and an excellent central location. A sundowner on the fifth-floor terrace is a memorable treat. $130

Riverside 18–20 Ton Duc Thang ☎08 3822 4038, ⊛riversidehotelsg.com; map p.93. This modernized grand colonial pile proudly eyes the river from the base of Dong Khoi, and offers spacious rooms with traditional furnishings at much cheaper prices than its famous neighbours, the *Majestic* and the *Grand*. $69

Sheraton 88 Dong Khoi ☎08 3827 2828, ⊛sheratongrandtower.com; map p.93. A towering monolith on Dong Khoi, ideally located for shopping and sights. Sumptuous rooms, but sky-high prices. $230

Sofitel Plaza 17 Le Duan ☎08 3824 1555, ⊛accorhotels.com/asia; map p.93. One of the jewels in Ho Chi Minh City's crown, firmly established as a favourite with business travellers. The hi-tech, open-plan lobby is a masterpiece and the rooftop pool is simply stunning. The rooms and facilities boast luxurious elegance with the most modern trimmings. $170

★ **Spring** 44–46 Le Thanh Ton ☎08 3829 7362, ⊛springhotelvietnam.com; map p.93. An excellent mid-range hotel with top-quality services, conveniently located just north of the centre. All the rooms are carpeted with cable TV and bathtubs. From the moment you step into the lobby to the warm greeting of the staff and the sight of the spiral staircase winding upstairs, you can tell there's something special about this place. Rates are way below what you'd pay for comparable rooms elsewhere in town. $37

Tan Hai Long 14–16 Le Lai ☎08 3827 2738, ⊛tanhailonghotel.com.vn; map p.93. One of a chain of mini-hotels offering comfortable, if cramped, mid-range rooms. This one is right next to the Ben Thanh market, ideal for shopping and well-positioned to get to most sights. $65

DE THAM AND AROUND

An An 40 Bui Vien ☎08 3837 8087, ⊛anan.vn; map p.104. This welcoming mini-hotel has 22 bright and airy rooms, all with a/c, bathtubs and internet connections. There's a second branch with slightly smaller and cheaper rooms at 216 De Tham. $40

★ **Beautiful Saigon** 62 Bui Vien & 40/19 Bui Vien ☎08 3836 4852, ⊛beautifulsaigonhotel.com; map p.104. These two mini-hotels in the heart of the budget district offer some of the best value around. Well-equipped rooms (most with computers), smartly dressed staff and free breakfasts come at budget prices. Number 2, tucked down an alley, is a bit quieter and has a good restaurant too. $30

Elios 231–235 Pham Ngu Lao ☎08 3838 5584, ⊛elioshotel.vn; map p.104. This swish place, with over ninety compact and snug rooms, could be the shape of things to come for the budget district. Efficient, helpful staff, a rooftop restaurant and wi-fi in all rooms. **$65**

Giang Son 283/14 & 283/24 Pham Ngu Lao ☎08 3837 7547, ✉giangson_guesthouse@hotmail.com; map p.104. It's worth splashing out on one of the bigger rooms here to appreciate the relaxing location (down a quiet alley) of this family-run guesthouse, which has been so successful that it's recently opened a second branch down the road. **$16**

Guest House California 171a Co Bac ☎08 3837 8885, ✉guesthousecaliforniasaigon@yahoo.com; map p.93. Away from the backpacker scene of De Tham, this friendly place has a range of fan and a/c rooms. It's a bit of a trek to the city's sights, but the trade-off is a quiet backstreet location in a real residential area. **$16**

Lac Vien 28/12–14 Bui Vien ☎08 3920 4899, ⊛lacvienhotel.com; map p.104. Enjoying a quiet location in the middle of an alley, the superior and VIP rooms at *Lac Vien* are some of the best choices in the budget district. Standard rooms are not such a good deal as they lack windows, but the superior upgrade is just $4 more. **$32**

★**Lan Anh** 252 De Tham ☎08 3836 5197, ✉nhutxuan1002@yahoo.com; map p.104. This friendly, family-run mini-hotel in the heart of De Tham has 23 bright, clean rooms with a/c that bring a high rate of returning visitors. For its combination of desirable amenities (efficient showers, satellite TV and so on), super-helpful staff, central location and competitive room rates, this is one of the best deals in town. Ask for a room at the back to escape the street noise. **$18**

Le Le 171 Pham Ngu Lao ☎08 3836 8686, ✉lelehotel @saigonsportshotel.com; map p.104. This ageing but popular mini-hotel was recently swallowed up by the *Sports Hotel* chain, which has at least another five budget hotels in the city. Rooms all have hot water, cable TV and IDD, and breakfast is included. **$20**

★**Madam Cuc** 127 Cong Quynh ☎08 3836 8761, ⊛madamcuchotels.com; map p.104. The genial Madam Cuc pays more attention to detail than most, resulting in a range of wholesome rooms, some sleeping up to four. Staff are well informed and helpful and breakfast, fruit, tea and coffee are included in the price of the room. They will also

BE OUR GUEST: EATING OUT IN HCMC

Hanoi may be Vietnam's administrative capital, but Ho Chi Minh City is without doubt its culinary capital. Besides **Vietnamese cuisine**, which these days enjoys global popularity, just about every other type of food you could imagine is served here, including Indian, Italian, Brazilian, Japanese, Mexican, Lebanese and German, though perhaps predictably **French** restaurants comprise the most formidable foreign contingent in town. The French legacy is also evident in the city's abundance of **cafés**, which are scattered throughout the city. Though you'll probably be tempted by a pizza or burrito at some time during your stay, it would be a crime to ignore the fabulous variety of indigenous food on offer, both in sophisticated **restaurants** and at **streetside stalls**. Owing to the transitory nature of foodstalls, it's impossible to make specific recommendations, but there are plenty to choose from – we give tips on how to spot a good one (see p.41). One area well worth checking out in the evening is around Ben Thanh market, where a cluster of foodstalls offer a bewildering variety of dishes, many specializing in seafood.

Also keep your eyes open for simple **eating houses**, where good, filling rice and noodle dishes are served for a pittance from buffet-style tin trays and vast soup urns; these are especially popular at lunchtime. Cheap **restaurants**, concentrated around De Tham, Pham Ngu Lao and Bui Vien, which cater exclusively for travellers, are fine if you want an inexpensive steak and chips or some fried noodles, but hardly in the league of the city's heavyweights, its **specialist restaurants**. Of course, by Vietnamese standards, these restaurants are incredibly expensive – eat at one and you'll probably spend enough to feed a Vietnamese family for a month – but by Western standards many of them are low-priced, and the quality of cooking is consistently high. What's more, ingredients are fresh, with vegetables transported from Da Lat, and meat often flown in from Australia.

Some of the swankier restaurants lay on reasonably priced **set menus** and also live **traditional music** in order to lure diners. Though there are many delectable dishes to discover in Ho Chi Minh City, keep an eye open for *chao bo*, slithers of beef grilled on sticks of lemon grass, which can be superb when the beef is well marinated. You'll find it on the menu of a few of the places listed below, such as *Vietnam House* and *Blue Ginger*.

Café culture, introduced by the French, is still very much alive in Ho Chi Minh City, and there are numerous places at which to round dinner off with an ice cream, crêpe or sundae. Earlier in the day, the same venues offer the chance to linger over a coffee and watch the world go by.

1

collect from the airport. If this place is full, they have three more branches at 123 Cong Quynh, 184 Cong Quynh and 64 Bui Vien, where you'll find a similarly warm welcome, efficient staff and good-value rooms. **$25**

Ly 8424b Bui Vien (down the lane next to 84b Bui Vien) ☏08 3836 4794, ✉hanhbtx@yahoo.com; map p.104. One of several budget dives tucked away in the narrow lanes north of Bui Vien. This one is cleaner and offers bigger rooms than most, and is run by a friendly, helpful family. **$10**

Miss Loi 178/20 Co Giang ☏08 3837 9589, ✉missloi @hcm.fpt.vn; map p.93. Located out of sight of the De Tham activity, this spotlessly clean and cosy guesthouse has a range of rooms in a quiet backstreet community. **$16**

New World 76 Le Lai ☏08 3822 8888, ⊕saigon .newworldhotels.com; map p.104. A benchmark on the Ho Chi Minh City hotel scene since its opening in 1993 – over five hundred luxurious rooms complemented by impressive sports and leisure facilities, cutting edge restaurants and a business centre. **$120**

Ngoc Minh 283/11–13 Pham Ngu Lao ☏08 3837 6407, ⊕ngocminh-hotel.com; map p.104. Located in a narrow alley and tucked away from the honking horns on Pham Ngu Lao, this place has a range of competitively priced rooms, all with a/c, cable TV and wi-fi. **$18**

Orient 274–276 De Tham ☏08 3920 3993, ⊕orienthotel.vn; map p.104. Decent mini-hotel with small but comfy rooms and friendly, helpful staff, right in the heart of the budget district. **$17**

Que Huong–Liberty 4 265 Pham Ngu Lao ☏08 3836 4556, ⊕libertyhotels.com.vn; map p.104. Run by the reliable Liberty group, this place offers stylish rooms with wi-fi, satellite TV and tea- and coffee-making facilities, plus a decent buffet breakfast served in its ninth-floor restaurant. **$82**

Saigon Sports 2 82 Le Lai ☏08 3925 3873, ⊕saigonsportshotel.com; map p.104. Formerly *Sen Hotel*, this is another recent acquisition of the *Sports Hotel*

chain. Rooms are small but all have wi-fi in the room, satellite TV, minibar, safety box and hairdryer and it's just far enough from the budget district to not feel enveloped by it. **$22**

Spring House 221 Pham Ngu Lao ☏08 3837 8312, ⊕springhousehotel.com.vn; map p.104. Set in the middle of noisy Pham Ngu Lao, this place is a decent budget alternative, with bamboo furnishings and friendly staff, but ask for a room at the back. **$20**

Vinh Guesthouse 269 De Tham ☏08 3836 8585, ☏08 3920 8127; map p.104. Located at the heart of the action on De Tham, this tiny place has just a few fan and a/c rooms, plus a dorm at the top of a seemingly endless staircase. Dorm **$6**, double **$15**

WEST OF DE THAM

Equatorial 242 Tran Binh Trong ☏08 3839 7777, ⊕equatorial.com; map pp.74–75. This palatial hotel offers very comfortable rooms with the full gamut of facilities. It has a pool on the fourth floor as well as a gym, sauna and beauty salon, plus an excellent restaurant (*Orientica*, see p.102). **$150**

★ **Four Roses** 790/5 Nguyen Dinh Chieu ☏08 3832 5895, ✉roseminne@hcm.vnn.vn; map pp.74–75. Located in no-man's-land between Cho Lon and the city centre, the *Four Roses* is full of character. Set in a tranquil garden bordered by bougainvillea, it has just six immaculately clean, pleasantly furnished rooms all with balconies. Family-run with a distinctly French flavour, it offers the perfect antidote to hectic Ho Chi Minh City; there's a beauty salon in the basement (the owner is a beautician) and meals can also be rustled up on request. **$20**

Windsor Plaza 18 An Duong Vuong ☏08 3833 6688, ⊕windsorplazahotel.com; map pp.74–75. It may be a short distance from the city centre in District Five, but the *Windsor* has a lot going for it. The rooms are luxurious and most have fantastic views, and there are good shopping, entertainment and dining options in the same building. **$120**

EATING

CENTRAL HO CHI MINH CITY

3T Quan Nuong 29–31 Ton That Tiep; map p.98. This hugely popular rooftop spot serving Vietnamese barbecue is located right above the *Temple Club* (see p.99). Order up your choice of meat, seafood and veg, and cook it to your taste at the table. Best to go with a group, and best to book ahead at weekends (do it through a Vietnamese friend as little English is spoken). Most dishes $3–8. Daily 5–11pm.

Al Fresco's 27 Dong Du; map p.98. Huge portions of everything here – pizzas, steaks, burgers and barbecued ribs (the speciality; a jumbo plate of ten to twelve ribs costs $30) – keep customers coming back for more. There's an upstairs room if downstairs full. Daily 10am–11pm.

Amigo 55 Nguyen Hué; map p.98. Upmarket grill restaurant, recommended for its T-bone steaks and seafood prepared on an open grill, plus a good salad bar. Mains around $30. Daily 11am–11pm.

Ashoka 17/10 Le Thanh Ton; map p.98. Smart Indian restaurant offering authentic Moghul Indian dishes – some, such as *cho cho tikka* (chicken marinated in yoghurt), cooked in the tandoor – and a satisfying range of veggie dishes. Mains $3–5. Daily 11.30am–2pm & 5–10pm.

Augustin's 10 Nguyen Thiep; map p.98. Hidden down a narrow lane linking Dong Khoi and Nguyen Hué, this intimate bistro serves well-cooked but pricey French dishes. Mains $3–12. Mon–Sat 11.30am–2pm & 6–10.30pm.

★ **Au Parc** 23 Han Thuyen ☎ 08 3829 2772; map p.98. Stylish place, conveniently located between Notre Dame Cathedral and Reunification Palace, serving great breakfasts and salads, with a good deli counter and home delivery too. Gets a bit busy downstairs, so head upstairs for a more relaxed environment. Mains $4–12. Mon–Sat 7.30am–10.30pm, Sun 8am–5pm.

Bitter Sweet Coffee House 81 Le Thanh Ton; map p.98. This cozy café serves good coffee, juices, beer and cocktails as well as a small selection of cakes and muffins. It's handy for a break from shopping in the boutiques along Pasteur. Daily 7am–11pm.

★ **Blue Ginger** 37 Nam Ky Khoi Nghia; map p.98. Refined, low-ceilinged dining room with eye-catching artwork on the walls and traditional live evening music as you tuck into quality Vietnamese dishes (main courses around $5–6). Popular with tour groups but still worth checking out for its agreeable ambience and great food. 7am–2pm & 5–10pm.

Ciao Café 40 Ngo Duc Khe & 74–76 Nguyen Hué; map p.98. These smartly decorated, popular venues serve steaks, spaghetti and Asian food, and have a kids' menu too. Mains around $4–6. Daily 7am–11pm.

Elbow Room 52 Pasteur ☎ 08 3821 4327; ⓦ elbowroom.com.vn; map p.98. Under the same management as *Skewers* (see p.99) and also offering delivery service, this cosy diner specializes in comfort food like battered fish and chips and baked Cajun meatloaf at around $10–15 a dish. There's also a well-stocked bar and live music on Fri evening. Daily 8am–11pm.

Fanny's Ice Cream 29–31 Ton Thap Thiep; map p.98. With its mustard-coloured walls, wrought-iron chairs and magazines to read, this is an ideal spot to enjoy a peach melba or maybe even a cocktail. Daily 8am–11pm.

Gartenstadt 34 Dong Khoi; map p.98. High-quality German bar-restaurant; generous portions, imported sausages and a good selection of German beers, some on draught. Main courses $7–13. Daily 10.30am–midnight.

Gloria Jean's 131 Dong Khoi; map p.98. Formerly known as *Brodard's*, this popular spot on Dong Khoi serves coffee, sandwiches and pastries. Daily 7am–11pm.

Hoi An 11 Le Thanh Ton ☎ 08 3823 7694; map p.98. Refined, traditional Vietnamese food is served in a sumptuous wooden house, run by the owners of *Mandarine* (see opposite). Set menus start at $35; book ahead to reserve a table. Daily 11am–2pm & 5.30–10.45pm.

Jaspa's 33 Dong Khoi; map p.98. Under the same management as *Al Fresco's* and *Pepperoni*, this place is a bit classier, featuring international fusion cuisine such as salt and pepper steak with wasabe mash ($19). Daily 7.30am–late.

Java Coffee Bar 38 Dong Du; map p.98. Welcoming coffee bar in the heart of the downtown area, serving a few main dishes such as pizzas and spaghetti plus sandwiches and smoothies. Daily 7am–11.30pm.

Kem Bach Dang 26 & 28 Le Loi; map p.98. Twin open-fronted ice-cream parlours, revered for extravagant creations, some of which feature fruits from Da Lat; unfortunately, it's a magnet for beggars who periodically stray inside. Daily 9am–midnight.

La Dolce Vita Bar Hotel Continental, 132–134 Dong Khoi; map p.98. Café, restaurant, bar and *gelateria* rolled into one, set in the refined courtyard surroundings of this Ho Chi Minh City institution. Daily 7am–10pm.

★ **La Fenetre Soleil** 1st floor, 44 Ly Tu Trong (near junction with Pasteur); map p.98. Though forced to move recently, this quirky café has managed to recreate the offbeat feel of the original, with a mismatch of furniture and bare brick walls. Apart from good coffee and shakes, they serve good set lunches (around $7) and cocktails, with shisha pipes too. It's just next to the Ho Chi Minh City Museum in case you need a rest after that. Daily 10am–midnight.

La Fourchette 11 Ngo Duc Ke; map p.98. Ho Chi Minh City's oldest French restaurant boasts an intimate atmosphere at this two-floor restaurant (non-smoking upstairs). The short menu features imported steaks and set lunches at around $15. Daily 11.30am–2.30pm & 6.30–10pm.

Le Jardin 31 Thai Van Lung ☎ 08 3825 8465; map p.98. Excellent French food at very reasonable prices ($3–8) served in a pleasant garden setting. Very popular so advance booking is advisable. Daily 11am–2pm & 6–9pm.

Lemongrass 4 Nguyen Thiep; map p.98. A decent, upmarket establishment where the highly rated Vietnamese food is eaten to the lilting strains of traditional live music. Main courses $5–15. Daily 11am–2pm & 5–10pm.

Mali Thai 37 Dong Du; map p.98. Most central of the Thai restaurants in town, with spicy curries and *tom yam* soup that are sure to bring tears to your eyes. Good set lunches around $4. Daily 11am–10pm.

Mandarine 11a Ngo Van Nam ☎ 08 3822 9783; map p.98. This established upmarket restaurant, beautifully decorated in traditional Vietnamese style, serves well-prepared Vietnamese standards. Set menus starts from $35. Live traditional music in evenings; reservations essential. Daily 11.30am–2pm & 5–10pm.

Maxim's Nam An –17 Dong Khoi; map p.98. One of the few venues in HCMC where you can enjoy traditional Vietnamese dishes, either from set menu or a la carte, in a plush environment and with a performance of classical Vietnamese music and dance to accompany it. Main courses $7–12. Daily 7am–midnight.

Mogambo 50 Pasteur; map p.98. Fish and chips, home-made pies, bangers and mash and big burgers attract a steady stream of resident expats and tourists to this small but cosy place. Mains $6–14. Daily 10am–10.30pm.

★ **Nam Giao** 136/15 Le Thanh Ton; map p.98. Excellent Hué food served in this hugely popular but simple place

1

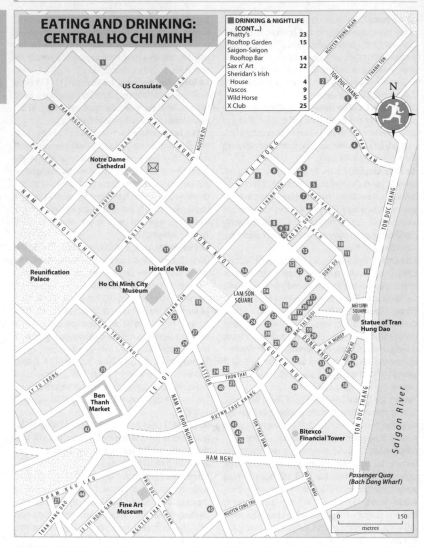

EATING AND DRINKING: CENTRAL HO CHI MINH

■ DRINKING & NIGHTLIFE (CONT...)

Phatty's	23
Rooftop Garden	15
Saigon-Saigon Rooftop Bar	14
Sax n' Art	22
Sheridan's Irish House	4
Vascos	9
Wild Horse	5
X Club	25

US Consulate

Notre Dame Cathedral

Reunification Palace

Hôtel de Ville

Ho Chi Minh City Museum

LAM SON SQUARE

MEI LINH SQUARE

Statue of Tran Hung Dao

Ben Thanh Market

Bitexco Financial Tower

Saigon River

Passenger Quay (Bach Dang Wharf)

Fine Art Museum

N

0   150
metres

● RESTAURANTS

3T Quan Nuong	40	La Dolce Vita Bar	14	Sandals	15	Apocalypse Now	11
Al Fresco's	17	La Fenetre Soleil	11	Sen Hue	32	Blue Gekko	3
Amigo	39	La Fourchette	31	Skewers	7	Chu	7
Ashoka	5	Le Jardin	6	Sushi Bar	1	Dai Ly Bia Hoi	10
Au Parc	8	Lemongrass	19	Tandoor	10	Drunken Duck	24
Augustin's	24	Mali Thai	18	Temple Club	40	Factory	21
Bitter Sweet Coffee House	23	Mandarine	4	Tin Nghia	44	Ice Blue	19
Blue Ginger	45	Maxim's Nam An	38	Vietnam House	26	La Habana	6
Ciao Café	21/37	Mogambo	43	Warda	30	Le Caprice	13
Elbow Room	41	Nam Giao	35	Wrap & Roll	12	Level 23	16
Fanny's Ice Cream	40	Napoli Café	2	Xu	15	Liberty	18
Gartenstadt	28	Ngon	13	ZanZBar	20	Liquid	1
Gloria Jean's	22	Paris Deli	33			Lush	2
Hoi An	3	Pho 2000	42	**■ DRINKING & NIGHTLIFE**		Number 5 Bar	26
Jaspa's	36	Pho 24	25	17 Saloon	27	O'Briens Factory	8
Java Coffee Bar	16	Refinery	9	Amber Room	17	Pacharan	12
Kem Bach Dang	27/29	Restaurant 13	34			Palace Club	20

tucked away down an alley behind Ben Thanh market. Join the throng of locals and a smattering of tourists to sample the famous *bun bo hué* or a *tasty banh khoai* for a dollar or two a dish. Daily 7.45am–10pm.

Napoli Café 7 Pham Ngoc Thach; map opposite. This place, a short stroll northwest of the cathedral, is hugely popular among locals for a short break in the day or to listen to the band in the evening. Choose from a modest selection of main dishes, cakes, pastries and sundaes or indulge in the *mangia e bevi* – a sensational blend of ice cream, orange juice and fresh fruit (68,000đ). Daily 7.30am–11pm.

★ **Ngon** 138 Nam Ky Khoi Nghia ☎ 08 3825 7179; map opposite. An experience not to be missed – delicious regional specialities served in a renovated colonial building at very reasonable prices. It's extremely popular, so be prepared to wait for a table at peak eating times. Mains $2–12. Daily 7am–11pm.

Paris Delii 35 Dong Khoi; map opposite. This place is a real find, and an ideal lunch stop downtown. Order up a croissant and coffee or a $5 set lunch with fresh juice at the counter, then head upstairs to the comfortable dining/lounge area and enjoy. Daily 7am–10.30pm.

Pho 24 5 Nguyen Thiep; map opposite. If the thought of eating from a street stall makes you shudder, sample your first bowl of pho, the nation's signature dish, in this spotless diner. *Pho 24* has over a dozen branches in District One alone, including those at 271 Pham Ngu Lao and on the third floor of Diamond Plaza. Mains $2–3. Daily 6.30am–10pm.

Refinery 74/7c Hai Ba Trung; map opposite. This cute little bistro set back from busy Hai Ba Trung has a relaxed vibe and serves an appealing range of dishes such as barbecued lamb ($14) as well as beers and cocktails. Daily 11am–late.

Restaurant 13 15 Ngo Duc Ke; map opposite. Simple but clean and a/c spot which serves some of the cheapest food downtown – a seafood or meat and rice dish will set you back around $4, and the beers are relatively cheap too. Daily 6.30am–11.30pm.

Sandals 93 Hai Ba Trung; map opposite. This swish place, operated by the famed *Sailing Club* from Nha Trang and Mui Ne, makes a good retreat for a light lunch while shopping or sightseeing downtown. Imaginative sandwiches and salads as well as delicious juices. Most dishes around $10. Daily 8am–midnight.

Sen Hue 48 Nguyen Hué; map opposite. Hué specialities occupy most of the menu at this smart but simple eatery with a convenient downtown location. Go for a bowl of *bun bo Hué* ($2.50) or the grilled beef *Sen* style ($6.50). Daily 10.30am–10.30pm.

Skewers 9a Thai Van Lung ☎ 08 3822 4798, ⓦ skewers -restaurant.com; map opposite. Award-winning Mediterranean cuisine using simple and healthy ingredients. Try the pan-fried salmon with nicoise salad ($15). Free delivery in Districts One and Three. Mon–Fri 11.30am–2pm & 6–10pm, Sat & Sun 6–10pm.

★ **Sushi Bar** 2 Le Thanh Ton ☎ 08 3823 8024, ⓦ sushibar .com.vn; map opposite. Highly rated sushi or sashimi mix in the heart of HCMC Japantown for around $14–17, plus Japanese beer and sake. Daily 10am–11.30pm.

Tandoor 74/6 Hai Ba Trung ☎ 08 3930 4839, ⓦ tandoorvietnam.cm; map opposite. An excellent range of Indian dishes, from biriyani to vindaloo, with several vegetarian options, in a convenient central location, with delivery service too. Popular set lunches from around $7. Daily 11am–2.30pm & 5–10.30pm.

Temple Club 29–31 Ton That Thiep; map opposite. Excellent Vietnamese food at around $15 a dish is served in a wonderful, relaxed atmosphere with tasteful decor. There's also a comfy lounge bar out back. Daily 11.30am–midnight.

Vietnam House 93–95 Dong Khoi; map opposite. Occupying a splendid louvred colonial building, *Vietnam House* offers a cracking introduction to Vietnamese food, featuring a wide a la carte menu as well as set lunches and dinners (from $15). There's a pianist on the ground floor and traditional folk music upstairs from 7–9pm. Daily 10am–11pm.

Warda 71/7 Mac Thi Buoi; map opposite. Middle-eastern dishes such as kefta kebab and duck with apricot tajine for around $10, with shisha pipes on hand as well. The exotic setting features flowing drapes and big cushions to lounge on. It's tucked away down a narrow alley off Mac Thi Buoi. Daily 11am–midnight.

Wrap & Roll 62 Hai Ba Trung; map opposite. Handy outlet of a chain doing for spring rolls what *Pho 24* does for pho – serving street food (most dishes $3–5) in a sanitized, a/c environment. Choose from a host of ingredients, peel off a rice wrapper and get rolling. Daily 10am–11pm.

Xu 71–75 Hai Ba Trung ☎ 08 3824 8468, ⓦ xusaigon .com. map opposite. This super-cool, minimalist venue has quickly developed a reputation as one of the city's most innovative fusion restaurants. For the full-on experience, pick the chef's set menu at $42.50 (or $80 with free-flow wine and cocktails). The main restaurant is upstairs, while downstairs is more a bar, and a DJ spins tunes here on weekends. Daily 11am–midnight.

★ **ZanZBar** 41 Dong Du; map opposite. This place has really taken off, both as a restaurant that offers some highly original dishes, and as a welcoming bar where you can make friends. Set lunches are around $10 and there's tasteful background music too. Daily 7am–1am.

DE THAM AND AROUND

Allez Boo 195 Pham Ngu Lao; map p.104. It may be better known as a watering hole (see p.105), but this place also turns out very acceptable Vietnamese, Thai and Western dishes at about $5 each. Daily 24hr.

Asian Kitchen 185/22 Pham Ngu Lao; map p.104. Tucked away down the narrow alley east of De Tham, this laidback

1

place features well-priced Vietnamese, Japanese and vegetarian dishes (around $2–5). Daily 7am–midnight.

Bobby Brewer's 45 Bui Vien ⓦ bobbybrewers.com; map p.104. If you're having a coffee break, then why not take in a movie too? All-day movies (many Vietnam-related) show at this movie lounge – check out the website for what's on now. Daily 8am–11pm.

Café 333 201 De Tham; map p.104. One of many travellers' cafés on De Tham, this one stands out for its friendly service and huge menu of Vietnamese and international dishes. Main courses $3–7. Daily 6.30am–midnight.

Café Sinh To 231 De Tham; map p.104. A no-frills but remarkably good-value juice bar bang in the centre of De Tham. Serves sandwiches and cakes too. Daily 6am–10pm.

Café Zoom 169a De Tham; map p.104. The place for Vespa and Lambretta fanatics to hang out, with a close-up view of the action at one of the city's busiest junctions. Daily 7am–2am.

Cappuccino 258 De Tham ☏ 08 3837 4114; map p.104. Serves up good pizzas at around $5 as well as reasonable Mexican and Vietnamese fare and wines by the glass too. There's another branch at 86 Bui Ven, and delivery service too. Daily 8.30am–midnight.

★ **Chi's Café** 40/31 Bui Vien ☏ 08 3836 7622; map p.104. It's worth tracking down this place, which is hidden in a narrow alley east of De Tham, for its build-your-own breakfasts, tasty and cheap Vietnamese food, and helpful travel advice. Delivery service too. Most dishes $3–5: Daily 7am–11pm.

Coriander 185 Bui Vien; map p.104. Great Thai food at reasonable prices ($3–5) at this tiny restaurant on a busy stretch of Bui Vien. Daily 7am–11pm.

Dinh Y 171b Cong Quynh; map p.104. Cheap but tasty vegetarian food prepared by Cao Dai adherents in a convenient location by Thai Binh market. Dishes $1–4. Daily 6.30am–9pm.

Dynasty New World Hotel, 76 Le Lai; map p.104. The decor is elegant (porcelain and bonsai), and the food is splendid, featuring delicious *dim sum* at lunchtime. Set menus start at around $30, but the sky's the limit if you plump for delicacies like bird's-nest soup or shark's fin. Mon–Sat 11.30am–2.30pm & 6–10pm; Sun 11.30am–2.30pm.

Good Morning Vietnam 197 De Tham; map p.104. Part of an Italian-run chain of restaurants that serves dependably good pizza and pasta ($3–5) in a welcoming environment. Daily 9am–midnight.

Highlands Coffee 187 Pham Ngu Lao; map p.104. Located at the hectic junction of De Tham and Pham Ngu Lao, this cool, a/c place has comfy armchairs and a flashy internet terminal, and serves cakes, sandwiches, smoothies and coffee. Daily 7.30am–11pm

Kim Café 268 De Tham; map p.104. Besides breakfasts and veggie meals galore, there's garlic bread, mashed potatoes and a fantastic chicken curry ($4). The bright

lights and no-frills, bustling atmosphere don't encourage diners to linger, but it's a good spot to get a filling meal for next to nothing. Daily 7am–late.

Margherita 175/1 Pham Ngu Lao; map p.104. Some of the cheapest and tastiest pizzas and pasta dishes in town ($3–4), not to mention the burritos and chicken Kiev that make this a good choice for cheap eats. Daily 7am–midnight.

Minh Duc 35 Ton That Tung; map p.104. It's worth escaping the tourist enclave around De Tham at lunchtime to join the scrum of locals at this point-and-eat place, where a wide range of well-prepared local dishes is on display (around 35,000đ a dish). Daily 10am–10pm.

New Pearl 205–207 Pham Ngu Lao and 259–265 De Tham; map p.104. This restaurant and bar has hit the scene in a big way, with two huge venues just near the corner of Pham Ngu Lao and De Tham. Both places have extensive menus of Vietnamese and Western dishes, and while prices are a bit higher than elsewhere ($5–10), you do get a/c, comfortable seating and attentive staff. They have a DJ on the decks at the Pham Ngu Lao branch after 9pm. Daily 7am–midnight.

Ngoc Suong 106 Suong Nguyet Anh ☏ 08 3925 6939; map pp.74–75. The most atmospheric branch of this hugely popular chain of seafood restaurants, drawing big crowds every evening. Mains $5–15. Reservations recommended. Daily 10am–10.30pm.

Pepperoni's 111 Bui Vien ☏ 08 3920 4989; map p.104. Above the *Spotted Cow* bar, this place serves pizzas, pasta, steaks and daily specials ($4–6), with frequent offers such as two pizzas for the price of one. Daily 8.30am–11pm.

Pho 2000 1–3 Phan Chu Trinh; map p.98. A great value spot, located next to Ben Thanh market. Clean surroundings and big bowls of delicious noodle soup and other Vietnamese staples for around $2–3. Daily 6.30am–11pm.

Pho Quynh 323 Pham Ngu Lao; map p.104. Whenever you feel the need to slurp down a bowl of beef noodle soup, the staff at *Pho Quynh* are ready and waiting with some of the tastiest broth in town ($2). Daily 24hrs.

Punjabi 40/3 Bui Vien; map p.104. One of HCMC newest and best Indian restaurants, this simple restaurant serves up generous portions of delicious North Indian cuisine. Lots of vegetarian dishes too and prices are around $2–4 a dish. Daily 11am–11pm.

Sasa Café 242 De Tham; map p.104. Not exactly gourmet food, but it has a huge menu of international dishes at cheap prices ($3–5), and the standard is generally fine. Daily 6.30am–midnight.

Sozo 176 Bui Vien; map p.104. A great place for a slow and relaxing breakfast or a midday break, this café serves excellent cakes and cookies, and employs under-privileged kids; all profits go into staff training. Head upstairs to escape the street noise. Daily 6.30am–10.30pm.

BUYING YOUR OWN FOOD: MARKETS AND SUPERMARKETS

With baguettes, cheese and fruit in such abundant supply in Vietnam, making up a picnic is easy. All the basics can be found at any of the city's **markets**, though if you're homesick for peanut butter, Vegemite or other such exotica, you'll need to head for a specialist **supermarket** or **provisions store**.

MARKETS

A stroll through a wet or fresh market in Vietnam, gazing at all the familiar and unfamiliar items on sale, is an essential activity for every visitor to the country. Don't be surprised if you get dragged into a conversation either, as Vietnamese do much of their socializing in the markets.

The handiest market for De Tham is **Thai Binh market**, down at the southwestern end of Pham Ngu Lao. Just about as near, and larger, is **Ben Thanh market** (see p.81), the central market in the city centre. Cho Lon is served by **Binh Tay market** (see p.84) on its southwestern border and by **An Dong market**, northeast of it at the junction of Tran Phu and An Duong Vuong.

SUPERMARKETS AND PROVISIONS STORES

Annam Gourmet Shop 16–18 Hai Ba Trung. Huge deli located downtown, pandering to the whims of expats and visitors alike.

Co-op Mart 189c Cong Quynh. Huge Western-style supermarket within easy walking distance of De Tham, selling clothes, toys, household goods, cosmetics and a good selection of Western foods. There's also a large branch at 168 Nguyen Dinh Chieu.

Minimart 250 De Tham. Snacks, drinks and basic toiletries on sale in the budget district.

Nhu Lan Bakery 66–68 Ham Nghi. Famed bakery selling bread, croissants and cakes.

Parkson Plaza 39–45 Le Thanh Ton. On the fourth floor of this shopping mall is a supermarket selling a good range of imported goods.

Thuong Xa Supermarket 135 Nguyen Hué. On the first floor of this centrally located shopping plaza, this large supermarket sells, amongst other things, Western tinned and dairy products.

Veggy's 29a Le Thanh Ton. Well-stocked with imported meats, cheeses and cereals, this place is a popular shopping spot for local expats.

Tin Nghia 9 Tran Hung Dao; map p.98. Mushrooms and tofu provide the backbone to the inventive menu in this friendly vegetarian restaurant. Most dishes $1–3. Daily 7am–2pm & 4–8.30pm.

Villa FB 79 Syong Nguyet Anh; map pp.74–75. Housed in a lovely old 1930s colonial house and its garden, this elegant restaurant features a variety of Vietnamese and Western dishes on its menu ($7–14), as well as a good range of wines; in fact, if you like, you can dine in the wine cellar. Daily 10am–10pm.

Zen 185/30 Pham Ngu Lao; map p.104. One of the few really authentic vegetarian options around De Tham. Cheap and tasty dishes such as burritos, wild red rice and Chinese mushrooms; delicious fruit shakes too. Mains $3–5. Daily 6.30am–10.30pm.

GREATER HO CHI MINH CITY

An Vien 178a Hai Ba Trung; map pp.74–75. Tucked away from the main road, this place is extremely intimate, with many different alcoves and corners on three floors, all sumptuously decorated, and with high-quality Vietnamese food to match. Main courses $5–12. Daily 9am–11pm.

⭐ **Au Manoir de Khai** 251 Dien Bien Phu ☎08 3930 3394; map pp.74–75. This is the nearest you're likely to get to feeling like a colonial of consequence, as the staff treat all guests with great deference. Stunning surroundings, tranquil atmosphere, sensational French food, such as grilled lamb tenderloin with Dijon mustard sauce ($17), and an extensive wine list. Daily 11am–2pm & 6–9.30pm.

Banh Xeo 46a Dinh Cong Trang; map pp.74–75. Vietnamese pancakes, stuffed with a mixture of shrimps, pork, beans, bean sprouts and egg are the speciality at this streetside eatery off Hai Ba Trung that has become a must-visit spot for many travellers. At around 40,000đ a throw, they'll fill you up for most of the day, though there are plenty of other worthy dishes to do the job. Daily 10am–9.30pm.

⭐ **Café Central** 4th floor, 18 An Duong Vuong; map pp.74–75. Located in District Five a couple of kilometres west of De Tham (in the same building as the *Windsor Plaza Hotel*). Fantastic lunch and dinner buffet (around $15 and $20 respectively), featuring over 150 Vietnamese, Japanese and Western culinary treats that will have you re-filling your plate time and again. Daily 6am–10pm.

Camargue 191 Hai Ba Trung; map pp.74–75. A colonial-style modern villa with rattan furniture and wooden ceiling fans, sets the scene of a bygone era for this expensive French restaurant. The menu is constantly changing, but features dishes like beef carpaccio and lamb tenderloin with couscous. It's set back from the main road down a narrow lane. Main courses $12–24. Daily 6–11pm.

Dat 16 Truong Dinh; map pp.74–75. It's worth trekking out to the wilds of District Three to check out this popular

1

place that specializes in wrap-and-roll dishes with yummy dips, but can also rustle up a cheap and tasty beefsteak with fries. Mains $3–5. Daily 10am–11pm.

Loving Hut (Hoa Dang) 38 Huynh Khuang Ninh; map pp.74–75. This is a great find for vegetarians, particularly vegans, as it features a wide menu of vegetarian dishes, including pizza, salad and hotpot ($2–8). Even carnivores would enjoy their fabulous pho, and the smart, a/c environment is pretty cool too. Daily 9.30am–2pm & 4.30–9pm.

Ocean Palace 2 Le Duan; map pp.74–75. This elegant, high-ceilinged Chinese restaurant just opposite the History Museum is a great place to relax after filling your mind with Vietnam's complex past. Order up a few dim sum baskets (some of the best in Saigon, around $2 each), or go for the roasted suckling pig or crispy duck, both of which are excellent. Wash it down with a beer or glass or two of wine, then walk it off in the Botanical Gardens, just across the road. Main courses $5–10. Daily 10am–2.30pm & 6–10.30pm.

Orientica Equatorial Hotel, 242 Tran Binh Trong, District Five; map pp.74–75. Super-stylish restaurant on the second floor of the *Equatorial*, specializing in seafood prepared in a variety of ways, plus steaks and hotpots. Main dishes cost between $20–35. Daily 11.30am–2.30pm & 6.30–10.30pm.

Pho Binh 7 Ly Chinh Thang; map pp.74–75. A must-see for all war buffs: a wartime safe house for Communists, it was from here that the command was given to kick off the 1968 Tet Offensive. Don't make the trip for the soup alone, though. Main dishes $2–3. Daily 6am–10pm.

Pho Hoa 260c Pasteur; map pp.74–75. High-quality pho shops proliferate along Pasteur, none better than *Pho Hoa*. On offer are huge bowlfuls of soup complemented with chunks of chicken or beef and plenty of fresh greens on the tables to add yourself. You'll pay around 50,000đ but it's well worth it. Daily 6am–midnight.

Pho Hung 241–243 Nguyen Trai; map pp.74–75. The path in front of this pho shop is constantly jammed with motorbikes of aficionados who might drop by for a bowl of broth at any time of day or night. It's a short walk west of the budget district; drop by and decide if it's the best in town, as some would argue. Main dishes $2–3. Daily 6am–3am.

Spice 27c Le Quy Don ☎ 08 3930 7873; map pp.74–75. Stylishly furnished Thai restaurant with menu that looks like a magazine, featuring classics like *tom yam* and *som tam*. Well worth going out of your way for. Main courses $5–10. Daily 11am–2pm & 5.30–10.30pm.

DRINKING AND NIGHTLIFE

Ho Chi Minh City boasts a good range of nightlife, so there's no need to head back to your hotel once dinner is through, although an ongoing crackdown on late opening means you'll probably be tucked up in bed by midnight unless you're in the De Tham area. Later at night, a number of **clubs** get going, though they often have short lifespans unless they are under the protection of a major hotel. Things seem a bit looser around the budget district, where several places open all night. The free monthly magazines *The Word* and *Asia Life* carry up-to-the-minute listings of the city's latest bars, plus the hottest new clubs and any more highbrow entertainment on offer.

Bars and pubs in Ho Chi Minh City range from hole-in-the-wall dives to elegant cocktail lounges that would not be out of place in a European capital. The area around Dong Khoi is predictably well endowed, and another boozy enclave exists around Le Thanh Ton, Hai Ba Trung and Thi Sach, where a glut of places, ranging from slick yuppie haunts to watering holes that hark back to the raunchy GI bars of the 1960s, has developed to cater for expats renting apartments nearby. At the other end of the scale, all the cheap restaurants and cafés around De Tham turn their hand to drink at night – fine if you're willing to forego atmosphere in order to save a dollar or two on a beer, and great for meeting like-minded tourists. Many of the bars listed below feature **live music** either every night or at the weekend. In most places, such as *17 Saloon*, you'll

---

TRADITIONAL ENTERTAINMENT

Few places cater for Westerners wanting an insight into Vietnamese culture, though there is the odd exception. About 8km north of the city, **Binh Quoi Village** (☎ 08 3556 5891, ⓦ binhquoiresort.com.vn) features Tuesday, Thursday and Saturday evening programmes of dinner followed by **folk music and traditional dancing**, organized by Saigontourist (tickets for meal and show around $25). For Western and Vietnamese classical music, ask the Conservatory of Music (☎ 08 3824 3774) at 112 Nguyen Du about the HCMC Youth Chamber Music Club's performances, which can be scheduled on demand. It's also worth checking out what's on at Lam Son Square's Municipal Theatre (☎ 08 3829 9976), which occasionally hosts fashion shows, **traditional drama** and dance. Water-puppetry isn't as big in Ho Chi Minh City as it is in Hanoi, though if you aren't going to the north you might want to attend one of the shows laid on at the Golden Dragon Theatre (see box, p.80) or at the History Museum (hourly 10am–4pm, except 1pm; $2).

BIA HOI BARS

If you can't afford the price of a bottle of Saigon beer, you might try a **bia hoi bar**, where locals glug cheap local draught beer at around 5000đ a litre. These spit-and-sawdust bars tend to open in the afternoon and close around 8–9pm, though some stay open later. They crop up all over the city, but the two listed below are convenient for Dong Khoi and De Tham.

Dai Ly Bia Hoi 4 Thi Sach; map p.98. If the restaurants and bars around Dong Khoi seem too expensive, duck in here and drown your sorrows in a jug of the local special. They serve some tasty snacks as well.

Bia Hoi Bar 102 Bui Vien; map p.98. Tiny place but an excellent spot to watch the world wander by while chilling out with a cool beer.

find Filipino bands performing well-rehearsed covers of current hits and old favourites, though there's also a growing base of local musicians who are making a name for themselves in venues like *Thi Café* and *Yoko*. It isn't unheard-of for big showbiz names from the West to make appearances in HCMC (Bob Dylan was here recently), so check out the local press for details. **Prices** vary wildly: a Saigon beer at a streetside café in De Tham will cost you around $1, but you can multiply that by four or five in a more upmarket bar on Dong Khoi. One way to economize while downtown is to take advantage of early-evening **happy hours**, or check out the surprisingly cheap and tasty **bia hoi** (see box above).

CENTRAL HO CHI MINH CITY

Amber Room 59 Dong Du; map p.98. This upstairs room located right across from the Sheraton is the kind of comfortable lounge bar you might find in Europe's top cities, with comparable prices too. Daily 3pm–midnight.

Apocalypse Now 2c Thi Sach; map p.98. A pioneer of the city's nightlife scene, always rowdy and sweaty at weekends with an eclectic crowd, though can be rather dull during the week. Dark and cavernous, with two dance floors and a compact garden. Daily 7pm–late.

Blue Gekko 31 Ly Tu Trong; map p.98. Expat hangout offering pub atmosphere with pool, darts and sports TV. Happy hour is 5–7.30pm, but at other times drinks are pricey. Daily 5pm–late.

Chu 158 Dong Khoi; map p.98. A convenient and inexpensive venue for evening entertainment, with live music (mostly 60s and 70s songs) from 9pm–1am, plus an eclectic menu that includes beef pie, spaghetti, Asian dishes and ice creams. Daily 8am–1am.

Drunken Duck 58 Ton That Tiep; map p.98. One of several bars along Ton That Tiep that is making this street a magnet for HCMC nightlife, offering a huge range of shooters, cocktails with aptly themed names like Aquackalypse Now and a full range of beers. Daily 6pm–late.

Factory 102 Mac Thi Buoi; map p.98. New nightclub furnished like a factory, featuring DJs playing mostly hip-hop. Daily 9pm–late.

Ice Blue 54 Dong Khoi; map p.98. Traditional English pub-style bar, with a dartboard, a friendly atmosphere and a range of international beers; 4–8pm is happy hour. Daily 4pm–late.

La Fenetre Soleil 1st floor, 44 Ly Tu Trong; map p.98. Functioning as a chill-out café (see p.97) during the day, this little gem turns its hand to mixing cocktails and filling shisha pipes in the evenings. Daily 11.30am–midnight.

★ **La Habana** 6 Cao Ba Quat; map p.98. A touch of Cuba in HCMC in the form of a friendly bar serving a good range of beers and cocktails as well as Spanish food and tapas. Live music most nights and salsa dancing on Mon and Thurs. Daily 10am–late.

Le Caprice 15th floor, Landmark Building, 5b Ton Duc Thang; map p.98. A pricey and stylish restaurant, but it's worth splashing out on an expensive cocktail to enjoy the view along the river. Daily 11am–2pm & 5–10.30pm.

Level 23 Sheraton Hotel, 88 Dong Khoi; map p.98. This is a great spot for after-dinner cocktails while enjoying panoramic views of the city, and if you're in the mood, the band might get you dancing too. 7pm–midnight.

Liberty 80 Dong Khoi; map p.98. A largely Vietnamese crowd waltzes along to the smoochy live music in this dark upstairs club; disco music takes over later. Daily 8.30pm–late.

Liquid 104 Hai Ba Trung; map p.98. Western and local pop both feature at this venue that draws a lively local crowd. It's located a bit north of the centre and attracts few tourists, but is a good spot to check the beat of modern HCMC. Daily 8pm–late.

Lush 2 Ly Tu Trong; map p.98. This elegant club is one of the top places for the city's movers and shakers, both expats and locals, to let their hair down at the weekend, when it gets packed. Weekdays it can be pretty dead though. Daily 6pm–late.

Number 5 Bar 44 Pasteur; map p.98. This place has a similar formula to *Phatty's* round the corner – a big bar area with plenty of bar stools, pretty waitresses, comfort food and sports on TV. Daily 3pm–1am.

O'Briens Factory 74a 3 Hai Ba Trung; map p.98. *O'Briens Factory* isn't a world away from a smart London pub, and is popular with expats for its good atmosphere, pool table, well-stocked bar and comforting Western

1

menu. Happy hour 3–7pm (except Sun). Mon–Sat 11am–late, Sun 6pm–late.

Pacharan 97 Hai Ba Trung; map p.90. Smart, three-floored Spanish place just behind the Municipal Theatre, serving tapas and a wide range of drinks. Live music (mostly Spanish) some nights. Daily 10am–late.

Palace Club Palace Hotel, 55 Nguyen Hué; map p.98. One of HCMC's most enjoyable nightclubs for its sophisticated but unpretentious vibe, attracting an interesting mix of locals and foreign visitors, this club is located in the *Palace Hotel*. Daily 6pm–late.

Phatty's 46–48 Ton That Tiep; map p.90. This sports bar and grill is currently one of the city's most popular bars, and is often packed with punters watching rugby or Australian Rules Football. There are enough screens, it seems, for every customer to be watching a different channel, even if the result is a bit cacophonous. Daily 9am–11pm.

Rooftop Garden Rex Hotel, 141 Nguyen Hué; map p.98. A drink amidst the fairy-lit topiary and clumsy model animals of the *Rex* fifth-floor terrace is still *de rigueur* on a trip to the city. Daily 7am–late.

Saigon–Saigon Rooftop Bar Caravelle Hotel, 19 Lam Son Square; map p.98. Romantic views of the city and nightly live music in a stylish ambience more than compensate for the pricey drinks list in this lofty (tenth floor) hotel bar. Popular with local expats. Daily 9am–midnight.

Sax n' Art 28 Le Loi; map p.98. Slick jazz club with mellow sounds from the house band, led by saxophonist

Tran Manh Tuan, starting at 9pm, sometimes featuring good vocalists. Full marks for atmospheric decor, zero marks for the sneaky 65,000đ cover charge slipped on to the bill without warning. Daily 5pm–midnight.

Sheridan's Irish House 17/13 Le Thanh Ton; map p.98. Live music most nights in this typical Irish bar which also has an extensive menu. It attracts a regular crowd of expats with its pies and other comfort food, and the music is mostly covers of hit songs. Daily 8am–late.

Vascos 74/7d Hai Ba Trung; map p.98. Live bands on Fri and DJs on Thurs and Sat, plus a good range of food (French, Italian and Asian) at this hip bar with a casual/smart ambience in a former opium refinery set back from the main road. Daily 11am–midnight.

Wild Horse 8a1/d1 Thai Van Lung; map p.98. Saloon-type place, complete with swinging doors and trophy heads, specializing in imported steaks and international dishes. Live music too – mostly covers of Western pop hits. Daily 10am–2pm & 4–11.30pm.

X Club 21–27 Ton That Tiep; map p.98. One of the city's newest discos, located in the trendy Ton That Tiep area, this place gets crowded on a Fri and Sat night. Daily 8pm–late.

★ **Yoko** 22a Nguyen Thi Dieu; map pp.74–75. If you get fed up with the lack of variety in music bars, head on round to *Yoko*, named after John Lennon's mrs, where you'll catch a different theme (blues/rock, reggae, jazz, etc) each night of the week. Bands play from 9.30–11.30pm and

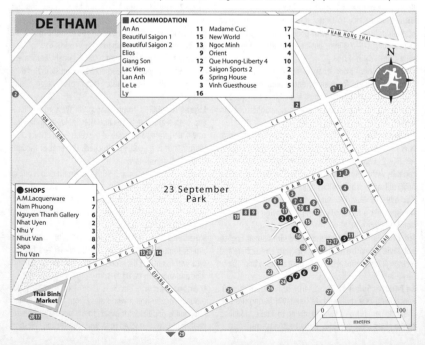

1

BOOGIE NIGHTS

Ho Chi Minh City's **club scene** has been floundering for the last few years as midnight closing is enforced throughout the city. Traditional nightclubs, where the practice of employing hostesses in slit gowns, are still prevalent and some establishments continue to cater for the locals' love of **ballroom dancing** – a tradition which is fading out as MTV turns local youngsters on to Viet pop and the latest Western sounds. Western visitors tend to steer clear of the more disco-like places with flashing lights in favour of more dimly lit clubs like *Apocalypse Now*, *Factory* and *Lush*. Most places levy a **cover charge** (normally $4–5), though some just charge higher prices for drinks. Again, see local listings magazines for the hottest new clubs.

---

some musicians here have bags of talent. Add to this the warm atmosphere of the place and comparatively cheap prices for drinks, and you've got one of HCMC's best live music venues. Daily 6pm–late.

DE THAM AND AROUND

17 Saloon 103a Pham Ngu Lao; map p.90. Wild West-style bar occupying two floors near the budget hotel district. Its competent Filipino band draws a mixed and enthusiastic audience. Daily 7pm–1am.

Allez-Boo 187 Pham Ngu Lao; map p.98. Bamboo and thatch decor, loud music, great food (see p.99) and a good selection of cocktails make this place hugely popular and it's heaving most nights. Daily 24hr.

Crazy Buffalo 212 De Tham; map p.98. Directly opposite *Go 2 Bar* (see below), this huge place is clearly trying to emulate the success of its neighbour, with two-for-one offers on drinks and loud rock music, but so far hasn't quite made it. Daily 24hr.

Cyclo Bar 163 Pham Ngu Lao; map p.98. This congenial place with dartboard and pool table offers draught beer and cocktails as well as comfort food such as bangers and mash. Three floors and sports on TV. Daily 9am–late.

Go 2 187 De Tham; map p.98. This large, four-storey bar and restaurant on the corner of Bui Vien, run by the

owners of *Allez Boo*, is packing them in, with a little help from a small army of barkers who steer passers-by inside. Daily 24hr.

Le Pub 175/22 Pham Ngu Lao; map p.98. Tucked away down a lane off Pham Ngu Lao, this place stands out for its attractive decor, cheap beer, good selection of food and cool sounds played by the resident DJ. Daily 7am–late.

Spotted Cow 111 Bui Vien; map p.98. This smart sports bar, located in the heart of the budget district, is a good place to meet up with other travellers or expat residents while enjoying a glass of grog. Daily 9am–midnight.

Thi Café & Lounge 224 De Tham; map p.98. In the daytime this place functions as a chill-out café, a good place to check email or have a chat. However, around 9pm on most nights it morphs into one of the city's most interesting bars for live acoustic music, performed by locals and itinerant musicians. Well worth checking out. Daily 7.30am–late.

GREATER HCMC

America 3rd Floor, 18 An Duong Vuong, District Five; map pp.74–75. Located in the same building as the *Windsor Plaza Hotel*, this swish disco attracts an upmarket clientele with its big dance floor, nightly DJs and impressive light show. 7pm–1am.

MARKETS AND SHOPPING

Ho Chi Minh City can be a dangerous place to go **shopping**, as you'll likely buy more than you intended once you see the prices. Paintings on rice paper, silk *ao dai*, lacquerware, embroidered cloth, musical instruments and ethnic garments are all popular gifts and souvenirs, as are **curios** such as opium pipes, antique watches, French colonial stamps and banknotes, while the cheapest items are the ubiquitous T-shirts and conical hats. Visitors interested in Vietnam's history will find a wealth of copied **books** on the subject, sold in tourist areas by wandering vendors with a metre-high stack on their hip. Sadly the range of English-language books available in regular bookshops is very limited. For cheap and cheerful **souvenirs**, head for Ben Thanh market, Le Loi or De Tham; for something precious and pricey, browse the upmarket boutiques along Dong Khoi and its tentacles, such as Dong Du and Mac Thi Buoi. **Bargaining** is an essential skill to cultivate if you're going to be doing much shopping. **Shopping malls** attract curious crowds with their glitz and glamour; some offer distractions other than shopping in the form of cinemas and bowling alleys. For something different, intriguing **model ships** are sold on Cao Ba Quat, north of the Municipal Theatre, just east of the *Caravelle Hotel*. Generally speaking, shops **open** daily 10am to dusk, while larger stores often stay open beyond 8pm.

DEPARTMENT STORES AND SHOPPING MALLS

An Dong Plaza 18 An Duong Vuong, District Five; map

pp.74–75. Occupying three floors below the *Windsor Plaza Hotel* and infrequently visited by tourists, this place has several outlets selling jewellery, clothes and handicrafts.

1

MARKET SHOPPING

The local **markets** are well worth checking out, both as a source of bargains and as a window on Vietnamese culture. The biggest is **Ben Thanh market** (see p.81), at the junction of Tran Hung Dao, Le Loi and Ham Nghi, which has a huge variety of cheap clothes (*ao dai* under $30) and all kinds of souvenirs like chopstick sets and carved seals, though unfortunately all stalls there are now fixed price. **Dan Sinh market**, 104 Yersin (p.82), has a section specializing in army surplus, both American and Vietnamese, though most items are likely to be fake. For other smaller souvenirs, check out the shops along Le Loi and Dong Khoi for old **coins**, **stamps**, notes and **greetings cards** featuring typical Vietnamese scenes hand-painted onto silk.

Diamond Plaza 34 Le Duan; map p.93. Probably the city's most diverse mall, featuring department store, supermarket, fitness centre, hospital, swimming pool, bowling alley, cinemas and serviced apartments.

Parkson Department Store 39–45 Le Thanh Ton; map p.93. Upmarket department store in the heart of the hotel district, selling expensive handicrafts, jewellery and cosmetics among other things. There are other branches at Hung Vuong Plaza (District Five) and beside the airport.

Saigon Centre 65 Le Loi; map p.93. Cafés, souvenir shops, boutiques, small department store and supermarket in convenient location between downtown and the budget area.

Saigon Square 7–9 Ton Duc Thang; map p.93. There are now two outlets for this vendor of cheap knock-offs of designer-brand clothing and accessories.

Thuong Xa Tax Shopping 135 Nguyen Hué; map p.93. Known locally as the Russian Market and located opposite the *Rex*, this is a sprawling department store selling electronic goods, cameras, watches, pirate CDs and DVDs, jewellery, leather goods and lacquerware.

Vincom Centre 70–72 Le Thanh Ton; map p.93. The latest shopping mall to open in HCMC (though it won't be the last) sells most designer labels and houses a few cafés and restaurants.

Zen Plaza 54–56 Nguyen Trai; map p.93. Black and white eight-storey shopping complex, packed with cosmetics, toys, electrical and household goods and video games. A cafeteria on the top floor has stunning views of the city.

BOOKS, NEWSPAPERS AND MAGAZINES

Artbook 43 Dong Khoi; map p.93. While most books here are art or architecture-related, there's lots more as well and titles are well displayed.

Bookazine 28 Dong Khoi; map p.93. Stocks a range of newspapers and magazines, as well as detailed maps of Vietnamese provinces and an intriguing hotchpotch of secondhand books, some of which look like collectors' items.

Fahasa 40 Nguyen Hué and 60 Le Loi; map p.93. Probably the best-stocked bookshops in town for English-language titles, including guide books, maps, some novels and magazines.

Thu Van 40/4 Bui Vien; map p.104. A wide selection of secondhand books on sale. The shop is tucked away down the narrow alley to the east of De Tham.

HANDICRAFTS, FABRICS AND ANTIQUES

A.M. Lacquerware 185 Pham Ngu Lao; map p.104. Lacquerware, ceramic, stone, bamboo, shell and horn products at affordable prices.

Art Arcade 151 Dong Khoi; map p.93. Paintings, lacquerware and ceramics, plus Buddha statues, old watches and trinkets.

Bich Lien 125 Dong Khoi; map p.93. General souvenirs-cum-handicrafts, plus a good range of Tin Tin paintings on lacquer.

Khai Silk 107 Dong Khoi; map p.93. One of several downtown outlets for the creations of one of the city's top designers, selling exclusive outfits at high prices.

Mai O Mai 67 Mac Thi Buoi; map p.93. Sells an eye-catching range of hand-made jewellery, including bags, necklaces and earrings.

Nga 41 Mac Thi Buoi; map p.93. Some stunningly decorated lacquerware furniture and items of home decor that will become conversation pieces back home.

Nhat Uyen 237 De Tham; map p.104. Striking designs on bags, scarves, cushion covers and silks.

Nhu Y 257 De Tham; map p.104. Tasteful pieces of lacquerware, Buddha images and reproduction art.

Sapa 209 De Tham & 7 Ton That Thiep; map p.104. Attractive garments and artefacts from Vietnamese ethnic minority groups.

Song 76d Le Thanh Ton; map p.93. Beautifully designed garments made with natural materials and organic dyes but big prices.

Tay Son 198 Vo Thi Sau; map pp.74–75. Frequented by tourist groups, since you can watch processes such as making lacquerware as well as browse their large warehouse of furniture, wooden carvings and lacquered art.

PAINTINGS

Apricot Gallery 50–52 Mac Thi Buoi; map p.93. One of the city's most exclusive galleries, with intriguing, original oils by local artists from $650 upwards.

Lotus Gallery 67 Pasteur; map p.93. If you're in the market for original Vietnamese art, be it traditional or contemporary, there's a good range on show here over two floors.

Nam Phuong 105 Bui Vien; map p.104. One of many artists making a living by reproducing classic images in the travellers' quarter; good work and reasonable prices.

Nguyen Thanh Gallery 53 Bui Vien; map p.104. Some original paintings by Nguyen Thanh, but mostly reproductions.

TAILORS

Chuong 270 Hai Ba Trung; map pp.74–75. A long-established and reliable tailor located a few blocks north of downtown.

Nhut Van 107 Bui Vien; map p.104. Long-standing tailor in the budget district with many satisfied customers.

T&V 39 Dong Du; map p.93. Slightly more expensive than other places but worth it for the fresh and original designs.

Zakka 134 Pasteur; map p.93. High-quality tailor, also sells divine ready-to-wear silk creations.

DIRECTORY

Banks and exchange Most banks have ATMs and exchange cash or travellers' cheques. Sacombank at 211–213 Pham Ngu Lao (Mon–Fri 7.30–11.30am & 1–4.30pm, Sat 7.30–11am) is convenient for those staying around Pham Ngu Lao. Otherwise, foreign exchange kiosks on Nguyen Hué and Le Loi have extended daily opening times. Also, most gold and jewellery shops will exchange dollars for dong at a slightly better rate than the bank.

Cinema Diamond Cinema complex on the thirteenth floor of Diamond Plaza (see opposite; ☎08 3822 7897); Galaxy Cinema, 116 Nguyen Du (☎08 3822 8533); Bobby Brewer's Movie Lounge, 45 Bui Vien (☎08 3920 4090, ⓦ bobbybrewers.com.

Consulates Australia, Landmark Building, 5b Ton Duc Thanh ☎08 3821 8100; Cambodia, 41 Phung Khac Khoan ☎08 3829 2751; Canada, 235 Dong Khoi ☎08 3827 9899; China, 39 Nguyen Thi Minh Khai ☎08 3829 2459; Indonesia, 18 Phung Khac Khoan ☎08 3825 1888; Laos, 93 Pasteur ☎08 3829 7667; Malaysia, 2 Ngo Duc Ke ☎08 3829 9023; New Zealand, Suite 804, Level 8, The Metropolitan Building, 235 Dong Khoi ☎08 3822 6907; Singapore, Saigon Centre, 65 Le Loi ☎08 3822 5174; Thailand, 77 Tran Quoc Thao ☎08 3932 7637; UK (& British Council), 25 Le Duan ☎08 3825 1380; US, 4 Le Duan ☎08 3820 4200.

Courier services DHL, 4 Phan Thuc Duyen, Tan Binh District ☎08 3844 6203; FedEx, 146 Pasteur, close to the *Rex Hotel* ☎08 3829 0995.

Dentists Starlight Dental Clinic, 2 Bis Cong Truong Quoc Te (☎08 3822 6222), is an international-standard dental clinic. The International SOS Dental Clinic (☎08 3829 8424) at 163a Nam Ky Khoi Nghia has a 24hr emergency centre.

Emergencies Dial ☎113 for the police, ☎114 in case of fire or ☎115 for an ambulance; if possible, get a Vietnamese speaker to call on your behalf.

Hairdressers 143 Salon, 143 Bui Vien. Haircut, highlights, manicure, pedicure, etc.

Hospitals and clinics International SOS Clinic, 167a Nam Ky Khoi Nghia (☎08 3829 8424), has international doctors, can arrange emergency evacuation and has a 24hr emergency service (☎08 3829 8520). Columbia Saigon, 8 Alexandre De Rhodes (☎08 3823 8888), and Columbia Gia Dinh at 1 No Trang Long, Binh Thanh (☎08 3803 0678), have multinational doctors with 24hr emergency cover and evacuation. HCM City Family Medical Practice, Diamond Plaza, 34 Le Duan (☎08 3822 7848), is an international clinic with multinational doctors and specialist knowledge of vaccinations, as well as 24hr emergency cover and evacuation. International Medical Centre, 1 Han Thuyen (☎08 3827 2366), is a French-run, non-profit, 24hr hospitalization centre with in-patient wards, intensive care and emergency surgery. Cho Lon's Cho Ray Hospital, at 201 Nguyen Chi Thanh (☎08 3855 4137) has an outpatients' room for foreigners and a foreigners' ward. The Hospital of Traditional Medicine, 187 Nam Ky Khoi Nghia (☎08 3932 6579), has acupuncture treatment.

Internet access Most hotels now provide free wi-fi or internet access, but there are still a few shops offering internet access for around 6000–8000đ an hour, such as at 53 Bui Vien.

Laundry Most hotels and guesthouses will wash clothes for you, but rates vary wildly so check first; upmarket hotels can do dry-cleaning; there are also a number of laundry and dry-clean operators around Pham Ngu Lao such as at 203 Bui Vien, where rates are 10,000đ per kilo.

Pharmacies There are several pharmacies in and around the De Tham area, such as 65 Bui Vien, while the one at 389 Hai Ba Trung is reputed to be the best stocked in the city.

Police Main police station is at 73 Yersin ☎08 3829 7073. You must first go to the police station in the ward where the crime took place to obtain an initial report before coming here; try to avoid lunchtime visits, as there's likely to be nobody on duty.

Post offices The GPO (daily 6am–10pm) is beside the cathedral at the head of Dong Khoi; poste restante is kept here.

Telephone services Several places, especially in the budget district, offer phone services from which you can call the US or UK for under 20 cents a minute. There are IDD, fax and telex facilities at the GPO (see above).

Visas Visa extensions and re-entry visas must be organized through an agent or tour operator; the process takes about four days and costs $25.

1

ACTIVITIES

GOLF

Vietnam Golf and Country Club Long Thanh My Village, District Nine ☎08 6280 0124, ⓦvietnamgolfcc.com. Has two high-quality courses and a driving range.

MASSAGE AND SPAS

For unbridled pampering, check out ⓦspasvietnam.com for a complete listing of the city's many spas and treatments on offer.

Traditional Vietnamese Massage Institute 185 Cong Quynh ☎08 3839 6697. To ease aches and pains, head for where blind masseurs and masseuses will smoothen your kinks for 45,000đ/hr (fan room) or 55,000đ/hr (a/c). 9am–9pm.

RUNNING

For runners and walkers, the **Hash House Harriers** (ⓦsaigonh3.com) meet every Sun at the *Caravelle Hotel* at 1.30pm.

SWIMMING AND LEISURE FACILITIES

Many upmarket hotels have excellent sport and leisure facilities that non-residents can generally use – at a price – but it's wise to check ahead first.

California Wow Queen Ann Building, 28–32 La Lai ☎08 6222 0355. California Wow has a branch of its good quality fitness centres here.

Hotel Pools Park Hyatt, Renaissance and Sofitel. For a daily fee of between $5 and $10 you can use the facilities at these pools if you are not a guest. Some include use of sauna and steam bath. Diamond Plaza shopping centre (see p.106) also has a pool.

Lam Son 242 Tran Binh Trong. An inexpensive but busy pool.

Lan Anh Country Club 291 Cach Mang Thang ☎08 3862 7144. Favoured by expats, try the relatively cheap pool and international-standard tennis courts, squash courts and gym here.

Workers' Club In the northern corner of the Cong Vien Van Hoa Park, on Nguyen Thi Minh Khai. There are tennis courts and a swimming pool, though they're often crowded.

WATER PARKS

Dai The Gioi 600 Ham Tu in Cho Lon. This attractive park has pools and slides. Entry 65,000đ, children 45,000đ. Mon–Fri 8am–9pm, Sat & Sun 10am–6pm.

Dam Sen A little further north of Dai The Gioi. The water park here has 25 different types of water games. Entry 100,000đ. Mon–Fri 9am–6pm, Sat & Sun 8.30am–6pm.

Around Ho Chi Minh City

When Ho Chi Minh City's blaring horns and pushy vendors become too much for you, you'll find you can get quite a long way **out of the city** in a day. With public transport slow and erratic, day-trips are best arranged through a tour operator (see box, p.90). The single most popular trip out of the city takes in one or both of Vietnam's most memorable sights: the **Cu Chi tunnels**, for twenty years a bolt hole, first for Viet Minh agents, and later for Viet Cong cadres; and the weird and wonderful **Cao Dai Holy See** at Tay Ninh, the fulcrum of the country's most charismatic indigenous religion. While it's possible to see both places in a day (indeed, most people do), be prepared to spend most of the day on the road.

Another enjoyable day (or half-day) out can be had at one of the **water parks** that are located on the fringe of the city and make a great antidote to the dust and heat of Ho Chi Minh City (see Listings above). Southwest of the city, a new highway runs down to **My Tho** (see p.120), where you can catch a glimpse of the Mekong River; while to the northeast, it breezes up to the dreary orbital city of **Bien Hoa**, from where Highway 51 drops down to the beaches around **Vung Tau** (see p.213).

The Cu Chi tunnels

1

During the American War, the villages around the district of **Cu Chi** supported a substantial **Viet Cong** (VC) presence. Faced with American attempts to neutralize them, they quite literally dug themselves out of harm's way, and the legendary **Cu Chi tunnels** were the result. Today, tourists can visit a short stretch of the tunnels, drop to their hands and knees and squeeze underground for an insight into life as a tunnel-dwelling resistance fighter. Some sections of the tunnels have been widened to allow passage for the fuller frame of Westerners but it's still a dark, sweaty, claustrophobic experience, and not one you should rush into unless you're confident you won't suffer a subterranean freak-out.

There are two sites where the tunnels can be seen – **Ben Dinh** and, 15km beyond, **Ben Duoc**, though most foreigners get taken to Ben Dinh.

A brief history

When the first spades sank into the earth around Cu Chi, the region was covered by a rubber plantation tied to a French tyre company. Anti-colonial **Viet Minh** dug the first tunnels here in the late 1940s; intended primarily for storing arms, they soon became valuable hiding places for the resistance fighters themselves. Over a decade later, VC activists controlling this staunchly anti-government area, many of them local villagers, followed suit and went to ground. By 1965, 250km of tunnels crisscrossed Cu Chi and surrounding areas – just across the Saigon River was the notorious guerrilla power base known as the **Iron Triangle** – making it possible for the VC guerrilla cells in the area to link up with each other and to infiltrate Saigon at will. One section daringly ran underneath the Americans' Cu Chi Army Base.

Though the region's compacted red clay was perfectly suited to tunnelling, and lay above the water level of the Saigon River, the **digging parties** faced a multitude of problems. Quite apart from the snakes and scorpions they encountered as they laboured with their hoes and crowbars, there was the problem of inconspicuously disposing of the soil by spreading it in bomb craters or scattering it in the river under cover of darkness. With a tunnel dug, ceilings had to be shored up, and as American bombing made timber scarce the tunnellers had to resort to stealing iron fence posts from enemy bases. Tunnels could be as small as 80cm wide and 80cm high, and were sometimes four levels deep; **vent shafts** (to disperse smoke and aromas from underground ovens) were camouflaged by thick grass and termites' nests. In order to throw the Americans' dogs off the scent, pepper was sprinkled around vents, and sometimes the VC even washed with the same scented soap used by GIs.

Tunnel life

Living conditions below ground were appalling for these "human moles". Tunnels were foul-smelling, and became so hot by the afternoon that inhabitants had to lie on the floor in order to get enough oxygen to breathe. The darkness was absolute, and some long-term dwellers suffered temporary blindness when they emerged into the light. At times it was necessary to stay below ground for weeks on end, alongside bats, rats, snakes, scorpions, centipedes and fire ants. Some of these unwelcome guests were co-opted to the cause: boxes full of scorpions and hollow bamboo sticks containing vipers were secreted in tunnels, where GIs might unwittingly knock them over.

Within the multi-level tunnel complexes, there were latrines, wells, meeting rooms and dorms. Rudimentary **hospitals** were also scratched out of the soil. Operations were carried out by torchlight using instruments fashioned from shards of ordnance, and a patient's own blood was caught in bottles and then pumped straight back using a bicycle pump and a length of rubber hosing. Such medical supplies as existed were secured by bribing ARVN soldiers in Saigon. Doctors also administered herbs and acupuncture – even honey was used for its antiseptic properties. **Kitchens** cooked whatever the tunnellers could get their hands on. With rice and fruit crops destroyed, the diet consisted largely of tapioca, leaves

CU CHI: THE GUIDED TOUR

The **guided tour** of Ben Dinh kicks off in a thatched hut, where a map of the region, a cross-section of the tunnels and a black and white movie bristling with national pride fill you in on the background. From there, you head out into the bush, where your guide will point out lethal booby-traps, concealed trap doors and an abandoned tank. There are several models showing how unexploded ordnance was ingeniously converted into lethal mines and traps, and a demonstration of how smoke from underground fires was cleverly dispersed far from its source.

When you reach the shooting range, you have the chance to shoulder an M16 or AK47 and shoot off a few rounds, or stop at the adjacent souvenir and snack stalls. Finally, you get the chance to stoop, crawl and drag yourself through a section of the tunnels about 140 metres long (with frequent escape routes for anyone who can't hack it). It only takes 10–15 minutes to scramble through, but the pitch blackness and intense humidity can be discomforting, so when you emerge, you'll be glad you don't have to live down there for weeks on end as the VC did.

and roots, at least until enough bomb fragments could be transported to Saigon and sold as scrap to buy food. Morale was maintained in part by **performing troupes** that toured the tunnels, though songs like "He who comes to Cu Chi, the Bronze Fortress in the Land of Iron, will count the crimes accumulated by the Enemy" were not quite up to the standard set by Bob Hope as he entertained the US troops.

The end of the line

American attempts to **flush out** the tunnels proved ineffective. Operating out of huge bases erected around Saigon in the mid-Sixties, they evacuated villagers into strategic hamlets and then used defoliant sprays and bulldozers to rob the VC of cover, in "scorched earth" operations such as January 1967's **Cedar Falls**. Even then, tunnels were rarely effectively destroyed – one soldier at the time compared the task to "fill[ing] the Grand Canyon with a pitchfork". GIs would lob down gas or grenades or else go down themselves, armed only with a torch, a knife and a pistol. Die-hard soldiers who specialized in these underground raids came to be known as **tunnel rats**, their unofficial insignia *Insigni Non Gratum Anus Rodentum*, meaning "not worth a rat's arse". Booby-traps made of sharpened bamboo stakes awaited them in the dark, as well as "bombs" made from Coke cans and dud bullets found on the surface. Tunnels were low and narrow, and entrances so small that GIs often couldn't get down them, even if they could locate them. Maverick war correspondent Wilfred Burchett, travelling with the NLF in 1964, found his Western girth a distinct impediment: "On another occasion I got stuck passing from one tunnel section to another. In what seemed a dead end, a rectangular plug was pulled out from the other side, and, with some ahead pulling my arms and some pushing my buttocks from behind, I managed to get through...I was transferred to another tunnel entrance built especially to accommodate a bulky unit cook."

Another American tactic aimed at weakening the resolve of the VC guerrillas involved dropping leaflets and broadcasting bulletins that played on the fighters' fears and loneliness. Although this prompted numerous desertions, the tunnellers were still able to mastermind the **Tet Offensive** of 1968. Ultimately, the Americans resorted to more strong-arm tactics to neutralize the tunnels, sending in the B52s freed by the cessation of bombing of the North in 1968 to level the district with **carpet bombing**. The VC's infrastructure was decimated by Tet, and further weakened by the **Phoenix Programme**. By this time, though, the tunnels had played their part in proving to America that the war was unwinnable. At least twelve thousand Vietnamese guerrillas and sympathizers are thought to have perished here during the American War, and the terrain was laid waste – pockmarked by bomb craters, devoid of vegetation, the air poisoned by lingering fumes.

ARRIVAL AND INFORMATION

With a tour The most convenient way to visit the Cu Chi Tunnels is with a tour, and every tour operator in HCMC offers a similar itinerary. Signing up through your hotel will please them and give you some kind of come-back should things go wrong.

By taxi If you don't want to join a crowd in a bus, four people will pay around $60 for a taxi following the same itinerary.

By boat and bus Another option is to go by boat and return by bus ($18) – contact Delta Adventure Tours (see box, p.90) for details.

Information Both sites daily 7am–5pm; about $5 entrance, not generally included in tour price (about $8). The shooting range costs about $15 per clip of bullets, depending which rifle you choose.

CAO DAI

The basic tenets of **Cao Dai** were first revealed to **Ngo Van Chieu**, a civil servant working in the criminal investigation department of the French administration on Phu Quoc Island, at the beginning of the 1920s. A spiritualist, Ngo was contacted during a seance by a superior spirit calling itself Cao Dai, or "high place". This spirit communicated to him the basics of the Cao Dai creed, and instructed him to adopt the Divine Eye as a tangible representation of its existence. Posted back to Saigon soon afterwards, Ngo set about evangelizing, though according to French convert and chronicler Gabriel Gobron the religion didn't gather steam until late in 1925, when Ngo was contacted by a group of mediums sent his way by the Cao Dai.

At this stage, **revelations** from the Cao Dai began to add further meat to the bones of the religion. Twice already, it informed its mediums, it had revealed itself to mankind, using such vehicles as Lao-tzu, Christ, Mohammed, Moses, Sakyamuni and Confucius to propagate systems of belief tailored to suit localized cultures. Such religious intolerance had resulted from this multiplicity, that for the **third alliance** it would do away with earthly messengers and convey a universal religion via spirit intermediaries, including Louis Pasteur, William Shakespeare, Joan of Arc, Sir Winston Churchill and Napoleon Bonaparte. The revelations of these "saints" were received using a *planchette* (a pencil secured to a wooden board on castors, on which the medium rests his hand, sometimes known as a *corbeille-à-bec*).

Though a fusion of Oriental and Occidental religions, propounding the concept of a **universal god**, Cao Dai is primarily entrenched in Buddhism, Taoism and Confucianism, to which cause-and-effect creeds, elements of Christianity, Islam and spirituality are added. By following its five commandments – Cao Dai followers must avoid killing living beings, high living, covetousness, verbal deceit and the temptations of the flesh – adherents look to hasten the evolution of the soul through reincarnation.

The religion was effectively **founded** in October 1926, when it was also officially recognized by the French colonial administration. Borrowing the structure and terminology of the Catholic Church, Cao Dai began to grow rapidly, its emphasis upon simplicity appealing to disaffected peasants, and by 1930 there were five hundred thousand followers. In 1927, Tay Ninh became the religion's Holy See; Ngo opted out of the papacy, and the first pope was **Le Van Trung**, a decadent mandarin from Cho Lon who saw the error of his ways after being visited by the Cao Dai during a seance.

Inevitably in such uncertain times, Cao Dai developed a **political agenda**. Strongly anti-French during World War II, subsequently the Cao Dai militia turned against the Viet Minh, with whom they fought, using French arms, in the French War. By the mid-Fifties, the area around Tay Ninh was a virtual fiefdom of Cao Dai followers. In *The Quiet American*, Graham Greene describes the Cao Dai militia as a "private army of 25,000 men, armed with mortars made out of the exhaust-pipes of old cars, allies of the French who turned neutral at the moment of danger". Even then, however, they were feuding with the rival Hoa Hao sect, and in a few years their power had waned.

Post-liberation, the Communist government confiscated all Cao Dai land, though it was returned ten years later. Today, the religion continues to thrive in its twin power bases of Tay Ninh District and the Mekong Delta.

1

Trang Bang

Several kilometres northwest of Cu Chi, Highway 22 slices through idyllic paddy flatlands before reaching **TRANG BANG**, where the photographer Nick Ut captured one of the war's most horrific and enduring images – that of a naked girl with her back in flames running along the highway, fleeing a napalm attack. The girl, Phan Thi Kim Phuc, now married and living in Canada, was named in 1997 as a goodwill ambassador for UNESCO. Despite third-degree burns covering half of her body, she remains remarkably unembittered, stating "I am happy because I am living without hatred."

Long Hoa

A few kilometres off the highway lies **LONG HOA**, the site of the enigmatic **Cao Dai Great Temple**, or Cathedral, of the Holy See of Tay Ninh District. **Joss-stick factories** line the road into Long Hoa, their produce bundled into mini-haystacks by the roadside to dry. Around 4km later you reach Long Hoa's **market**, from where the cathedral itself is another 2km.

Cao Dai Great Temple

A grand gateway marks the entrance to the grounds of the 1927-built Cao Dai Great Temple. Beyond it, a wide boulevard escorts you past a swathe of grassland used on ceremonial occasions, to the wildly exotic temple itself, over whose left shoulder rises distant **Nui Ba Den**, Black Lady Mountain.

The temple's exterior

On first sighting, the **Great Temple** seems to be subsiding, an optical illusion created by the rising steps inside it, but your first impressions are more likely to be dominated by what Graham Greene described as a "Walt Disney fantasia of the East, dragons and snakes in Technicolor". Despite its Day-Glo hues and rococo clutter, this gaudy construction somehow manages to bypass tackiness. Two square, pagoda-style **towers** bookend the front facade, whose central portico is topped by a bowed, first-floor balcony and a **Divine Eye**. The most recurrent motif in the temple, the eye, is surrounded by a triangle, as it is on the American one-dollar bill. A figure in semi-relief emerges from each tower: on the left is Cao Dai's first female cardinal, Lam Huong Thanh, and on the right, Le Van Trung, its first pope.

The temple's interior

The eclectic ideology of Cao Dai is mirrored in the **interior**. Part cathedral and part pagoda, it draws together a potpourri of icons and elements under a vaulted ceiling, and daubs them all with the primary colours of a Hindu temple. Men enter the

---

CAO DAI SERVICES

A major attraction is attending one of the daily **services** at the temple (daily 6am, noon and 6pm), and most tours usually arrange their visit to coincide with the midday one. Though other times are inconvenient, they do offer the opportunity to concentrate on what's happening without the accompanying roadshow of hundreds of flashing cameras. Before services, visitors are shepherded upstairs and past the traditional **band** that plays behind the front balcony, and on into the gods, from where they can look down on proceedings and take photographs. Most worshippers dress in white robes, though some dress in yellow, blue and red, to signify the Buddhist, Taoist and Confucian elements of Cao Dai. Priests don square hats emblazoned with the Divine Eye. At the start of a service, worshippers' heads nod, like a field of corn in the breeze, in time to the clanging of a gong. Then a haunting, measured **chanting** begins, against the insect whine of the string band playing its own time. As prayers and hymns continue, incense, flowers, alcohol and tea are offered up to the Supreme Being.

cathedral through an entrance in the right wall, women by a door to the left, and all must take off their shoes. Inside the lobby, a **mural** shows the three "signatories of the 3rd Alliance between God and Mankind": French poet Victor Hugo and the fifteenth-century Vietnamese poet, Nguyen Binh Khiem, are writing the Cao Dai principles of "God and humanity, love and justice" in French and Chinese onto a shining celestial tablet. Beside them, the Chinese nationalist leader Sun Yat Sen holds an inkstone, a symbol of "Chinese civilization allied to Christian civilization giving birth to Cao Dai doctrine", according to a nearby sign.

Outside of service times (see box opposite) tourists are welcome to wander through the **nave** of the cathedral, as long as they remain in the aisles, and don't stray between the rows of **pink pillars**, entwined by green dragons, that march up the chamber. Cut-away windows punctuate the outer walls, their grillework consisting of the Divine Eye, surrounded by bright pink lotus blooms. Walk up the shallow steps that lend the nave its litheness, and you'll reach an **altar** that groans under the weight of assorted vases, fruit, paintings and slender statues of storks. The **papal chair** stands at the head of the chamber, its arms carved into dragons. Below it are six more chairs, three with eagle arms, and three with lion arms, for the cardinals. Dominating the chamber, though, and guarded by eight scary silver dragons, a vast, duck-egg-blue **sphere**, speckled with stars, rests on a polished, eight-sided dais. The ubiquitous Divine Eye peers through clouds painted on the front. You'll see more spangly stars and fluffy clouds if you look up at the sky-blue **ceiling**, with mouldings of lions and turtles.

ARRIVAL AND DEPARTURE   CAO DAI

By tour Most people visit the temple on a tour that also takes in the Cu Chi Tunnels (see p.109).

By bus If you'd rather go it alone, infrequent buses to Tay Ninh depart from Ho Chi Minh City's An Suong station; ask the driver to drop you off at the front gates of the temple.

The Mekong Delta

FLOATING MARKET, CAN THO

The Mekong Delta

Touring the orchards, paddy fields and swamplands of the Mekong Delta, you could be forgiven for thinking you've stepped into the pages of a geography textbook. A comma-shaped flatland stretching from Ho Chi Minh's city limits southwest to the Gulf of Thailand, the delta is Vietnam's rice bowl, an agricultural miracle that pumps out more than a third of the country's annual food crop from just ten percent of its total land mass. Rice may be the delta's staple crop, but coconut palms, fruit orchards and sugar-cane groves also thrive in its nutrient-rich soil, and the sight of conical-hatted farmers tending their land is one of Vietnam's most enduring images. To the Vietnamese, the region is known as Cuu Long, "Nine Dragons", a reference to the nine tributaries of the Mekong River, which dovetail across plains fashioned by millennia of flood-borne alluvial sediment.

Surprisingly, agriculture gripped the delta only relatively recently. Under **Cambodian** sway until the close of the seventeenth century, the region was sparsely inhabited by the *Khmer krom*, or "downstream Khmer", whose settlements were framed by swathes of marshland. The eighteenth century saw the Viet **Nguyen** lords steadily broaden their sphere of influence to encompass the delta, though by the 1860s **France** had taken over the reins of government. Sensing the huge profits to be gleaned from such fertile land, French *colons* spurred Vietnamese peasants to tame and till tracts of the boggy delta; the peasants, realizing their colonial governors would pay well for rice harvests, were quick to comply. Ironically, the same landscape that had served the French so well also provided valuable cover for the Viet Minh resistance fighters who sought to overthrow them; later it did the same for the Viet Cong, who had well-hidden cells here – inciting the Americans to strafe the area with bombs and defoliants.

A visit to the Mekong Delta is so memorable because of the region's **diversity**. Everyday scenes include children riding on the backs of water buffalo or cycling to school through country lanes clad in white *ao dai*; rice workers stooping in a sea of emerald; market vendors grinning behind stacks of fruit; bright yellow incense sticks drying at the roadside; flocks of storks circling over a sanctuary at dusk; Khmer monks walking mindfully in the shadow of pastel pagodas; locals scampering over monkey bridges or rowing boats on the delta's maze of channels.

THE MEKONG RIVER

By the time it reaches Vietnam, the Mekong River has already covered more than four thousand kilometres from its source high on the Tibetan Plateau; en route it traverses southern China, skirts Burma (Myanmar), then hugs the Laos–Thailand border before cutting down through Cambodia and into Vietnam – a journey that ranks it as Asia's third-longest river, after the Yangtse and Yellow rivers. **Flooding** has always blighted the delta; ever since Indian traders imported their advanced methods of irrigation more than eighteen centuries ago, networks of canals have been used to channel the excess water, but the rainy season still claims lives from time to time.

It's difficult to overstate the influence of the river: the lifeblood of the rice and fruit crops grown in the delta, it also teems with craft that range in size from delicate rowing boats to hulking sampans, all painted with distinctive eyes on the prow. These continue an ancient tradition and were originally intended to scare off "river monsters", probably crocodiles.

PHU QUOC ISLAND

Highlights

❶ Boat trips Drift along narrow canals, visiting floating markets and fruit orchards around Can Tho. **See p.122**

❷ Home-stays Stay in rural communities, observing daily aspects of Vietnamese culture, and getting to know your hosts. **See p.132**

❸ Khmer pagodas Marvel over the rich colours of temples around Tra Vinh. **See p.132**

❹ Bird sanctuaries Watch flocks of storks and migrating cranes wheeling in the sky at Bang Lang near Long Xuyen and Tram Chim near Cao Lanh. **See p.150 & p.127**

❺ Chau Doc Visit a Cham village and fish farms on the river, and explore nearby Sam Mountain. **See p.151**

❻ Mui Ca Mau Stand at the southeastern tip of mainland Southeast Asia at Cape Ca Mau and imagine the thrill of early explorers on spotting this mangrove-lined coast. **See p.147**

❼ Phu Quoc Island Sprawl on its gorgeous beaches, ride a motorbike through its mountainous interior and dive or snorkel around the coastline. **See p.164**

HIGHLIGHTS ARE MARKED ON THE MAP ON P.118

MEKONG DELTA

HIGHLIGHTS
1 Boat trips
2 Home-stays
3 Khmer pagodas
4 Bird sanctuaries
5 Chau Doc
6 Mui Ca Mau
7 Phu Quoc Island

PROVINCES
1 An Giang
2 Dong Thap
3 Long An
4 Tien Giang
5 Kien Giang
6 Can Tho
7 Hau Giang
8 Vinh Long
9 Ben Tre
10 Tra Vinh
11 Ca Mau
12 Bac Lieu
13 Soc Trang

CAMBODIA

SOUTH CHINA SEA
(EAST SEA)

Con Dao
Archipelago

Gulf of Thailand

Ho Chi Minh City

Ho Chi Minh City
Tan An
My Tho
Ben Tre
Cai Lay
Cai Mon
Tra Cu
Moc Hoa
Cao Lanh
An Huu
Vinh Long
Tra Vinh
Binh Minh
Soc Trang
Sa Dec
Can Tho
Chau Thanh
Thanh Tri
Hong Ngu
Long Xuyen
Phung Hiep
Vinh Quoi
Bac Lieu
Vi Thanh
Long My
Chau Doc
Sam Mountain
Nha Ban
Tri Ton
Oc Eo
Rach Gia
Rach Soi
Gia Rai
Vinh Xuong
Ba Chuc
Tap Duc
Ca Mau
Nam Can
Tinh Bien
U Minh
Kien Luong
Ba Hon
Binh An
Hon Chong Peninsula
Ha Tien
Mui Ca Mau
Phu Quoc Island
Duong Dong

Tien Giang
Hau Giang
MY THUAN Bridge

HWY-1
HWY-1
HWY-63

N

0   50
kilometres

GETTING AROUND THE RIVER AND DELTA

Inevitably the best way to experience river life is on a **boat trip**. Day-trips can be organized in Ho Chi Minh City, My Tho, Cai Be, Vinh Long, Can Tho or Chau Doc, while some tour operators offer 2–3 day live-aboard trips (see box, p.122). Since most day tours follow a similar itinerary (a visit to a floating market and stops at cottage industries on the shore), you'll probably want to choose just one. Though Can Tho is most popular for its good range of hotels and restaurants, you're likely to see more tourists than locals in the nearby floating markets. A good alternative is Vinh Long, from where boats head out in many directions through the canals of An Binh Island to the floating market at Cai Be.

Most visitors hurtle around the delta on a **tour bus** out of Ho Chi Minh City, denying themselves the chance to sink into the languid life of the region. With time in hand, it's far more satisfying to **hire a vehicle** or take **local transport** – not nearly as daunting a prospect as it is up the coast, since the number of settlements with hotels means journeys can be kept relatively short. Traffic has to stop occasionally at the **ferries** that make road travel in the delta possible, though completion of some long-awaited bridges is speeding up travel times. The enforced halts at the ferries are at least enlivened by strolling hawkers. Locals used to do much of their travelling on the **passenger and cargo boats** that crawl around the delta's waterways, but the increased prevalence of motorbikes has led to many routes being cut, so this is no longer a viable way of getting around for visitors.

If you really want to do the delta in style, sign up for an overnight trip on one of the *Bassac* boats (☎0710 382 9540; ⍟transmekong.com; around $230 per person). These are former rice barges converted into floating hotels, offering a cosy cabin and gourmet meals to accompany the classic delta sights. The most popular trip is from Cai Be to Can Tho, stopping off at a few rural villages along the way and joining the throng at Cai Rang floating market in the morning.

Another luxury option, with similar itinerary and rates, is the Song Xanh **sampan** cruise (☎091 227 0058, ⍟vietnamluxurytravel.com). If these rates sound a bit steep, Saigon-based Delta Adventure Tours (☎08 920 2112, ⍟deltaadventure.info) offer a more basic 3-day, 2-night Mekong cruise, taking in Cai Be, Sa Dec, Long Xuyen and Chau Doc for just $55 per person.

There are over a dozen towns in the delta with facilities for tourists, though some are rarely visited as they are not on the way to anywhere. **My Tho** is well geared up for boat trips, and near enough to Ho Chi Minh City to be seen on a day-trip: it affords an appetizing glimpse of the delta's northernmost tributary, the Tien Giang. From My Tho, laidback **Ben Tre** and the bounteous fruit orchards besieging it are only a hop and a skip away. **Cao Lanh** is strictly for bird enthusiasts, but **Sa Dec**, with its timeless river scenes and riotously colourful flower nurseries, has a more universal appeal, while just down the road, **Vinh Long** is another jumping-off point for boat trips.

Many visitors spend a day or two in **Can Tho**, the delta's biggest settlement, to take advantage of its decent hotels and restaurants and to recharge batteries before venturing out to the **floating markets** nearby. From Can Tho, there's something to be said for dropping down to the foot of the delta, where the swampland that surrounds **Ca Mau** can be explored by boat, and **Mui Ca Mau** signals journey's end in Vietnam. Pulling up, en route, at the Khmer stronghold of **Soc Trang** is especially rewarding if your trip coincides with the colourful Oc Om Bok festival (Nov or Dec), during which the local Khmer community takes to the river to stage spectacular longboat races. Northwest of Can Tho meanwhile, and a stone's throw from the Cambodian border, is the ebullient town of **Chau Doc**, south of which **Sam Mountain** provides a welcome undulation in the surrounding plains. The opening of the border here has brought a steady stream of travellers going on to Phnom Penh by boat, and several of them rest up a few days here before leaving the country.

Ha Tien, a remote border town surrounded by Khmer villages, is the best place to hop on a boat to Phu Quoc. The town has also become popular for its **international border**

crossing, which allows beach bums to slide along the coast from Phu Quoc Island to Sihanoukville in Cambodia or vice versa.

Given its seasonal flooding, **the best time to visit** the delta is, predictably enough, in the dry season, which runs from December to May.

My Tho

Southwest of Ho Chi Minh City, buses emerge from the city's unkempt urban sprawl and into the pastoral surrounds of the Mekong Delta's upper plains. The delta is too modest to flaunt its full beauty so soon, but glimpses of rice fields hint at things to come, their burnished golds and brilliant greens interspersed with the occasional white ancestral grave. Seventy kilometres out of Ho Chi Minh City lies **MY THO**, an amiable market town that nestles on the north bank of the Mekong River's northernmost strand, the Tien Giang, or Upper River.

My Tho's proximity to Ho Chi Minh City means that it receives the lion's share of day-trippers to the delta, resulting in a scrum of pushy vendors crowding round each tour bus that arrives. Nevertheless, the town comes as a great relief after the onslaught of Ho Chi Minh City, its uncrowded boulevards belying a population of around 220,000, and you can easily escape the melee by hopping onto a boat or wandering into the backstreets.

This daily influx of visitors seems appropriate, given the town's **history**. Chinese immigrants fleeing Formosa (modern-day Taiwan) after the collapse of the Ming dynasty established the town in the late seventeenth century, along with a Vietnamese population keen to make inroads into this traditionally Khmer-dominated region. Two centuries later the French, wooed by the district's abundant rice and fruit crops, rated it highly enough to post a garrison here and to lay a (now-defunct) rail line to Saigon; while the American War saw a consistent military presence in town. Today My Tho's commercial importance is as pronounced as ever, something a walk through the busy town market amply illustrates.

The river's traffic – which ranges from elegant sampans to vast, lumbering cargo boats, unpainted and crude – is best viewed from Lac Hong Park at the eastern end of 30 Thang 4 street, where you're sure to catch sight of the most characteristic feature of the boats in the delta – feline eyes painted on their prows. In the evenings, especially at weekends, this corner of town is packed as families stroll up and down, interspersed with sellers of balloons, popcorn and even tropical fish. At night, young lovers huddle on their motorbikes, while men play shuttlecock football on the street under the intent gaze of a statue of nineteenth-century anti-French hero Nguyen Huu Huan, who studied in My Tho.

The market

Beside Bao Dinh canal, between Le Dai Hanh and Thu Khoa Huan streets • Sunrise to sunset

Follow the direction of the canal up along Trung Trac and you'll soon be gobbled up by My Tho's vast **market**, which is at its busiest early in the morning. As well as the usual piles of fruit, cereals and tobacco, several stalls sell ships' chandlery, their heaped fishing nets almost indistinguishable from the fresh noodles on sale nearby.

Cao Dai Temple

Ly Thuong Kiet • Sunrise to sunset • Free

Head west of the town centre on Ly Thuong Kiet for the **Cao Dai Temple**, which is worth a look for its colourful architecture. It is a small-scale replica of the Holy See in Tay Ninh, with the all-seeing Divine Eye above the entrance, dragons writhing up columns and images of the odd mix of characters, such as Victor Hugo and Sun Yat Sen, that comprise the religion's saints. Note also the herb garden to the right of the temple, which is used to concoct remedies for ailments of the poor.

The Chinese Quarter

To the east of the Bao Dinh Canal, the region just south of Dinh Bo Linh Street is home to My Tho's modest **Chinese Quarter**, though there's little to betray its existence other than a feverish sense of commerce. Shopfronts here are piled to the rafters with sugar-cane poles, watermelons and fish awaiting transportation to Ho Chi Minh City, as well as half-hatched eggs (containing chick embryos), prized as the perfect complement to a *bia hoi*.

Vinh Trang Pagoda

60a Nguyen Trung Truc • Cyclo should cost about 15,000đ

A worthwhile side-trip is making the short journey on foot or cyclo up Nguyen Trung Truc to the attractive **Vinh Trang Pagoda**, with its rajah's palace-style front facade. Since its construction in 1849 it has been renovated several times, most recently in 2002. The entrance, round to the right, leads into the heart of the temple, where a tiny courtyard is flanked by the cubicles where the monks sleep. The main

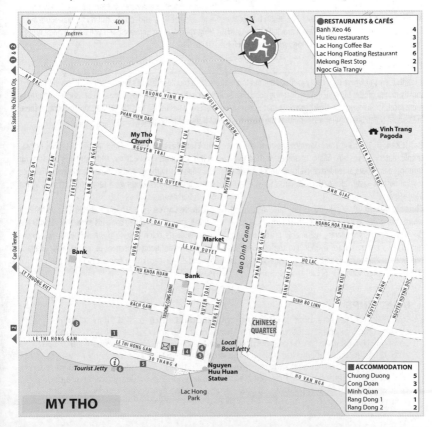

RESTAURANTS & CAFÉS

Banh Xeo 46	4
Hu tieu restaurants	3
Lac Hong Coffee Bar	5
Lac Hong Floating Restaurant	6
Mekong Rest Stop	2
Ngoc Gia Trangv	1

ACCOMMODATION

Chuong Duong	5
Cong Doan	3
Minh Quan	4
Rang Dong 1	1
Rang Dong 2	2

MY THO

chamber, beyond the miniature mountain to your left, is characterized by dark-wood pillars and tons of gilt woodwork, but of more interest are the eclectic influences at play in the pagoda's decor – classical pillars, Grecian-style mouldings of urns and bowls of fruit and glazed tiles similar to Portuguese *azulejos*. Outside, the tombs of several monks stand near a pond patrolled by huge elephant-ear fish, while a tall, standing Buddha and a more jovial seated Buddha watch over the front gate.

ARRIVAL AND DEPARTURE   MY THO

By bus Buses terminate at Tien Giang station, 3km northwest of town, from where xe om shuttle into the centre (about 15,000đ).

Destinations: Can Tho (2hr 30min); Cao Lanh (2hr); Ho Chi Minh City (1hr 30min).

ACCOMMODATION

Chuong Duong Opposite the GPO at 10, 30 Thang 4 📞073 387 0875. With prime views of the river, this has long been the town's smartest place to stay; its tidy rooms all have a/c, hot water and TVs, and those upstairs have riverfront balconies. $24

Cong Doan Beside the GPO at 61, 30 Thang 4 📞073 387 4324. This ageing edifice has spartan but light double rooms which can accommodate up to four people. $7

Minh Quan 69, 30 Thang 4 📞073 397 9979. One of My Tho's newest hotels, the *Minh Quan* provides some stiff competition for the Chuong Duong with its tasteful furnishings and modern fittings, and rooms at the front have good river views too. $20

Rang Dong 1 25, 30 Thang 4 📞073 387 4400. The older branch of this reliable, though rather plain, hotel has simple, functional rooms, and its location is more central than the newer, second branch. $8

Rang Dong 2 40/5 Section 3, Ward 6, Le Thi Hon Gam 📞073 397 0085, 🌐rangdonghotel.net. With river views west of the centre, the *Rang Dong 2* has rooms with a/c, cable TV and fridges, but try to get a room away from the adjacent karaoke bar if you want a good night's sleep. $10

EATING AND DRINKING

Though there's nowhere to get very excited about in town, there are a couple of **places to eat** just out of town that cater mostly to tour groups but turn out consistently good dishes, including the locally famous elephant-ear fish. For something more local, stroll round the **night market** that opens up each evening beside the tour boat offices on 30 Thang 4. There are several cheap but popular restaurants at the southern end of Nam Ky Khoi Nghia.

Banh Xeo 46 11 Trung Trac. Down by the riverside, this simple eatery serves up filling pancakes stuffed with shrimp, beansprouts, shredded chicken and pork, as well as several other tasty alternatives. Mains $1–3. Daily 9am–9pm.

Chuong Duong 10, 30 Thang 4. This hotel restaurant, which specializes in seafood, is the best dining option in the town centre, with large, reasonably priced portions served on a breezy terrace overlooking the Mekong. It's very popular among locals and domestic visitors, so can be crowded at times. Mains $3–6. Daily 6am–11pm.

Hu Tieu Restaurants 24 and 44 Nam Ky Khoi Nghia. Both these places serve filling and nutritious bowls of *hu tieu* (noodles with seafood and meat), the key difference being that number 24 serves a vegetarian version. Mains $1–2. Daily 6am–3pm.

Lac Hong Coffee 63, 30 Thang 4. There's little nightlife in My Tho, though this coffee bar adds a touch of class to the town with its colonial-style shuttered windows, comfy armchairs and good selection of coffee and cocktails (around $1–2 each). The bar occasionally features live music. Daily 6–11pm.

BOAT TRIPS

Several companies offer boat trips from the **tourist boat centre** (6–8, 30 Thang 4) to the islands in the Mekong; most tours head for Thoi Son, Phung and Qui islands. Tien Giang Tourist Company (📞073 387 3184, 🌐tiengiangtourist.com), and Ben Tre Tourist Company (📞073 387 9103, 🌐bentretourist.vn) are the most reliable. Both charge $18–35 per person for a tour of about three hours, depending how many people are in the group. Local boats, which you can find at the small jetty on Trung Trac, are much cheaper, and $20 should get you an entire boat for a two- to three-hour trip. However, bear in mind that the owners of these boats are not licensed or insured to carry tourists, so it's a bit of a risky business.

Lac Hong Floating Restaurant 30 Thang 4. Right in front of the tour boat offices, this floating restaurant is quite classy, and offers a good range of dishes accompanied (usually) by a breeze off the river. Mains $1–10. Daily 10am–10pm.

Mekong Rest Stop About 8km along the road to HCMC. The *Mekong Rest Stop* is a purpose-built restaurant for tourist buses on their way to the delta. It is set in a beautifully landscaped garden with lotus ponds and offers set menus for two people at around $8–10. Daily 7am–10pm.

Ngoc Gia Trang 196a Ap Bac. About 2km northwest of the centre, *Ngoc Gia Trang* is set in a quiet, green compound back off the road and offers a range of tasty dishes at reasonable prices, though they're often busy with tour groups. Set menu $7.50 per person. Daily 8am–9pm.

DIRECTORY

Banks There's an ATM next to the *Cong Doan* hotel, 61, 30 Thang 4 and another at Vietinbank, at the western end of Thu Khoa Huan. The Agribank at the opposite end of Thu Khoa Huan on the corner of Le Loi will change dollars for dong.

Post office The post office is conveniently located opposite the boat jetties on Le Thi Hong Gam, where you can also find internet access.

Around My Tho

Day-trippers tend to see little of My Tho as they disgorge from tour buses and embark on a **boat trip** (see box opposite) round two or three of the **islands** in the Tien Giang branch of the Mekong River. Upstream at **Cai Be** it's a similar story, with fleets of buses from Ho Chi Minh City descending on the village at around 11am for boat tours of the **floating market**. Arranging trips locally tends to lead to a more relaxed and enjoyable experience, but you'd probably need to sleep over at least one night. In contrast to Cai Be, the quirky **snake farm** at Dong Tham sees few foreign visitors.

Tan Long

Beyond its chaotic shoreline of stilthouses and boatyards, **TAN LONG** ("Dragon Island"), the least frequently visited island, boasts bounteous sapodilla, coconut and banana plantations, as well as highly regarded longan orchards. As with the other islands, Tan Long is sparsely inhabited, by small communities of farmers and boat-builders.

Thoi Son

THOI SON ("Unicorn Island") is the largest of the four islands and many of the organized tours out of Ho Chi Minh City stop here for lunch and fruit sampling. Narrow canals allow boats to weave through its interior. Gliding along these slender waterways, overhung by handsome water-palm fronds that interlock to form a cathedral-like roof, it's easy to feel you're charting new territory. Swooping, electric-blue kingfishers and sumptuously coloured butterflies add to the romance. Local tours do not always include **lunch** in the price, but all tours will stop somewhere you can get refreshment.

Qui Island

QUI ("Turtle") **Island** is the newest of the group, having been formed by sediment in the river then stabilized by planting mangroves, and is overflowing with longans, dragon fruit, mango, papaya, pineapple and jackfruit. There is a small, family-run **coconut candy factory**, just opposite here along the Ben Tre coastline, where you can watch the coconut being pressed and the extracted juice being mixed with sugar and heated, then dried and cut into bite-size pieces. You can buy a box to take home.

2

ONG DAO DUA, THE COCONUT MONK

Ong Dao Dua, the **Coconut Monk**, was born Nguyen Thanh Nam in the Mekong Delta, in 1909. Aged 19, he travelled to France where he studied chemistry until 1935, when he returned home, married and fathered a child. During a lengthy period of meditation at Chau Doc's Sam Mountain (see p.155) he devised a new religion, a fusion of Buddhism and Christianity known as **Tinh Do Cu Si**. By the 1960s, this new sect had established a community on Phung Island, where the monk lorded it over his followers from a throne set into a man-made grotto modelled on Sam Mountain. The monk became as famous for his idiosyncrasies as for his doctrine: his name, for instance, was coined after it was alleged he spent three years meditating and eating nothing but coconuts.

Unfortunately, the Coconut Monk never got to enjoy his "kingdom" for long: his belief in a peaceful reunification of North and South Vietnam (symbolized by the map of the country behind his grotto, on which pillars representing Hanoi and Saigon are joined by a bridge) landed him in the jails of successive South Vietnamese governments, and the Communists were no more sympathetic to his beliefs after 1975. Ong Dao Dua died in 1990.

Phung Island

PHUNG ("Phoenix") **ISLAND** is famed as the home of an offbeat religious sect set up three decades ago by the eccentric **Coconut Monk**, Ong Dao Dua (see box above), although there's not much left to see from his era, and only the skeleton of the open-air **complex** he established remains. Among its mesh of rusting staircases and platforms, you'll spot the rocket-shaped elevator the monk had built to whisk him up to his private meditation platform. Elsewhere are nine dragon-entwined pillars, said to symbolize the Mekong's nine tributaries and betraying a Cao Dai influence. The Coconut Monk's story is told (in Vietnamese) on a magnificent **urn**, which he is said to have crafted himself out of shards of porcelain from France, Japan and China.

Dong Tam Snake Farm

10km west of My Tho • Daily 7am–5pm • 20,000đ • A xe om to the farm costs around 20,000đ

Run by the military, the **Dong Tam Snake Farm** breeds snakes for their meat and skins. Watching the sluggish pythons and cobras sleeping in cages is not a particularly pretty sight, though there are several other animals on display in a small zoo, including porcupines, monitor lizards, otters, monkeys, eagles, peacocks and an enormous albino turtle. One of the farm's most popular products is Cobratox – a cream that includes cobra venom and stings on application, but is rated by many as an effective cure for rheumatism.

Cai Be Floating Market

40km west of My Tho, just south of Highway 1

Cai Be's floating market is one of the most popular in the delta, and also the most distinctive because of its backdrop of a slender cathedral spire. Throughout the day boats of all sizes throng in the waters of the Tien Giang, with fruit vendors displaying a sample of their produce suspended from a stick. The market reaches its busiest at around midday when busloads of visitors on organized tours roll in to Cai Be village from Ho Chi Minh City, 110km away. They are shepherded on to boats for a few hours to explore the market and fruit orchards on nearby islands before zipping back to the city. While this may be convenient for those who are short of time, it's all a bit rushed and the midday heat can be oppressive. If you have a more relaxed schedule, meandering through the picturesque channels of An Binh Island between Vinh Long and Cai Be market, or overnighting in a home-stay (see box, p.132) before visiting the market in the morning, offers a more rewarding experience.

Ben Tre Province

The few travellers who push on beyond My Tho into **BEN TRE PROVINCE** are rewarded with some of the Mekong Delta's most breathtaking scenery. Until recently this province was isolated by the Mekong's wide arms around it, but the new Rach Mieu Bridge from My Tho (opened in 2009) is starting to bring a rush of visitors. Famed for its fruit orchards and coconut groves (Vietnamese call it the "coconut island"), the province has proved just as fertile a breeding ground for revolutionaries, first plotting against the French, and later against the Americans, and was one of the areas seized by the Viet Cong during the Tet Offensive of 1968.

BEN TRE

EATING
Ben Tre Floating Restaurant 2
Ham Luong Hotel 3
Hung Vuong 1

HAI BA TRUNG
Truc Giang Lake
30 THANG 4
DONG KHOI

Bank
NGUYEN DINH CHIEU
LE LOI
LE DAI HANH
Market
HUNG VUONG

& Bus Station

ACCOMMODATION
Dong Khoi 2
Ham Luong Hotel 4
Hung Vuong 3
Thao Nhi Guest House 1

0   200
metres

Ben Tre

Of the US bombing campaign on the provincial capital of **BEN TRE**, a US major was quoted as saying, "It became necessary to destroy the town in order to save it." – a classic wartime analysis. Today, Ben Tre is a pleasant and industrious town displaying none of the wounds of its past (apart from a heavily populated cemetery and proud war memorial), and makes an agreeable contrast to the tourist bustle of nearby My Tho. Though short on specific sights, the surrounding countryside is lush and photogenic. It's a relaxing and friendly place to hole up for a couple of days, with a buzzing **town market** and a new **riverside promenade**, which makes a pleasant place to stroll in the morning or evening. With a bicycle or motorbike, you can explore the maze of trails on both sides of the river. For more of an adventure, head out of town on a boat trip along the **Ben Tre coastline**, where labyrinthine creeks afford marvellous scope for exploring, and sometimes include stops at apiaries, rice-wine and sugar-processing workshops.

ARRIVAL AND DEPARTURE

BEN TRE

By bus The opening of the new bridge to Ben Tre means that all visitors now arrive by road: buses terminate at the new bus station on Highway 60 about 2km northwest of the town centre.

INFORMATION

Tourist information Located at 65 Dong Khoi to the north of the centre, Ben Tre Tourist Company (daily 7–11am & 1–5pm; ☎075 382 9618) can organize car rental, bicycles and some tours, including boat trips along the coast; for motorbikes, contact the *Hung Vuong Hotel*. The Vietinbank on Nguyen Dinh Chieu exchanges dollars.

ACCOMMODATION

Dong Khoi 16 Hai Ba Trung ☎075 382 2501. On the north bank of Truc Giang Lake, the state-run *Dong Khoi* has decent rooms at very cheap rates, though you might have to share your space with cockroaches and the place can get rowdy when they host a wedding, as they often do. **$9**

Ham Luong Hotel 200c Hung Vuong ☎075 356 0560, ⓦhamluongtourist.com.vn. This is one of Ben Tre's newest and smartest hotels, located along the riverfront. Rooms have traditional furnishings with smart fixtures and fittings and the fourth floor café overlooking the river is a great spot to relax. **$22**

Hung Vuong Hotel 166 Hung Vuong ☎075 382 2408. The riverside *Hung Vuong Hotel* has the best location and some of the best facilities of Ben Tre's hotels. Its large,

2

well-equipped rooms all have a/c and TVs and some have bathtubs and river views. **$24**

★ **Thao Nhi Guest House** Hamlet 1, Tan Thach village ☎ 0908 123488, ✉ thaonhitours@yahoo.com. A cheap and adventurous option is the *Thao Nhi Guest House*, set in the grounds of a longan orchard some distance from town. It has a range of rooms, including wooden cabins with fan and shared bathroom, and larger ones with a/c. The boss, Phat, is extremely friendly and helpful, and organizes cheap and enjoyable boat trips to watch a sunrise or sunset over the Mekong River. Bicycles are available for free to guests. The atmosphere is very relaxing – the kind of place to settle in for a few days – and its restaurant has a good menu that features elephant-ear fish and huge prawns. It's about 6km from the new bus station, but if you call ahead they'll arrange a pick-up. **$6**

EATING

Ben Tre Floating Restaurant Hung Vuong, about 3km west of the centre. This is a fine venue for a sunset drink or dinner, though the menu of Vietnamese dishes is rather limited. Don't forget your mosquito repellent. Main courses cost around $4.50. Daily 10am–10pm.

Ham Luong Hotel 200c Hung Vuong.The ground-floor restaurant here is a reliable stand-by, serving up a good range of Vietnamese stir-fries and soups as well as steak and chips, though it's sometimes booked by wedding parties; the fourth-floor café is the place to kick back with a coffee or cocktail (over 300 drinks to choose from) and enjoy views over the river. Mains $4–10. Daily 6am–10pm.

Hung Vuong Hotel 166 Hung Vuong. This place serves up a decent range of Vietnamese and Western dishes, even if the decor is somewhat uninspiring, and like the nearby *Ham Luong*, it occasionally gets overrun with business conventions or wedding parties. Mains $3–9. Daily 6am–10pm.

Cao Lanh and around

West of My Tho, and Cai Be, Highway 1 crosses the My Thuan Bridge on its way to Vinh Long and Can Tho. Just before the bridge, however, at An Huu, Highway 30 branches north, rolling into modest **CAO LANH** 34km later. The town is no oil painting and offers little unless you're charmed by **wading birds**; its location beside the western edge of the **Plain of Reeds** makes Cao Lanh an ideal launching pad for trips out to the storks and cranes that nest in the nearby swamplands. Coming from Ho Chi Minh City, you'll pass the two great concrete tusks (intended to resemble lotus petals) of the **war memorial** as you veer onto the main drag, Nguyen Hué. One tusk bears a hammer and sickle, the other a Vietnamese red star.

The burial place of Nguyen Sinh Sac

Pham Huu Lau, about 1km west of the town centre • Free

On the southwestern outskirts of town, a landscaped park contains a monument, shaped like an open clam, which marks the burial place of Ho Chi Minh's father, **Nguyen Sinh Sac**. The park's area has recently been expanded to include several examples of stilted houses typical of the south, as well as a replica of Ho Chi Minh's house in Hanoi. With a lake and benches in shady areas, it's a pleasant place to pass an hour or so.

Dong Thap Museum

Just off Pham Huu Lau, to the left beyond the first bridge • Tues–Sun 7–11.30am & 1.30–5pm, Mon 7–11.30am • Free

While in town, it's worth having a look around the **Dong Thap Museum**. Though there are no English signs, there is a well-organized display of fossils, skulls, farming tools, fishtraps, basketware and textiles, as well as the inevitable paintings of heroic Vietnamese forces repelling French and American troops.

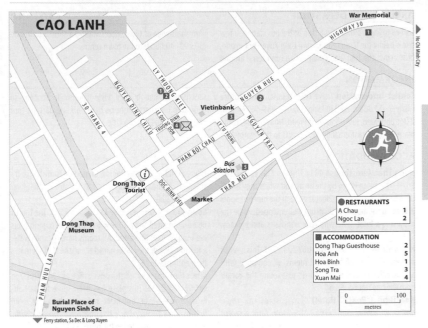

Ferry station, Sa Dec & Long Xuyen

Tram Chim National Park

45km northwest of Cao Lanh

Of the 220 species of birds nesting at **Tram Chim National Park** (previously called the Tam Nong Bird Sanctuary), it's the sarus cranes, with their distinctive red heads, that most visitors come to see, though numbers have sadly declined drastically in recent years, and there's not much to be seen outside the months of December to May. In flight above the marshland of the sanctuary, the slender grey birds reveal spectacular black-tipped wings. **Cranes** feed not from the water but from the land, so when the spate season (July–Nov) waterlogs the delta, they migrate to Cambodia. Visiting the park, however, can be very expensive (over $100 per day for a small group), so this is a trip for committed bird enthusiasts only: if you're keen, ask at the office of Dong Thap Tourist in Cao Lanh for details (see p.128).

Xeo Quyt Relic Area

You'll need to approach the tourist office (see p.128) if you want to take a trip out to **Xeo Quyt Relic Area**, deep in the cajeput forest 30km southeast of Cao Lanh. Day tours here used to go by boat but now it's a road trip. The district's dense cover provided the perfect bolthole for Viet Cong guerrillas during the American War, and from 1960 to 1975 the struggle against America and the ARVN was masterminded from here. The boggy nature of the terrain made a tunnel system similar to that of Cu Chi (see p.109) unfeasible, so they made do with six submerged metal chambers sealed with tar and resin. Suspecting the base's existence, Americans bombed the area regularly, and even broadcast propaganda from the air to demoralize its occupants, but by developing a policy of "going without trace, cooking without smoke, speaking without noise", the cadres residing here escaped discovery throughout the war.

2

ARRIVAL AND DEPARTURE

CAO LANH

Buses to and from Cao Lanh stop at the bus station, a few paces below the town centre. From Long Xuyen or beyond, buses cross the Tien Giang via the Cao Lanh ferry, around 4km southwest of town, necessitating a short xe om ride (30,000–40,000đ) to the town centre.

INFORMATION

Tourist information Dong Thap Tourist, whose office (daily 7–11.30am & 1.30–5pm; ☎067 385 5637) is at 2 Doc Binh Kieu, just off the main road, Nguyen Hué, is the place for tourist information about visits to the nearby bird sanctuaries, though very little English is spoken, so dedicated twitchers might be better off approaching tour operators in Ho Chi Minh City.

ACCOMMODATION

Dong Thap Guesthouse 48 Ly Thuong Kiet ☎067 387 2670. This place is run by the army and when they aren't chanting in the yard next door it's one of the quietest spots in town. Basic rooms are small but well equipped, while the biggest is a huge suite with cosy armchairs and balcony. **$15**

Hoa Anh 38-42 Ly Tu Trong ☎067 224 0567. This newish mini-hotel has small but smart rooms, all equipped with a/c, satellite TV and wi-fi, and it's just round the corner from the bus station. **$8.50**

Hoa Binh ("Peace" Hotel) 1km east of the town centre on Highway 30 ☎067 385 1469. After a recent renovation, this place is one of the smartest choices in town, with bright, tiled floors and modern furnishings. It's situated, rather symbolically, across from the war memorial. **$20**

Song Tra 178 Nguyen Hué ☎067 385 2624. The tourist board-accredited *Song Tra* is where those on birding tours are usually accommodated. All rooms have a/c, hot water and cable TV, but they lack character and the staff seem less than enthusiastic. **$24**

Xuan Mai Just west of the post office at 33 Le Qui Don ☎067 385 2852. This place has been subject to a half-hearted make-over, but make sure you check the room first, as some are very dingy. Its larger rooms have bathtubs and breakfast is included in the price. **$13**

EATING

A Chau 42 Ly Thuong Kiet. Almost next door to the *Dong Thap Guesthouse*, the *A Chau* is popular for parties, and features a good range of dishes such as rice with fried pork and vegetables for around $2.50. Daily 7am–9pm.

Ngoc Lan 210 Nguyen Hué. If you walk down Cao Lanh's main street at lunchtime, this place is likely to be most crowded. Plenty of rice and noodle dishes and cheap prices. Mains $1–3. Daily 7am–10pm.

Song Tra 178 Nguyen Hué. There's an in-house restaurant at the *Song Tra* hotel though it's a rather uncharismatic affair serving Vietnamese staples. Mains $2–5. Daily 7am–9pm.

Vinh Long

Ringed by water and besieged by boats and tumbledown stilthouses, the island that forms the heart of **VINH LONG** has the feel of a medieval fortress. However, if you find yourself yearning for a peaceful backwater, first impressions will be a let-down; central Vinh Long is hectic and noisy, its streets a blur of buses and motorbikes. Make for the waterfront, though, and it's a different story, with hotels, restaurants and cafés conjuring up something of a riviera atmosphere. From here you can watch the **Co Chien River** roll by, dotted with sampans, houseboats and the odd raft of river-weed. Though there's little to see or do in town, Vinh Long offers some of the most interesting **boat trips** in the delta – to the Cai Be floating market, coconut candy workshops, fruit orchards or even overnighting in home-stays.

Vinh Long Museum

Phan Boi Chau, opposite the boat jetty • Tues–Thurs 8–11am & 1.30–4.30pm, Fri & Sat 6–9pm • Free

Vinh Long has few specific sights, though the **Vinh Long Museum**, facing the waterfront, is worth a look if you haven't already visited war museums elsewhere. Displays in various buildings include historical finds from the region, farming

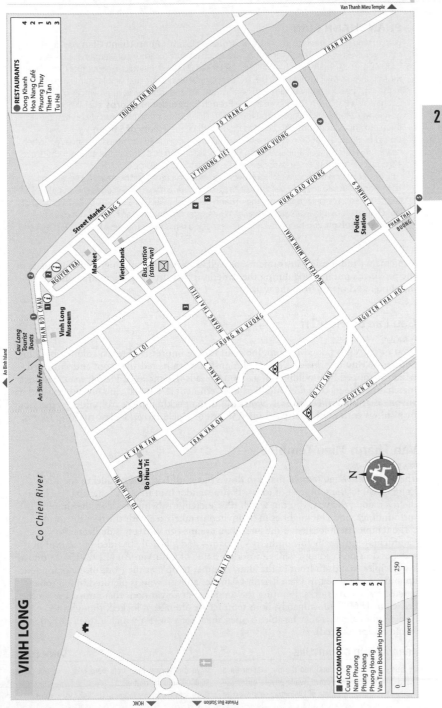

VINH LONG

Van Thanh Mieu Temple

RESTAURANTS
Dong Khanh	4
Hoa Nang Café	2
Phuong Thuy	1
Thien Tan	5
Tu Hai	3

Co Chien River

An Binh Island

Cuu Long Tourist Boats

An Binh Ferry

Vinh Long Museum

Street Market

Market

Vietinbank

Bus station (state-run)

Police Station

Cao Lac Bo Huu Tri

ACCOMMODATION
Cuu Long	1
Nam Phuong	3
Phung Hoang	4
Phuong Hoang	5
Van Tram Boarding House	2

TRAN PHU

TRUONG TAN BUU

30 THANG 4

HUNG VUONG

LY THUONG KIET

HUNG DAO VUONG

2 THANG 9

PHAM THAI BUONG

NGUYEN THI MINH THAI

NGUYEN THAI HOC

HOANG THAI HIEU

TRUNG NU VUONG

NGUYEN DU

VO THI SAU

3 THANG 2

LE LOI

1 THANG 5

NGUYEN TRAI

PHAN BOI CHAU

LE VAN TAM

TRAN VAN ON

TO THI HUYNH

LE THAI TO

Private Bus Station

HCMC

0   250   metres

N

2

PHAN THANH GIAN

Born in Vinh Long Province in 1796, the mandarin diplomat **Phan Thanh Gian** was destined to be involved in a chain of events that was to shape over a century of Vietnamese history.

On August 31, 1858, French naval forces attacked Da Nang, citing persecution of Catholic missionaries as their justification. The French colonial land-grab, that would culminate in 1885 in the total conquest of Vietnam, had begun. By 1861, the three eastern provinces of Cochinchina had been conquered by the **French Expeditionary Corps**, and although there were popular anti-French uprisings Emperor Tu Duc sold out the following year, when the three provinces were formally ceded to the French by the **Treaty of Saigon**, which was signed by Phan Thanh Gian. A year later he had the opportunity to redress the situation, when he journeyed to Paris as ambassador to Emperor Napoleon III, to thrash out a long-term peace – the first Vietnamese ambassador ever to be despatched to Europe.

However, efforts to reclaim territory given up under the terms of the treaty failed, and by 1867 France moved to take over the rest of Cochinchina. Unable to persuade the spineless Tu Duc to sanction popular uprisings, Phan Thanh Gian embarked on a hunger strike in protest at French incursions and Hué's ineffectuality. When, after fifteen days, he had still not died, he swallowed **poison**, and his place among the massed ranks of Vietnamese heroes was assured.

implements and musical instruments, as well as a gruesome photographic catalogue of the province's pummelling during the American War. In the gardens are tanks, a helicopter and planes from the war.

Cau Lac Bo Huu Tri

Le Van Tam

West of the Vinh Long Museum, look out for the impressive French colonial building, **Cau Lac Bo Huu Tri**. This oddly shaped mansion, with its red-tiled roof and shuttered windows topped by mouldings of garlands, recalls the ghosts of French *colons* and rice merchants. The place is now run by the government as a social club for retirees, and if anyone is around, they probably won't mind you peeking in the front door at the fancy furnishings with mother-of-pearl inlay, a bust of Uncle Ho and a few meeting rooms.

Van Thanh Mieu Temple

Daily 5–11am & 1–7pm

The **Van Thanh Mieu Temple** sits 2km down the road that runs parallel to the Rach Long Canal to the southeast of town. If you wander into the tiny lanes that back onto the river along the way, you can watch tiles and coffins being made in the simplest of surroundings, and you might even be invited to take a tea with the friendly locals.

The temple itself, located at the end of an avenue of tall trees, is dedicated to Confucius – unusually for southern Vietnam – and a heavily bearded portrait of him watches over proceedings, while a wooden statue of Chu Van An (1292–1370), one of his disciples, stands in front of the altar. Another temple at the front of the compound honours local mandarin Phan Thanh Gian (see above), who is pictured in red robes, flanked by slender storks. Fronting the temple are two cannons that rained fire on the French in 1860. Unfortunately, both temples are often kept locked, though the gardener or caretaker may be able to open them for you (for which a small donation would be appreciated).

ARRIVAL AND DEPARTURE	VINH LONG

By bus State-run buses pull into the bus station on 3 Thang 2 in the centre of town, while private buses use another bus station a couple of kilometres southwest of town on Nguyen Hué; from here take a xe om (about 30,000đ) into the centre.

Destinations: Sa Dec (50min); Tra Vinh (1hr 30min).

INFORMATION

Tourist information For information about boat trips or home-stays, check the state-run Cuu Long Tourist (☎070 382 3616), whose main office is in the *Cuu Long Hotel*, or the private Mekong Travel 8, 1 Thang 5 (☎070 383 6252): both charge around $25–40 per person for a 4–5 hour tour of Cai Be floating market, fruit orchards and the narrow waterways of An Binh Island.

ACCOMMODATION

Most of Vinh Long's accommodation options are located near the boat jetty on the northern edge of town. Where boat trips operate in the Mekong Delta, notably around Vinh Long, the local tourist board can also arrange for visitors to stay with the owners of fruit orchards, allowing a close-up view of rural life (see box, p.132).

2

Cuu Long Phan Boi Chau ☎070 382 3656. This government-run place is looking rather faded now, and details like polyester sheets and thin aluminium doors don't impress. However, it's got an ideal location and some rooms have fine views of the Vinh Long riviera; all include satellite TV, a/c, hot water and breakfast. $15
Nam Phuong 11 Le Loi ☎070 382 2226. A smart mini-hotel near the town centre. Although some rooms don't have windows, they all come with a/c, hot water and cable TV, and breakfast is included. $14
Phung Hoang 2h Hung Vuong ☎070 382 5185. This mini-hotel represents some of the best value in town. It has

a dozen or so rooms with varying sizes and facilities, all with chintzy furnishings, and the staff are very friendly. $6
Phuong Hoang 2r Hung Vuong ☎070 382 2156. Just twenty metres south of its almost-namesake, this place has slightly less fancy rooms at marginally higher prices. All rooms are a different size and layout, so it's worth looking at a few before deciding. $8
Van Tram Boarding House 4, 1 Thang 5 ☎070 382 3820. Just five rooms here, but all are a good size and well equipped with TVs, fridges, hot water and a/c. Add in its prime location and the result is great value. $15

EATING AND DRINKING

Dong Khanh 49 2 Thang 9. Located just south of the town centre, this place produces standard Vietnamese stir-fries, soups and grilled dishes, with menus in English. Mains $1–3. Daily 6am–8pm.
Hoa Nang Café 1 Thang 5. With a long river frontage, this is a perfect place to sip a cool drink while watching the sun sink into the Mekong. However, you're likely to be driven away by the screaming karaoke soon after. Daily 7am–11pm.

Phuong Thuy Phan Boi Chau, opposite the Cuu Long Hotel. The Cuu Long Tourist-owned *Phuong Thuy*, built out over the river, boasts the best location of the town's restaurants, though the Vietnamese food is only average and service is indifferent. Mains $2–6. Daily 6am–10pm.
Thien Tan South of town, at 56/1 Pham Thai Buong. This big place set back from the road is the best place for barbecued dishes in town, and draws a faithful following of locals. Mains $3–10. Daily 10am–10pm.

BOAT TRIPS FROM VINH LONG

The cheapest and simplest way to see the river is to hop on the An Binh Ferry on Phan Boi Chau, and cross the Co Chien River (5min; 5000đ) to reach **An Binh Island**. Sometimes called Minh Island, it's a jigsaw of bite-sized pockets of land, skeined by a fine web of channels and gullies, eventually merging, to the east, with the province of Ben Tre. This idyllic landscape is crisscrossed by a network of dirt paths, making it ideal for a morning's rambling or cycling, though you'll need to take your own refreshments.

However, most people fork out for a day or half-day boat trip to see several aspects of delta life, organized either through Cuu Long Tourist or Mekong Travel (see above), or through local boatmen always on the look-out for customers near the tourist jetty. These tours often include the option of overnighting in a **home-stay** (see box, p.132) in a totally rural environment, though as they increase in popularity, some start to resemble guest houses rather than home-stays, with visitors put up in custom-built bamboo huts separated from the family home.

Most tour itineraries head upriver to the floating market at **Cai Be** (see p.124), stopping to visit fruit orchards, and rice-paper and candy factories en route; some tours also stop for a fish lunch at a rural outpost. Watching the river traffic, from the tiny rowing boats to huge sampans loaded with rice husks (fuel for the nearby brick kilns), is fascinating, and stepping ashore from time to time reveals insights into the lifestyles of the locals.

2

HOME-STAYS IN THE DELTA

While the Vietnamese are generally gregarious people, it's unusual for foreigners to be invited into their homes. However, most visitors are curious about local culture, so it's not surprising that home-stays are becoming ever more popular and widely available. Though there are **home-stays** all around the country, those located on tranquil islands of the delta, surrounded by acres of orchards, are particularly attractive.

For around $25 a head, you are transported by boat to your host's (usually isolated) abode, shown around the gardens, given a tasty dinner (most likely including the delicious elephant-ear fish – a delta speciality) and lodgings for the night, either in a bed or hammock in a spare room. Bathroom facilities are basic, sometimes with squat toilets and bucket baths, but generally clean. If you book your home-stay with a tour operator like Sinhbalo Adventures (see p.90), you can also spend the day kayaking between water palms along narrow canals, or cycling along narrow lanes between coconut, mango and papaya trees.

Tu Hai 29 2 Thang 9. A no-frills shophouse producing standard Vietnamese stir-fries, soups and grilled dishes, with menus in English. Closes early when it's quiet. Mains $1–3. Daily 7am–8pm.

DIRECTORY

Banks Vietinbank at 143 Le Thai To exchanges travellers' cheques and cash and has an ATM.
Post office and internet The post office is in the middle of town at 12c Hoang Thai Hieu, where there's also internet access.

Tra Vinh

It's only another 65km southeast through some classic delta scenery – vivid green rice paddies, backed by coconut and water palms – to **TRA VINH**, an outback market town whose broad, tree-lined streets and smattering of colonial piles have yet to see tourists in any numbers. Even if you don't plan to stay here, it makes an interesting day out from Vinh Long. This region of the delta is Khmer country; as you get nearer to Tra Vinh, distinctive pagodas begin to appear beside the road, painted in rich pastel shades of lilac, orange and turquoise, their steep horned roofs puncturing the sky. Altogether there are over 140 Khmer pagodas scattered around the province.

Most visitors come here to visit the storks at nearby Hang Pagoda (see p.134), although the town's low-key charm makes it an intriguing place to spend a day or two. Unusually, Tra Vinh isn't ostensibly dominated by a branch of the Mekong – you'll have to journey a couple of hundred metres east of the 800-metre-square grid forming the town centre to find the river. A hike through the **market** to riverside Bach Dang makes the most engaging approach. The bridge 100m north of the fish market commands great views of the **Tra Vinh River**, whose eddying waters run canal-straight to the north. In places the river is almost corked by boats moored seven or eight deep.

Just south of the market, at the junction of Pham Thai Buong and Tran Quoc Tuan, the Chinese **Ong Pagoda** is worth a visit as it's a very active place of worship and there's always something interesting going on. North of the town centre up Le Loi, the **Ong Met Pagoda** is very different, with a Khmer-style roof above colonial arches and shutters: you're assured of a friendly reception here from the monks studying at its English school. Immediately north is the pretty **Tra Vinh Church**, an imposing buttressed construction, fronted by a statue of Christ above the entrance, with waves of stonework rippling up its spire.

ARRIVAL AND DEPARTURE

By Bus Buses from Vinh Long and beyond hit the southwest corner of Tra Vinh, terminating about 800m from the centre of town at the bus station on Nguyen Dang, off Dien Bien Phu. Buses take about an hour and a half and xe om are waiting to ferry passengers around town.

INFORMATION

Tourist information The extremely helpful Tra Vinh Tourist Company at 64–66 Le Loi (☎074 385 8556, ☎074 385 8768) can provide local information.

ACCOMMODATION

Cuu Long Hotel 999 Nguyen Thi Minh Khai (on the main road just before entering town) ☎074 386 2615, ☎074 386 6027. This hotel has some of the smartest rooms in Tra Vinh, and brings an aura of prosperity to the small town (though it's a bit of a trek to the centre) with its surprisingly well-equipped rooms that have a touch of elegance. $18

Hoan My 105a Nguyen Thi Minh Khai ☎074 386 2211, ☎074 386 6600. Located almost opposite the *Cuu Long Hotel*, this mini-hotel looks very ordinary from the outside, but inside it has tastefully furnished rooms, some with massage showers. The most expensive rooms are huge and have private balconies. $17

Palace 3 Le Thanh Ton ☎074 386 4999. One of the smartest places in the town centre, the *Palace* seems to have been transported from a bygone era with its chunky traditional furniture and high ceilings. Even the polite welcome from the staff harks back to a time when courtesy counted above all. $25

Thanh Tra 1 Pham Thai Buong ☎074 385 3626, ☎074 625 0658. This recently refurbished hotel has a central location and reasonable restaurant, which make it the most popular choice for business people. Rooms are smart but lack character and some are rather dingy, so take a look first. $25

EATING

Ben Co About 5km from the town centre, on the right-hand side of Highway 53 (the road to Vinh Long) about half a kilometre after the turning for Ba Om. The popular *Ben Co* serves up huge bowls of delicious *banh canh* – a noodle soup with pork, for about $2. Daily 6am–4pm.

Thanh Tra Hotel 1 Pham Thai Buong. The top-floor restaurant of the *Thanh Tra Hotel* serves an unexciting but reliable range of Vietnamese and Western dishes. It may not be gourmet food, but it's one of the few places in town with an English menu and it is in a very convenient location in the town centre. Mains $2–6. Daily 6am–9pm.

Tuy Huong 8 Dien Bien Phu. Opposite the front of the market, the *Tuy Huong* offers a range of Chinese and Vietnamese dishes, such as sweet and sour prawns or fresh spring rolls, in a no-frills, open-air café environment. Good spot for people watching. Mains $1–4. Daily 7am–8pm.

Viet Hoa 80 Tran Phu. The *Viet Hoa* specializes in seafood, served up in the form of kebabs, smothered with a sauce or as a steaming hotpot (best to eat with a group); to get there walk south of the front of the market along Dien Bien Phu and turn right on to Tran Phu. Mains $2–5. Daily 8am–8pm.

DIRECTORY

Bank The Agribank, one block west of the market at 70–72 Le Loi, will change US dollars, and has an ATM.

Post office Hung Vuong, just opposite the *Thanh Tra Hotel*.

Ba Om Pond

Daily 24hr • Free • 5km southwest of town, a signposted road on the left runs down to the pond; buses to and from Vinh Long pass the short approach road here, or a xe om from the centre of Tra Vinh costs around 30,000đ

Ba Om Pond is beloved of Tra Vinh picnickers and courting couples. Around the pond, drinks and snack vendors lie in wait for visitors, but although it can get crowded at weekends, on weekdays it is usually restful. Bordered by grassy banks, and shaded by towering, aged trees whose roots clutch at the ground, Ba Om is cloaked with plants that attract flocks of birds in the late afternoon.

Ang Pagoda

Behind Ba Om Pond • Sunrise to sunset • Free

The area across the far side of the pond has been a Khmer place of worship since the eleventh century, and today it's occupied by **Ang Pagoda**. Steep roofed and stained with age, the pagoda makes an affecting sight, especially when it echoes with the chants of its resident monks. Fronting it is a nest of stupas guarded by stone lions, while murals inside depict scenes from the Buddha's life. In season, rice from the pagoda's paddy fields is heaped next to the altar, where it's guarded by an impressive golden Sakyamuni image and a host of smaller ones. Several Cambodian monks are resident here, who are eager to practise their English with visitors.

Khmer Minority People's Museum

Daily 7–11am & 1–5pm • Free

Probably the most interesting of the attractions by Ba Om Pond is the **Khmer Minority People's Museum**, just in front of the Ang Pagoda. The display includes musical instruments, a depiction of Khmer daily life, Buddha statues and samples of traditional dress. For students of cultural differences, here's an opportunity to note differences between Khmer and Vietnamese lifestyles.

Hang Pagoda

Hang Pagoda is around 6km south of town along Dien Bien Phu • There's no public transport to the pagoda, so you'll have to take a xe om: about 50,000đ for the return trip

The sight of the hundreds of **storks** that nest in the grounds of this Khmer pagoda is one that will linger in the memory. Timing, however, is all-important, and you should aim to catch these magnificent creatures before dusk, when they wheel and hover over the treetops, their snowy wings catching the evening's sunlight. It's a stirring sight, though you might find yourself distracted by the saffron-robed monks who clamour to practise their English. They may also show you their wood-carving workshop, where there's usually someone at work on a wooden rat or tiger. Hang Pagoda itself – an arched stone gate to the left of the main road betrays the entrance to the compound – is nothing to write home about. Dominating it is a **Sakyamuni statue**, hooped by a halo of fairy lights and flanked by murals depicting scenes from his life.

Sa Dec

A cluster of brick and tile kilns on the riverbank announces your arrival in the charming town of **SA DEC**, a little over 20km upriver of Vinh Long. French novelist Marguerite Duras lived here as a child (see below), and decades later the town's stuccoed shophouse terraces, riverside mansions and remarkably busy stretch of the rumbling Mekong provided the backdrop for the movie adaptation of her novel *The Lover*.

MARGUERITE DURAS

Marguerite Duras (1914–96) was born to French parents in a suburb of Saigon, and lived in various locations in Vietnam and Cambodia before going, aged 18, to study at the Sorbonne in France. She wrote many novels, plays and film scripts including the autobiographical novel *The Lover* (1984), which sold over three million copies and was translated into forty languages. Its subject is an interracial affair between a 15-year-old French girl and her middle-aged Chinese lover, set in 1930s' Indochina. Duras had little sympathy for her peers, of whom she wrote "I look at the (French) women in the streets of Saigon. They don't do anything, just save themselves up… Some of them go mad…some are deserted for a young maid." Duras clearly had no intention of letting life pass her by in this way, even if it meant becoming the subject of the town's gossip.

Though her novels are principally about the inner thoughts of her characters, she also describes the landscape around Sa Dec as it still appears today: "In the surrounding flatness, stretching as far as the eye can see, the rivers flow as if the earth slopes downward."

If you visit Sa Dec with a tour guide, they will almost inevitably take you to look at her former house beside the river – an old colonial villa that now belongs to the People's Committee.

It's worth wandering along **Nguyen Hué**, whose umbrella-choked lanes hide Sa Dec's extensive riverside market as well as the former home of Dumas' lover. Waterfront comings and goings are observed by rheumy old men playing chequers, and women squat on their haunches, selling fruit from wicker baskets.

The home of Huynh Thuy Le

225a Nguyen Hué • Open daily 8am-5pm • 20,000đ • ☎ 067 377 3937

Nestled among the tumbledown homes along Nguyen Hué on the riverside stands the former home of Huynh Thuy Le, who became the lover of Marguerite Duras in the 1930s (see box opposite). The old family home, now administered by Dong Thap Tourism, features some elaborate carved panels and lashings of gold lacquer work, as well as some photos of the couple in question, though interestingly none of them together. There are even a couple of rooms available for rent here, though they are more like cubbyholes and can't be recommended as good value lodgings.

Tu Ton Rose Garden

Daily 8–11am & 1–5pm

A few kilometres north of town by the river, Sa Dec's famed **flower nurseries** consist of more than a hundred farms cultivating a host of ferns, fruit trees, shrubs and flowers. The expansive grounds of **Tu Ton Rose Garden** get the lion's share of tourists visiting the area. In addition to the varieties of roses cultivated here (among them the *Brigitte Bardot*, the *Jolie Madame* and the *Marseille*), over 580 species of plants are grown, ranging from orchids, carnations and chrysanthemums, through to medicinal herbs and pines grown for export around Asia. Bear in mind that the nurseries are overrun on Sundays by tourists from Ho Chi Minh City, who come to pose for photos among the blooms; and that things get particularly busy and colourful in the run-up to Tet, as farms prepare to transport their stocks to the city's flower markets.

ARRIVAL AND DEPARTURE
SA DEC

By bus Buses terminate 300m southeast of the town centre. As you come in from the bus station, the town's three main arteries – Nguyen Hué, Tran Hung Dao and Hung Vuong – branch off to your right.

ACCOMMODATION

Huong Thuy 58 Le Thanh Ton ☎ 067 386 8963. The best value in town is this family-run, mini-hotel just north of the market. It's centrally located with immaculately clean, a/c rooms which all have hot water, TVs and fridges. $7

Sa Dec 108/5a Hung Vuong ☎ 067 386 1430. The *Sa Dec*, at the northern end of the street, is a reasonable if uninspiring place to stay. Some rooms are in dire need of a lick of paint, but the fan-cooled rooms go for less than $10 and breakfast is included. $9

EATING

Chanh Ky 193 Nguyen Sinh Sac. This little family-run joint doles out noodle and rice dishes such as *pho bo* (beef noodle soup) and *com ga* (rice with chicken) in a no-frills environment for around $2 that you can wash down with cold beer. Daily 7am–8pm.

Com Thuy 439 Hung Vuong. A popular lunch spot that serves up Vietnamese staples and has an English menu. Order up a plate of spring rolls, a steamy soup or a stir-fry from the friendly staff, and pay less than a couple of dollars for each dish. Daily 7am–9pm.

DIRECTORY

Post office and internet The post office, at the corner of Nguyen Sinh Sac and Hung Vuong, has internet.

Can Tho

A population of around a million makes **CAN THO** the delta's biggest city, and losing yourself in its commercial thrum for a few days is the perfect antidote to time spent in the quiet backwaters of the delta. However, first impressions are rather less than encouraging: Can Tho is a hefty settlement but, once the oppressive urban sprawl encasing the town has been negotiated, its breezy waterfront comes as a pleasant surprise.

At the confluence of the Can Tho and Hau Giang rivers, the city is a major mercantile centre and transport interchange. The recent re-opening of the former US air base for commercial flights, as well as the enormous effort of completing the biggest bridge in the delta, shows that this city features large in government plans for future development.

But Can Tho is no mere staging post. Some of the best restaurants in the delta are located here; what's more, the abundant **rice fields** of Can Tho Province are never far away, and at the intersections of the canals and rivers that thread between them are some of the delta's best-known **floating markets**. Can Tho was the last city to succumb

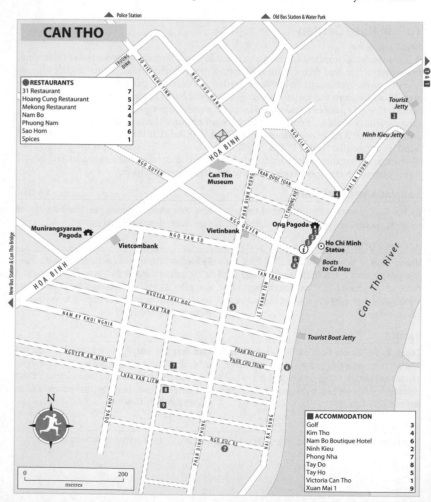

to the North Vietnamese Army, a day after the fall of Saigon, on May 1, 1975 – the date that has come to represent the reunification of the country.

Though its **boat trips** (see box, p.140) are the main reason for visiting Can Tho, a handful of lesser diversions on dry land will help keep you amused in the meantime.

Can Tho Museum
1 Hoa Binh • Tues–Thurs 8–11am & 2–5pm, Sat & Sun 8–11am & 6.30–9pm • Free

Broad Hoa Binh is the city's backbone, and the site of the impressive **Can Tho Museum**, which presents "the history of the resistance against foreign aggression of Can Tho people" as well as local economic and social achievements. Despite the enormity of the place and the extensive signs in English, it's all a bit drab apart from a few highlights like models of a teahouse and a herbalist treating patients.

Munirangsyaram Pagoda
36 Hoa Binh • Sunrise to sunset • Free

Two hundred and fifty metres southwest of the Can Tho Museum, the 1946-built **Munirangsyaram Pagoda** warrants examination only if the more impressive Khmer pagodas around Tra Vinh or Soc Trang aren't on your itinerary. Entrance into the pagoda compound is through a top-heavy stone gate weighed down with masonry reminiscent of Angkor Wat, but there is little to see inside apart from a few plaster Buddha images.

The waterfront
Walking east along Nguyen Thai Hoc deposits you bang in the middle of the city's **riverside promenade**, which extends along Hai Ba Trung. The whole riverfront is now lined by beds of plants and stone seats: the old market has also been replaced by a covered area with souvenir stalls and an excellent restaurant. As with most delta towns, this riverside area gets crowded in the evenings as locals come out for a stroll in the cooler air. Waterfront **cafés** will rustle up a fresh coconut or a pot of green tea and from your seat you can watch the relentless sampan traffic of the Can Tho River.

As you head north from the covered market along Hai Ba Trung, an imposing silver **statue** of a waving Uncle Ho greets you on the promenade.

Ong Pagoda
Just north of the Uncle Ho statue, Ong Pagoda is a colourful place built in the late nineteenth century by wealthy Chinese townsman Huynh An Thai. Inside, a ruddy-faced Quan Cong presides, flaunting Rio Carnival-style headgear. On his left is Than Tai, to whom a string of families come on the first day of every month, asking for money and good fortune. On his right is Thien Hau, Goddess of the Sea. There's also a small chamber dedicated to Quan Am to the left of the main hall.

ARRIVAL AND DEPARTURE   CAN THO

By plane In early 2011, the former Binh Tuy US military airbase at Tra Noc, about 6km from the city centre, re-opened for civilian passengers. Inside the airport are a cafeteria, souvenir shops, currency exchange, hotel booking and tourist information desks. Taxis and xe om await arriving planes. Though it only offers a few domestic flights at present, there are hopes that it will receive international flights in the future.
By bus In 2010 the much-touted bridge across the Hau Giang River to Can Tho (see box, p.138) was finally completed, making the archaic ferry service redundant and cutting travel time to and from Ho Chi Minh City. The bridge brings traffic to the south side of the city, where a new bus station on 3 Thang 2 (to the southwest of the city centre) accommodates most long-distance buses. However, the old bus station, on Nguyen Trai (to the northwest of the city centre) is still functioning so you might find yourself dropped here. Both are just a short xe om ride (10,000–20,000đ) from the centre.

2

BRIDGING THE DELTA

The **Mekong River** deposits tons of fertile earth on the delta each year, making the region's produce so abundant, but it also provides a barrier to swift travel, forcing drivers to queue for hours to cross its countless channels by slow, lumbering ferries. In the late 1990s a plan was hatched to build huge **bridges** at three key points in the delta – My Thuan, My Tho and Can Tho – in order to cut down journey times. The first of these, at My Thuan, crossing the Tien Giang, opened in 2000 and immediately slashed hours off journey times. The second, linking My Tho and Ben Tre, suffered delays but finally opened in early 2009. The third and biggest project, crossing the widest of the Mekong's nine arms (the Hau Giang) at Can Tho, was the scene of a tragic accident in September 2007 when a 90-metre section of an approach ramp collapsed, killing more than fifty workers. Construction was delayed for a while but was finally completed in 2010, and now visitors arriving by land pass over the longest cable-stayed bridge in Southeast Asia as they approach Can Tho.

Destinations: Bac Lieu (3hr); Ca Mau (5hr); Chau Doc (2hr 30min); Ha Tien (5hr); Ho Chi Minh City (4hr); Long Xuyen (1hr 30min); My Tho (2hr 30min).
Airlines Vietnam Airlines' main office is at 66 Nguyen An

Ninh (☎ 0710 384 4320).
Destinations: Ho Chi Minh City (daily; 45 min); Hanoi (daily; 2hr); Phu Quoc (daily; 45 min); Con Dao (4 weekly; 1hr).

INFORMATION AND TOURS

Tourist office For information about boat trips and other local attractions, drop in at the helpful Can Tho Tourist at 50 Hai Ba Trung (☎ 0710 382 1852, ⊛ canthotourist.com .vn), who can organize tour boats along the river and to the

floating markets. Boats depart from the tourist jetty ("Ben Tau Du Lich"), as do evening river cruises (daily 8–9.30pm; 10,000đ), which feature Vietnamese music.

ACCOMMODATION

Hai Ba Trung and Chau Van Liem together form the axis of Can Tho's healthy **hotel** scene, with the more expensive and mid-range properties clustered around the northern end of Hai Ba Trung, and budget places located around Chau Van Liem and streets further south.

Golf 2 Hai Ba Trung ☎ 0710 381 2210, ⊛ vinagolf.vn. With over a hundred rooms, a first-floor pool and all the appropriate facilities, not to mention fabulous river views, this place stands at the head of the pack in Can Tho, even though it's all a bit soulless and international. $150
Kim Tho 1a Ngo Gia Tu ☎ 0710 222 2228, ⊛ kimtho .com. Squeezing in beside the established hotels along the riverfront, this twelve-storey place is giving stiff competition with its state-of-the-art fixtures and fittings, plus sweeping river views. $45
Nam Bo Boutique Hotel 1 Ngo Quyen ☎ 0710 381 9138. This renovated colonial building now accommodates not only the new *Nam Bo* restaurant, but also a boutique hotel with just seven rooms. They are not particularly spacious but they are well-equipped with the latest gadgetry. $140
Ninh Kieu 2 Hai Ba Trung ☎ 0710 382 4583. Attractive place offering good-value, well-appointed rooms off coolly tiled halls; all rates include breakfast. Opt for the A3 building, a newer extension that has slightly more expensive rooms that enjoy great river views. $48
Phong Nha 70 Nguyen An Ninh ☎ 0710 382 1615. Located in a smart new building, this is the best of three

hotels of the same name in town, and represents one of Can Tho's best budget options. All rooms have a/c and bathrooms are spotless. $15
Tay Do 61 Chau Van Liem ☎ 0710 382 1009. A reliable mid-range option in town, with over forty cosy rooms boasting all mod cons, including satellite TV. $35
★ **Tay Ho** 42 Hai Ba Trung ☎ 0710 382 3392. After a thorough renovation, this cheap and cheerful place right on the riverfront stands out as the best budget deal in town, especially if you can get one of the two rooms with riverfront views for around $15. $10
Victoria Can Tho Cai Khe Ward ☎ 0710 381 0111, ⊛ victoriahotels-asia.com. Built and furnished in classic French-colonial style but with all the modern facilities you'd expect from the delta's first international standard hotel. It's set in a grand riverside location across a bridge to the north of the town centre and surrounded by lush tropical growth. $220
Xuan Mai 1 17 Dien Bien Phu ☎ 0710 382 3578. Tucked away down a side street off Chau Van Liem, this is a decent budget option, with large, bright rooms, some with fan and others with a/c. If this is full, they have two similar places around the corner at 94 and 60 Nguyen An Ninh. $8

EATING

Can Tho is well endowed with good, affordable restaurants, most serving Vietnamese food, though there are plenty that also offer international dishes. Those along Hai Ba Trung target a primarily foreign market, while locals tend to patronize places around the **market** and along Nam Ky Khoi Nghia.

31 Restaurant 31 Ngo Duc Ke. Simple café serving up tasty and cheap Vietnamese dishes enjoyed by all in a no-frills environment. However, it's not a place to relax as there's a bustle of tour groups constantly coming and going from the attached hotel. Mains $2–5. Daily 6am–11pm.

Hoang Cung Restaurant 55 Phan Dinh Phung. Located on the ground floor of the *Saigon Can Tho* hotel, this place serves decent Western and Vietnamese dishes in a stylish environment at reasonable prices. Mains $3–8. Daily 6am–11pm.

★ **Mekong Restaurant** 38 Hai Ba Trung. This long-established favourite is still hard to top for its cheap, flavoursome Vietnamese and Chinese meals, as well as succulent chateaubriand steaks for around $6. There is also a good vegetarian selection, and another room out back if it's packed out front. Daily 8am–2pm & 4–10pm.

Nam Bo 1 Ngo Quyen ☎ 0710 381 9138. Recently moved across the street, this French café-inspired place with attractive furnishings has managed to retain an intimate atmosphere in its new location. Innovative dishes like prawn with mango sauce, tempting salads, sandwiches and desserts make up the menu; main dishes cost around

$5–6. There's also a neat bar area on the roof that's ideal for a pre- or post-dinner drink. Daily 6am–11pm.

Phuong Nam 48 Hai Ba Trung. This place enjoys a great riverfront location right next to the *Mekong Restaurant*, and benefits from occasional overspill from that popular venue. It serves a good range of cheap and tasty Western and Vietnamese dishes, with an upstairs balcony too, which is ideal for people watching. Mains $3–6. Daily 10am–2pm & 5–10pm.

★ **Sao Hom** Hai Ba Trung. This tastefully decorated open-sided riverfront place has the ideal location – right next to where hungry tourists disembark from boat trips. It serves an appealing menu of Vietnamese and Western dishes that features items such as sauteed pumpkin flowers with garlic. Draft beer, wines, cocktails, coffee and ice cream on offer too. Mains $3–10. Daily 5am–11pm.

Spices Victoria Can Tho hotel, Cai Khe Ward. Fine dining in a tasteful ethnic interior, or outside on the romantic riverside terrace and the extensive menu, with appetizers such as *banh cuon* (rice pancakes stuffed with pork, shrimp and salmon eggs) ($7) and main courses for $9–21, make the detour to this hotel restaurant worth the effort. Daily 6am–10pm.

DIRECTORY

Banks Vietcombank, 7 Hoa Binh (Mon–Fri 7–11am & 1–5pm), changes cash and travellers' cheques and has an ATM. Vietinbank at 9 Phan Dinh Phung (Mon–Fri 7.30am–noon & 1–6pm) changes travellers' cheques and cash for similar rates.

Bicycle and motorbike rental Enquire at the *Huy Hoang* hotel, 35 Ngo Duc Ke. Rates are around $3 a day for a bicycle, $7–10 a day for a motorbike.

Hospital The general hospital is located 3km west of the centre on Highway 91B.

Internet Most hotels offer internet access, and there are hundreds of free wi-fi spots around town. There is also an independent operator at 199 Phan Dinh Phung charging 6000đ/hr.

Pharmacy 31b Chau Van Liem; and 78 Hai Ba Trung.

Police 67–69 Hung Vuong, northwest of the city centre.

Post office 2 Hoa Binh (daily 6am–9pm). IDD, internet, poste restante, fax and express mail service.

Sports Non-residents can use the swimming pool and tennis courts at *Victoria Can Tho* hotel (floodlit in the evening) for a few dollars.

Supermarket There is a huge Co-op Mart at the junction of Hoa Binh and Ngo Quyen.

Waterpark Can Tho Water Park (☎ 0710 376 3343; Mon–Fri 8.45am–5.30pm, Sat & Sun 7.45am–5.30pm; 40,000đ), in Cai Khe Ward to the north of town, has several pools, water chutes and slides in a large, landscaped area.

Binh Thuy Temple

Daily 7.30–10.30am & 1.30–5.30pm • Free • Journey from Can Tho costs about 50,000đ return by xe om

Six kilometres north of Can Tho along the road to Long Xuyen, the **Binh Thuy Temple** began life in the nineteenth century as a *dinh*, or communal house for travellers to rest in. The present building dates back to 1909, and immediately catches the eye with its green-tiled eaves framed by frangipani trees. Though it appears small from outside, the cool interior runs very deep, and the walls are decorated with images of Chinese gods and Vietnamese heroes. Between the sturdy wooden pillars are several altars, with some ghoulish characters guarding one of them with axes raised.

2

BOAT TRIPS AND FLOATING MARKETS

Every morning an armada of boats takes to the web of waterways spun across Can Tho Province and makes for one of its **floating markets**. Everything your average villager could ever need is on sale, from haircuts to coffins, though predictably fruit and vegetables make up most of what's on offer. Each boat's produce is identifiable by a sample hanging off a bamboo mast in its bow, but it's difficult to get colourful pictures as the produce is stored below.

CAI RANG

Of the two major nearby markets, the most commonly visited, 7km out of Can Tho, is **Cai Rang**, but you'll have to be prepared to queue up with all the other tourist boats before you can weave among the fervent waterborne activity, with drinks vendors clamouring to make a sale. Nevertheless it's a fun experience, especially if you can get there between 7–8am. This market is particularly active on Sundays.

PHONG DIEN

Another 10km west and you're at modest **Phong Dien**, whose appeal is that it sees relatively few tourists and so the locals are correspondingly friendly. If you wish to stay longer here, the purpose-built *My Khanh Village* (☎0710 384 6260, ⊚ mykhanh.com; $30), is nearby at 335 Lo Vong Cung, with wooden bungalows in a shady setting and a good-sized pool. Its attractions (geared mostly to domestic visitors) include an ancient house, a pond full of crocodiles, caged monkeys and a pig-racing track, plus a pony and trap to take visitors round the site. Animal-rights activists might not enjoy it, but conditions here are better than at most such places in Vietnam. There are also demonstrations on making rice cakes and brewing wine, and traditional musicians perform in the evenings. Few Western visitors stay here so it's a good way to meet some Vietnamese.

VISITING THE MARKETS

Most organized tours take you to Cai Rang or Phong Dien early in the morning, then make a leisurely return to the city, via the maze of picturesque canals and orchards that surround it, usually stopping to sample star fruit and sapodilla, longan and rambutan along the way. Can Tho Tourist (see p.138) charges between 200,000 and 250,000đ per person for such a tour, depending on the itinerary and type of boat. As usual, unofficial boat operators are cheaper, charging about 80,000đ per hour for a simple sampan: women prowl for customers along Hai Ba Trung, and some can be friendly and informative, but be on the lookout for scams, and check out the boat as some have no shelter from sun or rain. Phong Dien is more easily reached by **hiring a xe om** (about 60,000đ), then renting a sampan for an hour's rowing (about 60,000–80,000đ) among the buyers and sellers.

The Duong Home

144 Bui Huu Nghia • Daily 8am–noon & 2–5pm • Donation

Down a side street opposite Binh Tuy Temple is the beautiful **Duong Home**, which was used in the 1992 filming of *The Lover* (see p.488). A classic example of French colonial architecture, its shuttered windows and elaborate stucco decorations conceal a spacious living room featuring period furnishings with mother-of-pearl inlay. Note the intricately carved panels beside the pillars, where a bat sits at the summit of a menagerie of animals; unlike in the West, where bats symbolize vampires, in the East they are seen as a portent of good luck. The current residents are often on hand to show visitors round, and the adjacent orchid garden contains what is thought to be the tallest cactus in the country.

Soc Trang

Straddled across an oily branch of the Mekong, **SOC TRANG** lacks the panache of other delta towns, though on the fifteenth day of the tenth lunar month (Nov–Dec) the

2

town springs to life as thousands converge to see traditional Khmer boats (*thuyen dua*) racing each other during the **Oc Om Boc festival**.

Khleang Pagoda

In the middle of town on Nguyen Chi Thanh • Sunrise to sunset • Free

Khmer pagodas are ten-a-penny in this region of the delta, but the **Khleang Pagoda**, located in the heart of Soc Trang, is one of the most impressive. It is surrounded by a two-tiered terrace and the doors and windows are adorned with traditional Khmer motifs in greens, reds and golds. Inside is a wonderful golden Sakyamuni statue, though unfortunately, the doors are often locked.

Khmer Museum

23 Nguyen Chi Thanh • Mon–Sat 7.30–11.30am & 1.30–4.30pm • Free

Directly opposite the Khleang Pagoda, the **Khmer Museum** houses some low-key exhibits including stringed instruments made of snakeskin and coconut husks, and some wonderfully colourful food covers, shaped like conical hats, but with a stippled surface.

Dat Set Pagoda

163 Mau Than 68 • Sunrise to sunset • Free

Head north from the Khleang Pagoda along Mau Than 68 for a few minutes, and you'll see the Dat Set pagoda on the right. Also known as the Buu Son Tu Pagoda, it is constructed almost entirely from clay, with a smart sheet-metal roof to keep the rain off. Dat Set makes a welcome change from the more numerous Khmer pagodas in this region of the delta. Chinese visitors flock here to see the pagoda's impressive and highly colourful collection of clay statues; many are life-size, with animals and figures from Chinese mythology being the most popular subjects. The pagoda is also home to some truly gargantuan candles that look like pillars, weigh around 200kg each and are said to last for seventy years of continuous burning.

Mahatup Pagoda

To get to the Mahatup pagoda, go 2km south of town along Le Hong Phong, then turn right at a fork beside a small market and continue another 800m. Cars are not allowed on the last few hundred metres, so you'll have to walk or hop on one of many waiting xe om

Mahatup Pagoda, aka Bat Pagoda, is famed for its vast community of golden-bodied fruit bats, which spectacularly take to the skies at dusk. A fire in 2007 destroyed much of the main building, but reconstruction is now complete, and a large pond has also been added behind the temple. Plan to get here around 5.30pm – as the drop in temperature wakes them, you'll see the bats spinning, preening and flapping their matt-black wings, some spanning 1.5m.

Khmer monks have worshipped at this site for four hundred years, and it is often busy with Vietnamese visitors. Inside, bright murals bearing the names of the Khmer communities around the world that financed them recount the life of the Buddha. Outside, look out for the graves of four pigs behind the large hall to the right opposite the pagoda, each of which had five toenails (pigs usually have four). Since such animals are believed to bring bad luck, they are honoured with well-tended resting places to ward off any evil tendencies. The tombstones are painted with their likenesses and the dates of their passing on.

ARRIVAL AND DEPARTURE

The waterway running roughly west to east splits Soc Trang in two, with most of the town nestling on its south bank. The town's spine is Hai Ba Trung, which runs across the water, before becoming Tran Hung Dao on the southern outskirts.

By bus The bus station is at the northern end of town on Nguyen Chi Thanh. Buses to HCMC leave every half hour and less regularly to other destinations in the Delta. Xe om are on hand to ferry arriving passengers into the town centre.

INFORMATION

Tourist information Soc Trang Tourist, at 104 Le Loi (daily 7–11am & 1.30–5pm; ☎ 079 382 2024), can usually help with local information.

ACCOMMODATION

Khanh Hung Hotel 17 Tran Hung Dao ☎ 079 382 1026. Located in the centre of town, this place has 53 rooms ranging from basic and cheap to carpeted suites that have seen better days. Its central location, friendly staff and handy restaurant make it the most convenient base in town, but check a few different rooms before deciding. $10
Ngoc Thu 3km out of town at km 2127 on Highway 1 ☎ 079 361 3108, ⓦ ngocthuhotel.com. If you have your own transport, this is the best place to stay in Soc Trang. It has a range of comfortable rooms, with two pools and a tennis court; the cheaper rooms at the back are particularly good value. $18
Que Huong 128 Nguyen Trung Truc ☎ 079 361 6122. This is a newish place set on a quiet backstreet with spacious, well-equipped rooms that include ADSL cables, while there's also wi-fi in the lobby. $14

EATING

Hung North of the river at 24 Hung Vuong (down a small lane). One of Soc Trang's most popular places among locals, this place serves various dishes with rice; its specialities are goat curry and pickled shrimp. Take your phrase book or point to dishes on display as there's no English menu. Mains $2–5. Daily 8am–8pm.
Khanh Hung Hotel 17 Tran Hung Dao. This hotel restaurant serving Vietnamese dishes like chicken and rice ($2) and spare ribs and rice ($1.50) wins no prizes for attractive decor, nor is eating here a gourmet experience, but the big attraction is the English menu – about the only one in town. The set menu ($3.50) is a decent option. Daily 6am–10pm.

DIRECTORY

ATM There's an ATM in front of the *Khanh Hung Hotel*.

Post office and internet The post office is in the centre of town at 1 Tran Hung Dao, and has internet access.

Bac Lieu

Beyond Soc Trang the landscape becomes progressively more waterlogged and water palms hug the banks of the waterways that crisscross it. A little over 40km southwest of Soc Trang, Highway 1 dips south towards the crown of **BAC LIEU**, before veering off west to Ca Mau. It may be the back end of nowhere, but Bac Lieu's prosperity is evident in new shopping complexes and upmarket homes around the centre. The source of this prosperity is overseas Vietnamese, many of whom hail from this region. Although there are few sights to set the pulse racing, the town's got the only accommodation between Soc Trang and Ca Mau and is in good proximity to the nearby Bac Lieu Bird Sanctuary.

Bac Lieu Bird Sanctuary

Daily 7.30am–5pm • 15,000đ • Arrange transport through Bac Lieu Tourist Company (see p.144)

Well worth the visit, the sanctuary is 6km southwest of Bac Lieu towards the coast. There is an observation tower and paths among the cajeput forest, along which local guides can lead you. Lots of birds can be seen here from July to December, including herons and egrets, but there is little to see from January to June. Guides are necessary and will appreciate a tip, even though their English skills are limited.

ARRIVAL AND DEPARTURE BAC LIEU

By bus The bus station is 1.5km west of town, and xe om shuttle back and forth to the centre. There are frequent departures to HCMC (about 4.5hr) and less regular departures to other destinations in the Delta.

INFORMATION

Tourist information The Bac Lieu Tourist Company, at 2 Hoang Van Thu (daily 7–11am & 1–5pm; ☎0781 382 4272, ☎0781 382 4273), is conveniently situated next to the *Bac Lieu* hotel, though the staff are not terribly helpful.

ACCOMMODATION

Bac Lieu 4–6 Hoang Van Thu ☎0781 395 9697. The town's main hotel was undergoing some major renovation at the time of writing. Rooms are a decent size, complete with a/c, cable TV and hot water, but only some have a view, so ask to take a look first. **$18**

Cong Tu 13 Dien Bien Phu ☎0781 395 3304. For a bit of character, head to the *Cong Tu*, right next to the *Bac Lieu Hotel* (main entrance is on the riverside). This palatial colonial villa has just ten rooms with fancy furnishings and high ceilings, as such it's quite popular so best to book ahead. **$15**

EATING AND DRINKING

Bac Lieu 4–6 Hoang Van Thu. The *Bac Lieu*'s ground-floor restaurant offers set menus of Vietnamese cuisine starting at $5, as well as a la carte dishes such as fish prepared with various sauces at around $3–4. Service is reasonably efficient but the atmosphere is somewhat sterile. Daily 6am–10pm.

Cong Tu 13 Dien Bien Phu. The café at the *Cong Tu* is atmospheric, with tables ranged around a covered courtyard, and its wide-ranging menu includes lots of fish dishes, making this the best dining venue in town. Mains $3–5. Daily 7am–10pm.

Kitty On the corner of Ba Trieu and Tran Phu. Your best option for nightlife in Bac Lieu is to join the overseas Vietnamese at *Kitty*, a first-floor bar that wouldn't look out of place in Ho Chi Minh City and serves expensive cocktails, beers and coffee, as well as a reasonable range of Vietnamese dishes ($3–8). Daily 10am–11pm.

DIRECTORY

Bank Sacombank is at no. 82 Tran Phu where you can exchange money. There's an ATM conveniently located in front of the *Bac Lieu*.

Post office The post office is in the centre of town at 20 Tran Phu.

Ca Mau

With its left shoulder braced against the Bac Lieu Canal, Highway 1 heads westwards from Bac Lieu towards the **Ca Mau Peninsula**, which constitutes not only the end of mainland Vietnam but of Southeast Asia as well. In this part of the country, **waterways** are the most efficient means of travel – a point pressed home by the slender ferries moored in all the villages the road passes. Much of this pancake-flat region of the delta is composed of silt deposited by the Mekong, and the swamplands covering portions of it are home to a variety of wading birds. In addition to rice cultivation, shrimp farming is a major local concern – along the way you're sure to spot shrimp ponds, demarcated by mud banks that have been baked and cracked crazily by the sun.

CA MAU itself, Vietnam's southernmost town of any size, has a frontier feel to it, though rapid development is changing that fast. Things have changed since 1989 when travel writer Justin Wintle described it as a "scrappy clutter...a backyard town in a backyard province", though there are still pockets of squalor between the glitzy new buildings. Ca Mau sprawls across a vast area, with broad boulevards connected by potholed lanes and a couple of busy bridges spanning the Phung Hiep Canal that splits the town in two. To the west, the town is bordered by the Ganh Hao River, which snakes past as though trying to wriggle free before the encroaching stilthouses squeeze the life from it.

Although few Western travellers currently visit Ca Mau, there are now speedboats to Rach Gia that cover the journey in less than three hours, and improvements to Highway 63 make the journey by road less arduous, so incorporating Ca Mau in a circular tour of the delta is now a tempting possibility, as it takes you off the tourist trail and through classic delta scenes.

2

The Market

Le Loi • Sunrise to sunset

Along the north bank of the Phung Hiep Canal, which divides the town, is the rag-tag squall of the **market** that lurks on the banks of the canal. A shantytown of corrugated iron, canvas and sacking, it is a bustling centre for packing fish for sale and shipment. As such, it doesn't have the photogenic appeal of most delta markets. Current moves to clean up the riverbank may see this market moved elsewhere in the near future.

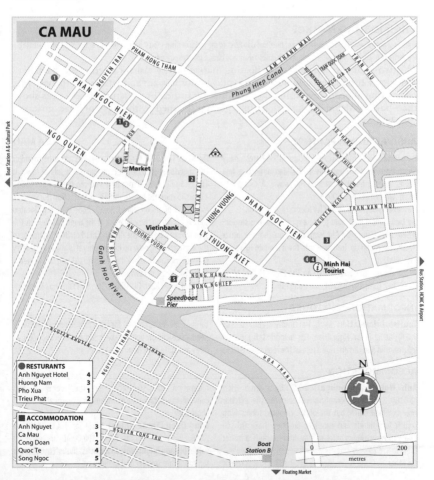

CA MAU

● RESTURANTS	
Anh Nguyet Hotel	4
Huong Nam	3
Pho Xua	1
Trieu Phat	2

■ ACCOMMODATION	
Anh Nguyet	3
Ca Mau	1
Cong Doan	2
Quoc Te	4
Song Ngoc	5

Cao Dai Temple

Phan Ngoc Hien • Sunrise to sunset • Free

Worth a look for its ornate towers, Ca Mau's Cao Dai temple is evidence of how deeply rooted the religion is in the Mekong Delta; these temples are a distinctive feature of many delta towns and add a playful splash of colour with their Disneyesque decorations. A couple of parks opposite the temple offer shady areas to escape the bustle of town near the canal.

2

Cultural Park

2km west of Ca Mau • Daily dawn–dusk • 10,000đ • About 30,000đ for a xe om

This is one of the town's most intriguing attractions, at least during the rainy season (July–Nov), though its name is something of a misnomer. It is, in fact, a bird sanctuary teeming with storks and many other birds that nest in the trees in easily observed fenced-off areas. The huge park also has a mini zoo featuring elephants, monkeys, deer and other animals, as well as lots of pavilions and picnic spots. Arrive about 4pm to explore the park then watch the birds arriving to roost.

The Floating Market

Boat from boat station B, on the west bank of the Ganh Hao River to the south of town • You'll need to turn up at the pier and negotiate a fee with the boatmen for the 30–40 minute trip downstream and back. Expect to pay around $10

The two-kilometre journey to the floating market gives a taste of riverine life, passing factories, a fish market and warehouses, plus lots of flotsam and jetsam, on the way to see a string of boats advertising their produce by suspending a sample from sticks above their bows. A definite risk on this trip is getting splashed by the wake of huge ferries speeding by.

ARRIVAL AND DEPARTURE   CA MAU

By plane Vasco Airlines (ⓦvasco.com.vn) operates a daily flight from Ho Chi Minh City to Ca Mau airport, a few kilometres southeast of town on Highway 1. A xe om into town will cost about 30,000đ.
Destinations: Ho Chi Minh City (daily; 1hr).

By bus Almost next door to the airport is the bus station, where buses from Ho Chi Minh City, Can Tho and other destinations pull up. Transport into town is again by xe om (30,000đ)
Destinations: Bac Lieu (2hr); Can Tho (5hr); Ho Chi Minh City (7hr); Long Xuyen (6hr); Soc Trang (3hr).

By boat The most useful boat services are to be found at the speedboat jetty, located on the south side of town at 162 Phan Boi Chau. From here you can get to Nam Can in 1 hour 15 minutes for around $3, or to Dat Mui (for Cape Ca Mau) in 3 hours for about $6.50. Boat Station B, located south of town on the east bank of the Ganh Hao River, is the spot to take a boat to the floating market. Boat Station A, to the west of town, now no longer operates any regular ferry service. For Can Tho, you'll need to go to Cong Ca Mau jetty, about 3km east of town.
Destinations: Rach Gia (daily; 3hr; $6), Can Tho (3hr; $6).

INFORMATION AND TOURS

Tourist information Minh Hai Tourist (ⓣ0780 383 1828), at 62 Pham Ngoc Hien, has helpful staff for local information and can arrange a tour of the region, as well as car and speedboat rental for trips to outlying areas. You'll need a sizeable group to make hiring a boat economical, as rates are quite high (around $150/day).

ACCOMMODATION

Anh Nguyet (Moonlight) 207 Phan Ngoc Hien ⓣ0780 356 7666, ⓦanhnguyet.com.vn. The exterior may not look much, but the plush, carpeted rooms with stylish furnishings and excellent facilities make this Ca Mau's most luxurious place to stay. Rates include a buffet breakfast. $29
Ca Mau 20 Phan Ngoc Hien ⓣ0780 383 1165. A recent renovation has smartened up the rooms at this conveniently located hotel, making it a reasonable budget choice. $9
Cong Doan (Trade Union) 9 Luu Tan Tai ⓣ0780 383 3245. Top-priced rooms here (300,000đ) are excellent value; big and bright with all facilities, though the cheaper fan rooms are smaller and gloomier. $7

Quoc Te (International) 179 Phan Ngoc Hien ☎0780 382 6745, ✉quoctehotel@yahoo.com.vn. Top-end rooms here are big, clean and comfy with all facilities, while cheaper rooms are a bit smaller. **$19**

Song Ngoc 2b Hung Vuong ☎0780 381 7303,

☎0780 381 7307. All rooms in this mini-hotel situated near the roundabout south of the canal have bathtubs as well as a/c, hot water, TVs and mini-bars. Rooms on the upper floors have a good view of the town. **$11**

EATING

Anh Nguyet Hotel 207 Phan Ngoc Hien ☎0780 356 7666, ⓦanhnguyet.com.vn. The restaurant at the town's best hotel has tasty food and a relaxing ambience, though sometimes it's booked by wedding parties. There are a few Western dishes as well as a comprehensive range of Vietnamese cuisine. Mains $3–6. Daily 6am–9pm.

Huong Nam 21 De Tham. If you're looking for a snack in town, head for this shop, where you can get a sandwich or cake to take away (about $0.50–1), then drop into the nearby coffeeshop at 17 or 19 De Tham and wash it down with a strong coffee or soft drink. Daily 7am–6pm.

Pho Xua 239 Phan Ngoc Hien. On the north side of town, *Pho Xua* is set in traditional pavilions with wooden pillars around a shady garden, and is the best spot in town for a meal. It has a fairly extensive menu of Vietnamese dishes in English and plenty of appealing seafood options, such as shrimp stir-fry for $4. Daily 7am–10pm.

Trieu Phat 22 Phan Ngoc Hien. For basic and cheap ($1–2) rice and noodle dishes, it's difficult to beat the central *Trieu Phat*, though you'll need your phrasebook to understand the menu. Daily 7am–9pm.

DIRECTORY

Bank To exchange travellers' cheques or cash, Vietinbank is at 94 Ly Thuong Kiet (Mon–Fri 7.30–11am & 1.30–4.30pm); it also has an ATM.

Post office and internet The main post office (daily 6am–10pm) is opposite Vietinbank, on Luu Tan Tai; internet is available here.

Around Ca Mau

The **marshes** circling Ca Mau form one of the largest areas of swampland in the world, covering about 150,000 hectares. The Ca Mau Peninsula was a stronghold of resistance against France and America, and for this it paid a heavy price, as US planes dumped millions of gallons of Agent Orange over it to rob guerrillas of jungle cover. Further damage has been done by the shrimp-farm industry, but pockets of mangrove and cajeput forests remain, inhabited by sea birds, wading birds, waterfowl and also honey bees, attracted by the mangrove blossoms.

Mui Ca Mau National Park

About 100km south of Ca Mau • 10,000đ • Take a speedboat from the speedboat jetty in Ca Mau to Dat Mui. On arrival in Dat Mui, either rent a local boat or hop on a xe om (about 40,000đ return) to Mui Ca Mau (Cape Ca Mau) through a mangrove swamp for the last few kilometres

This voyage to the end of the earth may not quite be a Jules Verne epic, but it's a fun and satisfying way to pass a day, as you get to visit not only the southernmost point of Vietnam but also the end of mainland Southeast Asia. The speedboats (see opposite) that take you through the throng of life in the delta can get pretty crowded, but if you're lucky you might get a window seat to look out on the houses, shacks and boats that line the river.

Once inside the national park, you can take a photo of yourself standing beside a boat-shaped monument marking the latitude (8 degrees north) and longitude (104 degrees east) of this remote location, then gaze out over the endless ocean and the mountainous Khoai Island just off the coast. There's even a **look-out tower** from where you can get good views over the mangrove forests, and a restaurant on stilts over the water.

U Minh Forest and National Park

100km from Ca Mau • 10,000đ • There are no longer public ferries serving this route, so your options are to fork out for a day-trip with Minh Hai Tourist, which includes a visit to Da Bac (an offshore island), or take a local bus heading towards Rach Soi along Highway 63 to the turn-off for the national park, then stick your thumb out and hope for the best

U Minh is famous for its cajeput forests. Lining the nearby canals are water palms, modest groves of cajeput and fish traps consisting of triangles of bamboo sticks driven

2

GET YOUR KICKS ON HIGHWAY 63

Of all the roads that crisscross the Mekong Delta, few have such a strong sense of what this watery world is all about as **Highway 63**, which zigzags north from Ca Mau to Minh Luong, just south of Rach Gia – a distance of a little over 100 kilometres. The road is sealed all the way, though it's often no wider than a single track road, and for most of its journey it follows narrow canals that carry a real hotchpotch of vessels going about their business. At **Vinh Tuan** it crosses a wide canal, allowing great views of river life, though parking on the bridge is illegal, so park near and walk on to it. There are also several **monkey bridges** across the canals – fragile structures consisting of narrow tree trunks, which require the assured balance of a monkey to cross them (thus the name). Like many other aspects of local culture, monkey bridges are disappearing fast, but Highway 63 still offers a fascinating glimpse of traditional life in the delta. Near the end of the highway, you need to cross a wide river by ferry at Tac Cau, where you'll see huge fishing ships loading ice to freeze their catch. If you don't have your own transport, take a bus from Ca Mau to Rach Gia to follow this highway.

---

into the riverbed. The slender white trunks of the cajeput thrive in U Minh's marshy, coffee-coloured waters, and gliding through them in a boat would be a truly tranquil experience if it were not for the racket of the boat engine. Along the way, you may spot bright blue birds flitting over the water, or, depending on the season, apiarists collecting honeycombs from the trees, which attract bees in huge numbers when they are in flower.

Long Xuyen

Some 60km (an hour's drive) northwest of Can Tho, **LONG XUYEN** attracts few foreign visitors, though the unusual cathedral, the well-organized museum, Tiger Island and the nearby stork garden and crocodile farm are all worth a look.

The Cathedral

Nguyen Hué

Dominating the town is the spire of the concrete **cathedral**, shaped in the form of two upstretched arms whose hands clasp a cross. Unfortunately the church is often locked, but if you can get inside check out the numerous tiny portals that shed light on the dim-lit interior, illuminating gilt Stations of the Cross, and another giant pair of hands over the altar, clutching a globe.

My Phuoc Communal Hall

Nguyen Hué

At the other end of Nguyen Hué from the church, the dragon-stalked roofs of the grandest building in town, the **My Phuoc Communal Hall**, shelter carved pillars and embroidered banners in the temple-like interior. Nearby is a very large statue of a meek-looking **Ton Duc Thang**: born locally, he was successor to Ho Chi Minh as president of the Democratic Republic of Vietnam, giving the town its main claim to fame.

Tiger Island

Ton Duc Thang Exhibition House • daily 7–11am & 1–5pm • Free

You can visit Ton Duc Thang's birthplace and childhood home at **My Hoa Hung Village** on **Tiger Island**. Here you will find the **Ton Duc Thang Exhibition House**, which displays well-presented photos and memorabilia such as the leg irons he wore in Con Dao prison, the prime-ministerial bicycle and the plane that took him from Hanoi to

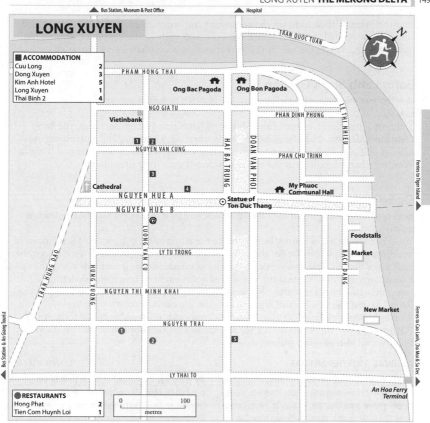

LONG XUYEN

■ ACCOMMODATION	
Cuu Long	2
Dong Xuyen	3
Kim Anh Hotel	5
Long Xuyen	1
Thai Binh 2	4

TRAN QUOC TUAN

PHAM HONG THAI

Ong Bac Pagoda   Ong Bon Pagoda

NGO GIA TU

Vietinbank   PHAN DINH PHUNG

LE THI NHIEU

NGUYEN VAN CUNG

HAI BA TRUNG

DOAN VAN PHOI

PHAN CHU TRINH

Cathedral

NGUYEN HUE A

My Phuoc
Communal Hall

NGUYEN HUE B   Statue of
Ton Duc Thang

LUONG VAN CU

Foodstalls

Market

BACH DANG

LY TU TRONG

HUNG VUONG

NGUYEN THI MINH KHAI

Ferries to Tiger Island ▶

Ferries to Cao Lanh, Cho Moi & Sa Dec ▶

New Market

TRAN HUNG DAO

NGUYEN TRAI

Bus Station & An Giang Tourist

LY THAI TO

An Hoa Ferry
Terminal

● RESTAURANTS	
Hong Phat	2
Tien Com Huynh Loi	1

0   100
metres

2

Saigon in 1975 to celebrate victory. The island is very tranquil and unspoilt, and home-stays here can be arranged (see p.151).

An Giang Museum

11 Ton Duc Thang on the corner of Ly Thuong Kiet • Tues–Sun 7.30–11am & 1.30–5pm • About 15,000đ

Also worth a look, particularly for its display of Oc Eo relics (see box, p.150), is the **An Giang Museum** housed in a grand edifice in the northern part of town. On the first floor the focus is on the different religions practised in the region – Catholicism, Buddhism and Hoa Hao. On the second floor is a treasure trove of remnants of Oc Eo culture. Among the exhibits are a large lingam and a wooden Buddha that is so decayed it is now almost unrecognizable, as well as delicate items of gold jewellery. Other displays focus on minority culture, particularly the Cham, and the inevitable documenting of the local revolutionary movement and battles against the French and Americans. Unfortunately, there are no signs in English.

Blue Sky Crocodile Land

44/1a Tran Hung Dao (about 2km south of the town centre) • Daily 7.30am-10pm • Admission 10,000đ

At this crocodile farm, you can watch crocs lying around doing nothing (except for feeding time, when they practise their jaw-snapping on unsuspecting ducklings released into their pens). Then head for the restaurant and order up croc fried rolls, sweet and sour croc or curried croc, and round out your visit with a purchase of a croc-skin bag, wallet or belt. As you can see, at this eco-friendly set-up, there's no waste at all.

Bang Lang Stork Garden

About 15km south of Long Xuyen on Highway 9 • Daily 6am–6pm • 20,000đ • Xe om from Long Xuyen will cost around 120,000đ round-trip

South of Long Xuyen is one of the Mekong Delta's best stork sanctuaries, the **Bang Lang Stork Garden**, with thousands of birds wheeling, swooping and squabbling over nesting places at dusk. Turn up an hour before sunset to witness the memorable sight. Wearing a hat might help as the site is smothered with their droppings.

Oc Eo

40km west of Long Xuyen on Highway 943 • As it's difficult to find alone, you're best off arranging a trip through An Giang Tourist (see opposite)

You'd need to be a real history buff to make the effort to see the modest foundations of buildings that remain at **Oc Eo**, though the ride itself is an enjoyable diversion into the back lanes of the delta, passing rice fields, lotus ponds and fruit orchards along the way. Excavations in 1998/9 at this site uncovered gold jewellery, bowls and skeletons in vases, though all such precious objects are now on display in museums at Long Xuyen, Rach Gia and Ho Chi Minh City. The covered site consists of low walls and foundations of buildings over one thousand years old. It's possible to continue on Highway 943 to Tup Duc (see p.154) and Chau Doc (see opposite), though it's a bumpy road and progress is slow.

ARRIVAL AND DEPARTURE LONG XUYEN

By bus Most buses stop on Pham Cu Luong, off Tran Hung Dao a couple of kilometres south of town, though local buses, including some from Chau Doc, pull up at the bus station about 2km to the north of town, also on Tran Hung Dao. Destinations: Ca Mau (6hr); Chau Doc (1hr); Ha Tien (5hr); Ho Chi Minh City (5hr).

By ferry Travelling to and from Cao Lanh by ferry, you'll come via Choi Moi Isle – to the east – and the An Hoa Ferry terminal, at the end of Ly Thai To in the centre of town. Destinations: Infrequent ferries connect Long Xuyen with Sa Dec and Cao Lanh (both about 1hr).

OC EO AND THE FUNAN EMPIRE

Between the first and sixth centuries AD, the western side of the Mekong Delta, southern Cambodia and much of the Gulf of Siam's seaboard came under the sway of the Indianized **Funan Empire**, an early forerunner of the great Angkor civilization. The heavily romanticized annals of contemporary Chinese diplomats describe how the Funan Empire was forged when an Indian Brahmin visiting the region married the daughter of a local serpent-god, and how the serpent rendered the region suitable for cultivation by drinking down the waters of the flood plains. Such fables are grounded in truth: Indian traders would have halted here to pick up victuals en route from India to China, and would have disseminated not only their Hindu beliefs, but also their advanced irrigation and wet-rice cultivation methods.

One of Funan's major trading ports, **Oc Eo**, was located between Long Xuyen and Rach Gia. In common with other Funan cities, Oc Eo was ringed by a moat and consisted of wooden dwellings raised off the ground on piles. Given the discovery of Persian, Egyptian, Indian and Chinese artefacts (and even a gold coin depicting the Roman Emperor Marcus Aurelius) at Oc Eo sites, the port must have played host to a fair number of traders from around the world. To view **artefacts** from the site, visit the museums at Long Xuyen and Rach Gia, or the Fine Arts Museum in Ho Chi Minh City (see p.81).

The Funan Empire finally disappeared in the seventh century, when it was absorbed into the adjacent **Chen La** Empire.

INFORMATION AND GETTING AROUND

Tourist information The main office of An Giang Tourist is at 80e Tran Hung Dao (daily 7–11am & 1–5pm; ☎076 384 1036, ⓦangiangtourimex.com.vn); the staff are helpful with local information and can arrange home-stays on Tiger Island. **Getting around** Access to Tiger Island by ferry (1000đ, 2000đ with bike) is from the eastern end of Nguyen Hué.

ACCOMMODATION

Cuu Long 21 Nguyen Van Cung ☎076 394 1427, ⓔcuulonghotel@gmail.com. This recently renovated government hotel is Long Xuyen's best bet at the moment. Most rooms are spacious and bright with modern furnishings and tubs in the bathrooms, though the cheapest rooms have no windows. $20

Dong Xuyen 9a Luong Van Cu ☎076 394 2260, ⓔdongxuyenag@hcm.vnn.vn. The fanciest-looking place in town occupies almost an entire block and boasts sauna, jacuzzi and carpeted rooms with all facilities, though the service is rather sloppy. $22

Kim Anh Hotel 5–9 Thi Sach ☎076 394 2551, ⓔkimanh-hotel@hcm.vnn.vn. The *Kim Anh Hotel* is an eight-storey block in a central location with comfy rooms and a palatial suite on the top floor. Rooms are equipped with a/c, satellite TV, minibar and hair dryers. $20

Long Xuyen 19 Nguyen Van Cung ☎076 384 1927, ⓔlongxuyenhotel@hcm.vnn.vn. There are cheap, well-maintained rooms in this ageing, government-run place that's overdue a renovation. Advantages are friendly staff and the best restaurant in town on the premises. $15

Thai Binh 2 4–8 Nguyen Hué ☎076 384 1859, ☎076 384 6451. You'll find some of the cheapest rooms in town here (some with fan), but don't expect much in the way of service and try to avoid proximity to the karaoke rooms. $5

EATING

Hong Phat 242/4 Luong Van Cu. The smart *Hong Phat* has tasty Chinese and Vietnamese fish and meat dishes in a clean, brightly lit dining room. Try the ribs stewed with pepper ($2). Daily 9am–9pm.

Long Xuyen See above. The most reliable restaurant in town is at the *Long Xuyen* hotel, which serves tasty dishes such as shrimp fried with cauliflower (80,000đ) and steak and chips for just $2.50. Daily 6am–10pm.

Tien Com Huynh Loi 252/1 Nguyen Trai. *Tien Com Huynh Loi* has delicious, cheap, rice dishes and *bun bo Hué* ($2–3) served in clean surroundings, but there's no English menu. Daily 10am–10pm.

DIRECTORY

Airlines Vietnam Airlines' office (☎076 843 248) is located in the *Dong Xuyen* hotel, which also has an ATM.

Banks Vietinbank, just north of the *Long Xuyen* hotel on Luong Van Cu, can exchange money and also has an ATM.

Hospital The town's hospital is north of the centre on Le Loi.

Internet There is internet access at 81 Nguyen Hué, though the entrance is round the corner on Luong Van Cu.

Post office Long Xuyen's post office (daily 6am–10pm) is at 106 Tran Hung Dao, to the north of the centre.

Chau Doc

Since the opening of the border to Cambodia a few kilometres north of town, **CHAU DOC** has boomed in popularity, and is the only place apart from Can Tho where you are likely to see foreigners in any numbers. Snuggled against the west bank of the Hau Giang River, the town came under Cambodian rule until it was awarded to the Nguyen lords in the mid-eighteenth century for their help in putting down a localized rebellion. The area sustains a large Khmer community, which combines with local Cham and Chinese to form a diverse social melting pot. Just as diverse is Chau Doc's religious make-up: as well as Buddhists, Catholics and Muslims, the region supports an estimated 1.5 million devotees of the indigenous Hoa Hao religion (see box, w00). Forays by Pol Pot's genocidal Khmer Rouge into this corner of the delta led to the Vietnamese invasion of Cambodia in 1978.

On Doc Phu Thu and a few other streets in town, colonial relics are still evident, but their grand shophouse terraces, flaunting arched upper-floor windows and awnings propped up by decorous wrought-iron struts, are interspersed with characterless new edifices.

2

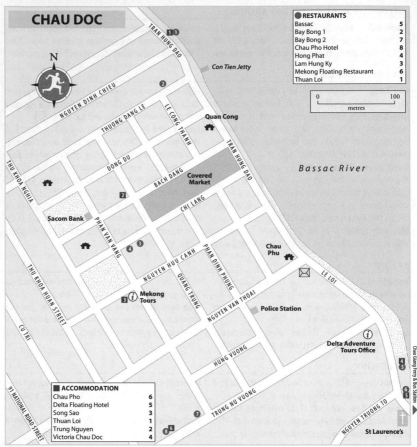

CHAU DOC

N

Con Tien Jetty

Bassac River

Quan Cong

Covered Market

Sacom Bank

Chau Phu

Mekong Tours

Police Station

Delta Adventure Tours Office

Chau Giang Ferry & Bus Station

St Laurence's

Sam Mountain

● RESTAURANTS	
Bassac	5
Bay Bong 1	2
Bay Bong 2	7
Chau Pho Hotel	8
Hong Phat	4
Lam Hung Ky	3
Mekong Floating Restaurant	6
Thuan Loi	1

0	100
metres	

▮ ACCOMMODATION	
Chau Pho	6
Delta Floating Hotel	5
Song Sao	3
Thuan Loi	1
Trung Nguyen	2
Victoria Chau Doc	4

The covered market and around

The obvious place to begin an exploration of Chau Doc is at its **covered market**, where the overspill of stalls and street vendors spreads from Quang Trung to Tran Hung Dao, and from Dong Du to Nguyen Van Thoai. This is one of the delta's biggest markets and is packed with a phenomenal range of produce, much of which is unfamiliar to Western eyes. Even if you have explored other markets in the region, it's well worth picking your way through the rows of neatly stacked stalls of fresh produce, household goods, fish and flowers.

To the east of the covered market, stalls are crammed into narrow alleyways that run towards the river, where you're greeted by a multitude of bobbing boats and waterside activities.

If you wander south by the river from here, you'll find a narrow park bordering the river that features a tall statue celebrating the local catfish and makes a pleasant place for a breezy stroll in the morning or evening.

Quan Cong Temple

A four-tiered gateway deep in the belly of the open market announces **Quan Cong Temple**. Beyond the courtyard, two rooftop dragons oversee its entrance and the outer walls' vivid murals. Inside the temple is the red visage of Quan Cong, sporting green robe and bejewelled crown, and surrounded by a sequin-studded red velvet canopy.

Chau Phu Temple
A few steps southeast through the covered market stalls along Tran Hung Dao, the lofty chambers of **Chau Phu Temple** offer a cool respite from the heat outside, and fans of gilt woodwork will find much to divert them. It was built in 1926 to honour Thoai Ngoc Hau (1761–1829), a local hero whose elaborate tomb is located at the base of Sam Mountain (see p.155).

2

St Laurence's Church
1km south of the tourist jetty, on the west side of Le Loi • Free

Built over the site of its previous namesake, the church was established by a French missionary in the late nineteenth century. A small statue of the saint stands in the garden, while a bust of him peers out from behind a glass panel set in the spire, and statues of two local Catholic martyrs oversee the courtyard.

ARRIVAL AND DEPARTURE   CHAU DOC

By Bus The bus station is roughly 3km southeast of town on Le Loi, from where xe om run into town (about 20,000đ). Destinations: Ca Mau (7hr); Can Tho (2hr 30min); Ha Tien (4hr); Ho Chi Minh City (6hr); Long Xuyen (1hr).

By ferry The tourist jetty where most boat tours leave from is immediately south of the *Victoria* Chau Doc hotel. Chau Giang is reached by a car ferry, which departs from the jetty opposite St Laurence's church on Le Loi.

THE HOA HAO RELIGION

Sited 20km east of Chau Doc, the diminutive village of Hoa Hao lent its name to a unique religious movement at the end of the 1930s. The **Hoa Hao Buddhist sect** was founded by the village's most famous son, Huynh Phu So. A sickly child, Huynh was placed in the care of a hermitic monk under whom he explored both conventional Buddhism and more arcane spiritual disciplines. In 1939, at the age of 20, a new brand of Buddhism was revealed to him in a trance. Upon waking, Huynh found he was cured of his congenital illness, and began publicly to expound his breakaway theories, which advocated purging worship of all the clutter of votives, priests and pagodas, and paring it down to simple unmediated communication between the individual and the Supreme Being. The faith has a fairly strong **ascetic** element, with alcohol, drugs and gambling all discouraged. Peasants were drawn to the simplicity of the sect, and by rumours that Huynh was a faith healer in possession of prophetic powers.

Almost immediately, the Hoa Hao developed a **political agenda**, and established a **militia** to uphold its fervently nationalist, anti-French and anti-Communist beliefs. The Japanese army of occupation, happy to keep the puppet French administration it had allowed to remain nominally in charge of Vietnam on its toes, provided the sect with arms. For themselves, the French regarded the Hoa Hao with suspicion: Huynh they labelled the "Mad Monk", imprisoning him in 1941 and subsequently confining him to a psychiatric hospital – where he promptly converted his doctor. By the time of his eventual release in 1945, the sect's uneasy alliance with the Viet Minh, which had been forged during World War II in recognition of their common anti-colonial objectives, was souring, and two years later Viet Minh agents assassinated him. The sect battled on until the mid-Fifties when **Diem's purge** of dissident groups took hold; its guerrilla commander, Ba Cut, was captured and beheaded in 1956, and by the end of the decade most members had been driven underground. Though in the early Sixties some of these resurfaced in the Viet Cong, the Hoa Hao never regained its early dynamism, and any lingering military or political presence was erased by the Communists after 1975.

Today there are thought to be somewhere around two million Hoa Hao worshippers in Vietnam, concentrated mostly around Chau Doc and Long Xuyen. Some male devotees still sport the distinctive long beards and hair tied in a bun that traditionally distinguished a Hoa Hao adherent.

2

Destinations: Chau Giang (every 10min); Phnom Penh (daily; 4hr).

By minibus Mekong Tours (☎076 386 8222, ⊛mekongvietnam.com), 14 Nguyen Huu Canh, and Delta

Adventure (☎076 358 4222, ⊛deltaadventure.info) at 53 Le Loi sell minibus tickets, as does the tour desk at *Vinh Phuoc* hotel.

Destinations: Can Tho ($6); Ho Chi Minh City ($10).

INFORMATION AND TOURS

Tourist information The state-run An Giang Tourist does not have an office in Chau Doc, but most hotel and guesthouse owners can help out with local information, as well as arrange local excursions and onward travel, including boat services to and from Phnom Penh. The tour desk at *Vinh Phuoc* hotel is another good source of local information.

Tours Both Mekong Tours (☎076 386 8222, ⊛mekongvietnam.com), 14 Nguyen Huu Canh, and Delta

Adventure (☎076 358 4222, ⊛deltaadventure.info) at 53 Le Loi offer half-day trips to the local floating market, a fish farm and Cham village (about $12/person), and day-trips to Tup Duc (about $25/person). To get to Tra Su, Tup Duc and Ba Chuc, either join a tour with one of the companies mentioned above, or rent a motorbike and be prepared to get lost a few times before arriving at your destination, as road signs are few and far between.

ACCOMMODATION

★ **Chau Pho** 88 Trung Nu Vuong ☎076 356 4139, ⊛chauphohotel.com. Spacious, well-maintained rooms with expansive views from the upper floors make this the best mid-range option in town, though it is several blocks from the riverside action. It also has tennis courts and a classy restaurant. $30

Delta Floating Hotel Just south of the tourist jetty, ☎076 356 3810, ⊛deltaadventure.info. Basic rooms over the river (fixed, in fact, not floating), all with en-suite bathrooms and a ringside view of the action on the water. Check the room first as some are a bit musty and the noise from the restaurant upstairs can filter down. $15

Song Sao 12–13 Nguyen Huu Canh ☎076 356 1777. Smart but compact rooms, all fully equipped with hot water, a/c and so on, with front rooms overlooking a square. Staff are keen to help but have limited English. Its central location is probably its biggest pull. $12

Thuan Loi 275 Tran Hung Dao ☎076 386 6134. This riverside mini-hotel near the market offers some of the best value in town. Both fan and a/c rooms are clean and comfortable (try to get one overlooking the river), and the wooden restaurant over the water affords a great front-seat view of the Mekong. $10

Trung Nguyen 86 Bach Dang ☎076 356 1561, ⊛trungnguyenhotel.com.vn. Very smart mini-hotel, right in the town centre, with fifteen smallish but well-furnished rooms, all with small balconies. Staff are very helpful and efficient, and they rent out bicycles and motorbikes ($2 and $8 per day respectively) too. $15

Victoria Chau Doc 1 Le Loi ☎076 386 5010, ⊛victoriahotels-asia.com. Just 300m southeast of the town centre, this colonial-style hotel lords it over the river. The rooms are tastefully furnished with *Indochine* elegance and some have glorious river views. $185

EATING

Chau Doc has more places to **eat** than most Mekong Delta towns, catering to diners looking for something tasty and cheap as well as those looking for some ambience. A snack at one of the food stalls around the market, particularly on Tran Hung Dao, Chi Lang and Le Cong Thanh, is a good option if you're feeling adventurous.

Bassac Victoria Chau Doc, 1 Le Loi. Imaginative Western and Asian dishes, such as rack of lamb and roasted duck breast, served in a romantic riverside dining terrace overlooking the Mekong, with dishes averaging around $12–15. There's also an attractive adjoining bar with pool table and backgammon, ideal for a sundowner. Daily 11am–2pm & 6–10pm.

Bay Bong 1 22 Thuong Dang Le. This place looks like any other hole-in-the-wall eatery with plastic stools and tables, but the food is wonderfully prepared. The speciality is catfish in clay pot. Mains $2–4. Daily 7am–9pm.

★ **Bay Bong** 2 Trung Na Vuong. Bay Bong 1 was so popular among both locals and visitors that the owners have now opened a smart second branch, using china

instead of plastic plates, and it has an a/c room too. Everything is good, including the sour fish soup. Mains $2–4. Daily 7am–9pm.

Chau Pho Hotel 88 Trung Nu Vuong. This smart, ground-floor dining area may lack riverside views, but the food, mostly Vietnamese with a few Western options, is excellent and the service is very attentive. Main dishes $6–15. Daily 7am–9pm.

Hong Phat 77 Chi Lang. Above-average rice and noodle shop with an English menu, a stone's throw from the market and usually busy, serving Vietnamese staples such as shrimp in spicy sauce ($3.50). Daily 8am–8pm.

Lam Hung Ky 71 Chi Lang. Friendly, family-run eatery opposite the market, whose imaginative

Chinese-influenced menu features beef with bitter melon and black beans; a full meal, including a beer, will come to around $3. Daily 8am–8pm.

Mekong Floating Restaurant Just south of the tourist jetty on Le Loi. Located on the riverbank above the Floating Hotel operated by Delta Adventure, this place is popular among backpackers for its cheap prices and wide choice of dishes. Mains $2–5. Daily 7am–10pm.

Thuan Loi 275 Tran Hung Dao. Enjoy the riverside action at this guesthouse restaurant and choose from a huge range of dishes, most of which cost around $2–3. Sometimes gets busy with tour groups. Daily 7am–10pm.

DIRECTORY

Banks Sacombank, 88 Dong Du, can exchange foreign currency and travellers' cheques, and also has an ATM.

Bicycle and motorbike rental Available at *Trung Nguyen* hotel ($2 & $8 per day respectively).

Hospital Opposite the *Victoria Chau Doc* on Le Loi.

Pharmacy 14 Nguyen Huu Canh.

Post office and internet On the corner of Le Loi and Nguyen Van Thoai (daily 6am–10pm); it also has internet access.

Around Chau Doc

There are several places of interest to visit in the area **around Chau Doc**, including a **Cham community** and the brooding **Sam Mountain** with its kitsch pagodas. Further afield are a bird sanctuary, a battlefield from the American War and the scene of a Khmer Rouge massacre. If you're making the journey up to Chau Doc from Long Xuyen on Highway 91, look out for the **incense factories**, where the sticks are spread out to dry along the roadside, often arranged in photogenic circles.

Chau Doc Floating Market

Opposite the tourist jetty on the Bassac River • Any boatman will row you there for a small fee

Since this floating market was only established recently, you have to wonder whether it's more for the benefit of tourists than locals. Nevertheless, if you've managed to get this far through the delta without visiting any of the other floating markets along the way, it's certainly worth a look. As usual, boats advertise their products by hanging a sample from a stick on the deck.

Con Tien Island and Chau Giang District

Two settlements a stone's throw away from Chau Doc across the Hau Giang River are worth venturing out to, and most people visit both on a half-day **tour** (see opposite). One is the cluster of **fish-farm houses** floating on the river next to **Con Tien Island**, above cages of catfish that are fed through a hatch in the floor. Fish farming is big business in the delta, and some of these cages can be over 1000 cubic metres in size.

The other settlement is a **Cham community** in **Chau Giang District**, which you can visit independently via a ferry from a jetty south of the tourist jetty on Le Loi. Here you'll discover kampung-style wooden houses, sarongs and white prayer caps that betray the influence of Islam, as do the twin domes and pretty white minaret of the **Mubarak Mosque**.

Sam Mountain

Arid, brooding **Sam Mountain** rises dramatically from an ocean of paddy fields. It's known as *Nui Sam* to Vietnamese tourists, who flock here in their thousands to worship at its clutch of pagodas and shrines. Even if the temples don't appeal, the journey up the hill is good fun. As you climb, you'll pass massive boulders that seem embedded in the hillside, as well as some plaster statues of rhinos, elephants, zebras and a Tyrannosaurus rex near the top. From the top, the **view** of the surrounding, pancake-flat terrain is breathtaking, though the hill is, in fact, only 230m high. In the rainy season, the view is particularly spectacular, with lush paddy fields scored by hundreds of waterways, though in the dry season the barren landscape is hazy and less inspiring. There's a tiny military outpost at the summit, from which you can gaze into Cambodia on one side, Chau Doc on the other.

2

Tay An Pagoda

At the foot of Sam Mountain the first pagoda you'll see is kitsch, 1847-built **Tay An Pagoda**, the pick of the bunch, its frontage awash with portrait photographers, beggars, incense-stick vendors and bird-sellers (releasing one from captivity accrues merit, though some clever vendors train the birds to fly back later). Guarding the pagoda are two elephants, one black, one white, and a shaven-headed Quan Am Thi Kinh. The number of gaudy statues inside exceeds two hundred: most are of deities and Buddhas, but an alarmingly lifelike rendering of an honoured monk sits at one of the highly varnished tables in the rear chamber. To the right of this room an annexe houses a goddess with a thousand eyes and a thousand hands, on whose mound of heads teeters a tiny Quan Am.

Chua Xu Temple

Fifty metres west of Tay An, **Chua Xu Temple** honours Her Holiness Lady of the Country, a stone statue said to have been found on Sam's slopes in the early nineteenth century, though the present building, with its four-tiered, glazed green-tile roof, dates only from 1972. Inside, the Lady sits in state in a marbled chamber, resplendent in colourful gown and headdress. Glass cases in corridors either side of her are crammed to bursting with splendid garb and other offerings from worshippers, who flood here between the 23rd and 25th of the fourth lunar month, to see her ceremonially bathed and dressed. Shops in front of the temple sell colourful baskets of fruit that locals buy to offer to Her Holiness.

Chua Hang

A few hundred metres west and then south around the base of Sam Mountain, the multi-storey **Chua Hang** (Cave Pagoda), is a popular stopping-off point for local tourists, although the tiny grotto after which the pagoda is named is rather a let-down after the sweaty ascent.

Tra Su Bird Sanctuary

Just north of Chi Lang on Highway 948

Beyond Sam Mountain, the varied attractions at Tra Su, Tup Duc and Ba Chuc could all be covered in a busy day's travelling, though this remote area is not a place for hurrying. This bird sanctuary is located about 23km from Chau Doc and consists of a protected forest of cajuput trees and wetlands that attract a great variety of birds including storks, egrets, cormorants, peafowl and water cocks. A boat ride around the sanctuary combined with a walk to a viewing tower takes a couple of hours and costs around $7 per person depending on how many in the group. Even if you're not a dedicated birder, you'd probably enjoy floating around this watery wonderland with its huge lily pads and moss-shrouded trees.

Tup Duc

50km southwest of Chau Doc, near Tri Ton • Daily 7.30am–5pm • 12,000₫ • Museum daily 7.30–11am & 1–5pm

During the American war, **Tup Duc** gained the rather ignominious moniker "Two Million Dollar Hill", a reference to the amount the US military is said to have spent trying to dislodge the Viet Cong from its slopes.

Now the Vietnamese government has ploughed in money of its own in an attempt to turn it into a **tourist resort**, by installing pedal boats on a lake, an ostrich-breeding farm, a flower garden, a shooting range, a restaurant and refreshment kiosks at the foot of the hill. There is also a small museum here, an electronic mock-up of the battle and dummies in a cave on the hill, re-creating a Viet Cong briefing scene. Kids will probably latch onto you and lead you up a stairway past the huge boulders that provided such effective cover to the Viet Cong. Squeezing through the narrow passageways formed by the jumble of boulders, it is easy to see how it made such a perfect hide-out.

Ba Chuc

40km southwest of Chau Doc • Take Highway 91 and then Highway N1 along the border towards Ha Tien and turn sou[ ] for the last few kilometres

Both Tup Duc and Ba Chuc are located in a sweep of staggeringly beau[ ] countryside southwest of Chau Doc, though their significance is far from pe[ ] Refugees fleeing Pol Pot's Cambodia boosted the Khmer population here in the late 1970s, and pursuit by the Khmer Rouge ended in numerous indiscriminate massacres; a grisly **memorial** to the worst of these, at the village of Ba Chuc, stands as testament to that horrific era.

Ba Chuc Memorial and Phi Lai Pagoda

The **memorial** in the centre of the village pays homage to to the 3157 villagers massacred, most of them clubbed to death, in two weeks in April 1978. Only two villagers survived the tragedy. An unattractive concrete canopy fails to lessen the impact of the eight-sided memorial: behind its glass enclosure, the bleached skulls of the dead of Vietnam's own "killing fields" are piled in ghoulish heaps, grouped according to age to highlight the youth and innocence of many of the dead.

Many of the victims were killed in the adjacent **Phi Lai Pagoda**, where bloodstains on the walls and floor can still be easily seen. A signboard in Vietnamese beside a tiny door below the altar notes that forty villagers perished here when a grenade was thrown into the cramped space.

Between the memorial and the pagoda is a small room, where a horrific set of black-and-white photos taken just after the massacre shows buckled, abused corpses scattered around the countryside. Some of the images on display are extremely disturbing and you should not enter if you are a sensitive type. There are also a few cafés and food stalls set up to cater to visitors to the site.

Ha Tien

Of all Delta towns, **HA TIEN**, at the extreme northwest on the border with Cambodia, has been changing the fastest in recent years: where once it received only a trickle of visitors, it now buzzes with Western travellers. Two major factors have caused this: first, the **opening of the border** to foreigners at Xa Xia, just north of Ha Tien, meaning that it's now possible to head directly to Cambodia's coastal towns of Kep and Sihanoukville without passing through Phnom Penh; and the second factor is the beginning of **hydrofoil services to Phu Quoc**, offering a shorter and cheaper route to the island than from Rach Gia. Thus this town, which until recently had an end-of-the-line feel, is coming to terms with its newfound popularity.

A BRIEF HISTORY OF HA TIEN

Founded by Chinese immigrant **Mac Cuu** in 1674, with the permission of the local Cambodian lords, **Ha Tien** thrived thanks to its position facing the Gulf of Thailand and astride the trade route between India and China. By the close of the seventeenth century, Siam (later Thailand) had begun to eye the settlement covetously, and Mac Cuu was forced to petition Hué for support. The resulting alliance, forged with Emperor Minh Vuong in 1708, ensured Vietnamese military backup, and the town continued to prosper. Mac Cuu died in 1735, but the familial fiefdom continued for seven generations, until the French took over in 1867. Subsequently, the town became a resistance flash-point, with Viet Minh holing up in the surrounding hills, and even sniping at French troops from the **To Chau Mountain**, to the south.

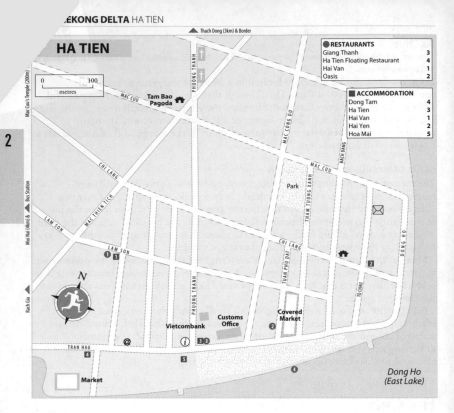

HA TIEN

● RESTAURANTS	
Giang Thanh	3
Ha Tien Floating Restaurant	4
Hai Van	1
Oasis	2

■ ACCOMMODATION	
Dong Tam	4
Ha Tien	3
Hai Van	1
Hai Yen	2
Hoa Mai	5

The riverside park

Central Ha Tien still has a few quaint, shuttered, colonial buildings in its backstreets, though the original **market**, now moved west along the riverbank, has been razed to make way for a new **riverside park**. The former pontoon bridge that made the corner of Tran Hau and Dong Ho a busy area has also been removed, leaving the only access to town via the huge bridge to the southwest of town. The riverside is now an enjoyable place to stroll, watching fishing boats unloading on the opposite bank, and by following Tran Hau eastwards and then continuing north on Dong Ho, you can enjoy pleasant views and often an agreeable breeze blowing off the so-called East Lake (Dong Ho). In fact, it is not a lake but a large inlet where the To Chau River flows out to the sea.

The temple dedicated to Mac Cuu

Take a walk up Mac Thien Tich and west along Mac Cuu to where the temple stands at the foot of the hill where he and his relatives lie buried in semicircular Chinese graves. Inside the temple, electric "incense" sticks glow constantly before Mac Cuu's funerary tablet, keeping the memory of Ha Tien's founding father alive. Mac Cuu's actual **grave** is uppermost on the hill, guarded by two swordsmen, a white tiger and a blue dragon. From this vantage point, there are good views from the hill over the mop-tops of the coconut trees below and down to the sea.

Tam Bao Pagoda

At the junction of Mac Thien Tich and Phuong Thanh

The colourful **Tam Bao Pagoda** is set in tree-lined grounds dominated by an attractive lotus pond, a huge statue of Quan Am and a large reclining Buddha. Out the back of the pagoda, said to have been founded by Mac Cuu himself, is a pretty garden tended by the resident nuns, its colourful flowers interspersed with tombs. In the rear chamber of the pagoda, a statue of the goddess with a thousand hands and a thousand eyes sits on a lurid pink lotus, while behind her are photos and funerary tablets remembering the local dead.

2

ARRIVAL AND DEPARTURE
HA TIEN

By bus Buses terminate at the new bus station on Highway 80 a couple of kilometres north of town and just a few kilometres from the Cambodian border post at Xa Xia: to get into town from here take a xe om (about 15,000đ). Destinations: Can Tho (5hr); Chau Doc (4hr); Ho Chi Minh City (8hr); Long Xuyen (6hr); Rach Gia (2hr 30min).

By boat Hydrofoils to and from Ham Ninh on Phu Quoc's east coast (1hr 30min) dock on the south bank of the To Chau River, and tickets (230,000đ) can be bought at any hotel.

GETTING AROUND

Getting around Though nowhere officially rents vehicles, most hotels can help out. Rates should be around $2.50 for a bike and $8 for a motorbike. Failing that, hire the services of a xe om (about 200,000đ for a half-day trip).

THE MUI NAI LOOP

A pleasant half or full day can be spent exploring the countryside around Ha Tien, with a convenient circular route northwest of town meaning you won't need to backtrack. This makes an ideal bike ride when the weather is good.

Strike off west along Lam Son. At the end of the road, turn left and continue straight at a small roundabout. A **war cemetery** serves as a landmark on the right 2.5km from town, and where the road forks, branch left, signposted Nui Den (lighthouse). Follow this road to the coast and along a winding stretch of road with some beautiful views until you reach the entrance to Mui Nai beach (5000đ per person, 1000đ per bike).

A pleasant – if not idyllic – four-hundred-metre curve of sand, shaded by coconut palms and backed by lush green hills, **Mui Nai beach** offers reasonable swimming in clean, shallow waters. The beach is very popular among Vietnamese, and there are several resorts here, though they're all overpriced and poorly maintained. The best of the bunch is the *Hong Phat* (❶077 395 1661; 400,000đ), with reasonable air-conditioned rooms and a restaurant too.

There are a few other restaurants and beachside cafés, so you can kick back and crack open a few crabs while enjoying a fresh coconut juice or a refreshing slice of watermelon.

Leave the beach at the far end and turn left on to the coast road, weaving your way between rice fields, shrimp farms, water buffalo wallowing in ponds and signs reading 'Frontier Area'. You'll see the 48m-high granite outcrop housing **Thach Dong**, or Stone Cave, long before you reach it; 3–4km past Mui Nai the road reaches a junction, where a left turn leads to the Cambodian border.

Turn right at this junction and very shortly the road passes a cluster of food stalls that mark the entrance to Thach Dong (daily 6.30am–6pm; 5000đ per person, 1000đ per bike). A **monument** shaped like a defiant clenched fist stands as a memorial to 130 people killed by Khmer Rouge forces near here in 1978. Beyond this, steps lead up to a **cave pagoda** that's home to a colony of bats. Its shrines to Quan Am and Buddha are unremarkable, but balconies hewn from the side of the rock afford great views over the hills, paddy fields and sea below. Look to your right and you're peering into Cambodia.

From here, continue along the circular road that will bring you after a few kilometres back into Ha Tien.

2

INFORMATION

Tourist information There's a new tourist office at 1 Phuong Thanh (☏077 395 9598), though as yet they seem more interested in selling bus tickets and breakfasts than giving sound travel advice. It's best to rely on staff at your hotel for local information.

ACCOMMODATION

As part of Ha Tien's construction boom, several **new hotels** have opened recently, giving visitors plenty of options. Many are clustered around the market, and although they are mostly geared to Vietnamese guests, they drop their rates radically in the off-season (May–Oct).

Dong Tam 83 Tran Hau ☏077 395 0555. This smart new place, also known as Du Hung 2, has a variety of rooms, all with a/c, cable TV and wi-fi, and the enthusiastic staff can help with travel plans. Bikes and motorbikes for rent too. $15

Ha Tien 36 Tran Hau ☏077 385 1563. The plush, carpeted rooms here are the smartest in town and the place is tastefully designed, but ask to see the room first as some are a bit dingy. $20

Hai Van 55 Lam Son ☏077 385 2872. This long-established hotel has simple but clean rooms in the old wing as well as smart a/c rooms in a new wing, with friendly staff. They have some large suites that are a steal at 250,000đ. $8

Hai Yen 15 To Chau ☏077 385 1580. An efficiently run place with helpful and informative staff. The bright, decent-sized rooms are good value and those on the upper floors have good views of Dong Ho. $13

Hoa Mai 1–3 Tran Hau ☏077 385 0849. One of the best budget options in town, this place has a range of well-maintained rooms, some with good river views, in a central location. $7

EATING AND DRINKING

In the evening, a **night market** sets up along Tran Hau, some stalls selling souvenirs and others selling seafood, attracting crowds of locals and visitors alike.

Da Ha Tien Floating Restaurant On the riverbank in front of the covered market. This is the real deal – a wooden vessel full of character; friendly, helpful waiters; and a menu of traditional Vietnamese and popular Western dishes such as beefsteak ($2.50) and spaghetti with seafood ($3). Best of all, the kitchen is up to scratch, and everything tastes great. Daily 6am–10pm.

Giang Thanh In front of the Ha Tien Hotel, Tran Hau. For something a little classy, the *Giang Thanh* serves Vietnamese, Chinese and Western dishes in a traditional, open-sided building. It's a popular spot for locals to dine and looks over the riverside promenade. Mains $3–10. Daily 6am–10pm.

Hai Van 57 Lam Son. The long-standing *Hai Van* is a good choice for eating, even though they've been squeezed out of their former riverside location and pushed into the backstreets. Now next door to (and run by) the hotel of the same name, it serves up decent Western breakfasts and an extensive menu of Vietnamese dishes. Mains $2.50–10. Daily 6am–10pm.

Oasis 42 Tuan Phu Dat. If you're looking for nightlife in Ha Tien, nothing can compare with *Oasis*, largely because there's no competition. This Western-run bar serves beer and cocktails, though no food at the time of our visit. Closes early when it's quiet – sometimes around 9pm. Daily noon–midnight.

DIRECTORY

Banks The Vietcombank at 4 Phuong Thanh can exchange cash or travellers' cheques, and also has an ATM.

Internet The post office has internet access, as does the shop at 54 Tran Hau.

Post office The post office (daily 6.30am–9pm) is on To Chau, a short walk north of the river.

Visas If you're heading onto Cambodia, visas are available at the border at Xa Xia ($25), but it's better to get one in Ho Chi Minh City to avoid any overcharging, which is a common occurrence.

Hon Chong Peninsula

Just 30km south of Ha Tien lies the **Hon Chong Peninsula**. A string of offshore isles has earned this region the moniker "mini-Ha Long", but it's as a coastal resort that it draws throngs of Vietnamese and a smattering of foreigners. The approach to the peninsula is blighted by unsightly cement factories belching out clouds of smoke, and while Hon

2

BOAT TRIPS AROUND THE ISLANDS

For a small fee (15,000đ) you can join a 45-minute boat tour out to Hon Phu Tu and the nearby **Hang Tien Grotto**, which has some attractive stalactites and stalagmites. Nguyen Anh (later to become Gia Long) hid here while on the run after the Tay Son Rebellion, and locals have dubbed its stone plateaux as his throne, sofa, bed and so on. If there's no one else around, you can rent the entire boat for about 300,000đ for this short trip.

For a more luxurious boat trip around local islands, the *Hon Trem Resort* (see below) can organize a full day-trip, including fishing and lunch as well as a visit to **Nghe Island** and the **Ba Lua Archipelago**, for about $150 per person. It may also be worth speaking to Hung at *Tan Phat* restaurant (☎016 6735 8168) as they have boats for rent and are sometimes amenable to negotiating the price, so it should work out cheaper than a day out with the *Hon Trem Resort*.

Chong has yet to suffer any significant environmental degradation as a result of these factories, their ugly presence looms over the area and certainly detracts from its appeal. For the moment, Hon Chong's calm waters and beaches fringed with palms and casuarinas remain among the most attractive in the delta, though they cannot compare with the beaches on Phu Quoc.

The beaches

Admission to Bai Duong 5000đ

The sweep of **beach** in front of most of the resorts on the peninsula is fine for sunbathing and enjoys a decidedly unspoilt feel with few signs of tourist trappings, but is too shallow and spongy for swimming. Things are better nearer the *Hon Trem Resort* (see below), though the most picturesque beach is **Bai Duong**, named after the casuarina trees that line its sands. After passing pandanus, tamarind and sugar-palm trees, the coastal track ends at a towering cliff, in front of which stands **Sea and Mountain Pagoda** ("Chua Hai Son") and a cluster of souvenir and food stalls. Go into the temple grounds, and look for an opening in the rock that leads into **Cave Pagoda** ("Chua Hong"). A low doorway leads from its outer chamber to a grotto in the cliff's belly, where statues of Quan Am and several Buddhas are lit by coloured lights. The cramped stone corridor that runs on from here makes as romantic an approach to a beach as you could imagine, though the stench of the resident bats somewhat spoils the atmosphere.

As you hit the sand of Duong Beach, the rugged rocks out to sea in front of you constitute **Father and Son Isle** ("Hon Phu Tu"), though it is now rather a misnomer as "Father", the bigger of the two pillars of rock, fell crashing in to the sea in 2006 (unfortunately, Kien Giang Tourism, who use these islands for their logo, have yet to come up with an alternative). The beach here is reasonably attractive, though still too shallow for swimming.

ARRIVAL AND DEPARTURE   HON CHONG

By bus Irregular buses ply the route between Hon Chong and Rach Gia (about 30,000đ). Coming from Ha Tien, you'll have to take a Rach Gia-bound bus and get off at Ba Hon, then take a xe om (about 60,000đ) the last few kilometres.

ACCOMMODATION

An Hai Son Binh An Village ☎077 375 9226. Located in the centre of Hon Chong Bay facing the sea, this place is well-managed and has smart rooms with a/c, TVs and fridges, as well as decent restaurants. There are also tennis courts and free bicycles for guests' use. **$17**
Green Hill Guesthouse 905 Road 11 ☎077 385 4369. Perched on the hillside at the north end of the beach, this family-run hotel lives up to its billing, its handful of beautifully furnished rooms all commanding sweeping views of the bay and representing a good deal. **$17**
★ **Hon Trem Resort** Binh An Village ☎077 385 4331. The *Hon Trem Resort* boasts a prime location with all its compact villas enjoying great views from a steep hillside, as well as spacious rooms in a new block that are extremely

comfortable and well equipped. Add a gorgeous swimming pool, great beach views and the two best dining options on the peninsula, and you've got the best spot to lay your head. $35

EATING

Hon Trem Resort ☎ 077 385 4331. Even if you choose not to stay here, it's worth visiting the *Hon Trem Resort*'s smart restaurant on top of the hill, both for its fantastic view of the islands in the bay and for its wide range of dishes priced at $3–5 each. Daily 7am–9pm.

Tan Phat At the southern end of Binh An Village, about half a kilometre north of the Green Hill Guesthouse. For straightforward fare, this simple eatery serves up tasty seafood dishes as well spaghetti and steak and chips on a deck overlooking a fishing harbour. Mains around $4. Daily 6am–11pm.

Rach Gia

About 100km southwest of Ha Tien, though also easily accessible from Long Xuyen, Can Tho or Ca Mau, the thriving port of **RACH GIA** teeters precariously over the Gulf of Thailand. The capital of Kien Giang Province, it's home to a community of around two hundred thousand people, many of whom live in new housing on reclaimed land on the coast just south of the centre. A small islet in the mouth of

RACH GIA

Police Station

NGUYEN CONG TRU

Vietcombank

🏴 1, 🏴 2, ▲ & Bus Station

TRAN PHU

Cai Lon River

NTT Temple, Phu Quoc & Jetty

BACH DANG

THANH THAI

N

Nguyen Trung
Truc Statue

PHAN CHU TRINH

3

NGUYEN DU

HAM NGHI

HUYNH TINH CUA

TRAN PHU

(i) Kien Giang
Tourist

NGUYEN HUNG SON

LY TU TRONG

HUNG VUONG

NGUYEN HUNG SON

4

TRAN PHU

0   50
metres

Museum

NGUYEN VAN TROI

LE LOI

2

NGUYEN TRUNG TRUC

TRAN HUNG DAO

NGUYEN THAI HOC

Cai Lon River

Riverside
Cafés

■ ACCOMMODATION	
Hong Nam	2
Hong Yen	1
Kim Co	4
Sealight	5
Wild Rose	3

● RESTAURANTS	
Hai Au	3
Tay Ho	1
Vinh Hong	2

🏴 3, 🏴 5, Airport & Rach Soi (7km) ▼

Ben Tau Rach Meo (Quay) & Rach Soi (7km) ▼

THE HEROICS OF NGUYEN TRUNG TRUC

From 1861 to 1868, **Nguyen Trung Truc** spearheaded anti-French guerrilla activities in the western region of the delta: statues in the centre of Rach Gia and at the temple dedicated to him depict him preparing to unsheathe his sword and harvest a French head. In 1861, he masterminded the attack that culminated in the firing of the French warship *Esperance*; as a wanted man, he was forced to retreat to Phu Quoc, from where he continued to oversee the campaign. Only after the French took his mother hostage in 1868 did he turn himself in and in October of the same year he was executed by a firing squad in the centre of Rach Gia. Defiant to the last, his final words could have been lifted from a Ho Chi Minh speech: "So long as grass still grows on the soil of this land, people will continue to resist the invaders."

2

the Cai Lon River forms the hub of the town, but the urban sprawl spills over bridges to the north and south of it and onto the mainland. The town has little in the way of historical and cultural attractions, and for most foreign visitors it is simply a place to overnight en route to Phu Quoc Island.

It's worth taking a walk along **Bach Dang** or **Tran Hung Dao** to watch the activity on the boats of all sizes that clutter the port. Men and women darn and fold nets, charcoal-sellers hawk their wares to ships' captains and roadside cafés heave with fishermen – many of whom have seen the bottoms of a few beer bottles – awaiting the next tide.

The museum

27 Nguyen Van Troi • Mon–Fri 7.30–11am & 1.30–5pm • Free

Rach Gia's museum is the single worthwhile sight in the town centre, and even that probably won't distract you for more than half an hour. It's housed in a recently renovated colonial house that displays wartime photos and souvenirs, along with relics from nearby Oc Eo – shards of pottery, coins and bones, and the skeleton of a whale in a mesh-fronted shed to the right of the main building.

Nguyen Trung Truc Temple

18 Nguyen Cong Tru

Of Rach Gia's handful of pagodas, only the **Nguyen Trung Truc Temple** is really worth making an effort to see. It's also conveniently located right next to the jetty from which hydrofoils leave for Phu Quoc, so if you arrive early, you can take a quick look before leaving town.

In front of the temple is a statue of local hero **Nguyen Trung Truc** (see box above) drawing his sword. Inside, a portrait of Nguyen in black robe and hat provides the main chamber with its centrepiece. Up at the main altar, a brass urn labelled "Anh hung dan toc Nguyen Trung Truc" and flanked by slender storks standing on turtles, is said to hold the **ashes** of Nguyen Trung Truc himself.

ARRIVAL AND DEPARTURE	RACH GIA

By plane Arriving at the airport, it's a 7km taxi ride into town (about 80,000đ). If you're heading to Phu Quoc, it's worth considering the daily flight (8.15am; about $40), which saves the journey from the jetty at Vong Beach to the west coast beaches, as well as a bumpy crossing when the weather is rough. The same flight continues to Ho Chi Minh City ($60). For tickets or information, contact Vietnam Airlines at 16 Nguyen Trung Truc (☎ 077 392 4320).

By bus Buses to and from points north (such as Ha Tien and Hon Chong) pull up at Rach Gia's local bus station on Nguyen Binh Kiem, 500m north of the town centre; a taxi or xe om into town should cost no more than 20,000đ. Arrivals and departures from other destinations use the bigger bus terminal at Rach Soi, 7km southeast of Rach Gia; a taxi or xe om either way costs around 50,000–80,000đ.

By boat Arriving and departing boats use one of two piers. Several companies operate express boats to and from Phu Quoc Island (see below), at around 8am and 1pm (2hr 30min; around $15) from Phu Quoc quay, 200m west of the Nguyen Trung Truc Temple. It's better to buy a ticket for the speedboat in advance; the Superdong office at 14 Tu Do (☎077 387 7742, ☎077 387 7741) is just round the corner from the pier. From Rach Meo quay, 5km south of town on Ngo Quyen, express boats and regular boats leave for and arrive from Ca Mau and other destinations in the delta.

Destinations: Ca Mau (daily; 3hr); Phu Quoc (several daily; 2hr 30min).

INFORMATION

Tourist information Kien Giang Tourist at 11 Ly Tu Trong (7.30–11.30am & 1–5pm; ☎077 396 2024) is nowadays perhaps the least helpful of all provincial tourist offices in the delta, so you'll need to rely on your hotel for local information.

ACCOMMODATION

As far as accommodation goes, there's nowhere outstanding, but few people spend more than a night here but it is a useful stop on the way to or from Phu Quoc Island.

Hong Nam Block B1, Ly Thai To ☎077 387 3090. Near the bus station, this place has clean, tiled rooms with cable TV and wi-fi, though it's a bit tricky to find and many rooms have a restricted view, so look at a few rooms before choosing. $̲1̲0̲
Hong Yen 259–261 Mac Cuu ☎077 387 9095. A kilometre north of the centre, this hotel has an inconvenient location but it makes up for it with spacious rooms equipped with desks and bathtubs, free wi-fi and the friendliest staff in town. $̲8̲
Kim Co 141 Nguyen Hung Son ☎077 387 9610. The centrally located *Kim Co* is probably the most convenient option, and the brightly painted, good-sized rooms come with cable TV and wi-fi. $̲1̲3̲

Sealight A11, 3 Thang 2 ☎077 625 5777, ⓦsealighthotel.vn. Towering nineteen storeys over the Rach Gia coastline, this glitzy hotel looks sadly misplaced. Just where they plan to find enough guests to fill its 93 smallish and over-priced rooms is a mystery, but if you need comfort at any cost, here's your spot. $̲3̲3̲
Wild Rose (Tam Xuan) 19 Tran Quang Dieu ☎077 392 0325. Overlooking the northern branch of the Cai Lon River, this place is worth considering for its well-equipped and attractively furnished rooms. You could even splash out $20 for the enormous 3-bed room and have enough room to throw a party. $̲1̲0̲

EATING

Hai Au 2 Nguyen Trung Truc. This is probably the best of the seafood options, serving steamboat and fish specialities in a prime open-terraced riverside location, just across the bridge to the southeast of town. Prices are a bit steep ($3–8 for main courses), but the quality is good and service is attentive. Daily 6am–10pm.
Tay Ho 6 Nguyen Du. This no-frills eatery has an English menu and is popular with locals, serving a variety of traditional Vietnamese dishes. It's down a little sidestreet east of the park and makes a good lunch stop if you're exploring the town. Mains around $4. Daily 10am–9pm.
Vinh Hong 31 Tran Hung Dao. This seafood restaurant faces the southern branch of the Cai Lon River and your options for dinner eye you warily from tanks mounted on the walls as you enter. The friendly staff can help with recommendations. Mains $3–5. Daily 7.30am–9pm.

DIRECTORY

Bank You can exchange travellers' cheques and cash at Vietcombank, which also has an ATM, north of the river on Mac Cuu.
Hospital The hospital is at 46 Le Loi, and there's a pharmacy, north of the centre, at 14a Tran Phu.
Post office and internet Just north of here on Mau Than is the post office (daily 6.30am–10pm), which also has internet access.

Phu Quoc Island

Located just 15km off the coast of Cambodia in the Gulf of Thailand, **PHU QUOC ISLAND** rises from its slender southern tip like a genie released from a bottle. Virtually unknown by outsiders a decade ago, it has now cast a spell on enough visitors, with its soft-sand beaches, swaying palms and limpid waters, to challenge Nha Trang as Vietnam's top beach destination. Spanning 46km from north to south, it's Vietnam's largest offshore island (593 square kilometres), though Cambodia also claims the island, calling it Ko Tral. Phu Quoc is just 45km from Ha Tien, and a little under 120km from Rach Gia.

The topography and vegetation are quite unlike the rest of the delta, and give the place a totally different feel. Phu Quoc's isolation made it an attractive hiding place for two of the more famous figures from Vietnam's past. **Nguyen Anh** holed up here while on the run from the Tay Son brothers in the late eighteenth century, and so too, in the 1860s, did **Nguyen Trung Truc** (see box, p.163). Today, over eighty thousand people – and a sizeable population of indigenous dogs (recognizable by a line of hair running up the spine instead of down) – dwell on the island, famous throughout Vietnam for its black pepper and its fish sauce (*nuoc mam*), which is graded like olive oil.

Like Mui Ne, Phu Quoc is a favourite bolt-hole for expats living in Ho Chi Minh City and, with work almost complete on an international airport in the centre of the island, slated to open in 2012, its future looks rosy. Yet while resorts and bars are springing up fast and access roads are being sealed, for the moment Phu Quoc still retains something of a pioneer outpost feel. Many places can only be reached via dirt tracks and the beaches are largely free of vendors. In the rainy season (May–Oct) Phu Quoc is relatively quiet, and room rates become more easily negotiable, though in peak season (Dec–Jan), accommodation prices can increase sharply and advance booking is necessary.

Duong Dong

You'll probably find no need to go into the only town of any size on Phu Quoc – **DUONG DONG** – since most resorts provide all basic needs. However, it's worth dragging yourself off the beach to spend a few hours here; early morning or evening are the best times. There is a small **lighthouse** and **temple** (Dinh Cau) situated on a promontory at the entrance to the harbour, which is of no great consequence but does provide good **views** down the northern part of Long Beach. The town's **market**, on Ngo Quyen, to the left across the rickety bridge in the centre of town, is always bustling and photogenic with its displays of fruit and flowers, and it's well worth joining the throng of shoppers, especially early in the morning. There's also a **night market** that sets up each evening along Vo Thi Sau near the lighthouse, where you can pick up a few souvenirs and check out the good-value Vietnamese food stalls.

SNORKELLING AND DIVING

There's a reason why visitors come in droves from November to May, and why resorts raise their rates then. It's because during those months the waters surrounding the island become limpid and ideal for diving and snorkelling. Some visitors snorkel optimistically in front of resorts on Ong Lang Beach, but the best locations are around the **An Thoi Islands** to the south or **Turtle Island** off the northwest coast, both of which can be visited by boat trip from Phu Quoc. At these reefs – the former of which is rated by some as the best dive site in Vietnam – you can float above brain and fan corals, watching parrot fish, scorpion fish, butterfly fish, huge sea urchins and a host of other marine life.

REPUTABLE OPERATORS

Most resorts can sort out snorkelling trips to the offshore islands, charging around $15–20 per person (depending on number in the group), which includes snorkelling, fishing and lunch.

John's Tours 143 Tran Hung Dao ☎091 910 7086.
Rainbow Divers 11 Tran Hung Dao ☎091 340 0964, ⓦdivevietnam.com. The well-organized Rainbow Divers run diving trips with hotel pick-up at about 7am on most days during the diving season (early Nov–late May), charging $25 for snorkelling, $55

for one dive or $75 for two dives, and including all equipment and lunch or fruit. It also offers PADI courses in open-sea and advanced diving.
Tony Travel 100 Tran Hung Dao ☎090 744 1616, ⓦhttp://tonyislandtour.com.

2

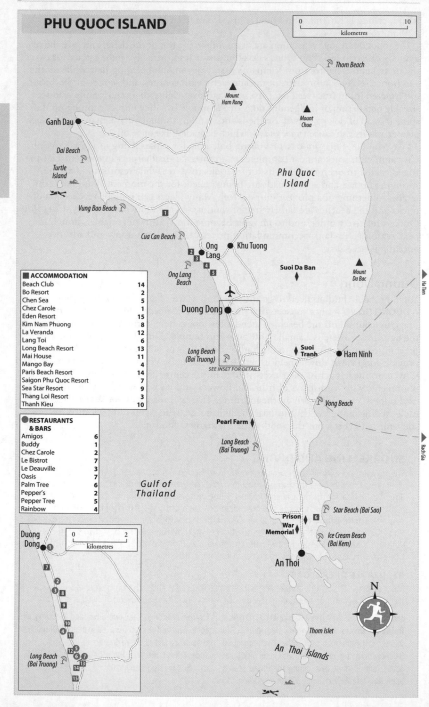

PHU QUOC ISLAND

0   kilometres   10

Thom Beach

Mount
Ham Rong

Mount
Chua

Ganh Dau

Dai Beach

Turtle
Island

Phu Quoc
Island

Vung Bao Beach

Cua Can Beach

1

Ong
Lang

Khu Tuong

2
3

4

5

Suoi Da Ban

Mount
Da Bac

Ong Lang
Beach

Duong Dong

Ha Tien

ACCOMMODATION

Beach Club	14
Bo Resort	2
Chen Sea	5
Chez Carole	1
Eden Resort	15
Kim Nam Phuong	8
La Veranda	12
Lang Toi	6
Long Beach Resort	13
Mai House	11
Mango Bay	4
Paris Beach Resort	14
Saigon Phu Quoc Resort	7
Sea Star Resort	9
Thang Loi Resort	3
Thanh Kieu	10

Long Beach
(Bai Truong)

SEE INSET FOR DETAILS

Suoi
Tranh

Ham Ninh

Vong Beach

Rach Gia

**RESTAURANTS
& BARS**

Amigos	6
Buddy	1
Chez Carole	2
Le Bistrot	7
Le Deauville	3
Oasis	7
Palm Tree	6
Pepper's	2
Pepper Tree	5
Rainbow	4

Pearl Farm

Long Beach
(Bai Truong)

Gulf
of
Thailand

Star Beach (Bai Sao)

6

Prison
War
Memorial

Ice Cream Beach
(Bai Kem)

An Thoi

N

Duong
Dong

1

0   kilometres   2

7

2

3
8

9

10

4
11

12
5
6
7
13

14

15

Long Beach
(Bai Truong)

Thom Islet

An Thoi Islands

Hung Thanh Fish Sauce Factory

Daily 8–11am & 1–5pm · Free

Phu Quoc is famed throughout the country for producing top-quality **fish sauce** – a key ingredient in most Vietnamese dishes. **Hung Thanh** factory, located down an alley on the left of Nguyen Van Troi, the road to the left just beyond the market, welcomes visitors, though you might need a peg for your nose as the aroma is rather pungent. It would also be helpful if you take along a Vietnamese speaker to explain things as the staff there speak no English.

2

Long Beach

The main attraction of Phu Quoc is its fabulous beaches, and the **west coast** has some of the best. The majority of resorts and guesthouses are strung out to the south of Duong Dong, on **Long Beach** (Bai Truong) – an appropriate name, as it stretches almost to the southern tip of the island some 20km away. Most resorts are fronted by fine stretches of soft yellow sand and swaying coconut palms and the beach is ideal for sunbathing, sunset watching and swimming. Beyond the first 7–8 kilometres south of town the beach is completely deserted, and the coast road southward provides some classic tropical beach views.

If you're here for rest and relaxation, you need do nothing more than saunter back and forth between resort and the beach. If you get restless, you can always rent a motorbike to explore the island or sign up for a boat trip.

Coi Nguon Museum

149 Tran Hung Dao · Daily 7am–5pm · 20,000đ · ☎ 077 398 0206, ⓦ coinguonmuseum.com

This museum, the only privately owned one in the Mekong Delta, is located on the main road behind the resorts on Long Beach and about 5km south of Duong Dong; it is well worth a visit to get an overview of Phu Quoc's natural and political history. The carefully arranged exhibits include whale, dugong and swordfish skeletons, samples of sand and petrified wood, a fantastic variety of shells, a potted history of the island's past, pottery from shipwrecks and, if you make it up to the fifth floor, sweeping views along the coast. There are also handicrafts made of local materials on sale, though a shell-encrusted chair might be a bit big for the backpack.

Phu Quoc Pearl Farm

Daily 8am–5pm · ⓦ treasuresfromthedeep.com

About halfway down Long Beach, the **Phu Quoc Pearl Farm** is worth a look to see how pearls are cultured or to pick up a souvenir. There's an interesting display on the complex process, and some stunning (and pricey) jewellery on sale. Look out for the Aussie flag on the sign out front, as some of owner Grant's ex-employees have set up rival farms nearby and pay taxi drivers to lead visitors their way.

Ong Lang and the beaches further north

The west coast north of Duong Dong is a bit more rugged, but the beautiful bays tucked along **Ong Lang Beach** (Bai Ong Lang) are certainly worth visiting, and a few cosy resorts, separated from each other by rocky headlands, offer the chance to really get away from it all. Ong Lang Beach is much quieter than Long Beach, and has a few coral reefs just off the coast, though for really good snorkelling you'd need to join a boat trip to the north or south end of the island. North of Ong Lang, there are a few more attractive beaches called **Cua Can**, **Vung Bao** and **Dai**. Resorts are beginning to spring up here too, though the region still has a feel of splendid isolation.

2

EXPLORING THE INTERIOR

Phu Quoc is the kind of island that is ideal for exploration, and there is little traffic, making it easy to ride a motorbike around. Over seventy percent of the island is forested at present, and the hills of the north are particularly verdant. If you do this, be aware that few roads are surfaced, so you are likely to return to your resort at the end of the day covered in a film of red dust – wearing a helmet is compulsory and a face-mask is a good idea too.

All over the island, and especially in the north, you will pass by **pepper plantations**, the plants easily identifiable as climbers on three-metre-high poles – at places like **Khu Tuong**, a few kilometres inland from Ong Lang Beach (see map); they welcome visitors to look around. There are also two cleansing **streams** in the centre of Phu Quoc: **Suoi Da Ban** and **Suoi Tranh**. A walk beside them reveals moss-covered boulders, tangled vines and small cascades, though they tend to dry up between January and May, when the trip is not worth it.

The east-coast beaches

The **east coast** is, so far, largely undeveloped, though it does have a good surfaced road running halfway up it (from An Thoi to Ham Ninh and Duong Dong) that offers some respite from the constant dust kicked up off the dirt roads throughout the rest of the island.

Signposted just north of the T-junction where the road from Long Beach meets the road up the east coast, **Star Beach** (Bai Sao) is a hot contender for best beach on the island. Its dazzling white sand and pale blue water are mesmerizing and while the waves crash on Long Beach during the monsoons, Star Beach is often calm. A few **beach restaurants** do a healthy trade, particularly at weekends when the beach gets overrun with locals, and there are even a couple of places offering lodgings. In season there are kayaks for rent and half-day snorkelling trips by boat.

A little south of Bai Sao, **Ice Cream Beach** (Bai Kem) is also a blinding white colour, but the military generally prohibit entry to foreigners unless arriving on a boat tour.

In the middle of the east coast, **Vong Beach** and Ham Ninh provide jetties for hydrofoils arriving from Rach Gia and Ha Tien. There's no beach to speak of at Vong Beach – just mudflats. The only other beach on the east coast is **Thom Beach**, in the extreme northwest of the island, which is only reached after a wearing, 35-km motorbike ride over rough roads from Duong Dong, and has virtually nothing in the way of facilities.

The war memorial and former prison

Prison Tues–Sun 7.30–11am & 1.30–5pm

In the south of the island, two unusual attractions are located almost opposite each other, the **war memorial** and the former **prison** (Nha Tu Phu Quoc). The war memorial, perched on a slight rise beside the main road about a kilometre south of the junction of the roads down the west and east coasts, marked on the map (see p.166), consists of three abstract forms, in one of which is cut the shape of a human form, while the prison's small museum chronicles its use to detain enemies of the state, though there is no English signage.

ARRIVAL AND DEPARTURE   PHU QUOC

Whether you arrive by air or by sea, you will likely be besieged by touts trying to drag you off to their favoured hotel or guesthouse, so it's a good idea to have somewhere in mind before arrival. If you have made a prior booking, most resorts provide a free airport transfer, saving you a lot of hassle and expense.

By plane Flights from Ho Chi Minh City land at Phu Quoc Airport, currently on the edge of Duong Dong town, from where it is a short trip to the resorts on Long Beach, or a seven-kilometre ride to those at Ong Lang Beach. However, a new international airport located further south near the centre of the island will open in 2012, which will benefit some resorts on Long Beach but will involve a longer drive to resorts at Ong Lang and Cua Can. Reservations can

currently be made through your resort or at the Vietnam Airlines office at 122 Nguyen Trung Truc (☎077 399 6677), in front of the airport gate, although this is set to change when the new airport is completed.
Destinations: Ho Chi Minh City (several daily; 1hr); Can Tho (daily; 40min).
By speed boad It's advisable to book your ticket in

advance: boats run between Rach Gia and Vong Beach, and Ha Tien and Ham Ninh. Ask your hotel or guesthouse to help you, or, when buying tickets back to the mainland, visit the offices at the top of Tran Hung Dao, just behind the northern end of Long Beach.
Destinations: Rach Gia/Vong Beach (several daily; $15; 2hr 30min); Ha Tien/Ham Ninh (daily; $11; 1hr 30min).

GETTING AROUND

By xe om or taxi There is currently no organized bus service so you'll have to take a taxi or xe om to get around the island, unless you opt, as many do, to rent a motorbike for complete freedom of movement.
By motorbike Prices range from $6–10 a day depending on the type of motorbike you rent. This is an exciting option,

but not a good place for first-time riders to test their skills as you can suddenly come across dangerous conditions such as potholes or torrential downpours. Most resorts and guesthouses rent motorbikes – check yours over carefully, as many of these machines are falling apart. Wear a helmet, face-mask (for the dust) and plenty of sunscreen.

ACCOMMODATION

Accommodation options are expanding fast and many new places were under construction at the time of writing. Not all mid-range places include air conditioning, TV and fridge, so check before booking if these are important. While resorts on **Ong Lang Beach** are quieter, they are separated from each other by headlands, so there's no choice when it comes to eating, as there is on **Long Beach**. Bear in mind that during the rainy season (May–Oct), many small places close for several months and those that are open reduce their prices. By contrast, it can be difficult to get a room in some places in the high season, so advance booking is advised for more upmarket places. Most resorts and guesthouses can also arrange boat tours, including visits to the local pearl farm on Long Beach (Bai Truong) or an evening's cuttlefish fishing, using coloured plastic shrimps as bait.

LONG BEACH (BAI TRUONG)

★ **Beach Club** ☎077 398 0998, ⓦbeachclubvietnam .com. Under English management, this small, well-run place offers simple, pleasant rooms and bungalows in one of the most tranquil spots on Long Beach. There's a low-key, friendly vibe to the place and the kitchen turns out some excellent food, both Vietnamese and Western. $30
Eden Resort ☎077 398 5598, ⓦedenresort.com.vn. This stylish resort features well-equipped, spacious rooms in the main building and bungalows set in beautifully landscaped gardens, as well as a spa and good-sized pool. The resort fronts a wild stretch of beach, and the capable staff can help make travel and tour arrangements. $140
Kim Nam Phuong ☎077 384 6319. One of the few remaining budget resorts on Phu Quoc, this place is located near the top end of Long Beach; some bungalows come with a/c and hot water, while cheaper rooms are smaller with fans and cold water. $10
★ **La Veranda** ☎077 398 2988, ⓦlaverandaresort .com. The presence of this Accor property on Long Beach is a clear sign of developers' confidence in the island's appeal. It occupies a lovely, French-colonial-style building with luxurious rooms, a small pool, spa, a delightful restaurant, and super-efficient staff. $150
Long Beach Resort ☎077 398 1818, ⓦlongbeach -phuquoc.com. This new, top-end resort takes ancient architecture as its theme, and indeed the entrance looks like the gateway to Hue's Imperial City. Rooms continue the

theme with traditional furnishings, long drapes and simple tiled floors. At the back of the resort is a pool and bridge leading over a lotus pond to the beach. $170
Mai House ☎077 384 7003, ⓔmaihouseresort @yahoo.com. Mai House consists of attractive thatched bungalows set far apart from each other in a lush garden under towering palms. Rooms are stylishly furnished and feel very cosy, with thick mattresses on the canopied beds and bamboo chairs on a secluded veranda. There's no a/c here but the sense of privacy sets it apart from cheaper lodgings. $70
Paris Beach Resort ☎077 399 4548, ⓦphuquocparisbeach.com. Snuggled up to the Beach Club, this place offers clean bright rooms or bungalows, some with beach views, though some are very cramped together. The restaurant here with its huge and varied menu is a definite bonus. $30
Saigon Phu Quoc Resort ☎077 384 6999, ⓦvietnamphuquoc.com. This government-run resort is the top choice for domestic tourists, and features well-equipped villas in manicured grounds and useful facilities like shuttle bus and swimming pool. It can get busy with tour groups at times but the efficient staff cope with it gracefully. $206
Sea Star Resort (Sao Bien) ☎077 398 2161, ⓦseastarresort.com. This attractive, well-managed place with competitively priced rooms, and a nice shady patch of beach in front, is excellent value as the decent-sized rooms have all facilities. $40

2

Thanh Kieu (Coco Beach) ☎ 077 384 8394. One of the cheapest options along this stretch of beach with basic but clean brick bungalows, though they are set back a bit from the beach. All rooms have a small veranda with hammock and it's a friendly, family-run place with free internet for guests. Breakfast is included in the rate and they can arrange airport transfers. $55

ONG LANG BEACH (BAI ONG LANG)

Bo Resort ☎ 077 398 6142, ⓦ boresort.com. Pleasant, tastefully furnished bungalows made of wood and thatch on a steep hill overlooking a gorgeous stretch of beach, with a well-appointed restaurant too. The bungalows enjoy some privacy, so it's ideal for an escape, but it's a bit of a clamber to those at the top of the hill. $50

Chen Sea ☎ 077 399 5895, ⓦ centararesorts.com. The southernmost and most expensive resort on Ong Lang Beach has now been taken over by the Central Group. It features luxurious rooms in a mixed traditional and modern style, some with private pool. There's also a large, beachfront, communal pool, a diving and watersports centre, a solarium deck, a spa, a mini library and a recreational activities programme too. $295

★ **Mango Bay** ☎ 0903 382207, ⓦ mangobayphuquoc .com. This place enjoys a lovely tranquil location and offers spacious, stylish bungalows, made with local soil using eco-friendly techniques, with fans and large verandas (no a/c or TV). The coast is rocky in front but there are deserted sandy bays on each side. $90

Thang Loi Resort ☎ 077 398 5002, ⓦ phu-quoc.de. A remote setting, with simple bamboo and wood huts nestled on a hillside. Facilities are basic, with no hot water or fans and electricity in the evening only, but it's a great place to get away from it all; the snorkelling is excellent too. It closes from May-Oct. $30

OTHER BEACHES

Chez Carole Cau Can Beach ☎ 077 370 3793, ⓦ chezcarole.com.vn. This newish resort features just a few luxurious wooden bungalows with indoor/outdoor bathrooms, comfortable furnishings and great beach views, as well as some smaller rooms close together and further back from the beach. It's certainly a place to get away from it all, and fortunately the house restaurant (see below) is one of the best places to eat on the island. $80

Lang Toi Star Beach ☎ 077 397 2123, ⓔ langtoi -restaurant@yahoo.com.vn. This is currently your best bet if you want to set up camp on Star Beach on the east coast. This place is basically a beachfront restaurant, has four decent rooms for rent, each with a spacious balcony and bathtub. Unfortunately, it's prone to power cuts and staff are not always on the ball. $45

EATING AND DRINKING

Duong Dong's night market (see p.165) is a great place to sample authentic **Vietnamese dishes** at very cheap prices. Not surprisingly, every beach resort, apart from the cheapest guesthouses, has its own restaurant; most have reasonable menus and some have sea views, but the quality is erratic and prices are often inflated. Bear in mind if you stay anywhere but **Long Beach**, you'll be limited to the restaurant at your resort unless you have a rented motorbike. Long Beach may be busier, but you do get several dining choices in a small area.

Amigos On Long Beach immediately south of La Veranda. This place seems more set up as a bar than a restaurant, with cold beers, lots of cocktails and pool tables. However, it also serves burritos, enchiladas, pizzas (about $5–6) and Vietnamese fare ($3–4). Daily 8am–11pm.

Buddy 26 Nguyen Trai, Duong Dong. Good place for a cooling ice cream or shake if you make a trip to town. Sandwiches (about $2), fish and chips ($3) and reliable local info if the Kiwi owner happens to be there. Daily 8am–10pm.

Chez Carole 88 Tran Hung Dao, on the main road near the north end of Long Beach. This place covers all the bases, from varied breakfasts to Western dishes like hamburgers and steaks and Vietnamese favourites, and even includes Carole's suggestions for best pick. Main dishes cost around $3–5. Daily 10am–midnight.

Le Bistrot On the lane leading to La Veranda resort, Long Beach. Relaxing place with pool table offering French and international dishes ($3–4), and with a children's playground in the garden. Popular for dining in the day and choosing a drink from the well-stocked bar in the evening. Daily 10am–midnight.

Le Deauville In front of Kim Nam Phuong guesthouse, Long Beach. French-style preparation of many dishes, such as cassolette of stuffed squid and barbecued chicken Deauville-style. Good prices, around $3–5 for a main course, and some wines on offer too. Opens for lunch only in the low season (May–Nov). Nov–May daily 11am–10pm.

Oasis 118/5 Tran Hung Dao, on the lane leading to La Veranda, Long Beach. Pizzas, pasta, curries and Vietnamese dishes are all served at this bar/restaurant that's popular among visitors. It also features sports on TV and a pool table. Daily noon–midnight.

Palm Tree On the lane leading to La Veranda, Long Beach. Great traditional Vietnamese dishes plus a seafood barbecue every evening in the high season. It's just opposite the entrance to *La Veranda* and doesn't enjoy beach views, but this place is all about taste, not ambience, and prices seem just a bit cheaper here ($3–4 for main courses) than anywhere else. Daily 7am–11pm.

Pepper's 89 Tran Hung Dao, on the main road near the north end of Long Beach, ☎ 077 384 8773. The place to go for pizzas, grills and jumbo salads, with a delivery service too. Most dishes are around $4. Though it doesn't have beach views, it's a pleasant, breezy spot and staff are very welcoming. Daily 10am–11pm.

★ **Pepper Tree** La Veranda resort, Long Beach. The ideal place for a splurge is at this classy, first-floor restaurant in a colonial-style building. Plenty of seafood on offer, such as steamed sea bass with artichokes in clam butter ($20), in a refined atmosphere. Daily 11.30am–2pm & 6.30–10.30pm.

Rainbow In front of Thanh Kieu resort (but not connected), Long Beach. Classic beach bar (just a shack really with tables and chairs under thatched shades on the beach), serving up burgers and steaks, at around $4, as well as beers and cool sounds. Attracts people looking to party in the high season. Daily 8am–late.

DIRECTORY

Bank The Vietcombank at 20, 30 Thang 4 in Duong Dong will exchange money and cash travellers' cheques; it also has an ATM.

Post office The post office (7am–8pm) is also on 30 Thang 4, where internet access is available. There is a hospital towards the eastern end of 30 Thang 4, and there are pharmacies along Ngo Quyen beside the market.

The central highlands

MARKET, KON TUM

The central highlands

If you'd like to get off the beaten track in Vietnam, this is the place to do it. The bulk of travellers shoot along the coast to the east, and even those who prefer mountains to beaches usually head to the larger, more spectacular ranges to the north of the country. The central highlands can't quite match the northern mountains for scenic beauty, and its minority groups are far less colourful, but there's a lot to see here – thundering waterfalls, mist-laden mountains, immense longhouses and barely a tourist in sight. Bounded to the west by the Cambodian border, and spreading out over the lofty peaks and broad plateaux of the Truong Son Mountains, the central highlands stretch from the base of Highway 1 right up to the bottleneck of land that squeezes past Da Nang towards Hanoi and the north. The region's fertile red soils yield considerable natural resources – among them coffee, tea, rubber, silk and hardwood. Not all of the highlands, though, have been sacrificed to plantation-style economies of scale – pockets of primeval forest still thrive, where wildlife including elephants, bears and gibbons somehow survived the days when the region was a hunting ground for Saigon's idle rich and Hué's idle royalty.

For most visitors who ascend to these altitudes, the main target is **Da Lat**, an erstwhile French mountain retreat that appears very romantic from afar, when the mists roll over its pine-crested hilltops, though some find it disappointing close-up, with its dreary architecture and tacky tourist trappings. The city itself is not without its charms, among them a bracing climate, some beguiling colonial buildings, picturesque bike rides and a market overflowing with delectable fruits and vegetables.

Heading north from Da Lat, you'll pass pretty **Lak Lake**, an attractive body of water surrounded by minority villages. Then comes a series of gritty highland towns whose reputations rest less on tourist sights than on the villages and open terrain that ring them. First comes **Buon Ma Thuot**, a surprisingly busy place considering its far-flung location. While the city itself has little to detain the visitor, the surrounding waterfalls and E De minority villages certainly do; it's also the gateway for treks into **Yok Don National Park**.

Pleiku to the north is another less-than-lovely city, though again encircled with a ring of delightful minority villages – this time Jarai and Bahnar. Further north again is **Kon Tum**, by far the most attractive and relaxing of these three provincial capitals; you'll be able to take in three **Bahnar villages** on an afternoon's walk from the city centre, and mop up a few other minority groups farther afield.

The Jarai and Bahnar are merely the major chunks of the highlands' patchwork of **ethnic minorities**. Cocooned in woolly jumpers, scarves and bobble hats, the highlanders exude a warmth unsurpassed elsewhere in the country, and are the undoubted highlight of a trip through the area. However, many groups are struggling to maintain their identities in the face of persistent pressure from Hanoi to assimilate – a number of rather large protests have taken place since the turn of the 21st century, with the central government's reactions widely criticised by international governments and human rights groups (see p.466). Sensitive to the minority rights issue, the Vietnamese authorities only opened this region to foreigners in 1993, and while you're free to travel

COFFEE GROWING

Highlights

❶ **Trekking** Trek along forest trails at Yok Don National Park, home to a glittering array of flora and fauna. **See p.196**

❷ **Dambri Waterfalls** The most impressive waterfalls in the highlands – stand right below them and feel the spray on your face. **See p.178**

❸ **Da Lat** Abseil down a waterfall or pose for pictures on a pony in the capital of adventure sports and kitsch. **See p.179**

❹ **Ride the rails** Chug your way through highland scenery on the short train ride to Trai Mat village, 7km east of Da Lat. **See p.190**

❺ **Lak Lake** Paddle around Lak Lake in a dug-out canoe at dawn and watch the sunrise shimmer across its surface. **See p.191**

❻ **Coffee country** Enjoy a cup of fresh coffee in Vietnam's capital of caffeine, Buon Ma Thuot. **See p.192**

❼ **Bahnar villages** Overnight in a dramatically tall communal *rong* in a Bahnar village near Kon Tum. **See p.199**

HIGHLIGHTS ARE MARKED ON THE MAP ON P.177

independently between the major cities, visiting one of the highlands' many minority villages independently can be difficult: in most cases you'll need to go through a local tourist office (and pay handsomely for the privilege). In each area, it's best to double-check the current regulations, especially concerning overnight stays in villages.

Your highland experience will vary enormously depending upon **when you visit**. The dry season runs from November through to April. To see the region at its atmospheric best, it's better to go in the wet season, May to October, although at this time the rain can make some outlying villages inaccessible.

The southern central highlands

The southern section of the central highlands is its most-travelled region, though the vast majority pass straight through from Ho Chi Minh City to Da Lat, the only city in the area that appears on open-tour bus schedules. It's also possible to fly into Da Lat, but there are actually a few sights on the overland route from Ho Chi Minh City. The route follows Highway 1 for about 70km before branching northeast on **Highway 20**, which starts a steady climb. The rubber trees corralling its traffic occasionally reveal tantalizing views of the valleys below. Buses sometimes screech to a brief halt on the causeway traversing **La Nga Lake**, from where the **houseboats** cast adrift on its waters are only a zoom lens away. Locals use foot-powered rowing boats to access their homes, which double as fish farms. East of La Nga, Highway 20 passes wooded slopes whose verdant greens are flecked occasionally by the red-tiled roofs of farmsteads and the roving figures of grazing cattle. Look out for unusual rock formations at the roadside in **Dinh Quan**, 112km from Ho Chi Minh City, where enormous smooth boulders are scattered beside the highway in the southern part of town, and volcanoes with symmetrical slopes and flat tops are visible from the road both south and north of town.

In time the hills yield to the tea, coffee and mulberry plantations of the **Bao Loc Plateau**. The town of **Bao Loc** is the best place for a pit stop between Ho Chi Minh City and Da Lat, and it's also a jumping-off point for visits to nearby **Cat Tien National Park** and **Dambri Waterfalls**. Another 100km further northeast, Highway 20 switchbacks up the considerable climb to **Da Lat** at an altitude of just under 1500 metres.

Bao Loc

The undulating hills around **BAO LOC** provide fertile soil for the cultivation of **tea** and **coffee**, while locals also cultivate the mulberry bushes, of whose leaves **silkworms** are so fond. There are no sights of interest in the town itself, but it offers a convenient place to break the long journey between Ho Chi Minh City and Da Lat – all buses linking these cities pass through Bao Loc on the way. Those with their own transport will be able to scoot around the surrounding countryside, which is very attractive.

ACCOMMODATION   BAO LOC

Bao Loc 795 Tran Phu ☎063 386 4107. South of the centre, this is a remarkably good place to stay for the price – an extra few bucks will buy you a/c instead of a fan. Rooms at the back have nice views over the countryside. $9

Seri Bank Hotel 5 Road 28/3 ☎063 386 4150. The smartest and most comfortable hotel in town, set back from the main highway behind a small lake. It's a far larger place than you'd expect in this neck of the woods, and has a good range of facilities, including a small sauna. $30

EATING

Nam Hue 821 Tran Phu. A few steps away from the *Bao Loc Hotel*, and good for the Vietnamese staples; you'll pay less than $5 for a meal.

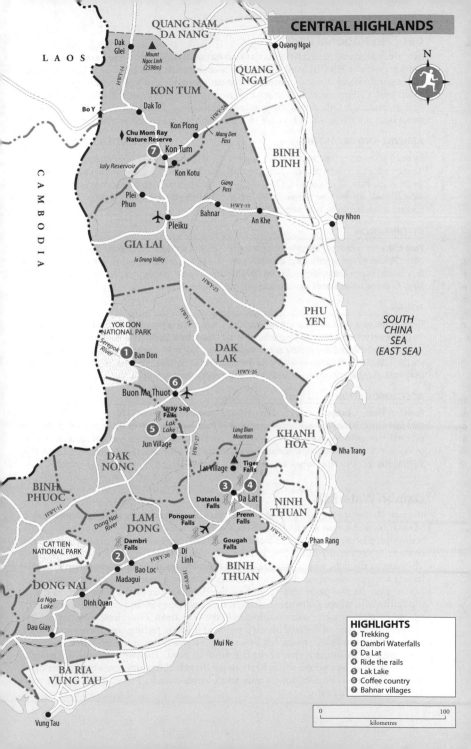

LAOS

QUANG NAM
DA NANG

Dak Glei

Mount
Ngoc Linh
(2598m)

Quang Ngai

QUANG
NGAI

KON TUM

Bo Y

Dak To

HWY-14

Kon Plong

Mang Den
Pass

BINH
DINH

Chu Mom Ray
Nature Reserve

❼ Kon Tum

Ialy Reservoir

Kon Kotu

HWY-24

Giang
Pass

Plei
Phun

Bahnar

An Khe

HWY-19

Quy Nhon

CAMBODIA

Pleiku

GIA LAI

Ia Drang Valley

HWY-14

HWY-25

PHU
YEN

SOUTH
CHINA
SEA
(EAST SEA)

YOK DON
NATIONAL PARK

Serepok
River

❶ Ban Don

DAK
LAK

HWY-26

❻

Buon Ma Thuot

Dray Sap
Falls

Lak
Lake

❺

Jun Village

HWY-27

Lang Bian
Mountain

KHANH
HOA

DAK
NONG

Lat Village

Tiger
Falls

Nha Trang

BINH
PHUOC

HWY-14

Dong Nai River

LAM
DONG

Pongour
Falls

❸
Datanla
Falls

❹ Da Lat

Prenn
Falls

NINH
THUAN

CAT TIEN
NATIONAL PARK

❷

Dambri
Falls

HWY-20

Di
Linh

Gougah
Falls

Phan Rang

HWY-27

DONG NAI

Bao Loc

Madagui

La Nga
Lake

Dinh Quan

HWY-28

BINH
THUAN

Dau Giay

Mui Ne

BA RIA
VUNG TAU

Vung Tau

HIGHLIGHTS
❶ Trekking
❷ Dambri Waterfalls
❸ Da Lat
❹ Ride the rails
❺ Lak Lake
❻ Coffee country
❼ Bahnar villages

0 ————————— 100
kilometres

Cat Tien National Park

The area's outstanding attraction is **Cat Tien National Park**, a protected area situated 150km north of Ho Chi Minh City and about 50km west of Bao Loc. The park covers the largest lowland tropical rainforest in south Vietnam, and hosts nearly 350 species of birds, over 450 species of butterflies and over one hundred mammals, including wild cats, elephants, monkeys and the rare Javan rhinoceros. Don't bank on seeing a rhino, though, as the few residing here are in a secluded reserve closed to visitors.

ARRIVAL AND DEPARTURE — CA TIEN NATIONAL PARK

By bus If you're coming from Ho Chi Minh City by public transport, take a bus for Da Lat from Mien Dong station; tell the driver you want "Vuon Quoc Gia Cat Tien" (Cat Tien National Park), and you'll be dropped at the km125 junction at Tan Phu town. From here, xe om (about 100,000đ) cover the final 24km to the park along a narrow surfaced road. If you're arriving from the north, a signposted road (also surfaced) to the park branches right just before the small town of Madagui.

3

INFORMATION

Park office You need to pay the entrance fee at a park office (50,000đ) located on stilts about 100m before the ferry crossing to park headquarters, across the Dong Nai River. As the park places limits on visitor numbers, it's important to book ahead (T 061 366 9228, W namcattien.org). You can also hire vehicles and boats for travel to the park's more remote areas, but there are few English-speaking guides.

TOURS

Tours of the park Though a dozen walking trails exist, the catch is that you need to hire a jeep or pick-up to get to the start of most of them ($10–25), plus a guide to go with you ($15–25), so a day out can easily cost $40–50. There's also a night safari ($10), though few people spot more than a flash of deer eyes before the panicked creatures flee.

Tours from HCMC Some tour operators in Ho Chi Minh City, such as Sinhbalo tours (see p.90) and Da Lat, such as Phat Tire Ventures (see box, p.187) can organize tours that include a visit to the park.

ACCOMMODATION

Forest Floor Lodge T 061 366 9890, W **vietnamforesthotel.com.** A spectacular, resort-style affair, with rooms either in well-appointed wooden lodges, or "deluxe tents" that are more like treehouse dwellings. Staff can also organize a range of park activities, even if you're not staying here. **$130**

Park accommodation There are a few simple rooms with a/c and a campsite with two-person tents, which you can book through the park office. Camping **$8**, double **$12**

Dambri Waterfalls

18km north of Bao Loc • Daily 7am–5pm • 10,000đ, lift costs 5000đ • A xe om from Bao Loc should cost around 120,000đ return • From Da Lat, take an "Easy Rider" xe om (see box, p.184), which works out at about $60 for the round-trip

Surrounded as they are by dense forest, **Dambri Falls** are much more attractive than any of those in the vicinity of Da Lat, and the only ones worth visiting in the dry season. The road to the falls, which branches north from Highway 20 just east of Bao Loc, bisects rolling countryside carpeted by coffee, tea and pineapple plantations. Once you arrive, there are two paths leading to the falls. The main one to the right leads to the top of the falls, where some ugly fencing stands between you and a precipice over which a torrent of white water tumbles over the 80m drop. From here, you can descend to the base of the falls by steep steps, or if you're feeling lazy, there's a lift available. A second path, to the left by a restaurant, leads down a steep stairway among towering trees to a superb view of the falls from in front. The two paths are linked by a bridge over the river, where you're likely to get drenched in spray, even during the dry season. The path continues downstream to a smaller cascade, Dasara Falls, but the trail can be slippery after rain.

Pongour and Gougah Waterfalls

Undulating tea plantations abound along the road around **Di Linh**, the biggest town between Bao Loc and Da Lat. From here, Highway 28 branches right and heads down to Phan Thiet. Around 25km beyond Di Linh on Highway 20, pine trees begin to feature in the landscape and it's at this point you'll see signs for two of the region's most impressive waterfalls, **Pongour** to the left, and **Gougah** to the right. The former are about 7km off the main road, and are a wide affair more impressive for the rock formations than falling water – imagine a miniature Niagara with most of the taps turned off. The **Gougah** falls, a little beyond the turning to Pongour, are just 400m off the highway, and are worth stopping for a look in the wet season when a thundering cascade pours over them. From here it's about 40km to **Da Lat**, of which the final ten-kilometre stretch cuts steeply through heavily wooded slopes.

Da Lat and around

3

Vietnam's premier hill station, **DA LAT**, sits tucked into the mountain folds of the **Lang Bian Plateau** at an altitude of around 1500m. A beguiling amalgam of winding streets, picturesque churches, bounteous vegetable gardens and crashing waterfalls, this quaint colonial curio is a great place to chill out, literally and metaphorically; if its cool air gets you in the mood for action, you could try trekking to minority villages, mountain-biking and rock-climbing (see box, p.187).

By tacit agreement during the American War, both Hanoi and Saigon refrained from bombing the city and it remains much as it was half a century ago. However, it's important to come to Da Lat with no illusions. With a population of around 200,000, the city is anything but an idyllic backwater: sighting its forlorn architecture for the first time in the 1950s, Norman Lewis found the place "a drab little resort", and today its colonial relics and pagodas stand cheek by jowl with some of the dingiest examples of East European construction anywhere in Vietnam. Moreover, attractions here pander to the domestic tourist's predilection for swan-shaped pedal-boats and pony-trek guides in full cowboy gear, while at night the city can be as bleak as an off-season ski resort.

Central Da Lat forms a rough crescent around the western side of man-made **Lake Xuan Huong**, created in 1919 when the Cam Ly River was dammed by the French, who named it the "Grand Lac". The city escaped bomb damage, and a French influence is still evident in its central area, whose twisting streets and steps, lined with stone buildings rising to red-tiled roofs, cover a hillock located between the streets of Bui Thi Xuan and Phan Dinh Phung.

THE FRENCH IN DA LAT

It was **Dr Alexander Yersin** who first divined the therapeutic properties of Da Lat's temperate climate on an exploratory mission into Vietnam's southern highlands, in 1893. His subsequent report on the area must have struck a chord: four years later Governor-General Paul Doumer of Indochina ordered the founding of a convalescent hill station, where Saigon's hot-under-the-collar *colons* could recharge their batteries, and perhaps even take part in a day's game-hunting. The city's Gallic contingent had to pack up their winter coats after 1954's Treaty of Geneva, but by then the cathedral, train station, villas and hotels had been erected, and the French connection well and truly forged.

The French elite who once maintained **villas** in Da Lat preferred to site their homes on a hill to the southeast of the city centre, rather than in the maw of its central area. The villas that they built along Tran Hung Dao survive today, some renovated and others in a sad state of disrepair, but they evoke the feel of the colonial era more than anywhere else in Da Lat.

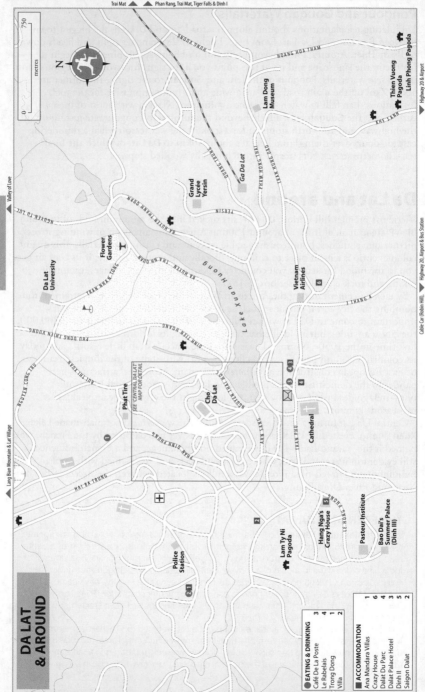

DA LAT & AROUND

● **EATING & DRINKING**
Café De La Poste	3
Le Rabelais	4
Trong Dong	1
Villa	2

■ **ACCOMMODATION**
Ana Mandara Villas	1
Crazy House	6
Dalat Du Parc	4
Dalat Palace Hotel	3
Dinh III	5
Saigon Dalat	2

Lake Xuan Huong

Flower gardens daily 7.30am–5pm • 15,000d

Just down the slopes from the market you'll find the glassy lake of **Xuan Huong**. At 7km in circumference it's perfect for a bike ride, and parts of the promenade are great for walkers. Head eastwards around the north side of the lake along **Nguyen Thai Hoc**, and you'll soon leave the bustle of the city behind as you pass between the lake and the extensive grounds of Da Lat's **golf club** (see box, p.187). After this, you'll soon reach Da Lat's **flower gardens**, inside which paths lead you past hydrangeas, roses, orchids, poinsettia, topiary and a nursery. There's nothing outstanding on display here, but on weekends the place is packed with Vietnamese taking photos of each other posing in front of the flowerbeds.

Continue along **Ba Huyen Thanh Quan** and trace its broad arc around the lake. As you double back, you'll see the slate belfry of the **Grand Lycée Yersin** peeping out from the trees above and to your left. Note that at the time of writing this area resembled a construction site, due to the creation of a huge new museum and culture complex.

Ga Da Lat

Where Ba Huyen Thanh Quan turns into Yersin, you can head one of two ways: west, and back into the city centre; or east up Nguyen Trai to **Ga Da Lat**, the city's train station, built in 1938 and a real time capsule. Below its gently contoured red-tiled roof and behind the multicoloured Art Deco windows striping its front facade, its ticket booths are reminiscent of a provincial French station. Outside, the rail yard is in a charming state of dilapidation, with cattle grazing on the grass and flowers that grow among its tracks and ancient locomotives.

Trains ran on the rack railway linking Da Lat to Thap Cham (see p.225) and beyond from 1933 until the mid-Sixties, when Viet Cong attacks became too persistent a threat for them to continue. Nowadays, the only services are those heading 7km across horticultural land and market gardens to the village of **Trai Mat**, a few kilometres away (see p.190).

Dinh I

1 Tran Quang Dieu • Daily 7.30–11.30am & 1.30–4.30pm • 5000d

About 1km east of the train station, a small lane to the right leads to **Dinh I**, one of Bao Dai's many palaces in the region. A number of its features and 1930s furnishings are very similar to Dinh III – Bao Dai's Summer Palace (see p.182) – which is perhaps the most popular attraction in town. As such, you might want to give this a miss, although

---

COUNTRYSIDE DETOURS

From Tran Hung Dao two roads wiggle south, offering pleasant detours out into the countryside – the half-day bike ride outlined below will put a little definition on your calves. **Khe Sanh** branches south off Tran Hung Dao, opposite Pham Hong Thai, and further south leads back to Highway 20. The focus of this detour is **Thien Vuong Pagoda**, remarkable for its trio of four-metre-tall sandalwood statues (Sakyamuni, in the centre, rubs shoulders with the Goddess of Mercy and the God of Power), imported from Hong Kong in 1958, and for the huge **statue of Buddha** seated on a lotus, 100m up the hill above the pagoda. Stalls in front of Thien Vuong hawk the usual candied strawberries, artichoke tea and *cu ly* to the Vietnamese tourists who flock here, many of whom are young girls who come from all over Vietnam to pray for good fortune and a successful marriage.

Further east, **Hoang Hoa Tham** leads to colourful **Linh Phong Pagoda**, which is fronted by a gateway bearing a fierce, panting dragon face with protruding eyes. Behind its gaudy yellow doors, the pagoda exudes a peaceful aura. Its resident nuns are very friendly and the remote location affords peerless views of the cultivated and wooded valley below.

Dinh I enjoys better views over the city and is in a more peaceful setting and receives fewer visitors, so you can wander round without hordes of other tourists. This building was used as Bao Dai's workplace, and the conference room upstairs, with its large map of the country, has a business-like air to it. There are several interesting photos on the walls of the other rooms, including one of Bao Dai in a racing car and another of his concubines. Other points of interest include a doorway to a secret tunnel and an archaic phone switchboard at the entrance to the building.

Dalat Palace Hotel

12 Tran Phu • ☎ 063 382 5444, ⓦ dalatpalace.vn

Running west to east just south of the city centre, **Tran Phu** cradles two of the city's most memorable French-era buildings. One is the splendidly restored 1920s **Dalat Palace Hotel**, the social heart of colonial-era Da Lat. Still a great place to stay (see p.185), it has great views of Lake Xuan Huong, and enjoying a long, cool drink overlooking its manicured lawns is a luxury that's worth the expense.

The cathedral

Tran Phu • Surise to sunset • Free

Across the road from the Dalat Palace Hotel and a few steps west along Tran Phu, Da Lat's dusty pink **cathedral**, consecrated in 1931 and completed eleven years later, is dedicated to St Nicholas, protector of the poor; a statue of him stands at the opposite end of the nave to the simple altar, with three tiny children loitering at his feet. Light streaming in from the cathedral's seventy stained-glass windows, mostly crafted in Grenoble, teases a warm, sunny glow from the mellow pink of the interior walls. A tiny metal cockerel perched almost invisibly at the top of the steeple has earned the cathedral its rather unglamorous moniker, "Chicken Church".

Bao Dai's Summer Palace (Dinh III)

Daily 7.30–11am & 1.30–4.30pm • 5000d • You'll find the palace by bearing left onto Le Hong Phong 500m west of the cathedral

Also known as **Dinh III**, the erstwhile summer palace of Emperor Bao Dai evokes one of two reactions from visitors: love or boredom. Built between 1933 and 1938, it provided Bao Dai with a bolt-hole between elephant-slaughtering sessions. The building is palatial, though not in a traditional style – Art Deco would be a better description.

Etched with stark white grouting, its mustard-coloured bulk is set amid rose and pine **gardens**. Nautical portholes punched into its walls give it the distinct look of a ship's bridge, as does the mast-like pole sprouting from its roof.

Past the two large blue metal lanterns flanking the front entrance, the first room to your right is Bao Dai's **working room**, dominated by a bust of the man himself, and home both to the imperial motorbike helmet, and to a small book collection. Buffalo horns in the **reception room** come from animals bagged by Bao Dai himself on one of his hunting forays into the forests around Da Lat. His queen preferred more sedate pastimes, and would have tinkled on the piano here. The palace's most elegant common room is its **festivities room** or dining room, though catching a whiff of furniture polish in this dark, echoing chamber, it's hard to imagine the royal revelries that once went on here.

The bedrooms

Royal ghosts are far easier to summon upstairs, where the musty **imperial bedrooms** seem just to have had the dustsheets whipped back for another royal season. Princes and princesses all had their quarters, as did the queen, whose chamber features a chaise longue that looks unnervingly like a dentist's chair. But the finest room, predictably enough, went to Bao Dai, who enjoyed the luxury of a balcony for his "breeze-getting and his moon-watching". Out on the landing, look out for a bizarre mini-sauna, labelled a *Rouathermique*. The place is surrounded by the usual attractions – pony rides and dressing up in minority costume, and the exit forces you to pass through a gauntlet of souvenir stalls.

The Crazy House

3 Huynh Thuc Khang • Daily 7am-7pm • 12,000₫ • ☎ 063 382 2070

Easily combined with a visit to Bao Dai's Summer Palace (see opposite) is **Hang Nga's Crazy House**, shaped to resemble the knotted trunks of huge trees and another place that visitors – not to mention the citizens of Da Lat – either love or hate. While most merely pop by for a visit, it also functions as a guesthouse (see p.185); day-visitors are welcome to look around any unoccupied rooms, most of which have entertaining *Alice in Wonderland*-style interiors with mirrors and mushrooms in abundance. A selection of photographs on the walls inside the entrance provide clues as to how such a bizarre construction got planning permission – its owner, Hang Nga, is the daughter of former president Truong Chinh, and as such is above the usual planning constraints.

3

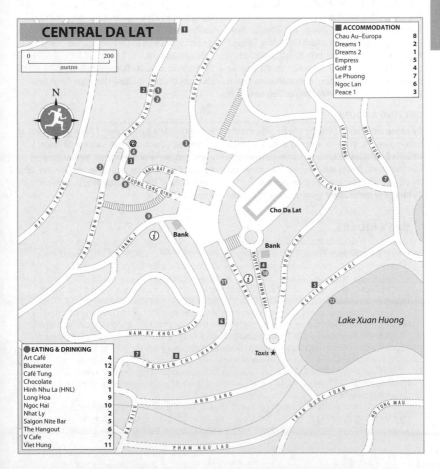

Lam Dong Museum

4 Hung Vuong • Mon–Sat 7.30–11.30am & 1.30–4.30pm • 4000đ

Set on a hill beyond the eastern end of Tran Hung Dao near the beginning of Hung Vuong, the **Lam Dong Museum** is the best museum in the central highlands and well worth visiting. Located in a new building, the displays are thoughtfully laid out and give a tantalizing taste of the region's rich history. Exhibits include Cham artefacts from recent archeological digs as well as a collection of rice jars, ceramics and jewellery found in tombs, and some vicious-looking spears. The museum also gives a thorough introduction to the lifestyles of the local minority groups such as the Ma, Koho and Churu, along with a map showing their distribution in the province and many of their handicrafts and household implements. There's also a display covering the French and American Wars, though it is little different to similar displays around the rest of the country.

ARRIVAL AND DEPARTURE   DA LAT

By plane Lien Khuong Airport (☎ 063 384 3373) is 29km from town south of the city, off the road to Ho Chi Minh City. Vietnam Airlines buses meet each flight (40,000đ), or you can hop in a taxi for $12–15. The Vietnam Airlines Booking Office is at 2 Ho Tung Mau (daily 7.30–11.30am & 1–4.30pm; ☎ 063 383 3499).

Destinations: Da Nang (daily; 1hr 20min); Hanoi (2–3 daily; 1hr 40min); Ho Chi Minh City (5 daily; 50min).

By train The only services from Da Lat' station, which constitutes a sight in itself (see p.181) are the irregular ones to Trai Mat village (5 daily; 40min). Although there is a schedule in place, in practice trains are very unlikely to run with fewer than fifteen passengers.

By bus Buses from Ho Chi Minh City, Nha Trang and elsewhere arrive at Da Lat bus station, located about 1km south of the city centre on 3 Thang 4. Most of the reliable open-tour operators run shuttle services into town; failing that, it's a short xe om or taxi ride, and also within walking distance. Regular travellers rate *Sinh Café* buses the best to and from Ho Chi Minh City, and Orange Bus to and from Nha Trang.

Destinations: Buon Ma Thuot (4hr); Da Nang (16 hr); Ho Chi Minh City (7hr); Nha Trang (4hr); Phan Rang (3hr).

GETTING AROUND

By xe om and taxi Da Lat is too hilly for cyclo, and the horse-drawn carts that were once one of the city's more attractive features are pretty much a thing of the past (apart from trots around the lake in high season), so for journeys of any distance you'll have to rely on xe om and taxis.

By bicycle or motorbike If you're fit, you might consider renting a bicycle or tandem (about $2 a day), though with all the steep hills, a motorbike makes more sense (around $5–7 a day): both are available from hotels and tour operators.

By car Renting a car and driver for the day (also easily arranged through hotels or tour operators) costs around $50.

EASY RIDERS

Those travelling through central Vietnam will surely, at some stage, hear references to the famed **Easy Riders**. Though the term is now used to describe pretty much any motorbike driver willing to go beyond day-trip distance, the concept started life in Da Lat; the success of the initial Easy Riders group spawned a glut of copycat operators (this is Vietnam, after all), many of which now go under totally different names and, on occasion, are said to be better than the originals.

The machinations of Vietnamese tour operations mean that it's hard to give any cast-iron recommendations. However, the best place to go shopping for a budding Vietnamese Dennis Hopper is the bottom end of **Truong Cong Dinh**, where several competing outfits vie for your affections. Most are able to produce telephone directory-size books filled with glowing recommendations, but copying is rife and these are to be taken with a pinch of salt.

Prices range from around $15 a day for a tour of the main sights in the city to around $75 a day for a longer trip, usually including accommodation and entrance fees to sights; feel free to suggest your own itinerary.

The standards and prices of local operators change like the wind, however, there is a simple trick for those planning to go on a long tour – go on a short one first. Spending a day, or even a half-day, with your prospective driver will give you a good indication of what they'll be like on a week-long trip.

INFORMATION

Tourist information The handful of tourist offices in Da Lat can all arrange guides, bus tickets, car hire and tours; the main one is Da Lat Travel Services, though *Sinh Café* and TM Brothers have offices here too. If you plan to go trekking to minority villages, you may need to get a permit from the police and be accompanied by a certified guide. You can skirt around the red tape by signing up for a tour of one or several days with one of Da Lat's adventure sports operators which also offer mountain-biking, rock-climbing and abseiling outings. Phat Tire Ventures is a reliable outfit (see box p.187).

ACCOMMODATION

Enduringly popular with both Western and domestic tourists, Da Lat has a wide range of **places to stay**, from cheap, windowless rooms to luxury, international-standard hotels. However, if your visit coincides with a public holiday, especially Tet, be warned that prices increase by up to fifty percent, and you'll need either to arrive early or **book ahead**. The densest concentrations of budget hotels lie on Phan Dinh Phung; ask for a room at the back, as the main road can be noisy. Several classy hotels operate downtown, but there are many more out in the open spaces south and west of the city centre. Check that prices include hot water – a luxury in much of southern Vietnam, but a necessity in Da Lat. Air-conditioning is neither necessary nor usually provided in Da Lat.

CENTRAL DA LAT

Chau Au–Europa 76 Nguyen Chi Thanh ☎ 063 382 2870, ✉ europa@hcm.vnn.vn; map p.183. Professionally run place with a range of rooms. All are dazzlingly clean with homely touches – an extra $5 secures a front room with view. Staff are extremely helpful and there's free internet and wi-fi. $12

★ **Dreams 1 & 2** 151 and 164b Phan Dinh Phung ☎ 063 383 3748, ⓦ dreamshoteldalat.com; map p.183. The reputation of this hotel is such that it has become the default accommodation setting of Da Lat's budget travellers – you're advised to book at least a couple of days ahead. Its good name is well deserved, with helpful and highly friendly staff, clean rooms with modern bathrooms, free use of the jacuzzi and sauna upstairs and unbeatable fresh passion fruit juice at breakfast. $25

Empress 5 Nguyen Thai Hoc ☎ 063 383 3888, ⓦ empresshotelvn.com; map p.183. Attractive colonial-style building overlooking the lake, with tastefully furnished rooms and all facilities. Although only a few minutes' walk from dozens of places to eat, it feels set apart from the rest of Da Lat. $70

Golf 3 4 Nguyen Thi Minh Khai ☎ 063 382 6042, ⓦ vinagolf.vn; map p.183. Part of the *Golf* empire, an upmarket tower-block hotel situated slap-bang in the centre of town. Choose from a selection of comfortable suites or cheaper standard rooms. $77

Le Phuong 80d Nguyen Chi Thanh ☎ 063 382 3743, ✉ lephuonghotel@gmail.com; map p.183. Put this one in the "flashpacker" category – a mid-ranger with good-looking, well-equipped rooms. Staff speak little English but are willing to please and keep the place spick and span. $30

Ngoc Lan 42 Nguyen Chi Thanh ☎ 063 382 2136, ⓦ ngoclanhotel.vn; map p.183. Spacious, well-equipped rooms with good views over the lake at this four-star hotel, whose halls have been given a mauve makeover. It's a bit overpriced, but facilities are excellent; in addition, the ground-floor restaurant is a good place to eat whether you're staying here or not. $85

Peace 1 64 Truong Cong Dinh ☎ 063 382 2787; map p.183. Budget hotel that's reliably popular with backpackers. All rooms have hot water and private bathrooms, and some have balconies with views of the busy street below – or opt for quieter rooms with a terrace at the back. There's also a cheap and popular café downstairs. $10

OUTER DA LAT

Ana Mandara Villas Le Lai ☎ 063 355 5888, ⓦ anamandara-resort.com; map p.180. This new complex of luxury villas located in spacious grounds just outside the city centre. While boasting every conceivable comfort inside, the complex is in a humble village area, offering a good opportunity to connect with local society. $240

Crazy House 3 Huynh Thuc Khang ☎ 063 382 2070; map p.180. Da Lat's quirkiest sight is also its quirkiest place to stay. Rooms are small for the price, and it's worth noting that you'll have tourists crawling around from 7am–7pm, but it's not too much of a problem if you plan the day accordingly. $30

★ **Dalat Du Parc** 7 Tran Phu ☎ 063 382 5777, ⓦ hotelduparc.vn; map p.180. A sympathetically restored colonial edifice that makes the ideal place to stay if your budget won't stretch to a room at the nearby *Dalat Palace*. The cage-lift creaks up to pleasant, well-ventilated rooms with elegant interiors and polished wooden floors. Outside peak season it's possible to get some superb deals on their website. $50

★ **Dalat Palace Hotel** 12 Tran Phu ☎ 063 382 5444, ⓦ dalatpalace.vn; map p.180. Da Lat's most magnificent colonial pile sits in manicured grounds, still radiating its 1920s splendour. All rooms are lavishly appointed and decked out with period furnishings, including clunky telephones and massive bathtubs. Simply gorgeous, but it often feels a little empty. Book online for the best deals. $170

3

Dinh II 12 Tran Hung Dao ☎ 063 382 2092; map p.180. If you fancy living like a colonial but can't afford the rates at the *Dalat Palace* or *Ana Mandara*, then this place, also known as the Palace 2, is your spot. The huge rooms in the main house, once home to the French governor, are beautifully furnished and the complex is surrounded by pines. **$35**

Saigon Dalat 2 Hoang Van Thu ☎ 063 355 6789, ⓦ saigondalathotel.com; map p.180. This new four-star hotel makes a reasonable attempt at capturing a bygone era with its traditional furnishings, though it includes modern touches like flat-screen TVs. You're likely to pay just over half the advertised rates. **$125**

EATING

Da Lat has abundant food stalls and a broad range of restaurants serving Vietnamese, Chinese and international **cuisines**. Head to the **central market** for pho, com and the like, as well as one or two vegetarian stalls, signed as *com chay*, or even picnic provisions of bread, cheese and cake, complemented by fresh local berries. Note that you'll also see a fair few places serving *bun bo* and other types of Hué cuisine – apparently, sixty percent of Da Lat's current population can trace their origins there.

Art Café 70 Truong Cong Dinh; map p.183. Located in the heart of the budget hotel district, this place has stylish, bamboo-themed decor, and appealing dishes, such as capsicum stuffed with pork and minced beef wrapped in a herbal leaf, for around $2.50 each. Spaghetti and vegetarian dishes are served too, plus cheap cocktails. Daily 10am–9.30pm.

Bluewater 2 Nguyen Thai Hoc; map p.183. An attractive restaurant perched over the lake, which, considering the location, serves good-value authentic Chinese seafood dishes – the soups (around $6) are particularly good, and usually made for sharing. Also functions as a café and bar (see opposite). Daily 6.30am–11.30pm.

Chocolate Truong Cong Dinh; map p.183. There are two places with this name on Truong Cong Dinh (AKA Easy Rider Alley). The upper one is a so-so restaurant, while this one at the bottom of the road is a trendy café that serves decent breakfasts (from $1) and sinfully tempting pancakes. Daily 9am–11pm.

Hinh Nhu La (HNL) 94 Phan Dinh Phung; map p.183. Convenient for the budget hotels, this place is smartly furnished and offers pizzas (from $2.50) as well as a good range of Vietnamese dishes. However, do note that it can often take some time to get served. Daily 11.30am–11pm.

Le Rabelais The Dalat Palace Hotel, 7 Tran Phu ☎ 063 382 5777, ⓦ dalatpalace.vn; map p.180. This place can be quite a treat, since for much of the day, you'll have it almost entirely to yourself. Given the palatial setting, replete with waitresses clad in beautiful *ao dai*, this gives one licence to play emperor or empress over High tea ($15), served from 3–5.30pm. In the evening, mains from the largely French menu usually go for around double that. Daily 9am–9pm.

★ **Long Hoa** 3 Thang 2; map p.183. With a French-café ambience and attentive staff, *Long Hoa* serves tasty and filling Vietnamese dishes – kick off with a strawberry wine aperitif, while for dessert the home-made yoghurt takes some beating. Two can dine for $7–10. Daily 11am–9pm.

Ngoc Hai 6 Nguyen Thi Minh Khai; map p.183. Tasty Vietnamese dishes, such as fried deer with curry ($4), in a convenient location between the market and the lake. Daily 9am–10pm.

Nhat Ly 88 Phan Dinh Phung; map p.183. Hugely popular with Vietnamese and foreigners alike for its wide menu of dishes at very reasonable prices (from $2.50). Often packed to the gills at mealtimes, but do note that there's an overflow room out back. Daily 9am–9pm.

★ **Trong Dong** 220 Phan Dinh Phung; map p.180. Simple-looking restaurant with unusual tartan-effect tablecloths and year-round tinsel, but some of the best home cooking in the city. Try their tasty sugar-cane prawns and a Vietnamese special salad (shrimps, peanuts, lotus gourd, pork and herbs; $2), or their more adventurous venison dishes. Daily 10am–9pm.

★ **V Cafe** 1/1 Bui Thi Xuan; map p.183. A bit removed from the budget hotel district, but worth tracking down for its cosy atmosphere and good cooking, including some great home-made pies and cakes, at affordable prices – a big slab of cake will set you back around $1.50. Daily 7am–10.30pm.

Viet Hung 7 Nguyen Chi Thanh; map p.183. One of a clutch of cafés offering partial views across the lake. They cater to Western tastes with a range of fast food (fruit shakes, soups, pizzas and pancakes) as well as some Vietnamese dishes. Also has wi-fi. Daily 6.30am–11pm.

DRINKING AND NIGHTLIFE

For most locals, **nightlife** means a cup of coffee in one of the city's atmospheric **cafés**. For visitors, there's not much more unless you fancy a game of pool or a dance at one of the hotel discos.

Bluewater 2 Nguyen Thai Hoc; map p.183. This lakeside restaurant is also a great place for coffee or something stronger – you may struggle to get a seat during sunset hours. Daily 6.30am–11.30pm.

Café De La Poste 12 Tran Phu. See map, p.180. Modern, French-style café opposite the *Dalat Du Parc* hotel. Colonial in style, it's grand but a tad pricey (buffet breakfast $8, set lunch or dinner $13.50), yet just about worth the splurge. If your budget allows, it's also a good place for cocktails ($8). Daily 6am–10pm.

Café Tung 6 Khu Hoa Binh; map p.183. Leather upholstery, dark varnished wood and 1950s French crooners on the sound system: truly a café lost in time. It's perhaps at its most atmospheric in the evening, over a bottle of beer. Daily 6am–10pm.

Saigon Nite Bar 11a/1 Hai Ba Trung; map p.183. Da Lat's long-standing Western-style bar with friendly, welcoming staff, pool table, darts and a reasonable selection of CDs. The guest books chronicle a stream of drunk but contented customers. Daily 3pm–late.

The Hangout 71 Truong Cong Dinh; map p.183. Easy Rider-affiliated place aimed at travellers, with a pool table, cheap beers and motorbikes for rent. A good place to take the pulse of Da Lat and make some local friends. Daily 9am–midnight.

SHOPPING

The market, **Cho Da Lat**, stands on top of a hill in the city centre. A charmless reinforced-concrete structure it may be, but it houses a staggering range of fruit and vegetables. Strawberries, beetroot, fennel, artichokes, avocados, blackberries and cherries grown in the market gardens surrounding the city are all sold here, along with a riot of flowers. Artichoke teabags, with their diuretic properties, make quirky **souvenirs**, and candied Da Lat strawberries are also sold at many stalls. **Montagnards** carrying their chattels in backpacks are a fairly common sight at the market, especially early in the morning when they come to trade with stallholders.

DIRECTORY

Banks Vietcombank, 6 Nguyen Thi Minh Khai, and Sacombank on Hoa Binh Square change travellers' cheques and cash, and have ATMs.

Hospital Lam Dong Hospital, 4 Pham Ngoc Thach ☎063 383 4158.

Internet access These days most hotels and guesthouses provide internet access and wi-fi, free to guests. Otherwise, it's a Vietnamese city – there are internet cafés everywhere.

Police 9 Tran Binh Trong ☎063 382 2032.

Post office 14 Tran Phu (daily 7.30am–5.30pm), with poste restante, IDD, fax and DHL courier services.

ACTIVITIES IN AND AROUND DA LAT

There is some spectacular scenery in the vicinity of Da Lat, which lends itself to challenging treks, bike rides and other **adventure activities**. A number of local tour operators can help to organize most of the following; the two with the best reputation are ★ Phat Tire Ventures, 109 Nguyen Van Troi (☎063 382 9422, ⊛ptv-vietnam.com); and Groovy Gecko, 65 Truong Cong Dinh (☎063 383 6521, ⊛groovygeckotours.net). Hotel pick-up usually comes as part of the package.

Bike riding There are a number of excellent day- and half-day bike routes around Da Lat. Many head north to Lat Village (p.188), or south into the countryside (see box, p.181), but it's also possible to organize trips to further-flung locations such as Buon Ma Thuot, Nha Trang or even Hoi An.

Canyoning There's a beautiful canyon fifteen minutes from Da Lat by car; the adventurous course requires ropes and a bit of bravery. Half-day trips from $40 per person.

Golf The eighteen-hole course just off central Da Lat (see map, p.180) boasts inspiring views from some tees. Starts at around $95 per person, including caddy.

Hiking Most local tour operators will be able to organize a guided hike, with everything from half-day to week-long walks and treks; figure on around $30 per person per day. Again, Lat Village and the surrounding area is a popular destination, while the above operators will be able to take you into more uncharted territory.

Tennis Both the *Dalat Palace* and *Dalat Du Parc* have tennis courts, available to guests for free, and non-guests for a small fee.

Whitewater rafting Phat Tire Ventures run rafting and kayaking trips on routes including rapids of class 2, 3 and 4. Kayaking from $37 per person, rafting from $57 per person.

Around Da Lat

The spectacular scenery around Da Lat lends itself to challenging **treks**, **bike rides** and other **adventure activities** (see box, p.187). None of the local waterfalls is worth visiting in the dry season (Dec–May), with the possible exception of **Tiger Falls**, though you might enjoy a **boat ride** on one of the local lakes or a **cable-car ride** from Robin Hill to Lake Tuyen Lam, where kayaks are available for rent. Another popular jaunt is by **train** to **Trai Mat**, taking time out to admire the adornments on the **Linh Phuoc Pagoda**.

The Valley of Love

Daily 7am–5pm • 10,000đ

Thung Lung Tinh Yeu, or the **Valley of Love**, sits five kilometres north of Da Lat. Bao Dai and his courtiers used to hunt here in the 1950s, before a dam project in 1972 flooded part of the valley and created **Lake Da Thien**. The valley's still waters and wooded hills are actually quite enticing, though the music blasting from souvenir stalls and the buzzing of rented motorboats do not enhance the aura of romance. Kitsch diversions such as pony rides round the lake escorted by a cowboy are also on offer.

XQ Historical Village

Opposite entrance to Valley of Love • Daily 8am–5pm • 10,000đ

More a tourist trap than a place of historical worth, though worth popping into if you're visiting the adjacent Valley of Love. Here you'll find several traditional houses displaying the process and product of silk embroidery picture-making. You can watch the girls painstakingly producing images thread by thread, then walk through an exhibition of landscapes, still lifes, portraits and more surreal compositions, all woven from silk.

Lat Village

14km north of Da Lat along Xo Viet Nghe Tinh • To get to Lat Village, take one of the hourly green buses heading up Phan Dinh Phung in Da Lat (2000đ). Alternatively, it's not too far to cycle

The village's thatch-roofed bamboo stilthouses are occupied by Chill and Ma, but mostly Lat, groups of Koho peoples eking out a living growing rice, pulses and vegetables. The various paths running through the village are easy to follow so a guide is not essential, though one can be easily arranged through any of Da Lat's tour operators.

Ankroet lakes and falls

If you go it alone and hire a motorbike for the day, you could combine a visit to Lat Village with a jaunt out to **Ankroet lakes and falls**, signposted 8km along the road to Lat. The falls are more secluded and attractive than most in the area but there is little water during the dry season.

Lang Bian Mountain

From Lat Village, you'll see the peak (2169m) of **Lang Bian Mountain** looming above you to the north. It's a 4hr ascent on foot, though by car you can drive up to the canopy of pines on the lower peak. Inevitably, a schmaltzy legend has been concocted to explain the mountain's formation. The story tells of two ill-starred lovers, a Lat man called Lang and a Chill girl named Bian, who were unable to marry because of tribal enmity. Broken-hearted, Bian passed away, and the peaks of Lang Bian are said to represent her breast heaving its dying breath. Bian's death seems not to have been wholly in vain: so racked with guilt was her father, that he called a halt to tribal unrest by unifying all of the local factions into the Koho.

FROM TOP LAK LAKE (P.191); DAMBRI FALLS (P.178)>

Robin Hill and Lake Tuyen Lam

Cable-car rides daily 7.30–11.30am & 1.30–5pm • 50,000đ one way • Boat trips 200,000đ for up to five people

As you leave Da Lat to the south on Highway 20, a slip road to the right leads to the top of **Robin Hill**, crowned by a huge **cable-car** terminus. Rides in the cable car once offered fantastic views over the slopes around the city, which are now marred by construction work. The twelve-minute trip deposits you at **Lake Tuyen Lam**, a placid and attractive expanse of water on which you can take a **boat trip**. Any taxi or xe om driver in town will be willing to take you here, but it's also possible to get to the falls independently with your own wheels.

Datanla Falls

200m south of Lake Tuyen Lam, signposted on the right of the road as "Thac Datanla" • Daily 7am–5pm • **Luge rides** 20,000đ

The **Datanla Falls** are some of the most impressive in the area, and can easily be combined with a visit to nearby Lake Tuyen Tam. In Koho, *datanla* means "water under leaves", and that pretty much sums up the place: from the car park, it's a steep fifteen-minute clamber down to the falls, probing some splendidly lush forest. The falls themselves are not terribly thrilling, their muddy waters cascading onto a plateau spanned by a wooden footbridge that provides a hackneyed photo opportunity. The more famous **Prenn Falls** are a further 6km out of town, but though extremely popular with local tourists a visit cannot be recommended – the park's attractions include bears, deer and monkeys kept in wretched conditions.

Chicken Village

18km south of Da Lat and just west of Highway 20

CHICKEN VILLAGE (ask for Lang Con Ga) is just like any other Vietnamese village, apart from the bizarre, 5m-high cement cockerel that stands proudly on a plinth in the centre, its mouth open in mid-squawk. Whether you're a potential buyer of textiles or not, it's interesting to take a look at the rudimentary looms that the women need to strap themselves into to operate. It's also possible to go rambling through the nearby fields and foothills without a permit.

Trai Mat

Train shuttle services daily at 7.45am, 9.50am, 11.55am, 2pm, 4.05pm • Round-trip 90min • 80,000đ

The nearby village of **TRAI MAT** is just 7km from Da Lat, and ideally placed for a short excursion. Most head there by **train** (see p.184), the line taking you east past some interesting, if not terribly beautiful, countryside. The village itself rewards exploration – Linh Phuoc Pagoda is the main draw, but if you have more time (or are willing to get a xe om back), grab a bite to eat or hunt down the beautiful Cao Dai temple on a rise just east of the village.

Linh Phuoc Pagoda

The highlight of Trai Mat is **Linh Phuoc Pagoda**, an incredibly ornate building which showcases the art of tessellation, whereby small pieces of broken china or glass are painstakingly arranged in cement. The first thing to catch the eye is the huge dragon in the courtyard to the right of the main building, constructed from over twelve thousand carefully broken beer bottles. Artwork inside the pagoda is even more intricate, with mosaic dragons entwined around the main hall's pillars, while stairs lead up on the left to colourfully inlaid galleries, shrines and good views. The deep sound of resonating bells, rung by devotees, makes the main hall very atmospheric.

Tiger Falls

4km east of the train station along Trai Mat • Daily 7.30am–5pm • 10,000đ

Located at the end of a precarious switchback road are the **Tiger Falls**, the most popular in the area with visitors. A steep concrete stairway leads down to the base of the falls, which tumble from a great height and offer good photo opportunities. The falls are a very popular destination for Vietnamese, so you're unlikely to be able to enjoy the place alone. Pools and boulders around the base of the falls make ideal spots for a picnic. By the restaurants you'll see a statue of a primitive hunter and another of a huge hollow tiger, whose mouth you can climb into for a photo.

Lak Lake

Gong performances $100 per group • **Canoe rides** $20

A hundred and fifty kilometres north of Da Lat and 40km south of Buon Ma Thuot, Highway 27 passes serene **LAK LAKE**, a charming spot that has become very popular with tourists. Five thousand people, mostly from the Mnong community, once lived on the lake itself, but have since moved into distinctive longhouses in shoreside villages. There are a number of (slightly cheesy) activities available here, including musical gong performances and elephant rides; note that the latter can no longer be recommended, since you'll be sitting atop a metal cage that's doubtless extremely painful for the poor pachyderm. Still, the lake itself is a glorious place, as once attested by Emperor Bao Dai himself – he grabbed some of the best sites in southern Vietnam for his many palaces, so it comes as no surprise to learn that he had one here, in a prime spot on a small hill overlooking the lake. The palace is long gone, but the site is now home to a small hotel (see below).

3

Jun Village

Located on the southern side of the lake

If you're intent on getting the whole minority village experience, complete with grunting pigs and squawking chickens waking you in the morning, head on round to **Jun Village**, a thriving Mnong community on the west side of the hill, whose longhouses crowd together near the shore – to say hello in their local tongue, use "kuro-me" to men and "kuro-e" to women. Dak Lak Tourist (see below) has a branch office here, and a longhouse where it's possible to stay overnight.

ARRIVAL AND INFORMATION   LAK LAKE

By bus Although Lak Lake is mostly geared towards organized tour groups, it's possible to arrive here independently, on the local buses heading between Da Lat and Buon Ma Thuot; it's a shorter ride from the latter, from which tickets cost 20,000đ. Buses set down and pick up at Jun Village, to the south of the lake, leaving Buon Ma Thuot approximately once an hour.

Dak Lak Tourist Office For bookings and enquiries, contact Dak Lak Tourist Office (☎ 0500 385 2246, ⓦ daklaktourist.com.vn).

ACCOMMODATION

Staff at the following will likely speak little English, but you'll be able to book through Dak Lak Tourist Office (see above).

★ **Bao Dai Residence** On a rise off the southeastern shore of the lake. The walls of Bao Dai's old palace boasts some intriguing snaps of Vietnam's last emperor and a few well-equipped rooms that enjoy fabulous views over the lake. With a decent restaurant too, it's far and away the best place to stay hereabouts. $30

Jun Village To the south of the lake. Accommodation is available at 15 longhouses in homely Jun Village itself.

Mosquito nets and mattresses are provided, and there are outside toilet facilities. $7

Lak Resort To the east of the lake. Snuggled into a protected bay to the east of the hill, the *Lak Resort* consists of both smart, brick bungalows with a/c, TV and fridge in the rooms, and two longhouses ($5) beneath a grove of trees. Staff in traditional Mnong dress dish up reasonable food at the floating restaurant. $35

Buon Ma Thuot and around

The city of **BUON MA THUOT** itself has little to offer, its central sprawl of modern buildings being splayed across a grid of characterless streets. With a jeep protruding from its central column, the town's dramatic **Victory Monument** on Le Duan is the hub from which all the town's main roads radiate. The town grew big on coffee and rubber, and is surprisingly affluent with a spate of buildings under construction and flash cars buzzing around its streets. However, in a neat reversal of the norm, urban renewal is occurring from the outside in, and the centre is still appealingly grubby.

The main draw of Buon Ma Thuot is what can be found in its environs: nearby minority villages with **longhouses**; traditional minority communities (mostly E De people) at **Ako Dhong** on the northern outskirts of town and in the surrounding countryside at **Ban Don** near **Yok Don National Park**; and some wonderful waterfalls. Between April and July you'll see the city surrounded by millions of lemon-coloured butterflies, wafting through the air like yellow petals.

3

Brief history

During French colonial times, the town developed on the back of the coffee, tea, rubber and hardwood crops that grew in its fertile red soil, and was the focal point for the **plantations** that smothered the surrounding countryside: plantation owners and other *colons* would amuse themselves by picking off the elephants, leopards and tigers once prevalent in the area. In later years Americans superseded the French, but they were long gone by the time the North Vietnamese Army (NVA) swept through in March 1975, making Buon Ma Thuot the first "domino" to fall in the Ho Chi Minh Campaign.

Khai Doan Pagoda

89a Phan Boi Chau • Sunrise to sunset • Free

Of central Buon Ma Thuot's few sights, the **Khai Doan Pagoda**, built in 1951, is an interesting fusion of E De longhouse and Hué Imperial architecture; it stands on a slope beside a large bo tree, underneath which sits a Buddha image in meditation posture. The front of the building, approached by steps, is made of huge slabs of glossy, painted wood, with the approximate dimensions of a longhouse, but the ornate, double-layered roof is classic Hué architecture. Just below the roof at the front runs a frieze of gold-painted panels depicting scenes from the life of the Buddha. A more recent extension of brick and cement at the back houses the altar with several more Buddha images, while the bright pillars have dragons leaping off them. The pagoda was built to honour Emperor Khai Dinh's wife, Hoang Thi Cuc, who was also mother of the last emperor, Bao Dai.

Ethnographic Museum

Le Duan • Daily 7–11am & 1.30–5pm • 10,000đ

To find out more about the cultures of the local minority groups, check out the **Ethnographic Museum**, originally set in a crumbling edifice surrounded by peaceful gardens to the south of the centre. At the time of writing, the museum was set to move to a rather spectacular building just to the north of the original structure – a bizarre, and rather impressive, fusion of tribal and contemporary styles. Among the exhibits are a waistcoat made of bark, traditional clothing of the various ethnic groups of the region, funerary statues of peacocks and tusks, and instruments for taming elephants, like vicious mahouts' spikes and two thorny harnesses.

Ako Dhong

About 2km from the city centre, and best approached by xe om (10,000đ). Otherwise, follow Phan Chu Trinh towards the northeast, then turn left on Tran Nhat Duat

On the town's northern fringes, the tidy E De weaving village of **Ako Dhong**, is also worth a visit. Not that this will give you any real insights into tribal culture – the sturdy longhouses have clean-swept yards and trim hedges, giving the feel of an affluent suburb. The tantalizing aroma of roasting coffee beans often fills the air, and the gentle clack-clack emanating from the buildings signals the weavers at work.

Dak Lak Water Park

Nguyen Chi Thanh, 4km northeast of Buon Ma Thuot • 35,000đ • ☎ 0500 395 0381

If you're in need of cooling down, head for the pools and water flumes of **Dak Lak Water Park**, which can come as a blessed relief on one of Buon Ma Thuot's many scorching summer days. The complex is rather smaller than similar facilities in other

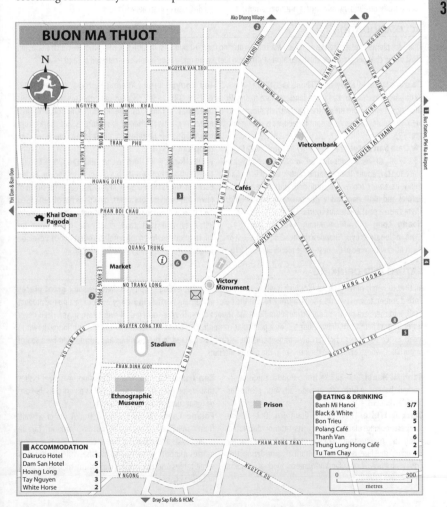

BUON MA THUOT

ACCOMMODATION
Dakruco Hotel	1
Dam San Hotel	5
Hoang Long	4
Tay Nguyen	3
White Horse	2

EATING & DRINKING
Banh Mi Hanoi	3/7
Black & White	8
Bon Trieu	5
Polang Café	1
Thanh Van	6
Thung Lung Hong Café	2
Tu Tam Chay	4

countries, and centred on an artificial mountain, from which the slides race down: best to come during the week when it is less busy.

ARRIVAL AND DEPARTURE BUON MA THUOT

By plane The airport is 8km east of town on the road towards Da Lat; a taxi into town costs around $7. Vietnam Airlines (☎0500 395 4442) is at 19 Ama Thanh Long.
Destinations: Da Nang (daily; 1hr 10min); Hanoi (2 daily; 1hr 40min); Ho Chi Minh City (5–6 daily; 1hr).

By bus The bus station (☎0500 387 6833) is 3km northeast of town on Nguyen Tat Thanh; several a/c express services arrive daily from Nha Trang and Ho Chi Minh City.
Destinations: Da Nang (12hr); Ho Chi Minh City (7hr); Nha Trang (4hr); Pleiku (4hr).

INFORMATION

Tourist information Although Dak Lak Province is fairly relaxed about visits to surrounding villages, some, particularly those near the Cambodian border, are still theoretically off limits, while others are not permitted to house foreign guests overnight. Check with the Dak Lak Tourist Office at 53 Ly Thuong Kiet (☎0500 385 2246, ⒲daklaktourist.com.vn), who can also arrange car rental, guides, visa extensions and tours.

ACCOMMODATION

There are plenty of places to **stay** in Buon Ma Thuot, catering for most budgets, though few of them have much character. Most of the cheaper places are clustered along Ly Thuong Kiet, while mid-range hotels are scattered around town.

Dakruco Hotel 30 Nguyen Chi Thanh ☎0500 397 0889, ⒲dakrucohotels.com. By far the fanciest place to stay in the city, set apart from the centre in a relatively prosperous area. The rooms are very pleasant indeed, as is the on-site spa. $95

★ **Dam San Hotel** 212–214 Nguyen Cong Tru ☎0500 385 1234, ⒲www.damsanhotel.com.vn. A good-value place to stay, about 1km from the centre, which is no bad thing. Its smart rooms are furnished with tasteful local textiles and most have lovely views across a lush hillside. There's also a pool and tennis courts. $35

Hoang Long 168 Hung Vuong ☎0500 384 1841, ⒲hoanglonghotel.vn. A nondescript building to the east of the centre, with some of the best-value rooms in town. $10

Tay Nguyen 110 Ly Thuong Kiet ☎0500 385 1009, ☎0500 385 2250. Located near the town centre, this place has a range of ageing but functional rooms; mercifully, this L-shaped building is set back from the road and therefore quieter than much of the competition. $16

White Horse 7–13 Nguyen Duc Canh ☎0500 381 5656, ⒠whitehorsehotelvn@yahoo.com. Also known as the Bach Ma, this is tucked away in a backstreet to the north of town. Although it looks smart, questions have been raised over how professionally it is run – rooms are occasionally left dirty, and staff can't exactly be relied upon for information. However, the hotel still offers good mid-range value. $28

EATING AND DRINKING

All the big hotels have restaurants, which is where many visitors end up eating – a pity, as there are some **great places** dotted around town. It would also be a crime to visit the heart of Vietnam's **coffee industry** without tasting the product itself, and there are plenty of opportunities in Buon Ma Thuot's cafés. They're scattered all over town, so you need never suffer from caffeine withdrawal, but there's a particular concentration along the south end of Le Thanh Tong, known to locals as "Coffee Street". Not terribly atmospheric, these cafés are packed in the evenings and surrounded by a sea of motorbikes, whose owners sip their drinks in the dim-lit interiors.

Banh Mi Hanoi 123–127 Le Hong Phong. Large, well-stocked bakery, which can provide all your picnic (or breakfast) needs.

Black & White 171 Nguyen Cong Tru. One of the sharpest-looking places in town, its interior decorated along the monochrome lines hinted at by the name. However, the fare is pleasingly normal considering the arty ambience – regular Vietnamese food at regular Vietnamese prices.

Bon Trieu 33 Hai Ba Trung. Cooks up tasty beef dishes that are perennially popular as well as a very passable *cari de* (goat curry), for around $2 a dish.

Polang Café G26 Tran Khanh Du. A bit of a walk from anywhere, this café has a striking facade resembling a longhouse entrance; inside, the decor utilizes minority patterns and motifs, while the bases of some tables and chairs are made of the gnarled stumps of coffee bushes.

ELEPHANT RACE FESTIVAL

If you're in town in spring, don't miss the **Elephant Race Festival**, which takes place on the banks of the Serepok River near Ban Don. It's usually held in the third lunar month but preparations take place for weeks beforehand – those who own elephants in the area spend time fattening up their beasts on local fruit and crops. The race itself is usually brief but blazing, the elephants encouraged (or distracted) by the loud drumming of gongs. Ask at Dak Lak Tourist for dates and details.

Thanh Van 20 Ly Thuong Kiet. Friendly joint famed locally for its fine *nem* (spring rolls), which go for $2 a portion and are absolutely delicious. There's a similar place right next door if this one's full.

★ **Thung Lung Hong Café** Hem 153 Phan Chu Trinh. Snuggled at the base of a steep valley at the end of a sidestreet off Phan Chu Trinh. It's hugely popular among locals and, given the dearth of nightlife in Buon Ma Thuot, a godsend for visitors too. Also a bit of a walk away from the centre.

Tu Tam Chay 103 Quang Trang. Although the food on display here looks meaty and fishy, all the dishes here are one hundred percent vegetarian; point, sit and eat. Prices are extremely low – $1.50 should be enough for a small meal.

DIRECTORY

Banks Vietcombank, 6 Tran Hung Dao, changes travellers' cheques and foreign currency and has an ATM – there are many more around the town centre.

Internet The post office has internet access, or try the cheap shop at 36 Ly Thuong Kiet.

Post office (daily 7am–8.30pm) is on Le Duan just south of Victory Monument.

Waterfalls around Buon Ma Thuot

Several waterfalls near Buon Ma Thuot Thuot are worth visiting, especially in the wet season, though unless you're a real falls fan you can be selective. **Dray Sap** and **Dray Nur**, situated side-by-side, are the most impressive and most popular.

Trinh Nu Falls
8am–6pm • Free

Comprising a narrow chute of water approached by a steep path, these small falls are less spectacular than Dray Sap and Dray Nur a little further down the road (see below), but still worth a visit – the boulders lining the river are highly picturesque. The area is in the process of turning into a resort of sorts, and may soon make a more appealing place to stay than central Buon Ma Thuot. At the top of the falls is a restaurant with small, inviting pavilions overlooking the river – a good spot to rest up for refreshment or lunch.

Dray Sap and Dray Nur Falls
8am–6pm • 8000đ ticket gives access to both falls

The crescent-shaped **Dray Sap** and neighbouring **Dray Nur Falls** are among the most spectacular waterfalls in the central highlands. After a short descent down steps from the car park, a wooden **suspension bridge** to the left leads to Dray Nur Falls, which, though not as wide as Dray Sap, carry more water in the dry season. On the other hand, at the end of the wet season, in September, water levels are usually too high for the short walk to the falls to be accessible. Almost 15m high and over 100m wide, Dray Sap doesn't mean "waterfall of smoke" for nothing: a fug of invigorating spray sags the air around. The area round the falls can get very crowded at weekends and on public holidays, but midweek a trip here makes a pleasant outing for a half or full day. Just after passing the ticket office at the approach to Dray Sap Falls, a road branching to the right leads another 7km to **Gia Long Falls**, yet another waterfall in the region, where there's also the chance of **camping**.

PARK ACTIVITIES

There are a number of **activities** on offer in Ban Don, an increasingly switched-on national park. Basic **hiking** is the most popular, though you'll need a guide ($40 full-day; $20 half-day). One interesting variation is a night hike ($10; seven-person minimum); at certain times of year, shine a torch into the darkness and you'll see the eyes of thousands and thousands of frogs staring back at you. During daylight hours, it's also possible to take a short **boat-ride** along the Serepok ($20 per boat), or have an **elephant trekking tour**; the latter cannot be recommended due to the unfriendly metal cages plonked atop the beasts.

ARRIVAL · WATERFALLS AROUND BUON MA THUOT

To get to the falls, follow Highway 14 for 20km southwest of town, then turn left at the village of Ea Ting. Just 1km down this road, a left turn leads to Trinh Nu Falls; Dray Sap and Dray Nur are a further 9km along. Most go as part of a tour, which will cost around $10 per person.

Yok Don National Park

Vietnam's largest wildlife preserve, **Yok Don National Park**, stretches 115,000 hectares between the hinge of the Cambodian border and the **Serepok River**. If you start off early in the morning you might see E De and other minority peoples leaving their split-bamboo thatch houses for work in the fields, carrying their tools in raffia backpacks. In addition, over sixty species of animals, including tigers, leopards and bears, and more than 450 types of birds, populate the park; most, however, reside deep in the interior. Of all its exotic animals, **elephants** are what Yok Don is best known for; the tomb of the greatest elephant hunter of them all – Y Thu Knu (1850–1924), who had a lifetime tally of 244 – is located beyond the final hamlet from the park entrance.

Ban Don

The three sub-hamlets that comprise the village of **BAN DON** lie a few kilometres beyond Yok Don's park HQ, on the bank of the crocodile-infested Serepok River. Khmer, Thai, Lao, Jarai and Mnong live in the vicinity, though it's the **E De** that make up the majority. They adhere to a matriarchal social system, whereby a groom takes his bride's name, lives with her family and, should his wife die subsequently, marries one of her sisters so that her family retains a male workforce. Houses around the village, a few of which are longhouses, are built on stilts, and some are decorated with ornate woodwork.

However, village life in Ban Don has become overwhelmingly commercial as the Ban Don Tourist Centre has organized its residents into a tourist-welcoming taskforce. It's possible to spend the night here, though you'll only truly appreciate Yok Don by heading further into the park; one exception is during March, when the annual elephant festival is held (see box, p.195).

ARRIVAL · YOK DON NATIONAL PARK

By bus Ban Don is about 45km from Buon Ma Thuot. Most people visit the park on an organized tour (see box above), but there are hourly public buses (10,000đ) from Phan Boi Chau in Buon Ma Thuot; these terminate a few kilometres from the park entrance, and the remaining distance is easily covered by xe om.

By taxi It's also possible to get a taxi from Buon Ma Thuot for around $35, including 2hr waiting time.

ACCOMMODATION

Park Accommodation Overnight accommodation in the park includes the twin-bedded cabin-style rooms in the guesthouse by the park office, a campground or forest stations in the park. While it's possible to just turn up at the park office, you'll certainly save time – and likely have more luck – by booking through Dak Lak Tourist office (see p.194). $10

Pleiku

Though it's not terribly easy on the eye, the regional capital of **PLEIKU** possesses a carefree air quite in keeping with its far-flung location. The city was wrecked during the war (see box below), and so little of it was left standing that a near-total reconstruction was required when hostilities ceased. The 1980s reincarnation that you'll see lacks charm, but given the distances between central highlands cities you'll most likely want to stay anyway – a range of nearby minority villages further sweeten the deal, though note that you'll need a guide to visit any of them. If you're keen to explore minority villages without a government chaperone, it makes sense to push on 50km north, just an hour's journey, to Kon Tum, where there are fewer restrictions.

Ho Chi Minh Museum

1 Phan Dinh Phuong • Mon–Fri 7.30–11am & 1–5pm • Free

The **Ho Chi Minh Museum**, to the north of the town centre, features swords, crossbows, bamboo xylophones, a weaving loom and a pair of Uncle Ho's sandals, but no English signs. Of all the country's Ho Chi Minh museums, few score more highly on the glorifying scale than the one in Pleiku, which focuses largely on the local ethnic communities' uncompromising adoration for Uncle Ho.

Gia Lai Museum

Tran Hung Dao • Mon–Fri 7.30–11am & 1–5pm • 10,000đ

The **Gia Lai Museum** is a little better, with a gong and rice-wine jar collection in one gallery and, in another, replicas of a Bahnar grave and longhouse are displayed. However, there's no real reason to come here if you're visiting the local Bahnar villages.

ARRIVAL AND DEPARTURE

PLEIKU

By plane The airport (☎ 059 382 5097) lies 7km northeast of the city, from where taxis (about 100,000đ) and xe om (about 50,000đ) make the journey to the centre; Vietnam Airlines, at 18 Le Lai (Mon–Sat; ☎ 059 382 3058), can arrange onward flight reservations.
Destinations: Da Nang (daily; 50min); Hanoi (2 daily; 1hr 25min); Ho Chi Minh City (4 daily; 1hr 25min).

By bus The bus station is below the three-way crossroads 600m southeast of the centre, a short xe om ride into the city along Hung Vuong.
Destinations: Buon Ma Thuot (4hr); Da Nang (10hr); Kon Tum (1hr); Quy Nhon (4hr).

INFORMATION

Tourist office Gia Lai Tourist (☎ 059 387 4571, ⓦ gialaitourist.com) is inside the *Hung Vuong Hotel* (see opposite), and can provide information as well as arrange expensive, tailor-made trekking and battlefield tours and overnight stays in minority villages (see opposite).

THE ROLLING THUNDER CAMPAIGN

The band of peaks to the west of Highway 14 en route to Pleiku, and the rugged terrain buttressing them, constituted one of the American War's major combat theatres. It was an NVA (North Vietnamese Army) attack on Pleiku, in February 1965, that elicited the "Rolling Thunder" campaign (see p.446); the war's first conventional battle of any size was fought in the **Ia Drang Valley**, southwest of Pleiku, eight months later. Hundreds of Americans died at Ia Drang, but many times more Communists perished, spurring America to claim victory by dint of a higher body count. A decade later, in March 1975, Pleiku was abandoned when NVA troops overran Buon Ma Thuot. As the South's commanding officers flew by helicopter to safety, two hundred thousand Southern soldiers and civilians were left to make their own way down to the coast, hounded at every step by NVA shells.

ACCOMMODATION

Accommodation in Pleiku is decidedly uninspiring; there's a smattering of near-identical cheap options in the city centre, though almost nothing at the middle or higher end.

Duc Long 95–97 Hai Ba Trung ☎059 387 6303. The best budget option in town is a couple of blocks west of the market. The big, carpeted rooms have pine furnishings and represent good value; choose yours carefully, since some are, shall we say, less private than others. $12

HAGL Hotel 1 Phu Dong ☎059 371 8450, ⊛hagl.com .vn. By far the most comfortable option around: its rooms are spacious and well-equipped with desks and bathtubs,

and those on the upper floors have good views across the countryside. Good value, and a nice place to treat yourself if you've been on a central highland slog. It's about 1km east of the town centre. $50

Hung Vuong 2 Le Loi ☎059 382 4270. The home of Gia Lai Tourist (see opposite), and not a terrible place to stay – cheap, with decent, simple rooms, and a fairly good on-site restaurant. $15

EATING

Acacia Restaurant At the HAGL Hotel. The *Acacia Restaurant* serves up a good range of Vietnamese, and a few Western, dishes. Considering the fact that it's in the city's poshest hotel, prices are surprisingly reasonable, and service fast. The downside is that, unless you're staying here, it's a fair walk from the centre.

Café Tennis 61 Quang Trang. Reasonable place for a decent coffee. It is, in fact, located next to a tennis court – come at the right time and you may even be able to see a few games.

Nem Ninh Hoa 66 Nguyen Van Troi. Small place churning out delicious *nem*. Expect to pay around $2.50 for a good plateful of these roll-your-own spring rolls.

Thien Thanh 1km north of the town centre. *Thien Thanh* is a pleasant garden restaurant, at the end of a steep lane off Le Loi: look for the sign on the right. This attractive place has a landscaped garden with small ponds and sweeping views over rice fields, as well as a good range of Vietnamese food. Service can be painfully slow.

DIRECTORY

Bank Vietcombank at 62 Phan Boi Chau can change travellers' cheques and has an ATM.

Internet Available across town, including the shop at 80 Nguyen Van Troi.

The Villages Around Pleiku

This far north in the highlands, the **Jarai** (see p.470) and, to a lesser extent, the **Bahnar** (see p.470) outnumber the E De, though many of them have been assimilated into mainstream Vietnamese culture. You'll need a guide to tour any of these villages (see opposite).

The Jarai villages

It's possible to visit a number of Jarai villages in the area and, as is common with this particular tribe, the incredibly ornate graveyards are the main focus of interest. In the past the Jarai would stick bamboo poles through the earth and into a fresh grave, through which to "feed" the dead, though now they tend to leave fruit and bowls of rice on top of the grave. **Plei Phun** is by far the most commonly visited of the local Jarai villages. Your guide will show you around the headman's house, the local graveyard and village spring. The graveyard is particularly interesting, and you'll see roughly hewn **hardwood statues** depicting figures in a range of moods placed around each family grave.

The Bahnar villages

A group of four secluded but easily accessible **Bahnar** settlements lie 38km east of Pleiku, en route to Quy Nhon. The villages of **Dek Tu**, **De Cop**, **De Doa** and **Dek Rol** all rub shoulders with one another across a small area of forests and streams. Small split-bamboo and straw houses on stilts proliferate through these orderly communities, and each one boasts an impressive, steeply thatched *rong*, or communal house, where ceremonies are performed, local disputes are resolved and decisions taken. Again, the graveyards are particularly interesting, particularly that of Dek Tu, where the practice of feeding the dead is prevalent. Unlike the Jarai, each of the deceased has his own individual grave complete with a small sloping roof. Ladders made out of bamboo poles are leant against the graves to aid the journey to a new life; some are adorned with surprising ornaments, including wooden American fighter jets.

INFORMATION AND ACCOMMODATION

Tourist information Pleiku's tourist board, Gia Lai Tourist, is notoriously defensive of the region's few remaining traditional settlements and doesn't approve of individuals making forays into the wilds, insisting that you should always be with a licensed guide when visiting villages. If you try to bypass this regulation and just turn up in villages, you'll get little cooperation from the locals, who receive a cut from visitor fees – and their own share of the blame, even when it all lies with the renegade tourist. To visit the Jarai or Bahnar villages,

VILLAGES AROUND PLEIKU

you'll need to be with an official guide from Gia Lai Tourist (see p.198); these cost from $10 for a half-day and $20 for a whole one, and you'll have to fund their transportation.

Home-stays It's possible to arrange a home-stay in the largest Bahnar village, De Cop. Gia Lai Tourist have commandeered a house on stilts here, from where you can visit each village on a one-day hike. A two-day programme visiting both Plei Phun and these villages works out about $30–35 a head for a group of five people.

Kon Tum

The sleepy, friendly town of **KON TUM** sits on the edge of the Dakbla River, and is one of the best bases in the central highlands – unlike busy Buon Ma Thuot and concrete-heavy Pleiku, this provincial capital makes a highly pleasant place to stay. It also has a few sights of its own, including some sterling colonial-era architecture – some of the most beautiful buildings in the country. However, most are here to use Kon Tum as a springboard for jaunts to outlying villages of the **Bahnar** and other minorities such as the **Sedang** (see p.471), **Gieh Trieng** and **Rongao**. There are about 650 minority villages in the province, of which only a few have been visited by foreigners, so the scope for adventure here is broad.

Kon Tum's riverside promenade along the Dakbla River is a fine place for a stroll – especially on fair-weather evenings, when it seems as if half the town stops by. It would also be the perfect place for a beer, but only the bars on the other side of the road seem to sell bottles – and even then, they're usually warm and only for on-site drinking.

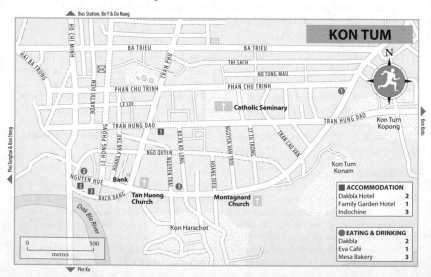

■ ACCOMMODATION	
Dakbla Hotel	2
Family Garden Hotel	1
Indochine	3

● EATING & DRINKING	
Dakbla	2
Eva Café	1
Mesa Bakery	3

Tan Huong Church

92 Nguyen Hué • Sunrise to sunset • Free

At the junction of Nguyen Hué and Tran Phu, you can't miss the grand bulk of **Tan Huong Church**, with colourful bas reliefs in pastel shades on its facade. Considering Kon Tum's remote location, the church is a surprisingly elegant building; the original structure was completed in the 1850s but has been restored several times since.

Montagnard Church

Nguyen Hué • Sunrise to sunset • Free

Also known as the "Wooden Church", this stunning edifice was built by the French in 1913 and has been frequently restored since then. A statue of Christ stands over the front entrance; below him, a stained-glass window neatly fuses the classic Christian symbol of the dove with images of local resonance – a Bahnar village and an elephant. In the grounds is a statue of nineteenth-century French bishop Stephen Theodore Cuenot, who established the diocese of Kon Tum. Mass is held in the Bahnar language – they don't mind curious foreigners popping their heads in, but be respectful if taking any pictures.

There's also an **orphanage** behind the church, which looks after children of all ages in spartan but well-cared-for surroundings. Visitors are welcome, as are donations.

3

Catholic seminary

56 Tran Hung Dao • Sunrise to sunset • Free

Kon Tum's **Catholic seminary** is certainly worth a look for its impressive architecture. Set in the middle of garden-filled grounds, its appearance is far more European than Vietnamese. The soft cream colour of the seminary walls is offset by dark wood, and though few of the rooms are open to visitors, the gardens are a great place to relax for half an hour.

ARRIVAL AND DEPARTURE   KON TUM

By plane The nearest airport is less than an hour down the road in Pleiku (see p.198), though you'll need to use your initiative to get to Kon Tum without hitting Pleiku first. Highway 14 is around 1km west of the terminal; either wait for one of the irregular Kon Tum-bound buses, or prepare to haggle with a xe om driver.

By bus The bus station is to the northwest of town on Phan Dinh Phung. From here, it's best to take a xe om (20,000đ) to the town centre, which is about 3km away.
Destinations: Da Nang (5hr); Pleiku (1hr); Quang Ngai (5hr); Attapeu, Laos (8hr).

INFORMATION

Tourist office Kon Tum Tourist (📞 060 386 3334, 🌐 kontumtourist.com) is open daily 7–11am & 1–5pm, on the ground floor of the *Dakbla Hotel* (see below). They rent bikes and can organize a wide range of tours, including trekking, river trips and traditional dance performances, and offer information on new areas opening up in the surrounding region. Even if you don't book a tour through them, they're happy to give independent advice.

ACCOMMODATION

Dakbla Hotel 2 Phan Dinh Phung 📞 060 386 3333. Kon Tum's state-owned monstrosity has relatively cheerful rooms. It's great for solo travellers too, as single rates are typically half that of doubles. **$20**

★ **Family Garden Hotel** 235 Tran Hung Dao 📞 060 386 2448, 🌐 familyhotelvietnam.com. A good budget option on one of Kon Tum's main roads. The rooms are clean and brightly decorated, there's an attractive garden and the owners are friendly. **$17**

Indochine 30 Bach Dang 📞 060 386 3335, 📠 060 386 2762. The town's fanciest hotel enjoys a prime riverside location. Perhaps not as grand as the wistful name may lead you to believe, but rooms are cosy and those facing the river have great views. **$45**

3

VISITING THE MINORITY VILLAGES

There are dozens of Bahnar villages encircling Kon Tum. As most are free from the official restrictions that hang over Pleiku, you're at liberty to explore this area at will, although for **overnight stays** it's best to check first with the tourist office (see p.201); if you opt for their guided tours it'll work out at around $25 per person per day.

All Bahnar villages have at their centre a longhouse known as a *rong*. Built on sturdy **stilts** with a platform and entrance at either end (or sometimes in the middle); the interior is generally made of split bamboo and protected by a towering thatched roof, usually about 15m high. The *rong* is used as a venue for festivals and village meetings, and as a **village court** at which anyone found guilty of a tribal offence has to ritually kill a pig and a chicken, and must apologize in front of the village.

WITHIN KON TUM

One good thing about Kon Tum is that you don't have to go far to get a feel of a minority village, as there are a couple of Bahnar villages within the town itself. First comes **Kon Harachot**, whose immaculate *rong* faces a football field – if you're lucky, you may even get to see an all-Bahnar game. To get there, head east along Nguyen Hué, and take any right turn up until Hoang Dieu; Ly Thai To will bring you straight to the *rong*. Following Nguyen Hué to its eastern end brings you to **Kon Tum Konam**, while following Tran Hung Dao to the east takes you directly to **Kon Tum Kopong**, where there is another wonderful example of a *rong*. Villagers at Kon Tum Kopong are big on **basket-weaving**, and you might chance upon locals cutting bamboo into thin strips and crafting them into sturdy baskets, which they sell very cheaply in the local market.

PLEI THONGHIA AND KON HONGO

The villages of **Plei Thongia** and **Kon Hongo**, respectively 1km and 4km west of Kon Tum, are inhabited by members of the Rongao, one of the smaller minority groups in the region. Women are often busy weaving in the shade of their simple, wooden huts, **ox carts** trundle along the dusty road and children splash about in the Dakbla River down below. It's possible to walk to Plei Tonghia – heading north from the Dakbla bridge, turn left at Ba Trieu and just keep going. Kon Hongo is within cycling distance but a little tricky to find – it's easier to take a xe om there (20,000d) and work your way back on foot.

KON KOTU

About 5km to the east of Kon Tum is the most frequently visited of Bahnar villages, **Kon Kotu**. Though now linked to Kon Tum by a surfaced road, it makes a pleasant walk to go there by **country paths** (contact the local tourist office for details) and it's possible to overnight in the village *rong*. To get there **by road**, follow Tran Hung Dao east out of town until you reach a suspension bridge over the river at **Kon Klor**. Turn left 200m beyond the bridge and follow the road to Kon Kotu. Though the village church is absolutely huge, and fairly pretty to boot, it's still the immaculate *rong* that commands the most attention. No nails were used in the construction of the bamboo walls, floor and the impossibly tall thatch roof of this lofty communal hall. It also doubles as an occasional **overnight stop** for local trekking tours organized by Kon Tum Tourist (see p.201), either in a simple guesthouse ($12 per person), or the longhouse itself ($10).

YA CHIM

About 17km southwest of Kon Tum is the village of **Ya Chim**, where there are a few Jarai cemeteries that can be visited, though it's best to go with a guide from Kon Tum Tourist as they are tricky to find. Wooden posts, some of them carved in the form of mourning figures, surround the graves and personal possessions such as a bicycle or TV are placed inside. The graves are carefully tended for a period of three to five years after death and offerings are brought to the site daily. At the end of this period a buffalo is sacrificed to make a feast for the villagers and the grave is abandoned in the belief that the spirit of the deceased has now departed.

MOVING ON TO LAOS

The **international border crossing** from the central highlands to Laos, open at Bo Y 80km northwest of Kon Tum, provides access to the rarely visited region of southern Laos. Heading on west it takes you to Isaan, in the forgotten northeast of Thailand – three off-the-beaten track Southeast Asian destinations in one. Though in theory you can obtain a fifteen-day Lao visa at the border ($30; two passport photos required), it's best to get your visa in advance at the Lao consulate in either Ho Chi Minh City (see p.90) or Da Nang (p.274) or their Hanoi embassy (p.373), as border officials are notorious for extorting unscheduled payments from travellers in order to prevent administrative delays. There are irregular bus departures from Kon Tum to Attapeu and Pakse in Laos: check at the bus station for times.

EATING AND DRINKING

Dakbla 168 Nguyen Hué; see map p.200. Very popular with foreign visitors, offering a range of well-priced Vietnamese and Western dishes, as well as selling a selection of ethnic souvenirs.

★ **Eva Café** 1 Phan Chu Trinh; see map p.200. The place to savour the excellent local coffee is the *Eva Café*, run by a local sculptor, whose work is also displayed here; the three-storey café has been built to resemble a stilthouse, and its surrounding garden yields fountains, wooden sculptures of distorted faces and a waterfall trickling down the back wall.

Mesa Bakery 80 Nguyen Hué; see map p.200. Just the ticket if you're looking for a few provisions to pop in your bag on a village hike, this bakery produces mountains of decent bread, mini-pizzas, cookies and the like.

DIRECTORY

Banks It's possible to change money at the BIDV Bank at 1 Tran Phu, where there's also an ATM; there's another at the Agribank at 88 Tran Phu.

Internet There are several places offering internet access, including an outlet at 202 Ba Trieu.
Post office 205 Le Hong Phong.

The northern central highlands

From Kon Tum, travellers have the choice of heading for the **Laos** border at Bo Y (see box above), down to the coast at **Quang Ngai** on Highway 24 or continuing north on the picturesque Highway 14, also know as the **Ho Chi Minh Highway**, which is a pleasure to travel on.

Dak To

Around 42km north of Kon Tum, the district of **DAK TO** witnessed some of the most sustained fighting of the American War; to the west of the road to Dak To is Rocket Ridge, a brow of hills that earned its name from the heavy bombing – napalm and conventional – it received during this time. To the south of town is Charlie Hill, which was the scene of one of the fiercest battles of the war, ending in a VC victory over Southern troops. There's a *rong* right in the middle of Dak To, where the inhabitants are mostly Sedang, and with a little exploration you should be able to find more Sedang longhouses in the settlements surrounding Dak To.

Dak Glei and beyond

Heading north along the route from Dak To, the road passes through **Dak Glei**, where there's another spectacular *rong*. Directly east is virgin jungle surrounding Mount Ngoc Linh (2598m), the highest peak in the central highlands. Beyond here, the route takes you through wonderfully verdant and unpopulated countryside before Highway 14B branches off to the right at **Nam Giang**, taking you down to the coast at Hoi An or Da Nang.

The southern coast

THE RED SAND DUNES NEAR MUI NE

The southern coast

Vietnam's convex southern coastline is lined with seemingly endless beaches that, for many, are reason enough to visit the country. The main resort areas of Nha Trang and Mui Ne have seen their popularity explode, and are now adding culinary sophistication and top-drawer accommodation to their coastal charms. There are also a number of less-heralded beaches to track down, and even a few islands, but the region also has historical significance – this was once the domain of the kingdom of Champa, whose magnificent ruins still dot the coast.

An Indianized trading empire, **Champa** was courted in its prime by seafaring merchants from around the globe, but steadily marginalized from the tenth century onwards by the march south of the Vietnamese. These days a few enclaves around Phan Thiet and Phan Rang are all that remain of the Cham people, but the remnants of the towers that punctuate the countryside – many of which have recently been restored – recall Champa's former glory (see p.343).

Despite the influx of tourism, **sea fishing** is the region's lifeblood and provides a living for a considerable percentage of the population. Fleets of fishing boats jostle for space in the cramped ports and estuaries of the coastal towns, awaiting the turn of the tide; and fish and seafood drying along the road are a common sight. The fertile soil blesses the coastal plains with coconut palms, rice paddies, cashew orchards, sugar cane fields, vineyards and shrimp farms. One of the most commonly seen fruits here, especially around Phan Thiet, is the dragon fruit, which grows on plants with distinctive, octopus-like tentacles.

Vietnam's southernmost beaches are not on the southern coast at all, but on the former French prison islands of **Con Dao**. While many beaches are now experiencing high-octane development, Con Dao retains a laidback, unhurried air that tempts many to stay far longer than they'd planned. Back on the mainland, the first town of note is **Vung Tau**, once a French seaside resort, and now a smart, oil-rich town with passable beaches; much better beaches can be found further up the coast at places like **Ho Coc**. In reality, few travellers have the time or inclination to meander along the beaches between Vung Tau and Mui Ne, but with your own transport and an adventurous spirit you'll find somewhere to pace out a solitary set of footprints in the pristine sand.

You'll never be alone at **Mui Ne**, a short skirt up the coast. Very recently, this was virtually unheard of, but its transition from being the country's best-kept secret to one of its most high-profile resorts happened almost overnight. It's perhaps a sign of things to come for Vietnamese tourism – slick resorts rubbing shoulders along a fine sweep of soft sand, looking out over aquamarine waters. This tourist enclave attracts a steady stream of overseas visitors, as well as providing an idyllic short break for Ho Chi Minh City's expats and growing middle-class. Those for whom a day sunbathing is a day wasted will prefer to make a little more headway, and rest up around **Phan Rang**, site of **Po Klong Garai**, the most impressive of the many **tower complexes** erected by the once-mighty empire of **Champa**. The nearby beaches at **Ninh Chu** and **Ca Na** aren't quite in the same league as Mui Ne, but both make appealing options for a bit of peace and quiet.

North of Phan Rang, Highway 1 ploughs through sugar-cane plantations, blinding white salt flats and shrimp farms on its way into **Nha Trang**. Here travellers can enjoy the best of both worlds – a combination of Cham towers and beach activities, the latter including diving and snorkelling trips. Nha Trang also has the southern coast's greatest range of accommodation and restaurants, and is a deservedly popular place. Other

BEACH AT NHA TRANG

Highlights

1 Con Dao Islands Discover the site of Vietnam's most feared prison, which now welcomes divers, trekkers and beach bums. **See p.209**

2 Ca Na beach Everyone knows about Nha Trang and Mui Ne, but the southern coast still has a few virtually deserted beaches – this pristine stretch being one such example. **See p.225**

3 Mui Ne Stay in a fancy resort at Mui Ne and go kitesurfing in the breezy bay. **See p.220**

4 Cham monuments Get up close to the impressive Po Klong Garai towers, just outside Phan Rang, and other other Cham towers in the region. **See p.226**

5 Underwater activities Snorkel or dive in the clear waters off the islands near Nha Trang. **See p.229**

6 Mud baths Wallow in a mud bath at the Thap Ba Hot Springs near Nha Trang. **See p.233**

7 Quy Nhon Spend a couple of days meandering around this relatively unsung beach city with a pleasant chilled-out vibe, great seafood and some of the coast's best Cham ruins. **See p.240**

HIGHLIGHTS ARE MARKED ON THE MAP ON P.208

THE SOUTHERN COAST

more secluded beaches that warrant an expedition further north include **Doc Let** and **Sa Huynh**, while for a little more civilization, **Quy Nhon** makes a useful halt above Nha Trang. The scars of war tend not to intrude too much along this stretch of the country, though many visitors make time to visit **Quang Ngai**, where Vietnam's south-central arc of coastline culminates, and view the sombre site of the notorious **My Lai** massacre perpetrated by US forces in 1968.

The Con Dao Archipelago

Vietnam is book-ended to the south by the admirably unspoilt **Con Dao Archipelago**, a confetti-like spray of sixteen emerald-green islands, cast adrift in the South China Sea some 185km south of Vung Tau. The sleepy nature of the archipelago belies some tumultuous history – under French occupation, Con Dao was home to the most feared prison in the country, and haunting remnants of that time are still visible. However, more come here to get away from such negative thoughts, and since regular flights began early this century, the archipelago has taken its first steps to welcoming tourists.

Con Son island, the largest in the group, is a laidback get-away with some striking colonial buildings, alluring beaches and challenging treks in the rugged hills of the national park. **Trekking** in the national park, **diving** off the surrounding islands, watching **sea turtles** laying eggs and lounging on the uncrowded **beaches** are some of the alternative activities.

4

Brief history

The British East India Company established a **fortified outpost** on Con Son in 1703. Had this flourished, the island may by now have been a more diminutive Hong Kong or Singapore, given its strategic position on the route to China. But within three years, the Bugis mercenaries (from Sulawesi) drafted in to construct and garrison the base had murdered their British commanders, putting paid to this early experiment in colonization. Known then as Poulo Condore, Con Son was still treading water when the American sailor John White spied its "lofty summits" a little over a century later, in 1819. White deemed it a decent natural harbour, though blighted by "noxious reptiles, and affording no good fresh water".

The island finally found its calling when decades later the French chose it as the site of a **penal colony** for anti-colonial activists. Con Son's savage regime soon earned it the nickname "Devil's Island". Prisoners languished in squalid pits called "tiger cages", which featured metal grilles instead of roofs, from which guards sprinkled powdered lime and dirty water on the inmates. As the twentieth century progressed the colony developed into a sort of unofficial "revolutionary university". Older hands instructed their greener cell-mates in the finer points of Marxist-Leninist theory, while the dire conditions they endured helped reinforce the lessons.

Con Son Island

The biggest island in the archipelago, **CON SON** is its undisputed hub of activity, and the only place with any tourist facilities whatsoever. Bar diving and perhaps a short trip to a neighbouring island, for now this is the only place people get to see in Con Dao – no bad thing, since Con Son itself is an arrestingly beautiful place.

Con Son Town

Village-like Con Son Town is the largest settlement, and home to almost all of the island's accommodation and restaurants. Its peaceful promenade makes a beautiful place for a walk, past the huge gnarled trunks of the malabar almond trees as colourful

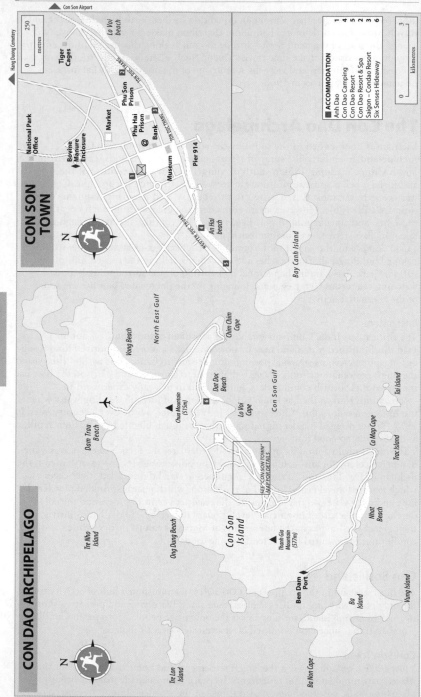

CON DAO ARCHIPELAGO

CON SON TOWN

Con Son Airport

Hang Duong Cemetery

Lo Voi beach

Tiger Cages

Phu Son Prison

Phu Hai Prison

Market

Bank

National Park Office

Bovine Manure Enclosure

Museum

Pier 914

An Hai beach

TON DUC THANG

TON DUC THANG

NGUYEN DUC THUAN

ACCOMMODATION

Anh Dao 1
Con Dao Camping 4
Con Dao Resort 5
Con Dao Resort & Spa 2
Saigon – Condao Resort 3
Six Senses Hideaway 6

kilometres

metres

Vong Beach

North East Gulf

Chim Chim Cape

Dat Doc Beach

La Voi Cape

Con Son Gulf

Bay Canh Island

Tai Island

Ca Map Cape

Trac Island

Dam Trau Beach

Chua Mountain (515m)

Tre Nho Island

Ong Dung Beach

Con Son Island

SEE "CON SON TOWN" MAP FOR DETAILS

Thanh Gia Mountain (577m)

Nhat Beach

Ben Dam Port

Ba Island

Vung Island

Tre Lon Island

Ba Non Cape

fishing boats bob in the bay. The promenade is punctuated by Pier 914, whose curious name derives from one estimate of the number of prisoners who died during its construction; nowadays it's a great place to listen to the sea at night, perhaps with a beer in hand.

Few come to Con Dao for its sightseeing potential, but in and around the town centre are a few historical sights should you ever tire of diving, eating and lazing around.

The Revolutionary Museum
Mon–Sat 7.30–11.30am & 1.30–5pm • Free

The island's museum located directly behind Pier 914 is rarely visited, and staff are likely to be surprised when you turn up – if they're awake. The pictures of old Con Dao are unlikely to detain you for too long; also look out for the poorly stuffed black squirrel, the island's most distinctive animal, in the first hall.

The prison
Daily 7.30–11.30am & 1.30–5pm • 20,000đ

The many cells in the now-defunct prison remain littered with shackles, placed painfully close together. In a couple of exhibition cells, emaciated statues show how the Vietnamese inmates spent their days crowded together, unless they were selected for the "tiger cages" or the "solariums", where they were exposed to the elements in roofless rooms.

Hang Duong Cemetery
About 1km northeast of town on Nguyen An Ninh

The graves in the **Hang Duong Cemetery** add a tangible layer to the island's tragic past. All are unmarked, but one stands out – bright-coloured combs lie deposited on the grave of revolutionary heroine Vo Thi Sau, who in 1952 became the first woman to be executed here, at the age of nineteen.

Bovine manure enclosure
If the morbid mood gets you, you could even visit the **bovine manure enclosure**, located just off Vo Thi Sau on the way to the national park headquarters. The prison warders used to march prisoners into this windowless room, then pump it full of manure as a form of torture or execution, depending on their whim.

HIKING AND BIKING ON CON SON

A hike along one of the island's many trails in the national park may be more appealing than a tour of the prison. Some trails, such as one heading straight north to Ong Dung Beach, are well marked and can be followed independently, while others, such as to Thanh Gia Mountain, the island's highest peak at 577m, require the services of a guide. Birdwatchers might be lucky enough to spot rare species such as the Red-billed Tropicbird or the Pied Imperial Pigeon. Make sure to take plenty of water and food, as there is nothing available outside the town. The **Con Dao National Park** headquarters are located north of the town centre at 29 Vo Thi Sau, and have information about hiking trails – it's also possible to hire a guide here.

It's also quite tempting to rent a scooter for the day, particularly if the relentless traffic elsewhere in Vietnam has so far put you off the idea. The roads are virtually empty, even in the middle of the village, for most of the day. You basically have two options: heading north from Con Son Town, you'll pass the *Six Senses* resort and the airport before reaching Dam Trau beach, located down a side-trail branching off to the west. Alternatively, it's an easy journey south to Ca Map Cape, at which point you'll swing northwest towards the small settlement of Ben Dam where most of the fishing boats dock. Its population is an interesting mix of mostly sailors and prostitutes.

ACTIVITIES

MOTORBIKES

Renting a bike is a piece of cake; most hotels charge $5–7 per day, though do note that there are almost no petrol stations on the island – one has been marked on the map (see p.210).

DIVING

The best diving months are April and May, when visibility can be over twenty metres. There are two good diving operators on the island, both of whom have a full range of services from snorkelling trips to full PADI courses.

★ **Dive! Dive! Dive!** Just west of Pier 914 ☎ 064 383 0701, ⓦ dive-condao.com.
Rainbow Divers Operates from the *Six Senses* resort ☎ 090 557 7671, ⓦ divevietnam.com.

EXPLORING THE ISLANDS

Renting a boat to explore other islands in the archipelago can be incredibly tricky, not to mention expensive if you're not travelling in a group. Dive! Dive! Dive! will be able to advise on boat hire, and join you up with any other travellers who happen to have the same plans – at the very worst, you may get to be dropped off and picked up at a good point on the daily diving trip.

Beaches

After visiting the historic monuments and trekking across the island you may want to focus on some serious relaxation. **Lo Voi** and **An Hai** beaches, which front the town, are not bad, though the bay is often cluttered with fishing boats. Other good beaches around the island are **Dam Trau** and **Bai Ong Dung** in the north and **Bai Dat Doc** to the east of town, but you'll need to trek or **rent a motorbike** (see box above) to get there.

Other islands

You'll find plenty of deserted beaches and healthy coral reefs on some of the outlying islands. From June to October it is possible to watch sea turtles laying eggs at night on nearby **Bay Canh Island**; less predictable are occasional sightings of dugongs, which are endearing mammals (also known as sea cows) that feed only on seagrass, grow up to three metres long and weigh up to four hundred kilos.

ARRIVAL AND DEPARTURE   CON SON

By plane Two airlines now fly to Con Son from Ho Chi Minh City: the Vietnam Air Services Company (VASCO; ☎ 08 3842 2790; best booked through the Vietnam Airlines website, ⓦ vietnamairlines.com.vn) have a few small, propeller-driven planes, but far preferable are the modern jets of Air Mekong (ⓦ airmekong.com.vn), which started service in 2011. The airport is around 15km northeast of town. Most of the major hotels run shuttle services, which meet the planes and drop back off before flights; you can still catch a ride with one for a $2 fee. The journey into town gives a tantalizing glimpse of the island's rugged beauty and windswept, deserted beaches.

Destinations: Can Tho (daily; 1hr); Ho Chi Minh City (4 daily; 1hr).

By boat The only services from mainland Vietnam leave from Vung Tau (2 weekly; 14hr), and arrive at Ben Tam Port on the west of the island. Few travellers take these services any more, and they don't save all that much money when transport to Vung Tau and lost time are factored in. If you're still keen, contact Vung Tau Tourist in Vung Tau (see p.216).

ACCOMMODATION

Be warned that you'll pay far more here than you would for similar facilities on the mainland. This is not a great place for budget travellers – there are a few family guesthouses just to the north of *Con Dao Camping*, but none can be wholeheartedly recommended.

Anh Dao 22 Tran Phu ☎ 064 363 0170. This mini-hotel is the most reliable budget option in town – not saying much, but rooms are comfortable enough and the service friendly. $25

Con Dao Camping 2 Nguyen Duc Thuan ☎ 064 383 1555, ⓦ condaocamping.com. The best mid-range choice, with passable rooms set inside distinctive triangular buildings. In peak season, you'll likely be able to talk them into allowing you to pitch a tent in the small pine glade just to the north. $30

Con Dao Resort 8 Nguyen Duc Thuan ☎ 064 383 0939, ⓦ condaoresort.vn. Probably the best beach location on Con Son, this hotel has a good swimming pool, comfortable rooms and large buffet breakfasts. Staff can also arrange boat trips. $70

Con Dao Resort & Spa 16b Ton Duc Thang ☎ 064 383 0456, ⓦ atcvietnam.com. Also known as *Resort ATC*, this has a few rooms in thatched stilt-houses and others in brick bungalows, though the bungalows offer little privacy. $40

Saigon – Condao Resort 18–24 Ton Duc Thang ☎ 064 383 0336, ⓦ saigoncondao.com. Not a bad choice at all for those on a moderate budget, with a small pool and most rooms offering good views of the beach. They have a few cheaper (slightly stuffy) villas set apart from the main building, and boast one of the town's best restaurants (see below). $90

Six Senses Hideaway Dat Doc Beach ⓦ sixsenses .com. One of Vietnam's most exclusive resorts, a few minutes' drive up the coast from Con Son Town. The super-modern, timber-framed villas are rather gorgeous – the bamboo-covered outdoor showers are a particularly nice touch, as is the fact that islanders form a healthy chunk of the staff. There's also a pristine stretch of private beach, and a private butler to take care of guests' every need. $480

EATING

Con Dao Resort 8 Nguyen Duc Thuan ☎ 064 383 0939, ⓦ condaoresort.vn. The outdoor bar/restaurant at this hotel is the best place on the beach for an evening drink. The food's good too, and prices are reasonable – simple dishes go from $3.50. Daily 8am–11pm.

★ **Saigon–Condao Resort** 18–24 Ton Duc Thang ☎ 064 383 0336, ⓦ saigoncondao.com. This hotel's open-air on-site restaurant is by far the best in Con Dao Town, and prices are surprisingly reasonable – by way of example, $5 will get you a coralfish steak with chilli and lemongrass, a plate of sliced bitter melon and a glass of fresh lemonade. Daily 8am–10pm.

Six Senses Hideaway Dat Doc Beach ⓦ sixsenses.com. So secluded is the *Six Senses* that if you're staying here, you'll be eating here anyway. The on-site restaurant and juice/cocktail bar are superb and also open to non-guests, but bring money – you'll have to add a zero to prices that you'd expect to pay elsewhere. Daily 8am–10pm.

DIRECTORY

Bank There's an ATM outside the Vietinbank at the junction of Le Duan and Le Van Viet

Internet The free terminals in the lobby of the *Con Dao Resort* are the most reliable option for a quick email check

(even if you're not staying there). There are also a couple of hit-and-miss cafés on Le Duan.

Post office Nguyen Thi Minh Khai.

Vung Tau

Connected by hydrofoil to Ho Chi Minh City, and therefore a default weekend bolt-hole for its stressed-out inhabitants, **VUNG TAU** is a scruffy, and slightly seedy, but likeable place. "The Bay of Boats", as its name translates, is located some 125km southeast of Ho Chi Minh City on a hammerheaded spit of land jutting into the mouth of the Saigon River. Once a thriving riviera-style beach resort, the city's **offshore oil** industry and steadily growing port have transformed it into a more business-oriented conurbation, though residents of Ho Chi Minh City still flock to on weekends, when hotel rates rise. Locals are fond of swimming on the town's **beaches**, but they're all second-rate despite recent attempts to clean them up. However, the boardwalk along **Bai Sau**, known to seasoned expats as "Back Beach", remains a pleasant place for an evening stroll, and perhaps a light seafood meal; "Front Beach", where the ferries arrive, has more traffic and less appeal.

Brief history

Portuguese ships are thought to have exploited the city's deep anchorage as early as the fifteenth century. By the turn of the twentieth, French expats, who knew the place as "Cap Saint-Jacques", had adopted it as a retreat from the daily rigmarole of Saigon, and set to work carving colonial villas into the sides of **Nui Lon** and **Nui Nho**, two low hills

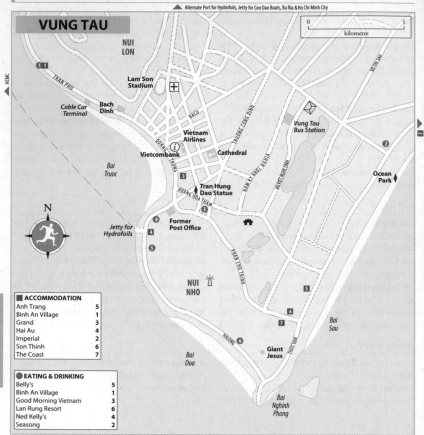

near the coast. Shifts in Vietnam's political sands duly replaced French visitors with American GIs. With them gone, and the Communist government in power, the city became a favoured launch pad for the vessels that spirited away the **boat people** (see p.451) in the late 1970s.

Nui Lon

Cable car daily 7.30am–6pm · 100,000đ

Two hundred and one metres high and accessible by **cable car**, this is the highest peak in Vung Tau, and commands predictably sweeping views. There's a small park at the top, which is particularly good for families; known officially as the Ho May Tourism Resort, it includes a cherry blossom orchard and a peacock garden.

Bach Dinh

12 Tran Phu · Daily 7am–5pm · Small admission fee

One of the few remaining colonial structures worth a look is the imposing **Bach Dinh** peeping out from behind a vanguard of frangipani and bougainvillea. Built at the end of the nineteenth century, it served as a holiday home to Vietnam's political players, hosting such luminaries as Paul Doumer, governor-general of Indochina (for whom it was originally erected), emperors Thanh Thai and Bao Dai and President Thieu. Inside you can see the building's collection of "valuable antique items", excavated from a seventeenth-century shipwreck off Con Dao; among the exhibits are such unmissables as "dry burned fruits", "beard-tweezers" and "pieces of stone in the ship". Upstairs is a display of Cambodian Buddhist statuary and shards of old pottery, but they are eclipsed by the commanding views of the bay.

Nui Nho
To get there, turn up a small lane called Hai Dang, just north of the hydrofoil jetty

On Nui Nho hill stands the town's **lighthouse**. Built in 1910, it seems to have been based on a child's sketch of a space-rocket, and is a popular place for locals to walk or jog to in the morning and evening. The views from here out to sea and across town make for good photos. Note that the foothills in these parts are studded with almost a dozen pagodas, all accessible to the public.

Giant Jesus
Approach via a stairway from the southern end of Ha Long • Daily 7.30–11.30am & 1.30–5pm • Free

Vung Tau's own little touch of Rio, the 28m-high **Giant Jesus**, which sits on a low peak a few hundred metres further south of Nui Nho, boasts excellent views. Cherubs wielding harps and trumpets herald your approach to the outstretched arms of the city's most famous landmark. Climb the steps inside the wind-buffeted statue and you can perch, parrot-like, on Jesus's shoulder, from where you'll enjoy giddying views of the surrounding seascape.

Bai Sau
If swimming and sun-seeking brought you to Vung Tau, your best bet is to head for the sands of **Bai Sau** ("Back Beach"), far and away Vung Tau's widest, longest (5km) and best, which is still not saying much. Backed by hotels, it's not exactly a tropical paradise, though on weekends, when it's cluttered with kids, deckchairs and umbrellas, and the fruit- and seafood-vendors are out in force, it's pleasant enough.

ARRIVAL AND DEPARTURE   VUNG TAU

By bus All buses terminate at the bus station at 192 Nam Ky Khoi Nghia, where xe om and taxis will be on hand to ferry you to a hotel.
Destinations: Da Lat (6hr); Ho Chi Minh City (2hr).

ACTIVITIES IN VUNG TAU
There are a couple of interesting ways to while away the time in Vung Tau.

WATERSPORTS
Other than hiking on top of the hills of Nui Lon or Nui Nho, you can head to **Ocean Park** (daily 6.30am-5.30pm; free), which occupies a 700m beach frontage on Bai Sau, rents out watersports equipment, offers beach games, lifeguards, showers and a smart restaurant.

GREYHOUND RACING
If you enjoy a flutter and are in town on a Saturday night, head for the **Lam Son Stadium** at15 Le Loi, Vietnam's only venue for greyhound racing.

GOLF
The Paradise golf course (☎064 382 3366) is a decent eighteen-hole range off Bai San; a round will cost about $95, including caddy.

By boat and hydrofoil Hydrofoils from Ho Chi Minh City dock at a large terminal at the south end of Bai Truoc (also known as "Front Beach"). It's within walking distance of a number of hotels, and a lot of restaurants, though seemingly half the town will be waiting to take you away in a taxi. In bad weather, the hydrofoils occasionally have to use a more sheltered location 12km away; in such instances, free shuttle buses will be provided. This is also the departure point for ferries to Con Dao though at the time of writing these services were becoming less and less reliable. Destinations: HCMC (every 30min; 1hr 15min); Con Dao (2 weekly; 14hr).

GETTING AROUND

By xe om Once in Vung Tau, you can get around by cyclo, xe om or taxi. Given the city's sprawling layout, it's hard to give specific prices, though such is the level of competition that you'll be able to ascertain the right amount by simply asking a few drivers.

By bike For more independence, you can pay slightly more than the average in the rest of Vietnam to rent a bicycle (up to $4 per day) or motorbike (from $7 per day) through most hotels.

INFORMATION

Tourist information For local maps and information, go to Vung Tau Tourist (☎064 385 6445, ⓦvungtautourist.com.vn) at 29 Tran Hung Dao, which can also help book ferry tickets to Con Dao. A few doors along is the Vietnam Airlines office (☎064 385 6099) at 21 Tran Hung Dao, where you can book domestic or international flights.

ACCOMMODATION

Most of Vung Tau's classier (and more expensive) places tend to be clustered around Front Beach (Bai Truoc), with a wider range of options on Back Beach (Bai Sau). Weekend rates are higher than weekdays, as the town is invaded by swarms of escapees from Ho Chi Minh City.

FRONT BEACH (BAI TRUOC)

Binh An Village 1 Tran Phu ☎064 351 0016, ⓦbinhanvillage.com. Although it's a stretch from town, this is the most appealing place in the area. Ten individually furnished and decorated rooms enjoy fabulous sea views, and some have private gardens as well. $100

Grand 2 Nguyen Du ☎064 385 6888, ⓦgrandhotel.com.vn. The swanky *Grand* has smart, attractive rooms, attentive staff and good facilities for business travellers. The hotel is right on the front and many of its rooms boast delightful sea views. $90

Hai Au 124 Ha Long ☎064 385 6178, ⓔhaiauhotel@hcm.vnn.vn. Right opposite the ferry terminal, this aging beast was Vung Tau's first proper hotel, and it shows in its faded decor, empty banqueting halls and minimal staff. However, the rooms aren't too bad at all, and rates have dropped to the degree that it's now one of the best-value places in town. $20 Back Beach (BAI sau)

Anh Trang 67a Thuy Van ☎064 352 3535. One of the better budget options on Back Beach; its en-suite rooms are nothing to write home about, but they're safe and do the job. The few facing the sea are almost double the price. $20

Imperial 159–163 Thuy Van ☎064 362 8888, ⓦimperialhotel.vn. One of the most attractive hotels on the Back Beach strip, with Roman stylings in the lobby and smart, modern-looking rooms; the ones on upper floors have good sea views. $150

Son Thinh 153 Phan Chu Trinh ☎064 352 3492, ⓦsonthinhhotel.com. Good, friendly option just off the main drag – and therefore a fair bit quieter than its competition. Free buffet breakfast and wi-fi access. $20

The Coast 300a Phan Chu Trinh ☎064 362 7778, ⓦthecoasthotel.com.vn. One of the only good upper-to-mid-range places in town, with a secluded location, though very near the beach. Rooms are every bit as good as at more expensive competitors, and there's a good restaurant on site. $55

EATING AND DRINKING

With a large number of resident expats, Vung Tau supports a more cosmopolitan span of restaurants than your average Vietnamese town; French cuisine weighs in heavily, but it's also possible to find spaghetti and burgers as well as delicious Vietnamese seafood – Bai Sau beach is a good place to head for the latter. In addition, there are a number of bars in the town centre catering to the expat community – many are open until the last customers leave.

Belly's 94a Ha Long. A great place for western breakfast or a light Vietnamese dish for lunch, not to mention a beer in the evening. There's a small book exchange upstairs.

Binh An Village 1 Tran Phu. Something a little different – here you can enjoy seafood or steaks in a sumptuous setting for around $20, accompanied by live jazz on Sat night and Sun lunchtime.

4

Good Morning Vietnam 6 Hoang Hoa Tham. Yet another branch of the Italian chain. Like the others, it's a reliable place to load up on Western fare – the pizzas are particularly good. The only downside is its location, set back in the gritty area off Front Beach.

Lan Rung Resort 3–6 Ha Long. This hotel may be aimed more at honeymooning locals than foreign tourists, but its seafront restaurant is a quality affair – try the seafood, or guzzle down a microbrewed beer.

Ned Kelly's 128 Ha Long. The best of two or three expat-owned places on the same stretch of road. Good for cold beer (proof: the owner's an Aussie), a game of pool and a bit of banter with locals.

Seasong 163 Thuy Van. On the fourth floor of the flash Imperial Shopping Mall, this restaurant has a refined atmosphere and serves up dishes like wok-fried tiger prawn with hazelnut for around $6.

DIRECTORY

Banks Vietcombank, 27 Tran Hung Dao (Mon–Fri 7–11.30am & 1.30–4pm), changes travellers' cheques and has a 24hr ATM.

Internet Several hotels have internet access and wi-fi, though for cheaper rates, try the shops on Bacu.

Post office The post office (7am–8.30pm) is at 408 Le Hong Phong.

The Ba Ria coast

As you move up the coast of Ba Ria province from Vung Tau, the beaches gradually get more enticing. Since the region is near to Ho Chi Minh City, you have to go quite a way before you escape the hordes of domestic tourists who head for the area at weekends and on public holidays, though weekdays can be blissfully quiet.

4

GETTING AROUND   BA RIA COAST

Public transport is scarce on this stretch, and unless you have your own wheels you may have to hit Ba Ria city to get to or from Vung Tau. However, with a rented vehicle you can explore more fully the road that hugs the coast much of the way from Vung Tau to Mui Ne, throwing up glimpses of rural life as well as the salty tang of the nearby sea.

Long Hai

The first town along the coast is **LONG HAI**, set below a wall of impressive mountains some 20km from Vung Tau. It's very popular with Vietnamese, many of who find its wide beach and fishing-village atmosphere more appealing than Vung Tau. Dunes fringe the town's eastern extreme; to the west stands a fishing village, complete with a huge flotilla of fishing boats and assorted coracles sporting brightly coloured flags.

Minh Dam caves

To get to the caves, take the coastal road east from Long Hai, then a signed left turn just beyond the *Thuy Duong Resort*

The Minh Dam caves, just around the cape from Long Hai, were a Communist bolt-hole from 1948, from where you can enjoy prodigious views of the rice fields that quilt the coastal plain stretching to the horizon to the northeast, and of the boulder-strewn coastline below. The caves are not much more than gaps between piled boulders, yet with a little imagination it's still possible to picture Viet Minh and Viet Cong soldiers lounging, cooking and sleeping here. Bullets have left pockmarks on some of the rocks, and joss sticks are still lodged in crevices in memory of those who fell here. Since there are many forks in the path, however, you really need a guide to find your way around – they're best organized through one of the nearby resorts.

ARRIVAL AND DEPARTURE   LONG HAI

By bus Long Hai is served by buses from Ho Chi Minh City's Mien Dong station; coming from Vung Tau, you'll need to take a bus to Ba Ria and then change, or take a xe om direct for about $5.

ACCOMMODATION AND EATING

Few foreigners stay here, and those that do so tend to bypass the town altogether and head straight along to the **resort area** east of town. There are also a fair few resorts heading northeast up the coast; all places listed here see prices rocket at weekends. This being a resort area, most people eat where they stay, but there are a few **food stalls** by the road leading up to the *Military Guest House*. All the hotels listed below are on Road 44.

CENTRAL LONG HAI

★**Anoasis Beach Resort** ☎064 386 8227, ⓦanoasisresort.com.vn. This lovingly restored former residence of Emperor Bao Dai overlooking a deserted coastline has won awards. The thatch-roofed bungalows discreetly set amongst pine-studded hills are very special, with gorgeous bamboo furnishings and fittings, and huge bathtubs. Facilities also run to a business centre, swimming pool and charming open-air terraced restaurant. Non-residents can enjoy its facilities for $10 a day at weekends, $6 in the week. $130

Long Hai Beach Resort ☎064 366 1351, ⓦlonghaibeachresort.com. A step down in quality and largely geared towards domestic or East Asian tourists, this resort has tastefully furnished rooms, a large swimming pool, a casino and fitness centre, but mostly caters for large groups. You can expect a 30–40 percent discount from the rack rate at most times of the year – check online. $170

Military Guest House 298 Doan An Dieu ☎064 386 8316. The pick of Long Hai's smattering of budget guesthouses, located at the end of the road that runs into the village. It has basic rooms with a choice of fan or a/c, and looks out over a wide expanse of beach shaded by casuarinas. $15

Thuy Duong Resort ☎064 388 6215, ⓦthuyduong resort.com.vn. A good mid-range option, standing behind a fine beach lined with casuarinas: its accommodation ranges from pleasant beach huts to luxurious suites in the main hotel, with leisure facilities including a pool and tennis courts. $50

ALONG THE COAST

★**Ho Tram Beach Resort** ☎064 378 1525, ⓦhotramresort.com. A thoroughly classy resort in which the rooms ooze character, their elegant furnishings and fittings augmented by luxurious on-site spa facilities, and a superb restaurant. It's a full 22km northeast of Long Hai, though the hotel does operate (costly) shuttle buses. $135

Loc An Resort ☎064 388 6377, ⓦlocanresort.com. Budget resort nestled 14km northeast of Long Hai, beside a lagoon cut off from the sea by a line of sand dunes: it has cosy rooms with all facilities, and bicycles and tandems are available for guests' use. Unless you have your own wheels, you'll need to take a taxi or xe om to get here. $45

Ho Coc Beach

The new road continues to wind along the coast, fringed by casuarinas and sand dunes, until it reaches **Ho Coc Beach**. Ho Coc is a spellbinding, 5km stretch of wonderfully golden sand, dotted with coracles and large boulders, lapped by clear waters and backed by fine dunes. It's still in the early stages of development, but you'll be able to find a simple place to stay. As with most places around here, it gets crowded with day-trippers at the weekend but is practically deserted during the week.

ARRIVAL AND DEPARTURE   HO COC BEACH

Buses Services from Ho Chi Minh City, Vung Tau and Ba Ria trundle as far as Xuyen Moc, about 10km north of here, from where you'll need to take a xe om; drivers will start the bidding at 100,000đ, though you should be able to halve this with a little effort.

ACCOMMODATION

Saigon-Ho Coc Resort ☎064 379 1036, ⓦsaigonbinhchauecoresort.com. On the beach itself, this resort boasts good-sized and well-furnished brick bungalows; guests get free entry to the nearby Binh Chau Hot Springs (see below). $40

Binh Chau Hot Springs

15km northeast of Ho Coc Beach • Entry 20,000đ; communal pool 30,000đ; private mini-pools 50,000đ per person per hour • ☎064 379 1036, ⓦsaigonbinhchauecoresort.com

The **Binh Chau Hot Springs** have been developed into a kind of theme park with the addition of a golf-driving range, tennis courts, sand volleyball court, billiards and ox-cart rides around the site. The sulphurous waters bubbling hellishly in the streams and wells here vary greatly in temperature. Old people soothe their aching limbs in the foot-soaking stream, while elsewhere visitors boil eggs sold on site to make up ad hoc picnics. You can bathe in the mineral waters of the "Dreaming Lake", a communal **swimming pool**, but renting your own **mini-pool** is a more tempting option. There are also a sauna, massage and mud baths in the main complex.

ARRIVAL AND DEPARTURE   BINH CHAU HOT SPRINGS

There's no public transport to the springs; guests tend to arrive on package tour buses or with their own vehicle. However, it's only 6km from Binh Chau village, accessible on highly irregular coastal buses linking Mui Ne and Vung Tau. From here you can pick up a xe om for the final stretch.

ACCOMMODATION

Saigon-Ho Coc Resort ☎064 387 1131, ⓦsaigonbinhchauecoresort.com. Part of the eponymous operation on Ho Coc Beach (see p.218), this is an equally good place to stay – it's a question of whether you'd like to be closer to the springs or the beach. There's no public transport here – call ahead to arrange pick-up. **$40**

The southern Binh Thuan coast

Binh Thuan province boasts but one popular tourist draw – the sands and resorts of **Mui Ne** (see p.220). Most bypass the southern Binh Thuan coast entirely, but for those with their own wheels – or willing to brave the scarce public transport – there are a few things to see. From the Ba Ria coast (see p.217), **Highway 55** follows the windswept coast to **Ham Tan**, passing through cashew orchards with glimpses of huge sand dunes to your right. This route is so far off the beaten track that ox carts are almost as common as motorized vehicles. Occasional dirt tracks lead down to some fantastic stretches of **deserted beach**, where a few coracles pulled up beyond the tide level hint at human habitation. After passing Ham Tan, the coast road continues eastward; the landscape is beautiful, with remote fishing villages sheltered by coconut palms, and dragon-fruit orchards lining the road. This eventually veers away from the coast in the form of Highway 712 to join the unrelenting traffic of Highway 1 about 30km before **Phan Thiet**, a bustling yet essentially uninteresting city that few give any regard to on their way to Mui Ne.

Cape Ke Ga

If you're enjoying the coast road, it's possible to branch off Highway 712 about 15km after Ham Tan and follow the coast all the way to **Cape Ke Ga**, where a lighthouse built by the French in the late nineteenth century still stands.

ACCOMMODATION   CAPE KE GA

⭐ **Princess D'Annam** ☎062 368 2222, ⓦprincessannam.com. Tucked away in this unknown corner of the country, this hotel comes as something of a surprise with its fabulously furnished villas and calming, minimalist decor. Facilities include four pools, a spa, two restaurants and 24hr butler service. **$260**

Ta Cu Mountain

Signposted about 2km south of the junction of Highway 719 and Highway 1, approximately 40km west of Phan Thiet • Cable car 100,000đ return

Ta Cu Mountain is home to Vietnam's largest reclining Buddha (49m). It makes an interesting trek to climb the mountain, probably in the company of Buddhists on pilgrimage, though there is also a cable car that stops near the summit, leaving just a short climb. Resorts in Phan Thiet and Mui Ne can organize tours here, though it's easy to find if you have your own transportation.

Phan Thiet

The unassuming capital of Binh Thuan Province, **PHAN THIET** has little of interest for foreigners, who prefer the sands of Mui Ne just along the coast (see below). However, the very absence of tourists is, for some, a draw in itself and the town is likeable enough, particularly where Highway 1 crosses the Tran Hung Dao bridge, beside which lies a fleet of picture-perfect fishing boats. In addition, Phan Thiet has **Doi Duong**, its own perfectly acceptable stretch of beach, and one very popular with the Vietnamese – to get to the best bit, head around 700m northeast from the main entrance point on Nguyen That Thanh.

Ho Chi Minh museum

Museum and school Tues–Sun 7.30–11.30am & 1.30–4.30pm • 10,000đ

Trung Trac skirts the city centre en route to the sedate riverside **Ho Chi Minh Museum**. As with other such museums around the country, its exhibits include memorabilia of Ho's life from his early days abroad up to his death in 1969, such as his white tunic, walking stick, sandals and metal helmet. Next door is a school where Ho once taught; its rooms have remained unchanged since his brief spell here, and effortlessly conjure up another age.

ARRIVAL AND DEPARTURE   PHAN THIET

By train There's a small train station in town, with a single daily service to Ho Chi Minh City (3hr). Far less prone to traffic jams than the buses, seasoned expats view this as the best way to get to Mui Ne. The nearest stop on the main line is Muong Man, a 200,000đ ride away by xe om, and near double that by taxi.
Destinations: Da Nang (5 daily; 12–17hr); Ho Chi Minh City (5 daily; 3–5hr); Hué (5 daily; 14–18hr); Nha Trang (5 daily; 4–6hr).

By bus The bus station is 2km north of the centre on Tu Van Tu. If you're really set on staying here, you should be able to get Mui Ne-bound open-tour buses to drop you off, rather than taking local services. Note that there's also a shuttle bus linking Phan Thiet and Mui Ne (every 15min; 8000đ).
Destinations: Ho Chi Minh City (4hr); Nha Trang (5hr).

ACCOMMODATION AND EATING

There are plenty of places to stay in Phan Thiet, though the culinary scene isn't terribly exciting. As you'd expect, there's plenty of seafood on offer, but no specific establishments stand out from the crowd – most travellers end up eating at their hotel.

The Palms ⊕ 062 381 0226, ⓦ thepalmsvietnam.com. Swish new mid-ranger overlooking the *Novotel* golf course. The design of both the rooms and the complex in general is a cut above what you'd expect at this price range, and the on-site restaurant is excellent – they're proud of their steaks, but also serve good Vietnamese food. $55

Novotel Ocean Dunes ⊕ 062 382 2393, ⓦ novotel .com. A mammoth, but attractive, resort with two swimming pools and free use of bicycles, as well as the wonderful *Sea Horse* restaurant. However, its main draw is a superb eighteen-hole golf course. $130

Mui Ne

Many Vietnamese beach areas have seen recent surges in popularity, but **MUI NE** takes the biscuit. Not so long ago this was a sleepy backwater ignored by domestic and international tourists alike, but the beach is now largely invisible from the coastal road, thanks to 10km of wall-to-wall resorts. The fact that Highway 1 juts inland before Mui Ne was the main factor behind it keeping off the radar for so long, but the secret was fully unveiled during an eclipse of the sun in the mid-1990s, which had its

---

ANYONE FOR GOLF?

There are two decent golf courses in the Mui Ne area. First is the **Ocean Dunes Golf Club**, on the grounds of the Novotel in Phan Thiet (see above). Larger and newer is the **Sealinks Golf and Country Club**, which sprawls across the hills at the entrance to Mui Ne. Both boast fabulous ocean views, and cost a shade under $100 per round, including caddy.

OUTDOOR ACTIVITIES

Though the number one activity at Mui Ne is **relaxing on the beach**, the place also attracts **wind- and kitesurfers** when the wind is up between August and April, and Mui Ne even hosts an event in the Asian Windsurf Tour each February. There are a number of establishments that offer equipment rental; the following also give lessons in windsurfing and kitesurfing, with an hour's instruction costing around $40 for the former, and $60 for the latter.

Jibes 90 Nguyen Dinh Chieu ⓦ windsurf-vietnam.com.

Storm Mia Resort ⓦ stormkiteboarding.com.

Xuan Uyen 78 Nguyen Dinh Chieu ☎ 062 384 7476.

optimum viewing spot here. Now it's popular as a weekend retreat for expats living in Ho Chi Minh City, as well as a favourite with upmarket visitors happy to pay $70 or more per day to lounge around in a luxurious resort. Many of these visitors are Russian – this is one of the only places in South East Asia in which Cyrillic text vies for supremacy with Roman.

There's no doubt that its laidback atmosphere is one of its best features, but Mui Ne is also something of a tourist enclave, separated as it is from any Vietnamese community. This probably won't bother you if you're looking for unadulterated beachside relaxation, but if you crave interaction with locals or a higher-octane nightlife scene, you'd be better off heading on up to Nha Trang. Another potential problem at Mui Ne is that the strong winds and surf tend to erode parts of the beach between August and December, so you might just find the waves lapping onto the garden of your chosen resort. However, good stretches of soft sand can always be found with a little exploration.

Mui Ne is stretched along one main road – resorts make up most of the seaward side of the road, especially to the west of the curl; these peter out further east, where budget hotels start to pop up. All along, the non-seaward side of the road is made up of restaurants and cheap hotels. Heading further east, the beach finally disappears too, before the road reaches the actual **village and harbour of Mui Ne**, where fishing boats cluster together in their hundreds.

Po Shanu Towers

Daily 7am–5pm • Small admission fee

On the western fringe of Mui Ne are the Po Shanu Towers, which date from the eighth century. While they can't compare with monuments like Po Klong Garai near Phan Rang (see p.225), they are worth a look as the towers – two big, one small – are in reasonable repair, and the site occupies a pretty hilltop location with good views.

Fairy Spring

North of Mui Ne, signed from the main road

Fairy Spring is in fact a narrow stream running through a psychedelic landscape of white and red **sand dunes**, which are also accessible via an uphill, inland turn at the village of Mui Ne. The softness of the sand makes the dunes difficult to climb, but the resulting views are ample reward. The sand can also get very hot, so it makes sense to go early or late in the day, when the colours are also at their most spectacular.

ARRIVAL AND DEPARTURE   MUI NE

By bus The majority of travellers arrive in Mui Ne on open-tour buses, which drop off outside the relevant company offices. Most hotels will be able to book an onward ticket, often for buses that pick up right outside the front door.

Local buses are few and far between, bar the shuttle buses linking Phan Thiet and Mui Ne (every 15min; 8000đ); there's also a single, juddering, daily service down to Vung Tau. **Destinations:** Ho Chi Minh City (4hr); Nha Trang (5hr).

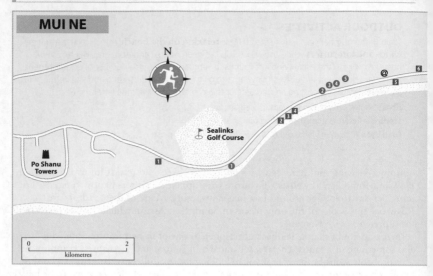

By train Many expats go by train from Ho Chi Minh City to Phan Thiet (see p.220). Getting back this way can be hard, since tickets often sell out and the station is some distance from the beach – buy your return ticket in Ho Chi Minh City, if you're sure about your dates. If you're heading to or from the north, the nearest station is in remote Muong Man (see p.220), a tiny village that's a minimum 200,000đ from Mui Ne on a xe om.

GETTING AROUND

By xe om Mui Ne is long and hard to cover on foot. You'll be endlessly badgered by xe om drivers, who will charge from 15,000đ for a short ride.

By bike It's easy to rent a bicycle ($2/day) or motorbike ($6–7/day) from your resort or guesthouse; first check details like the brakes to avoid unnecessary accidents.

INFORMATION AND TOURS

Local **tour operators** offer day tours of the region taking in the sand dunes, Fairy Spring, the Po Shanu Towers, and Ta Cu Mountain (see p.219). However, it has to be said that Mui Ne's local attractions are limited, and these tours often include missable destinations such as the guide's uncle's dragon fruit orchard. For more in-depth **information** on the local area, visit ⓦ muinebeach.net.

ACCOMMODATION

Since the main activity in Mui Ne is lazing on the beach, choosing where to stay is the biggest decision to make while here. Budget options are limited, as the resort's upmarket image means that many places that previously offered cheap rooms have now upgraded their facilities and prices, though this means more choice in the moderate and expensive categories. Bear in mind that many places bump their prices up at weekends. Not all places along the beach have street numbers; in these cases places are identified by kilometre distance along the road from Phan Thiet.

Blue Waves 94a Nguyen Dinh Chieu ☎ 062 384 7989, ⓦ tiendatresort.com.vn. Also known as the "Tien Dat", this is about as cheap a resort as you'll find along the strip. Rooms aren't super-swish but they're comfortable and fairly priced; you'll pay about twenty percent more for those facing the sea. $40
Cham Villas 32 Nguyen Dinh Chieu ☎ 062 374 1234, ⓦ chamvillas.com. Relative newcomer with just a handful of luxurious, well-appointed villas – just about representing value for money. A good place to go if you're seeking some peace and quiet; spa treatments are also available. $150
Coco Beach 58 Nguyen Dinh Chieu ☎ 062 384 7111, ⓦ cocobeach.net. This French-run resort has 28 tasteful, thatched wooden bungalows and some family-size villas, complete with verandas, Cham-style fabrics, a/c and all modern comforts, set among tropical gardens off the beach. The relaxed style and friendly staff have made this an established favourite. $135
Dynasty 140A Nguyen Dinh Chieu ☎ 062 384 7816,

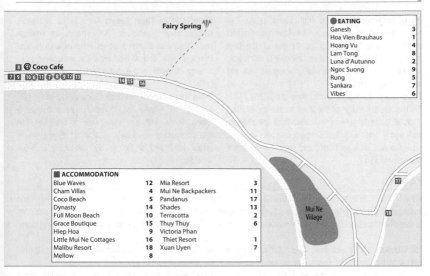

● EATING	
Ganesh	3
Hoa Vien Brauhaus	1
Hoang Vu	4
Lam Tong	8
Luna d'Autunno	2
Ngoc Suong	9
Rung	5
Sankara	7
Vibes	6

Fairy Spring

@ Coco Café

■ ACCOMMODATION			
Blue Waves	12	Mia Resort	3
Cham Villas	4	Mui Ne Backpackers	11
Coco Beach	5	Pandanus	17
Dynasty	14	Shades	13
Full Moon Beach	10	Terracotta	2
Grace Boutique	15	Thuy Thuy	6
Hiep Hoa	9	Victoria Phan	
Little Mui Ne Cottages	16	Thiet Resort	1
Malibu Resort	18	Xuan Uyen	7
Mellow	8		

Mui Ne Village

ⓦdynastyresorts.com. The elegantly furnished rooms, attentive staff and filling buffet breakfasts make this a comfortable place to stay. Many rooms face the beach, as does the on-site swimming pool, which is up there with the best in Mui Ne. **$70**

Full Moon Beach 84–90 Nguyen Dinh Chieu ☎062 384 7008, ⓦwindsurf-vietnam.com. Attractive and sturdy beachfront establishment, featuring thatched bamboo huts with verandas and spacious rooms, some on stilts and with attached bathrooms; rates include breakfast. Also note that this is also the location of Jibe's, one of Mui Ne's best bars. **$60**

Grace Boutique 144a Nguyen Dinh Chieu ☎062 374 3357, ⓦgraceboutiqueresort.com. One of Mui Ne's friendliest resorts, which is one reason why it has become a real favourite with Ho Chi Minh City-fleeing expats, many of whom return again and again (there are only fourteen rooms, so it helps to book ahead). Almost uniquely in Vietnam, smoking is prohibited across the resort, which also features a small infinity pool and an equally minuscule restaurant. **$100**

Hiep Hoa 80 Nguyen Dinh Chieu ☎062 384 7262, ⓦmuinebeach.net/hiephoa. Just eight smart but basic rooms and a handful of bungalows, some with fans and others a/c, in this tiny, friendly compound facing a fine stretch of beach. **$15**

Little Mui Ne Cottages 10b Huynh Thuc Khang ☎062 384 7550-1, ⓦlittlemuineresort.com. Large bungalows and cosy rooms with bamboo furnishings in a tidy compound with a good-size pool, free internet access and bikes. The attention to detail makes this place very appealing. **$75**

Malibu Resort Ward 5 ☎062 384 9669, ⓦmalibu-resort.com. Located to the east of the main bay, this place

feels extremely secluded – come here if you want to relax. Rooms are spacious and smartly furnished, and in addition to the modest swimming pool there's a small bar-restaurant on site – a good thing, given the location. **$70**

Mellow 117c Nguyen Dinh Chieu ☎062 374 3086. Basic hostel, a chill-out venue that's particularly popular with windsurfers, some of whom end up staying for weeks. Dorm **$6**

★ **Mia Resort** 24 Nguyen Dinh Chieu ☎062 384 7440, ⓦsailingclubvietnam.com. Delightfully landscaped resort featuring rooms and bungalows with thatched roofs and mustard-coloured walls, plus imaginative interiors with good use of local textiles. Swimming pool, popular bar and restaurant too. **$95**

★ **Mui Ne Backpackers** 88 Nguyen Dinh Chieu ☎062 384 7047, ⓦmuinebackpackers.com. Extremely well-run hostel, good for both dorm accommodation and private rooms, plus a few bungalows at the back, with all guests free to use the small on-site pool and join in the inevitable night-time bar-crawl. Dorm $6, double **$20**

Pandanus Km 5 ☎062 384 9849, ⓦpandanusresort.com. Pretty homely for a Mui Ne resort, with staff that genuinely seem eager to please. Though a tiny bit rough around the edges, this is a good place to stay as it boasts elegant rooms and a landscaped garden, plus pool, spa and restaurant overlooking the beach. **$110**

★ **Shades** 98A Nguyen Dinh Chieu ☎062 374 3237, ⓦshadesmuine.com. You'll have to book early to stay in this fantastic boutique hotel. There are just seven individual apartments here, all super-hip in design; rooms include neat touches like double glazing, flat-screen TVs and kitchen facilities. **$50**

4

★ **Terracotta** 28 Nguyen Dinh Chieu ☎ 062 384 7610, ⓦ terracottaresort.com. One of the newer resorts on the strip, yet it already boasts one of the best reputations. With gardens that could double as golf lawns, elegant rooms and amiable staff, it's a great pick and competitively priced. **$100**

Thuy Thuy 123 Nguyen Dinh Chieu ☎ 062 384 7357. On the opposite side of the road to the beach, but a grand place to stay nonetheless. Staff are amiable and you'll find a beautiful garden, pool and spa alongside the well-positioned and tastefully-equipped bungalows. **$50**

Victoria Phan Thiet Resort Km 9 ☎ 062 381 3000, ⓦ victoriahotels-asia.com. The cottages set amongst tropical gardens feature spacious interiors with tasteful European decor and all mod cons. The management can arrange excursions and guests have free use of mountain bikes. **$190**

Xuan Uyen 78 Nguyen Dinh Chieu ☎ 062 384 7476. A range of simple but incredibly cheap bungalow rooms, some with sea view. One of Mui Ne's few real backpacker hang-outs, it also serves reasonably priced food and drinks in the beachside chill-out area. **$8**

EATING

What Mui Ne lacks in terms of cultural attractions, it makes up for with gastronomic diversity. As well as the resorts and hotels, all of which have their own restaurants, there's no shortage of independent eating joints and bars along the strip. All of the following restaurants are open through the day, though note that you'll struggle to find anywhere to eat after 10pm.

★ **Champa** 58 Nguyen Dinh Chieu. On a delightful terrace at the *Coco Beach Resort*, *Champa* serves up top-class French cuisine (dinner only) with impeccable service and prices from about $10 for a main dish.

Ganesh 57 Nguyen Dinh Chieu. This small but attractive restaurant is Mui Ne's only Indian option, and is just as authentic as its sister restaurants elsewhere in Vietnam. Thali platters start at $6.50.

Hoa Vien Brauhaus 2a Nguyen Dinh Chieu. Way out on the western edge of the strip, this serves a tasty mix of Czech and Asian dishes – the Czech dishes tend to be heavy, meaty affairs, while the tempura veggies stand out from the Asian menu. However, as the name might suggest, many are more interested in the beer – brewed on site, and absolutely delicious.

Hoang Vu 121 Nguyen Dinh Chieu. The dark-panelled room is more enticing than the bright, new place next door, but both turn out delicious Vietnamese cuisine – try the red snapper in pepper sauce ($4).

Lam Tong 92 Nguyen Dinh Chieu. This no-frills place is right on the beach and has some of the lowest prices on the strip (around $5 per main dish) for decent Vietnamese and international food, plus cheap wine – good place to sample some Vang Dalat, the local favourite.

Luna d'Autunno 51a Nguyen Dinh Chieu. Beautiful bamboo decor sets the scene for devouring a wood-fired pizza (around $7) and washing it down with a bottle of wine from the extensive list.

Rung 65b Nguyen Dinh Chieu. "Rung" means forest, which is exactly what it feels like inside this cavernous eatery, which is decorated to look like a forest. A grilled fish will set you back $5, while a dish of snake or crocodile (served with fried veggies) will cost about $7.50.

DRINKING AND NIGHTLIFE

Mui Ne's nightlife is improving in direct proportion to the number of visitors looking for action. Most staying at the resorts tend to drink there too, but if you're at the budget end of the scale and looking for some drinking buddies, head to *Mui Ne Backpackers* before sundown and join one of their infamous bar crawls. Bars often close at dawn in peak season, while at quieter times you may find many of them closed.

DJ Station 120c Nguyen Dinh Chieu. This bar draws a young, energetic crowd of expats and visitors, all here to drain a few cheap drinks. It's one of the best places to head for if you feel like a dance – occasionally around a fire-spinning performance.

Guava 53 Nguyen Dinh Chieu. On the "wrong" side of the road, but still a great place to hang out, with a super-comfortable lounging area and a huge cocktail menu. Also does decent Western-style snack food.

Jibes 90 Nguyen Dinh Chieu. The main base of the local kitesurfing community, and for good reason – the drinks are good and cheap, the comfy seating encourages chatting with friends old or new, and the atmosphere is uber chilled. The sea views help, too.

Sankara 90 Nguyen Dinh Chieu. This rather pricey cocktail bar is by far the trendiest in Mui Ne; its various nooks and crannies surround an open-air pool, and the whole joint is illuminated with gentle lighting in the evening.

Xuan Uyen 78 Nguyen Dinh Chieu. The tiny beachside terrace at the back of this hotel makes cheap cocktails and is about as close in feel to "old" Mui Ne as you're going to get – rickety chairs, hole-dotted umbrellas and a wonderful beach view.

DIRECTORY

Banks There are plenty of ATMs along the strip, mostly in front of the big resorts.

Internet Computers and wi-fi are available at many resorts; some may allow you to use their terminals even if you're not staying there (try the *Terracotta* resort).

Ca Na

Given its proximity to the highway, **CA NA** is a more relaxing place than you would ever think. Hardly more than a wide spot in the road, this small town might even tempt you into staying overnight. Beyond the coracles parked along the beach the water is invitingly clear and snorkelling is a possibility, though you'd be wise to ask locals where to wade in as the coral here is razor sharp. If you crave a little more solitude, a spine of decent dunes back up another good stretch of sand 2km south; a fifteen-minute walk east of the resort area is Ca Na village itself, characterized by the blue fishing boats typical of coastal Vietnam.

ARRIVAL AND DEPARTURE   CA NA

By train Ca Na's station is on the main line, 2km north of the beach and village.

By bus Buses stop right next to the beach resort. You should be able to get open-tour buses to drop you off, though arranging a pick-up can be troublesome. The only regular services are to Phan Rang (1hr).

ACCOMMODATION AND EATING

Ca Na has a few cheap places to stay, and that's about that; both establishments listed here have attached restaurants, which are your best bet for food. Both lie in between highway and beach, a short walk east of the bus stop, and about 1.7km south of the train station.

Ca Na ☎ 068 376 1320. Cheap and a little scruffy, this guesthouse has rooms set in distinctive, high-roofed bungalows – a nice idea, but one that makes things a little cramped in the part of the room that doubles as the ceiling. **$10**

Pandaran ☎ 068 376 1955. Almost next door to the *Ca Na*, this is slightly more salubrious, though again don't go expecting too much. The family that run the guesthouse are extremely friendly to foreign guests, and have made an admirable effort to make the place look good – however, given the calibre of the sea views, you may not even notice. **$12**

Phan Rang and Thap Cham

Although **PHAN RANG** is an unlovely place, whose western limits have fused with the neighbouring town of **THAP CHAM**, the area is rich in historical attractions. The name of the latter, meaning "Cham Towers", gives a clue to the primary reason for stopping here. This region of Vietnam once comprised the Cham kingdom of Panduranga (see box, p.226), and the nearby remnants of **Po Klong Garai** are some of the best preserved in the country. The excellent **Po Re Me** towers – nearly as good – are also in the area. **Tuan Tu**, one of Vietnam's most appealing Cham villages, lies near Phan Rang, as does **Ninh Chu Beach**, a glorious sweep of wide sand that is sometimes deliciously quiet on weekdays, but often overrun with Vietnamese at weekends.

Quan Cong Temple

In the centre of town on Thong Nhat • Sunrise to sunset • Free

The only thing to see in Phan Rang itself is **Quan Cong Temple**, dating from the 1860s. It has faded, pink-wash walls that rise to three consecutive roofs, each draped upon huge red wooden piles imported from China, and laden with fanciful figurines and dragons. Quan Cong is at the head of the third and final chamber, framed by ornate

CHAM ARCHITECTURE

The weathered but beguiling **towers** that punctuate the scenery upcountry from Phan Thiet to Da Nang are the only remaining legacy of **Champa**, an Indianized kingdom that ruled parts of central and southern Vietnam for over fourteen centuries (see p.434). From murky beginnings in the late second century, Champa rose to unify an elongated strip from Phan Thiet to Dong Hoi, and by the end of the fourth century Champa comprised four provinces: **Amaravati**, around Hué and Da Nang; **Vijaya**, centred around Quy Nhon; **Kauthara**, in the Nha Trang region; and **Panduranga**, which corresponds to present-day Phan Thiet and up to Phan Rang. The unified kingdom's first capital, established in the fourth century in Amaravati, was **Simhapura** ("Lion City"); nearby, just outside present-day Hoi An, **My Son**, Champa's holiest site and spiritual heartland, was established (see p.264).

To honour their gods, Cham kings sponsored the construction of the **religious edifices** that still stand today; the red-brick ruins of their towers and temples can be seen all along the coast of south-central Vietnam. While they never attained the magnificence of Angkor, their greatest legacy was a striking architectural style characterized by a wealth of exuberant sculpture. The typical Cham **temple complex** is centred around the **kalan**, or sanctuary, normally pyramidal inside, and containing a lingam, or phallic representation of Shiva, set on a dais that was grooved to channel off water used in purification rituals. Having first cleansed themselves and prayed in the **mandapa**, or meditation hall, worshippers would then have proceeded under a **gate tower** and below the *kalan's* (normally) east-facing vestibule into the sanctuary. Any ritual objects pertaining to worship were kept in a nearby repository room, which normally sported a boat-shaped roof.

Cham towers crop up at regular intervals all the way up the coast from Phan Thiet to Da Nang, and many of them have been restored in recent years. A handful of sites representing the **highlights** of what remains of Champa civilization would include: Po Klong Garai towers (see below); Thap Doi towers (see p.242); Po Re Me Tower (see opposite); My Son (see p.264); Po Nagar towers (see p.232).

gilt woodwork and rows of pikes. There's a decent market just south of the temple, one popular with local Cham people.

ARRIVAL AND DEPARTURE
PHAN RAN AND THAP CHAM

Note that though fused together with a few stringy roads, Phan Rang and Thap Cham are separate entities whose centres are around 7km apart. Trains arrive in Thap Cham to the west, and buses in Phan Rang to the east, and you'd be wise to plan accordingly – the train station is right next to the Cham towers, though the bus station is closer to most accommodation and Tuan Tu village.

By train The train station (Ga Thap Cham) sits on the main line, though not all services stop here – you'll find out which ones do when booking your ticket.
Destinations: Ho Chi Minh City (2 daily; 6hr 30min); Nha Trang (2 daily; 2hr).

By bus The bus station is 300m north of Phan Rang town centre. Local buses to Ca Na leave from outside the *Ho Phong* hotel.
Destinations: Ca Na (1hr); Da Lat (3hr); Ho Chi Minh City (7hr); Nha Trang (2hr); Phan Thiet (3hr).

Po Klong Garai

Daily 7am–5pm • 10,000đ

Elevated with fitting grandeur on a granite mound known as Trau Hill, the **Po Klong Garai Cham towers** are a cut above anything in the town centre. Dating back to around 1400 and the rule of King Jaya Simharvarman III, the complex comprises a *kalan*, or sanctuary, a smaller gate tower and a repository, under whose boat-shaped roof offerings would have been placed. It's the 25m-high *kalan*, though, that's of most interest. From a distance its stippled body impresses; up close, you see a bas-relief of six-armed Shiva cavorting above doorposts etched with Cham inscriptions and ringed by arches crackling with stonework flames, while other gods sit cross-legged in niches elsewhere around the exterior walls.

Push deeper into the *kalan*'s belly and there's a *mukha* lingam fashioned in a likeness of the Cham king, Po Klong Garai, after whom the complex is named. In days gone by, the statue of Shiva's bull (Nandi) that stands in the vestibule would have been "fed" by farmers wishing for good harvests; nowadays it gets a feed only at the annual **Kate Festival** (the Cham New Year), a great spectacle if you're here around October. On the eve of the festival, there's traditional Cham music and dance at the complex, followed, the next morning, by a lively procession bearing the king's raiment to the tower.

ARRIVAL AND DEPARTURE   PO KLONG GARAI TOWERS

By train Train is the best way to arrive here, since the complex is visible from Thap Cham station – just 20,000đ away by xe om, and even walkable (though you'll have to head south and take the road under the tracks). In fact, with some clever scheduling you won't even need to stay in the area at all, merely get on the next train – there are places to eat around the station. In addition, most open-tour buses pull in for a short stop.

By xe om From Phan Rang itself, it's about $5 return by xe om.

Po Re Me Tower

Daily 7.30am–6pm • Free

If Po Klong Garai inspires further interest in Cham towers, you could make the trickier journey out to **Po Re Me Tower**. Like its near-neighbour, the tower (which draws its name from the last Cham king) enjoys a fine hilltop location, though its four storeys tapering to a lingam are sturdier and less finished than Po Klong Garai. Its high point is the splendid bas-relief in the *kalan*'s entrance, depicting Shiva manifest in the image of mustachioed King Po Re Me waggling his arms, and watched over by two Nandis. Po Re Me is also a focus of Cham festivities during the Kate Festival (see p.51).

ARRIVAL AND DEPARTURE   PO RE ME TOWER

By xe om The tower is 8km south of Phan Rang and Thap Cham on Highway 1; the track is hard to find, so a xe om (about $6 return from Phan Rang) is a wise option.

Tuan Tu Village

There's still a Cham presence around Phan Rang. **Tuan Tu Village** is home to more than a thousand Cham people, whom you'll recognize by the headcloths that they favour over conical hats. Largely Muslim, they maintain an unpretentious, 1966-built mosque free of any trappings, not even a minaret. Also keep any eye out for the distinctive **Cham text**, dotted liberally about the place and, with its Southeast Asian swirls, rather more beautiful than Vietnam's somewhat messy Roman writing. Locals are friendly and not used to seeing visitors – don't be surprised to find yourself invited for tea or coffee.

ARRIVAL AND DEPARTURE   TUAN TU VILLAGE

By xe om Tuan Tu is 3–4km from central Phan Rang – certainly within range by bike or on foot, though not signed at all, and very hard to track down by yourself. A xe om shouldn't be more than 100,000đ for the round-trip. The mosque is behind a well, to the right of the settlement's only road.

Ninh Chu Beach

5km northest of Phan Rang is Ninh Chu beach, a more indolent alternative to trekking around Phan Rang's Cham towers. The beach is a reasonably clean and wide crescent of sand – soft, if not exactly golden. Ninh Chu doesn't have the same pulling power for foreigners as Mui Ne or Nha Trang, but its beach is popular for swimming, sunbathing, beach games and jogging too. With several resorts located here, it's worth considering as a place to rest up, particularly midweek, when it can be very quiet. If you're here at a weekend, be prepared for crowds of families and noisy teenagers.

4

Accommodation in Phan Rang itself is limited; you're better off avoiding the town completely and heading for Ninh Chu Beach, where the options are much more appealing. There are a few cheap options near the train station in Thap Cham, if you need to stay that way. As for eating, there are plenty of snack shacks around the train station, but nothing notable in town. Many decent establishments are located on Ninh Chu Beach; the *Den Gion* is closest to Phan Rang town (approximately 3km away), with the *Hoan Cau* 2km further north, and the *Saigon Ninhchu* 2km north again.

PHAN RANG

Ho Phong 353–363 Ngo Gia Tu ☎ 068 392 0333. The best option in the town centre, with bare but spacious rooms and (occasionally) an English-speaker at reception. It's at the south end of town, near the bridge. Breakfast not included. ̄$25
Thong Nhat 343 Thong Nhat ☎ 068 382 7201. A little cheaper than Ho Phang, but almost as good. It's at the north end of town, and therefore convenient for the bus station; in addition, there's a restaurant on the ground level. ̄$16

NINH CHU

Den Gion Resort ☎ 068 387 4047, ⓦ dengion-resort .com. In the centre of the beach and itself centred on a wonderful swimming pool, this resort draws heavily on the region's Cham heritage for its design. Rooms are smartly decorated, if rather small; conversely, the size of the

complex as a whole can make it feel deserted outside peak season. ̄$45
Hoan Cau ☎ 068 389 0077, ⓦ hoancautourist.com.vn. One of the strangest hotels in Vietnam, with rooms made to look like old tree stumps and statues of Snow White characters dotted around the complex. Luridly cheesy, the rooms are ugly and cramped together. Nevertheless, they're spacious, clean and good value on the inside. ̄$16
★ **Saigon Ninhchu** ☎ 068 387 6000, ⓦ saigonninhchuhotel.com.vn. At the far north end of the bay, this hotel has beautifully furnished, thick-carpeted, spacious rooms, and the executive suites even have beach views from the bath. There's also a big pool, tennis courts, a spa and a classy restaurant that's the best place to eat for miles around and reasonably priced to boot – a bucketful of oysters, steamed over lemongrass will set you back 90,000d. ̄$75

Nha Trang

Big enough to bustle, yet small enough to retain its relaxed air, the delightful city of **NHA TRANG** has, despite increasingly stiff competition, earned its place as Vietnam's top beach destination. A grand 6km scythe of soft yellow sand is lapped by rolling waves on one side and fringed on the other by cafés, restaurants, hotels and some unusual modern sculptures. Hawkers are on hand to supply paperbacks, fresh pineapple and massages, while **scuba-diving** classes and all kinds of **watersports** are available. Local companies also offer popular day-trips to Nha Trang's outlying **islands**, combining hiking, **snorkelling** and an onboard feast of seafood. Bear in mind that the rainy season, around November and December, sees the sea get choppy and the beach loses much of its appeal.

There's far more to Nha Trang than sea and sand. The culinary scene is noteworthy, as is the range of accommodation amongst some stylish boutiques and bars. Then there are a few sights, both in and around the city, with the intriguing **Po Nagar Cham towers** of greatest appeal – by the time Nguyen lords wrested this patch of the country from Champa in the mid-seventeenth century, the towers had already stood here for over seven hundred years. Beyond the centre, you'll find hot springs in which you can wallow in mud, the world's longest cross-sea cable-car ride, and more besides. Last, but not least, is the city's huge and hugely photogenic fishing fleet, which moors just north of the centre – a place of salty, local appeal in a city that has been embracing change for decades.

Beach-bumming certainly takes precedence over sightseeing in Nha Trang, but there are a clutch of worthwhile places to visit in the city itself, including the Alexandre Yersin museum (see box, p.232), and a beautiful pair of religious buildings.

Nha Trang Cathedral

Thai Nguyen • Sunrise to sunset • Free
Thread your way southwest from the Pasteur Institute, and after a few minutes you'll hit **Thai Nguyen**, home to two of Nha Trang's best-known sights. Presiding

---

ACTIVITIES IN THE SOUTH CHINA SEA

DIVING

Nha Trang is the **dive centre of Vietnam**, as is well evidenced by the number of dive companies that operate here. It's best avoided October to December, when the strong currents stir up the silt and reduce visibility, but during the dry season (Jan–May) there are dive boats kitting out and casting off every day to one of over twenty dive sites in the region. A typical day out, including a couple of dives and lunch, costs around $80, with snorkelling around $25; PADI courses are also available, from basic Discover packs (around $100) to Open Water (4 day; $360).

There are well over a dozen operators in Nha Trang and some are downright dangerous – there have been cases of divers left behind, and even a couple of deaths since the turn of the millennium. The places listed below have stellar reputations; both also offer PADI courses.

Rainbow Divers 90a Hung Vuong ☎ 058 352 4351, ⓦ divevietnam.com.
Sailing Club Divers 72-74 Tran Phu ☎ 058 352 1629, ⓦ sailingclubdivers.com.

WATERSPORTS

If you'd rather get your kicks above water, various points on the beach rent out watersports equipment (the section by the *Louisiane Brewhouse* is best). For a mere $10 you can scare the wits out of swimmers by zapping them with a **jet-ski** spray for thirty minutes, but keep in mind that you will be held responsible for any injuries or damages. Less environmentally disastrous are the sports of **parasailing** ($16), **windsurfing** ($30) and riding a **banana boat** ($35/boat), with prices varying according to activity.

4

over the street's eastern end, the stolid, grey-brick **Nha Trang Cathedral**, built in the 1930s, casts its shadow over the sloping cobbled track that winds round to its front doors from Nguyen Trai. Under the lofty, vaulted ceilings within the cathedral's dowdy exterior, vivid stained-glass windows depict Christ, Mary, Joseph, Joan of Arc and St Theresa.

Long Son Pagoda

Sunrise to sunset • Free

If you feel as if you're being watched as you climb up to the cathedral, 800m along Thai Nguyen from the Nha Trang Cathedral, it's probably the huge white Buddha statue seated on a hillside above **Long Son Pagoda**. Stone gateposts topped by lotus buds mark the entrance to the 1930s-built pagoda. An impressive bronze Buddha stands at the head of the altar, and there are the usual capering dragons on the eaves, but it's the huge **White Buddha**, 152 steps up the hillside behind, that's the pagoda's greatest asset – and Nha Trang's most recognizable landmark. Crafted in 1963 to symbolize the Buddhist struggle against the repressive Diem regime, around its lotus-shaped pedestal are carved images of the monks and nuns who set fire to themselves in protest, among them Thich Quang Duc (see box, p.80). Note that in recent years, the pagoda has become a popular haunt for local beggars.

North of the centre

Just to the north of Nha Trang are a couple of wonderful sights – the evocative Cham towers of **Po Nagar**, and the joyous mud-pools of the **Thap Ba Hot Springs**. Heading a little further north will bring you to the **Hon Chong Promontory**, a finger of granite boulders dashed by the sea; it's quite possible to clamber down to the rocks. Immediately up the coast is **Hon Chong Beach**, less refined than the city beach but more secluded. Cheap seafood restaurants proliferate at its far end. At night, the views from here across the bay to the central beach zone are very impressive.

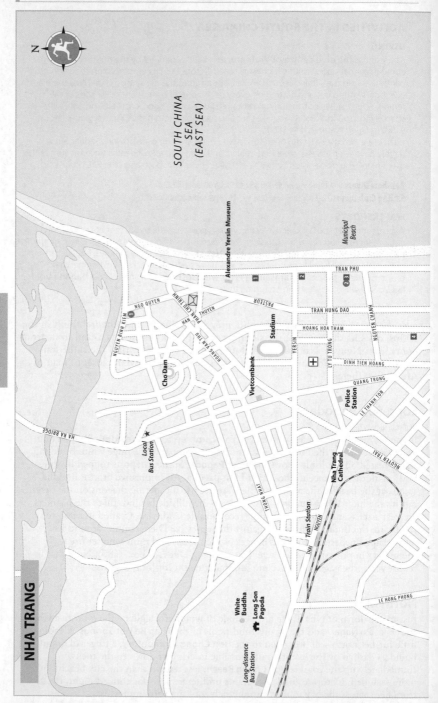

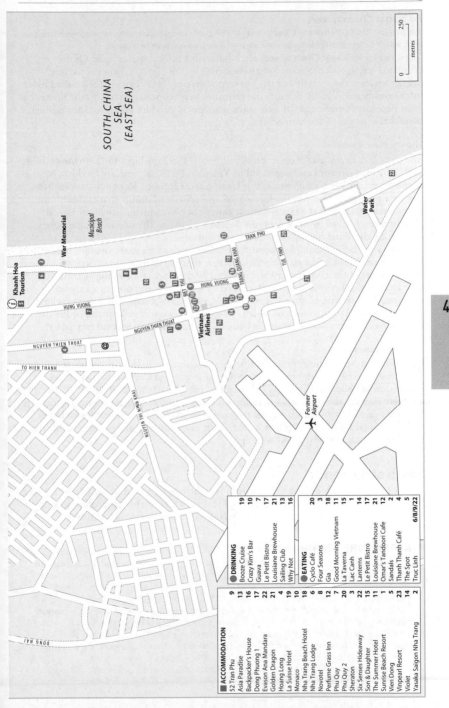

SOUTH CHINA
SEA
(EAST SEA)

4

■ ACCOMMODATION		● DRINKING		● EATING	
52 Tran Phu	9	Booze Cruise	19	Cyclo Café	20
Asia Paradise	13	Crazy Kim's Bar	10	Four Seasons	3
Backpacker's House	16	Guava	7	Gia	18
Dong Phuong 1	17	Le Petit Bistro	17	Good Morning Vietnam	11
Evason Ana Mandara	22	Louisiane Brewhouse	21	La Taverna	15
Golden Dragon	21	Sailing Club	13	Lac Canh	1
Hoang Long	4	Why Not	16	Lanterns	14
La Suisse Hotel	19			Le Petit Bistro	17
Monaco	10			Louisiane Brewhouse	21
Nha Trang Beach Hotel	18			Omar's Tandoori Cafe	12
Nha Trang Lodge	8			Sandals	5
Novotel	3			Thanh Thanh Café	4
Perfume Grass Inn	12			The Spot	23
Phu Quy	7			Truc Linh	5
Phu Quy 2	20				
Sheraton	3				
Six Senses Hideaway	22				
Son & Daughter	15				
The Summer Hotel	11				
Sunrise Beach Resort	1				
Vien Dong	5				
Vinpearl Resort	23				
Violet	14				
Yasaka Saigon Nha Trang	2				

6/8/9/22

Po Nagar Cham towers

Daily 6am–6pm • 16,000đ • The towers are 1.2km from central Nha Trang, and it's quite possible to walk – keep heading north from the beach, and take the first left after the bridge. Otherwise, any xe om driver in town will be willing to take you.

The glorious **Po Nagar Cham towers** are Nha Trang's most popular sight. Of the estimated ten towers, or *kalan*, constructed here by the Hindu Cham people (see p.472) between the seventh and twelfth centuries, only four remain. Their baked red bricks weathered so badly through the centuries that restoration work on the towers has been necessary; nevertheless, the complex manages to produce an age-old atmosphere, despite the gaggles of souvenir sellers.

The northern tower

The complex's largest and most impressive tower is the 25m-high **northern tower**, built in 817 by Harivarman I and dedicated to Yang Ino Po Nagar, tutelary Goddess Mother of the Kingdom and a manifestation of Uma, Shiva's consort. Restored sections stand out for their lighter hue, but the lotus-petal and spearhead motifs that embellish the tower are original, as is the lintel over the outer door, on which a lithe four-armed Shiva dances, flanked by musicians, on the back of an ox. The two sandstone pillars supporting this lintel bear spidery Cham inscriptions.

Inside, a vestibule tapering to a pyramidal ceiling leads to the main chamber, where a fog of incense hangs in the air. The golden statue that originally stood in here was pilfered by the Khmer in the 10th century and replaced by the black stone statue of Uma still here today – albeit minus its head, plundered by the French and now in a Parisian museum. The ten arms of cross-legged Uma are nowadays obscured by a gaudy yellow robe, and a doll-like face has been added. Yang Ino Po Nagar is still worshipped as the protectress of the city and the statue is bathed during the **Merian Festival** each March.

The other towers

Possessing neither the height nor the intricacy of the main *kalan*, the **central tower**, dating back to the seventh century, is dedicated to the god Cri Cambhu, and sees a steady flow of childless couples pass through to pray for fertility at its lingam. The **southern tower** is the smallest of the four, and also features a lingam inside. Beneath its boat-shaped roof, half-formed statues in relief are still visible at the **northwest tower**, and the frontal view of an elephant is just about discernible on the western facade, its serpentine trunk now blackened with age.

South of the centre

Unmissable just south of Nha Trang is **Hon Tre**, the biggest island in the bay by far, and home to one of the country's largest amusement parks. Near the jump-off points of ferry and cable-car is the rather interesting **National Oceanographic Institute**.

ALEXANDRE YERSIN

A Swiss-French scientist who travelled to Southeast Asia in 1889 as a ship's doctor, **Alexandre Yersin** developed a great love for Vietnam and learned to speak Vietnamese fluently. He was responsible for the founding of Da Lat (he recognized the beneficial effects of the climate there for Europeans), and settled in Nha Trang in 1893. By the time of his death in 1943, Yersin had become a local hero, thanks not to his greatest achievement – the discovery of a **plague bacillus** in Hong Kong in 1894 – but rather to his educational work in sanitation and agriculture, and to his ability to predict typhoons and thus save the lives of fishermen. Significantly, his name is still given to streets, not only in Nha Trang but around the country, sharing an honour generally only granted to Vietnamese heroes.

There's a **museum** (Mon–Fri 7.30–11am & 2–4.30pm; 26,000đ) in the centre of Nha Trang, and it's worth visiting, stuffed as it is with books and other paraphernalia formerly belonging to Yersin.

MUD MUD, GLORIOUS MUD

A side-road heading west just to the north of the Po Nagar Cham towers takes you through suburban Nha Trang to the **Thap Ba Hot Springs** (Daily 7am–7.30pm; ☎058 383 4939, ⓦthapbahotspring.com.vn). The main attraction here is the opportunity to wallow in mineral-enriched mud – allegedly good for the skin, but great fun too. You'll be encouraged to buy a "private" bath (around 250,000đ per person), though in practice foreigners going for the "communal" bath option (100,000đ per person) get exactly the same thing. After washing off, you're free to have a swim in pools filled with water rich in sodium silicate chloride, said to have beneficial effects on stress, arthritis and rheumatism. There are a number of other options available, including spa treatment, massage, and meals – it's even possible to stay the night. To get here, it's best to grab a cab from the Po Nagar towers.

Vinpearl Land Amusement Park

Park open 8am–9pm (to 10pm Sat & Sun); cable car (10min) daily 9am–10pm • 360,000đ • ☎058 359 0111, ⓦvinpearlland.com

Hon Tre is dominated by this massive amusement park, which includes a hotel (see p.235), a waterpark with slides and flumes, a mini-oceanarium, 4-D movies, a shopping mall and some rides – great fun, especially for those travelling with children. You can get here by speedboat or "canoe-taxi", but it's more enjoyable by cable car, which, at 3.3km long, is the longest such ride in the world. The mainland station is just south of central Nha Trang.

The National Oceanographic Institute

Beside Cau Da Wharf, 4km south of Nha Trang • Daily 6am–6pm • 15,000đ

Established in 1923 and housed in a colonial mansion, this is a veritable Frankenstein's lab of pickling jars and glass cases yielding crustaceans, fish, seaweed and coral. In one room an 18m-long humpback whale skeleton is displayed, plus a hammerhead shark and bow-mouth guitarfish. If you've been out snorkelling you might spot some recent acquaintances in the aquarium's twenty or so tanks of primary-coloured live fishes and sea horses. There are three large open ponds in the forecourt, home to horseshoe crabs, zebra sharks and various local species of fish.

ARRIVAL AND DEPARTURE   NHA TRANG

By plane Flights into the city land at Cam Ranh International Airport (☎058 398 9918), 35km south of the city. From here take a bus (25,000đ) or taxi (around $12) to Nha Trang. Despite the airport's name, and the wishes of local businesses, there are no scheduled international flights – apparently due to the local authorities' refusal to fund the necessary firemen. Vietnam Airlines have an office at 91 Nguyen Thien Thuat (daily 7–11.30am & 1.30–5pm; ☎058 352 6768).
Destinations: Da Nang (2 daily; 1hr 15min); Hanoi (3 daily; 1hr 45min); Ho Chi Minh City (4 daily; 1hr).
By train Ga Nha Trang (ticket office daily 7.30–11am & 1.30–9pm; ☎058 382 2113) is just west of the city centre on Thai Nguyen. Though walkable, it's tempting to take a

cab; as always, stepping out of the station and flagging one down on the main road will help you avoid the cowboys. Just about any hotel or travel agency in Nha Trang will get you a ticket, though since commission rates vary widely, it pays to shop around.
Destinations: Da Nang (5 daily; 9hr–12hr 30min); Hanoi (5 daily; 24hr–32hr); Ho Chi Minh City (6 daily; 7hr 10min–11hr 15min); Hué (5 daily; 12hr–16hr 10min).
By bus Most visitors arrive on open-tour buses, which drop off centrally outside affiliated offices or hotels. The long-distance bus station (☎058 382 2192) sits 1km west of the city centre, and around 700m west of the train station.
Destinations: Buon Ma Thuot (4hr); Da Lat (4hr); Da Nang (12hr); Ho Chi Minh City (10hr); Hué (15hr).

GETTING AROUND

On foot Nha Trang isn't a very large city, so walking may well be your means of covering the ground – especially if a daily pilgrimage to the municipal beach marks the extent of your travels.
By bicycle and xe om Should you plan to stray a little

further afield, bicycle rental is the most efficient and enjoyable way to go. Bicycles are available for around $2 per day at most of the city's hotels, though xe om are everywhere if you need them (and even if you don't).
Car tours Fully fledged car tours of the region (around

BOAT TRIPS TO THE ISLANDS

Several companies in Nha Trang (see "Listings" opposite) offer day-trips to a selection of islands, including a stop for **snorkelling** and a **seafood lunch** on board – all for around $6–8 per person. However, to fully enjoy the day, you'll need to fork out for several extras if you don't want to sit on the boat and wait till everyone comes back. Some boat rides, particularly those booked through backpacker guesthouses, can be quite wild and alcohol-fuelled, while other operators run gentler tours.

On a typical island day tour, you'll be picked up from your hotel, taken to Cau Da Wharf, 6km south of the town centre, and shuffled on to one of many boats jostling in the harbour. As the boat casts off at around 9.30am, you'll pass beneath the cable car to Hon Tre (see below), then chug between islands for about half an hour to **Hon Mun** (Black Island), named after the dark cliffs that rear up from it. There's no beach to speak of on Hon Mun, but the island boasts one of the best places for snorkelling in the area, with some great coral. Boats hang around for an hour or so while people snorkel over the corals or sunbathe on the boat, and there are frequently diving groups here too. There's a 40,000đ charge to snorkel in this "protected area", though it's not clear quite how it's being protected.

After a break for lunch in the shelter of Hon Mot, boats head for Hon Tam, where there's a small beach (10,000đ entry), and you get the chance to stretch on the sand or splash about in the sea for an hour before heading for the final destination, the **Tri Nguyen Aquarium** (25,000đ) on **Hon Mieu**. The setting here is wonderfully kitsch: visitors approach the site through giant lobsters and past cement sharks, and the strange building that houses the aquarium looks like a galleon dragged up from the depths and draped in seaweed. Inside, the tanks feature black-tipped sharks, bug-eyed groupers, hawksbill turtles and colourful sea anemones. Finally the boat heads back to the mainland and visitors are whisked back to their hotels.

$50/day) can be arranged by tour operators (see p.238), who also offer day-trips to the islands off Nha Trang and minibus tours of the central highlands.

ACCOMMODATION

The fact that Nha Trang is chock-full of hotels doesn't seem to be discouraging developers, and the city's already wide **choice of accommodation** just keeps on growing. Beachfront monoliths are gradually blocking out any sea view from the backstreet mini-hotels. Even so, it's worth bearing in mind that the city draws Vietnamese as well as foreign tourists, and that there can be difficulties finding a room over public holidays, when prices rise. **Backpackers** should head straight for "Hostel Alley", opposite the Vietnam Airlines office on Nguyen Thien Thuat.

52 Tran Phu 52 Tran Phu ☎058 352 4228, ⓦ52tranphuhotel.com. One of the few remaining mid-range options on the central beachfront. Though perhaps a little institutional, rooms are simple but comfortable and all have a/c and hot water. **$25**

Asia Paradise 6 Biet Thu ☎058 352 4686, ⓦasiaparadisehotel.com. Decent mid-ranger, right in the middle of things, with smallish but elegant rooms, all of which have balconies. **$40**

Backpacker's House 54g Nguyen Thien Thuat ☎058 352 4500, ⓦbackpackershouse.net. Good backpacker option, set off the main road in the thick of the bar area. Nothing spectacular, but a fine place to meet travel buddies. Dorm **$7**, double **$12**

Dong Phuong 1 101–103 Nguyen Thien Thuat ☎058 352 6896, ⓔdongphuongnt@dng.vnn.vn. This family-run hotel is one of the most popular of the area's many budget options. Functional but spacious rooms, ranging from small fan rooms to the enormous, a/c penthouse. **$6**

Evason Ana Mandara Southern end of Tran Phu ☎058 352 2222, ⓦsixsenses.com. Nha Trang's most luxurious resort comes with its own slice of beach and features dreamy bungalows with all mod cons and some traditional touches, including ethnic-minority tapestries. Facilities include two pools, tennis courts, a beach restaurant, and the superb Six Senses spa. **$370**

Golden Dragon 78/36 Tue Tinh ☎058 352 7117, ⓦgoldendragonhotel.com.vn. A cosy and welcoming mini-hotel tucked away down a quiet backstreet in the south of town, just 5min from the beach, with good-value a/c rooms. There's a tiny pool and sundeck on the fourth floor. **$20**

Hoang Long 30/12 Hoang Hoa Tham ☎058 352 5316. Tucked away down an alley opposite the *Chi Thanh*, this place offers compact fan or a/c rooms at very competitive prices. On a quiet road and feels far from the action, though in reality it's just a short walk away from all the restaurants and bars. **$10**

★ **La Suisse Hotel** 34 Tran Quang Khai ☎058 352 4353, ⓦlasuissehotel.com. Perhaps the most popular budget hotel in the city, allying great service with cheap but well-appointed rooms. The semi-secluded location is also a bonus, since you're largely off the radar of hawkers and xe om drivers. **$20**

Monaco 4a Ton Dan ☎058 352 2398, ⓦmonaconha trang.com. The best option in a small alley full of smart, modern mini-hotels, its rooms simply but elegantly decorated, and all with a/c. Some rooms have sea views – for now. **$25**

Nha Trang Beach Hotel 4 Tran Quang Khai ☎058 352 4468, ⓦnhatrangbeachhotel.com.vn. Smart mini-hotel in the budget district with a/c, hot water, TV and comfortable furnishings in all the rooms. **$22**

Nha Trang Lodge 42 Tran Phu ☎058 352 1500, ⓦnhatranglodge.com. A twelve-floor hotel that was once one of the best in town. Its rooms are now slightly dated, but larger than those in most modern hotels; in addition, they still boast the same fantastic sea views. **$60**

Novotel 50 Tran Phu ☎058 322 1027, ⓦnovotel.com. Beautiful beachfront hotel, whose rates often drop below $100 – five-star rooms at three-star prices. There's not too much in the way of facilities, bar, a small pool and spa, though this adds to the relaxed air. **$150**

Perfume Grass Inn 4a Biet Thu ☎058 352 4286, ⓦperfume-grass.com. This reasonably priced place has lots of "character" – a double-edged compliment, if ever there was one, but rooms are cheerful enough, some coming with reclining chairs and bathtubs. Staff are friendly, and there's a relaxing rooftop terrace. **$18**

Phu Quy 54 Hung Vuong ☎058 352 1609, ⓔphuquyhotel@dng.vnn.vn. Welcoming, reasonably priced family-run mini-hotel. Rooms, with either a/c or fans, are small, but all are spotlessly clean. There's also a small terrace with sun-loungers on the roof. **$15**

Phu Quy 2 1 Tue Tinh ☎058 352 6060, ⓦphuquyhotel .com.vn. A very smart mid-range option, this 15-storey building offers good beach views, especially from the upper-floor rooms and the tiny rooftop pool. Rooms are well-furnished and have wooden floors. **$33**

★ **Sheraton** 26–28 Tran Phu ☎058 388 0000, ⓦsheraton.com. A relative newbie and already the flashiest city-centre option by far. Rooms have been decorated with soothing colours and local art, and you'll be able to see the sea from most shower cubicles. You should be able to lop a fair chunk off the rack rates. **$220**

Six Senses Hideaway Ninh Van Bay ☎058 372 8222, ⓦsixsenses.com. Choose from beach villas, rock villas, hill-top villas, over-water villas or spa-suite villas on an idyllic island off the coast, but make sure you can handle the price tag before you come ashore. **$500**

Son & Daughter 54a Nguyen Thien Thuat ☎058 352 1709. On the same sidestreet as the *Backpacker's House*, this is slightly cheaper, and slightly more relaxed, though staff are less likely to speak English. Dorm **$5**, double **$12**

The Summer Hotel 34 Nguyen Thien Thuat ☎058 352 2186, ⓦthesummerhotel.com.vn. A cool 3-star mini-hotel. The rooms are modern and comfortable, if a little on the small side. Staff are helpful and there's a swimming pool on the roof. **$30**

Sunrise Beach Resort 12–14 Tran Phu ☎058 382 0999, ⓦsunrisenhatrang.com.vn. Enjoying a superb location towards the northern end of the beach, this elegant, rambling hotel boasts a classical colonial design. Some rooms are a little small, but move up to a suite and you'll be drinking in the sea views from the jacuzzi on your balcony. **$210**

Vien Dong 1 Tran Hung Dao ☎058 352 3606, ⓔviendonghtl@dng.vnn.vn. Ageing but well-run operation, counting a swimming pool, tennis courts and satellite TV among its amenities. Rooms in the main building are scrupulously clean, but those in the poolside annexe are less polished. **$22**

Vinpearl Resort 7 Tran Phu ☎058 391 11166, ⓦvinpearlresort-nhatrang.com. This luxurious resort is actually located on Hon Tre out in the bay, and features nearly 500 well-equipped rooms as well as the biggest pool in Southeast Asia (5000sqm). It is accessed by speedboat or cable car from the southern end of Tran Phu. **$260**

Violet 12 Biet Thu ☎058 352 2314, ⓦviolethotel .com.vn. This well-maintained mini-hotel on trendy Biet Thu has a small pool and restaurant, as well as smart rooms with new furnishings and all mod cons. Importantly, it's also just a hop, skip and jump to the beach. **$22**

Yasaka Saigon Nha Trang 18 Tran Phu ☎058 382 0090, ⓦyasanhatrang.com. Impressive high-rise hotel, whose facilities include a fitness centre, swimming pool and tennis courts. Rooms are spacious and boast full amenities; all face the sea, with fabulous views from the upper floors. **$75**

EATING

Finding a decent **place to eat** presents no problem in Nha Trang, with seafood its speciality – it's cheapest, and at its best, in the out-of-town area north of Tran Phu bridge. You don't need to leave the beach to eat during the day, as **strolling vendors** are on hand with their tempting snacks. There's also a night market south of the water park with many cheap food stalls.

PAMPER YOURSELF

Spa, massage and beauty services are now big business in Nha Trang, and there are a host of places to choose from. Some are more proficient than others, but the two have a great reputation. Both offer a huge range of services, including facials (from $16), body scrubs ($15), hot-stone massages ($25); given the prodigious length of the "menus", it may help to avoid any unnecessary stress by plumping for an all-in package.

Lotus 28 Tran Quang Khai ☎ 058 352 6457.
Su Spa 93 Nguyen Thien Thuat ☎ 058 352 3242.

Cyclo Café 130 Nguyen Thien Thuat. A friendly ambience along with a solid menu of Vietnamese and Italian food (from $2.50 per dish), plus locally brewed beer make this place worth checking out. Daily 7.30am–10pm.

Four Seasons 40 Tran Phu. This smart beachfront restaurant serves seafood specials from around $5, plus a good range of shakes and ice creams. If it's just coffee you're after, however, the place next door is a little more attractive. Daily 7am–11pm.

Gia 30 Tran Quang Khai. One of the better-looking Vietnamese restaurants in town, its tree-cloaked courtyard tables best at night when illuminated by lantern-light. Mains from $3. Daily 10am–10pm.

La Taverna 115 Nguyen Thien Thuat. Authentic Italian atmosphere and food at this welcoming place in the budget district. Pizzas for around $5.50, pasta a little less. Daily 10am–11pm.

★ **Louisiane Brewhouse** Tran Phu Beach. This beachfront place has it all – an excellent range of Vietnamese and Western dishes (such as red snapper fillet for $5.50), a sushi corner, a pizza corner, home-made cakes and pastries and a swimming pool that's free for customers. Also one of the city's best places to drink (see p.238). Daily 8am–late.

Lac Canh 44 Nguyen Binh Kiem. A table-side grill that's hugely popular among locals. Not the most salubrious place in town, but the food ($2–4) more than compensates. Daily 9am–9.30pm.

★ **Lanterns** 72 Nguyen Thien Thuat. This charming restaurant serves delectable Vietnamese food, with burgers, pasta dishes and local specialities starting from $3.50, but that's not the end of the story – their proceeds help to support local orphanages, from which many of the staff are sourced for work experience. They also run half-day cooking classes for $14. Daily 10am–10pm.

Le Petit Bistro 26b Tran Quang Khai. Good-looking French bistro, doling out superb dishes at surprisingly reasonable prices – $5.50 will get you a full belly. The daily special board is usually the best place to start, though ensure you've room for one of their delectable desserts. Good cheese and cold cuts of meat round out the picture. Daily 10am–10pm.

Omar's Tandoori Cafe 89b Nguyen Thien Thuat and 96a/8 Tran Phu. Not the most attractive restaurant in Nha Trang – or even on this side of the road – but this remains the place to go should you get the urge for an Indian curry. Most will set you back a shade under $5. Daily 7am–10pm.

★ **Sandals** 26–28 Tran Phu ☎058 388 0000, ⓦ sheraton.com. Inside the Sheraton, this stylish Hong Kong-style restaurant allows you to experience the high life on a moderate budget – you'll be able to eat well for under $5. Dim sum, salads and desserts fill an extensive pick 'n' tick menu; all are lovingly prepared, and absolutely delicious. Daily 11am–2pm & 6–10pm.

Thanh Thanh Café 10 Nguyen Thien Thuat ☎058 382 4413. Extensive menu of reasonably priced Vietnamese, Western and vegetarian dishes, but the range of wood-fired pizzas is their forte; also offers city deliveries. Daily 7am–9pm.

The Spot 17b Hung Vuong. A good place to head if your travels through Vietnam have left you hankering for some Western food. This small place whips up hearty breakfasts, pies and roast spuds, as well as Vietnamese dishes. Daily 9am–10pm.

Truc Linh 11 and 18 Biet Thu, 80 Hung Vuong and 83 Tran Phu. Very successful operation serving up a good range of Western and Vietnamese dishes, with seafood the speciality. Prices are a little above average (most dishes cost over $6) but the food is still good value – for now, since the chain's popularity has seen standards dropping. The branch at 18 Biet Thu is the most atmospheric. Daily 8am–10pm.

DRINKING & NIGHTLIFE

Nha Trang has a **buzzing nightlife** scene. There are plenty of chillout and party places around the budget district, and pricier nightspots along the beachfront; many places have generous happy hours, sometimes lasting all day. Occasional **crackdowns** have the bars closing at midnight, but left to their own devices, most bar-owners will stay open till the wee hours.

Booze Cruise 110 Nguyen Thien Thuat; map pp.231–232. Super-cheap cocktails and an often raucous atmosphere. Happy hour tends to run from 2–11pm, with this fact alone convincing a fair proportion of passers-by to pop in for a drink. Daily 11am–late.

Crazy Kim's Bar 19 Biet Thu; map pp.231–232. Two-foot-tall cocktails, happy hour that runs noon-midnight, great selection of CDs, hedonistic party atmosphere and hangover breakfasts make this place very popular with expats, tourists and brave locals, who rave till late. Proceeds from the bar go towards helping Nha Trang's street children. Daily 9.30am–late.

Guava 34f Nguyen Thien Thuat; map pp.231–232. Well-designed bar, with pool table, sports on TV, jumping beats and some weird cocktails, many of which feature local ingredients (passion fruit juice being a particular favourite). They have two bars in town, with the newer one on Nguyen Thien Thuat the more appealing. Daily 11am–late.

Le Petit Bistro 26b Tran Quang Khai; map pp.231–232. This charming restaurant (see p.236) is notable for its extensive wine menu – an unexpected delight, particularly at the more affordable end of the scale. Daily 10am–10pm.

★ **Louisiane Brewhouse** Tran Phu Beach; map pp.231–232. Not just an excellent restaurant (see p.236), but a terrific place to drink. They make a pilsener, a dark lager, a witbier and seasonal ales, all of which can be tried in a cute (and fairly priced) sampler set. After that, pick a pint of your favourite one, and enjoy it on the beach or over a game of pool. Daily 8am–late.

Sailing Club 72–74 Tran Phu; map pp.231–232. This has been a favourite spot for an eclectic group of party animals for some years. It draws a well-heeled expat crowd and hordes of tourists to its refined beachfront bar, which gets progressively less refined as the night wears on. Daily 7am–late.

Why Not 24 Tran Quang Khai; map pp.231–232. Big place with inside and outside seating, pool table, dance floor and comfy lounge area. Serving beer and spirits, with live music some nights. Daily 9am–late.

SHOPPING

Andy's Book Exchange 4d Biet Thu. Small store with a fairly decent selection of used books.

Bambou 15 Biet Thu. Offers original-design T-shirts at $10 each, plus other bright and colourful souvenirs.

Lac Viet 4c Biet Thu. Specializes in lacquerware ornaments and wood carvings.

Vietnam Pure Silk 19 Le Thanh Ton. Has ready-to-wear silk garments and tailor shop plus embroidery, artwork and ethnic souvenirs.

XQ Arts and Crafts Centre 64 Tran Phu. Displays and sells embroidered pictures, some of which are stunning works of art, from $30 upwards.

DIRECTORY

Bank Vietcombank, 17 Quang Trung, changes cash and travellers' cheques, and has an ATM. There's also a convenient branch of Agribank at 2 Hung Vuong.

Car rental Most tour operators, including Khanh Hoa Tourism at 1 Tran Hung Dao (☎ 058 352 8100), can arrange car rental with driver for $40–45 per day; minibuses are also available at a slightly higher rate.

Hospital 19 Yersin, below the city stadium ☎ 058 382 2168.

Internet There are hundreds of places offering internet access in Nha Trang, including 24d Nguyen Thiet Thuat, where rates are a standard 100đ per minute.

Mini–markets Branches of A Mart can be found all over town; all have cheap drinks and a wide range of snack food.

Pharmacy 27 Le Thanh Ton.

Police 5 Ly Tu Trong ☎ 058 382 2400.

Post office 4 Le Loi (daily 7am–9pm), has fax, IDD facilities, internet access, poste restante and DHL courier desk (closed Sun); there are also several other small post offices scattered around town.

Tour operators Con Se Tre Tourist, 100/16 Tran Phu ☎ 058 352 7522; Hanh Café, 10 Hung Vuong ☎ 058 352 7467, ✉ hanhcafe@dng.vnn.vn; Khanh Hoa Tourism, 1 Tran Hung Dao (☎ 058 352 8100, ⓦ nhatrangtourism.com.vn) is the official government office, so the best place to go for visa extensions; Mama Linh, 23c Biet Thu ☎ 058 052 2844; Sinh Café, 2a Biet Thu ☎ 058 352 2982, ✉ info@sinhcafevn .com; TM Brothers Café, 34 Nguyen Thien Thuat ☎ 058 352 3556, ✉ tmbrotherscafevietnam@yahoo.com.

The coast north of Nha Trang

Most tourists leapfrog the 400km-plus of coastline between Nha Trang and Hoi An on a tour bus, but swathes of splendid coastline do exist along this stretch of the country, many of which remain relatively untouched. Visitors to places like **Doc Let**, **Whale Island** and **Bai Dai** will find good accommodation options and uncrowded beaches in front of their resort.

Ba Ho Falls

9am–6pm • 5,000đ • Take a bus headed for Ninh Hoa District from Nha Trang's local station, and tell the driver your destination; a xe om from the turn-off should cost around 10,000đ. It's easy to find the falls if travelling under your own steam – the turning for the falls is signposted to the left from the highway

Therapeutic properties are attributed to the waters of the three pools at **Ba Ho Falls**, around 20km from Nha Trang. At the lowest of the falls, the water is beautifully clear, and ideal for a refreshing dip. From there, a steep track leads through lush forest to two more pools.

Hon Khoi Peninsula

At Ninh Hoa, about 33km north of Nha Trang, Highway 26 branches off left from Highway 1 to Buon Ma Thuot, then about 5km later, a signposted turning on the right leads 12km to the splendid **Hon Khoi Peninsula**, on which you'll find pristine **Doc Let Beach**. You'll probably be keen to linger here awhile: the casuarinas and white sands of the beach are perfect for a day's beach-bumming, although you do have to pay a small entrance fee for the privilege unless you are staying at one of the resorts here.

4

ARRIVAL AND DEPARTURE   HON KHOI PENINSULA

The turn-off to Hon Khoi is signed from the highway about 38km north of Nha Trang, just north of the village of Ninh Hoa.

By bus or train Ninh Hoa itself is accessible by bus from Nha Trang (every 30min; 14,000đ), and has a small train station on the main line (served by most trains from north and south); all resorts will be able to arrange pick-up from here, or from Nha Trang (usually $25 per vehicle).

ACCOMMODATION

Doc Let Beach Resort ☎058 384 9152, ☏058 384 9506. A reasonable budget option at the south end of the beach. Mainly used by local tourists, it has pleasant huts with a/c or fans, plus some cheaper fan rooms set back from the beach in a single concrete block. $12

★ **Jungle Beach Resort** ☎091 342 9144, ⓦjunglebeachvietnam.com. On a separate beach, this is one of the most secluded places to stay on the entire Vietnamese coast – many guests have come for a day and spent a week or two. There are basic rooms and bungalows for rent; all meals are included in the room price, and the food is excellent. Trails on the hillside behind are ripe for exploring and the beach is pristine. $25

★ **Ki-em Art House Resort** ☎058 367 0952, ⓦki-em.com. In the middle of the beach, this place is in a class of its own. Run by an artist couple, it's a dreamy compound with a handful of individually decorated bungalows, a meditation room, art gallery and huge picnic tables in the garden. $175

Paradise Resort ☎058 367 0480, ⓔparadise _doclech@hotmail.com. The resort has a few huge rooms and some simple bungalows, plus a shady terrace overlooking the beach. Rates include three meals a day. $35

White Sand Resort ☎058 367 0670, ⓦwhitesandresort.com.vn. Just south of the *Doc Let* is the newest arrival on the scene, the *White Sand Resort*, an attractive low-rise development with beautifully furnished rooms, all with balconies. The resort also has a spa, a pool, tennis courts and free wi-fi. Book online for the best deals. $85

Hon Gom Peninsula and Hon Ong (Whale Island)

Another 50km or so north along Highway 1 from the Hon Khoi Peninsula, a road branches off to the right along the **Hon Gom Peninsula**, accessing the endless beaches on both sides of this swan's neck of land. About 15km down the peninsula, the road reaches the **Dam Mon jetty**, from where it's a five-minute hop by speedboat to **Hon Ong (Whale Island)**. Humpback whales and whale sharks are often seen in the area from May to August and Rainbow Divers (see box, p.229) runs dives from here.

ACCOMMODATION   HON ONG

Whale Island Resort ☎058 384 0501, Ⓦwhaleislandresort.com. On Whale Island itself, this place has a wonderfully relaxing feel, with simple but tasteful bungalows peeking out over dense vegetation at a fabulous view of the bay. However, you have to pay extra for transfers from Nha Trang, and compulsory meals ($25 per person) which can work out as much as your room. The resort has catamarans, canoes and snorkelling equipment available for guests' use for a nominal fee. **$50**

Dai Lanh

Back on Highway 1, the main road also passes some impressive but empty beaches. You can get a taster 83km from Nha Trang, just beyond the Hon Gom Peninsula at the tiny fishing village of **DAI LANH**, whose appeal lies in the fact that there's absolutely nothing to do. With its patchwork of clay-tile roofs and modest fleet of blue fishing boats, the village lies at the northern end of the 1km-long beach curving around Vung Ro Bay, a **beach** whose casuarinas and white sands are hemmed between the clear, turquoise waters of the South China Sea and a mantle of green mountains.

Beyond Dai Lanh, you'll have to wait until just before **Quy Nhon** to get more glimpses of idyllic beaches. Highway 1D branches off to the right from Highway 1 about 30km south of town, and passes some sheltered pristine bays as it squiggles up the coast.

Quy Nhon

A likeable little seaport town, **QUY NHON** is set on a narrow stake of land harpooning the South China Sea. It's a good place to get away from tourists – few come here, thanks in no small part to the fact that the local beach is both less dazzling than others along this coast, and a bit shallow for swimming. For more adventurous travellers, however, the lack of foreigners only adds to the town's intrigue, and there are a few places worth checking out in the nearby area, including some superbly restored Cham towers. The beach makes a lovely place for a breezy evening stroll.

North of Quy Nhon, and within easy day-trip distance, are the Banh It towers, and the Cha Ban Citadel – both important remnants of Cham rule.

Brief history

Quy Nhon's origins lie in the Cham migration south, at the start of the eleventh century, under pressure from the Vietnamese to the north. They named the empire they established in the area Vijaya, meaning "Victory"; its epicentre was the citadel of Cha Ban (see p.243), though it was Quy Nhon – then known as Sri Bonai – that developed into its thriving commercial centre. Centuries later, the Tay Son Rebellion (see p.437) boiled over in this neck of the woods. During the American War the city served as a US port and supply centre, and was engorged by refugees from the vicious bombing meted out to the surrounding countryside.

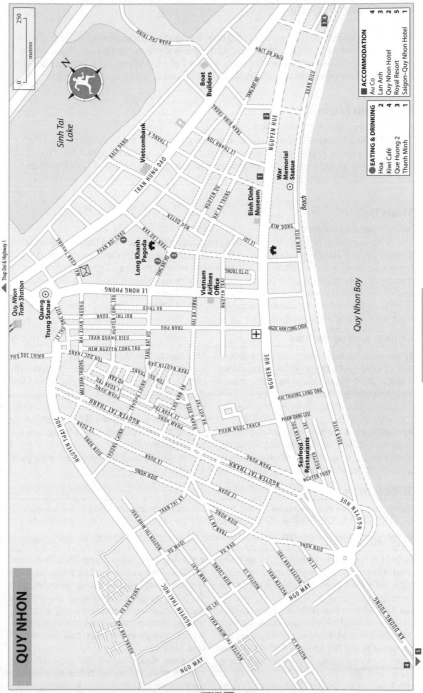

QUY NHON

4

Sinh Tai Lake

Quy Nhon Bay

Beach

War Memorial Statue

Binh Dinh Museum

Long Khanh Pagoda

Vietnam Airlines Office

Quang Trung Statue

Vietcombank

Boat Builders

Seafood Restaurants

Quy Nhon Train Station

Thap Doi & Highway 1

Bus Station

Long Khanh Pagoda

141 Tran Cao Van

Right in the middle of the city, the **Long Khanh Pagoda** is an imposing structure, its nine-tiered roof dominating the skyline. On either side of the main building stands a turret – one containing a drum, the other a giant bell. In the grounds, look out for the tall statue of Buddha, which is currently painted a rather sickly shade of green.

Binh Dinh Museum

28 Nguyen Hué • Mon–Fri 7–11am & 2–5pm • 15,000đ

The **Binh Dinh Museum** contains some superb examples of Cham masonry – exactly what you'd expect, given the prevalence of such sites in the nearby area. Other items in the collection include ethnic dress worn by minority groups in Binh Dinh Province, and the usual war memorabilia.

Thap Doi

2km west of town on Tran Hung Dao

The most accessible of Quy Nhon's Cham monuments are the **Thap Doi**, or "Double Towers", which have been the subject of an extensive restoration in recent years. Their former shabby backstreet setting has been transformed into a small green park where the slender towers, framed by palms, command attention. Both date from around the end of the twelfth century, and embellishments such as sandstone pilasters, spearhead-shaped arches and the sandstone statues of winged Garuda, the vehicle of Vishnu, give the buildings a spiritual aura.

ARRIVAL AND DEPARTURE · QUY NHON

By plane Phu Cat Airport 35km north of Quy Nhon. A Vietnam Airlines minibus shuttles passengers into and out of town (25,000đ), and the company has an office at 55 Le Hong Phong (☎ 056 382 5313).
Destinations: Hanoi (2 daily; 1hr 40min); Ho Chi Minh City (2 daily; 1hr 10min).
By train Quy Nhon's branch-line train station is beside the Quang Trung statue at the north end of town, though service is irregular, so you'd be better off taking a taxi or xe om (around 50,000–60,000đ) to the nearby station at Dieu

Tri for trains to Ho Chi Minh City or Hanoi.
Destinations: (from Dieu Tri) Ho Chi Minh City (5 daily; 14hr); Nha Trang (5 daily; 4hr); Quang Ngai (5 daily; 3hr).
By bus Buses pull up at Quy Nhon's long-distance bus station, a short xe om ride west of the city centre, at the corner of Tay Son and Nguyen Thai Hoc (though open-tour buses bypass the town).
Destinations: Da Nang (8hr); Nha Trang (4hr); Quang Ngai (4hr).

INFORMATION

Tourist information and bike rental The best place for local travel information and bicycle ($2/day) or motorbike ($10/day) rental is the Kiwi Café (see opposite).

ACCOMMODATION

Au Co 24 An Duong Vuong ☎ 056 374 7699. The best of several mini-hotels clustered together opposite the beach to the west of town. The a/c rooms have TVs and are kept spotlessly clean. **$12**
Lan Anh 102 Xuan Dieu ☎ 056 389 2921, ✉ nzbarb @yahoo.com. One of the better budget choices in town, this is managed by a Kiwi who knows the local area well and runs a tight ship. There's a variety of a/c and fan rooms as well as a dorm (50,000đ). Some rooms have balconies and sea views. **$10**
Life Resort ☎ 056 384 0132, ⍟ life-resorts.com. An

immaculate resort sitting around 18km from central Quy Nhon. There are pleasing Cham frills to the design of common areas and rooms alike; the bathrooms in the latter are particularly striking. There are spa facilities and wonderful restaurants on site, and staff can arrange everything from watersports to tai chi sessions. Reserve online and you can almost halve the advertised rates. **$165**
Quy Nhon Hotel 8 Nguyen Hué ☎ 056 389 2402, ⍟ quynhonhotel.com.vn. Not bad for the price – the spacious rooms with bathtubs on the ground floor are good

value, though the smaller, cheaper rooms upstairs are less appealing. **$25**

★ **Saigon–Quy Nhon Hotel** 24 Nguyen Hue ☎ 056 382 9922, ⓦ saigonquynhonhotel.com.vn. This high-rise hotel is centrally located, and boasts a pool and health club. The rooms themselves are carpeted and well-equipped, and good value for money. **$50**

Royal Resort 1 Han Mac Tu ☎ 056 374 7100, ⓦ royalquynhon.com. Luxurious rooms strung along the seafront at the very western edge of Quy Nhon. Rooms are supremely comfortable, but you'll have to pay $10 extra for a sea view; there's also a pool and a great café on site. **$65**

EATING AND DRINKING

Hoa 124 Tang Bat Ho. *Nem* lovers should head straight here – cheap, cheerful and thoroughly appropriate to Quy Nhon's laidback atmosphere. It should cost around $1.50 for a good plateful of the spring rolls.

Kiwi Café 102 Xuan Dieu. Also known as "Barbara's", the homely – if slightly scruffy – *Kiwi Café* next to the *Lan Anh* turns out cheap and cheerful backpacker staples, as well as beer, soft drinks and cocktails. Kiwi by nature as well as name, it's a good place to head for local information.

★ **Que Huong 2** 125 Tang Bat Ho. The two-storey *Que*

Huong 2 has a formidable local reputation and is regularly full to bursting in the early evenings: its sister branch is at 185 Le Hong Phong. Some of the dishes are fancifully named, such as the "fried cracky noodle and roughly-fried snake head", but everything tastes great.

Thanh Minh 151 Phan Boi Chau. This reliable, hole-in-the-wall restaurant continuously doles out dirt-cheap, simple vegetarian fare. Simply point at what you'd like, and try to suppress your surprise when the final bill arrives – eating so much for under $2 just doesn't seem right.

DIRECTORY

Bank The Vietcombank, 152 Le Loi, will exchange dollars and has a 24hr ATM.

Internet Many hotels offer free internet or wi-fi, and there's also internet access at 2g Nguyen Hué.

Banh It

Daily 7am–5pm • 10,000đ • The towers lie about 20km north of Quy Nhon, a distance best spanned by xe om – or, if you have your own wheels, on your way in or out of town. Those arriving at Dieu Tri train station may be able to talk a xe om driver into dropping you by the towers on your way to Quy Nhon – figure on around 90,000đ

The superbly restored **Banh It** Cham towers, known locally as Thap Bac, cut a dash on a hilltop over the river from Quy Nhon. Their site is little visited, relative to other Cham towers in the area, but the short climb from the access road yields tremendous views of the surrounding countryside, enhanced by the giant white statue of a seated Buddha below.

Cha Ban Citadel

The citadel is only accessible if you have your own wheels, or are able to rent some. 2km west of the highway, around 21km north of Quy Nhon, look out for a small lane on the left signposted "Canh Tien"

If you are travelling under your own steam you could search for the last vestiges of **Cha Ban Citadel**, the erstwhile capital of Vijaya; this site constituted the political centre of Champa from the early eleventh century until 1471, when Le Thanh Ton finally seized it, killing fifty thousand Cham people in the process. The Tay Son brothers renamed the site Hoang De and made it their base in the mid-1770s (see p.437). It's undergoing restoration, but you'll be able to see the **Canh Tien Tower**, standing on a slight rise: its distinctive shape is visible from afar, a rectangular brick and sandstone edifice framed by sandstone pilasters.

Quang Ngai

Slender **QUANG NGAI**, clinging to the south bank of the Tra Khuc River some 130km south of Da Nang, is about as pleasant as you could expect of a town skewered until recently by Vietnam's main highway. Though Highway 1, which once ripped through Quang Ngai, now skirts it to the east, the town is still a buzzing little place. The area had a long tradition of resistance against French rule, one that was to find further focus during American involvement. The reward was some of the most extensive bombing meted out during the war: by 1967, American journalist Jonathan Schell was able to report that seventy percent of villages in the town's surrounding area had been destroyed. A year later, the Americans turned their focus upon **Son My Village**, site of the My Lai massacre (see box opposite).

ARRIVAL AND DEPARTURE QUANG NGAI

By train Quang Ngai has a station on the main line about 2km west of town, and most services stop by.
Destinations: Da Nang (4 daily; 2hr 40min); Quy Nhon (4 daily; 3hr); Nha Trang (4 daily; 7hr).

By bus The bus station is a little over 500m south of the centre, and 50m east of Quang Trung on Le Thanh Ton.
Destinations: Da Nang (4hr); Nha Trang (7hr); Quy Nhon (4hr).

INFORMATION

Tourist office Quang Ngai Tourist is 150m north of Hung Vuong at 310 Quang Trung (☎055 381 7811, ⓦ quangngaitourist.com.vn), though to be honest you're better off asking for information at one of the hotels.

ACCOMMODATION AND EATING

Hung Vuong 45 Hung Vuong ☎055 371 0477. Slightly shabby mid-ranger with good-value rooms, some with carpets and bathtubs. There are two places with the same name on this road; the other is a fair bit cheaper. **$35**
Petro Song Tra 1 An Duong Vuong ☎055 371 4468. Again, there are two of these in the same part of town, near the river (what is it with Quang Ngai?). The one you'll be after is the one marked "Petrosetco", which is newer and sports delightful rooms, many with a river view. The older one has a pool, but you'll be free to use this even when staying at the newer place. **$70**

EATING AND DRINKING

If you're up for a beer, head for the snack-shacks that line the river at night, outside the *Petro Song Tra* – also note that at 5,000đ per bottle, Quang Ngai's own brews are about the cheapest in Vietnam.

Nhung Com Ga 474 Quang Trung. The best place in town for the local speciality of *com ga* – chicken and rice, which costs around $2 for a plateful.

DIRECTORY

Bank There's an ATM at the *Hung Vuong Hotel*, and several others along Quang Trung.
Internet Internet access is unusually difficult to find; try 634/01 Quang Trung, down an alley off the main road.
Post The post office is about 100m west of the highway, at the junction of Hung Vuong and Phan Dinh Phung.

Son My Memorial Park

The park is 12km east of Quang Ngai • Daily 7am–5pm • 10,000đ • Distance best covered by xe om (100,000đ, including waiting time) or taxi (usually a little over 400,000đ for four people, including waiting time)

In the sub-hamlet of Tu Cung, the site of an infamous massacre of civilians by American soldiers on March 16, 1968 is remembered at the **Son My Memorial Park**. Pacing through this peaceful and dignified place, set within a low perimeter wall, you'll be accompanied by a feeling of blanched horror, and a palpable sense of the dead all around you. Wandering the garden, visitors can see bullet holes in trees, foundations of homes burnt down (each with a tablet recording its family's losses), blown-out bomb shelters, and cement statues of slain animals. One path ends at a large, Soviet-style statue of a woman cradling a dead baby over her left arm while raising her right fist in defiance. Once you've seen the garden, step into the museum to view the grisly display upstairs, though be warned that it's a disturbing place for anyone with a sensitive disposition. Here, beyond a massive marble plaque recording the names of the dead, family by family, and a montage of rusting hardware, a **photograph gallery** documents the event.

THE MY LAI MASSACRE

The massacre of civilians in the hamlets of **Son My Village**, the single most shameful chapter of America's involvement in Vietnam, began at dawn on March 16, 1968. US Intelligence suggested that the 48th Local Forces Battalion of the NVA, which had taken part in the Tet Offensive on Quang Ngai a month earlier, was holed up in Son My. Within the task force assembled to flush them out was **Charlie Company**, whose First Platoon, led by Lieutenant William Calley, was assigned to sweep through **My Lai 4** (known to locals as **Tu Cung Hamlet**). Recent arrivals in Vietnam, Charlie Company had suffered casualties and losses in the hunt for the elusive 48th, and always found themselves inflicted by snipers and booby-traps. Unable to contact the enemy face to face in any numbers, or even to distinguish civilians from Viet Cong guerrillas, they had come to feel frustrated and impotent. Son My offered the chance to settle some old scores.

At a briefing on the eve of the offensive, GIs were told that all civilians would be at market by 7am and that anyone remaining was bound to be an active Viet Cong sympathizer. Some GIs later remembered being told not to kill women and children, but most simply registered that there were to be no prisoners. Whatever the truth, a massacre ensued, whose brutal course Neil Sheehan describes with chilling understatement in *A Bright Shining Lie*:

The American soldiers and junior officers shot old men, women, boys, girls, and babies. One soldier missed a baby lying on the ground twice with a .45 pistol as his comrades laughed at his marksmanship. He stood over the child and fired a third time. The soldiers beat women with rifle butts and raped some and sodomised others before shooting them. They shot the water buffalos, the pigs, and the chickens. They threw the dead animals into the wells to poison the water. They tossed satchel charges into the bomb shelters under the houses. A lot of the inhabitants had fled into the shelters. Those who leaped out to escape the explosives were gunned down. All of the houses were put to the torch.

In all, the Son My body count reached 500, 347 of whom fell in Tu Cung alone. Not one shot was fired at a GI in response, and the only US casualty deliberately shot himself in the foot to avoid the carnage. The 48th Battalion never materialized. The military chain of command was able temporarily to suppress reports of the massacre, with the army newspaper, *Stars and Stripes*, and even the *New York Times* branding the mission a success. But the awful truth surfaced in November 1969, through the efforts of former GI Ronald Ridenhour and investigative journalist Seymour Hersh, and the incontrovertible evidence of the grisly colour slides of army photographer Ron Haeberle. When the massacre did finally make the cover of *Newsweek* it was under the headline "An American Tragedy" – which, as John Pilger pointed out, "deflected from the truth that the atrocities were, above all, a *Vietnamese* tragedy".

Of 25 men eventually charged with murder over the massacre, or for its subsequent suppression, only Lieutenant William Calley was found guilty, though he had served just three days of a life sentence of hard labour when Nixon intervened and commuted it to house arrest. Three years later he was paroled.

It's all too easy to dismiss Charlie Company as a freak unit operating beyond the pale. A more realistic view may be that the very nature of the US war effort, with its resort to unselective napalm and rocket attacks, and its use of body counts as barometers of success, created a climate in which Vietnamese life was cheapened to such an extent that an incident of this nature became almost inevitable. If indiscriminate killing from the air was justifiable, then random killing at close quarters was only taking this methodology to its logical conclusion.

Michael Bilton and Kevin Sim, whose *Four Hours in My Lai* remains the most complete account of the massacre, conclude that "My Lai's exposure late in 1969 poisoned the idea that the war was a moral enterprise." The mother of one GI put it more simply: "I gave them a good boy, and they made him a murderer."

My Khe Beach

3km east of Son My • Can usually be added to a xe om or taxi trip to Son My for another 30,000đ

In stark contrast to the chilling Son My site, secluded **My Khe Beach** consists of 7km of powder-soft sand, backed by casuarinas, and is very good for swimming. Hamlets stand along the back of the beach, while fishing boats are sometimes moored off it, and there's a handful of restaurants that only get busy at the weekend. The area is still slowly gearing up for tourism, and could not really be recommended as a place to stay at the time of writing.

The central coast

CITADEL WALL, TUCÉ

5

The central coast

The narrowest bit of the country holds an astonishingly dense collection of sights. From the south, you'll come first to the town of Hoi An, highly traditional and hugely popular on account of its wonderful architecture, laidback air and superb culinary scene. Further north is Da Nang, whose bars, restaurants and sleek new buildings make it enjoyable in a more contemporary sense; however, it too boasts a wealth of nearby sights. Then there's Hué, erstwhile capital of the Nguyen dynasty. A visit to the old Imperial City, with its splendid palace buildings and manicured gardens is like a taking a step into the past. Lastly are the sights pertaining to the American War in the famed Demilitarized Zone (DMZ). The area marked the divide between North and South Vietnam, which, some would argue, still exists today.

You'll notice great differences in weather, cuisine, language and even local character to the north and south of the Ben Hai River, which runs through the DMZ (see box, p.303). However, Vietnam was not always divided along this point – it was previously the Hoanh Son Mountains, north of Dong Hoi (p.314) that formed the cultural and political line between the Chinese-dominated sphere to the north, and the Indianized Champa kingdom to the south. As independent Vietnam grew in power in the eleventh century, so its armies pushed southwards to the next natural frontier, the Hai Van Pass near Hué. Here again, the Cham resisted further invasion until the fifteenth century, when their great temple complex at **My Son** was seized and their kingdom shattered.

Since then, other contenders have battled back and forth over this same ground, among them the Nguyen and Trinh lords, whose simmering rivalry ended in victory for the southern Nguyen and the emergence of **Hué** as the nation's capital in the nineteenth century. The Nguyen dynasty transformed Hué into a stately Imperial City, whose palaces, temples and grand mausoleums now constitute one of the highlights of

---

THE NORTH-SOUTH DIVIDE

Although Vietnam was reunified in 1976, there still exists a palpable north-south divide, one that many tourists end up picking up on as they head across the DMZ. Of course, many of the differences stem from the **ideological division** that followed World War II, and the protracted, bloody war between the two sides; however, there have long been other factors at work.

One of these is the relative **fertility of the soil** – parts of the south get three rice harvests per year, while in the north it's usually one. This is said to feed into a great difference in character between north and south – northerners are said to be more frugal and southerners more laidback, partly because the latter have historically had less work to do for the same reward.

There are also notable differences in **tradition**. Ho Chi Minh City flaunts its Westernisation, while Hanoians are just as proud of their city's colonial- and dynastic-era structures.

Then there are **dialectical** differences – ask a traditionally-clad Hanoian girl what she's wearing, and she'll say it's "ao zai". Ask a lady from Ho Chi Minh City the same thing, and it would be an "ao yai". Trained ears will also hear that there's another dialect at work in the centre of Vietnam.

However, for visitors, the most enjoyable aspect of the north-south divide is likely to be the **food**. The quintessential northern food is pho bo – this beef noodle soup is found throughout Vietnam, but originated in Hanoi, where it's still at its best. Other northern dishes include hotpots, rice gruels and sweet and sout soups. Southern flavours include curries and spicy dipping sauces, often married with a touch of sugar and coconut milk to balance the heat. However, most renowned nationwide is central cuisine – both Hoi An and Hué boast dishes of astonishing variety.

NINH BINH PROVINCE

Highlights

❶ Hoi An Sip a latte by lantern-light while waiting for your tailor-made clothes to measure up in this laidback city. **See p.251**

❷ My Son Majestic Cham ruins covered in moss, grass and leaves – rise early to see them before the crowds. **See p.264**

❸ Da Nang Amiable city providing a jump-off point for lofty Ba Na Hill Station and the fabled Marble Mountains. **See p.269**

❹ Hué's Imperial City Cross the Perfume River to meander through the intricately decorated buildings that emperors once called home. **See p.282**

❺ Local cuisine Locals agree that central Vietnam does it best – try the assorted specialities of Hoi An and find out why. **See p.261**

❻ Vinh Moc tunnels The most interesting sight in the famed DMZ: a warren of dens where tenacious locals sheltered during the war, often for weeks on end. **See p.307**

HIGHLIGHTS ARE MARKED ON THE MAP ON P.250

5

a visit to Vietnam, despite the ravages they suffered during successive wars. In 1954, Vietnam was divided at the Seventeenth Parallel, only 100km north of Hué, where the Ben Hai River and the **DMZ** marked the border between North and South Vietnam until reunification in 1975. Though there's little to see on the ground these days, the desolate battlefields of the DMZ are a poignant memorial to those who fought here on both sides, and to the civilians who lost their lives in the bitter conflict.

Da Nang and nearby **China Beach** are other evocative names from the American War, but the region has more to offer. The compact riverside town of **Hoi An**, with its core of traditional, wood-built merchants' houses and jaunty Chinese Assembly Halls, is a particularly captivating place. Inland from Hoi An, the Cham spiritual core, **My Son**, survives as a haunting array of overgrown ruins in a hidden valley, while heading the other way you'll find a succession of pristine beaches that are now the subject of mass development.

This region has a particularly complicated **climate** as it forms a transitional zone between the north and south of Vietnam. In general, around Da Nang and Hué the **rainy season** lasts from September to February, with most rain falling between late September and December; during this season it's not unusual for road and rail links to be cut. Hué suffers particularly badly and, even during the **"dry season"** from March to August, it's possible to have several days of torrential rain, giving the city an annual average of three metres. Overall, the best time to visit this southern region is in spring, from February to late May, before both temperatures and humidity reach their

THE CENTRAL COAST

QUANG BINH

THE DMZ

Ben Hai River

Dong Ha

QUANG TRI ⑥ Quang Tri

Lao Bao

HWY-9 Khe Sanh

SOUTH CHINA SEA (EAST SEA)

N

THUA THIEN-HUÉ ④ Hué

HWY-1

LAOS

A Luoi

Cau Hai

Lang Co

Hai Van Pass

Hai Van Tunnel

Monkey Mountain

BACH MA NATIONAL PARK

Ba Na Hill Station

Da Nang ③

Non Nuoc Beach

Cham Islands

BA NA NATURE RESERVE

① ⑤ Cua Dai Beach

Hoi An

Tra Kieu

Thu Bon River

My Son ②

QUANG NAM

HWY-1

HIGHLIGHTS
① Hoi An
② My Son
③ Da Nang
④ Hué's Imperial City
⑤ Local cuisine
⑥ Vinh Moc Tunnels

0   50
kilometres

summer maximum (averaging around 30°C), or just at the end of the summer before the rains break.

Hoi An

Stubbornly traditional and jam-packed with sights, the small city of **HOI AN** also exudes a laidback, almost dreamy atmosphere that makes it an essential stop on any tour of the country. This intriguing place, with its narrow streets comprising wooden-fronted shophouses topped with moss-covered tiles, has much to recommend it, not least the fact that a concerted effort has been made to retain the city's old-world charm: by way of example, it's the only place in Vietnam that places restrictions on motorbike use, and the only place that forces local businesses, by law, to dangle **lanterns** from their facades. These come to the fore as evening encroaches, and by nightfall you'll see them shining out from narrow alleys and the riverbank in their hundreds, the light reflecting in the waters of the Thu Bon River. Also notable are the city's many cheap **tailors**, who will whip up made-to-measure clothes in no time, and a **culinary scene** that ranks among the best in Asia.

Hoi An's ancient core is a rich architectural fusion of Chinese, Japanese, Vietnamese and European influences dating back to the sixteenth century. In its heyday, the now drowsy channel of the Thu Bon River was a jostling crowd of merchant vessels representing the world's great trading nations (see p.253), and the mellow streets of this small, amiable town still emanate a timeless air.

The city's most photographed sight is, without doubt, the beautiful **Japanese Covered Bridge**. However, the most noteworthy monuments in town stem from Hoi An's resident Chinese population. First are the **merchant homes**, some of them more than two hundred years old, and still inhabited by the descendants of prosperous Chinese traders. Between their sober wooden facades, riotous confections of glazed roof tiles and writhing dragons mark the entrances to **Chinese Assembly Halls**, which form the focal point of civic and spiritual life for an ethnic Chinese community that, today, constitutes one quarter of Hoi An's population.

Granted UNESCO World Heritage status in 1999, Hoi An is now firmly on most visitors' agendas. For some it's already too much of a tourist trap, with its profusion of tailors' shops and art galleries and its rapidly proliferating hotels – try telling those who come for a day and stay for a week. It's easy to while away the time, taking day-trips to the atmospheric Cham ruins of **My Son**, biking out into the surrounding country or taking a leisurely sampan ride on the Thu Bon River. If possible, try to time your visit to coincide with the **Full-Moon Festival**, on the fourteenth day of the lunar calendar every month, when the town centre is closed to traffic and traditional arts performances take place in the lantern-lit streets. Notable in a different way is the flooding which hits every year, usually in October – at this time the riverside roads can be under several feet of water, and if you've brought your wellies along, it actually makes for a great time to visit.

FAI FO SPRING FAIR

Although long since swallowed up by the sands of time, the spring fair of Fai Fo, the former name of Hoi An, had a measurable influence on the city of today. From humble beginnings in the sixteenth century, the event grew into an exotic showcase of world produce. From Southeast Asia came silks and brocades, ivory, fragrant oils, fine porcelain and a cornucopia of medicinal ingredients. The Europeans brought their textiles, weaponry, sulphur and lead – as well as the first Christian missionaries in 1614. During the four-month fair, travelling merchants would rent local lodgings and warehouses; many went on to establish a more permanent presence through marriage to Vietnamese women, who were (and still are) renowned for their business acumen.

5

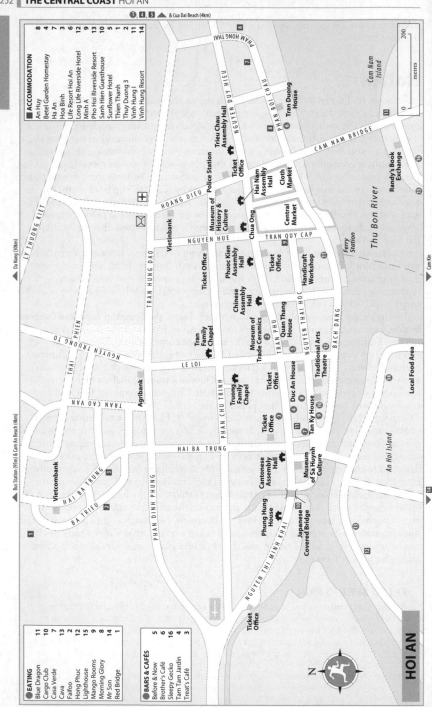

❶, ❹, ❺, ▲ & Cua Dai Beach (4km)

ACCOMMODATION
An Huy	8
Betel Garden Homestay	4
Ha An	7
Hoa Binh	3
Life Resort Hoi An	6
Long Life Riverside Hotel	12
Minh A	9
Pho Hoi Riverside Resort	13
Sanh Hien Guesthouse	10
Sunflower Hotel	5
Thien Thanh	1
Thuy Duong 3	2
Vinh Hung I	11
Vinh Hung Resort	14

EATING
Blue Dragon	11
Cargo Club	10
Casa Verde	7
Cava	13
Faifoo	2
Hong Phuc	12
Lighthouse	15
Mango Rooms	9
Morning Glory	8
Mr Son	14
Red Bridge	1

BARS & CAFÉS
Before & Now	5
Brother's Café	6
Sleepy Gecko	16
Tam Tam Jardin	4
Treat's Café	3

HOI AN

N

My Son (40km) ▲

▲ Bus Station (95m) & Cam An Beach (4km)

◄ Da Nang (30km)

Cam Nam Island

Thu Bon River

Cam Kin ►

An Hoi Island

Local Food Area

5

Brief History

For centuries, Hoi An played an important role in the **maritime trade** of Southeast Asia. This goes back at least as far as the second century BC, when people of the so-called Sa Huynh culture exchanged goods with China and India, but things really took off in the sixteenth century when Chinese, Japanese and European vessels ran with the trade winds to congregate at a port then called Fai Fo, whose annual spring fair brought in traders from far and wide (see box, p.251). Tax collectors arrived to fill the imperial coffers, and the town swelled with artisans, moneylenders and bureaucrats as trade reached a peak in the seventeenth century.

Commercial activity was dominated by Japanese and Chinese merchants, many of whom settled in Fai Fo, where each community maintained its own governor, legal code and strong cultural identity. But in 1639 the Japanese shogun prohibited foreign travel and the "Japanese street" dwindled to a handful of families, then to a scattering of monuments and a distinctive architectural style. Unchallenged, the Chinese community prospered, and its numbers grew as every new political upheaval in China prompted another wave of immigrants to join one of the town's self-governing "congregations", organized around a meeting hall and place of worship.

In the late eighteenth century, silt began to clog the Thu Bon River just as markets were forced open in China, and from then on the port's days were numbered. Although the French established an administrative centre in Fai Fo, and even built a rail link from Tourane (Da Nang), they failed to resuscitate the economy, and when a storm washed away the tracks in 1916 no one repaired them. The town, renamed Hoi An in 1954, somehow escaped damage during both the French and American wars and retains a distinctly antiquated air.

Japanese Covered Bridge

Linking Nguyen Thi Minh Khai and Tran Phu • 24hr • Free • Temple under ticket scheme (see box, p.254)

The western extremity of Tran Phu is marked by a small arched bridge of red-painted wood, popularly known as the **Japanese Covered Bridge**, which has been adopted as Hoi An's emblem. It was known to exist in the mid-sixteenth century, and has subsequently been reconstructed several times to the same simple design. According to local folklore, the bridge was erected after Japan suffered a series of violent earthquakes which geomancers attributed to a restless monster lying with its head in India, tail in Japan and heart in Hoi An. The only remedy was to build a bridge whose stone piles would drive a metaphorical sword through the beast's heart and fortuitously provide a handy passage across the muddy creek. Inside the bridge's narrow span are a collection of stelae and four statues, two dogs and two monkeys, which suggest that work began in the year of the monkey and ended in that of the dog. The small **temple** suspended above the water is a later addition dedicated to the Taoist god Tran Vo Bac De ("Emperor of the North"), a favourite of sailors as he controls wind, rain and other "evil influences".

The Chinese assembly halls

Historically, Hoi An's ethnic Chinese population organized themselves according to their place of origin – Fujian, Guangdong, Chaozhou or Hainan. Each group maintained its own assembly hall as both community centre and house of worship, while a fifth hall also provided assistance to all the local groups and to visiting Chinese merchants.

Cantonese Assembly Hall

176 Tran Phu • Under ticket scheme (see box, p.254)

The westernmost of the Chinese assembly halls sits just east of the Japanese Bridge, and belonged to Hoi An's Cantonese population. You can't miss its gaudy entrance arch, a recent embellishment to the original late eighteenth-century hall built by immigrants from

5

VISITING HOI AN'S SIGHTS

Hoi An has a **ticket scheme** covering the majority of its most famous sights, the proceeds of which contribute to the preservation of the old centre. A ticket costing 90,000đ (valid for one day), allows access to five places:

- Either Chua Ong or the temple on the Japanese Covered Bridge (the bridge itself is free)
- One of the museums (see p.256)
- One of the three Chinese Assembly Halls requiring tickets (see p.253)
- One of the merchants' houses or family chapels requiring tickets (see opposite)
- The Hoi An Handicraft Workshop at 9 Nguyen Thai Hoc

If you want to visit more sights in the scheme, you have to fork out for another ticket. If, like most, you're only aiming for one round, it's important to choose carefully – particular recommendations are the Japanese Covered Bridge, the Cantonese Assembly Hall, the Museum of Trade Ceramics and Tan Ky House. Also note that though "The Heritage Town" appears on your ticket, you walk on any Hoi An street for free.

Tickets are on sale at six **outlets**: 52 Nguyen Thi Minh Khai, 19 Ha Ba Trung, 5 Hoang Dieu, 12 Phan Chu Trinh, 37 Tran Phu and 78 Le Loi (see map, p.252). Groups of more than eight people are entitled to a free guide for the day; otherwise, you can hire one for around $15. The ticket outlets are **open** from 7am to 6pm, as are all the sights included in the scheme.

Guangdong. Though there's nothing of particular merit here, it's an appealing place, partly because of its plant-filled courtyard, ornamented with dragon and carp carvings (see box, p.257), and partly because of the fact that it's the least visited Chinese hall in Hoi An.

Chinese Assembly Hall

64 Tran Phu • Daily 7–11.30am & 2–5pm • Free

Plum in the centre of town, **the Chinese Assembly Hall**, or Chua Ba, was built in 1740 as an umbrella organization for all Hoi An's ethnic Chinese population. Thien Hau graces the altar, but the hall is nowadays used mainly as a language school where local ethnic Chinese children and adults come to learn their mother tongue. The school was closed in 1975 and only permitted to re-open in 1990.

Phuoc Kien Assembly Hall

46 Tran Phu • Under ticket scheme (see box above)

The most populous of Hoi An's Chinese groups hailed from Fujian, or Phuoc Kien, and their hall is a suitably imposing edifice with an ostentatious, triple-arched gateway added in the early 1970s. The hall started life as a pagoda built in the late seventeenth century when, so it's said, a Buddhist statue containing a lump of gold washed up on the riverbank. Almost a century later, the Chinese took over the decaying structure and rededicated it as a temple to Thien Hau, Goddess of the Sea and protector of sailors. She stands, fashioned in two hundred-year-old papier-mâché, on the principal altar flanked by her two assistants, green-faced Thien Ly Nhan and red-faced Thuan Phong Nhi, who between them can see or hear any boat in distress over a range of a thousand miles. A second sanctuary room behind and to the right of the main altar shelters a deity favoured by couples and pregnant women: the awesome Van Thien and her aides, the "twelve heavenly midwives", who decide the fundamentals of a child's life from conception onwards, including the fateful matter of gender. On the way out of the main building, take a look at the entrance porch decorated with colourful wooden friezes and delicate stone motifs.

Hai Nam Assembly Hall

10 Tran Phu • 7–11.30am & 2–5pm • Free

Heading east from the Phuoc Kien Assembley Hall, you'll pass the hall founded by Chinese from the island of Hainan, or Hai Nam, and also noted for its ornately carved, gilded altar table. Its unusual history is intriguing – in 1851 a Vietnamese general plundered three merchant ships, killing 107 passengers, after which the vessels were painted black to imply they were pirate ships. A lone survivor revealed the crime to King Tu Duc, who promptly condemned the general to death and ordered that the booty be returned to the victims' families. When the hall was built later in the century, it was dedicated to the unlucky passengers.

Trieu Chau Assembly Hall
157 Nguyen Duy Hieu • Under ticket scheme (see box opposite)

This hall is located just east of the market, and it's worth the stroll. Built in the late eighteenth century by Chinese from Chaozhou, or Trieu Chau, it's renowned for its remarkable display of woodcarving. In the altar niche sits the gilded Ong Bon, a general in the Chinese navy believed to hold sway over the wind and waves, surrounded by a frieze teeming with bird, animal and insect life so lifelike you can almost hear it buzz. The altar table itself depicts life on land and in the depths of the ocean, while panels on either side show two decorative ladies of the Chinese court modelling the latest Japanese hair fashions.

Merchant houses

The majority of Hoi An's original wooden buildings are found along Tran Phu and south towards the river, which is where you'll find the best-known **merchant's houses**.

Phung Hung House
4 Nguyen Thi Minh Khai • Under ticket scheme (see box opposite)

Just west of the covered bridge, this has been home to the same family since around 1780, since they moved from Hué to trade cinnamon and hardwoods from the central highlands, as well as silk and glass. The large two-storey house is Vietnamese in style, although its eighty ironwood columns and small glass skylights denote Japanese influence, and the gallery and window shutters are Chinese in style. An upstairs living area features an ancestral shrine as well as a large shrine to the protector deity Thien Hau, suspended from the ceiling; prayers were said here for the safe return of family members away on trading trips. A set of seven dice in a bowl on a table in front of the altar used to be thrown to determine the auspicious time to set out on a journey, although a plastic set has replaced the bone or marble originals.

Tan Ky House
101 Nguyen Thai Hoc • Under ticket scheme (see box opposite)

In the thick of things near the covered bridge, this is a beautifully preserved example of a two-storey, late eighteenth-century shophouse, amalgamating Vietnamese, Japanese and Chinese influences in an architectural style typical of Hoi An. The present house was built by a second-generation member of the Tan Ky family, who fled China as political refugees in the late sixteenth century, and took eight years to complete. The long, narrow building has shop space at the front, a tiny central courtyard and direct access to the river at the back, from where merchandise would be hauled upstairs to storerooms safe above the floods. The house, wonderfully cluttered with the accumulated property of seven generations grown wealthy from trading silk, tea and rice, is constructed of dark hardwoods, including termite-resistant jackfruit for its main columns. The skill of local woodcarvers is evident throughout, but most stunning is the inlay work: look out for two hanging poem-boards on which mother-of-pearl brush-strokes form exquisitely delicate birds in flight. Guides, speaking French and English, are on hand to answer questions, but at times the house is completely overwhelmed with visitors – far better to come, if you can, at a quieter time (early or late in the day) to appreciate the weight of history here.

5

Duc An House
129 Tran Phu • Hours vary, donation expected

A humble building, erected in the 1850s to house a family that had already been on the property for more than two centuries. It was once a highly successful bookshop, selling both Vietnamese and Chinese works, as well as a smattering from Europe. The bookshop then became a stockist of Chinese medicines, before becoming Hoi An's resistance headquarters in the colonial era.

Quan Thang House
77 Tran Phu • Under ticket scheme (see box, p.254)

A modest, single-storey shophouse, this was founded in the early eighteenth century by a captain from Fujian in China, and was home to a medicine-trading business. Frankly speaking, it's a mediocre affair – you'll find far more interesting places to visit under this section of the ticket scheme.

Family Chapels

On the face of it, Phan Chu Trinh is an unspectacular road but it hides two "family chapels", again houses built by wealthy Chinese merchants, but to a design reflecting their spiritual rather than commercial focus.

Tran Family Chapel
21 Le Loi • Under ticket scheme (see box, p.254)

On Phan Chu Trinh itself is the two hundred-year-old **Tran Family Chapel**, within a walled compound on the junction with Le Loi. Over home-made lotus-flower tea and sugared coconut you learn about the building and family traditions, going back thirteen generations (three hundred years) to when the first ancestor settled in Hanoi. The move to Hoi An came, so the story goes, when one son married a Vietnamese woman. Such was the parental disapproval that he fled south to make his fortune trading silk, pepper and ivory in Hoi An; one day, perhaps, a cynic might suggest, due to his new-found wealth, his forgiving family turned up on the doorstep. Succeeding generations continued to shine, with one mandarin to their credit – his portrait and ceremonial sword, bearing the Imperial insignia, are displayed in the reception room. On the altar itself, oblong funerary boxes contain a name-tablet and biographical details of deceased family leaders and their wives – carved lotus blossoms indicate adherents of Buddhism. Each year the entire family – more than eighty people – gather round the altar to venerate their ancestors and discuss family affairs.

Truong Family Chapel
Down an alley beside 69 Phan Chu Trinh • 7.30am–noon & 2–5pm • Small donation expected

The smaller, more elaborate of the two family chapels is the **Truong Family Chapel**, hidden down an alley. The Truong ancestors, like many ethnic Chinese now in Hoi An, fled China in the early eighteenth century following the collapse of the Ming Dynasty. The ground-breaking ceremony took place in 1840 at the auspicious moment of 5am on the fifth day of the eleventh lunar month – that is, on the hour of the cat and day of the cat, in the month and year of the mouse. This family also embraces mandarin forefathers and cherishes gifts from the Hué court, but more intriguing is an inscribed panel bestowed by Emperor Bao Dai on the wife of the fifth generation who, widowed at 25 and with three children, nevertheless remained faithful to her dead husband.

Museums

Hoi An has a clutch of fairly modest historical **museums**, none of which are especially interesting – they do, however, make for perfect rainy-day material.

Museum of Trade Ceramics
80 Tran Phu • Under ticket scheme (see box, p.254)

Hoi An's most rewarding museum is the **Museum of Trade Ceramics**, housed in a traditional timber residence-cum-warehouse. It showcases the history of Hoi An's ceramics trade, which peaked in the fifteenth and sixteenth centuries, with most of the exhibits from Vietnam, China and Japan. The rear room on the ground floor houses a small display about the architecture of Hoi An.

Museum of Sa Huynh Culture
149 Tran Phu • Under ticket scheme (see box, p.254)

The **Museum of Sa Huynh Culture**, occupying a two-storey French-era house, focuses on a distinct culture which flourished along the coast of central Vietnam between the second century BC and the second century AD; the name comes from the town 130km south of Hoi An where evidence was first discovered in 1902.

Museum of History and Culture
7 Nguyen Hué • Under ticket scheme (see box, p.254)

Behind Tran Phu temple lies Hoi An's **Museum of History and Culture**, attractively housed in another former pagoda. Apart from the copies of ancient maps of Fai Fo, the primary appeal of this small, informative museum is its quiet courtyard and carved, wooden door panels, depicting the four sacred animals: crane, dragon, turtle and the mythical *kylin*.

The market
Chua Ong • Under ticket scheme (see box, p.254)

Hoi An **market** retains an appealing, traditional atmosphere, despite the number of tourists. Like most, it's best in the early morning, especially among the fresh-food stalls that line the river. Look out for jars of tiny preserved tangerines, a regional speciality, amid neat stacks of basketware, bowl-shaped lumps of unrefined cane-sugar, liniments, medicinal herbs and every variety of rice.

Around the market
Wandering down through the market square brings you out by the ferry docks and Bach Dang, which regularly disappears each autumn under the swollen river. For most

---

UNRAVELLING THE ARCHITECTURAL FEATURES OF HOI AN

You can't walk far in Hoi An without confronting a **mythical beast** with a fish's body and dragon's head; though they're found all over northern Vietnam they seem to have struck a particular chord with Hoi An's architects. One of the most prominent examples tops a weather vane in the Phuoc Kien Assembly Hall, but there are plenty of more traditional representations about, carved into lantern brackets and beam ends, or forming the beams themselves. The **carp** symbolizes prosperity, success and, here, metamorphosing into a **dragon**, serves a reminder that nothing in life comes easily. To become a dragon, and thereby attain immortality, a fish must pass through three gates – just as a scholar has to pass three exams to become a mandarin, requiring much patience and hard work.

Another typical feature of Hoi An's architecture are "eyes" watching over the entrance to a house or religious building. Two thick wooden nails about 20cm in diameter are driven into the lintel as protection against evil forces, following a practice that originated in the pagodas of northern Vietnam. Assembly halls offer the most highly ornamented examples: that of Phuoc Kien consists of a yin and yang with two dragons in obeisance to the sun, while the Cantonese version is a fearsome tiger. The **yin and yang** symbol became fashionable in the nineteenth century and is the most commonly used image on houses, sometimes set in a chrysanthemum flower, such as at the Tan Ky House, or as the octagonal talisman representing eight charms.

5

ACTIVITIES IN AND AROUND HOI AN

There are a number of activities to enjoy in and around Hoi An – even more reason to make your stay here longer. Easiest to organize is **bicycle** or **motorbike** hire (see below), which will enable you to see some of the gorgeous surrounding countryside; with a motorbike, you can even make it to My Son (see p.264). Hoi An Motorbike Tours (🔵 motorbiketours-hoian.com) and Phat Tire Ventures (🔵 phattireventures.com) organize great trips around central Vietnam for motorbikes and bicycles respectively.

Slightly more taxing to arrange (but not much) are **boat rides** around the Thu Bon River; crowded ferry boats leave from the market end of Bach Dang every thirty minutes, and on the same road you'll be able to haggle with sampan-rowers (from 20,000đ for a short ride).

Then there are the **cooking classes**. A whole bunch of riverside restaurants offer these from $10 per person, slightly more for those including a visit to buy ingredients at the market. Most notable are the classes laid on by *Lighthouse* restaurant, which include a bike tour to fetch the ingredients from the countryside.

Lastly, from April–October it's possible to go **diving** around the Cham Islands (see p.264).

of the year it's dry, and the spectacle best captured between 6 and 7am when the fishing boats are unloading their catch. Towards the east end of Tran Phu, the north side of the market square is dominated by the colourful frontage of **Chua Ong**, a seventeenth-century pagoda-temple conversion dedicated to General Quan Cong.

Phan Boi Chau

Tran Duong House 25 Phan Boi Chau • Small donation expected

From the market, walk east along the river and you come to Phan Boi Chau, where the town takes on a distinctly European flavour – louvred shutters, balconies and stucco – in what was the beginnings of a **French quarter**. The interiors of these late nineteenth-century townhouses are characterized by vast, high-ceilinged rooms and enormous roof-spaces, markedly different from the Chinese abodes. You can take a brief tour round **Tran Duong House**, at no. 25, the home of an enterprising man who owns a smattering of period furniture.

ARRIVAL AND DEPARTURE   HOI AN

By train The nearest train station and airport are both 30km away in Da Nang (p.269), a distance easily covered by taxi (from $12) or xe om ($6). Bargain with your driver, and you'll be able to add a stop at the Marble Mountains, the beaches on route, or even Da Nang's Cham Museum for a small extra fee; either way, ask to take the new road to the east, which has more beautiful views and far less traffic.

By bus Open-tour buses usually drop you at their relevant

booking office (also the place to confirm your onward tickets), or affiliated hotel; some buses stop briefly at sights on their way north or south. To buy tickets, do some shopping around as prices vary; most hotels also sell tickets, with the free xe om ride to the bus handy for those with heavy luggage.

Destinations: Da Nang (45min); Hué (3hr); Quang Ngai (4hr); Nha Trang (11hr).

GETTING AROUND

By bicycle or motorbike Almost every hotel and many shops and tour agents have bicycles for rent ($2/day), or can arrange motorbikes (from $5) – the latter are a popular way to visit My Son (see p.264). Note that motorbikes are prohibited from the centre at peak tourist hours (bar a lunchtime trading break).

On foot While bikes are recommended for touring the outlying districts, Hoi An's central sights are all best approached on foot, especially since traffic restrictions apply in the town centre. The regulations are part of a much-needed effort to save the old town from the worst effects of fame.

INFORMATION

Tourist office and information For local information, ask in your hotel or try one of the dozens of private tour

agencies (see p.262). Most of the latter offer similar services – tours, transport, rail and air tickets – but prices and itineraries vary so it's worth shopping around. There's a tourist office of sorts on Le Loi, though the staff are more interested in selling tours than giving practical information.

ACCOMMODATION

The **number of hotels** in Hoi An continues to grow at an astonishing rate. The local authorities put a block on developments in the centre – too late to prevent some eyesores in the old streets – but a whole new enclave of pleasant and cheap mini-hotels has sprung up to the north of the centre along Ba Trieu; most of these have **swimming pools**, which provide welcome relief in warmer months. There are also a few new places on An Hoi Island. Competition means that, in general, **prices** have come down and standards have risen; most places will bargain and there's no longer a shortage of beds in peak season. If you do have difficulty, just head for the hotels further from the centre.

CENTRAL HOI AN

An Huy 30 Phan Boi Chau ☎0510 386 2116, ⓦanhuyhotel.com. This deceptively large place opens out behind a tiny entrance, concealing simple but well-equipped rooms. However, noise can be an issue near the back, and staff are not always the most helpful. $28

★**Ha An** 6 Phan Boi Chau ☎0510 386 3126, ⓦhaanhotel.com. Welcoming, family-run hotel set back from the street in a quiet residential area. Its 25 rooms are arranged in an L-shape around a relaxing communal garden; they're highly attractive, with petals strewn across the beds, and superior rooms have delightful stone floor showers. The breakfast buffet is another big selling point. $65

Hoa Binh 696 Hai Ba Trung ☎0510 391 6838. Large, clean rooms with satellite TV at this presentable hotel – rarely will you get a swimming pool at this price, but there it is on the ground floor. Note that service can be a little gruff. $10

★**Life Resort Hoi An** 1 Pham Hong Thai ☎0510 391 4555, ⓦlife-resorts.com. Luxurious, beach-style resort in central Hoi An, blending minimalist Japanese design with maximum service and facilities; these include a fantastic pool, massage rooms and restaurants exuding a sophisticated air. They also offer language and lantern-making classes free of charge, as well as affordable cooking courses. $150

Minh A 2 Nguyen Thai Hoc ☎0510 386 1368. This little guesthouse right by Hoi An market has just six rooms in an ancient shophouse. Facilities are basic – there's no a/c and access to the shared bathroom and toilet is through the kitchen – but it's a good opportunity to stay in a traditional family home. $15

Sanh Hien Guesthouse 7 Nguyen Thi Minh Khai ☎0510 386 3631. Just three doors down from the Japanese Bridge, this two hundred-year-old house offers real charm, although the rooms are very basic, with fans and shared bathrooms only. $15

★**Thien Thanh** 16 Ba Trieu ☎0510 391 6545, ⓦhoianthienthanhhotel.com. Comfortable and intimate mini-hotel with exceptionally attentive staff who try to make your stay as restful as possible. It has all mod cons,

such as cable TV, a/c and internet access; the more expensive rooms have balconies overlooking water-spinach fields. Many guests return again and again. $45

Thuy Duong 3 92–94 Ba Trieu ☎0510 391 6565, ⓦthuyduonghotel-hoian.com. Well placed for open-tour bus drop-offs, the rooms here are comfortable, well maintained and reasonably priced, though those on the ground floor around the courtyard pool can be noisy. $35

Vinh Hung I 143 Tran Phu ☎0510 386 1621, ⓦvinhhungresort.com. There are few more atmospheric places to stay in Hoi An than this broodingly dark old Chinese shophouse – come in the evening and it'll feel like you're entering an Oriental period drama. The rooms are also traditional in style; best are the two upstairs, complete with balcony, wood panelling, antique furniture and four-poster beds. $90

AN HOI, CAM NAM & OUTSIDE THE CENTRE

Betel Garden Homestay 161 Tran Nhan Tong ☎0510 392 4165, ⓦbetelgardenhomestay.com. In a small village a 15min walk from central Hoi An, this traditionally styled mini resort is a remarkably relaxing place to stay – great for those who would like to enjoy Hoi An without the crowds. Call for a pick-up. $45

★**Long Life Riverside Hotel** 61 Nguyen Phuc Chu ☎0510 391 1696, ⓦlonglifehotels.com. New hotel away from the crowds on An Hoi Island. Rooms are immaculate and have been given pleasant traditional flourishes, but are tuned into the modern day with flatscreen TVs and, in most, computers. There's also a lovely little swimming pool, and staff are attentive. $30

Pho Hoi Riverside Resort 7/2 Tran Phu ☎0510 386 1633, ⓦphohoiresort.com. Few tourists cross the bridge to peaceful Cam Nam Island, let alone stay there, but at this presentable resort you're just a short walk from central Hoi An, which you can see across the water from the outdoor bar or swimming pool. $70

Sunflower Hotel 397 Cua Dai ☎0510 393 9839, ⓔsunflowerhoian.com. This friendly hotel is on the way out to the beach, and therefore a bit of a stretch from town, but it's worth the hike for its cheap prices, lovely staff and large breakfasts. $15

5

Vinh Hung Resort An Hoi ☎0510 386 4074, ⓦ vinhhungresort.com. The latest addition to the Vinh Hung clan is over on An Hoi Island. It's essentially a budget resort, with moderately attractive rooms, though the location is quite wonderful – quiet, and with a lovely view of the Thu Bon River. **$70**

CUA DAI BEACH

Hoi An Beach Resort At the end of the road from Hoi An, to the south on the right ☎0510 392 7011, ⓦ hoianbeachresort.com.vn. Separated from the beach by a quiet road, this is slightly cheaper than nearby resorts. Rooms are elegant in cool, sand colours and bathrooms are generously proportioned; it's worth paying the extra for a room overlooking the river. Other attractions include two pools, a private beach and a restaurant recommended for its well-priced local dishes. Free shuttle bus to Hoi An. **$90**

Palm Garden Resort On the other side (north) of the Hoi An road, about 700m from the small bridge ☎0510 392 7927, ⓦ palmgardenresort.com.vn. This resort takes its name from the four hundred-odd trees dotting the complex;

some at beachside have hammocks for lazing or cocktail sipping. The rooms are spacious and well up to standard, while the seafood in the on-site restaurants is superb. **$210**

Swiss–Belhotel Golden Sand Resort 300m further along from the *Hoi An Beach Resort* ☎0510 392 7550, ⓦ swiss-belhotel.com. Aiming for a contemporary-traditional fusion, and largely getting the balance right, this resort has some of the best rooms on the strip, and by far the largest pool; little touches such as wafts of frangipani in the gardens make most stays special, though customer service is not always five-star. **$180**

Victoria Hoi An Resort Immediately alongside the *Hoi An Beach Resort* ☎0510 392 7040, ⓦ victoriahotels-asia.com. The ritziest hotel in town, right down to the named and signed "streets" within its large compound. Some of the top bungalows open onto a lovely stretch of beach, while the cheapest rooms occupy luxurious two-storey villas. There are also all the amenities you'd expect of an international-class resort, including a restaurant serving good but expensive meals, a free shuttle bus to Hoi An and a range of activities. **$190**

EATING

Hoi An is perhaps Vietnam's best food city – nowhere else are there so many **wonderful restaurants** within walking distance of each other. The divine array of **local delicacies** (see box opposite) has recently been augmented by places serving Thai, Turkish and Tex-Mex, as well as delectable French pastries. In the evenings, tables and chairs line Bach Dang, whose restaurants may look more Mediterranean than Vietnamese but largely focus on local produce; a few slightly cheaper places do likewise across the water on An Hoi Island. In addition to cut-price **set meals** featuring local specialities, many of Hoi An's restaurants also offer cooking classes, costing from $10 per person and best arranged a day in advance; some establishments will help you personally select your ingredients at the market.

Blue Dragon 46 Bach Dang. Offering a similar standard of Vietnamese food and service to many other restaurants on Bach Dang, but the *Blue Dragon* donates part of its profits to a charity that helps rural children stay in school. The fact that the tasty five-course meal is just $3.50 is a bonus.

Cargo Club 107–109 Nguyen Thai Hoc ☎0510 391 0489. Despite having a good selection of local and international dishes, the real draw is the French bakery downstairs, which offers decadent pastries (from just under $1) and an array of take-to-the-beach bread rolls. The home-made ice cream also has the crowds lining up.

★ **Casa Verde** 99 Bach Dang. American-run restaurant with a bewilderingly diverse menu (mains from $4). Particular picks include perfectly prepared steaks, Tex-Mex dishes and home-made pasta served with gigantic shrimps. All are superbly made, and the place is absolutely humming most evenings.

★ **Cava** 53 Nguyen Phuc. Try not to go here on your first day in Hoi An, or you may not get anywhere else. A winning location on An Hoi Island is further enhanced by the wonderfully prepared Vietnamese dishes on the menu (from $4), which is itself spiced up with a few Turkish choices. Superb.

Faifoo 104 Tran Phu. Locals rate the *banh bao* ($3) at this well-established and attractive restaurant as the best in town, though many travellers choose the cheap five-course sampler of Hoi An specialities (see box opposite).

Hong Phuc 86 Bach Dang. A friendly, good-value and popular riverside place run by two multilingual female cousins, serving scrumptious local food – if you want to know the secret, you can sign up for an afternoon cookery class, during which you learn how to make four dishes ($12). Get here early for a table on the balcony.

Lighthouse Cam Nam Island ☎0510 393 6235, ⓦ lighthousecafehoian.com. Out of the way on Cam Nam, this restaurant serves lovingly prepared Vietnamese dishes at decent prices – you'll be able to eat well for just over $5. Dutch owner Hans also runs interesting bike-plus-cooking tours in which you zoom through the countryside, stop off at a market or two to buy ingredients, then head back home in the evening to whip up your food. Diners can get a free ride here on their boat, which can be found off Bach Dang. Closed Tues.

★ **Mango Rooms** 111 Nguyen Thai Hoc. The menu at this chilled out restaurant is constantly changing but

HOI AN SPECIALITIES

Hoi An has a number of tasty specialities to sample. Most famous is *cao lau*, a mouthwatering bowlful of thick rice-flour **noodles**, bean sprouts and pork-rind croutons in a light soup flavoured with mint and star anise, topped with thin slices of pork and served with grilled rice-flour crackers or sprinkled with crispy rice paper. Legend has it that the genuine article is cooked using water drawn from one particular local well. Lovers of **seafood** should try the delicately flavoured steamed manioc-flour parcels of finely diced crab or shrimp called *banh bao*, translated as "white rose", with lemon, sugar and *nuoc mam*, complemented by a crunchy onion-flake topping, adding extra flavour. A local variation of *hoanh thanh chien* (fried wonton), using shrimp and crab meat instead of pork, is also popular. One less heralded dish (and one of the cheapest) is *mi quang*, which sees a simple bowl of meat noodles enlivened with the addition of flavoursome oils, a quail egg, fresh sprigs of leaves – few tourists order this dish, and your ordering it may be met with surprise. To fill any remaining gaps, try Hoi An **cake**, *banh it*, triangular parcels made by steaming green-bean paste and strands of sweetened coconut in banana leaves.

Many Hoi An restaurants serve these dishes, but one good place to head is the cheap, market-like area at the eastern end of An Hoi Island. It's a very cute place, with each section demarcated by the name of its chef, and their stated speciality.

always wonderfully creative – imagine red snapper with coriander and pineapple, or prawns in a passion fruit and chocolate sauce ($11) – and there's also an excellent wine list. Its sister restaurant – *Mango Mango* – is directly across the river from the Japanese Bridge, views of which make this a better choice for sampling maverick owner Duc's signature cocktails.

★ **Morning Glory** 106 Nguyen Thai Hoc. Succinctly described by one local expat as "street food with life-size furniture", this classy-looking restaurant has a menu full of reasonably priced Hoi An specialities such as *banh khoai* and green papaya salad with beef. There are also a few interesting fusion items – try the soy profiteroles ($1.50).

Mr Son An Hoi Island. Incredibly cheap local dishes, all served with a smile from what looks like, and in fact is, somebody's house. Mains start at $1, and they also make great shakes.

★ **Red Bridge** Thon 4, Cam Thanh ☎ 0510 393 3222, ⓦ visithoian.com. In just a short space of time, this restaurant has gained a reputation for serving some of Hoi An's finest modern Vietnamese cuisine (mains from $3.50), and also runs superb cooking classes. Situated 2km east of town, in incredibly scenic riverside surroundings, it will take you there on its own boat (see website for details).

NIGHTLIFE

Quiet Hoi An boasts a few bars nowadays, though beware of xe om drivers offering to take you to "secret" out-of-town venues; some are genuinely good, but more often than not it ends in extortion.

Before & Now 51 Le Loi. Double-storey Italian restaurant and bar inside a traditional shophouse. However, forget the food – it's far better as a venue for evening drinks, and about as lively as Hoi An gets.

Brother's Café 27 Phan Boi Chau. The garden setting on the banks of the Thu Bon River is reason enough to come to this Hoi An institution, though the food on the whole is overpriced. To experience the atmosphere without the cost, come for a coffee or sundowner.

Sleepy Gecko Cam Nam Island. Stride over the bridge to Cam Nam Island to drink in yet another picture-perfect

sunset at this chilled, English-owned bar. It can get nice and busy some evenings, but on other nights you'll be more or less on your own.

Tam Tam Jardin 121 Tran Phu. Stylish place serving good coffee and delicious French pastries; it's also good for a beer or cocktail in the evening.

Treat's Café 158 Tran Phu. Upbeat bar-restaurant with good music, a shady interior courtyard, pool and cheap happy-hour deals (4–9pm). A second, less popular outlet at 31 Phan Dinh Phung enigmatically promises to be "same same but different".

SHOPPING

Tourism has also led to a revival in local crafts, though there are plenty of second-rate **souvenirs** on sale as well. Dedicated browsers can occupy several hours in the shops and galleries along Tran Phu, Nguyen Thai Hoc and Le Loi, while just over the Japanese Bridge a cluster of old houses double as showrooms. Scattered here and there are workshops where you can see a range of **local crafts**, from embroidery, wood-carving and pottery to silk being made by traditional

5

methods; visits are free, though afterwards you'll be directed to the souvenir shop-cum-showroom, not that there's any obligation to buy. Hoi An is now well known for its **silk** and **tailoring**, with prices generally cheaper than in Hanoi or Ho Chi Minh City. You'll find shops all over town but the original outlet was the **market**, where even now rows of tailors sit at sewing machines next to rainbow-coloured stacks, and for a few dollars will make up beautiful garments in a matter of hours. It's worth shopping around – ask to see some finished articles before placing an order. If you have time, it's a good idea to have one item made first to check the quality and fit. To complete the outfit you can have **shoes** made to match, though be warned that, unlike clothing, you won't be able to alter any small errors in size. Such is the number of smaller-scale operations that it's unfair to single any out, but two more upmarket places with a good reputation for reliability are listed below.

HANDICRAFTS AND SOUVENIRS

49 Le Loi Look out for a tiny stall at this address, where the same family has been making silk lanterns for generations.

Hoi An Handicraft Workshop 9 Nguyen Thai Hoc. Part of the ticket scheme (see box, p.254), this is as good a place as any to get a handle on traditional craft, particularly the lanterns made out back. Concerts are held twice a day in the front (see box below).

House of Traditional Handicrafts 41 Le Loi. Fascinating shop with an ancient silk loom on the ground floor, and the silkworms themselves munching away upstairs – it's that much more tempting to buy when you've seen how your goods were made.

SILK AND TAILORING

A Dong Silk 62 Tran Hung Dao ⓦ adongsilk.com. One of the most renowned tailors in town, and therefore the country as a whole.

Lotus 82 Tran Phu ⓦ lotusjewellery-hoian.com. There's good handmade jewellery at this American-run shop – proof of its popularity lies in the fact that many local copycats are now using the same hardwood display cases.

Phuong Huy 9a Nhi Trung. Popular chain making a wide array of items such as suits and handbags. Other outlets at 25 and 26 Tran Phu.

Yaly Couture 358 Nguyen Duy Hieu ⓦ yalycouture .com. Another revered local tailor, particularly good for suits.

DIRECTORY

Banks and exchange You can exchange cash and travellers' cheques and get over-the-counter cash advances on credit cards at Vietcombank, 25 Hai Ba Trung, and Agribank, 2 Phan Dinh Phung and 92 Tran Phu. There are also several ATMs around town.

Books Randy's Book Exchange on Cam Nam Island may well be the best secondhand bookstore in Vietnam; if you can't face the walk, most guesthouses offer book exchange.

Hospital 4 Tran Hung Dao ☎ 0510 386 1218.

Laundry Places along Tran Hung Dao offer laundry services at around 15,000đ per kilo.

Pharmacies In addition to small pharmacies near the hospital, Bac Ai, at 68 Nguyen Thai Hoc, is well stocked.

Police 8 Hoang Dieu ☎ 0510 386 1204.

Post office The unusually fancy and well-organized GPO is at 4b Tran Hung Dao (daily 6am–10pm). There's a sub-post office at 89 Phan Chu Trinh.

Tour agencies Hotel booking desks and tour agents along Tran Hung Dao, Phan Dinh Phung and Hai Ba Trung offer outings to My Son and craft villages around Hoi An. All will also, for a commission, be able to arrange onward train and plane tickets from Da Nang, and handle visa extensions.

ARTS AND FESTIVALS

With the influx of tourists, Hoi An is becoming a centre for the **arts**. A delightful hour-long medley of **traditional music and dance** is performed most evenings in a cramped room rather grandly known as the Traditional Arts Theatre, 75 Nguyen Thai Hoc (Mon–Sat 9pm; 50,000đ). Folk musicians also play short concerts at the Hoi An Handicraft Workshop, 9 Nguyen Thai Hoc (Mon–Sat 10.15am & 3.15pm; included in ticket scheme).

Once a month vehicles are banned from the town centre, coloured silk lanterns replace electric lights and shopkeepers don traditional costume to celebrate the **Full-Moon Festival** (fourteenth day of the lunar calendar). It's a tourist event, but a great occasion nonetheless: there are traditional music performances, with food stalls selling local specialities by the Japanese Bridge and on the waterfront.

During the **Mid-Autumn Festival**, a much bigger affair celebrated nationwide on the fourteenth day of the eighth lunar month, people also float lanterns on the river. In recent years – usually in spring but dates vary – Quang Nam province has also staged a week-long **cultural heritage festival** in Hoi An and My Son, including Cham dances and folk songs.

Around Hoi An

5

From Hoi An you can bike out along meandering paths to the white expanse of **Cua Dai Beach** or hop on a sampan to one of the **islands** of the Thu Bon River. River tours take you to low-lying, estuarine islands and the **craft villages** along their banks, while it's also now possible to visit the distant **Cham Islands**, renowned for their sea swallows' nests.

The beaches

It's a popular bike ride to the clean, white sands of **Cua Dai Beach**. The inevitable hawkers patrol the area, but you can minimize the hassle by walking away from the main centre, or by taking an umbrella and deck chair for the day at one of the many beachfront café-restaurants; in return you'll be expected to buy at least a drink, though many also serve excellent seafood – just be sure to check the prices before ordering. En route by bike, you can take a detour through the beautiful, canal-riddled Cam Thanh area, which lies to the south of the main road; head east on Nguyen Duy Hieu and take a right when the road ends a couple of kilometres east of Hoi An.

Far less visited than Cua Dai is **Cam An Beach**, due north of Hoi An – hit Hai Ba Trung and just keep going, or follow the coastal road north-by-northwest from Cua Dai. Its ramshackle bars are where local expats go to hang out, and the whole stretch has a pleasantly scruffy vibe – sometimes tinged with marijuana smoke.

ARRIVAL

BEACHES AROUND HOI AN

By taxi or xe om Cua Dai is just 4km east of Hoi An, a distance easily covered by taxi (40,000đ) or xe om (from 20,000đ) – just tell the driver when to pick you up.

By bike Coming by bicycle or motorbike, you'll be asked to leave it at the beach entrance for a handful of dong; if you're staying at one of the Cua Dai hotels (or just claim to be), you'll be allowed to pass.

Cam Kim Island and the craft villages

A ten-minute ferry ride from the pier in Hoi An (10,000đ)

The large island of **CAM KIM** is famed for its **craft villages**, which have been inhabited by skilled artisans since the sixteenth century. Most carpenters have moved out of the village but a handful remain, building fishing boats (you'll find one of the few surviving boatyards right beside the island's jetty) or crafting furniture for export. The work of one famous community of wood-carvers, from Kim Bong Village, can be seen throughout Hoi An. Cam Kim is also a nice escape from Hoi An; it's worth taking a bike over and exploring the rest of the island. Cam Kim is also a stop on the boat trip back from My Son (see p.264).

The Cham Islands

Boat trips take an hour each way from Cua Dai Beach, and there are now hydrofoil services from here and (on weekends) Da Nang – all are best arranged through agencies in Hoi An. It's possible to camp on the island, though when large Vietnamese groups arrive (also usually weekends) you may not get much sleep.

A group of mountainous islands lying 10km offshore is clearly visible from the coast near Hoi An. Cu Lao Cham, or the **CHAM ISLANDS**, are inhabited by fishermen, the navy and collectors of highly prized birds' nests (see box, p.264). Three thousand people live on the main island, but until 1995 even Vietnamese people weren't allowed to visit because of the naval base – much of the island remains under military control, which means that only a couple of hiking trails are walkable. However, the island has become popular for its surrounding marine life, with 135 species of coral, 202 species of fish and 84 species of molluscs said to exist around the marine park.

5

NEST HARVESTS ON THE CHAM ISLANDS

Cham islanders have been harvesting **sea swallows' nests** since the late sixteenth century. Today the government-controlled trade contributes greatly to the local economy, with astronomical prices per kilo for the culinary delicacy, to which extraordinary medicinal virtues are also attributed. Each spring, when thousands of the tiny, grey-and-black birds nest among the islands' caves and crevices, villagers build bamboo scaffolding or climb up ropes to prise the diminutive structures, about the size of a hen's egg, off the rock.

DIVING

★ **Cham Island Diving Centre** 88 Nguyen Thai Hoc ☎0510 391 0782, ⊛chamislanddiving.com. Excellent operator offering diving trips to the islands from the *Dive* *Bar* in Hoi An. Snorkel trips from $40, two dives from $75, open-water PADI courses from $370.

My Son

Daily 6.30am–4.30pm • 60,000đ

Vietnam's most evocative Cham site, **MY SON**, lies 40km southwest of Hoi An, in a bowl of lushly wooded hills towered over by the aptly named Cat's Tooth Mountain. My Son may be no Vietnamese Angkor Wat, but it is now on UNESCO's World Heritage list and richly deserves its place on the tourist map. The riot of vegetation that until recently enveloped the site has now largely been cleared away, but the tangible sense of faded majesty still hangs over the mouldering ruins, enhanced by the assorted lingam and Sanskrit stelae strewn around and by the isolated rural setting, whose peace is broken only by the wood-gatherers who trace the paths around the surrounding coffee and eucalyptus glades. The groups of buildings labelled B, C and D most warrant your attention: viewing these, it's possible, with a little stirring of the imagination, to visualize how a functioning temple complex would have appeared in My Son's heyday.

Brief history

Excavations at My Son have revealed that Cham kings were buried here as early as the fourth century, indicating that the site was established by the rulers of the early Champa capital of **Simhapura**, sited some 30km back towards the highway, at present-day Tra Kieu. The stone towers and sanctuaries whose remnants you see today were erected between the seventh and thirteenth centuries, with successive dynasties adding more temples to this holy place, until in its prime it comprised some seventy buildings. The area was considered the domain of gods and god-kings, and living on site would have been an attendant population of priests, dancers and servants.

French archeologists discovered the ruins in the late nineteenth century, when the Chams' fine **masonry** skills were still evident – instead of mortar, they used a resin mixed with ground brick and mollusc shells, which left only hairline cracks between brick courses. After the Viet Cong based themselves here in the 1960s, many unique buildings were pounded to oblivion by American B52s, most notably the once magnificent A1 tower. Craters around the site and masonry pocked with shell and bullet holes testify to this tragic period in My Son's history.

Group B

Archeologists regard **Group B** as the spiritual epicentre of My Son. Of the central **kalan** (sanctuary), marked on maps as **B1**, only the base remains, along with a lingam discovered under the foundations a few years ago; but stone epitaphs found nearby reveal that it was dedicated to the god-king Bhadresvara, a hybrid of Shiva and fourth-century King Bhadravarman, and erected in the eleventh century, under King Harivarman IV, on the site of an earlier, wooden temple.

5

The repository room and around B1

Fortunately, other elements of Group B have fared rather better, particularly **B5**, the impressive **repository room**. Votive offerings and other ritual paraphernalia would have been stored in B5's chimney-shaped interior, while its outer walls support ornate columns and statues of deities. The carving on the southern facade is particularly well preserved; on the west look out for a fine bas-relief depicting two elephants with their trunks entwined around a coconut tree.

The carving of Vishnu sitting below the thirteen heads of the snake-god Naga that adorned the roof of **B6** was an early casualty of war, but the oval receptacle for the holy water used in purification rituals and statue-washing ceremonies is still intact inside. The two smaller temples flanking B1's south side, **B3** and **B4**, would have been dedicated to Skanda and Ganesha, the children of Shiva, while posted around the complex are the remains of seven tiny shrines honouring the gods of the elements and of the points of the compass.

Groups C

Originally separated from Group B by a wall, the **Group C** complex is quite distinct from it. This time the central *kalan*, **C1**, is standing and fairly well preserved, though the statue of Shiva that it was built to house long since went to Da Nang's museum, leaving only its base in place. The statues of standing gods around the walls have been allowed to stay, though, as has the carved lintel that runs across the entrance.

Group D

East of B and C, the two long, windowed *mandapa* (meditation halls) that comprise **Group D** have now both been converted into modest **galleries**. Precisely aligned with the foundations of B1 is **D1**, the **mandapa**, where the priests would meditate prior to proceeding through the (now ruined) gate **B2** to worship. It also contains a lingam, the remains of a carving of Shiva, and a statue of Nandi, Shiva's bull, while in **D2** you'll see a fine rendition of many-armed Shiva dancing, and, beside the steps up to its eastern entrance, an impressive statue of Vishnu's vehicle, Garuda. The ground between these two galleries was named the **Court of Stelae** by early archeologists, a reference to the stone tablets, etched with Sanskrit script, that litter it. As well as these stelae, altars and statues of deities would have stood in the court, though all that remain of these are their plinths, on whose sides are sculpted images of dancing women, arms raised to carry their gods.

Groups A and G

East of Group D, signs direct you to Groups A and G. Bomb damage was particularly cruel in the vicinity of **Group A**, reducing the once spectacular *kalan*, **A1**, to a heap of toppled columns and lintels that closely resembles a collapsed hall of cards. Unusually, A1 was constructed with both an eastern and a western entrance. Within, a huge lingam base is ringed by a number of detailed, fifteen-centimetre-high figures at prayer. You'll pass **A9**, the *mandapa*, and **A8**, the gate, en route from B, C and D; **A11** would have been the repository room.

The remains of hilltop **Group G**, 60m north of Group A, are equally poorly preserved. However, you can still pick out horned gargoyles, sporting fangs and bulbous eyes, carved into the corners of the main *kalan*. The base of a lingam stands at the *kalan*'s southwestern corner, with breasts around its base.

MINES

While we've outlined a handful of the site's particularly noteworthy edifices above, you'll get most out of My Son simply by wandering at your leisure – but don't stray far from the towers and marked paths, as **unexploded mines** may still be in the ground.

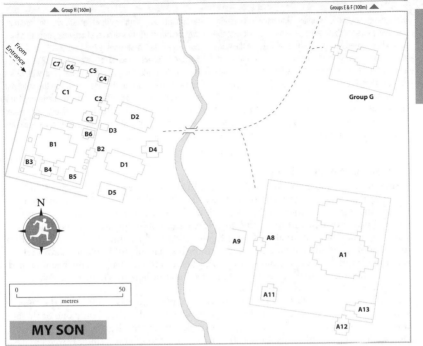

MY SON

ARRIVAL AND DEPARTURE

MY SON

By tour Most people visit on a guided tour from Hoi An (from \$8 per person); a popular variation is to return part of the way by boat, stopping at a couple of craft villages along the way (\$15).

By bike or taxi It's also possible to rent a taxi (\$35) or motorbike in Hoi An and travel to My Son independently; the road to the site strikes west from Highway 1 at Duy Xuyen, from where there are signs for My Son. Almost all tours go at around 8am, so to beat them leave a couple of hours earlier, or in the afternoon when most groups have departed.

Hoi An to Da Nang

Heading between **HOI AN** and **DA NANG** is a piece of cake, either by bus or rented vehicle. While most buses take the busy main road between the two cities, travelling by taxi or xe om – or under your own steam – gives you the chance to utilize the newer coastal road, and take in the Marble Mountains on the way. Since 2008 the long stretch of beach running parallel to the road, once unspoilt, has been the subject of huge development. Five-star resorts are springing up like mushrooms and there are now a couple of golf courses in the area, as advertised by Greg Norman and Colin Montgomerie, whose faces adorn billboards along the coastal road.

ACCOMMODATION

HOI AN TO DA NANG

Note that in addition to the following establishments, there are also **hotels** aplenty on China Beach up the coast, just east of Da Nang (see p.274).

Furama Resort ☎ 0511 384 7333, ⓦ furamavietnam .com. Set in lush gardens, this \$40m development stands out as one of Vietnam's top beach resorts. It offers luxuriously appointed rooms, international cuisine, two swimming pools plus a guarded beach and a range of recreational activities from tennis and golf to scuba-diving, ocean kayaking and windsurfing. **\$220**

Hoa's Place ☎ 0511 396 9216. Delightfully laidback

5

guesthouse near the Marble Mountains. It retains something of a cult reputation – some backpackers and surfers have stayed for months – but has been on the wane of late, partly thanks to the ongoing development of the area. Note that you're obliged to pay for meals here, since there's nothing in the area – they can work out as expensive as your room. $7

Life Resort ☎0510 391 4555, ⓦlife-resorts.com. A relative newbie, and highly attractive from top to toe. Rooms all have private balconies, and the on-site

restaurants are nothing short of superb. In addition, switched-on staff offer all sorts of activities, from romantic boat trips to tai-chi sessions. $205

Sandy Beach Resort ☎0511 383 6216, ⓦsandybeachdanang.com. A four-star hotel with prices to match, this is one of the older resorts on the strip, but still a relatively affordable option as you can usually lop a good 40 per cent off the rack rates. The rooms themselves are comfortable, if a little drab, but the common areas are quite appealing. $165

The Marble Mountains

Rising from the land between Hoi An and and Da Nang like an image from a Chinese painting are the fabled Marble Mountains, which have been revered for centuries by the Vietnamese. In addition to their auspicious shape (see box below), they have, for generations, resonated with the chink of stone masons chiselling away at religious statues, memorials and imitation Cham figures – hence the name. When Ho Chi Minh died, marble from these mountains was used for his mausoleum in Hanoi. Although the stone is still the area's life blood, quarrying the mountains has actually been banned locally – most of the marble used now comes from elsewhere in Vietnam, China or even places as far-flung as Afghanistan.

There's more to the Marble Mountains than shopping, however, riddled as they are with caves – a fact not lost on local tour agents. Despite all the fuss, only one of these caves rates above ordinary, but it's a good place to stretch your legs and admire the views. A torch is useful for exploring the caves and, although everything is well signposted, it's still worth picking up a sketch map (small charge) at the ticket desk.

Thuy Son

6am–5pm • 15,000đ or free after hours

Though only 107m high, this is both the highest and most important peak in the Marble Mountains. Two staircases, built for the visit of Emperor Minh Mang, lead up its southern flank; a lift was being installed at the time of writing. The main, westernmost entrance (the first you reach coming from the main road) brings you to the hollow summit, centred on pretty Tam Thai pagoda, itself surrounded by jagged rocks and grottoes.

The cave pagodas

The various visitable **cave pagodas** on Thuy Son are all a short walk from Tam Thai. From here, pass through a narrow defile, under a natural rock arch and you enter the antechamber to **Huyen Khong Cave**, the largest and most impressive on the mountain – descending steep, dark steps into the eerie half-light and swirling incense is quite an

---

THE TURTLE GOD

Most distinctive peaks in Vietnam tend to have their creation fixed in folklore, and the Marble Mountains are no different. Local mythology tells of the Turtle God hatching a divine egg on the shore; the shell cracked into five pieces, represented by the five small mountains. In Vietnamese these are named Ngu Hanh Son, meaning the five ritual elements: Thuy Son (water mountain) and Moc Son (wood) to the east of the road; Tho Son (earth), Kim Son (gold or metal) and Hoa Son (fire) to the west. Historically, Cham people came here to worship their Hindu gods and then erected Buddhist altars in the caves, which became places of pilgrimage, drawing even the Nguyen kings to the sacred site. When Ho Chi Minh died, marble from these mountains was used for his mausoleum in Hanoi, but quarrying has since been banned.

experience. Locals will point out stalactites resembling wrinkled faces and so on, but the cave's best feature is its roof through which sunlight streams like spotlights – you'll catch it in the hours either side of midday. A wall plaque commemorates a deadly accurate women's Viet Cong guerrilla unit, which during the war destroyed nineteen planes with just 22 rockets.

Backtracking to Tam Thai Pagoda, the path heading east under a couple more rock arches climbs slightly before starting to descend towards the eastern exit, affording expansive views over Non Nuoc Beach, the Cham Islands and north to Monkey Mountain. About halfway down you pass Linh Ung Pagoda behind which lurks **Tang Chon Cave**, in this case occupied by tenth-century Cham Hindu altars and two Buddhas, one sitting and one standing.

Non Nuoc

At the foot of the mountain is the dusty, unkempt village of **NON NUOC**. Since the fifteenth century, Non Nuoc has been inhabited by stone-carvers, who nowadays generally churn out mass-produced souvenirs using marble imported from Thanh Hoa Province, but it's fascinating to watch the masons at work – just follow your ears.

Follow the paved road east from Non Nuoc Village for about 500m, round a dogleg, and you reach **Non Nuoc Beach**. This, like the rest of the local coastline, is undergoing development, but it's still a pleasant place to kick back for an hour. A note of warning, however: there's a powerful **undertow** off this coast and when the northeast, winter monsoon blows up, riptides become particularly dangerous. Guards patrol the main swimming beaches during the day, where flags also indicate safe spots.

GETTING AROUND   **HOI AN TO DA NANG**

With a resort The vast majority of those staying at the area's five-stars do so on package deals, which include transport to and from Da Nang's airport or train station. **Independently** Those travelling independently will find a number of ways to travel between Hoi An and Da Nang (see the individual city accounts for more); the Marble Mountains sit almost in the middle, and if you can make a deal with a taxi or xe om driver you'll be able to stop by for an hour or so while travelling between the cities.

Da Nang

The largest city in Central Vietnam, **DA NANG** is primarily used by travellers as a jumping-off point for Hoi An, a city that has no airport or train station of its own. However, stick around a while and you'll find an unexpectedly amiable place, whose burgeoning middle class are seeing their cosmopolitan desires sated with a slew of trendy bars and cafés. The old French presence is also apparent in the leafy boulevards and colonial edifices along the riverfront promenade.

The elongated oval of Da Nang occupies a small headland protruding into the southern curve of Da Nang Bay. The city faces east, fronting onto Bach Dang and the Han River, across which the narrow Son Tra Peninsula shelters it from the South China Sea. The city itself harbours few specific sights of its own, beyond the wonderful **Cham Museum** with its unparalleled collection of sculpture from the period. However, there are a number of interesting sights in the area – just across the Son Tra Peninsula is **China Beach**, an increasingly developed stretch of sand from which you can see Monkey Mountain to the north and the Marble Mountains to the south.

Brief history

During the sixteenth and seventeenth centuries, trading vessels waiting to unload at Fai Fo (Hoi An) often sheltered in nearby Da Nang Bay, until Hoi An's harbour

5

began silting up and Da Nang developed into a major port in its own right. After 1802, when Hué became capital of Vietnam, Da Nang naturally served as the principal point of arrival for foreign delegations to the royal court. However, the real spur to the city's growth came in the American War when the neighbouring air base spawned the greatest concentration of US military personnel in South Vietnam (see box opposite).

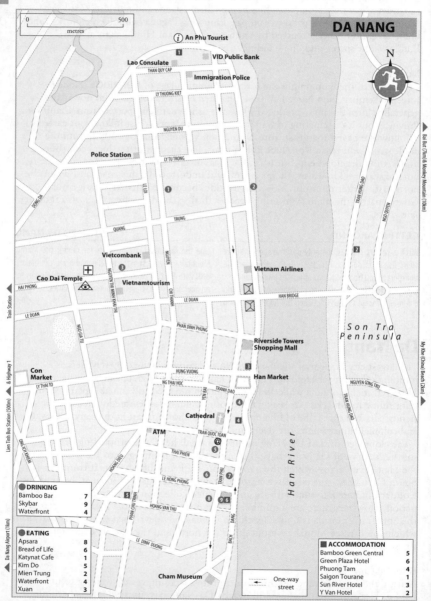

DA NANG

DRINKING
Bamboo Bar	7
Skybar	9
Waterfront	4

EATING
Apsara	8
Bread of Life	6
Katynat Cafe	1
Kim Do	5
Mien Trung	2
Waterfront	4
Xuan	3

ACCOMMODATION
Bamboo Green Central	5
Green Plaza Hotel	6
Phuong Tam	4
Saigon Tourane	1
Sun River Hotel	3
Y Van Hotel	2

One-way street

My Khe (China) Beach (3km), Non Nuoc Beach, Marble Mountains (15km) & Hoi An (32km) ▼

DA NANG DURING THE WAR

The city of Da Nang mushroomed after the arrival of the first American combat troops on March 8, 1965. An advance guard of two battalions of Marines waded ashore at Red Beach in Da Nang Bay, providing the press with a photo opportunity that included amphibious landing craft, helicopters and young Vietnamese women handing out garlands – not quite as the generals had envisaged. The Marines had come to defend Da Nang's massive **US Air Force base**; as the troops flew in so the base sprawled. Eventually Da Nang became "a small American city", as journalist John Pilger remembers it, "with its own generators, water purification plants, hospitals, cinemas, bowling alleys, ball parks, tennis courts, jogging tracks, supermarkets and bars, lots of bars". For most US troops the approach to Da Nang airfield formed their first impression of Vietnam, and it was here they came to take a break from the war at the famous **China Beach**.

At the same time the city swelled with thousands of **refugees**, mostly villagers cleared from "free-fire zones" but also people in search of work – labourers, cooks, laundry staff, pimps, prostitutes and drug pushers, all inhabiting a shantytown called Dogpatch on the base perimeter. Da Nang's population rose inexorably: twenty thousand in the 1940s, fifty thousand in 1955 and, some estimate, a peak of one million during the American years. North Vietnamese mortar shells periodically fell in and around the base, but the city's most violent scenes occurred when two South Vietnamese generals engaged in a little power struggle. In March 1966 Vice Air Marshal Ky, then prime minister of South Vietnam, ousted a popular Hué overlord, General Thi, following his open support of Buddhist dissidents. Demonstrations spread from Hué to Da Nang where troops loyal to Thi seized the airfield in what amounted to a **mini civil war**. After much posturing Ky crushed the revolt two months later, killing hundreds of rebel troops and many civilians. In the preceding chaos, the beleaguered rebels held forty Western journalists hostage for a brief period in Da Nang's largest pagoda, Chua Tinh Hoi, while streets around filled with Buddhist protesters.

When the North Vietnamese Army finally arrived to **liberate** Da Nang on March 29, 1975, they had less of a struggle. Communist units had already cut the road south, and panic-stricken South Vietnamese soldiers battled for space on any plane or boat leaving the city, firing on unarmed civilians. Many drowned in the struggle to reach fishing boats, while planes and tanks were abandoned to the enemy. Da Nang had been all but deserted by South Vietnamese forces, leaving the mighty base to, according to Pilger, be "taken by a dozen NLF cadres waving white handkerchiefs from the back of a truck".

The Cham Museum

2 Duong 2 Thang 9 • 7am–5pm • 30,000d

Even if you're just passing through Da Nang, try to spare an hour for the small **Cham Museum**, particularly if you plan to visit the Cham ruins at My Son (see p.264). The museum – whose design incorporates Cham motifs – sits in a garden of frangipani trees at the south end of Bach Dang, and its display of graceful, sometimes severe, terracotta and sandstone figures gives a tantalizing glimpse of an artistically inspired culture that ruled most of southern Vietnam for a thousand years. In the late nineteenth century French archeologists started collecting statues, friezes and altars from once magnificent Cham sites dotted around the hinterland of Da Nang, and opened the museum in 1916. Though this is undoubtedly the most comprehensive display of Cham art in the world, it's said that many of the best statues were carried off into European private collections.

The Exhibition Halls

The exhibits are grouped according to their place of origin and are positioned in two main halls. Be sure to make use of the excellent on-site reading material dotted around the exhibits.

In the **first hall**, a massive, square altar pedestal (late seventh century) from the religious centre of My Son is considered a masterpiece of early Cham craftsmanship, particularly its frieze depicting jaunty dancing girls, and a soulful flute player. However, experts and amateurs alike usually nominate two lithe dancers with Mona

5

> ## CHAM ART
>
> Recurring images in Cham **art** are lions, elephants and Hindu deities, predominantly Shiva (founder and defender of Champa) expressed either as a vigorous, full-lipped man or as a lingam, but Vishnu, Garuda, Ganesha and Nandi the bull are also portrayed. Buddhas feature strongly in the ninth-century art of Indrapura, a period when Khmer and Indonesian influences were gradually assimilated. The most distinctive icon is Uroja, a breast and nipple that represents the universal "mother" of Cham kings.
>
> As the Viets pushed south during the eleventh century, so the Chams retreated, and their sculptures evolved a bold, cubic style. Though less refined than earlier works, the chunky mythical animals from this period retain pleasing solidity and a playful charm.

Lisa smiles, their soft, round bodies seemingly clad in nothing but strings of pearls, as the zenith of Cham artistry. The piece also features two musicians on a fragment of capital produced by Tra Kieu sculptors in the late tenth century, just before the decline of the Champa kingdom.

The **second hall** is a new extension at the back; three times larger than the first hall, it includes a further 146 stone sculptures, dating from the seventh to the fourteenth centuries. There's also a small upstairs room; exhibits revolve around earthenware artefacts, though there's a collection of palanquins and other gilded woodwork (though these are from dynastic, rather than Cham, times).

Cao Dai Temple

63 Hai Phong opposite the hospital

Da Nang's **Cao Dai Temple** was built in 1956 and is Vietnam's second most important after Tay Ninh (see p.112). An elderly archbishop, assisted by fifteen priests, ministers to a congregation said to number fifty thousand here. The temple, which sees few tourists, is a smaller, simpler version of Tay Ninh, dominated inside by the all-seeing eye of the Supreme Being and paintings of Cao Dai's principal saints, Lao-tzu, Confucius, Jesus Christ and Buddha (see box, p.111). Services were banned between 1975 and 1986 and the building locked up, but now adherents gather to worship four times a day (6am, noon, 6pm & midnight). The occasional tourists who do turn up find it has more erratic opening times than its larger sister temple outside Ho Chi Minh City; you may find the gate locked when there is no service on.

ARRIVAL AND DEPARTURE
DA NANG

BY PLANE

The **Da Nang International** Airport is just 3km southwest of the city, and has connections to most major domestic airport, as well as scheduled services to Cambodia, China and Singapore. There are a couple of **taxi desks** inside the arrivals hall offering reasonable rates for Hoi An (from 50,000đ per person), but if you're going to the city centre, it's a little cheaper to take one of the metered taxis waiting outside (45,000đ or less). It's even walkable, if you have light luggage. **Airlines** include Jetstar, 137 Nguyen Van Linh (☎ 0511 358 3583); Vietnam Airlines, 58 Bach Dang (☎ 0511 382 1130). Both also have offices at the airport, as do Air Mekong (☎ 0511 381 8488).

Destinations: Buon Ma Thuot (daily; 1hr); Da Lat (daily; 1hr 30min); Hanoi (10 daily; 1hr 30min); Ho Chi Minh City (11 daily; 1hr 30min); Nha Trang (2 daily; 1hr); Pleiku (daily; 50min).

BY TRAIN

The **Ga Da Nang** is 2km west of town at 122 Hai Phong. There will be plenty of taxis (20,000đ to the centre) and **xe om** (10,000đ) drivers vying for your attention.

Destinations: Hanoi (6 daily; 15–20hr); Ho Chi Minh City (6 daily; 16–21hr); Hué (6 daily; 2hr 30min–3hr); Nha Trang (6 daily; 9–12hr).

BY BUS

Open-tour buses generally drop passengers at the Cham Museum, at the south end of Bach Dang, and there's usually another stop at the north edge of town, where most companies have their base. **Local buses** to Hoi An leave from Tran Phu, near the Cham Museum.

Destinations: Dong Ha (5hr); Hoi An (1hr 30min–2hr); Hué (3hr–4hr); Quang Ngai (5hr); Quy Nhon (11hr); Savannakhet, Laos (24hr).

GETTING AROUND

By bike and motorbike Da Nang is big enough and its sights sufficiently spread out to make walking round town fairly time-consuming. Most hotels either rent bikes or can direct you to somewhere that does (around $2/day); otherwise, there's no shortage of cyclo or xe om. Self-drive motorbikes (around $5/day) are available from tour agencies and most hotels.

INFORMATION

Tourist information There is no shortage of travel agencies in central Da Nang, all of whom will be able to advise on – and, they hope, sell – tours of the area. ⓦindanang.com is a useful resource; primarily aimed at expats living in the city, it's also good for listings information.

ACCOMMODATION

The majority of Da Nang's hotels are geared to business travellers or tour groups; these days, most are heading to the big resorts lining the beach between Da Nang and Hoi An. In Da Nang itself, a number of good-value mini-hotels have opened up along the riverfront.

Bamboo Green Central 158 Phan Chu Trinh ☎0511 382 2996, ⓦbamboogreenhotel.com.vn. Upmarket hotel popular with tour groups and business people. A good range of facilities, including money exchange, tour desk, restaurant and bar, plus decent – if rather bland – rooms, make this one of the best hotels in town. $40

★ **Green Plaza Hotel** 238 Bach Dang ☎0511 322 3399, ⓦgreenplazahotel.vn. It's hard to miss this new twenty-floor tower on the riverside; service is excellent and the rooms fresh and immaculate, though you'll pay extra for a river view. Non-guests are also welcome to use the *Skybar* on the top floor (see p.274). $105

Phuong Tam 174 Bach Dang ☎0511 382 4288. This riverside hotel is handy for the Cham Museum, and has well-appointed rooms with a/c and satellite TV. Those at the rear are quieter and slightly cheaper. $17

Saigon Tourane 5 Dong Da ☎0511 382 1021, ⓦsaigontourane.com.vn. Sitting away from the action, this old low-rise hotel still makes a comfortable, good-value choice. Facilities are numerous, including a restaurant serving international cuisine, piano-bar, health club and business centre. The rooms are very comfortable, equipped to three-star standards, albeit slightly soulless. $50

★ **Sun River Hotel** 132–136 Bach Dang ☎0511 384 9188, ⓦsunriverhoteldn.com.vn. Starting life in 2009, this gorgeous boutique hotel is the best mid-range option on the strip. Its modern rooms have wooden floors and furnishings and a cream-through-brown colour scheme. Rooms at the front cost a little more, and have river views from the curved windows. The café/bar also makes a good place to drink, even if you're not staying here. $45

Y Van Hotel 21 Tran Hung Dao ☎0511 393 6156, ⓔhotelyvan@vnn.vn. Situated on the quieter side of the Han River, this new fifteen-room mini-hotel is a shining beacon among Da Nang's lacklustre mid-range accommodation options. Rooms are luxuriously furnished with all amenities including full-size baths. The rooftop bar is a great spot to watch the city at night. $35

EATING

Da Nang has no shortage of places to eat, ranging from **food stalls** to full-blown, top-notch **restaurants**. Fruitful hunting grounds for local restaurants and food stalls are the west end of Hai Phong and streets to the south of Hung Vuong, particularly Nguyen Chi Thanh; the ground floor of the market also has a clutch of snack stands.

★ **Apsara** 222 Tran Phu. Prices are surprisingly reasonable at Da Nang's most attractive restaurant, with mains on the seafood-centred menu starting at $3.50, and soups going for half that. For an interesting change, try the *chao tom* – ground shrimp roasted on sugar cane. Traditional music is performed every night from 7–8pm. Daily 10am–2.30pm & 5pm–10pm.

★ **Bread of Life** 12 Le Hong Phong. A great place to throw down some Western comfort food. Baked goods, pancakes, pizza and a lot more are made and served by an all-deaf staff, and proceeds go towards a related local charity. Mains from $3. Daily 9am–8pm; closed Sun.

Katynat Cafe 51 Nguyen Chi Thanh. The most appealing of a recent glut of youth-focused, wi-fi-friendly cafés; fruit juices and small meals are available, while women get everything half-price on Wed. Daily 9am–8pm.

Kim Do 180 Tran Phu. This local favourite serves a broad range of Chinese cuisine and provides comfortable, a/c dining with attentive service. The portions can be on the small side, but with a bit of care you can eat reasonably well for around $6 per head. Daily 7am–9.30pm.

★ **Waterfront** 150–152 Bach Dang ⓦwaterfront danang.com. This super-stylish snack bar would look perfectly at home in Ho Chi Minh City's trendier quarters.

5

Sharply attired staff float around the two levels delivering tasty sandwiches ($3.50) and mezes. It's also a good place to drink (see below). Daily 10am–11pm.

Xuan 66 Hai Phong. This is what eating out in Da Nang used to be like. This cheap and cheerful street kitchen serves a mean *com ga* – chicken rice, a Da Nang speciality and yours for just $1. Daily noon–4pm & 6–10pm.

NIGHTLIFE

There are a few decent **bars** in Da Nang, as well as umpteen trendy **cafés**, most of which offer free wi-fi access. Also notable is a small selection of local beers to quaff – Da Nang Export and Bière la Rue.

★ **Bamboo Bar** 228 Bach Dang. Shoot some pool at this small, friendly bar, which can get very busy of an evening; a mainstay of the local expat community, it's also a good place to get a handle on all things Da Nang. Daily noon–1am.

Skybar Green Plaza Hotel 238 Bach Dang ☎0511 322 3399, ⓦgreenplazahotel.vn. Sitting atop the *Green Plaza Hotel*, this café and bar offers free high-speed internet access and wonderful river views. The music is generally far too loud, but you can always try asking staff to turn it down. Daily 8am–10pm.

★ **Waterfront** (See p.273). This swanky place is good for coffee during the day or alcohol by night – it's one of the only places in town that can make a decent latte, while they have a near-complete roster of Vietnamese beers. Music is usually of the typical lounge bar variety. Daily 10am–11pm.

DIRECTORY

Banks and exchange Vietcombank, 140 Le Loi; Incombank, 172 Nguyen Van Linh; VID Public Bank, 2 Tran Phu. ATMs now dot the city and are located in front of most higher-end hotels. There's also a bank and 24hr ATM at the airport.

Consulate The Lao consulate is located at 16 Tran Quy Cap (Mon–Fri 8–11.30am & 2–4.30pm; ☎0511 382 1208). A thirty-day tourist visa will cost $31 to $48, depending on your nationality; you'll need two passport photos, and visas are issued on the spot.

Hospital The Family Medical Practice at 50–52 Nguyen Van Linh (☎0511 358 2699, ⓦvietnammedicalpractice .com) has foreign staff and a dental clinic and offers 24hr emergency service.

Immigration police 7 Than Quy Cap. The place to go if you've lost your passport or have similar difficulties.

Post office Main office at 60 Bach Dang, poste restante at no. 66; other branches at 80 Hung Vuong, 41 Tran Quoc Toan and 20 Dong Da.

China Beach

The seaward side of the Son Tra Peninsula provides Da Nang with its nearest unpolluted beach – My Khe, the original **China Beach**, though its rival to the south, **Non Nuoc Beach**, also claims the same sobriquet (see p.269). My Khe is a long, if not exactly glorious, stretch of sand less than 3km southeast of central Da Nang. This was where US servicemen were helicoptered in for R&R during the American War, though these days it's far more popular with seafood-craving locals. A xe om ride here should cost 30,000đ (slightly more at night) for the ride from Da Nang.

ACCOMMODATION AND EATING   CHINA BEACH

It's quite possible to stay on or around China Beach, though the area has felt rather run-down since fancier hotels and resorts started to sprout up down the coast to the south (see p.267). Both hotels listed here are on the seafront, just to the right at the end of the the road from Da Nang.

My Khe Hotel II 233 Nguyen Van Thoai ☎0511 394 1095, ⓔmkbeach@vnn.vn. Long-standing China Beach favourite, built close to the ground yet with modern facilities. For most of the year you'll be able to halve the advertised prices – a good job, since the facilities and service do not do justice to the rack rates. **$60**

Tam's Pub 43 Ho Xuan Huong ☎09054 06905. Claims to have the "best burgers in town", and in the seafood-heavy China Beach area the lack of competition alone validates their point. They're pretty good, in any case, as is the Vietnamese food; they also rent out motorbikes and surfboards.

Tourane Hotel ☎0511 393 2666, ⓦtouranehotel .com.vn. A large renovated French colonial-style property that offers spacious yet simple rooms in villas. It's even less polished than the *My Khe II*, and has few facilities to speak of, but during low season you'll usually get a room for $35. **$60**

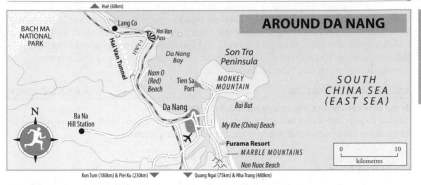

Monkey Mountain

A return trip to Bai But by xe om will cost around 120,000đ including a couple of hours' waiting time • Refreshments and reasonably priced seafood are on offer at a simple bar-restaurant behind the beach

A low-lying neck of land forms the Han River's east bank and then rises 700m in the north to rolling Nui Tien Sa. The name means "descending angels", a reference to heavenly creatures who apparently would often alight on the summit for a game of chess, but most people know it as **Monkey Mountain** on account of its wildlife population. Monkeys still inhabit the promontory, which is mostly a restricted military area. Head up to the observatories, or skirt round the northern tip where you can scramble down to coves and beaches in several places.

Bai But cove

A road along the promontory's south coast provides easier access to a sandy cove called **Bai But**, about 8km from the city centre. At weekends Da Nang day-trippers fill the beach, but at other times it's a good place to escape the noise and bustle of the city; also note the gigantic Buddha erected just uphill in 2010.

ACCOMMODATION   MONKEY MOUNTAIN

Son Tra Resort ☎ 0511 392 4924, ⌨ sontra.com.vn. This resort's curl of villas – all two-storey – is just about visible from China Beach, and they make a grand place to get away from it all. Service can be a little patchy, and though the villas are pristine and well-designed they're certainly a little overpriced. However, in general it's still a decent place to stay, and the facilities are excellent, most notably the private beach, swimming pool and on-site spa. $160

Ba Na Hill Station

48km west of Da Nang

Perched 1500m up a mountain and best attacked on a day-trip from Da Nang, **Ba Na Hill Station** provides a welcome change from the coast. The site was first developed by the French in the 1920s, who came in numbers to escape the summer heat and enjoy some cool, mountain air. After a brief heyday in the 1930s the resort was abandoned and soon fell victim to the ravages of war and the encroaching jungle. Thanks to a high annual rainfall together with temperatures at a constant 17–20°C, dense forest growth cloaks the mountain, which is home to over five hundred species of flora and 250 of fauna. Recently, local authorities have poured money into Ba Na, converting some of the old French villas into guesthouses and restaurants, laying forest trails and a new access road and even putting in a cable car – a great hit with the locals, who come up here at night to admire the lights of Da Nang twinkling far below. It is now something of a theme park and you will most likely be able to resist the temptation to stay the night.

But the **views** are indeed spectacular, taking in the Hai Van Pass, Son Tra Peninsula and Marble Mountains (depending on the weather – you may have to content yourself

5

with an atmospheric scene of mountains wreathed in mist, but while it's raining on the lower slopes, the summit can be above the clouds, enjoying brilliant sunshine).

Views apart, the main attraction is exploring the **forest paths** and wandering among the ruined villas, for which half a day will suffice. You may want to avoid summer weekends, when the place can be packed out.

ARRIVAL AND DEPARTURE   BA NA HILL STATION

By car or xe om A return trip by car or xe om from Da Nang will be pricey once waiting time is factored in – in theory, around $20 by cab and half that by xe om, but

bargain hard.

On a tour Da Nang tour agents offer various organized bus tours, mostly in summer.

Da Nang to Hué

Up the coast from Da Nang, Highway 1 zigzags over the **Hai Van Pass** (see box below), a wonderfully scenic ride by road or (especially) rail. These days, most buses cut out the pass via the Hai Van Tunnel, leaving a more peaceful journey for those that choose to take on the pass. From the top of the pass there are superb views, weather permitting, over the sweeping curve of Da Nang Bay, with glimpses of the rail lines looping and tunnelling along the cliff. The two routes converge again where the tunnel emerges, at the small beach town of **Lang Co**, whose beach boasts brilliant white sands – and is still, as yet, markedly undeveloped. To the west is **Bach Ma National Park**, a gorgeous place where the remains of another French-era hill station are swamped by some of the lushest vegetation in Vietnam.

Lang Co

Descending again into warmer air, a white-tipped spit of land comes into view round a hairpin bend, jutting into an aquamarine lagoon strung with fishing nets. Sadly, this much-photographed scene is marred by the road bridge marching across it. The original bridge spanning the lagoon has the dubious distinction of being the Viet Minh bomb squads' first target in 1947 and its ruined piles are still visible. Forty kilometres north of Da Nang, **LANG CO** village hides among coconut palms on the sandy peninsula, its presence revealed only by a white-spired church. It makes a popular lunch stop on the road between Da Nang and Hué, though a quick swim from the narrow beach will be spoilt by electricity pylons and a good deal of rubbish – head north away from the fishing village to find cleaner sand.

Lang Co has been earmarked for tourist development for years, yet it remains rather quiet, with only a few beach resorts in operation and a number of cheaper guesthouses on the other side of the highway.

ARRIVAL AND DEPARTURE   LANG CO

By train or bus The train station is on the lagoon's western side, or public buses will drop you off anywhere on the highway. Sinh Café open-tour buses stop at *Thanh Tam*,

while An Phu Tourist uses the very run-down *Tourist Hotel* towards the southern end of the strip.

PASS OF THE OCEAN CLOUDS

Thirty kilometres north of Da Nang, the first and most dramatic of three mountain spurs off the **Truong Son range** cuts across Vietnam's pinched central waist, all the way to the sea. This thousand-metre-high barrier forms a climatic frontier blocking the southward penetration of cold, damp winter airstreams, which often bury the tops under thick cloud banks and earn it the title **Hai Van**, or "Pass of the Ocean Clouds". These mountains once formed a national frontier between Dai Viet and Champa, and Hai Van's continuing strategic importance is marked by a succession of forts, pillboxes and ridge-line defensive walls erected by Nguyen-dynasty Vietnamese, French, Japanese and American forces.

ACCOMMODATION AND EATING

Though not yet over-busy, Lang Co has an array of options if you decide to stay. All places listed here will be able to serve food and is of a very high standard.

Lang Co Beach Resort ☎ 054 387 3555, ⊛ langcobeach resort.com.vn. Government-owned resort complex, with green-roofed, Hué-style villas, a landscaped pool and a replica covered bridge. The rooms are big, light and well equipped and the beach here is kept scrupulously clean. Notable are the few $40 "budget" rooms; these, and all other rooms on site, have their rates halved between Oct and March. **$100**

Nirvana Spa & Resort ☎ 054 387 3555, ⊛ nirvanaspavietnam.com. A series of twenty villas, strung out along the beach – the views are just what you'd expect. Don't be put off by the eyewatering rates – if you book online you can usually get a fifty percent discount. The pretty on-site spa has a wide range of massages, facials and other therapies. **$160**

Thanh Tam Resort ☎ 054 387 4456, ⊛ thanh tamresort.com.vn. Good-value, mid-range option, on the highway about 1500m north of the village. It's a surprisingly large place, with several restaurants to choose from. The rooms themselves are simple affairs, though all a/c and with free wi-fi; ask for one with a sea view. **$35**

Bach Ma National Park

Well off the beaten track, **Bach Ma National Park** is being developed as an eco-tourism destination, and dedicated ornithologists and botanists may want to make the effort to get here for the chance of seeing some of the region's 330 bird species and more than 1400 species of flora. Bach Ma is also home to 83 mammal species, including the Asiatic black bear, leopard and the recently discovered saola and giant muntjac (see p.478), as well as more visible deer and macaque monkeys. The highlands were previously the location of a French summer resort, where Emperor Bao Dai also kept several luxury villas. The majority of buildings, tennis courts and rose-beds are now in ruins, but a number of villas have been restored to provide tourist accommodation. It's just as easily accessible from Hué as it is from Da Nang.

ARRIVAL AND DEPARTURE   BACH MA

By car or bike By far the easiest way to get to Bach Ma is with your own transport – 26km west of Lang Co (and 40km south of Hué), look for a small green sign pointing south off Highway 1 in Cau Hai Village (Phu Loc District), then drive for another 3km to the park gate – or by rented car from Hué (around $80 for three people for the return journey).

THE TRAILS

Six short **nature trails** branch off the steep, tarmacked road which leads 16km from the entrance gate almost to the summit of Hai Vong Dai Mountain (1450m). Note that all marker distances refer to the distance from Highway 1 rather than from the park entrance.

Pheasant Trail (2.5km). Starts at the Km 8 marker to reach a series of waterfalls and pools, where you can swim. On the way you may hear the calls of white-cheek gibbons or some of the seven types of pheasant that inhabit the park, or see the fifty-centimetre-long earthworms which the locals cook and eat as a treatment for malaria.

Parashorea Trail (300m). At Km 14, a short but very steep trail named after this area's towering trees.

Rhododendron Trail (1.5km). Leads up 689 steps from Km 10 to a waterfall, with views over primary forest.

Five Lakes Trail (2km). Starts at Km 17.5, ends at a series of five pools fed by a waterfall, where you can also swim.

Summit Trail Leads 800m from the end of the road to the crest of Hai Vong Dai with good views over Cau Hai lagoon and surrounding mountains.

From here, instead of retracing your steps, you can walk back down the **Nature Exploration Trail** (2.5km). You can walk from the summit past ruined villas to rejoin the road at Km 17, beside the **Orchid House**, where nearly a hundred species are carefully nurtured.

is Both public and open-tour buses will drop you at the turning in Cau Hai, from where you can pick up a xe om for the final 4km stretch.

By xe om A xe om from Lang Co will cost a minimum of 250,000đ for the return trip. Note that, while cars are allowed inside the park, motorbikes and bicycles are not. Instead, you'll have to rent one of the park's jeeps, which will take you to the summit and back again, but can't drop off or pick up passengers en route.

INFORMATION

Visitors' Centre At the entrance to the park, stop first at the Visitors' Centre (7am–5pm; ☎054 387 1330, ⓦwww.bachma.vnn.vn) to buy your entrance tickets and arrange transport and accommodation (40,000đ entrance, 350,000đ for a four-seater jeep to the summit and back). If you are arriving outside these hours, phone in advance. Make sure you pick up a map of the trails, and it's also well worth investing in the excellent English-language booklet. While you're here, take a quick look round the exhibition; it's aimed at kids but is still very informative.

Hiring a guide Although it's not a requirement, it's definitely a good idea to take a guide ($12 for an English-speaker) when you're walking in the park, principally for your own safety – it's easy to get lost. Note that it's normal "forest etiquette" to share drinks, meals and carrying the loads.

Reforestation programme If you want to make a positive contribution to the onerous task of reforestation, there's a programme whereby you can buy a sapling and help plant it in one of the denuded areas of the park.

When to go Bach Ma is one of the wettest places in Vietnam, with a staggering eight metres of rainfall a year at the summit. The best time to visit is May–early Sept, but even then be prepared to get wet. Remember to take warm clothes since it can get chilly at the top.

Roadworks The top of the mountain was closed off at the time of writing, and roadworks in the area had been complicating transport practicalities – ask a Hué or Da Nang travel agency for the latest before setting off.

ACCOMMODATION

Should you wish to **stay** in the park, you can opt for the campsite (bring your own tent) at Km 18, or one of a number of guesthouses either near the summit or beside the entrance.

Do Quyen Villa. The five-room *Do Quyen Villa* is especially popular with its location near the summit, nestled amongst the trees. In peak season (June–Aug) it's advisable to book in advance; contact the Visitors' Centre for reservations. **$15**

EATING

There's a small **restaurant** at the park entrance, where you can also buy biscuits, water and snacks. Meals have to be ordered in advance if you're staying at the summit. Alternatively, you can bring your own food from Cau Hai market.

Hué

Still packed with the accoutrements of its dynastic past, **HUÉ** is one of Vietnam's most engaging cities. It boasts an unparalleled opportunity for historic and culinary exploration, thanks in no small part to its status as national capital from 1802–1945. Though the Nguyen dynasty is no more, Hué still exudes something of a regal, dignified air – its populace, indeed, are considered somewhat highbrow by the rest of the country. It's still a breeding ground for poets, artists, scholars and intellectuals, and you'll notice far more youngsters here than in other cities – largely because, unlike elsewhere in Vietnam, female students still wear the traditional *ao dai*.

Hué repays exploration at a leisurely pace, and contains enough in the way of historical interest to swallow up a few days with no trouble at all. The city divides into three clearly defined urban areas, each with its own distinct character. The nineteenth century walled **citadel**, on the north bank of the Perfume River, contains the once magnificent **Imperial City** as well as an extensive grid of attractive residential streets and prolific gardens. Across Dong Ba Canal to the east lies **Phu Cat**, the original merchants' quarter of Hué where ships once pulled in, now a crowded district of shophouses, Chinese Assembly Halls and pagodas. What used to be called the **European city**, a triangle of land caught between the Perfume River's south bank and

5

the Phu Cam Canal, is now Hué's modern administrative centre, where you'll also find most hotels and tourist services.

Pine-covered hills form the city's southern bounds; this is where the Nguyen emperors built their palatial Royal Mausoleums (see p.296). And through it all meanders the Perfume River, named somewhat fancifully from the tree resin and blossoms it carries, passing on its way the celebrated, seven-storey tower of Thien Mu Pagoda (see p.294). If you can afford the time, cycling out to Thuan An Beach (see p.292) makes an enjoyable excursion. Hué is also the main jumping-off point for day-tours of the DMZ (see p.301).

With all this to offer, Hué is inevitably one of Vietnam's pre-eminent tourist destinations. The choice and standard of accommodation are generally above average,

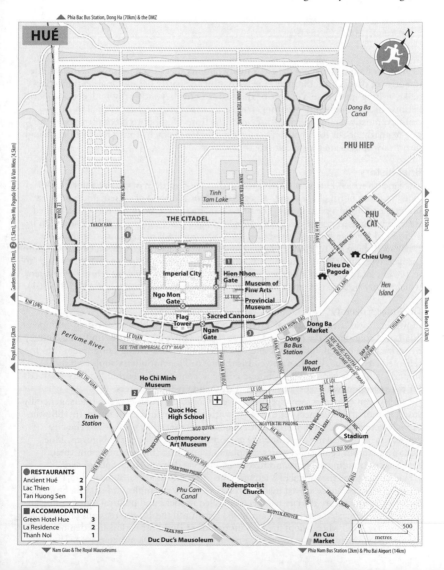

HUÉ

△ Phia Bac Bus Station, Dong Ha (70km) & the DMZ

Dong Ba Canal

PHU HIEP

◀ Garden Houses (1km), ▷ (1.5km), Thien Mu Pagoda (4km) & Van Mieu (4.5km)

Chua Ong (150m) ▶

Tinh Tam Lake

THE CITADEL

PHU CAT

THACH HAN

Imperial City

Hien Nhon Gate

Museum of Fine Arts

Dieu De Pagoda

Chieu Ung

Hen Island

Thuan An Beach (12km) ▶

Ngo Mon Gate

Provincial Museum

◀ Royal Arena (2km)

KIM LONG

Perfume River

Flag Tower

Sacred Cannons

Ngan Gate

SEE 'THE IMPERIAL CITY' MAP

Dong Ba Market

Dong Ba Bus Station

Boat Wharf

SEE 'HUÉ: SOUTH OF THE PERFUME RIVER' MAP

Ho Chi Minh Museum

Train Station

Quoc Hoc High School

Contemporary Art Museum

Stadium

RESTAURANTS
Ancient Hué	2
Lac Thien	3
Tan Huong Sen	1

ACCOMMODATION
Green Hotel Hue	3
La Residence	2
Thanh Noi	1

Phu Cam Canal

Redemptorist Church

An Cuu Market

0   500
metres

▽ Nam Giao & The Royal Mausoleums

Duc Duc's Mausoleum

▽ Phia Nam Bus Station (2km) & Phu Bai Airport (14km)

5

THE NGUYEN DYNASTY

In 1802 Prince Nguyen Anh, one of the southern Nguyen lords, defeated the Tay Son Dynasty with the help of a French bishop, Pigneau de Behaine. When Nguyen Anh assumed the throne under the title Emperor Gia Long he thus founded the **Nguyen Dynasty**, which ruled Vietnam from Hué until the abdication of Emperor Bao Dai in 1945. Eleven of the Nguyen emperors are buried in Hué (see p.296), the exceptions being Ham Nghi and Bao Dai; the latter died in Paris in 1997 after four decades in exile, while Ham Nghi was exiled to Algeria and eventually buried there.

Gia Long	1802–20	Ham Nghi	1884–85
Minh Mang	1820–41	Dong Khanh	1885–89
Thieu Tri	1841–47	Thanh Thai	1889–1907
Tu Duc	1847–83	Duy Tan	1907–16
Duc Duc	1883	Khai Dinh	1916–25
Hiep Hoa	1883	Bao Dai	1926–45
Kien Phuc	1883–84		

as are its restaurants serving the city's justly famous speciality foods. Nevertheless, the majority of people pass through Hué fairly quickly, partly because high entrance fees make visiting more than a couple of the major sights beyond many budgets, and partly because of its troublesome **weather**. Hué suffers from the highest rainfall in the country, mostly falling over just three months from October to December when the city regularly floods for a few days, causing damage to the historic architecture, though heavy downpours are possible at any time of year.

Brief history

The land on which Hué now stands belonged to the Kingdom of Champa until 1306, when territory north of Da Nang was exchanged for the hand of a Vietnamese princess under the terms of a peace treaty. The first Vietnamese to settle in the region established their administrative centre near present-day Hué at a place called Hoa Chan, and then in 1558 Lord Nguyen Hoang arrived from Hanoi as governor of the district, at the same time establishing the rule of the Nguyen lords over southern Vietnam which was to last for the next two hundred years. In the late seventeenth century the lords moved the citadel to its present location where it developed into a major town and cultural centre – **Phu Xuan**, which briefly became the capital under the Tay Son emperor Quang Trung (1788–1801).

The Nguyen dynasty

However, it was the next ruler of Vietnam who literally put Hué on the map – Emperor Gia Long, founder of the Nguyen Dynasty. From 1802, he sought to unify the country by moving the capital, lock, stock and dynastic altars, from Thang Long (Hanoi) to the renamed city of **Hué**. Gia Long owed his throne to French military support but his Imperial City was very much a Chinese concept, centred on a Forbidden City reserved for the sovereign, with separate administrative and civilian quarters.

The Nguyen emperors (see box above) were Confucian, conservative rulers, generally suspicious of all Westerners yet unable to withstand the power of France. In 1884 the French were granted land northwest of Hué citadel, and they then seized the city entirely in 1885, leaving the emperors as nominal rulers. Under the Nguyen, Hué became a famous centre of the arts, scholarship and Buddhist learning, but their extravagant building projects and luxurious lifestyle demanded crippling taxes.

Hué ceased to be the capital of Vietnam when Emperor Bao Dai abdicated in 1945; two years later a huge fire destroyed many of the city's wooden temples and palaces. From the early twentieth century the city had been engulfed in social and political unrest led by an anti-colonial educated elite, which simmered away until the 1960s. Tensions finally boiled over in May 1963 when troops fired on thousands of Buddhist nationalists demonstrating against the strongly Catholic regime of President Ngo Dinh Diem (see p.444). The protests escalated into a wave of self-immolations by monks and nuns until government forces moved against the pagodas at the end of the year, rounding up the Buddhist clergy and supposed activists in the face of massive public demonstrations.

Wartime

During the 1968 **Tet Offensive** Hué was torn apart again when the North Vietnamese Army (NVA) held the city for 25 days. Communist forces entered Hué in the early hours of January 31, hoisted their flag above the citadel and found themselves in control of the whole city bar two small military compounds. Armed with lists of names, they began searching out government personnel, sympathizers of the Southern regime, intellectuals, priests, Americans and foreign aid workers. Nearly three thousand bodies were later discovered in mass graves around the city – the victims were mostly civilians who had been shot, beaten to death or buried alive. But the killing hadn't finished: during the ensuing counter-assault as many as five thousand North Vietnamese and Viet Cong, 384 Southern troops and 142 American soldiers died, plus at least another thousand civilians. Hué was all but levelled in the massive fire power unleashed on NVA forces holed up in the citadel but it took a further ten days of agonizing, house-to-house combat to drive the Communists out, in what Stanley Karnow described as "the most bitter battle" of the entire war. Seven years later, on March 26, 1975, the NVA were back to liberate Hué in its pivotal position as the first major town south of the Seventeenth Parallel.

The mammoth task of **rebuilding** Hué has been going on now for more than twenty years but received a boost in 1993 when UNESCO listed the city as a World Heritage Site, which served to mobilize international funding for a whole range of projects, from renovating palaces to the revival of traditional arts and technical skills.

The citadel

Hué's days of glory kicked off in the early nineteenth century when Emperor Gia Long laid out a vast **citadel**, comprising three concentric enclosures, ranged behind the prominent flag tower. Within the citadel's outer wall lies the **Imperial City** (see p.282), containing administrative offices, parks and dynastic temples, with the royal palaces of the **Forbidden Purple City** at its centre. Though wars, fires, typhoons, floods and termites have all taken their toll, it's these Imperial edifices, some now restored to their former magnificence, that constitute Hué's prime tourist attraction. Apart from one museum, there are no specific sights in the outer citadel, but it's a pleasant area to cycle round, especially the northern sector where you'll find many lakes and the prolific **gardens** for which Hué is famed.

In accordance with ancient tradition, the citadel was built in an **auspicious location** chosen to preserve the all-important harmony between the emperor and his subjects, heaven and earth, man and nature. Thus the complex is oriented southeast towards the low hummock of Nui Ngu Binh ("Royal Screen Mountain"), which blocks out harmful influences, while to either side two small islands in the Perfume River represent the Blue Dragon's benevolent spirit in balance with the aggressive White Tiger. Just in case that wasn't protection enough, the whole 520 hectares are enclosed within 7m-high, 20m-thick brick and earth walls built with the help of French engineers, and encircled by a moat and canal. Eight villages had to be relocated when construction began in 1805, and over the next thirty years tens of thousands of workmen laboured to complete more than three hundred palaces, temples, tombs and other royal buildings, some using materials brought down from the former Imperial City in Hanoi.

The flag tower and the sacred cannons

The citadel's massive, 10km-long perimeter wall has survived intact, as has its most prominent feature, the **flag tower**, or *Cot Co* (also known as *Ky Dai*, "the King's Knight"), which dominates the southern battlements. The tower is in fact three squat,

5

brick terraces topped with a flagpole first erected in 1807, where the yellow-starred Viet Cong flag flew briefly during the 1968 Tet Offensive. Ten gates pierce the citadel wall: enter through Ngan Gate, east of the flag tower, to find a parade ground flanked by the nine **sacred cannons**, which were cast in the early nineteenth century in bronze seized from the Tay Son army. The cannons represent the four seasons and five ritual elements of earth, fire, metal, wood and water; originally they stood in front of Ngo Mon Gate, symbolizing the citadel's guardian spirits.

The Imperial City

7am–5pm • 55,000đ

A second moat and defensive wall inside the citadel guard the **Imperial City**, which follows the same symmetrical layout as Beijing's Forbidden City – though oriented northwest-southeast, rather than north-south. The Vietnamese version, popularly known as *Dai Noi* ("the Great Enclosure"), has four gates – one in each wall – though by far the most impressive is south-facing **Ngo Mon**, the Imperial City's principal entrance. In its heyday the complex must have been truly awe-inspiring, a place of glazed yellow and green roof tiles, pavilions of rich red and gilded lacquer and lotus-filled ponds – all surveyed by the emperor with his entourage of haughty mandarins. However, many of its buildings were badly neglected even before the battle for Hué raged through the Imperial City during Tet 1968, and by 1975 a mere twenty out of the original 148 were left standing among the vegetable plots. Some are in the midst of extensive restorations, and those which have been completed are stunning – notably **Thai Hoa Palace**, the **The Mieu** complex and **Dien Tho**. The rest of the Imperial City, especially its northern sector, is a grassed-over expanse full of birds and butterflies where you can still make out foundations and find bullet pockmarks in the plasterwork of ruined walls.

Ngo Mon Gate

In 1833 Emperor Minh Mang replaced an earlier, much less formidable gate with the present dramatic entrance way to the Imperial City, **Ngo Mon**, considered a masterpiece of Nguyen architecture. Ngo Mon (the "Noon" or "Southwest" Gate) has five entrances: the emperor alone used the central entrance paved with stone; two smaller doorways on either side were for the civil and military mandarins, who only rated brick paving, while another pair of giant openings in the wings allowed access to the royal elephants.

Five Phoenix Watchtower

The bulk of Ngo Mon is constructed of massive stone slabs, but perched on top is an elegant pavilion called the **Five Phoenix Watchtower** as its nine roofs are said to resemble five birds in flight when viewed from above. Note that the central roof, under which the emperor passed, is covered with yellow-glazed tiles, a feature of nearly all Hué's royal roofs. Emperors used the watchtower for two major ceremonies each year: the declaration of the lunar New Year; and the announcement of the civil service exam results, depicted here in a lacquer painting. It was also in this pavilion that the last Nguyen emperor, Bao Dai, abdicated in 1945 when he handed over to the new government his symbols of power – a solid gold seal weighing ten kilos and a sheathed sword encrusted with jade.

Thai Hoa Palace

Walking north from Ngo Mon along the city's symmetrical axis, you pass between two square lakes and a pair of *kylin*, mythical dew-drinking animals that are harbingers of peace, to reach **Thai Hoa Palace** ("the Palace of Supreme Harmony"). Not only is this the most spectacular of Hué's palaces, its interior glowing with sumptuous red and gold lacquers, but it's also the most important since this was the throne palace, where major ceremonies such as coronations or royal birthdays took place and foreign ambassadors were received (see box, p.284).

The palace was first constructed in 1805, though the present building dates from 1833 when the French floor tiles and glass door panels were added, and was the only major building in the Imperial City to escape bomb damage. Nevertheless, the throne room's eighty ironwood pillars, swirling with dragons and clouds, had been eaten away by termites and humidity and were on the point of collapse when rescue work began in 1991. During the restoration every column, weighing two tonnes apiece, had to be replaced manually and then painted with twelve coats of lacquer, each coat taking one month to dry. Behind the throne room a souvenir shop now sells books and tapes of Hué folk songs where once the emperor

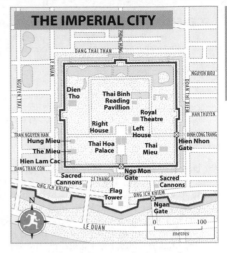

prepared for his grand entrance. It also contains two large dioramas depicting the Imperial City and flag tower in their heyday.

The Forbidden Purple City

From Thai Hoa Palace the emperor would have walked north through the Great Golden Gate into the third and last enclosure, the **Forbidden Purple City**. This area, enclosed by a low wall, was reserved for residential palaces, living quarters of the state physician and nine ranks of royal concubines, plus kitchens and pleasure pavilions. Many of these buildings were destroyed in the 1947 fire, leaving most of the Forbidden Purple City as open ground, a "mood piece", haunted by fragments of wall and overgrown terraces.

The Left House and Right House

However, a handful of buildings remain, including the restored **Left House** and **Right House** facing each other across a courtyard immediately behind Thai Hoa Palace. Civil and military mandarins would spruce themselves up here before proceeding to an audience with the monarch. Of the two, the Right House (actually to your left – the names refer to the emperor's viewpoint) is the more complete with its ornate murals and gargantuan mirror in a gilded frame, a gift from the French to Emperor Dong Khanh.

Thai Binh Reading Pavilion

Walking northeast from here you pass behind the Royal Theatre, built in 1826 and now belonging to the University of Fine Arts, to find the **Thai Binh Reading Pavilion**, an appealing, two-tier structure surrounded by bonsai gardens. The pavilion was built by Thieu Tri and then restored by Khai Dinh, who added the kitsch mosaics. This was where the emperor came to listen to music and commune with nature, but at the time of writing it was in a state of disrepair.

The Ancestral Altars

The other main cluster of sights lies a short walk away in the southwest corner of the Imperial City. Aligned on a south–north axis, the procession kicks off with **Hien Lam Cac** ("Pavilion of Everlasting Clarity"), a graceful, three-storey structure with some notable woodwork, followed by the **Nine Dynastic Urns**. Considered the epitome of Hué craftsmanship, the bronze urns were cast during the reign of Minh Mang and are ornamented with scenes of mountains, rivers, rain clouds and wildlife, plus one or two stray bullet marks. Each urn is dedicated to an emperor: the middle urn, which is also

5

CEREMONIES AT THE THAI HOA PALACE

On these occasions the emperor sat on the raised dais, wearing a golden tunic and a crown decorated with nine dragons, under a spectacular gilded canopy. He faced south across the **Esplanade of Great Salutations**, a stone-paved courtyard where the mandarins stood, civil mandarins to the left and military on the right, lined up in their appointed places beside eighteen stelae denoting the nine subdivided ranks. A French traveller in the 1920s witnessed the colourful spectacle, with "perfume-bearers in royal-blue, fan-bearers in sky-blue waving enormous yellow feather fans, musicians and guardsmen and ranks of mandarins in their curious hats and gorgeous, purple-embroidered dragons, kow-towing down, down on their noses amidst clouds of incense – and all in a setting of blood-red lacquer scrawled with gold".

the largest at 2600kg, honours Gia Long. They stand across the courtyard from the long, low building of **The Mieu**, the Nguyens' dynastic temple erected in 1822 by Minh Mang to worship his father. Since then, altars have been added for each emperor in turn, except Duc Duc and Hiep Hoa, who reigned only briefly, and Bao Dai who died in exile in 1997; the three anti-French sovereigns – Ham Nghi, Thanh Thai and Duy Tan – had to wait until after Independence in 1954 for theirs. Take a look inside to see the line of altar tables, most sporting a portrait or photo of the monarch. Behind each is a bed equipped with a sleeping mat, pillows and other accoutrements and, finally, a shrine holding funeral tablets for the emperor and his wife or wives. Anniversaries of the emperors' deaths are still commemorated at The Mieu, attended by members of the royal family in all their finery.

Hung Mieu

Exit The Mieu by its west door, beside a 170-year-old pine tree trained in the shape of a flying dragon, and follow the path north into the next compound to find **Hung Mieu**. This temple is dedicated to the Nguyen ancestors and specifically to the parents of Gia Long, and is distinguished by its fine carving.

Dien Tho

North again, **Dien Tho**, the queen mother's residence, is worth a look. Built in a mix of Vietnamese and French architectural styles, the palace later served as Bao Dai's private residence, and the downstairs reception rooms are now set out with period furniture, echoing the photos of the palace in use in the 1930s.

Royal Museum of Fine Arts

An Dinh Palace, Nguyen Khuyen • 7am–7pm • 50,000đ

From the eastern exit of the Imperial City (via Cua Hien Nhon – the "Gate of Humanity") it's a short walk to the **Royal Museum of Fine Arts**, which boasts an interesting display of former royal paraphernalia. Its most valuable exhibits are the lively paintings on glass that adorn the ironwood columns, a series of stone gongs and a wealth of furniture decorated with mother-of-pearl inlay. The museum is currently located inside An Dinh Palace, just to the south of central Hué, but may in time move back to its former location inside Long An Palace, just to the east of the Imperial City at 3 Le Truc.

Dong Ba Market

Tran Hung Dao

If crossing the Perfume River on Trang Thien Bridge, you'll pass **Dong Ba Market**, a rambling covered market at the southeast corner of the citadel, and one of the

5

epicentres of Hué's commercial life. Fruit, fish and vegetable vendors overflow into the surrounding spaces, while in the downstairs hall you'll find Hué's contribution to the world of fashion, the *non bai tho*, or **poem hat**. These look just like the normal conical hat but have a stencil, traditionally of a romantic poem, inserted between the palm fronds – and only visible when held up to the light. The market is within walking distance of the centre, but a more enjoyable way to get there is to hop on one of the sampans that shuttle back and forth from beside the Dap Da causeway.

Phu Cat

Hué's civilian and merchant quarter grew up alongside the citadel on a triangular island now divided into **Phu Cat**, Phu Hiep and Phu Hau districts. This part of town has a completely different atmosphere: it's a lively, crowded, dilapidated area centred on Chi Lang, in Phu Cat District, which still boasts some single-storey, wood and red-tiled houses as well as more ornate, colonial-era shophouses. The area was once home to the Chinese community, and five **Assembly Halls** still stand along Chi Lang. Old trees shade the Dong Ba Canal on the island's southwestern side, where Bach Dang was the site of anti-government demonstrations in the 1960s, centred around **Dieu De Pagoda**. There's nothing compelling to draw you onto the island, particularly if you've already seen the Chinese temples of Hoi An and Ho Chi Minh City, but the area provides a bustling contrast to the otherwise sedate streets of Hué.

The Chinese Assembly Halls

Chua Ong 319 Chi Lang • Chieu Ung 223 Chi Lang • Free

Chinese immigrants to Hué settled in five congregations around their separate **Assembly Halls**, of which the most interesting is **Chua Ong**. Founded by the Phuoc Kien (Fujian) community in the mid-1800s and rebuilt on several occasions, including after Viet Cong mortars hit a US munitions boat on the river nearby in 1968 and destroyed the pagoda plus surrounding houses. Surprisingly, there's no Buddha on the main altar but instead several doctors of medicine, along with General Quan Cong to the right and Thien Hau to the left, both protectors of sailors. The story goes that Quan Cong sat on the main altar until a devastating cholera epidemic in 1918 when he was displaced by the doctors, and the outbreak ended soon after. Of the other halls, **Chieu Ung** is worth dropping in to. The gilded altar displays some skilled carpentry. This pagoda was also founded in the nineteenth century by ethnic Chinese from Hai Nam, and has been rebuilt at least twice since.

The European city

Although the French became the de facto rulers of Vietnam after 1884, they left the emperors in the citadel and built their administrative city across the Perfume River on the south bank. The main artery of the **European city** was riverside Le Loi where the French Resident's office stood (now the *Le Residence* hotel), together with other important buildings such as **Quoc Hoc High School** and the *Frères Morin* hotel (now the *Saigon Morin*). Residential streets spread out south of the river as far as the Phu Cam Canal, and are linked to the citadel by Clemenceau Bridge, renamed Trang Tien Bridge after 1954. Apart from the high school, the only major sight is the **Ho Chi Minh Museum**, not just the obligatory gesture in this case as Ho did spend much of his childhood in Hué. The extraordinary, tiered spire of the **Redemptorist Church** dominates the southern horizon with its improbable blend of Gothic and Cubism created by a local architect in the late 1950s. The church caters to some of Hué's twenty thousand Catholics and is interesting to view in passing, though the interior is less striking.

Museum of Contemporary Art

1 Pham Boi Chau • 7.30–11am & 2–5pm • Free

Admirers of modern Vietnamese art should call in at the **Museum of Contemporary Art** – in fact an exhibition of the works of Diem Phung Thi, who was born in Hué in 1920. The old villa provides the perfect setting for her chunky "modules" developed from Chinese calligraphy.

The Ho Chi Minh Museum

7 Le Loi • Tues–Sun 7.30–11am & 2–4.30pm • 10,000đ

Ho Chi Minh was born near Vinh in Nghe An Province (see p.321), but spent ten years at school in Hué (1895–1901 and 1906–1909) where his father worked as a civil mandarin. The modern **Ho Chi Minh Museum** presents these years in the context of the anti-French struggle and then takes the story on to 1960s' peace protests in Hué and reunification. The most interesting material consists of family photos and rare glimpses of early twentieth-century Hué. You can still see the house where Ho lived for a time with his father in Duong No Village on the way to Thuan An Beach (see p.292).

ARRIVAL AND DEPARTURE   HUÉ

By plane Phu Bai Airport lies 15km southeast of the city centre. Arriving flights are met by a bus (50,000đ), which takes you to central hotels, and by metered taxis (around $15). The Vietnam Airlines office is at 23 Nguyen Van Cu (☎054 382 4709).

Destinations: Hanoi (3 daily; 1hr 10min); Ho Chi Minh City (6 daily; 1hr 20min).

By train The station lies about 1.5km from the centre of town at the far western end of Le Loi. Note that trains out of Hué get booked up, especially sleepers to Ho Chi Minh City and Hanoi, so make onward travel arrangements as early as possible (ticket office open daily 7–11.30am & 1.30–8pm).

Destinations: Da Nang (6 daily; 2hr 20min–3hr); Dong Ha (5 daily; 1hr 1hr 20min); Dong Hoi (6 daily; 2hr

40min–3hr 30min); Hanoi (6 daily; 13–16hr); Ho Chi Minh City (6 daily; 19–24hr); Nha Trang (6 daily; 11hr 20min–15hr); Ninh Binh (3 daily; 14hr).

By bus Public buses arrive at one of two stations – Phia Nam, just south of the city centre in An Cuu, for links with the south; and Phia Bac, off the citadel's northwest corner, for links with the north. However, almost no travellers use them, the vast majority arriving and departing either by train (recommended for long journeys) or on tour company buses. The latter pick up and drop off at various points around the main hotel district.

Destinations: Da Nang (3hr); Dong Ha (2hr 30min); Dong Hoi (5hr); Hoi An (4hr).

GETTING AROUND

By bicycle Hué's wide avenues become crowded during rush hour (7–9am & 4–6pm), but generally the most enjoyable way of getting around the city's scattered sights – and especially of touring the Royal Mausoleums – is by bicycle. Most hotels and guesthouses, plus a few cafés, offer bike rental (from $1/day) and motorbikes (from $5/day).

By bike and car tour Some places offer guided motorbike

tours of Hué and its environs, most pertinently Café on Thu Wheels and You & Me (see p.291), while most hotels and agencies can arrange car rental (around $35 per day).

By taxi There are countless xe om and taxis in Hué. Two reputable taxi companies are Mai Linh Taxi (☎054 389 8989) and Hué Taxi (☎054 381 8181).

REVOLUTIONARY EDUCATION

Ho Chi Minh was the most famous student to attend **Quoc Hoc High School**, which stands almost opposite his museum on Le Loi. The school was founded in 1896 as the National College, dedicated to the education of royal princes and future administrators who learnt the history of their European "motherland" – all in French until 1945. Ho studied here for at least a year before being expelled for taking part in anti-government demonstrations. Other revolutionary names that appear on the roster are Prime Minister Pham Van Dong, General Giap and Party Secretary Le Duan, while former president of South Vietnam Ngo Dinh Diem was also a student. Even during the 1960s Quoc Hoc had a justly earned reputation for breeding dissident intellectuals, and after reunification in 1975 some staff were sent for "re-education". Quoc Hoc is still a functioning school today – and, in fact, one of the most prestigious in the whole land.

5

INFORMATION AND TOURS

Tourist information The best bet for tourist information is either your hotel or one of the tour agents; staff at the *Mandarin Café* (see p.291) are particularly helpful. Every hotel and tour agent hands out photocopied maps, but for a detailed city plan try the big hotels and bookstalls on Le Loi.

Tours There are more travel agencies than it's possible to count in the Nguyen Tri Phuong and Pham Ngu Lao areas, and competition is cut-throat. However, it's good news for the traveller, as half-a-dozen prices can be checked with a few sideways steps – it certainly pays to shop around.

ACCOMMODATION

The majority of accommodation in Hué is located south of the Perfume River; **top-class establishments** overlook the river, while budget hotels and guesthouses are scattered in the streets behind, particularly the **backpacker enclave** of Hung Vuong and Nguyen Tri Phuong, and along Pham Ngu Lao. A few hotels have opened up within the citadel, though as yet you'll find better value south of the river.

Asia Hotel 17 Pham Ngu Lao ☎054 383 0283, ⓦasiahotel.com.vn; map p.289. Tall boutique-style hotel, with attractive, generously proportioned rooms and breakfasts with a view. There's also a tiny pool on site, as well as sauna facilities. Book online for some healthy discounts. **$80**

★ **Binh Duong III** 4/34 Nguyen Tri Phuong ☎054 383 0145, ⓔbinhduong1@dng.vnn.vn; map p.289. A wonderful place to stay – cheap, friendly and cosy. There are internet-ready computers in all rooms, and good city views from the upper levels. There's a slightly cheaper sister establishment just up the alley. **$15**

Binh Minh Sunrise 36 Nguyen Tri Phuong ☎054 382 5526, ⓦbinhminhhue.com; map p.289. Bright, welcoming hotel in a great location with a range of clean, homely rooms, some with balconies looking towards the mountains. A popular and good-value option, though rooms at the front will be noisy; it's worth an extra $5–10 for the better ones. **$15**

Green Hotel Hué 2 Le Loi ☎054 382 4668, ⓦgreenhotel -hue.com; map p.279. Large and architecturally adventurous hotel right next to the train station. Green is the theme in the fresh, rattan-furnished rooms, four levels of which curl around a central outdoor swimming pool. **$80**

Hué Backpackers 10 Pham Ngu Lao ☎054 382 6567, ⓦhanoibackpackershostel.com; map p.289. The only hostel in town, and it's a goodie. All dorm rooms are en-suite, while the ground-floor common area is always buzzing – especially so in the evening. Couples may be interested in the cheap "double dorm beds" for couples... which, it has to be said, occasionally result in predictable consequences. Dorm **$6**, double **$15**

★ **Huenino Hotel** 14 Nguyen Cong Tru ☎054 625 2171, ⓦhueninohotel.com; map p.289. Superb value, friendly staff and mouthwatering breakfasts at this small hotel, which has become a real favourite with budget travellers to the city. They have a habit of welcoming you back with a glass of juice – even if you've just popped to the shops. **$14**

Huong Giang 51 Le Loi ☎054 382 2122, ⓦhuong giangtourist.com; map p.289. Built in 1962 and renovated along a bamboo-and-rattan theme, with a pool, gardens, tennis court and other four-star facilities. It's cheaper and more homely than the next-door *Century Riverside*, but can't match the *Saigon Morin* for service and room size. Larger rooms overlooking the river offer better value for money. **$100**

Imperial Hotel 8 Hung Vuong ☎054 388 2222, ⓦimperial-hotel.com.vn; map p.289. The first five-star hotel in Hué dominates the skyline near the Perfume River; plush carpets lead the way to suitably well-appointed rooms, while the complex also includes a fitness centre, swimming pool and classy restaurant. Ask about discounts – the place often feels near-empty. **$180**

Impression Hotel 66/7 Le Loi ☎054 382 8403, ⓦhueimpressionhotel.com; map p.289. Also known as the *Dong Tam*, this is cheap yet looks rather plush from the outside, especially when the sun is shining on the pool in the front garden. The rooms are bare and don't quite match, but are still a steal. It's on a small alley off Le Loi. **$10**

★ **La Residence** 5 Le Loi ☎054 383 7475, ⓦla-residence-hue.com; map, p.279. Formerly the French governor's residence (hence the name), and overlooking the Perfume River, this intensively renovated hotel blends early-twentieth-century Art Deco design with excellent services. There's a palpable colonial air to the place, one best savoured with a cocktail by the riverside pool. **$160**

Mercure 38 Le Loi ☎054 393 6688, ⓦmercure.com; map p.289. Relatively new start-up whose stylish rooms alternate between plush carpets and wooden flooring – try to nab a room on the upper floors, especially those with a river view. Other facilities are somewhat minimal, though mention must be made of the upper-floor outdoor swimming pool. **$75**

★ **Orchid Hotel** 30a Chu Van An ☎054 383 1177, ⓦorchidhotel.com.vn; map p.289. Yet another contender for the friendliest hotel staff in the city – smiling attendants usher their customers to superbly stylish rooms, decorated with orchid petals and other attractive flourishes. Lastly, the breakfasts are astonishingly good – the staff must be tired of guests singing praises morning after morning. **$30**

★**Saigon Morin** 30 Le Loi ☎054 382 3526, ⓦmorinhotel.com.vn; map below. Hué's most famous French-era hotel has been renovated to four-star standards, but still retains some of its colonial charm, not least in the garden courtyard; swing by for a look, even if you're not staying. The rooms are a good size, if a little bland, and

kitted out with all the equipment you'd exp[...] mini-bar, bathtub and hairdryer. Facilities in[...] bar, two restaurants, a small pool ($5 to non[...] internet access. $115

Thanh Noi 57 Dang Dung ☎054 352 247[...] ⓔthanhnoi@dng.vnn.vn; map p.279. One of the few

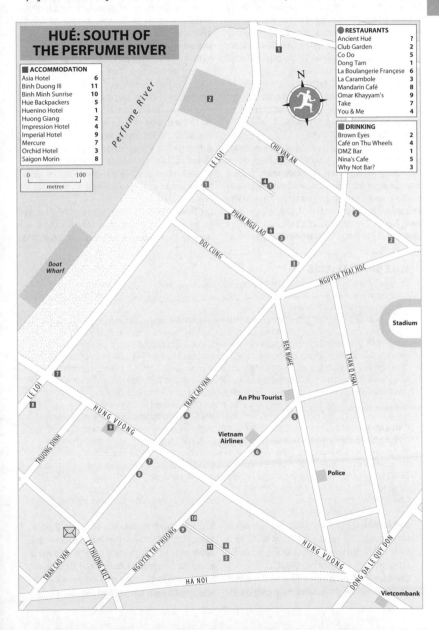

HUÉ: SOUTH OF THE PERFUME RIVER

ACCOMMODATION

Asia Hotel	6
Binh Duong III	11
Binh Minh Sunrise	10
Hue Backpackers	5
Huenino Hotel	1
Huong Giang	2
Impression Hotel	4
Imperial Hotel	9
Mercure	7
Orchid Hotel	3
Saigon Morin	8

RESTAURANTS

Ancient Hué	7
Club Garden	2
Co Do	5
Dong Tam	1
La Boulangerie Française	6
La Carambole	3
Mandarin Café	8
Omar Khayyam's	9
Take	7
You & Me	4

DRINKING

Brown Eyes	2
Café on Thu Wheels	4
DMZ Bar	1
Nina's Cafe	5
Why Not Bar?	3

tels north of the river, near the citadel, offering a touch of character in its Imperial-style decor and nice outdoor setting with pool and garden. There have been occasional problems with staff and cleanliness – check it out before you pay. $25

EATING

Ancient Hué 4/4/8 Lane 35 Pham Thi Lien; map p.289. Not in the city centre at all, but in the garden house district to the west (see p.279). However, this is the best of the few local restaurants serving a fusion of modern and Imperial-style cuisine, which is augmented by tranquil surroundings and attentive service. Set menus $20 per head, individual mains from $8. Tues–Sun 10am–9pm.

Club Garden 8 Vo Thi Sau ☏ 054 382 6327; map p.289. One of several garden restaurants along this street serving classic Vietnamese cuisine, with reasonably priced set menus – you'll be able to eat for under $5. Try and reserve a table outside. Daily 9am–11pm.

Co Do 22 Ben Nghe; map p.289. Small and inexpensive, no-frills restaurant offering a limited menu of local dishes. Lemongrass and chilli are the predominant flavours, accompanying squid, chicken or shrimps. Some people may find the seasoning on the heavy side, but the food is all very fresh and well prepared. Mains from $2.50. Daily 7am–8pm.

Dong Tam 48/7 Le Loi; map p.289. Vegetarian restaurant run by a Buddhist family. The short menu includes veggie banh khoai (see box below) and good-value combination plates, as well as decent set menus for $5 or so. It's best at lunchtime when the food's freshest and you can sit in the garden courtyard. Daily 10am–8pm.

La Boulangerie Française 46 Nguyen Tri Phuong; map p.289. A French charity runs this café and bakery school for local orphans in the hope that they gain employment after graduation. Their shop has an array of light and delicious French pastries (starting at around $1), perfect for breakfast or packed away for long boat rides. Daily 8am–8pm.

★ **La Carambole** 19 Pham Ngu Lao ☏ 054 381 0491; map p.289. The first foreign-owned restaurant in the city, and still the best. Prices are surprisingly reasonable (mains $5 and up), and the menu is full of tempting French goodies hard to find in Vietnam – cheese platters, quiche, banana flambé and so on. Reservations recommended. Daily 9am–9pm.

Lac Thien 6 Dinh Tien Hoang; map p.279. Restaurant run by a deaf-mute family who communicate by sign language. The food is cheap but pretty tasty, especially the

---

HUÉ SPECIALITIES

One good argument for staying in Hué an extra couple of days is its many speciality foods, best sampled at local stalls and street kitchens. Here are the main dishes, and the locals' tips for the best places to eat them:

Banh beo Order this afternoon dish and you get a whole trayful of individual plates, each containing a small amount of steamed rice-flour dough topped with spices, shrimp flakes and a morsel of pork crackling; add a little sweetened *nuoc mam* sauce to each dish and tuck in with a teaspoon. *Banh nam*, or *banh lam*, is a similar idea but spread thinly in an oblong, steamed in a banana leaf and eaten with rich *nuoc mam* sauce. Manioc flour is used instead of rice for *banh loc*, making a translucent parcel of whole shrimps, sliced pork and spices steamed in a banana leaf, but this time the *nuoc mam* is pepped up with a dash of chilli. Finally, *ram it* consists of two small dollops of sticky rice-flour dough, one fried and one steamed, to dip in a spicy sauce. You'll find good places in which to sample these dishes all over the city.

Banh khoai Probably the most famous Hué dish, a small, crispy yellow **pancake** made of egg and rice flour, fried up with shrimp, pork and bean sprouts and eaten with a special peanut and sesame sauce (*nuoc leo*), plus a vegetable accompaniment of star fruit, green banana, lettuce and mint. Amazingly, it's even more delicious than it sounds.

Bun bo Spicy rice-noodle beef soup flavoured with citronella, shrimp and basil; also called *bun ga* with chicken, or *bun bo gio heo* with beef and pork.

Chè A refreshing drink made from green bean and coconut (*chè xanh dua*), fruit (*chè trai cay*) or, if you're lucky, lotus seed (*chè hat sen*).

Bun Bo Hué 11b Ly Thuong Kiet. Of all the places serving bun bo, this simple affair has by far the most renown. Any local will confirm this, you should definitely sample it yourself for 15,000đ.

Chè Hém 29/31 Hung Vuong. For a local speciality there aren't as many places serving chè as you'd expect, but this is centrally located and as tasty as you'll get.

Hanh 11 Phu Duc Chinh. Here you'll find *banh khoai* freshly prepared throughout the day – 15,000đ will be enough for a plateful. It's another local favourite, and packed at mealtimes – many of the regulars will wonder what on earth you're doing on their turf.

TRADITIONAL ENTERTAINMENT

Under the Nguyen emperors, Hué was the cultural and artistic as well as political capital of Vietnam. A rich tradition of **dance** and **music** evolved from popular culture, from the complex rituals of the court and from religious ceremonies. Though much of this legacy has been lost, considerable effort has gone into reviving Hué folk songs, *Ca Hué*, which you can now sample, drifting down the Perfume River on a balmy Hué evening (tickets 60,000đ).

Historically the **Perfume River** was a place of pleasure where prostitutes cruised in their sampans and artists entertained the gentry with poetry and music. While the former officially no longer exist, today's folk-song performances are based on the old traditions, eulogizing the city's beautiful scenery or the ten charms of a Hué woman – including long hair, dreamy eyes, flowing *ao dai* and a conical hat – while she waits for her lover beside the river. This sounds great, but be warned that the experience can feel somewhat cheap – the fees given to performers are far too low to recruit those with genuine talent, and in 2009 the state of affairs was fiercely lambasted by local authorities.

The city authorities have also instigated a biennial arts festival (held in June) featuring not only folk songs, kite-flying, water-puppetry and other local traditions, but also international groups.

Hué staples (see box opposite); most plump for the *banh khoai* ($1.50), served with a mountain of leaves and lashings of peanut sauce. Daily 8am–7pm.

★ **Mandarin Café** 24 Tran Cao Van; map p.289. A leading light of Hué's backpacker business, this unassuming café off the main road rustles up cheap but very tasty Vietnamese and Western fare (mains from $2.50). Owner-photographer Mr Cu and his staff are also excellent sources of information and can assist with boat trips, bike and car rental and tours. Daily 7am–10pm.

Omar Khayyam's 34 Nguyen Tri Phuong; map p.289. Deservedly popular restaurant for its authentic Indian fare, which includes a good vegetarian and *thali* selection. You'll pay around $5 per head for a decent meal. Daily 7am–9pm.

Take 134 Tran Cao Van; map p.289. The best Japanese restaurant in town – okay, the only Japanese restaurant in town. However, it's not too bad at all, if a tiny bit pricey. The tempura (flash-fried comestibles) are particularly good. Daily 11am–9pm.

Tan Huong Sen 96b Nguyen Trai; map p.279. Just west of the citadel, and set in the middle of a small lagoon (complete with walking plank), the bamboo-decorated restaurant offers good-value, fresh seafood in unique surroundings. It's a popular dating spot for locals. Daily 8am–8pm.

You & Me 38 Tran Cao Van; map p.289. Backpacker favourite, with a good, cheap range of local dishes – meat, noodles, rice and other staples. Also a good place to ask about tours – their motorbike trips around the DMZ can be a blast. Daily 8am–10pm.

NIGHTLIFE

The bars listed here are open through the day, closing times are essentially based on demand – at least one place will be going until the wee hours.

Brown Eyes Chu Van An; map p.289. "Red Eyes" would be a more appropriate name for this bar – many a sozzled backpacker has stumbled from its doors into the light of early morning. Staff are fun, and there's a pool table to test your focus.

Café on Thu Wheels 3/34 Nguyen Tri Phuong; map p.289. Jot your own Thu-related pun on the wall at this tiny café-bar, which has long been a popular backpacker pit-stop. They also run good motorbike tours around Hué.

DMZ Bar 44 Le Loi; map p.289. Exactly what you'd expect of a Western bar – pool table, cold beers, Western grub and occasional live music. The clientele is a mix of

backpackers, expats and package tourists, and most seem to have a good time – you'll see missives to this end plastered across the walls.

Nina's Cafe 16/34 Nguyen Tri Phuong; map p.289. Simple, cheap and friendly affair up backpacker alley, with plastic chairs arrayed around a small courtyard. It's great for juice in the day, or as a quiet place for an evening beer – this is one place that will usually have closed by 9pm.

Why Not Bar? 21 Vo Thi Sau; map p.289. Comfy, open-air pub that often gets crowded at night when the music cranks up. Also serves good burgers, toasties and hotdogs, as well as standard Vietnamese fare.

5

Banks and exchange Vietcombank, 78 Hung Vuong, exchanges cash and travellers' cheques and has a 24hr ATM outside. More convenient is the exchange bureau outside the *Saigon Morin* hotel, which is also open longer hours (Mon–Sat 7am–10pm) with a 24hr ATM.

Hospital Hué Central Hospital, 16 Le Loi ☎ 054 382 2325.

Internet access If your hotel doesn't have internet access then head to the backpacker enclave of Hung Vuong and Nguyen Tri Phuong for internet cafés.

Pharmacies You'll find well-stocked pharmacies at 9 Hoang Hoa Tham (actually round the corner on Tran Cao Van) and 7 Ben Nghe.

Post office The GPO occupies a grand new building at 8 Hoang Hoa Tham, and also has internet facilities. Sub-branches are located at 38 Le Loi and in the station complex.

Around Hué

For the most part the Nguyen emperors lived their lives within Hué's citadel walls, but on certain occasions they emerged to participate in important rituals at symbolic locations around the city. Today these places are of interest more for their history than anything much to see on the ground, though the mouldering **Royal Arena** still hints at past spectacles. A visit to at least a couple of the **Royal Mausoleums**, however, is not to be missed – it's in these eclectic architectural confections in the hills to the south of Hué that the spirit of the Nguyen emperors lives on. Taking a boat along the **Perfume River** to get to the best mausoleums also offers the chance to stop off at the **Thien Mu Pagoda** and **Hon Chen Temple** on the way (see box, p.294).

Thuan An Beach is a bike-ride away, if you have the time and energy, making for an attractive journey across the estuary with views of fish farms to either side, though the beach itself is nothing spectacular. Further afield, one of the most popular excursions from Hué is a whirlwind day-trip round the **DMZ** (see p.301). **Bach Ma National Park** (see p.277) is also within striking distance.

West along the Perfume River

Hug the north bank of the Perfume River west of the citadel and you'll stumble across a few interesting sights, including the pagodas of **Thien Mu** and **Van Mieu**, the traditional garden houses of **Kim Long Village**, and the Temple of **Hon Chen**.

GETTING AROUND   WEST ALONG THE PERFUME RIVER

By bike These sights are most easily covered on a boat tour (see box, p.294), but all bar Hon Chen can be visited on an easy bike ride from the centre of Hué (6km; 30min). You can cross the river on the city centre bridges, but more exciting is the "footpath" that forms the eastern edge of the railway tracks. If you've got time it's a pleasant cycle ride on from Van Mieu (see p.294) along an empty country lane beside the river.

The Garden Houses

Donation (15,000đ)

Travelling by road to Thien Mu along the north bank of the river you pass through **Kim Long** village, a peaceful area of quiet lanes and canals where in the late nineteenth-century mandarins and other Imperial officials built their houses, surrounded by lush gardens. The seven most interesting of these "**garden houses**" have now been preserved, all of them lived in, and four remain open to the public. Recently a few have taken advantage of their fame and turned into decidedly unappealing cafés or restaurants.

The houses are strung along Phu Mong lane, which heads north from the riverbank just before 86 Kim Long; the turning is 1km west of the train tracks and a little hard to spot, so keep your eyes peeled. The first of the houses you come to, on the right behind an entrance arch at number 20, was built by one of Emperor Gia Long's most senior generals. It's now a café. Continuing along Phu Mong lane, take the first turning right to find the other houses.

Though there's not too much to see here these days, the side-road does contain one of Hué's best restaurants, *Ancient Hué* (see p.290).

An Lac Vien

1c Phu Mong • Head east from number 20 Phu Mong, taking the right fork and following the lane round to the end

Perhaps the most interesting of the garden houses is the last, **An Lac Vien**. It was built in 1888 by a junior mandarin under Thanh Thai. His grandson can give you an English-language leaflet and proudly show you round the house, full of family

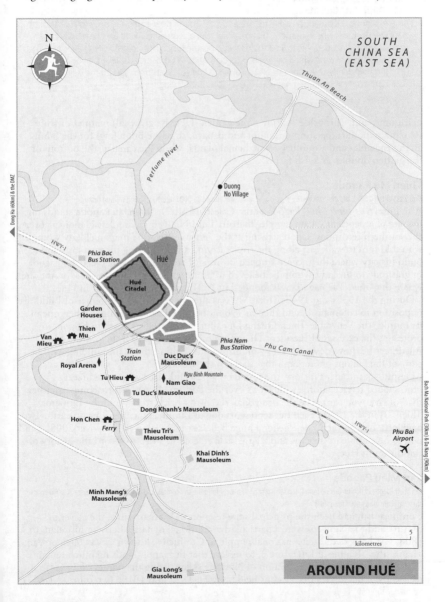

AROUND HUÉ

5

BOAT TRIPS ON THE PERFUME RIVER

A sizeable number of people still live in boats on the **Perfume River** and the waterways of Hué, such as the Dong Ba and Phu Cam canals, despite government efforts to settle them elsewhere. It's possible to join them, if only temporarily, by taking a boat trip, puttering about in front of the citadel on a misty Hué morning, watching the slow bustle of river life. A day's boating on the Perfume River is a good way to soak up some of the atmosphere of Hué and do a little gentle sightseeing off the roads. The standard **boat trip** takes you to **Thien Mu Pagoda**, **Hon Chen Temple** and the most rewarding mausoleums, usually those of **Tu Duc**, **Khai Dinh** and **Minh Mang**. However, if you want to visit some of the others or spend more time exploring, it's usually possible to take a bicycle on the boat and cycle back to Hué, though double-check this when you book the trip. Most tour agents (see p.288) and hotels offer river tours starting at $2 per person, including a very meagre lunch but no guide. However, all entrance fees are extra, which can work out costly at 55,000đ per mausoleum. If you'd rather do it independently, the same agents can arrange charter boats from $30 for the day, or hone your bargaining skills at the boat wharf beside the Trang Tien Bridge.

---

heirlooms, and – his pride and joy – the garden. Here he grows all manner of fruits (banana, sapodilla, persimmon, plum and papaya, to name but a few) for the family altar, vegetables and a number of medicinal plants, while the canal at the bottom of the garden doubles as a fish farm.

Thien Mu Pagoda

3km west of the citadel, and best reached by bicycle or xe om (latter around 45,000đ return including waiting time)

Also known as *Linh Mu* ("Pagoda of the Celestial Lady"), **Thien Mu Pagoda** stands on the site of an ancient Cham temple. In 1601 Lord Nguyen Hoang left Hanoi to govern the southern territories. Upon arriving at the Perfume River he met an elderly woman who told him to walk east along the river carrying a smouldering incense stick and to build his city where the incense stopped burning. Later Lord Hoang erected a pagoda in gratitude to the lady, whom he believed to be a messenger from the gods, on the site where they met. The pagoda was founded in 1601, making it the oldest in Hué.

During the 1930s and 1940s Thien Mu was already renowned as a centre of Buddhist opposition to colonialism, and then in 1963 it became instantly famous when one of its monks, the Venerable Thich Quang Duc, burned himself to death in Saigon, in protest at the excesses of President Diem's regime (see box, p.81); the powder-blue Austin car he drove down in is now on display just behind the main building, with a copy of the famous photograph that shocked the world.

Despite its turbulent history, the pagoda is a peaceful place where the breezy, pine-shaded terrace affords wide views over the Perfume River. Approaching by either road or river you can't miss the octagonal, seven-tier brick **stupa**, built by Emperor Thieu Tri in the 1840s; each tier represents one of Buddha's incarnations on earth. Two **pavilions**, one on each side, shelter a huge bell, cast in 1710, weighing over 2000kg and said to be audible in the city, and a large stele erected in 1715 to record the history of Buddhism in Hué.

Van Mieu Pagoda

Van Mieu Pagoda is 1km further on from Thien Mu Pagoda (4km away from the city centre), and will likely cost an extra 20,000đ on a xe om from there (or 65,000đ from Hué)

Confucianism had been the principal state religion in Vietnam since the eleventh century and the Nguyens were a particularly traditional dynasty. Early in his reign, in 1808, Gia Long dedicated a national temple to Confucius, known as **Van Mieu** or Van Thanh (the "Temple of Literature"), to replace that in Hanoi. Nothing much remains of the complex, beyond a collection of 32 stone stelae listing the names of 297 recipients of doctorates from exams held between 1822 and 1919. Two other stelae, under small shelters, record edicts from Minh Mang and Thieu Tri banning the "abuse of eunuchs and royal maternal relatives". You get a fine view of the royal landing stage and temple gate passing by on a Perfume River boat trip (see box opposite).

Hon Chen Temple

20,000đ • Hon Chen Temple is 9km from Hué and is only accessible from the river. If you don't want to take a tour, hire a sampan either from the ferry station directly opposite the temple (accessible from the riverside road), or from Minh Mang pier: it can be as cheap as 30,000đ per person for the return trip

Beyond Van Mieu boats head south to stop at the rocky promontory of **Hon Chen Temple**, named "Temple of the Jade Bowl" after the concave hill under which it sits. Again it's the scenery of russet temple roofs among towering trees that is memorable, though the site has been sacred since the Cham people came here to worship their divine protectress Po Nagar, whom the Vietnamese adopted as Y A Na, the Mother Goddess. Emperor Minh Mang restored Hon Chen Temple in the 1830s, but it was Dong Khanh who had a particular soft spot for the goddess after she predicted he would be emperor. He enlarged the temple in 1886, declared himself Y A Na's younger brother and is now worshipped alongside his favourite goddess in the main sanctuary, **Hué Nam**, up from the landing stage and to the right. Of several shrines and temples that populate the hillside, Hué Nam is the most interesting, particularly for its unique nine-tier altar table and a small, upper sanctuary room accessible via two steep staircases.

South of the river

You'll hit, or at least pass, a few sights on your way south to the mausoleums (bar that of Duc Duc, which sits immediately south of the city centre). Happily, all are easily accessible by bicycle, though many opt instead for a xe om tour. Directly west of the train station is the **Royal Arena**, once the site of much imperial merriment, but now sadly closed off. Heading south instead from the station, you'll come to **Nam Giao**, once the site of Imperial rites; swing a right and you'll soon find yourself at **Tu Hieu**, a gorgeous pagoda.

The Royal Arena

On the south bank of the Perfume River stands the **Royal Arena**, or Ho Quyen. Firstly, it's important to note that at the time of writing it had been **closed off** to visitors, with no apparent plans for its re-opening. However, such is the historical importance of the site that it's certainly worth asking around for the latest updates – it's also occasionally possible to track down a guard with the keys.

In Imperial times, Ho Quyen was where the emperors amused themselves with fights between elephants and tigers. Originally the contests were held on open ground in front of the citadel, but after a tiger attacked Minh Mang they were staged in the arena from 1830, until the last fight in 1904. This was not entirely sport: elephants symbolized the unequalled might of the sovereign while tigers represented rebel forces, and the arena was built on the site of an old Cham fort just to underline the message of Imperial power. It was, apparently, a pretty one-sided fight which the elephant was never allowed to lose, and contemporary accounts suggest that in later years the tigers were tied to a stake and had their claws removed.

THE HON CHEN TEMPLE FESTIVALS

Festivals at Hon Chen were banned between Independence and 1986 but have now resumed, taking place twice yearly in the middle of the third and seventh lunar month. The celebrations, harking back to ancient rituals, include trance-dances performed by mediums, usually females dressed in brightly coloured costumes, who are transported by a pulsating musical accompaniment. These events have proven popular with the few foreign tourists lucky enough to be here at the right time, and to hear that they're actually happening.

5

The Royal Arena still exists almost in its original state, though the royal pavilion has rotted away. If you can get in, climb up the staircase on the north wall to where the emperor would have sat facing south over the small arena. After they died, the elephants were worshipped nearby in a small temple, **Long Chau Dien**, which stands to the west of the arena, although almost completely hidden by undergrowth and with only a couple of elephant statues to see: follow the path round the arena's south side to find the temple, overlooking a small lake.

ARRIVAL AND DEPARTURE	ROYAL ARENA

The Royal Arena is 4km from central Hué, taking **Bui Thi Xuan** along the Perfume River's south bank through Phuong Duc, a famous metal-casting village. Each alley on the left has a sign; if you're on your own wheels, rather than the back of a xe om (roughly 25,000đ) Kiet 373 is the one to look for. If you want to combine the arena with the **Royal Mausoleums**, you can use a rough backroad from Phuong Duc village, though this takes a far steeper route than the main one via Dien Bien Phu.

Nam Giao

At the end of Dien Bien Phu, 3km from central Hué • Free

First and foremost in the ceremonial and religious life of the nation was **Nam Giao** ("Altar of Heaven"), where the emperor reaffirmed the legitimacy of his rule in sacred rituals, held here roughly every three years from 1807 to 1945. The ceremonies were performed on a series of terraces, two square-shaped and one round, symbolizing heaven, earth and man in descending order. Before each occasion the monarch purified himself, keeping to a strict regime of vegetarian food and no concubines for several days. He then carried out the sacrifices, with the assistance of some five-thousand attendants, to ensure the stability of both the country and the dynasty. Nam Giao makes a good place for a relaxing walk, though there's not too much to get your teeth into.

Tu Hieu Pagoda

About 1km west of Nam Giao on Le Ngo Cat • Free

The splendid **Tu Hieu Pagoda** is buried in the pine forests east of Nam Giao. Though not the most famous pagoda in Hué, it's one of the most attractive, and it does have an Imperial link since this is where royal eunuchs retired to and were worshipped after their deaths. The pagoda was founded in 1843 and still houses an active community of forty monks who extend a warm welcome to their occasional visitors. The main altar is dedicated to Sakyamuni, with the Buddhist trinity sitting up above, while a secondary shrine room behind contains altars to several famous mandarins and the eunuchs. Between the two buildings is a small courtyard festooned with orchids, and a star-fruit vine that has been here since the reign of Thanh Thai (1889–1907).

ARRIVAL AND DEPARTURE	TU HIEU PAGODA

Most get to the pagoda by xe om, thoug it's quite possible on a bicycle – take the road towards Tu Duc's Mausoleum from the Nam Giao T-junction and near the top of the hill look out for two tall columns announcing "Tu Hieu". Turn right here down a dirt road and then fork left to reach the pagoda's triple-arched gate behind which lies a peaceful, crescent-moon lake.

The Royal Mausoleums

These wise kings of Annam, who make death smile.   Charles Patris, late 1800s

Unlike previous Vietnamese dynasties, which buried their kings in ancestral villages, the Nguyen built themselves magnificent **Royal Mausoleums** in the valley of the Perfume River among low, forested hills to the south of Hué. For historical reasons only seven mausoleums were built, but each one is a unique expression of the monarch's personality, usually planned in detail during his lifetime to serve as his palace in death. More than anywhere else in Hué, it's here that the Nguyen emperors excelled in achieving a harmony between the works of man and his natural surroundings. Along with the Imperial City, these constitute Hué's most rewarding sights.

VISITING THE MAUSOLEUMS

The mausoleums are intoxicating places, occasionally grandiose but more often achieving an elegant simplicity, where it's easy to lose yourself wandering in the quiet gardens. Of the seven, the contrasting mausoleums of **Tu Duc**, **Khai Dinh** and **Minh Mang** are the most attractive and best-preserved, as well as being easily accessible. These are also the three covered by the boat trips, so they can get crowded; don't let this put you off – but if you do want something more off the beaten track then those of **Gia Long**, **Dong Khanh** and **Thieu Tri** are worth calling in on. Finally, **Duc Duc**'s temple and mausoleum are very modest but they are the closest to Hué and still tended by members of the royal family. Even if time allows, however, you probably won't want to visit all the mausoleums at a **ticket price** of 55,000đ each. If you are lucky enough to arrive on a public holiday, entry is free. Note that it's best to **avoid weekends** if possible.

The Mausoleum of Duc Duc

Daily 7am–5pm • 55,000đ • Opposite 74 Tran Phu (see map, p.293), head down Duong Duy Tan; the mausoleum is 100m along on the right • Unoffical guides will show you around for a small donation

Three emperors are buried at the **Mausoleum of Duc Duc**, which, although it's the closest to Hué, is rarely visited. Duc Duc (ruled 1883) and his wife are buried in a walled compound, while emperors Thanh Thai (ruled 1889–1907) and Duy Tan (ruled 1907–16) are interred in a separate row of graves behind the main temple, built in 1899. Duc Duc was forced to resign in 1883 by his senior courtiers after a mere three days as emperor, and died a year later in prison, while his son, **Thanh Thai**, was also removed in 1907 after a suspected anti-French conspiracy. The French then put Thanh Thai's 8-year-old son, **Duy Tan**, on the throne, but he fled the palace nine years later amid another revolutionary plot, and was eventually exiled with his father to the French territory of Réunion in the Indian Ocean. Duy Tan died in a World War II plane crash in 1945, fighting on the side of the Allies, but Thanh Thai was allowed back to Vietnam in 1947 and died in Saigon in the 1950s. Descendants of the Imperial family still live in the temple buildings, and possess a historic collection of family photos, including some of the funeral of Thanh Thai.

MAUSOLEUM DESIGN

It often took years to find a site with the right aesthetic requirements that would also satisfy the court cosmologists charged with interpreting the underlying supernatural forces. Artificial lakes, waterfalls and hills were added to improve the geomantic qualities of the location, at the same time creating picturesque, almost romantic, **garden settings** for the mausoleums, of which the finest examples are those of Tu Duc and Minh Mang.

Though details vary, all the mausoleums consist of three elements: a **temple** dedicated to the worship of the deceased emperor and his queen; a large, stone **stele** recording his biographical details and a history of his reign, usually written by his successor; and the royal **tomb** itself. The main temple houses the funerary tablets and possessions of the royal couple, many of which have been stolen, while nearby stand ancillary buildings where the emperor's concubines lived out their years. In front of each stele-house is a paved courtyard, echoing the Imperial City's Esplanade of Great Salutations, where officials and soldiers lined up to honour their emperor, but in this case the mandarins, horses and elephants are fashioned in stone; military mandarins are easily distinguished by their swords, whereas the civil variety clutch sceptres. Obelisks nearby symbolize the power of the monarch, and lastly, at the highest spot, there's the royal tomb enclosed within a wall and a heavy, securely fastened door. Traditionally the burial place was kept secret as a measure against grave-robbers and enemies of the state, and in extreme cases all those who had been involved in the burial were killed immediately afterwards.

5

The Mausoleum of Tu Duc

Daily 7am–5pm • 55,000đ • 7km from central Hué by road – easy by bicycle. It's 2km from the boat jetty to the west – walk on the dirt track, or take one of the xe om waiting on the riverbank (20,000đ)

With elegant pavilions and pines reflected in serene lakes, this walled, twelve-hectare park is the most harmonius of all the Nguyen mausoleums – quite a claim, considering their careful design, though not such a surprise at all considering the emperor in question – Tu Duc, who ruled from 1847–83, longer than any other Nguyen emperor (see box opposite).

Entering by the southern gate, **Vu Khiem**, brick paths lead beside a lake covered in water lilies and lotus to a small three-tiered **boating pavilion** which looks across to larger **Xung Khiem Pavilion**, where Tu Duc drank wine and wrote poetry; *khiem*, meaning "modest", appears in the name of every building. From the lake, steps head up through **Khiem Cung Gate**, the middle door painted yellow for the emperor, into a second enclosure containing the main temple, **Hoa Khiem**, which Tu Duc used as an office before his death. The royal funerary tablets here are unusual in that Tu Duc's, bearing a dragon, is smaller than the phoenix-decorated tablet of the queen. Beyond is a second temple, **Luong Khiem**, which served as the royal residence, and the elegant **royal theatre**, while behind the storerooms opposite once stood the quarters for Tu Duc's numerous concubines. Note that on the way into this mausoleum, you're likely to pass incense sticks laid out to dry, and people making – and selling – Hué's famous conical hats.

The emperor's tomb

The second group of buildings, to the north of the royal theatre, is centred on the emperor's tomb, preceded by the salutation court and stele-house. Tu Duc's stele, weighing twenty tonnes, is by far the largest; unusually, Tu Duc wrote his own self-critical eulogy, running to over four thousand characters, to elucidate all his difficulties. Behind the stele is a kidney-shaped pond, representing the crescent moon, and then a bronze door leading into a square enclosure where the unadorned tomb shelters behind a screen adorned with the characters for longevity. Emperor Kien Phuc, one of Tu Duc's adopted sons, is also buried here, just north of the lake.

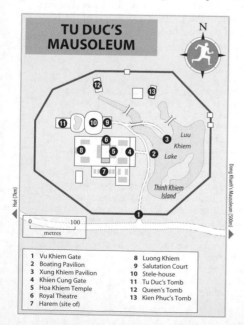

The Mausoleum of Dong Khanh

Daily 7am–5pm • 55,000đ • Only 500m from Tu Duc's mausoleum

Dong Khanh (ruled 1885–89) was put on the throne by the French as titular head of their new protectorate. A pliant ruler with a fondness for French wine, perfume and alarm clocks, he died suddenly at the age of 25 after only three years on the throne; having never got round to planning his final resting place he was buried near the temple he dedicated to his father. As a result this is a modest, countryside **mausoleum** with a rustic charm but is particularly well preserved.

The mausoleum consists of two parts: the main temple, and then the tomb and stele in a separate, walled

TU DUC'S MAUSOLEUM

N

Hué (7km)

0 — 100
metres

Dong Khanh's Mausoleum (500m)

Luu Khiem Lake

Thinh Khiem Island

1 Vu Khiem Gate	8 Luong Khiem
2 Boating Pavilion	9 Salutation Court
3 Xung Khiem Pavilion	10 Stele-house
4 Khien Cung Gate	11 Tu Duc's Tomb
5 Hoa Khiem Temple	12 Queen's Tomb
6 Royal Theatre	13 Kien Phuc's Tomb
7 Harem (site of)	

TU DUC

Emperor Tu Duc (ruled 1847-83) was a romantic poet trying to rule Vietnam at a time when the Western world was challenging the country's independence. Although he was the longest reigning of the Nguyen monarchs, he was a weak ruler who preferred to hide from the world in the lyrical pleasure gardens he created. The walled, twelve-hectare park took only three years to complete (1864–67), allowing Tu Duc a full sixteen years for boating and fishing, meditation, drinking tea made from dew collected in lotus blossoms and composing some of the four thousand poems he is said to have written, besides several important philosophical and historical works. Somehow he also found time for fifty-course meals, plus 104 wives and a whole village of concubines living in the park, though – possibly due to a bout of smallpox – he fathered no children. Perhaps it's not surprising that Tu Duc was also a tyrant who pushed the three thousand workmen building his mausoleum so hard that they rebelled in 1866, and were savagely dealt with.

enclosure on a slight rise 100m to the northwest. The complex was built mostly by Dong Khanh's son, Khai Dinh, after 1889, though has been added to since.

Follow the road round to the southeast or take a short cut over the hill by the footpath from between the refreshment stalls, forking left twice before you see Dong Khanh's tomb on your right and the temple straight ahead behind some trees

The main temple

The **main temple** holds most interest: the first thing you notice are the coloured-glass doors and windows, but the faded murals on each side wall showing scenes of daily life are far more attractive. Twenty-four glass-paintings, illustrated poems of Confucian love, hang on the temple's ironwood columns and, at either end of the first row, there are two engravings of Napoleon and the Battle of Waterloo. The three principal altars honour Dong Khanh with his two queens to either side, while his seven concubines have a separate altar in the back room. Finally, don't miss the altar to Y A Na in a small side-chamber, off to the right as you enter: Dong Khanh often consulted the goddess at Hon Chen Temple (see p.295) and dedicated an altar to her after she appeared in a dream and foretold that he would be emperor.

The Mausoleum of Thieu Tri

Daily 7am–5pm • 55,000đ • About 6km from the centre of Hué: head south from either Nam Giao or Tu Duc's mausoleum

Emperor Thieu Tri (ruled 1841–47) was the son of Minh Mang (see box, p.300) and shared his father's aversion to foreign influences – it's said he destroyed anything Western he found in the Imperial palaces – and his taste in architecture. His **mausoleum** follows the same basic pattern as Minh Mang's though without the attractive walled gardens, and is split into two sections placed side by side. As it's also smaller it took less than a year to build (1847–48), but its most distinctive feature is that it faces northwest, a traditionally inauspicious direction, and many people believed that this was the reason the country fell under the French yoke a few years later. Although the salutation courtyard, stele-house and tomb are suffering from serious neglect, the temple itself is in reasonable shape. It contains numerous poems, in mother-of-pearl or painted on glass, since Thieu Tri was a prolific poet who would pen a stanza or two at a moment's notice.

The Mausoleum of Khai Dinh

Daily 7am–5pm • 55,000đ • 10km from Hué by road. Arriving by boat, it's a 1.5km walk, heading eastwards up a valley with a giant Quan Am statue on your right until you see the mausoleum on the opposite hillside

This mausoleum is a monumental confection of European baroque, highly ornamental Sino-Vietnamese style and even elements of Cham architecture. Its most attractive feature is the setting, high up on a wooded hill, but it's worth climbing the 130-odd

5

steps to take a look inside the sanctuary itself, still in its original state. Khai Dinh (ruled 1916–25) was the penultimate Nguyen emperor and his mausoleum is a radical departure from its predecessors, with neither gardens nor living quarters and only one main structure. Khai Dinh was also a vain man, a puppet of the French very much taken with French style and architecture, and though he only reigned for nine years it took eleven (1920–31) to complete his mausoleum, and it cost so much he had to levy additional taxes for the project.

The principal temple

The approach is via a series of grandiose, dragon-ornamented stairways leading first to the salutation courtyard, with an unusually complete honour guard of mandarins, and on to the stele-house. Climbing up a further four terraces brings you to the **principal temple**, built of reinforced concrete with slate roofing imported from France, whose extravagant halls are a startling contrast to the blackened exterior. Walls, ceiling, furniture, everything is decorated to the hilt, writhing with dragons and peppered with symbolic references and classic imagery such as the Four Seasons panels in the antechamber. Most of this lavish display, not as garish as it might sound, is worked in glass and porcelain mosaic – even the central canopy, which looks like fabric. A life-size gilded bronze statue of the emperor holding his royal sceptre sits under the canopy, while his altar table and funerary tablet are up on the mezzanine floor behind. His portrait stands on the incense table in the antechamber. Khai Dinh was a particularly flamboyant dresser and it's rumoured that he brought back a string of fairy lights from France and proceeded to wear them around the palace, twinkling, until the batteries ran out.

The Mausoleum of Minh Mang

Daily 7am–5pm • 55,000đ • From Khai Dinh's tomb, follow the road to the highway, cross over the river and turn left after fifty metres. From the river jetties near the bridge, you can get to Gia Long's Mausoleum and Hon Chen Temple (see p.295) by sampan

Court officials took fourteen years to find the location for the **Mausoleum of Minh Mang** – for which the mandarin responsible was awarded two promotions; it then took only three years to build (1841–43), using ten thousand workmen. It was designed along traditional Chinese lines, with all the principal buildings symmetrical about an east–west axis. The mausoleum's stately grandeur is softened by fifteen hectares of superb landscaped gardens, almost a third of which is taken up by lakes reflecting the handsome, red-roofed pavilions.

Inside the mausoleum a processional way links the series of low mounds bearing all the main buildings. After the salutation courtyard and stele-house comes the **principal temple** (*Sung An*), where Minh Mang (ruled 1820–41) and his queen are worshipped. Though beautifully restored, the only point of interest about the temple itself is that local Christians vandalized it in 1885 to protest against Minh Mang's virulent anti-Catholicism. Continuing west you reach **Minh Lau**, the elegant, two-storey "Pavilion of Pure Light" standing among clouds of frangipani trees, symbols of longevity; beyond, two stone gardens trace the Chinese character for long life. From here the ceremonial pathway crosses a crescent lake and ends at the circular burial mound.

MINH MANG

Minh Mang, the second Nguyen emperor, was a capable, authoritarian monarch who was selected for his serious nature and distrust of Western religious infiltration. This revered emperor was also passionate about architecture – it was he who oversaw the completion of Hué citadel after Gia Long's death. Minh Mang's queen died at the age of 17, but despite this early loss Minh Mang managed to father 142 children with his 33 wives and 107 concubines.

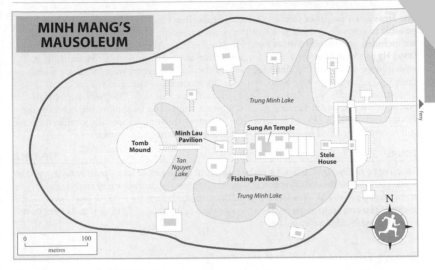

The Mausoleum of Gia Long

Daily 7am–5pm · 55,000đ · Best reached by sampan from the jetty near Minh Mang's mausoleum (20min each way; 100,000đ return)

As the first Nguyen ruler, Gia Long (ruled 1802–20) had his pick of the sites, and he chose an immense natural park 16km from Hué on the left bank of the Perfume River. Unfortunately his **mausoleum** – begun in 1814 and completed shortly after his death in 1820 – was badly damaged during the American War and there's not a great deal to see beyond some fine carving, and a double tomb with pitched roofs housing Gia Long and his wife. However, this is the least-visited of Hué's mausoleums and is recommended for the boat trip and the peaceful stroll through sandy pine forest, though some visitors complain of attracting a convoy of persistent soft-drink sellers for the duration of the two-kilometre walk. You approach the complex from the north to find the main temple, tomb and stele-house all aligned on a horizontal axis, looking south across a lake towards Thien Tho Mountain.

ARRIVAL AND DEPARTURE

ROYAL MAUSOLEUMS

On a tour A motorbike tour normally includes at least one mausoleum. Another popular option is a Perfume River boat trip (see box, p.294), though with one of these you'll face a couple of longish walks.

By bike and boat With your own wheels you'll have to negotiate your own ferry crossings, but will have more time to explore and won't be restricted to the three main mausoleums. A good compromise is to take a bike on board a tour boat and cycle back to Hué from the last stop, or vice versa.

The DMZ

During the American War, **Quang Tri** and **Quang Binh**, the two provinces either side of the **DMZ** (see box, p.303), were the most heavily bombed and saw the highest casualties – civilian and military, American and Vietnamese. Names made infamous in 1960s' and 1970s' America have been perpetuated in countless films and memoirs: Con Thien, the Rockpile, Hamburger Hill and Khe Sanh. For some people the DMZ will be what draws them to Vietnam, the end of a long and difficult pilgrimage; for others it will be a bleak, sometimes beautiful, place where there's nothing particular to see but where it's hard not to respond to the sense of enormous desolation.

North of the DMZ is one of the region's main attractions – the tunnels of **Vinh Moc**, where villages created deep underground during the American War have been preserved.

other points of interest lie south of the Ben Hai River, and while it's not
cover everything in a day, the most interesting of the places described here
d on **organized tours** from Hué (see p.288). Alternatively, it's possible to use
as a base or cover a more limited selection of sights on the drive north. If you
have limited time then the **Vinh Moc tunnels** should be high on your list, along with a
drive up Highway 9 to Khe Sanh, both for the scenery en route and the sobering
battleground itself. Note that, although you can now visit the DMZ without a **local
guide**, this is not recommended as most sites are unmarked and, more importantly, the
guides – arranged in Dong Ha (see p.304) – know which paths are safe; local farmers are
still occasionally killed or injured by **unexploded ordnance** in this area.

TOURS   **THE DMZ**

Considering the paucity of public transport in this area, most opt to go on a **guided tour** – guides usually do a good job
of relaying the essential historical information. Most come straight from Hué, from where tours usually cost $12–15 per
person; from Dong Ha it's a fair bit cheaper, though you'll likely be squashed onto one of the Hué buses anyway. If you're
heading north to Dong Hoi, it's usually possible to save a 3hr round-trip by getting off the bus on Highway 1 after the Vinh
Moc tunnels, and flagging down a public bus.

Quang Tri

Blink and you may well miss **QUANG TRI**, a town wiped off the map during the
American War, and indeed now officially called **Trieu Hai**. Keep your eyes peeled for

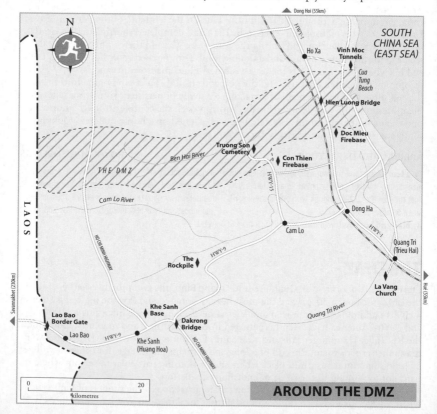

AROUND THE DMZ

5

THE HISTORY OF THE DMZ

Under the terms of the 1954 Geneva Accords, Vietnam was split in two along the Seventeenth Parallel, pending elections intended to reunite the country. The demarcation line ran along the Ben Hai River and was sealed by a strip of no-man's-land 5km wide on each side known as the **Demilitarized Zone**, or DMZ. All Communist troops and supporters were supposed to regroup north in the Democratic Republic of Vietnam, leaving the southern Republic of Vietnam to non-Communists and various shades of opposition. When the elections failed to take place, the river became the de facto border until 1975.

In reality both sides of the DMZ were anything but demilitarized after 1965, and anyway the border was easily circumvented – by the Ho Chi Minh Trail to the west (see box, p.316) and sea routes to the east – enabling the North Vietnamese to bypass a string of American fire bases overlooking the river. One of the more fantastical efforts to prevent Communist infiltration southwards was US Secretary of Defense Robert McNamara's proposal for an electronic fence from the Vietnamese coast to the Mekong River, made up of seismic and acoustic sensors that would detect troop movements and pinpoint targets for bombing raids. Though trials in 1967 met with some initial success, the "McNamara Line" was soon abandoned: sensors were confused by animals, especially elephants, and could be triggered deliberately by the tape-recorded sound of vehicle engines or troops on the march.

Nor could massive, conventional bombing by artillery and aircraft contain the North Vietnamese, who finally stormed the DMZ in 1972 and pushed the border 20km further south. Exceptionally bitter fighting in the territory south of the Ben Hai River (I Corps Military Region) claimed more American lives in the five years leading up to 1972 than any other battle zone in Vietnam. Figures for North Vietnamese losses during that period are not known, but it's estimated that up to thirty percent of ordnance dropped in the DMZ failed to detonate on impact and that these have, since 1975, been responsible for up to ten thousand deaths and injuries. So much fire power was unleashed over this area, including napalm and herbicides, that for years nothing would grow in the impacted, chemical-laden soil, but the region's low, rolling hills are now almost entirely reforested with a green sea of pine, eucalyptus, coffee and acacia.

one of its few identifying features – the small, pockmarked shell of **Long Hung Church** to the east of the road, 55km from Hué, kept as a memorial to victims of 1972 (see box above). Soon after, a track on the opposite side of the highway leads 4km southwest to the more impressive ruin of **La Vang Church**, beside which stands an extraordinary monument of *Alice in Wonderland* mushrooms supposedly representing the apparition of the Virgin Mary to persecuted Catholics on this spot in 1798. The town itself lies off to the east of the highway down Tran Hung Dao, the last surfaced road before you reach the Quang Tri River. There's not a lot to see, but if you've got your own transport the remains of **Quang Tri Citadel** are worth a look.

American troops weren't the first to suffer heavy losses in this region: during the 1950s, French soldiers dubbed the stretch of Highway 1 north of Hué as *la rue sans joie*, or "street without joy", after they came under constant attack from elusive Viet Minh units operating out of heavily fortified villages along the coast. Later, in the 1972 Easter Offensive, Communist forces overran the whole area, capturing **QUANG TRI** town, some 60km from Hué, from the South Vietnamese Army (ARVN) and holding it for four months while American B-52s pounded the township and surrounding countryside, before it was retaken at huge cost to both sides as well as civilians caught up in the battle.

Quang Tri Citadel

Just north of the town on Tran Hung Dao; entrance on Ly Thai To • Daily 7am–5pm • 12,000đ

This square, walled structure, resembling a smaller version of the citadel in Hué, was originally built from earth in 1806 by the Nguyen Dynasty, fortified with bricks in 1827, and served in turn as a base for the French and the ARVN before being overrun and destroyed in 1972. Parts of the wall and moat remain, and the south gate, through which visitors enter, has been rebuilt. Inside is a war memorial, the remains of a

5

nineteenth-century French prison consisting of fourteen tiny cells measuring 1m by 2m, and a small war **museum** with English captions (included in entrance fee). The museum houses some excellent photos of the fierce hand-to-hand fighting that took place towards the end of 1972 as ARVN troops eventually retook the city after 81 days. Stick to established paths, as unexploded ordnance may still lurk.

Dong Ha

As a former US Marine Command Post and then ARVN base, **DONG HA** was also obliterated in 1972, but unlike Quang Tri it has bounced back, thanks largely to its administrative status and location at the eastern end of Highway 9, which leads through Laos to Savannakhet on the Mekong River. The future looks rosy as well: a new deep-water port has been built to serve landlocked Laos, a number of special economic zones are under construction along the border, and Highway 9 has been upgraded as part of the massive Trans-Asian Highway project.

As the closest town to the DMZ, Dong Ha attracts a lot of tourist traffic, though few people choose to stay here, preferring the comfort and facilities of Hué. It is essentially a two-street town: Highway 1, known here as Le Duan, forms the main artery as it passes through on its route north, while Highway 9 takes off inland at a central T-junction.

ARRIVAL AND DEPARTURE
DONG HA

By train The station lies 1km south of town, just west of the highway.
Destinations: Dong Hoi (6 daily; 1hr 20min–2hr 10min); Hanoi (6 daily; 12–15hr); Hué (6 daily; 1hr 20min).
By bus The bus station is 500m south of the train station. A word of warning – many a traveller has come a cropper here, thanks to the strong-arm tactics of xe om drivers. If you're heading north, try to do so at the northernmost extremity of your tour (usually the Vinh Moc tunnels); if you're heading south to Hué, try to get on a tour bus. To get to Laos, it's best to use the direct buses to Savannakhet run on odd dates by Sepon Travel (see below).
Destinations: Dong Hoi (2hr); Hué (2hr); Lao Bao (2hr); Savannakhet (8hr).

INFORMATION

Tourist information Information, car rental and guides can be found at DMZ Tours (☎ 053 356 4056, ✉ dmzquangtri @gmail.com), 260 Le Duan; Sepon Travel (☎ 053 385 5289, ⓦ sepon.com.vn), 189 Le Duan; and Annam Tours (☎ 0905 140600, ⓦ annamtour.com), 207 Nguyen Du. Both sell tickets for DMZ tours (from $11), on which you join the coach originating in Hué. *Tam's Café* (see below) is also good for information, and can help to organize tours.

ACCOMMODATION AND EATING

Melody Hotel 62 Highway 1 ☎ 053 355 4664. A little gem that keeps its guests happy. Rooms are kept clean and have 24hr hot water (neither a given in these parts); in addition, all have a/c and satellite TV. Staff are also adept at helping with trips to DMZ attractions. $15
Phung Hoang 2 146 Le Duan ☎ 053 385 4567, ✉ phunghoanghotel2001@yahoo.com. Near the central crossroads, this is a welcome exception to the state-run guesthouses, with a range of en-suite rooms (all with a/c), as well as free internet access in the lobby. Have a look at a few rooms before making your choice. $15
Tam's Café 81 Tran Hung Dao, ⓦ tamscafe.co.nr. Charming café serving a range of coffees, juices, smoothies and teas – and, if you're lucky, ice cream. They donate much of their profits to charitable causes – most of the staff, in fact, are youths with impaired hearing.

DIRECTORY

Bank The town's bank at 1 Le Quy Don can exchange US dollars, and has an ATM.

West of Dong Ha

Heading west from Dong Ha on Highway 9 (also now known as Asian Highway 16, or AH16 for short), you begin to climb into the foothills of the Truong Son range. Where the highway veers south, a sheer-sided isolated stump 230m high dominates the valley: the **Rockpile**. For a while American troops, delivered by helicopter, used the peak for

5

THE BATTLE OF KHE SANH

The **battle of Khe Sanh** was important not because of its immediate outcome, but because it attracted worldwide media attention and, along with the simultaneous Tet Offensive, demonstrated the futility of America's efforts to contain their enemy. In 1962 an American Special Forces team arrived in Khe Sanh Town to train local Bru minority people in counter-insurgency, and then four years later the first batch of Marines was sent in to establish a forward base near Laos, to secure Highway 9 and to harass troops on the Ho Chi Minh Trail. Skirmishes around Khe Sanh increased as intelligence reports indicated a massive build-up of North Vietnamese Army (NVA) troops in late 1967, possibly as many as forty thousand, facing six thousand Marines together with a few hundred South Vietnamese and Bru. Both the Western media and American generals were soon presenting the confrontation as a crucial test of America's credibility in South Vietnam and drawing parallels with Dien Bien Phu (see p.412). As US President Johnson famously remarked, he didn't want "any damn Dinbinfoo".

The **NVA attack** came in the early hours of January 21, 1968; rockets raining in on the base added to the terror and confusion by striking an ammunition dump, gasoline tanks and stores of tear gas. There followed a seemingly endless, nerve-grinding NVA artillery barrage, when hundreds of shells fell on the base each day, interspersed with costly US infantry assaults into the surrounding hills. In an operation code-named **"Niagara"**, General Westmoreland called in the air battalions to silence the enemy guns and break the siege by unleashing the most intense bombing raids of the war: in nine weeks nearly a hundred thousand tonnes of bombs pounded the area round the clock, averaging **one airstrike every five minutes**, backed up by napalm and defoliants. Unbelievably the NVA were so well dug in and camouflaged that they not only withstood the onslaught but continued to return fire, despite horrendous casualties, estimated at ten thousand. On the US side around five hundred troops died at Khe Sanh (although official figures record only 248 American deaths, of which 43 occurred in a single helicopter accident), before a relief column broke through in early April, seventy-odd days after the siege had begun. NVA forces gradually pulled back and by the middle of March had all but gone, having successfully diverted American resources away from southern cities prior to the Tet Offensive. Three months later the Americans also quietly withdrew, leaving a plateau that resembled a lunar landscape, contaminated for years to come with chemicals and explosives; even the trees left standing were worthless because so much shrapnel was lodged in the timber.

directing artillery to targets across the DMZ and into Laos, but the post was abandoned after 1968. The highway continues over a low pass and then follows a picturesque valley past the **Dakrong Bridge**, which carries a spur of the Ho Chi Minh Highway before climbing among ever-more forested mountains to emerge at **KHE SANH** (now officially rechristened **Huang Hoa**), 63km from Dong Ha. In this area you'll still see a few stilthouses from the Bru and Co minorities, most of whom have been moved on – ostensibly for reasons of health and hygiene, though cynics would point to the fact that both the Bru and the Co helped the Americans during the war.

Khe Sanh

This bleak settlement, its frontier atmosphere reinforced by the smugglers' trail across the border to Laos only 19km away (see box, p.306), sits on the edge of a windswept plateau that was the site of a pivotal battle in the American War. Due to the high concentration of chemical and explosive contamination after the war, it's only recently that the soil around Khe Sanh has been able to support vegetation again, and the hills are now green with coffee plantations. Nothing else remains: when American troops were ordered to abandon Khe Sanh, everything was blown up or bulldozed.

The Museum

Daily 7am–5pm • 20,000đ

The only memorial is a small **museum**, 2km north of Khe Sanh Town, commemorating the siege – made even more poignant by the hauntingly beautiful mountains all

5

LAO BAO BORDER CROSSING INTO LAOS

Of the five **border crossings** open to foreigners between Vietnam and Laos, the most popular is still **Lao Bao**, 80km west of Dong Ha along Highway 9. It's an attractive ride, through misty mountains on a reasonable road, and the crossing is hassle-free beyond having to walk 1km between inspection posts. However, since reports of extortion are still common with travellers trying to do this route independently, or even from the bus station in Dong Ha, it's best to book a seat on one of the through-buses to Savannakhet from Dong Ha (see p.304) or Hué.

In theory you can obtain a fifteen-day **visa** for Laos at the border ($30; two passport photos required), but check beforehand for the latest situation. Otherwise, the safest option is to get your visa in advance at the Lao consulates in Da Nang (see p.274) or in Ho Chi Minh City (see p.107), or at their embassy in Hanoi (see p.388).

around. The small halls are dotted with photos and war paraphernalia, and surrounded by military vehicles and the contorted shapes of exploded bombs. On your way in you'll likely be offered "genuine" dog-tags – Khe Sanh coffee is a more worthwhile purchase. Be sure to peek over the fence at the red gash of the old airstrip.

North of Dong Ha

There are a few sights in and around the DMZ itself. Northwest of Dong Ha on Highway 15 are **Con Thien Firebase** and the **Truong Son Cemetery**, both notable wartime locations, while directly north of Dong Ha are another firebase and the **Vinh Moc Tunnels**, the latter being the most worthwhile sight in the whole area.

Con Thien Firebase

Roughly 12km out of Cam Lo, you pass the site of **Con Thien Firebase**. Again, there's precious little left to see, beyond a view north to what were once NVA positions, chillingly close on the opposite bank of the Ben Hai River. The largest American installation along the DMZ, Con Thien FireBase was first established by the Special Forces (Green Berets) and then handed over to the Marines in 1966, whose big guns could reach from here far into North Vietnam. In the lead-up to the 1968 Tet Offensive, as part of the NVA's diversionary attacks, the base became the target of prolonged shelling, followed by an infantry assault during which it was briefly surrounded. The Americans replied with everything in their arsenal, including long-range strafing from gunships in the South China Sea and carpet-bombing by B-52s. The North Vietnamese were forced to withdraw temporarily, but then completely overran the base in the summer of 1972.

Truong Son Cemetery

Thirty-odd kilometres northwest of Dong Ha along highways 9 and 15. There's no public transport to the cemetery, though it regularly features on DMZ tours. To get there under your own steam from Dong Ha, drive west on Highway 9 as far as Cam Lo Town (12km) and then turn north for 22km following signs along Highway 15.

Truong Son War Martyr Cemetery is dedicated to the estimated twenty-five thousand men and women who died on the Truong Son Trail, better known in the West as the Ho Chi Minh Trail (see box, p.316). A total of 10,036 graves lie in the fourteen-hectare cemetery among whispering glades of evergreen trees. Arranged in five geographical regions, the graves are subdivided according to native province, and centred round memorial houses listing every name and grave number in the sector. Each headstone announces *liet si* ("martyr"), together with as many details as are known: name, date and place of birth, date of enrolment, rank and the date they died.

Doc Mieu Firebase

The American front line comprised a string of firebases set up on a long, low ridge of hills looking north across the DMZ and the featureless plain of the Ben Hai River.

THE HISTORY OF THE TUNNELS

When American bombing raids north of the DMZ intensified in 1966 the inhabitants of Vinh Linh District began digging down into the red laterite soils, excavating more than fifty tunnels over the next two years. Although they were also used by North Vietnamese soldiers, the tunnels were primarily built to shelter a largely civilian population who worked the supply route from the Con Co Islands lying 28km offshore. Five tunnels belonged to Vinh Moc, a village located right on the coast where for two years 250 people dug more than 2km of tunnel, which housed all six hundred villagers over varying periods from early 1967 until 1969, when half decamped north to the relative safety of Nghe An Province. The tunnels were constructed on three levels at 10, 15 and 20–23m deep (though nowadays you can't visit the lowest level) with good ventilation, freshwater wells and, eventually, a generator and lights. The underground village was also equipped with a school, clinics and a maternity room where seventeen children were born. Each family was allocated a tiny cavern, the four-person space being barely larger than a single bed. They were only able to emerge at night and lack of fresh air and sunlight was a major problem, especially for young children who would sit in the tunnel mouths whenever possible. In 1972, the villagers of Vinh Moc were finally able to abandon their underground existence and rebuild their homes, rejoined by relatives from Nghe An a year later.

Although there's nothing much to see now, you pass the site of one of these, **Doc Mieu Firebase** to the east of Highway 1 about 14km north of Dong Ha. Before the NVA overran Doc Mieu in 1972, the base played a pivotal role in the South's defence. From here American guns shelled seaborne infiltration routes and, for a while, this was the command post for the "McNamara Line", calling in airstrikes from Da Nang to pound targets – both real and faked – along the Ho Chi Minh Trail.

Hien Luong Bridge

Just beyond Doc Mieu, Highway 1 drops down into the DMZ, running between paddy fields to the Ben Hai River, which lies virtually on the Seventeenth Parallel. You will see two bridges, the newly built one, which is open to traffic, and the unused **Hien Luong Bridge** that runs parallel to it. Until it was destroyed in 1967, the original Hien Luong Bridge was painted half red and half yellow as a vivid reminder that this was a physical and ideological boundary separating the two Vietnams. The reconstructed iron-girder bridge officially re-opened in 1975 as a symbol of reunification, and for many years represented an important psychological barrier between north and south.

The Vinh Moc tunnels

Daily 7am–5pm • 25,000d • The tour takes around fifty minutes and although these tunnels are bigger (the ceiling is almost 2m high in places) than those of Cu Chi it's not recommended for the claustrophobic

An amazing complex of tunnels where over a thousand people sheltered, sometimes for weeks on end, during the worst American bombardments (see box above). A section of the **Vinh Moc tunnels** has been restored and opened to visitors as a powerful tribute to the villagers' courage and tenacity, with a small museum at the entrance providing background information.

ARRIVAL AND DEPARTURE   VINH MOC TUNNELS

The tunnels feature on almost all DMZ tours but it's possible to get there independently if you have your own transport. In Ho Xa township, 7km north of the Ben Hai River and 28km from Dong Ha, a signpost opposite a petrol station indicates a right turn which takes you 15km to the tunnels. You may also end up approaching on a newer road, which crosses the Ben Hai River far to the east of the Hien Luong Bridge.

The Northern Coast

HALONG BAY AT SUNSET

The Northern Coast

Although largely devoid of beaches, Vietnam's northern coast boasts one of the country's foremost attractions, and one of the most vaunted spots in all of Southeast Asia – the mystical scenery of Ha Long Bay, where jagged emerald islands jut out of the sea in their thousands. Heading in by boat, you approach wave after wave of hidden bays, needle-sharp ridges and cliffs of ribbed limestone. The waters here are patrolled by squadrons of attractive, old-fashioned tourist junks, on which you'll be able to spend a night at sea; wonderful Cat Ba island is another great place to stay. You'll find similar karst scenery inland around the small city of Ninh Binh, while other notable sights in the area are the colonial buildings of Hai Phong and the caves around Dong Hoi.

The northern coast stretches all the way from the DMZ to the Chinese border. Heading north from the DMZ (the Demilitarized Zone) the first stretch is hemmed in by the jagged Truong Son Mountains, which separate Vietnam from Laos. Here, Vietnam shrinks to a mere 50km wide and is edged with sand dunes up to 80m high, marching inland at a rate of 10m per year despite efforts to stabilize them with screw-pine and cactus. The first place of note on this stretch is **Dong Hoi**, a largely uninteresting city, but one that serves as a jump-off point for the spectacular cave of **Phong Nha**. This was regarded as the largest cave in the land, until another was discovered nearby – **Son Doong** cave, yet to be fully charted but already held to be the largest in the world.

The area north of Dong Hoi is one of the poorest in Vietnam, and has little to detain the traveller; however, the mountains brushing the Lao border are home to a number of unique animal species, including the elusive **saola ox** and the more numerous **giant muntjac deer**. The only place that sees travellers in any number is **Vinh**, another rather dull place, but a logical stopover on this long stretch; you may care to track down **Ho Chi Minh's birthplace** in the nearby village of Kim Lien.

Despite the presence of these attractions, the vast majority of tourists make a bee-line from Hué to **Ninh Binh**. This is yet another unattractive northern city, but such is the wealth of nearby sights that visitors tend to stay for at least a couple of days; said attractions include majestic karst scenery, underground rivers that can be paddled through by boat, an ancient capital city and Vietnam's largest temple complex.

From Ninh Binh, most travellers push straight on north to Hanoi. However, it's quite possible to head directly from here towards Ha Long Bay, via the buzzing city of **Hai Phong** – one of the largest in Vietnam, and infinitely more appealing than most northern cities thanks to great colonial-era architecture and a young, friendly populace.

Then, of course, there's **Ha Long Bay** itself. A doyen of local tourist literature, you'll most likely have seen dozens of images of this unbelievably scenic place long before your arrival – happily, it really is that pretty. Tourism now rivals fishing as the prime activity, but the bay retains a certain authenticity, and its generous proportions are enough to swallow up the hordes or visitors, for the time being. Many overnight aboard a traditional wooden junk; their tea-coloured sails are just for show since almost all vessels are motor-driven, but there's a timeless, romantic air to floating amongst pristine moonlit peaks. By far the largest island in the bay, the wonderful **Cat Ba** makes an appealing base for exploring the area with some fine scenery as well as being home to **Cat Ba National Park**, a forest and maritime reserve that requires the usual mix of luck and dedication to see anything larger than a mosquito.

Highlights

❶ Phong Nha Cave Take a boat trip into the mouth of one of Asia's most extensive cave systems. **See p.315**

❷ Cycling from Tam Coc to Hoa Lu A fantasy landscape of limestone crags provides the backdrop for a leisurely cycle ride through Ninh Binh's prolific rice lands. **See p.324**

❸ Hai Phong's colonial architecture Hectic Hai Phong features a number of striking colonial-era buildings, which give hints as to this port city's importance under French rule. **See p.329**

❹ Cruising Ha Long Bay Passing through the maze of limestone pinnacles punctuating the turquoise waters is an unmissable experience. **See p.333**

❺ Overnighting on a junk Spend at least one night on board, taking a moonlight dip in the Bay's phosphorescent waters and waking far from the hustle and bustle of the cities. **See pp.334–335**

❻ Cat Ba With its cluttered harbour, lush interior and easy access to some of Ha Long Bay's most beguiling scenery, this is the best place to base yourself in the region. **See p.336**

HIGHLIGHTS ARE MARKED ON THE MAP ON PP.312–313

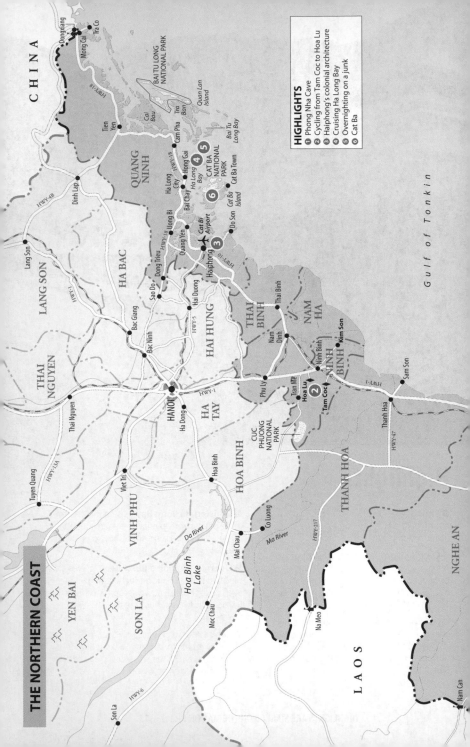

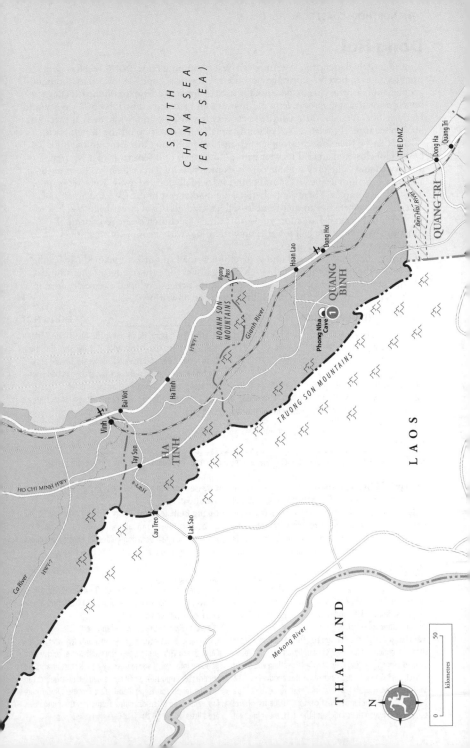

Dong Hoi

Almost entirely flattened in the American War's bombing raids, **DONG HOI** has risen from its ashes to become a prosperous, orderly provincial capital of over sixty thousand people. Tourists who pass by here usually use the town as a base for **Phong Nha Cave**, a hugely attractive system of caverns 30km away, and recognized by UNESCO as a World Heritage Site. As such, the town itself gets very few visitors and, while there is precious little to see here, the relative lack of tourists makes it a nice step off the beaten track.

The Nhat Le River oozes through town just before hitting the sea, with the bulk of Dong Hoi clustered around its west bank. Here you'll find remnants of a Nguyen dynasty **citadel** – the only notable part is its pretty south gate, which has been restored and now functions as the city's focal point; it's actually located away from the main body of the complex. There's a lively riverside **market** east of the gate and an area of covered stalls where in summer vendors sell ice-cold glasses of sweet-bean *chè*. Just to the north of the citadel are more ruins, this time of a church destroyed during the American War; only the bell tower is now standing, with a couple of small trees maintaining a lonely vigil on top.

Crossing the Nhat Le, you'll find yourself on a small spit of land, named My Canh. This is also the name of the small beach rifling down the eastern edge of the isthmus. As with sandy stretches up and down the land, it's being developed as a resort area; it was very much still under construction at the time of writing.

ARRIVAL AND DEPARTURE
DONG HOI

By plane Dong Hoi's small but surprisingly swish airport, Dong Hoi Airport, is 7km to the north of town.
Destinations: Hanoi (daily; 1hr 30min); Ho Chi Minh City (daily; 1hr 30min).
By train The station, Ga Dong Hoi, is in a scruffy area, 3km out of town west along Tran Hung Dao – it is not a particularly pleasant walk into the centre, but you'll easily find a taxi or xe om.

Destinations: Dong Ha (5 daily; 1hr 40min–2hr 35min); Hanoi (6 daily; 10hr–12hr); Hué (6 daily; 3hr–4hr); Ninh Binh (4 daily; 9hr–11hr); Vinh (6 daily; 3hr 30min–5hr).
By bus There's no long-distance bus station in Dong Hoi – just stand on the highway to flag buses down.
Destinations: Dong Ha (2hr); Hué (3hr 30min); Vinh (3hr).

TOURS

You'll find that most hotels run tours to Phong Nha, but the following independent outfits also come recommended.

Phongnha Discovery Tours 177 Hai Ba Trung ☎ 052 385 1661, ⓦ phongnhadiscovery.com. Small outfit able to book tickets and organize tours around Phong Nha-ke bang National Park (and, of course, to the cave itself). Also the best place to hunt up-to-date information about Son Doong, the world's largest known cave (see box opposite), which is in the area but not yet open to visitors.
Quang Binh Tourism 102 Ly Thuong Kiet ☎ 052 382 2669, ⓔ qbtouristcompany@dng.vnn.vn. Provides car rental and English-speaking guides for trips to the caves. They are also happy to book bus and train tickets.

ACCOMMODATION

Luxe Truong Phap ☎ 052 384 5959, ⓦ luxehotel.vn. Smart new hotel with English-speaking staff. Rooms are simple but immaculate, and some have a river view. Prices do not include breakfast. $25
Nam Long 22 Ho Xuan Huong ☎ 052 382 1851. One of the cheapest options in town; it's a family affair, and you're assured a friendly welcome. Rooms are larger than you might expect, but ask to see a few since some are windowless. $12
Saigon Quangbinh 20 Quach Xuan Ky ☎ 052 382 2276, ⓦ sgquangbinhtourist.com.vn. Quality hotel squashed between the citadel and the river, meaning that there are good views on both sides. The decor is chic, across the rooms and common areas alike, and you'll find a pool and tennis courts on site. $70
★ **Sun Spa Resort** My Canh ☎ 052 384 2999, ⓦ sunsparesortvietnam.com. Luxurious five-star on My Canh Beach. It's easily Dong Hoi's top hotel, and worth popping into even if you're not staying – its restaurants are superb (see opposite), while for a small fee non-guests can use the tennis courts, pool and other facilities. Rooms are fair value (and often discounted), though the bungalows are a little pricey. $120

EATING AND DRINKING

Hué specialities, such as *banh beo* and *banh khoai*, are available at a strip of small restaurants on Co Tam, one block north of the market. As usual, the market itself is home to a number of cheap and cheerful foodstalls. And look out for signs announcing the **local speciality** of *chao luon*, a thick eel soup sold at roadside restaurants.

QB Bar 3 Le Loi. More restaurant than bar, this trying-hard-to-be-flashy place uses pizzas, banana pancakes, fruit juices and even a couple of Korean dishes (from $3.50) to rope in every moderately affluent youth in the city. They also have the only espresso machine in the whole province – when it's working.

Saigon Quangbinh 20 Quach Xuan Ky. The stylish ground-floor lounge of this hotel is a good place for a drink.

From its comfy sofas you'll be able to take in partial river views – at their best during the day over a coffee, or at sundown with a cocktail in hand.

Sun Spa Resort My Canh. This hotel boasts a couple of reasonably priced restaurants: the *Sun Café* has an international a la carte menu, while the *Golden Lotus* serves perfectly prepared Vietnamese dishes, with seafood a speciality. Dishes start at around $6 at both venues.

Phong Nha and around

By the end of a trip to Vietnam, you may well be sick to death of caves – especially once you've been around Ha Long Bay – but if you see just one on your travels, make it **Phong Nha**, an otherworldly cavity only accessible by boat. It's a whopping 8km long, but only the first kilometre or so is open to the public, but this alone is beautiful enough to make a visit worthwhile. It was revered as the largest cave in Vietnam until the discovery of the nearby **Son Doong Cave**, now widely regarded as the largest in the whole world (see box below).

These caves form part of the **Phong Nha-Ke Bang National Park**, yet to be fully opened to international visitors. It's a place of intense beauty, at its best in the morning when banks of mist soften its jagged contours. There are other caves in the area, including the colossal **Thien Duong**, as well as the **Nuoc Mooc** eco-trail.

Brief history

Since time immemorial the underground river emerging at Phong Nha Cave has held a mystical fascination for the local population. The earliest-known devotees were ninth- and tenth-century Cham people, followed by Vietnamese who petitioned the **guardian spirits** during periods of drought, with great success by all accounts. When Europeans started exploring the caves early in the twentieth century it's said the rainmaker took everlasting umbrage. However, the explorers were undeterred and by the 1950s, tunnels 2km long had been surveyed and the number of visitors warranted the construction of a small hotel. Owing to the intervening wars, when Phong Nha provided safe warehousing – you can see evidence of an American rocket attack on the cliff above the cave entrance – nothing further happened until a British expedition was allowed to investigate in 1990. They began pushing upriver, eventually penetrating deep into the limestone massif.

THE WORLD'S LARGEST CAVE

Rarely can the word "cavernous" have been used with such justification. In 2009, a group of British cavers attempted the first-ever detailed survey of the **Son Doong cave**, in Phong Nha-Ke Bang National Park, finally giving up 4.5km in. Their records and photographs showed chambers large enough to swallow up whole city blocks – the largest found so far is over 250m high, and 150m wide. Subsequent investigations have added another 2km to the cave's charted length, and shown the presence of 70m-long stalactites, gigantic shards of crystal and grapefruit-sized calcite pearls. The cave is highly remote and, at the time of writing, had not yet been opened to the public, but it seems almost certain to become one of Vietnam's most alluring sights.

6

THE HO CHI MINH TRAIL

At the end of its "working" life, the Ho Chi Minh Trail had grown from a rough assemblage of animal tracks and **jungle paths** to become a highly effective **logistical network** stretching from near Vinh, north of the Seventeenth Parallel, to Tay Ninh Province on the edge of the Mekong Delta. Initially it took up to six months to walk the trail from north to south, most of the time travelling at night while carrying rations of rice and salt, medicines and equipment; in four years one man, Nguyen Viet Sinh, is reputed to have carried more than fifty tonnes and covered 40,000km, equivalent to walking round the world. By 1975, however, the trail – comprising at least three main arteries plus several feeder roads leading to various battlefronts and totalling over **15,000km** – was wide enough to take tanks and heavy trucks, and could be driven in just one week. It was protected by sophisticated anti-aircraft emplacements and supported by regular service stations (fuel and maintenance depots, ammunition dumps, food stores and hospitals), often located underground or in caves and all connected by field telephone. Eventually there was even an oil pipeline constructed alongside the trail to take fuel south from Vinh to a depot at Loc Ninh. All this absorbed thousands of men and women in maintenance work, as engineers, gunners and medical staff, while as many as fifty thousand Youth Volunteers repaired bridges and filled in bomb craters under cover of darkness.

The trail was conceived in early 1959 when **General Giap** ordered the newly created Logistical Group 559 to reconnoitre a safe route by which to direct men and equipment down the length of Vietnam in support of Communist groups in the south. Political cadres blazed the trail, followed in 1964 by the first deployment of ten thousand regular troops, and culminating in the trek south of 150,000 men in preparation for the **1968 Tet Offensive**. It was a logistical feat that rivalled Dien Bien Phu (see p.412) in both scale and determination: this time it was sustained over fifteen years and became a symbol to the Vietnamese of both their victory and their sacrifice. For much of its southerly route the trail ran through **Laos** and **Cambodia**, sometimes on paths forged during the war against the French, sometimes along riverbeds and always through the most difficult, mountainous terrain plagued with leeches, snakes, malaria and dysentery.

On top of all this, people on the trail had to contend with almost constant bombing. By early 1965, **aerial bombardment** had begun in earnest, using napalm and defoliants as well as conventional bombs, to be joined later by carpet-bombing B-52s. Every day in the spring of 1965 the US Air Force flew an estimated three hundred bombing raids over the trail and in eight years dropped over two million tonnes of bombs, mostly over Laos, in an effort to cut the flow. Later they experimented with seismic and acoustic sensors to eavesdrop on troop movements and pinpoint targets, but the trail was never completely severed and supplies continued to roll south in sufficient quantities to sustain the war.

Phong Nha Cave

Daily 6.30am–4.30pm · 40,000đ · boat 220,000đ

The only way to Phong Nha Cave is by boat. These seat up to fourteen people, and though it's theoretically possible to join other groups, you'll likely be told to charter one of your own. The boats wend their way 5km (30min) upstream to the cave entrance, after which the pilot cuts the engine and starts to paddle through. You'll drift awhile between rippling walls of limestone, and see immense stalactites and stalagmites, all lit by multicoloured spotlights. The boat eventually draws into a small subterranean beach, from which you follow an easy, 500m-long trail around the cave (flip-flops will be fine) – note that visitors must stick to the path to avoid any risk of rock damage. Your driver will be waiting for you at the end of the path.

Tien Son Cave

Daily 6.30am–4.30pm · ticket 40,000đ · boat 70,000đ

You can follow up your visit to Phong Nha by taking a steep, 330-step climb up to Tien Son Cave. From here you'll have a grand view of the valley, while inside there are Cham inscriptions dating as far back as the ninth century. Unfortunately, their magnificence is diluted somewhat by lurid lighting, presumably placed here to make for a more visually vivid experience – unless you're a true cave fanatic, you'll likely be happy with visiting Phong Nha alone.

Thien Duong Cave

Daily 7am–4pm• 120,000đ

Before the discovery of Son Doong (see box, p.315), Thien Duong, or "Paradise Cave", held a brief period in the limelight as the longest cavern in Vietnam. Under the same management as the *Sun Spa Resort* in Dong Hoi, the first kilometre or so has now been fully opened up to tourism – a truly baffling staff-to-visitors ratio shows that there are high hopes of making this one of Vietnam's major drawcards. This partially explains the high ticket price, though this also affords you a golf-buggy ride to the trailhead, and a (largely unnecessary) guide for the cave itself. It's a sweaty climb up, but the jaw-dropping beauty of the cavern makes such exertion worthwhile – there's nothing in particular to see, but it's simply a joy to be walking in a cavern of such unworldly size – in places, over 100m in both height and width.

Nuoc Mooc Eco-trail

Opening times vary • 50,000đ • Buy tickets at the Visitors' Centre near Phong Nha cave (see opposite), from where it's also possible to charter a boat (2hr; 350,000đ) to the trailhead

Sprawling along picturesque riverside territory and lassoed together with bamboo bridges, this 1km-long eco-trail shows the reassuring direction in which local tourism is heading. You're highly unlikely to see any animals, but there are a couple of opportunities to swim – the entry price will see your bags taken care of, though you'll have to pay extra for drinks.

ARRIVAL   PHONG NHA

On a tour Guided tours to the cave usually cost around $30 per person ($20 if in a small group), and are easy to organize with agencies or hotels in Dong Hoi (see p.314). Some do the same from Hué, though it's a hell of a long day-trip and not recommended.

By bus There are a few daily buses from Dong Hoi (20,000đ), though schedules are irregular; *Phong Nha Farmstay* (see below) should be able to give you up-to-date info.

By xe om If you can't track down a bus, try your luck with a xe om driver, though any deal will have to include at least two hours' waiting time; it'll cost a minimum of $25.

By motorbike With your own wheels, from Dong Hoi take Highway 1 north for 15km to Hoan Lao, where a signpost indicates a turn to Phong Nha. The national park is currently in the process of being opened up, and access is one big grey area; *Phong Nha Farmstay* (see below) runs great tours, and are the best to ask for park information.

INFORMATION

Tickets You'll have to buy tickets to all sights listed here at the Visitors' Centre, which is located in the centre of Son Trach village, right next to the boat departure point. Note, however, that the boats may not operate after heavy rain if the water level is too high.

ACCOMMODATION AND EATING

You'll find a fair number of near-identical budget hotels and simple restaurants lining the road around the Visitors' Centre.

★ **Phong Nha Farmstay** 35km from Dong Hoi ☎ 0944 759864, ⓦ phong-nha-cave.com. Superb hotel run by an affable Aussie and his Vietnamese wife. The setting is gloriously rural and highly picturesque, and though rooms are quite basic, the on-site swimming pool more than makes up for it. In addition, the kitchen churns out delectable, and fairly priced meals – a good thing, as there are no restaurants for miles around. A taxi here from Dong Hoi will cost $17, a xe om around half that. Dorm $8, double. $25

Saigon Phongnha ☎ 052 367 7016, ⓦ sgquangbinhtourist.com.vn. The only actual hotel in the area, though ageing without much grace. Rooms are a little institutional for some, and the reception is merely an outdoor desk; however, the adjacent dining area is a good place for coffee or beer after your trip to the caves. $25

6

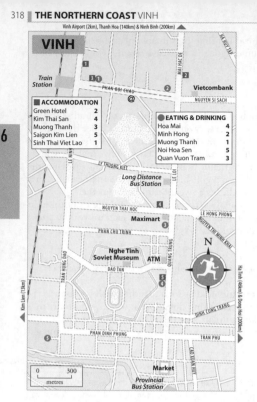

Vinh Airport (2km), Thanh Hoa (140km) & Ninh Binh (200km) ▲

VINH

Train Station

Phan Boi Chau

Vietcombank

Nguyen Si Sach

ACCOMMODATION
Green Hotel   2
Kim Thai San   4
Muong Thanh   3
Saigon Kim Lien   5
Sinh Thai Viet Lao 1

EATING & DRINKING
Hoa Mai   4
Minh Hong   2
Muong Thanh   1
Noi Hoa Sen   5
Quan Vuon Tram   3

Ly Thuong Kiet

Long Distance Bus Station

Nguyen Thai Hoc

Le Hong Phong

Maximart

Phan Chu Trinh

Nghe Tinh Soviet Museum

Dao Tan

ATM

Nguyen Thi Minh Khai

Quang Trung

N

Ha Tinh (46km) & Dong Hoi (200km)

Dinh Cong Trang

Phan Dinh Phung

Tran Phu

Market

0   300
metres

Provincial Bus Station

Kim Lien (13km)

Tran Hung Dao

Le Loi

Cao Xuan Huy

Vinh

If you want to see whole swathes of bleak, Soviet-style architecture, you could do worse than heading to **VINH**. Although a place of pilgrimage for Vietnamese tourists – Ho Chi Minh was born in the nearby village of **Kim Lien** – it receives very few foreign guests, most of whom use the city as a stop on the long journey between Hué and Hanoi, or a jumping-off point for the Lao border (see box below). Still, the place has its merits – plenty of cheap accommodation around the train and bus stations, and the chance to discover a real Vietnamese city, almost entirely unaffected by international tourism.

Brief history

Vinh fared particularly badly in the twentieth century. As an industrial port-city dominating major land routes, whose population was known for rebellious tendencies, the town became a natural target during both French and American wars. In the 1950s French bombs destroyed large swathes of Vinh, after which the Viet Minh burnt down what remained rather than let it fall into enemy hands; the

---

CAU TREO AND NAM CAN BORDER CROSSINGS INTO LAOS

There are border crossings into Laos at Cau Treo and Nam Can: since both are remote with haphazard bus connections, it's essential to get up-to-date advice from the bus station or local guesthouses before attempting either crossing.

Cau Treo is the crossing used by most buses heading from Hanoi to Vientiane. You may be able to pick one of these up in Vinh – they usually pass through town in the very late evening, making a stop at the long-distance bus station (see opposite). Making the same trip independently is possible, but frought with potential hazards – an internet search will bring up plenty of stories about the uncomfortable journey, and even a few pertaining to extortion. If you are willing to risk it, get on an early-morning public bus from Vinh to Tay Son, from where you'll have to pick up a minibus or xe om for the last 25km to Cau Treo; you could also try hitching to Lak Sao, 20km across the border in Laos.

There are now **direct buses** from Vinh to Phonsavan, via the **Nam Can** border crossing – comparatively devoid of complications, but still a rough ride. They leave from Vinh's long-distance bus station daily at 6am and take 12hr to get to Phonsavan; a couple per week continue straight through to Louang Prabang.

In theory, you can obtain Lao **visas** at both border posts ($30; two passport photos required), but check with the embassy for current information. Otherwise you can obtain Lao visas at the Lao consulates in Ho Chi Minh City (see p.107) or Da Nang (see p.274), or at their Hanoi embassy (see p.388).

rebuilt town was flattened once again during the American air raids. Reconstruction proceeded slowly after 1975, mostly financed by East Germany; the decrepit hulks of barrack-like apartment blocks, totally unsuited to the Vietnamese climate, still dominate the city centre. Things are beginning to improve, however, as trade with Laos brings more money into the region: Vinh's streets are being repaved and pavements laid; smart new villas and hotels are being built; and there's even a multi-storey supermarket stocked with all manner of goodies.

Nghe Tinh Soviet Museum

Daily 7–11am & 2–5.30pm • Free

Vinh's only sight, this celebrates a mass uprising against French rule in the 1930s (see p.440), relating the causes, development and aftermath of the uprising. It's located in the grounds of a Nguyen-dynasty citadel, which has seen better days; its only notable features are the old gates, which you'll pass through on your way to the museum.

ARRIVAL AND DEPARTURE   VINH

By plane Vinh Airport is 6km to the north of town (45,000đ by taxi; 25,000đ by xe om).
Destinations: Hanoi (2 daily; 1hr); Ho Chi Minh City (5 daily; 1hr 45min).
By train Ga Vinh is in Vinh's ugly northwestern suburbs, though it's an easy walk from a number of hotels. The city centre is also just about walkable, though xe om will be waiting in droves to spirit you away from the station.
Destinations: Dong Hoi (6 daily; 4hr–5hr); Hanoi (6 daily; 6hr–6hr 30min); Hué (6 daily; 6hr–9hr); Ninh Binh (4 daily; 4hr).

By bus The long-distance bus station (Ben Xe Vinh) is in the centre of the city while public buses from Trung Tam and the border with Laos terminate at the provincial bus station (Ben Xe Cho Vinh) at the south end of Quang Trung, behind Vinh market. Open-tour buses can set down passengers in Vinh en route, but confirm onward travel with the relevant company beforehand.
Destinations: Dong Ha (6hr–7hr); Dong Hoi (4hr); Hué (8hr–10hr); Ninh Binh (5hr); Tay Son (2hr); Vientiane (12hr–14hr).

INFORMATION

Tourist information Information is at a premium. Staff at the *Saigon Kim Lien hotel* (see below) can sometimes help out with the basics. Car and motorbike rental are available through most hotels, and you can pick up xe om anywhere in town (from 15,000đ for a short ride).

ACCOMMODATION

A transport hub, Vinh has a large number of hotels, which means places are willing to bargain. Many hotels, however, sit right on the highway, so wherever possible go for a room at the back.

Green Hotel 2 Mai Hac De ☎038 384 4788, ⓦ greenhotelnghean.com. If you're after a few creature comforts near the train station, this place has old-fashioned but decent-size rooms. Other plus points are the small pool and friendly welcome. **$25**
Kim Thai San 107 Nguyen Thai Hoc ☎038 384 4409. Very friendly mini-hotel, situated just off the busy streets yet in the thick of the action. Rooms are spacious, clean and all en suite. Each floor has a communal balcony. **$10**
Muong Thanh 1 Phan Boi Chau ☎038 353 5666, ⓦ muongthanhvinhhotel.com. Service is friendly and the rooms are smart and well-equipped at this large hotel, near the station. There's a swimming pool on the second floor. **$25**

Saigon Kim Lien 25 Quang Trung ☎038 383 8899, ⓦ saigonkimlien.com.vn. Vinh's top hotel opened in 1990 to commemorate the hundredth anniversary of Ho Chi Minh's birth. Prices are surprisingly affordable for comfortable and well-proportioned rooms. Facilities include a recommended restaurant, bar, pool, business centre and money exchange. **$40**
Sinh Thai Viet Lao 2 Le Ninh ☎038 353 8847. Right next to the train station, and a reasonable budget option if you're breaking a long journey; rooms are bare and beds a little hard, but all have satellite TV and en-suite bathrooms. **$10**

6

THE LIFE OF HO CHI MINH

So inextricably is the life of **Ho Chi Minh** intertwined with Vietnam's emergence from colonial rule that his biography is largely an account of the country's struggle for independence in the twentieth century. As Ho adopted dozens of pseudonyms and never kept diaries, uncertainty clouds his public life and almost nothing is known about the private man beneath the cultivated persona of a celibate and aesthete, totally dedicated to his family – a concept that embraced all the Vietnamese people.

Ho's **origins** were humble enough – he was born Nguyen Sinh Cung in 1890, the youngest child of a minor mandarin who was dismissed from the Imperial court in Hué for anti-colonialist sympathies. Ho attended high school in Hué but was expelled for taking part in a student protest; he left Vietnam for France in 1911, then spent several years wandering the world. He worked in the dockyards of Brooklyn and as pastry chef in London's *Carlton Hotel*, before returning to France in the aftermath of World War I, to earn his living retouching photographs. In Paris, Ho became an increasingly active **nationalist**, and caused quite a stir during the Versailles Peace Conference when he published a petition demanding democratic constitutional government for Indochina. For a while Ho joined the French Socialists, but when they split in 1920 he defected to become one of the founder members of the French Communist Party, inspired by Lenin's total opposition to imperialism.

Ho's energetic role in French Communism was rewarded when he was called to Moscow in 1923 to begin a career in **international revolution**, and a year later he found himself posted to southern China as a Comintern agent. Within a few months he had set up Vietnam's first Marxist-Leninist organization, the Revolutionary Youth League, which attracted a band of impassioned young Vietnamese eager to hear about the new ideology. But in 1927, Chiang Kai-shek, leader of the Chinese nationalists, turned against the Communists and Ho was forced to flee. For a while he lived in Thailand, disguised as a Buddhist monk, before turning up in Hong Kong in 1930 where he was instrumental in founding the **Vietnamese Communist Party**. By now the French authorities had placed a death sentence on Ho's head, for insurrection; he was arrested in Hong Kong but escaped with the help of prison hospital staff, who managed to persuade everyone, including the French police, that Ho had died of tuberculosis.

Ho disappeared again for a few years while the fuss died down, before reappearing on China's southern border in the late 1930s. In 1941, aged 51, he re-entered Vietnam for the first time in thirty years, wearing a Chinese-style tunic and rubber-tyre sandals, and carrying just a small rattan trunk and his precious typewriter. In the mountains of northern Vietnam, Ho, now finally known as Ho Chi Minh (meaning "He Who Enlightens"), was joined by Vo Nguyen Giap, Pham Van Dong and other young militants. Together they laid the groundwork for the anticipated national uprising, establishing a united patriotic front, the League for the Independence of Vietnam – better known by its abbreviated name, the **Viet Minh** – and training the guerrilla units that would eventually evolve into the Vietnamese People's Army. But events conspired against Ho: in 1942 he was arrested as a Franco-Japanese spy when he crossed back into China to raise support for the nationalist cause, and he languished for more than a year in various prisons, writing a collection of poetry later published as the "Prison Diary".

Meanwhile, however, events were hotting up, and when the Japanese occupation of Vietnam ended in August 1945, the Viet Minh were ready to seize control. Ho Chi Minh, by this time seriously ill, led them to a brief period in power following the August Revolution, and then ultimately to Independence in 1954. For the next fifteen years, as **President of the Democratic Republic of Vietnam**, Uncle Ho took his country along a sometimes rocky socialist path, continually seeking reunification through negotiation and then war. But he didn't live to see a united Vietnam: early in 1969 his heart began to fail and on September 2, Vietnam's National Day, he died. Since then, myth and fact have converged in a cult placing Ho Chi Minh at the top of Vietnam's pantheon of heroes, true to Confucian tradition – though against Ho's express wishes.

EATING

There's not much choice for places to eat in Vinh, although you'll find a whole host of street kitchens on Le Loi, with a group outside the bus station and another starting just east of the train station.

Hoa Mai 25 Quang Trung. The smartest option in town is this restaurant at the *Saigon Kim Lien* hotel, which serves fairly priced Asian and European dishes, starting at around $4.50. Daily noon–3pm & 6–9pm.

Minh Hong 3 Phan Boi Chau. Popular with the locals (always a good sign), this simple restaurant is worth tracking down if you're based near the train station, and serves standard Vietnamese rice, noodle and meat dishes for $2 and up. Daily 7am–7pm.

Noi Hoa Sen On a fine day this restaurant, set in the middle of a lake at the west end of Phan Dinh Phung, makes a pleasant and inexpensive place to eat. Their meat dishes (from $3) are recommended, though they'll likely point you to the fish first. Daily 9am–9pm.

★ **Muong Thanh** Come here for breakfast if you're staying in the area – a full buffet, including good fruit and freshly made omelettes, for just $2. Staff rarely get to see foreigners, and will likely make a fuss of you – expect to be plied with coffee and juice. Breakfast 8–10.30am.

Quan Vuon Tram 49b Le Loi. A popular choice for the evening, this beer garden serves jugs of bia hoi accompanied by chicken curry, spicy beef, pork skewers and the like. Daily 10am–10pm.

Kim Lien

Museum daily 7–11am & 1.30–5pm • Free

Ho Chi Minh was born in 1890 in Hoang Tru Village, **KIM LIEN** commune, 14km west of Vinh. The two simple houses made of bamboo wattle and palm-leaf thatch are 1959 reconstructions, now surrounded by fields of sweet potatoes. Ho's birthplace is said to be the hut by itself on the left as you approach, while behind stands the brick-built family altar. At the age of 6 Ho moved 2km west, to what is now called Lang Sen (Lotus Village), to live with his father in very similar surroundings. The two Sen houses are also replicas, built in 1955, with nothing much to see inside, but the complex is peaceful and alive with dancing butterflies. The **museum** nearby illustrates Ho's world travels with memorabilia and photos.

ARRIVAL AND DEPARTURE	KIM LIEN

By car or motorbike Take Phan Dinh Phung west from Vinh market. The road soon becomes Highway 46; follow this until you reach the signed turning south for Lang Sen and Kim Lien. The signed route takes you first to Ho's birthplace and then loops round to find the museum a little further back, down a path beside a small lotus pond.

By xe om A xe om to both sites from Vinh should set you back around 100,000đ, including waiting time.

Ninh Binh

At first glance, the provincial capital of **NINH BINH** appears to be yet another dusty, traffic-heavy northern town. However, glance to the west and you'll be beckoned to stay by a thousand fingers of limestone – a land-lubbing Ha Long Bay, with a clutch of historic and architectural sights to add to its geological beauty.

Despite the wealth of sights surrounding it (see box, p.323), Ninh Binh itself claims just one sight of its own: a kilometre to the north a picturesque little pagoda nestles at the base of **Non Nuoc Mountain**. This knobbly outcrop – no more than 60m high – is noted for an eminently missable collection of ancient poetic inscriptions and views east over a power station to the graphically named "Sleeping Lady Mountain".

6

ARRIVAL AND DEPARTURE
NINH BINH

Given Ninh Binh's small size, it's quite easy to cover the whole city on foot.

By train Ga Ninh Binh, Ninh Binh's pint-sized station, sits in a convenient location on the east side of town, an easy walk from the centre.
Destinations: Dong Hoi (4 daily; 10hr); Hanoi (4 daily; 2hr 30min); Hué (4 daily; 13hr–14hr); Vinh (4 daily; 4hr).

By bus The refreshingly well-organized bus station is also on the east side of town.
Destinations: Hai Phong (3hr); Hanoi (2hr); Kim Son, for Phat Diem (1hr); Son La (8hr); Vinh (5hr).

GETTING AROUND

Motorbike rental starts at around 100,000đ per day, while bicycles can be yours for just 25,000đ; almost every hotel will be able to sort you out.

INFORMATION

Tourist information All hotels and guesthouses can help with information, tours and transport; staff at the *Queen*, *Thanh Thuy* and *Xuan Hoa* hotels are particularly knowledgeable about the area and day-tours of the main sights can dip under $10 if you're in a group.

ACCOMMODATION

Queen 20–22 Hoang Hoa Tham ☎030 389 3535, ⓦqueenhotel.vn. Right next to the train station, the Queen has been housing budget travellers for years; with the addition of a spick-and-span new wing just across the road, it's now an even more appealing place to stay. Rooms in the old wing are a little worn, while those in the new one come with a higher price tag for flatscreen TVs and excellent en-suite facilities. $10

Thanh Binh 31 Luong Van Tuy ☎030 387 2439. Clean, well-equipped rooms off the highway make this a good alternative to the nearby *Thuy Anh* and *Thanh Thuy* if those are full. The meals here are also recommended. $20

Thanh Thuy 128 Le Hong Phong ☎030 387 1811, ⓦhotelthanhthuy.com. Another hotel with two distinct sections. Again, the new section is more salubrious; rooms are cheaper in the old wing, though rodent problems have been an issue. Breakfast is not included. $12

Thuy Anh 55a Truong Han Sieu ☎030 387 1602, ⓦthuyanhhotel.com. A hotel, rather than a guesthouse – a rarity in Ninh Binh. It boasts efficient service and a range of immaculately kept rooms, from a couple with fan and shared bathroom up to huge rooms furnished and equipped to a high standard. Prices are also quite reasonable, and there are good-quality bicycles and motorbikes for rent. $15

★ **Xuan Hoa** 31d Pho Minh Khai ☎030 388 0970, ⓦxuanhoahotel.com. Owner Xuan and his family provide the friendliest welcome in Ninh Binh. They have two hotels, situated almost side-by-side just off the main drag; relatively quiet by Ninh Binh standards, they overlook a lake. The rooms are spotless, modern and well equipped, and some have views of the mountains to the west. They also run excellent tours. $12

EATING

There are almost no restaurants of significant appeal in Ninh Binh, though on the plus side all hotels listed provide excellent food at surprisingly reasonable prices. Their kitchens are usually open from dawn until well into the evening.

Queen 20–22 Hoang Hoa Tham. This hotel turns out hearty meals, with the kitchen of the old wing slightly preferable. Were there an international award for banana pancakes ($1), this could serve as Vietnam's entry – perfect before a train ride, even if you're not staying here.

Rung & Bien 2 Tran Hung Dao. One of the only restaurants in central Ninh Binh to serve the regional speciality – goat meat (from 90,000đ). Stuffed animals are dotted around the place and show what else may be on the menu, but mercifully they can get the basics right too.

Thuy Anh 55a Truong Han Sieu. Good food in friendly surroundings, with some Chinese dishes on the menu – try the fried rice ($4). In addition, the rooftop bar provides a scenic spot to unwind at the end of a heavy day's sightseeing.

Xuan Hoa 31d Pho Minh Khai. Perhaps best in town for both value and quality, thanks to Hoa, the wife of owner Xuan, who whips up some excellent dishes. They can also serve goat dishes if given advance warning.

DIRECTORY

Bank Getting cash can still be a little tricky in Ninh Binh; the most useful ATM is the Techcombank at 75 Le Hong Phong.

MAKING THE MOST OF NINH BINH

While the town itself has little to detain you, the surrounding hills shelter **Tam Coc**, where sampans slither through the limestone tunnels of "Ha Long Bay on land", and one of Vietnam's ancient capitals, **Hoa Lu**, represented by two darkly atmospheric dynastic temples. On the way to Hoa Lu is **Trang Anh**, a less-touristed version of Tam Coc, while further on is **Bai Dinh Pagoda** – though decidedly non-ancient, this ranks as the largest Buddhist complex in Vietnam, and quite possibly the whole world, and is worth a look for its sheer scale alone. All of these places can be tackled in one day by car or motorbike, or by bicycle via the back lanes.

To the east, the stone mass of **Phat Diem Cathedral** wallows in the rice fields, an extraordinary amalgam of Western and Oriental architecture that still shepherds an active Catholic community. Heading west instead, **Cuc Phuong** is one of Vietnam's more accessible national parks and contains some magnificent, centuries-old trees.

More boat trips are in store at **Kenh Ga**, to visit a limestone cave, and at **Van Long** nature reserve, both on the Cuc Phuong road. These last sights are more distant: the cathedral requires a half-day outing, while Cuc Phuong and either Kenh Ga or Van Long can be combined in a long day-trip. Hanoi is only a couple of hours away, and the Hoa Lu/Tam Coc–Bich Dong circuit makes a popular and inexpensive day tour out of the capital. However, with more time, it's far better to take advantage of Ninh Binh's **hotels** and services to explore the area at a more leisurely pace.

Tam Coc

Boats 7am-5pm • Entry and boat hire 140,000đ

It's hard not to be won over by the mystical, watery beauty of the **Tam Coc "three caves" region**, which is effectively a miniature landlocked version of Ha Long Bay. The film *Indochine* helped to put it on the tourist map, and both good and bad have come of its burgeoning popularity – access roads have been improved, though some of the canal banks themselves have been lined with concrete. In addition, Tam Coc has become relentlessly commercial, with many travellers having a wonderful day spoiled by hard-sell antics at the end of their trip. Despite the over-zealous – occasionally aggressive – peddling of embroideries and soft drinks by the rowers, the two-hour sampan-ride is a definite highlight, meandering through dumpling-shaped karst hills in a flooded landscape where river and rice paddy merge serenely into one; keep an eye open for mountain goats high on the cliffs, and bright, darting kingfishers. Journey's end is **Tam Coc**, three long, dark tunnel-caves (Hang Ca, Hang Giua and Hang Cuoi) eroded through the limestone hills with barely sufficient clearance for the sampan after heavy rains. On the way back, you can ask to stop at **Thai Vi Temple**, a short walk from the river. Dating from the thirteenth century and dedicated to the founder of the Tran Dynasty, it's a peaceful, atmospheric spot.

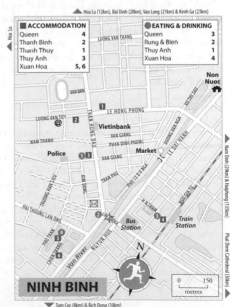

■ ACCOMMODATION		● EATING & DRINKING	
Queen	4	Queen	3
Thanh Binh	2	Rung & Bien	2
Thanh Thuy	1	Thuy Anh	1
Thuy Anh	3	Xuan Hoa	4
Xuan Hoa	5, 6		

NINH BINH

Tam Coc (8km) & Bich Dong (10km)

Bich Dong

If you have time after the boat trip, follow the road leading southwest from the boat dock for about 2km to visit the cave-pagoda of **Bich Dong**, or "Jade Grotto". Stone-cut steps, entangled by the thick roots of banyan trees, lead up a cliff face peppered with shrines to the cave entrance, believed to have been discovered by two monks in the early fifteenth century. On the rock face above, two giant characters declare "Bich Dong". The story goes that they were engraved in the eighteenth century by the father of Nguyen Du (author of the classic *Tale of Kieu*), who was entrusted with construction of the complex. The cave walls are now scrawled with graffiti but the three Buddhas sit unperturbed on their lotus thrones beside a head-shaped rock which purportedly bestows longevity if touched. Walk through the cave to emerge higher up the cliff, from where steps continue to the third and final temple and viewpoint over the waterlogged scene.

ARRIVAL AND DEPARTURE

TAM COC

To avoid the worst of the crowds at Tam Coc, it's best to set off either very early in the morning or in the late afternoon.

By bicycle or motorbike From Ninh Binh, the easiest and most enjoyable way to reach Tam Coc is to rent a bicycle or motorbike; the signed turning, replete with gigantic photo, is 4km south on Highway 1, before the cement factory. From Tam Coc, it's also possible to take a delightful 10km cycle ride through rice fields and limestone karst scenery to Hoa Lu (below) – a local map would come in handy (*Xuan Hoa* hotel hands out passable hand-drawn

ones), but you'll be able to ask locals.
By xe om Ninh Binh to Tam Coc will cost around $6, including waiting time. If you want to combine Tam Coc with other sights, it is more cost-effective to organize a tour.
On a tour Tours start at $10 on a bike or $20 per car, including Hoa Lu. Hanoi agencies also run day-trips, starting at $20 per seat in a minibus.

Hoa Lu

Twelve kilometres northwest of Ninh Binh, **Hoa Lu** makes another rewarding excursion. In the 10th century, this site was the capital of an early, independent Vietnamese kingdom called Dai Co Viet. The fortified royal palaces of the Dinh and Le kings are now reduced to archeological remains, but their dynastic temples (seventeenth-century copies of eleventh-century originals) still rest quietly in a narrow valley surrounded by wooded, limestone hills. Though the temple buildings and attractive walled courtyards are unspectacular, the inner sanctuaries are compelling – mysterious, dark caverns where statues of the kings, wrapped in veils of pungent incense, are worshipped by the light of candles.

Den Dinh Tien Hoang

Admission 10,000đ (includes Den Le Dai Hanh)

First stop at the site should be the imposing **Den Dinh Tien Hoang**, on the left as you approach from the car park and ticket office. It was dedicated to King Dinh Tien Hoang (also known as Dinh Bo Linh), who seized power in 968 AD and moved the capital south from Co Loa in the Red River Delta to this secure valley, far from the threat of Chinese intervention. Dinh Tien Hoang's gilded effigy can be seen in the temple's second sanctuary room, flanked by his three sons. Dinh was born near Hoa Lu, the illegitimate son of a provincial governor; he became known as a reforming monarch who ruled with a firm hand, and is reputed to have placed a bronze urn and caged tiger in front of his palace and decreed that "those who violate the laws will be boiled and gnawed". However, in 979 an assassin, variously rumoured to be a mad monk or a palace hitman, killed the king and his two eldest sons as they lay in a drunken sleep.

Den Le Dai Hanh
Admission 10,000đ (includes Den Dinh Tien Hoang)

The second temple in Hoa Lu, **Den Le Dai Hanh**, came about as the result of the anarchy that followed the death of King Dinh Tien Hoang. Le Hoan, commander of Dinh's army and supposed lover (and eventual husband) of his queen, wrested power and declared himself King Le Dai Hanh in 980. What's now known as the **Early Le dynasty** also spiralled into chaos 25 years later, while the king's three sons squabbled over the succession. Le Dai Hanh is enshrined in the temple's rear sanctuary with his eldest son and Queen Duong Van Nga. On the way out, signs direct you to an adjacent archeological dig where some tenth-century foundations have been unearthed, along with tiles and pottery shards.

Trang Anh
Boats 7am–5pm • Admission and boat hire 140,000đ

This complex of caves boasted "well-kept secret" status for a couple of years, but is now just as busy as its counterpart, Tam Coc (see p.323), if with slightly less pressure to buy drinks or embroidery at the end of your trip. Avoid weekends, when local tourists come down from Hanoi; the ensuing traffic-jams can make the caves quite claustrophobic.

Bai Dinh Pagoda
Free

Twelve kilometres from Hoa Lu is the jaw-dropping **Bai Dinh Pagoda**, which only opened up in 2010 and is yet to be fully completed. Bai Dinh's sheer scale makes it unique among Vietnamese Buddhist complexes – its numerous halls and courtyards sprawl up the mountainside for almost a kilometre. The front courtyard is lined with over five hundred arhat statues (each individually designed), while the largest bell and Buddha statue weigh in at 36 and 100 tons respectively. Although the temple is a functioning place of worship, it feels like a tourist trap, but one laid on primarily for locals – visit on a busy day and you'll run the gauntlet of camera sight-lines. It is nonetheless a spectacular thing to behold, particularly the wild extravagance of the three main hall interiors, all of which are filled with gigantic golden statues, and have their walls lined with dozens of smaller versions of the same.

ARRIVAL AND DEPARTURE   BAI DINH

By motorbike or bicycle If time allows, Hoa Lu is definitely one to do by bicycle in combination with Tam Coc (see p.323); allow at least one hour for the journey. The best route to Hoa Lu from Ninh Binh is to head up Tran Hung Dao, and turn left after #58 – from here, it's pretty much straight all the way.
By xe om From Ninh Binh, the quickest way to Hoa Lu is to rent a motorbike for the day or take a xe om (100,000đ for the round-trip). Bai Dinh is 20km from Ninh Binh, and you'll have to backtrack a bit from Hoa Lu to get there.
On a tour Hotels in Ninh Binh lay on tours from $10 per person on a bike, and $20 for a car; Hanoi agencies also run day-trips, costing from $20 per person in a minibus.

Phat Diem

Strike southeast from Ninh Binh and there's no mistaking that you've stumbled on a Christian enclave, where church spires sprout out of the flat paddy land on all sides; it's said that 95 percent of the district's population attend church on a regular basis. These coastal communities of northern Vietnam were among the first to be targeted by Portuguese missionaries in the sixteenth century. This area owes its particular zeal to the Jesuit Alexandre de Rhodes who preached here in 1627. The greatest monument to all this religious fervour is the century-old stone cathedral, **Phat Diem**, situated 30km from Ninh Binh in **Kim Son Village**.

The Cathedral

Opening times vary and often not open at all; check with your hotel in Ninh Binh before setting off

The first surprise is the cathedral's monumental **bell pavilion**, whose curved roofs and triple gateway could easily be the entrance to a Vietnamese temple save for a few telltale crosses and a host of angels. The structure is built entirely of dressed stone, as is the equally impressive cathedral facade sheltering in its wake; both edifices rest on hundreds of bamboo poles embedded in the marshy ground. Behind, the tiled double roof of the **nave** extends for 74m, supported by 52 immense ironwood pillars and sheltering a cool, dark and peaceful sanctuary. The **altar** table is chiselled from a single block of marble, decorated with elegant sprays of bamboo, while the altarpiece above glows with red and gold lacquers in an otherwise sober interior. Twelve priests conduct daily services here for a diocese that musters 140,000 Catholics.

ARRIVAL AND DEPARTURE   PHAT DIEM

By bus Frequent public buses depart from Ninh Binh bus station for the 1hr journey to Kim Son, though note that the last bus back leaves at around 3.30pm.

By bike or xe om Phat Diem is near enough to reach by rented motorbike or xe om. If you're riding here yourself, take the road heading straight east from Ninh Binh's Lim Bridge and, when you get to Kim Son Village, 100m after passing an elegant covered bridge, take a right turn to the cathedral.

INFORMATION

Follow the compound wall anticlockwise from the road to reach the entrance, where you can buy a small but informative booklet explaining the cathedral's colourful history. The bell is rung daily at noon, and visitors are allowed to accompany the bell-ringer up the stairs (block your ears, though).

Tran Me

TRAN ME, a town 23km from Ninh Binh on the road to Cuc Phuong, is the departure point for a couple of very different but worthwhile boat trips. It's possible to do them both in a day, or either one can be combined with a visit to Cuc Phuong or Hoa Lu.

Van Long Nature Reserve

90min boat trip 50,000đ

The more beguiling of the two boat trips in the area takes you round the shallow, reed-filled lagoons of **Van Long Nature Reserve**, signed to the right about 2km to the east of Tran Me. The road ends beside the ticket office (just past a new hotel complex)

FATHER SAU AND THE QUIET AMERICAN

The idea for Phat Diem cathedral was conceived and carried out by Father Tran Luc (also known as Father Sau), whose tomb lies behind the bell tower. It was more than ten years in the preparation, as stone and wood were transported from the provinces of Thanh Hoa and Nghe An, though it apparently took a mere three months to build in 1891. During the French War, the Catholic Church formed a powerful political group in Vietnam that stood virtually independent of the French administration but also opposed to the Communists. The then bishop of Phat Diem, Monseigneur Le Huu Tu, was outspokenly anti-French and an avowed nationalist, but, as his diocese lay on the edge of government-held territory, the French supplied him with sufficient arms to maintain a militia of two thousand men in return for containing Viet Minh infiltration. However, in December 1951 the Viet Minh launched a major assault on the village and took it – with suspicious ease for French tastes, who felt the Catholics were withholding information on enemy activities in the area, if not actually assisting them. When paratroopers came in to regain control, the Viet Minh withdrew, taking with them a valuable supply of weapons. The author Graham Greene was in Phat Diem at the time, on an assignment for *Life Magazine*, and watched the battle from the bell tower of the cathedral – later using the scene in *The Quiet American*.

where you are then poled across the wetlands and among the limestone outcrops in a low-slung bamboo sampan. Take your binoculars: the crags are home to a small, isolated population of Delacour's langur, and the reed beds provide refuge for migratory waterfowl. At present there's a good chance you'll have the place to yourself, with only the eerie cries of monkeys and birds to break the silence, but this is unlikely to last. **Hawkers** are banned from using boats, but already they gather round the ticket office whenever a tour bus appears and there is even talk about opening restaurants along the dyke.

6

Kenh Ga
Boat trips 50,000đ per person for a 45min ride

The village of **Kenh Ga** sits in a canal and is accessible only by water; though the trip may not be as scenic as others in the Ninh Binh area, it's still worth the journey. The village boasts houses and even an ornate church, but many families live on boats and the whole place seems to be engaged in watery pursuits: boatyards turn out concrete-hulled barges to take gravel and quarried stone downstream; there are fish farms and great flocks of ducks, and sampans bustle about, often propelled by people rowing with their feet. Kenh Ga (Chicken Canal) supposedly gets its name from the nearby hot spring where chickens were soaked in the near-boiling water to make them easier to pluck. The water is also said to be good for digestion, skin ailments and general recuperation and the site was developed for bathing, but the facilities are very run down.

Van Trinh grotto

Better to press on to the final destination, **Van Trinh grotto**, a little-visited cave system where the guide will point out gnarled rocky outcrops which conjure up images of turtles, dragons, elephants and wizened faces. The local tourist authority has now installed lighting and concrete pathways, but you'll still need **stout shoes**, especially during the dry season when boats can't pull up outside the cave and you may have to walk the final kilometre.

ARRIVAL AND DEPARTURE — VAN LONG AND KENH GA

By car or bike Van Long and Kenh Ga can be reached independently by car or motorbike, though you'll have to haggle with boat-owners to do justice to the area.
On a tour Hotels in Ninh Binh (and a few Hanoi tour agencies) also offer organized tours combining both places, usually roping in Hoa Lu and/or Tam Coc; prices start at around $12 per person for a one-day excursion, including all boat trips.

EATING

There are cheap food stalls in Tran Me, but the most convenient place to eat is the small **restaurant** next to the Kenh Ga ticket office. There is no menu but a good choice is the local fish and a dish of their excellent spring rolls. If you order before you set off on the boat trip, the meal will be ready on your return.

Cuc Phuong National Park

☎ 030 384 8006, 🌐 cucphuongtourism.com

In 1962 Vietnam's first national park was established around a narrow valley between forested limestone hills on the borders of Ninh Binh, Thanh Hoa and Hoa Binh provinces, containing over two hundred square kilometres of tropical evergreen rainforest. **Cuc Phuong** is well set up for tourism and sees a steady stream of visitors, attracted principally by the excellent primate rescue centre, but also by the easy access to impressively ancient trees. With more time, you can walk into the park interior, overnight in a Muong village and experience the multi-layered forest. The most enjoyable time for walking in these hills is October to January, when mosquitoes and leeches take a break and temperatures are relatively cool – but this is also peak season. Flowers are at their best February and March, while April and May are the months when lepidopterists can enjoy the "butterfly festival" as thousands of butterflies colour the forest.

Endangered Primate Rescue Center

Daily 9–11am & 1.30–4pm • ⓦ primatecenter.org

Some of the luckier victims of illegal hunting are now to be seen in the **Endangered Primate Rescue Center** located near the park gate. Opened in 1993, the centre not only cares for rescued animals, but also tries to rehabilitate them by releasing them into an adjacent semi-wild area. In addition, they run crucial research, conservation and breeding programmes. At any one time there may be between sixty and a hundred animals here, including Delacour's langur, with its distinctive black body and white "shorts", the Cat Ba, or Golden-headed langur, and the Grey-shanked douc langur, as well as various lorises and gibbons. It's a unique opportunity to see these incredibly rare species at close quarters.

The prehistoric caves

Much is made of Cuc Phuong's **prehistoric caves**, the most accessible of which is Dong Nguoi Xua, only 300m from the road, 7km from the park gate. Joss sticks burn in the cave mouth near three tombs estimated to be over seven thousand years old but there's nothing to see that justifies the steepish climb; if you decide to go, bring a torch for the upper reaches, and watch out for some decidedly dangerous steel staircases.

ARRIVAL AND DEPARTURE

CUC PHONG

By motorbike Cuc Phuong lies 45km north and west of Ninh Binh. There are no public buses, and since it's a little far by xe om it's best to go in a car or rent a bike from Ninh Binh; head north on Highway 1 for 10km to find the sign indicating "Cuc Phuong" to the left. From the gate it's a further 18km to the heart of the forest.

On a tour Day-trips from Hanoi start at $30 per person in a minibus and include lunch and guide. Or if you are already there it is easy to organize guided treks, including an overnight stay in a Muong village, through the Visitors' Centre or through hotels in Ninh Binh (see p.322).

INFORMATION

Visitors' Centre Daily 7–11am & 1.30–4pm. You'll find the Primate Center and Visitors' Centre just beyond the Cuc Phuong park gate. Entry tickets are on sale here (20,000đ, plus a further 10,000đ for an obligatory guide to the Primate Center) where you can also arrange accommodation.

ACCOMMODATION

Accommodation ranges from unexpectedly comfortable bungalows and bamboo chalets (from $20) to a basic hostel (singles from $6), located either at the headquarters or in the wild interior. Be aware that Cuc Phuong is some way above the plains and winter nights can get chilly.

CUC PHUONG'S FLORA AND FAUNA

Even now the park has not been fully surveyed but is estimated to contain approximately three hundred **bird species** and ninety **mammal species**, some of which were first discovered in Cuc Phuong, such as red-bellied squirrels and a fish that lives in underground rivers. Several species of bat and monkey, including the critically endangered Delacour's langur, inhabit the park, while bears and leopards roam its upper reaches. Hunting has taken its toll, though, and you're really only likely to see butterflies, birds and perhaps a civet cat or a tree squirrel, rather than the more exotic fauna. What you can't miss, though, is the luxuriant **vegetation** including 1000-year-old trees (living fossils up to 70m high), tree ferns and kilometre-long corkscrewing lianas, as well as a treasure-trove of medicinal plants.

WALKING IN CUC PHUONG

Of several **walks** in the park, one of the most popular starts at Car Park A, 18km from the park gate. For a steamy 7km (roughly 2hr), a well-trodden path winds through typical rainforest to reach the magnificent **cho xanh tree**, a 45m-high, 1000-year-old specimen of *Terminalia myriocarpa* – its dignity only slightly marred by a viewing platform. Dropping back down to the flat, take a left turn at the unmarked T-junction to bring you back to the road higher up at Car Park B. This second car park is also the start of the "Adventurous Trail", an 18-km hike through the park to Muong villages, noted for their gigantic wooden waterwheels, for which you'll need a guide and a night's accommodation (see opposite).

6

Hai Phong

Buzzing **HAI PHONG** is a great place to get a handle on urban Vietnam. A city of almost two million souls, it's the third largest in the land, though with just a fraction of the big two's tourists and expats, your presence is likely to be greeted with genuine surprise. Most travellers rifle straight past the city to Ha Long Bay, but those who choose to alight in Hai Phong will see a wholly Vietnamese city. Although a little scruffy around the edges, it's central broad and bustling avenues are shaded by ranks of flame trees and dotted with well-tended colonial villas. Most of these villas lie along the crescent-shaped nineteenth-century core that forms a southern boundary to today's city centre, where you'll also find some other superb specimens of **colonial architecture**.

Hai Phong is well connected to both Hanoi and Cat Ba and can function as a good stopping-off point for those who don't fancy joining a Ha Long Bay tour. It's a good place to hole up for a while, thanks in part to its strong café culture – there are clutches of *giai khat* on every major road, and most of the minor ones too.

Brief history

Hai Phong lies 100km from Hanoi on the Cua Cam River, one of the main channels of the Red River Estuary. Originally a small **fishing village** and military outpost, its development into a major port in the seventeenth century stems more from its proximity to the capital city than from favourable local conditions. In fact it was an astonishingly poor choice for a harbour, 20km from the open sea with shallow, shifting channels, no fresh water and little solid land. The first quay was only built in 1817 and it was not until 1874, when Hai Phong was ceded to the French, that a town began to develop. With remarkable determination, the first settlers drained the mosquito-ridden marshes, sinking foundations sometimes as deep as 30m into huge earth platforms that passed for building plots. Doubts about the harbour lingered, but then, in 1883, the nine-thousand-strong **French Expeditionary Force**, sent to secure Tonkin, established a supply base in Hai Phong and its future as the north's principal port was secured.

The 20th century

In November 1946 Hai Phong reappeared in the history books when rising tensions between French troops and soldiers of the newly declared Democratic Republic of Vietnam erupted in a dispute about customs control. Shots were exchanged over a Chinese junk suspected of smuggling, and the French replied with a **naval bombardment** of Hai Phong's Vietnamese quarter, killing many civilians (estimates range from one to six thousand), and only regained control of the streets after several days of rioting. But the two nations were now set for war – a war that ended, appropriately, with the citizens of Hai Phong watching the last colonial troops embark in 1955 after the collapse of French Indochina.

Barely a decade later the city was again under siege, this time by American planes targeting a major supply route for Soviet "aid". In May 1972 President Nixon

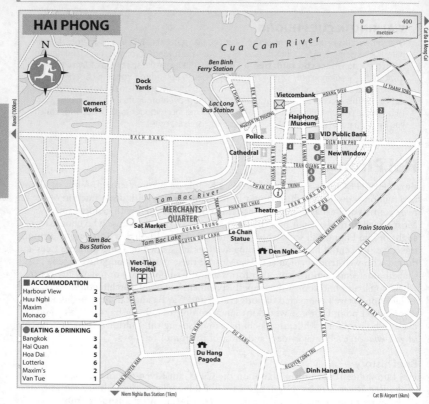

ordered the mining of Hai Phong harbour, but less than a year later America was clearing up the mines under the terms of the **Paris ceasefire agreement**. By late 1973 the harbour was deemed safe once more, in time for the exodus of desperate **boat people** at the end of the decade as hundreds of refugees escaped in overladen fishing boats (see box, p.451).

Hai Phong Museum

66 Dien Bien Phu • Tues & Thurs 8–10.30am, Wed & Sun 7.30–9.30pm • 2000đ

The best of Hai Phong's colonial-era structures are all found in the city centre. Furthest north is the wine-red **Hai Phong Museum**, whose motley collection of stuffed animals and colonial-era photos aren't really worth seeing, even on the rare occasions that the opening hours are being followed.

Hai Phong Cathedral

46 Hoang Van Thu • Sunrise to sunset

Just to the southwest of the Hai Phong Museum is the square tower of Hai Phong **Cathedral**, built in the late nineteenth century and recently renovated after years of neglect; it's European in style but with an altar decorated along the same burgundy-and-gold colours scheme as a Vietnamese pagoda. Enter via the east gate.

Hai Phong Theatre

27 Tran Hung Dao

South again is the buttermilk-yellow **theatre**; constructed of materials shipped from France in the early 1900s, it faces onto a wide, open square – a site remembered locally for the deaths of forty revolutionaries during the street battles of November 1946 "after a valiant fight against French invaders". Unfortunately, performances here are very irregular, usually only taking place when huge tour groups are in town.

6

Sea Dragon Park

It's impossible to miss **Sea Dragon Park**, the curl of green that slices through the city centre. In French times this was the Bonnal Canal, which once ran past the theatre, linking the Tam Bac and Cua Cam rivers. Nowadays the bulk of it is parkland; though cut up regularly by major roads, some sections remain good for a stroll. To its western end is Tam Bac Lake, the only surviving remnant of the canal; at its eastern end you'll see a massive bronze statue of the city's heroine, Le Chan (see below) made in a bold Socialist Realist style.

The merchants' quarter

To the north of the lake is Hai Phong's **merchants' quarter**, a lively area of street markets, chandlers and ironmongers. At its western end is **Sat Market**, whose nineteenth-century halls have been replaced by an ugly, six-storey block. Still, it's an interesting place to spend some time; the lower levels are home to literally hundreds of stalls, selling all sorts of food and clothing, while worm up to the top levels and you'll find a few ramshackle restaurants.

Den Nghe

Corner of Le Chan and Me Linh • Daily 7am–7pm

The central district of **Den Nghe** boasts an unusually cramped temple noted for its sculptures; you'll find the entrance on the northern side. The finest carvings are on the massive stone table in the first courtyard, but make sure you also look above the perfumed haze of incense for some detailed friezes. **General Le Chan**, who led the Trung Sisters' Rebellion (see p.435), is worshipped at the main altar; on the eighth day of each second lunar month she receives a birthday treat – platefuls of her favourite food, crab with rice noodles.

Du Hang Pagoda

2km south of the city on Chua Hanh

Located across the tracks, **Du Hang Pagoda** is a rewarding attraction. In its present form, the pagoda dates from the late seventeenth century and is accessed through an imposing triple-roofed bell tower. Interestingly, the architecture reveals a distinct Khmer influence in the form of vase-shaped pinnacles ornamenting the roof and pillars of the inner courtyard – according to Buddhist legend these contain propitious *cam lo*, or sweet dew. Beside it lies a small, walled garden of burial stupas.

Dinh Hang Kenh

It's worth going on to **Dinh Hang Kenh**, 1km east on Nguyen Cong Tru, if you haven't yet seen a *dinh*, or communal house. This one is a low, graceful building with a sweeping expanse of tiled roof facing across a spacious courtyard to an ornamental lake. Despite the surrounding apartment blocks, it's still an impressive sight. Thirty-two

6

monumental ironwood columns hold up the roof and populate the long, dark hall that is also noted for its carvings of 308 dragons sculpted in thirty writhing nests – now clothed in the dust of ages.

ARRIVAL AND DEPARTURE

By plane The Cat Bi Airport is 7km southeast of the city. Vietnam Airlines (ⓦ vietnamairlines.com.vn) and Jetstar (ⓦ jetstar.com) have flights in and out; the former have a booking office at 166 Hoang Van Thu (ⓣ 031 381 0890).
Destinations: Da Nang (daily; 1hr 45min); Ho Chi Minh City (6 daily; 2hr).

By train The station, Ga Hai Phong is an easy walk from the centre, and has services to Hanoi only; note that two of these services terminate at Hanoi's lesser-used Long Bien station. Take your pick between older carriages with wooden seats and cage-windows, or plusher new carriages, typically playing music at ear-splitting volumes.
Destinations: Hanoi (4 daily; 2hr 15min–3hr).

By bus Lac Long bus station is centrally located and

HAI PHONG

receives buses from Ha Long City's Bai Chay terminal (2hr), and the rest of the northeast. Niem Nghia, out in the southwest suburbs and a 20,000đ xe om ride from the centre, usually receives buses from Ninh Binh (4hr) and the south. Tam Bac, on the edge of the merchants' quarter, is the most common arrival point for buses from Hanoi (2hr); they leave every 10–20min.

By hydrofoil There are services to Cat Ba (1–3 daily; 45min) from the small Benh Binh Ferry Station; staff here are adept at charging tourists double the actual rate, so you may prefer to buy your ticket from the *Huu Nghi* hotel (see below). Also note that most of the bus-ferry-bus services from Hanoi to Cat Ba actually use another terminal, 30min to the east of the city centre.

GETTING AROUND

Xe om and cyclo are readily available and a good way of getting around the central district, although it's quite possible to tackle most of it on foot. There's no official bike or motorbike rental, but you might be able to arrange something through your hotel.

By taxi For longer distances a taxi or car rental is the only answer. For metered taxis call Hai Phong Taxi ⓣ 031 384 1999; Mai Linh Taxi ⓣ 031 383 3666; or VN Taxi ⓣ 031 383 8383.

INFORMATION

Tourist Information Centre 56 Hoang Van Thu (Daily 8am-5pm; ⓣ 031 356 9600, ⓦ Hai Phongtourism.org.vn). A

fairly useful little office, able to organize tours and sell maps of the area. There's usually an English-speaker present.

ACCOMMODATION

Hai Phong has a fair number of hotels, but – with a few noteworthy exceptions – prices tend to be high and the quality low. Budget accommodation of an acceptable standard is in particularly short supply and generally fills up early. Most hotels cluster on and around Dien Bien Phu, the city's main artery, with others dotted around town.

★ **Harbour View** 4 Tran Phu ⓣ 031 382 7827, ⓦ harbourviewvietnam.com. This mock-colonial, international-class hotel is as plush as central Hai Phong gets. It boasts two restaurants, a piano bar and a

pocket-sized pool, not to mention very stylish rooms and impeccable service. $200

Huu Nghi 60 Dien Bien Phu ⓣ 031 382 3244, ⓔ huunghihotel.vn. The largest hotel on the central strip is

THE BATTLES OF BACH DANG RIVER

The **Vietnamese navy** fought its two most glorious and decisive battles in the Bach Dang Estuary, east of Hai Phong. The first, in 938 AD, marked the end of a thousand years of Chinese occupation when General **Ngo Quyen** led his rebels to victory, defeating a vastly superior force by means of a brilliant ruse. Waiting until high tide, General Ngo lured the **Chinese fleet** upriver over hundreds of iron-tipped stakes embedded in the estuary mud, then counter-attacked as the tide turned and drove the enemy boats back downstream to founder on the now-exposed stakes.

History repeated itself some three centuries later during the struggle to repel **Kublai Khan's** Mongol armies. This time it was the great **Tran Hung Dao** who led the Vietnamese in a series of battles culminating in that of the Bach Dang River in 1288. The ingenious strategy worked just as well second time round when over four hundred vessels were lost or captured, finally seeing off the ambitious Khan.

housed in an unsympathetic eleven-storey block. Long one of the tallest buildings in town, it was, at the time of writing, already being dominated by a colossal new construction almost next door (set to be the *Imperial Boat Hotel*). Some rooms are a bit worn for the price, but facilities include a small pool, tennis court and fitness centre. $80

★ **Maxim** 3k Ly Tu Trong ☎031 374 6540, ⓦhotelhaiphong.com. Central, attractive and friendly, this has long been a magnet for budget travellers and as such you'd be wise to book ahead. It's also notable for being

on what passes for a quiet road in Hai Phong. Rooms come with satellite TV, a/c and fridges; it's worth paying a little extra for one with a window (especially on the upper levels). There's a decent restaurant downstairs (see below). $18

Monaco 103 Dien Bien Phu ☎031 374 6468, ⓔmonacohotel@vnn.vn. The most attractive of Dien Bien Phu's many hotels, with an art gallery-like reception hall and rooms designed with more attention than usual. Service can be a little off, but this is still excellent value. $28

EATING AND DRINKING

Hai Phong is well endowed with a fair **range of places** to eat and drink. Nowhere is particularly upmarket, but you'll find places serving good-value **seafood** and some increasingly fancy bia hoi outlets, including Hai Phong's very own microbrewery. In the evenings, hit the cafés and small restaurants **around the theatre**, or join the throng promenading up and down the gardens, pausing at ice-cream parlours or beneath the flickering lights of popcorn vendors. If you're looking for more action, there's a clutch of **live-music venues**, though even these shut up shop at midnight.

Bangkok 22a Minh Khai. Authentic Thai food in an attractive restaurant; they serve particularly good soups and curries ($3). Look for the sign saying "BKK". Daily 10am–9pm.

Hai Quan 41 Le Dai Hanh. Street venue serving delectable plates of *banh beo* ($1) – rice-cake sprinkled with lime and chilli slices, and eaten with a broth. Service is Hai Phong style – ie pleasantly gruff – but you'll most likely feel quite at home; there's a similar place right next door. Hours vary – early evening is your best bet.

Hoa Dai 39 Le Dai Hanh. Though it's almost like eating in the lobby of a cheap hotel, this place is popular with locals. There are no prices on the English-language menu, so try to cross-check with the Vietnamese one; on offer are eel, tortoise and cuttlefish, as well as more regular meat and veg dishes (from $3). Daily 9am–9pm.

Lotteria 88 Tran Phu. Korean-Japanese burger chain, usually serenading its young customers with incredibly loud pop music. The greasy fare here may sate those with a hankering for Western food. *Kimchi* burgers $1.50. Daily 24hr.

Maxim's 51 Dien Bien Phu. Decorated along contemporary Oriental lines, this restaurant bar is a great place for a drink when there's a bit of a crowd. There's often live music after 8.30pm. Daily 7.30am–midnight.

★ **Van Tue** 1a Hoang Dieu. A curious venue that's part restaurant, part beer-hall, with waiters bustling about with jugs of pilsner and great platters of food. The beer from the on-site microbrewery is excellent, and there's a veritable Noah's Ark of meat on the menu – this features good European dishes, but the Vietnamese ones are quite superb, and come out quite quickly despite the customer levels. Daily 9.30am–11pm.

DIRECTORY

Banks and exchange There are 24hr ATMs around almost every corner, including one outside Vietcombank, one outside the *Harbour View*, and another in the foyer of the *Huu Nghi*.

Hospital Ben Vien Viet–Tiep (Vietnam–Czech Friendship Hospital), 1 Nha Thuong ☎031 385 4185.

Post office The GPO is at the junction of Nguyen Tri Phuong and Hoang Van Thu.

Ha Long Bay

Drifting south from Vietnam's north coast in a wooden junk, your eyes will be riveted on what, at first, appears to be a jagged wall of emerald green. After an hour or so the wall swallows you up, and you find yourself in a fairyland of otherworldly limestone peaks, jutting from the water at sheer angles – this is **Ha Long Bay**, one of the most spectacular places in the whole of Vietnam.

From Guilin in China to Thailand's Phang Nga Bay, the limestone towers of the bay are by no means unique, but nowhere else are they found on such an impressive scale: an estimated 1969 islands pepper Ha Long Bay itself, with a further two thousand punctuating the coast towards China. Local legend tells of a celestial dragon and her children, sent by the Jade Emperor to stop an invasion, which spat out great quantities

6

of pearls to form islands and razor-sharp mountain chains in the path of the enemy fleet. After the victory the dragons, enchanted by their creation, decided to stay on, giving rise to the name *Ha Long* ("dragon descending"), and the inevitable claimed sightings of sea monsters.

In 1469, King Le Thanh Tong paid a visit to Ha Long Bay and was so inspired by the scenery that he wrote a poem, likening the islands to pieces on a chessboard; ever since, visitors have struggled to capture the mystery of this fantasy world. Nineteenth-century Europeans compared the islands to Tuscan cathedrals, while a local tourist brochure opts for meditative "grey-haired fairies". With so much hyperbole, some find Ha Long disappointing, especially since this stretch of coast is also one of Vietnam's more industrialized regions – a major shipping lane cuts right across the bay. The huge influx of tourism has, of course, added to the problem, not least the litter and pollution from fume-spluttering boats, but a sizeable proportion of tourist income does at least benefit the local communities.

The winter **weather** is another factor to bear in mind; from November to March there can be chilly days of drizzly weather when the splendour and romance of the bay are harder to appreciate.

Bar a clutch of gorgeous **caves**, conventional sights may be few on the ground, but even if you tire of the scenery there's a lot to do in the bay – **kayaking** across the tranquil waters, **swimming** amidst the twinkles of phosphorescent plankton, or even

---

ORGANIZED TOURS OF HA LONG BAY

Every Hanoi tour agent offers **Ha Long Bay excursions**, which work out easier – and usually cheaper – than doing the same thing yourself. There are a wide variety of trips available, including **day-tours**, though since the bay is a 6hr round trip from Hanoi these can feel very rushed. Most opt for a **two-day**, **one-night** tour, with the night spent at sea – this can be a delightful experience. Others go for a **three-day**, **two-night** trip, with the second night spent on wonderful Cat Ba Island (see p.336).

There's also the option of getting to Cat Ba by public transport (see p.338) – you'll miss out on a night at sea and a few caves, but from your hydrofoil seat you'll see the bay on the way (albeit in fast-forward).

BUDGET AND MID-RANGE TOURS

Competition among Hanoi tour operators is incredibly fierce, meaning that you can get an overnight trip for next to nothing – sometimes as low as $30. However, at this price range you really could be running the gauntlet, and many travellers encounter difficulties which sour their appreciation of the bay: vessels can be dirty, have poor facilities or be horribly overcrowded – it's always best to ask operators if they have a maximum group size (sixteen is the usual upper limit), though such promises are often broken. Some junks are also simply unsafe, though regulations have been tightened up since a boat went down in early 2011, killing eleven tourists and their local guide. Do also note that if your trip is cancelled – due to bad weather, for example – you are entitled to a full refund under Vietnamese law.

Compounding the confusion is the fact that very few operators have their own vessels – travellers tend to be shunted onto whichever junk has room. As such, you may find yourself sharing a vessel with people who have paid far more or less for the same thing. In short, it's almost impossible to give concrete recommendations for budget tour operators, but there are some good mid-range choices:

Ethnic Travel ☎ 04 3926 1951, ⊛ ethnictravel.com .vn. This outfit pride themselves on low-impact tours, and have a superb reputation. Some of their tours head to lesser-visited Bai Tu Long Bay; a three-day trip also including Ha Long Bay goes from $178 per person.

Hanoi Backpackers (see p.375). This hostel has been running hugely popular budget tours for years – these typically involve a bit of kayaking and swimming, and a lot of alcohol. From $80 per person.

Kangaroo Café ☎ 04 3828 9931, ⊛ kangaroocafe .com. This Aussie-owned outfit refuses to cut corners, and deserves its great reputation. In addition, the on-board meals are nothing short of superb. Two-day from $89 per person, three-day from $129.

climbing up a rocky cliff with your bare hands. The vast majority of visitors come on **organized tours** from Hanoi (see box below), travelling by road to Ha Long City, on the bay's northern shore, then transferring to cruise the bay on a replica wooden junk – it's not really any cheaper to do it by yourself. However, if you can do without the night on board, it's possible to hit Cat Ba – the largest and most beautiful island in the bay – from Hanoi using public transport (see p.338).

The caves

6

Bay entry 30,000đ (60,000đ if overnight) • Cave tickets 20,000đ in morning and 10,000đ in afternoon; all usually included in tour prices

The majority of travellers visit the bay on organized tours from Hanoi (see box below). These always include visits to one or more **caves**, which constitute the only actual sights in the area. Visually impressive though they are, busy days can see them rammed with tourists; unnatural lighting further detracts from their majesty, as can the tour guides' endless comparison of particular rock formations to animals or Buddhist deities.

Hang Dau Go

The bay's most famous cave is also the closest to Bai Chay, and as such a favourite for day-trippers, the "Grotto of the Wooden Stakes" is where General Tran Hung Dao amassed hundreds of stakes deep inside the cave's third and largest chamber before the

---

LUXURY TOURS

The sky's the limit on Ha Long Bay. The following are all reputable operators offering distinctive tours.

Buffalo Tours ☎04 3828 0702, ⓦbuffalotours .com. Impeccable tours on one of the best junks around – the *Jewel of the Bay*. The seafood is as delectable as you'll get on the bay, the wine list none too shabby and kayaking is included in the cost of the trip. Starts at $159 per person.

Emeraude ☎04 3934 0888, ⓦemeraude-cruises .com. A replica of a nineteenth-century paddle-steamer, the five-star *Emeraude* is one of the most luxurious vessels on the bay. Facilities include a restaurant, two bars, beauty salon and massage rooms and spacious sundecks where you can indulge in sunrise tai chi classes. From $169 per person.

Handspan ☎04 3926 0581, ⓦhandspan.com. Reliable operator with excellent vessels and a range of tours; perhaps of most interest is the trip around the less-visited Bai Tu Long Bay ($165 per person), which eschews the usual caves for excursions to fish farms and local schools.

Life Resorts ☎033 625 3000, ⓦlife-resorts.com. Fancy your own luxury vessel? On these tours it's just you and the crew – popular with honeymooners, for obvious reasons. From $600 for a night on board, much cheaper for day-trips.

Paradise Cruises ☎033 381 9999, ⓦ paradisecruises.vn. Sumptuously decorated cabins hint at high luxury – this is the only operator that expects guests to dress for dinner. Tai Chi sessions come as part of the package. From $190 per person.

DIY TOURS FROM HA LONG CITY

Most foreign tourists visit the bay on tours starting in Hanoi, but it's just about possible to do the same thing independently – however, it must be said that these are still tours, and not likely to save you much money when all's added up. First of all you have to get to Ha Long City (see p.341), then head to the Bai Chay tourist wharf, 2km west of town along Ha Long Avenue. From one booth here it's possible to take one of several **day-trips**, costing $5–10 per person and taking either 4, 6 or 8hr. However, these boats can get rather crowded and are not really recommended; if you go down this route, you'll also need to buy an **entry ticket** for the bay (30,000đ), as well as tickets to the caves (10,000–20,000đ).

If you're travelling in a group or want greater independence, you can always **charter** your own boat. Prices start at $50, excluding cave entry, for a 25-seater for 4hr. Meals on board cost extra, but can be excellent. Drinks tend to be pricey – it's best to take your own.

Bach Dang River battle of 1288 (see box, p.332). These are now long gone, but at the entrance to the cave keep an eye out for a stone stele with Chinese inscriptions – this was a paean written about the cave by King Khai Dinh, who visited in 1929.

Hang Thien Cung

On the same island as Hang Dau Go, a steep climb to the "Grotto of the Heavenly Palace" is rewarded by a rectangular chamber 250m long and 20m high, with a textbook display of sparkling stalactites and stalagmites – supposedly petrified characters of the Taoist Heavenly Court.

Hang Sung Sot and around

The most visited of all the caves in the bay, and featuring on almost all one- and two-day itineraries, is the "Surprise Cave". Inside its three echoing chambers, spotlights pick out the more interesting rock formations, including a "Happy Buddha" and rather surprising pink phallus. At the top you come out onto a belvedere with good views over the flotilla of junks below and sampans hawking souvenirs and soft drinks. Also in this area is **Ho Dong Tien** ("Grotto of the Fairy Lake") and **Dong Me Cung** ("Grotto of the Labyrinth") where, in 1993, ancient fossilized human remains were found; sadly, these only figure on a few tours.

Ho Ba Ham

Dau Be Island, on the southeastern edge of Ha Long Bay, encloses "Three Tunnel Lake", a shallow lagoon wrapped round with limestone walls and connected to the sea by three low-ceilinged tunnels that are only navigable by sampan at low tide. This cave is sometimes included in day-trips out of Bai Chay but is most easily visited from Cat Ba – as such it more commonly crops up on longer trips involving a stay on the island.

Cat Ba Island

Dragon-back mountain ranges mass on the horizon 20km out of Hai Phong as you approach **Cat Ba Island**. The island, the largest member of an archipelago sitting on the west of Ha Long Bay, boasts only one settlement of any size – Cat Ba Town, a fishing village now redefining itself as a tourist centre. The rest of the island is largely unspoilt and mostly inaccessible, with just a handful of paved roads across a landscape of enclosed valleys and shaggily forested limestone peaks, occasionally descending to lush coastal plains. In 1986 almost half the island and its adjacent waters were declared a **national park** in an effort to protect its diverse ecosystems, which range from offshore coral reefs and coastal mangrove swamps to tropical evergreen forest. Its value was further recognized in 2004, when the Cat Ba Archipelago was approved as an UNESCO Biosphere Reserve. However, change is coming – at the time of writing, a huge resort was under construction outside Cat Ba Town, and may be the first of many.

Brief history

Archeological evidence shows that humans inhabited Cat Ba's many limestone caves at least six thousand years ago. Centuries later these same caves provided the perfect wartime hideaway – the military presence on Cat Ba has always been strong, for obvious strategic reasons. When trouble with China flared up in 1979, hundreds of ethnic Chinese islanders felt compelled to flee and the exodus continued into the next decade as "boat people" sailed off in search of a better life, depleting the island's population to fewer than fifteen thousand. Now that prosperity has come in the form of tourism, the population is growing rapidly.

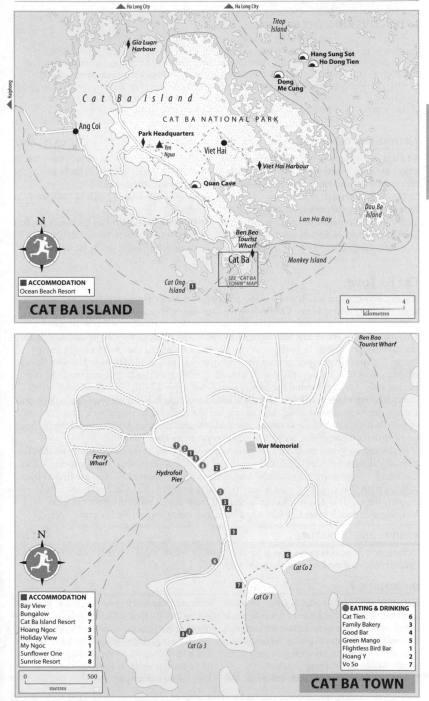

6

CAT BA ISLAND

Ha Long City   Ha Long City

Titop Island

Gia Luan Harbour

Hang Sung Sot
Ho Dong Tien

Dong Me Cung

C a t   B a   I s l a n d

CAT BA NATIONAL PARK

Haiphong

Ang Coi

Park Headquarters
Yen Ngua

Viet Hai

Viet Hai Harbour

Dau Be Island

Quan Cave

Lan Ha Bay

N

■ ACCOMMODATION
Ocean Beach Resort   1

Ben Beo Tourist Wharf

Cat Ba

Monkey Island

Cat Ong Island   1

SEE "CAT BA TOWN" MAP

0   4
kilometres

CAT BA TOWN

Ben Beo Tourist Wharf

War Memorial

Ferry Wharf

Hydrofoil Pier

1 2 1
3
4
2

5
3
4

5

6

6 Cat Co 2

7

Cat Co 1

N

■ ACCOMMODATION
Bay View   4
Bungalow   6
Cat Ba Island Resort 7
Hoang Ngoc   3
Holiday View   5
My Ngoc   1
Sunflower One   2
Sunrise Resort   8

8 7
Cat Co 3

● EATING & DRINKING
Cat Tien   6
Family Bakery   3
Good Bar   4
Green Mango   5
Flightless Bird Bar 1
Hoang Y   2
Vo So   7

0   500
metres

6

DISCOVERING THE ISLAND

One of the most rewarding ways to explore the area is by boat from Cat Ba Town, passing through the labyrinth of **Lan Ha Bay**, a miniature version of neighbouring Ha Long Bay but one which receives fewer visitors. There are **floating villages** and **oyster farms** in the area, which can be included in tour itineraries. Other options are **kayaking**, **rock-climbing** and visits to isolated **beaches** where the water is noticeably cleaner than elsewhere in the bay. Be warned, though: Cat Ba is by no means undiscovered and during the local summer holidays (June to mid-Aug) hotels and beaches in the area can be swamped.

ARRIVAL AND DEPARTURE   CAT BA ISLAND

On a tour The most popular way of getting to Cat Ba is on a tour from Hanoi – many companies offer three-day tours of Ha Long Bay with one night on board and the second on Cat Ba (see box, pp.334–335).

By ferry and bus If you'd rather travel independently, the quickest and most convenient option is a combined bus and high-speed ferry service from Hanoi run by Hoang Long Tourist Company (4–7 daily; 4hr; 170,000đ); buy tickets at Hanoi's Long Yen bus station. Getting back to Hanoi this way is easy: operators in Cat Ba town all sell tickets (with a 20,000đ mark-up).

Destinations: Hai Phong (2 daily; 2–3hr); Hong Gai (1 daily; 2hr).

By hydrofoil These depart from Hai Phong's Ben Binh ferry pier (1–4 daily; 1hr–1hr 30min; 130,000đ).

Destinations: Hai Phong (1–4 daily; 45min).

Cat Ba Town

Caught between green hills and a horseshoe bay alive with coracles scurrying among multicoloured fishing boats, **CAT BA TOWN**'s west-facing location makes it perfect for sunsets over outlying islands. Outside the summer peak, it retains a pretty laidback ambience despite the recent onslaught of tourism, which has seen a slew of new hotels and restaurants open along the harbour front. The town is divided into two sections: most tourist facilities are grouped around the new hydrofoil pier, while 800m to the west lies the original, workaday fishing village with a bustling market and its accompanying food and bia hoi stalls. Directly behind the pier is a small hill topped by the town's war memorial, erected during Ho Chi Minh's visit to the island in 1953; follow a path up the back to find a quiet, breezy spot from which to contemplate the harbour. If you prefer a close-up view of life afloat, hire one of the **coracles**, essentially water-taxis, that hover around the harbour steps; with hard bargaining an hour shouldn't cost more than 20,000đ.

To the east of town, on the far side of the peninsula, are three small, sandy **beaches**, romantically named Cat Co 1, Cat Co 2 and Cat Co 3. The two most southerly – Cat Co 1 and 3 – are more popular and home to resort developments: they are linked by a **cliffside path** that's a joy to walk at any time, day or night. Cat Co 2 is quieter and cleaner, with snacks and drinks available, but little shade; unfortunately, the cliff-hugging boardwalk from Cat Co 1 has been in a state of disrepair for some time.

ARRIVAL AND DEPARTURE   CAT BA

Minibuses meet almost all boats that arrive at one of the island's little ports, and in most cases a ride to Cat Ba Town is included in the price of your ferry or hydrofoil ticket or tour.

INFORMATION

Motorbike and bicycle rental To explore the island independently, your best bet is to rent a motorbike with or without a driver: xe om cruise around town and most hotels offer motorbike rental from $6 per day. You can also rent mountain bikes for $3 a day, but unless you're pretty fit, you may find the steep hills hard going in the heat.

Tourist information and post office Cat Ba's information office is on the main drag, though its owner is also the boss of a hotel and travel agency, so the advice given is far from impartial; instead, the People's Committee website (ⓦ catba.com.vn) provides the basics and most local hotels will help you out. The post office (7am–noon & 12.30–10pm) is beside *The Noble House* on the harbour front, near the hydrofoil pier.

ORGANIZED TOURS

Most hotels and agencies in Cat Ba Town arrange **tours**, with little to choose between them on price; to ensure that you have quality to match, it pays to ask fellow travellers for up-to-date advice on the best choices. Tours include boat trips ($12–20 per person per day), of which the most pleasant is the short sail north into **Lan Ha Bay**, including a visit to a floating village, and then either walk into the national park (see p.341) or a half-day cruise around the maze of limestone islands, stopping at one of the coral-sand beaches for a spot of swimming or kayaking. You can also explore **Ha Long Bay** (see p.333) from here, either as a one- or two-day trip, with the option of returning to Cat Ba or being dropped off in Bai Chay. Many opt instead to head to **Monkey Island** (from $7), an island that is, indeed, home to a small monkey population; most end up finding it a disappointment.

In addition to boat tours, hotels also arrange **trekking** in the national park. There are two standard excursions: a half-day "short trek" (from $6 per person) to Yen Ngua peak, perhaps stopping off for a swim on the way back, and a full-day "long trek" (from $12 per person) through the national park to Viet Hai village for lunch, then back by boat through fjord-like Lan Ha Bay with a stop for swimming and snorkelling or kayaking through cave tunnels to find secret lagoons. Pretty much every agency in Cat Ba will be willing to take you – hunt around on the harbour road.

Lastly, one of the most enjoyable activies on Cat Ba – and, indeed, the bay as a whole – is **rock-climbing**. ★ **Asia Outdoors** (☎091 376 0025, ⓦslopony.com), previously known as Slo Pony, pioneered rock-climbing in Vietnam and remain the best operator to go with; going with a copycat outfit may save you a couple of bucks, but none of them are certified. They take climbers on a phenomenal network of routes, including some on a deserted island off Cat Ba, and others which you simply climb until you fall into the sea.

ACCOMMODATION

Thanks to a building boom, **accommodation** on Cat Ba represents good value on the whole. The exception is during the peak summer holiday period of June through August, when the place is absolutely packed and prices can more than double. There are a couple of upper-range options in town, while budget hotels are popping up everywhere – booking in advance is a little dangerous, since you may end up sleeping next to a construction site. Note that there are also a couple of very noisy clubs and bars in the centre of town – at the time of writing, the worst offenders were on the streets up from the *Sunflower One*.

Bay View ☎031 368 8241. English-owned hotel that prides itself on providing good, clean rooms at rock-bottom prices. The food is excellent, and non-residents can make use of their cheap and reliable laundry facilities. Rooms with a view can be had for roughly double the price. $7

★ **Bungalow** ☎031 350 8408. Cat Ba Town lacks the remote feel of most of the island, but there's a real sense of mountain-sheltered isolation at this cluster of rustic bungalows on Cat Co 2 beach. Rooms contain nothing but mattresses and mosquito nets (communal showers only), but the setting is superb. $20

Cat Ba Island Resort ☎031 350 8798, ⓦcatbaislandresort-spa.com. Away from Cat Ba Town on the way to the beaches, this is a family-friendly hotel with swimming pools, water slides and the like. Rooms are a bit overpriced but stocked with all mod cons, and some have been refurbished with a fresh, modern design scheme. $110

Hoang Ngoc ☎031 368 8788. This new family-run guesthouse has that Cat Ba rarity – an elevator. The rooms are fresh and pleasant, and there's a communal balcony on every floor; in season, the eighth-floor rooftop also turns into a small bar at night. $12

Holiday View ☎031 388 7200, ⓦholidayviewhotel -catba.com. You can't miss this fourteen-storey monstrosity sticking up to the east of the pier. It does, however, boast three-star comforts, including a restaurant and terrace café, and its rooms are tastefully decorated, if a tad bland. $70

My Ngoc ☎031 388 8199, ⓦtuansailing.com. This hotel offers cheap rates for its seafront location. Ask for a room in the newer block – no balconies, but they're bigger and better equipped. It also arranges reasonable tours. $8

Ocean Beach Resort ☎04 3926 0463, ⓦoceanbeachresort.com.vn. Not in Cat Ba Town at all, but on a private island 15min away by boat – call to arrange a pick-up. The bamboo bungalows are extremely pleasant, and the food is excellent – good news, given the fact that there are no restaurants within walking distance. $90

Sunflower One ☎031 388 8429, ⓦsunflowerhotels .com.vn. Spacious and smartly furnished rooms make this a good choice if you're after a bit of comfort. Though not on the harbour, the upper floors get sea views. $25

★ **Sunrise Resort** ☎031 388 7360, ⓦcatbasunrise resort.com. If you want to feel the sand between your toes, head for this low-rise resort hotel, which has its own private chunk of Cat Co 3 beach. The burgundy-trimmed rooms all have seaview balconies; best value

are the deluxe rooms, whose "Extra King Size" beds are colossal. Hotel facilities include a restaurant, bar, pool and sauna. **$150**

EATING

The number of restaurants on Cat Ba is gradually expanding, with some offering tasty food – especially **seafood** – at reasonable prices. For a real challenge, order one of the huge crabs on display in some restaurants, and crack your way through to its succulent meat. The **floating restaurants** in Cat Ba harbour and off Ben Beo tourist wharf seem a nice idea but most are to be avoided owing to the staggering lack of value for money. All of the places listed below are open from morning until late into the evening.

Cat Tien A floating restaurant without the possibility of extortion, since it's connected to the Cat Co 3 road by gangplank – a rickety adventure in itself. The menu is extensive but you may need a few goes before landing on something that they actually have; recommended are the huge clam and shoot soups ($2).

Family Bakery Small, family-run place churning out round after round of delectable croissants, pains au chocolat and brioche, all for under $1. Unfortunately, they only serve instant coffee.

Green Mango Cat Ba's classiest restaurant has a pleasingly diverse menu – think green tea-smoked duck rolls with raspberry sauce, black barramundi with braised banana or pan-roast salmon with wasabi mashed potato.

Prices are lower than you might expect, and simple pizza, pasta or surf'n'turf dishes go from $4. The desserts are also unfairly good.

★ **Hoang Y** 197 Harbour Road. Friendly local joint with a well-deserved reputation for serving ultra-fresh seafood at reasonable prices; shrimp with lemon and garlic hits the spot, or try whole steamed fish with lashings of ginger ($4). Copycat restaurants with similar names have opened, so make sure you pick the original.

Vo So Located in the Sunrise Resort. Surprisingly reasonable prices given the opulent surroundings. Salads, soups and pasta dishes (from $4) are offered as well as the Vietnamese regulars, and some of the desserts are simply irresistible.

DRINKING AND NIGHTLIFE

In the evenings, locals and visitors stroll along the harbour front, stopping to enjoy a beer or juice at the drink stalls. If the moon is out, the path running between Cat Co 1 and Cat Co 3 makes for a spectacular place to drink. Bars are open all day, but closing time depends on how many tourists are in town –if there's enough of a crowd, things can easily go on to 4am.

Flightless Bird Bar Kiwi-run establishment known to locals as the "Penguin Bar", there being no word for Kiwi in Vietnamese. In addition to fairly priced drinks, they also offer good $3 pedicures.

★ **Good Bar** The most happening bar in town by a country mile; it gets pretty wild whenever there's a crowd. They serve strong cocktails, which you can enjoy over a game of pool, and play music suitable for dancing to.

DIRECTORY

Money exchange At the time of writing, the bank in Cat Ba Town does not handle foreign exchange, and there are no ATMs on the island. Your best option for changing money and travellers' cheques, therefore, is the Vu Binh gold shop (7am–10pm) on the main road by the market

– look for the giant credit card logos painted outside. It can exchange major currencies or travellers' cheques, and give credit card advances. Hotels and restaurants will also change cash and travellers' cheques, but at poor rates.

The rest of the island

One of Cat Ba's main draws is its rugged unspoilt scenery. A recommended outing is to rent a motorbike or a car for the day and explore the island's few paved roads and its isolated beaches.

Quan Y Cave

8km from Cat Ba Town • 15,000đ

The main cross-island road climbs sharply out of Cat Ba Town, giving views over distant islands and glimpses of secluded coves, and then follows a series of high valleys. After 8km look out on the right for the distinctive **Quan Y Cave,** a gaping mouth embellished with concrete, not far from the road. During the American War the cave became an army hospital big enough to treat 150 patients at a time.

Cat Ba National Park

16km from Cat Ba Town • 15,000đ • A xe om from Cat Ba to the park headquarters should cost under 50,000đ one way

Taking up much of the island is **Cat Ba National Park**, established in 1986 and little changed in decades. Its most famous inhabitant is a sub-species of the critically endangered **golden-headed langur**, a monkey found only on Cat Ba and now probably numbering fewer than sixty individuals. Considerably more visible will be the rich diversity of plant species, including some 350 of medicinal value, as well as birds, snakes and plenty of mosquitoes.

Ha Long City

Vietnam evidently has grand plans for **HA LONG CITY**. South-facing, and with Ha Long Bay raising its limestone fingers just across the sea, this place has great potential – unfortunately, development has been haphazard, and the vast majority of Western tourists hitting the bay do so on the express service from Hanoi, seeing the city only on the short walk between bus and junk. However, tourists from Vietnam and China pack the place out during the busy season, and the city now boasts several huge resort-style hotels.

Ha Long City is an amalgam of **Hong Gai** and **Bai Chay**, two towns merged in 1994, and now lassoed together by a bridge. For the moment, locals still use the old names – as do ferry services, buses and so on – as a useful way to distinguish between the two areas, each with its own distinct character, lying either side of the narrow Cua Luc channel. The hub of tourist activity and accommodation is Bai Chay, a rather unattractive beach resort and the main departure point for boat tours. For those in search of more local colour, or who are put off by Bai Chay's overwhelming devotion to tourism, Hong Gai provides only basic tourist facilities but has a more bustling, workaday atmosphere.

Bai Chay

Neon signs and flashing fairy lights blaze out at night along the **BAI CHAY** waterfront, advertising north Vietnam's most developed resort, with shoulder-to-shoulder hotels and a picturesque backdrop of wooded hills. While Bai Chay is swamped in summer

---

THE TRAILS

There are two main **trails** through the park. The "**short trek**" (2hr–3hr from the gates of the park) takes you to a viewpoint at the top of Yen Ngua peak. The path is easy enough to follow, but it's a steep climb, scrambling over tree roots and rocks in places, and extremely slippery in wet weather. Not everyone agrees that the views merit the effort. If you've got the time and energy, the "**long trek**" (4hr–5hr) is a more rewarding experience, especially if you finish up with a boat ride back to Cat Ba Town. It involves a strenuous eighteen-kilometre hike via **Frog Lake** (Ao Ech), over a steep ridge for a classic view over countless **karst towers**, then dropping down to Viet Hai village where you can buy basic foodstuffs. From there it's about an hour's walk through lush scenery to the jetty. The easiest way to tackle this walk is on an **organized tour** arranged by agents in Cat Ba (see p.338).

Remember to take repellent, good boots, a hat and lots of water if you plan to do any **walks** in the park. A **compass** wouldn't come amiss either, as people have got seriously lost. If you want to tackle the **trails** by yourself, you'll need to take a **guide** from the national park headquarters and arrange for a **boat** to meet you at the end.

with local holidaymakers and tourists from China, out of season it's a pretty sleepy place and decidedly less sleazy. Apart from strolling the seafront boulevard and taking a quick look at its very indifferent beach, Bai Chay has nothing to distract you from the main business of touring Ha Long Bay. If you're staying here, you can take a turn through the seafront **market**, a somewhat desultory array of tourist tat.

The Royal Amusement Park

6–10.30pm • 140,000đ

The only real attraction in Bai Chay is the **Royal Amusement Park**, which sits bay-side along the main road, just west of the *Novotel*. They show decent water-puppet performances and "cultural shows" offering a jazzed-up sampler of "traditional" song and dance. The park is a bit of a mess and the shows are nothing to write home about, but the puppet performances are certainly worth a look – some say that they're actually better than their more illustrious counterparts in Hanoi (see box, p.385).

Hong Gai

In contrast to Bai Chay, **HONG GAI** has a compelling, raw vitality plus an attractive harbour to the east, crowded with scurrying coracles. It's worth spending an hour or so wandering the harbour paths where a picturesque village lies strung out under the limestone knuckle of **Nui Bai Tho**. This mountain is named after a collection of poems (*bai tho*) carved into the rock, that detail Ha Long Bay's beauty, kicking off with King Le Thanh Tong's in 1468. Nowadays most are hidden behind houses clinging to the cliff edge, but keep an eye open as you follow Ben Tau lane from Long Tien, winding through the fishing village, and you might spot one or two of the weathered inscriptions; no one seems quite sure which are the royal verses.

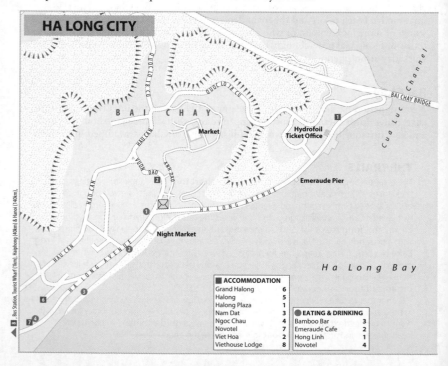

■ ACCOMMODATION	
Grand Halong	6
Halong	5
Halong Plaza	1
Nam Dat	3
Ngoc Chau	4
Novotel	7
Viet Hoa	2
Viethouse Lodge	8

● EATING & DRINKING	
Bamboo Bar	3
Emeraude Cafe	2
Hong Linh	1
Novotel	4

Also worth a look is the small but colourful **Long Tien Pagoda** on Long Tien. There are frequently ceremonies taking place in its small courtyard, offering fascinating glimpses into local rituals.

ARRIVAL AND DEPARTURE   HA LONG CITY

Two main **tourist wharfs** serve as junk-boat launchpads for the bay (see p.333): one 2km west of Bai Chay, and one just southeast of the bridge in Hong Gai. Most tourists hit the bay directly **from Hanoi**, but another nice option is to take the hydrofoil to Cat Ba.

By bus The bus station is on the Bai Chay side of the city on Highway 18, though it's a little far from anything. It's around 50,000đ into central Bai Chay by taxi, 30,000đ by xe om; double that for Hong Gai.
Destinations: Hanoi (3hr), Hai Phong (2hr) and Mong Cai (4hr).

By ferry and hydrofoil Ben Tau pier is tucked away down a sidestreet in Hong Gai, and serves slow ferries to Quan Lan in Bai Tu Long Bay (daily; 4hr). At the time of writing, there were no services to Cat Ba other than the tourist junks – it's usually possible to pay to join one of these, though since the amounts vary wildly, it's worth asking around.

INFORMATION

Tourist office There's a tourist information booth next to the *Emeraude Café* in Bai Chay, though since it's effectively a travel agency don't expect too much impartial advice.

Money changing There are ATMs all over the city (they're outside more or less every decent hotel in Bai Chay), as well as a few banks for changing money.

ACCOMMODATION

Despite a continuing increase in the number of hotels, especially in Bai Chay, there are still temporary room shortages during the Vietnamese summer season (June to early Sept) and holiday weekends; at other times, you'll be able to get good discounts. You'll find pretty much all of the more expensive places in **Bai Chay**, while there a few good cheapies on Vung Dao, and plenty more in **Hong Gai**. There's also an interesting eco-lodge on **Tuan Chau**, an island just to the west of Ha Long City proper.

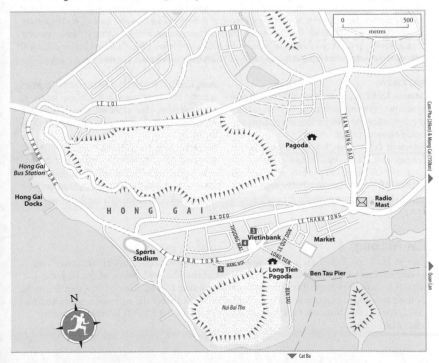

6

BAI CHAY

Grand Halong Off Ha Long Ave ☎033 384 4041. Charmingly retro in style, from the lobby to the rooms – the deluxe variety are particularly large, but all have a/c, satellite TV and small minibars. Huge breakfast buffets are laid out in the morning, and there's a pool. **$70**

Halong Plaza 8 Ha Long Ave ☎033 384 5810, ⓦhalongplaza.com. A smart four-star hotel offering all the usual upmarket facilities. The rooms are a good size and come with wi-fi; some command panoramic sweeps of the bay. Check their website for online deals. **$90**

★ **Novotel** Ha Long Ave ☎033 384 8108, ⓦnovotel .com. One of the most immaculately designed hotels in Vietnam – plush carpets lead to subtly lit and delicately scented rooms where you can see the outside world from every shower cubicle. The infinity pool outside is another nice touch and the on-site restaurant serves excellent food. **$150**

Viet Hoa 35 Vuon Dao ☎033 384 6035. One of the better budget hotels on Vuon Dao, this is a clean and welcoming place offering cheerful fan or a/c rooms. They're a decent size and all come with TVs and fridges as standard. **$15**

HONG GAI

Halong 80 Hang Noi ☎033 382 6509. Passable guesthouse within easy walking distance of the Ben Tau ferry pier. You may have to ask to see a few rooms before you're satisfied; if you'd like to see more, there are a couple of near-identical guesthouses next door. **$10**

Nam Dat 22 Cay Thap ☎033 361 1358. A step above most accommodation in the area, this new motel has huge rooms with flatscreen TVs and great en-suite facilities. The service is the only thing that sets it apart from a hotel. **$20**

Ngoc Chau 15b Cay Thap ☎033 362 0499. The best value of Hong Gai's numerous budget choices, with a bright, pine-panelled lobby, friendly staff and smart rooms, not to mention one of the only lifts in Hong Gai. **$12**

TUAN CHAU

Viethouse Lodge ☎033 384 2207, ⓦviethouselodge .com. Owned by a friendly German-Vietnamese couple, this cabin-style hotel is a great place to get away from it all and immerse yourself in a world of bamboo, lanterns, crackling stoves and serene gardens. The building itself is over one hundred years old, and was moved brick by brick from a Red Zao village in the northern mountains. They whip up tremendous food, too, and run bespoke tours of the area. **$50**

EATING AND DRINKING

Fresh **seafood** is the natural speciality of Ha Long Bay, with excellent lobster, crab and freshly caught fish on offer. Most tourists find themselves eating on or around Ha Long Avenue; off its southern edge there are a few overpriced restaurants, and a couple of good bars and cafés. There are no particularly notable restaurants in Hong Gai, though there are plenty of tiny places selling good *com binh danh* on the opposite side of the square from the *Ngoc Chau* hotel. You'll also find food stalls round the market, where ingredients come fresh from fishing boats in the harbour next door.

BAI CHAY

Bamboo Bar Off Ha Long Ave. Good-looking bar that can be hit or miss of an evening; even when it's a miss, staff and customers will be able to let you know where's best to go. Usually open past midnight.

Emeraude Cafe Ha Long Ave. The wonderful folks at *Emeraude* don't just run wonderful tours of the bay (see p.335), they can evidently fill your belly on dry land too. Pizzas and pasta dishes in this posh-looking venue start at around 130,000đ, or you can just pop in for coffee and a pastry. Daily 8am–9pm.

Hong Linh Ha Long Ave. The best of a clutch of cheapies opposite the market, serving Vietnamese staples at reasonable prices. A bowl of pho will set you back 20,000đ, while the seafood dishes are more like 100,000đ. Daily 8am–9pm.

Novotel Ha Long Ave ☎033 384 8108, ⓦnovotel.com. The ground floor of this hotel has, without doubt, the best-looking restaurant in town; all yours if you can stretch to $18 for a dinner buffet. In the summer, $25 will get you a barbeque buffet, plus a one-hour free flow of beer. Daily 6am–10pm.

Bai Tu Long

East of Ha Long Bay, stretching up towards the Chinese border, lies an attractive area of islands, known as **Bai Tu Long** or "Children of the Dragon". Some of the larger islands feature important forest reserves and are home to a number of rare species, such as the pale-capped pigeon, while dugong (sea cows) inhabit the surrounding waters. In 2001, **Bai Tu Long National Park** was created to protect the 15,700 hectares of marine and island habitat.

TO CHINA VIA MONG CAI

Of the three border crossings between Vietnam and China open to foreigners, the one at **Mong Cai** is by far the least used – the others have the advantage of rail connections on the Vietnamese side. Going via Mong Cai became even less appealing in 2011, when the hydrofoil services from Hai Phong and Ha Long City were cancelled; it's worth checking to see if they've reappeared, since for now the only way is by bus from Ha Long City (4hr) or Lang Son (4hr) – both arduous routes.

However, those that make it to Mong Cai will find a fun little frontier town, whose streets are lined with signs for karaoke and massage parlours – an interesting start or finish line to a trip through Vietnam. It thrives on cross-border trade with China: Vietnamese tourists flock here to snap up cheap Chinese clothes, while the Chinese come for gambling and girls. As such you'll find no shortage of places to stay, though local restaurant menus tend to have Chinese, rather than English, as a second language.

The border (7am–7pm) is just 1km from central Mong Cai, though this has been known to change. Just over the border is the small Chinese city of **Dongxiang**, which has bus connections to Nanning and Guangzhou.

Whichever way you're going, you'll need to have your **visa** organized in advance; the nearest Chinese embassy is in Hanoi and the nearest Vietnamese one in Nanning.

6

Quan Lan Island

Though there are few specific sights in the area, and consequently little tourist development, the odd intrepid tourist heads as far as **Quan Lan Island**, a long skinny island on the outer fringes of the bay. Although there has been much talk of developing the larger islands in Bai Tu Long as eco-tourism destinations, so far only Quan Lan has seen any development – and even this is fairly minimal.

The island's main attractions are the empty, sandy and relatively clean beaches fringing its east coast. A cycle ride on its only road makes a pleasant jaunt through rice paddies and over the dunes to the north tip. Otherwise, there's not much to do apart from enjoying simply being off the tourist trail – prepare to find yourself engaging even more closely with locals than you're used to.

ARRIVAL AND DEPARTURE   QUAN LAN ISLAND

By boat or hydrofoil Grubby boats (4hr 30min; 130,000đ) leave from Ben Tau pier on the Hong Gai side of Ha Long City. Infinitely preferable – and actually cheaper – were the hydrofoil services (1hr; 100,000đ) that left from Hong Gai's tour boat pier; these were cancelled abruptly in 2011, though it's worth checking to see if they've resumed services.

Onwards via xe om There are plenty of xe om and xe may (three-wheeler motorbike taxis) that wait at Quan Lan pier, on the island's southern tip, to take people 3km north to the main village (20,000đ).

ACCOMMODATION

Aside from the *Ngan Ha Hotel*, the other places to stay are spread out along the beach on the island's southeast coast.

ATI Resort signed off to the right 1500m from the ferry pier ☎033 387 7471, ☏033 387 7257. The smartest option on the island, its comfortable (but overpriced) wooden cabins are scattered among the dunes; water is heated by solar panels, so brace yourself for the possibility of cold showers. You can also rent bikes here, and there's a restaurant, though you're better off eating at the *com pho* places in the village. $45

Ngan Ha Hotel Opposite the post office ☎033 387 7296. Cheap and friendly, this is the budget place of choice for most travellers. Rooms are simple but perfectly adequate, while the meals are about as good as you'll get in the village. Bike rental also available. $15

Quan Hai At the southern end of the beach; phone in advance and someone will come to meet your ferry ☎0913 388632, ✉quanhai_baitulong@yahoo.com. Very basic wooden cabins, with bathrooms and (occasional) electricity – hot water only arrives when the sun has been shining, and runs out fast. However, it's friendly enough, and boasts a real end-of-the-world feeling. Basic meals also available. $15

Hanoi and around

MORNING EXERCISE, HOAN KIEM LAKE

Hanoi and around

By turns exotic, squalid, gauche and hip, the high-octane Vietnamese capital of Hanoi provides a full-scale assault on the senses. Its crumbly, lemon-hued colonial architecture is a feast for the eyes; swarms of buzzing motorbikes invade the ear, while the delicate scents and tastes of delicious street food can be found all across a city that – unlike so many of its regional contemporaries – is managing to modernize with a degree of grace. Despite its political and historical importance, and the incessant noise drummed up by a population of over six million, Hanoi exudes a more intimate, urbane appeal than Ho Chi Minh City.

7

Hanoi city centre comprises a compact area known as **Hoan Kiem District**, which is neatly bordered by the Red River embankment in the east and by the rail line to the north and west, while its southern extent is marked by the roads Nguyen Du, Le Van Huu and Han Thuyen. The district takes its name from its present-day hub and most obvious point of reference, **Hoan Kiem Lake**, which lies between the cramped and endlessly diverting **Old Quarter** in the north, and the tree-lined boulevards of the **French Quarter**, arranged in a rough grid system, to the south. West of this central district, across the rail tracks, some of Hanoi's most impressive monuments occupy the wide open spaces of the former **Imperial City**, grouped around Ho Chi Minh's Mausoleum on Ba Dinh Square and extending south to the ancient walled gardens of the Temple of Literature. A vast body of water confusingly called **West Lake** sits north of the city, harbouring a number of interesting temples and pagodas, but the attractive villages that once surrounded it have now largely given way to upmarket residential areas and a smattering of luxury hotels.

Modern Hanoi has an increasingly confident, "can do" air about it and a buzz that is even beginning to rival Ho Chi Minh City. There's more money about nowadays and the wealthier Hanoians are prepared to flaunt it in the ever-more sophisticated restaurants, cafés and designer boutiques that have exploded all over the city. Hanoi now boasts glitzy, multistorey shopping malls and wine warehouses; beauty parlours are the latest fad and some seriously expensive cars cruise the streets. Almost everyone else zips around on motorbikes rather than the deeply untrendy bicycle. The authorities are trying – with mixed success – to temper the anarchy with laws to curb traffic and regulate unsympathetic building projects in the Old Quarter, coupled with an ambitious twenty-year development plan that aims to ease congestion by creating satellite towns. Nevertheless, the city centre has not completely lost its old-world charm nor its distinctive character.

Hanoi, somewhat unjustly, remains less popular than Ho Chi Minh City as a jumping-off point for touring Vietnam, with many making the journey from south to

WHEN TO VISIT

The **best time to visit** Hanoi is during the three months from October to December, when you'll find warm, sunny days and levels of humidity below the norm of eighty percent, though it can be chilly at night. From January to March, cold winds from China combine with high humidity to give a fine mist, which often hangs in the air for days. March and April usually bring better weather, before the extreme summer heat arrives in late April, accompanied by monsoon storms which peak in August and can last until early October, causing serious flooding throughout the delta.

MAUSOLEUM OF HO CHI MINH

Highlights

❶ The Old Quarter Wander through the intoxicating tangle of streets that make up Hanoi's commercial heart. **See p.356**

❷ The Opera House Check out this stately signature-piece of French colonial architecture, modelled on the one in Paris. **See p.358**

❸ Ho Chi Minh's Mausoleum The ghostly figure of "Uncle Ho", embalmed against his wishes, remains a strangely moving sight. **See p.362**

❹ Temple of Literature Vietnam's foremost Confucian sanctuary and centre of learning provides a haven of green lawns amidst the hubbub of Hanoi. **See p.366**

❺ Museum of Ethnology Discover the staggering variety and creativity of Vietnam's ethnic minorities. **See p.370**

❻ Pho bo Join the locals and slurp on Hanoi's traditional beef-and-noodle breakfast soup. See p.380

❼ Bia hoi bars As night falls parties gather for a few refreshing jars of the local brew. See p.383

❽ Water-puppets Vietnam's quirky but charming art form developed in the floodlands of the Red River Delta. **See p.385**

HIGHLIGHTS ARE MARKED ON THE MAPS ON PP.352–353, 364–365

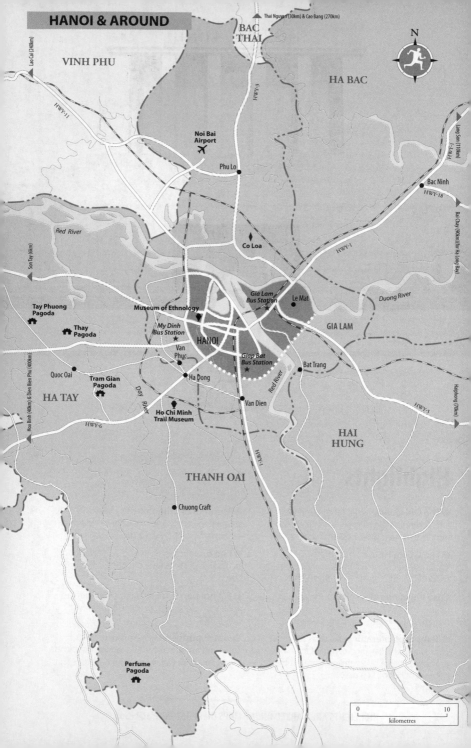

north. Nevertheless, it provides a convenient base for **excursions** to Ha Long Bay, and to Sa Pa and the northern mountains, where you'll be able to get away from the tourist hordes and sample life in rural Vietnam. There are also a few attractions much closer at hand, predominantly religious foundations such as the **Perfume Pagoda**, with its spectacular setting among limestone hills, and the spiral-shaped citadel of **Co Loa**, just north of today's capital. The Red River Delta's fertile alluvial soil supports one of the highest rural population densities in Southeast Asia, living in bamboo-screened villages dotted among the paddy fields. Some of these communities have been plying the same trade for generations, such as ceramics, carpentry or snake-breeding. While the more successful **craft villages** are becoming commercialized, it's possible, with a bit of effort, to get well off the beaten track to where Confucianism still holds sway.

Brief history

When Tang Chinese armies invaded Vietnam in the seventh century, they chose a small **Red River fort** as capital of their new protectorate, named, optimistically, *Annam*, the "Pacified South". Three centuries later the rebellious Vietnamese ousted the Chinese from their "Great Nest", *Dai La*, in 939 AD. After that, the citadel lay abandoned until 1010 when **King Ly Thai To**, usually credited as Hanoi's founding father, recognized the site's potential and established his own court beside the Red River. It seems the omens were on his side for, according to legend, when the king stepped from his royal barge onto the riverbank a golden dragon flew up towards the heavens. From then on **Thang Long**, "City of the Ascending Dragon", was destined to be the nation's capital, with only minor interruptions, for the next eight hundred years.

Ly Thai To and his successors set about creating a city fit for "ten thousand generations of kings", choosing auspicious locations for their temples and palaces according to the laws of geomancy. They built protective dykes, established a town of artisans and merchants alongside the **Imperial City**'s eastern wall, and set up the nation's first university, in the process laying the foundations of modern Hanoi. From 1407, the country was again under Chinese occupation, but this time only briefly before the great hero **Le Loi** retook the capital in 1428. The Le Dynasty kings drained lakes and marshes to accommodate their new palaces as well as a growing civilian population, and towards the end of the fifteenth century Thang Long was enjoying a **golden era** under the great reformer, King Le Thanh Thong. Shortly after his death in 1497, however, the country dissolved into anarchy, while the city slowly declined until finally Emperor Gia Long moved the royal court to Hué in 1802.

International intervention

By the 1830s Thang Long had been relegated to a provincial capital, known merely as *Ha Noi*, or "City within the River's Bend", and in 1882 its reduced defences offered little resistance to **attacking French forces**, led by Captain Rivière. Initially capital of the French Protectorate of Tonkin, a name derived from *Dong Kinh*, meaning "Eastern Capital", after 1887 Hanoi became the centre of government for the entire Union of Indochina. Royal palaces and ancient monuments made way for grand residences, administrative offices, tree-lined boulevards and all the trappings of a **colonial city**, more European than Asian. However, the Vietnamese community lived a largely separate, often impoverished existence, creating a seedbed of insurrection.

During the 1945 **August Revolution**, thousands of local nationalist sympathizers spilled onto the streets of Hanoi and later took part in its defence against returning French troops, though they had to wait until 1954 for their city finally to become the **capital of an independent Vietnam**. Hanoi sustained more serious damage during the air raids of the American War, particularly the infamous Christmas Bombing campaign of 1972. The subsequent political isolation together with lack of resources preserved what was essentially the city of the 1950s, somewhat faded, a bit battered and very overcrowded. These characteristics are still in evidence today, even as Hanoi is

7

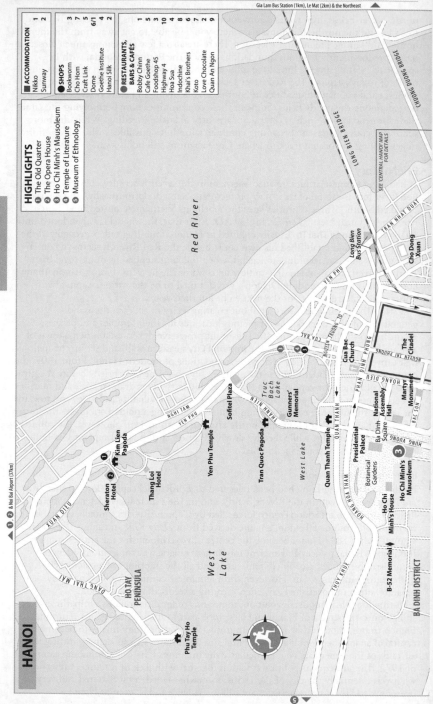

HANOI

Gia Lam Bus Station (1km), Le Mat (2km) & the Northeast

■ ACCOMMODATION	
Nikko	1
Sunway	2

● SHOPS	
Bookworm	3
Cho Hom	7
Craft Link	5
Dome	6/1
Goethe Institute	4
Hanoi Silk	2

● RESTAURANTS, BARS & CAFÉS	
Bobby Chinn	1
Cafe Goethe	5
Foodshop 45	3
Highway 4	10
Hoa Sua	4
Indochine	8
Khai's Brothers	6
Koto	7
Love Chocolate	2
Quan An Ngon	9

HIGHLIGHTS
1. The Old Quarter
2. The Opera House
3. Ho Chi Minh's Mausoleum
4. Temple of Literature
5. Museum of Ethnology

Red River

CHUONG DUONG BRIDGE

LONG BIEN BRIDGE

TRAN NHAT DUAT

SEE CENTRAL HANOI MAP FOR DETAILS

Cho Dong Xuan

Long Bien Bus Station

YEN PHU

The Citadel

NGUYEN TRI PHUONG

Cua Bac Church

HOANG DIEU

PHAN DINH PHUNG

Martyr Monument

BAC SON

National Assembly Hall

Ba Dinh Square

NGHI TAM

YEN PHU

Sofitel Plaza

Truc Bach Lake

Gunners' Memorial

QUAN THANH

HUNG VUONG

Presidential Palace

THANH NIEN

NGUYEN TRUONG TO

CUA BAC

Kim Lien Pagoda

Yen Phu Temple

Tran Quoc Pagoda

Quan Thanh Temple

West Lake

Botanical Gardens

Ho Chi Minh's House

Ho Chi Minh's Mausoleum

B-52 Memorial

BA DINH DISTRICT

HOANG HOA THAM

THUY KHUE

Sheraton Hotel

Thang Loi Hotel

XUAN DIEU

HO TAY PENINSULA

DANG THAI MAI

West Lake

Phu Tay Ho Temple

& Noi Bai Airport (37km)

N

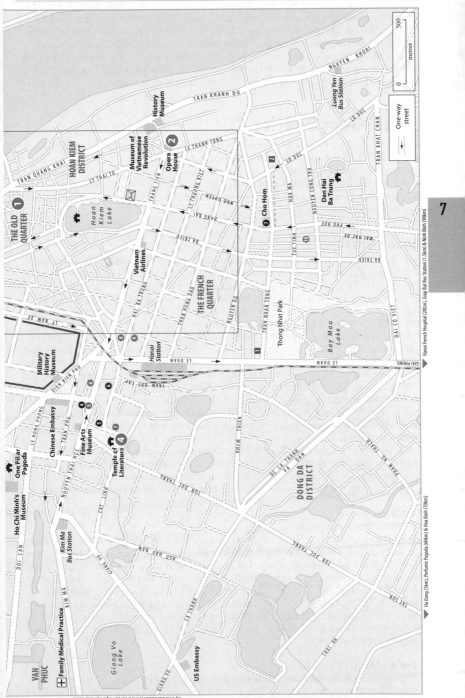

7

HANOI AND AROUND

THE OLD QUARTER

HOAN KIEM DISTRICT

History Museum

Museum of Vietnamese Revolution

Opera House

Hoan Kiem Lake

Vietnam Airlines

THE FRENCH QUARTER

Cho Hom

Den Hai Ba Trung

Thong Nhat Park

Bay Mau Lake

DONG DA DISTRICT

Military History Museum

Hanoi Station

One Pillar Pagoda

Ho Chi Minh's Museum

Chinese Embassy

Fine Arts Museum

Temple of Literature

Family Medical Practice

Kim Ma Bus Station

Giang Vo Lake

US Embassy

VAN PHUC

One-way street

500 metres

TRAN KHANH DU

NGUYEN KHOAI

Luong Yen Bus Station

LO DUC

TRAN KHAT CHAN

Hanoi French Hospital (200m), Giap Bat Bus Station (1.5km) & Ninh Binh (90km)

Ha Dong (5km), Perfume Pagoda (60km) & Hoa Binh (70km)

My Dinh Bus Station (8km) & Noi Bai Airport (37km)

reinventing itself as a dynamic international capital. New market freedoms combined with an influx of tourists since the early 1990s have led to a huge growth in privately run hotels and restaurants, several of international standard, and in boutiques, craft shops and tour agencies. As ancient – and antiquated – buildings give way to glittering high-rises, and as traffic congestion increases, the big question is how much of this historic and charming city will survive the onslaught of modernization.

Hoan Kiem District

The commercial core of Hanoi is **Hoan Kiem District**, home to the city's banks, airlines and the GPO, plus most of the hotels, restaurants, shopping streets and markets. But there's a lot more to the area, not least Hoan Kiem lake itself and the nearby **temples**, which date back to the earliest days of the city. Though you'll want to spend time on these individual sights, it's the abundant streetlife and architectural wealth that give the area its special allure.

7

Hoan Kiem Lake

Early morning sees **Hoan Kiem Lake** at its best, stirring to life as walkers, joggers and *tai chi* enthusiasts limber up in the half-light. Space is at a premium in this crowded city, and the lake's strip of park meets multiple needs, at its busiest when lunch-hour hawkers are out in force, and easing down slowly to evenings of old men playing chess and couples seeking twilight privacy on benches half-hidden among the willows. The lake itself is small – you can walk round it in thirty minutes – and not particularly spectacular, but to Hanoians this is the soul of their city.

The name of the lake, which means "Lake of the Restored Sword", refers to a legend of the great Vietnamese hero, Le Loi, who led a successful uprising against the Chinese in the fifteenth century. Tradition has it that Le Loi netted a gleaming sword while out fishing in a sampan and when he returned as King Ly Thai To, after ten years of battle, he wanted to thank the spirit of the lake. As he prepared the sacrifice there was a timely peal of thunder and the miraculous sword flew out of its scabbard, into the mouth of a golden turtle (Vietnamese use the same word for turtle and tortoise) sent by the gods to reclaim the weapon.

A good way to get your bearings in Hanoi is to make a quick circuit of the lake, a pleasant walk at any time of year and stunning when the flame trees flower in June and July. The sights below are given in a clockwise order, beginning at the iconic Huc Bridge (possibly the most photographed sight in the city) at the lake's northeast corner.

Den Ngoc Son
Daily 7.30am–5.30pm • 10,000đ

Crossing over the striking The Huc Bridge, an arch of red-lacquered wood poetically labelled the "place where morning sunlight rests", you find the secluded **Den Ngoc Son**, "Temple of the Jade Mound", sheltering among ancient trees. This small temple was founded in the fourteenth century and is dedicated to an eclectic group: national hero General Tran Hung Dao, who defeated the Mongols in 1288, sits on the principal altar; Van Xuong, God of Literature; physician La To; and a martial arts practitioner, Quan Vu. The temple buildings date from the 1800s and are typical of the Nguyen Dynasty; in the antechamber, look out for the dragon heads, carved with bulbous noses and teeth bared in manic grins.

Statue of King Ly Thai To
Heading south along the eastern side of the lake, you'll come to an imperious statue of Hanoi's founding father, King Ly Thai To, which was erected in 2004 in anticipation of

celebrations to mark the city's millennium in 2010. At dusk, the expanse of polished stone paving around it provides an incongruous venue for Hanoi's small but keen band of break-dancers.

The Tortoise Tower

A squat, three-tiered pavilion known as **Thap Rua**, or the **Tortoise Tower**, ornaments a tiny island at the southern end of Ho Hoan Kiem. It's illuminated after dark, and is another of Hanoi's most prevalent icons, with its reflection shimmering in the lake. It was built in the 19th century to commemorate the legend of the golden turtle and the restored sword, but is not accessible to the public.

The General Post Office

At the southeast corner of the lake stands the enormous **General Post Office**, which marks the northern fringe of the French Quarter. Opposite the post office, on the shore of the lake, stands a small and ancient brick tower. This is all that remains of an enormous pagoda complex, Chua Bao An, after French town planners cleared the site in 1892 to construct the administrative offices and residences of their new possession.

St Joseph's Cathedral

Nha Tho ("Big Church") Street • Daily 5–7am & 5–9pm

As you round the southern tip of the lake and head up its western shore you'll spot Hanoi's neo-Gothic cathedral over the rooftops to your left. Veer left along Hang Trong, then left into Nha Tho, to reach it. It was constructed in the early 1880s, partly financed by two lotteries, and though the exterior is badly weathered its high-vaulted interior is still imposing. Among the first things you notice inside are the ornate altar screen and the stained-glass windows, most of which are French originals. Over the black marble tomb of a former cardinal of Vietnam stands one of several statues commemorating martyred Vietnamese saints, in this case André Dung Lac who was executed in 1839 on the orders of the fervently anti-Christian emperor Minh Mang.

The cathedral's main door is open during services (the celebration of Mass was allowed to resume on Christmas Eve 1990 after a long hiatus); at other times walk round to the small door in the southwest corner. The cathedral is on Nha Tho, one of the most fashionable streets in the city for shopping, dining and drinking.

Ly Quoc Su Pagoda

52 Ly Quoc Su

Walking north from St Joseph's Cathedral along Ly Quoc Su brings you to **Ly Quoc Su Pagoda**, a small pagoda with a genuinely interesting collection of statues. Ly Quoc Su (sometimes also known as Minh Khong) was a Buddhist teacher, healer and royal adviser

---

GIANT TURTLES

At least one hardy giant turtle still lives in the lake. It was captured and examined in early 2011 when wounds on its leg and head were identified, though it still managed to elude captors twice before being netted. It is a rare species of enormous, **soft-shelled turtle** known as *rafetus swinhoei*, of which there are only a few other specimens in Vietnam and China. This one weighed in at around 200kg and scientists estimate its age at around 80-100 years, but of course Hanoians believe it is one and the same creature that took Ly Thai To's sword over five hundred years ago.

The turtle you're most likely to see, however, is a heavily varnished specimen captured in 1968. It's preserved and on view on a small island behind Den Son Ngoc, also accessible via the **The Huc Bridge**. Beside the bridge stands a nine-metre-high obelisk, the **Writing Brush Tower**, on which three outsized Chinese characters proclaim "a pen to write on the blue sky".

cured the hallucinating King Ly Than Tong of believing he was a tiger. Quoc Su's e resides alongside that of the white-bearded Tu Dao Hanh on the principal altar of this twelfth-century temple – when it later became a pagoda they simply added a few Buddhas behind. In front of the altar, two groups of statues face each other across the prayer floor: four secular, female figures sit opposite three perfectly inscrutable mandarins of the nineteenth century, clothed in rich red lacquer.

From Ly Quoc Su, make your way back to Hoan Kiem Lake and continue northwards to where *Thuy Ta* café (see p.383) offers respite from the traffic and a fine place to relax.

The Old Quarter

Walk north from Hoan Kiem Lake, across Cau Go, and suddenly you're in the tumultuous streets of the **Old Quarter**, a congested square kilometre that was closed behind massive ramparts and heavy wooden gates until well into the nineteenth century. Apart from one gate, at the east end of Hang Chieu, the walls have been dismantled, and there are few individual sights in the quarter; the best approach is simply to dive into the back lanes and explore. Alternatively, you might like to see it first from the seat of a cyclo or one of the new electric cars that zig-zag through its streets (see box, p.372) to help you pinpoint places you'd like to come back to.

Everything spills out onto pavements which double as workshops for stone-carvers, furniture-makers and tinsmiths, and as display space for merchandise ranging from pungent therapeutic herbs and fluttering prayer flags to ranks of Remy Martin and shiny-wrapped chocolates. With so much to attract your attention at ground level it's easy to miss the **architecture**, which reveals fascinating glimpses of the quarter's history, starting with the fifteenth-century merchants' houses otherwise found only in Hoi An (see p.255). As you explore the quarter you'll come across a great many sacred sites – temples, pagodas, *dinh* and venerable banyan trees – hidden among the houses.

Ma May and Hang Buom

Tube-house at no. 87 Ma May • Daily 8am–noon & 1.30–5pm • 5000đ • **Dinh** at no.64 Ma May

Walking north from Hang Bac along Ma May and onto **Hang Buom**, you pass a wealth of interesting detail typical of the quarter's patchwork architecture: simple one-storey shophouses, some still sporting traditional red-tiled roofs; elaborate plaster-work and Art Deco styling from colonial days; and Soviet chic of the 1960s and 1970s – each superimposed on the basic tube-house design.

To get a better idea of the layout of tube-houses, pop into the beautifully restored example at **87 Ma May**. Nowadays, the majority of facades bear distinctly European touches – faded wooden shutters, sagging balconies and rain-streaked moulding – dating from the early 1900s when the streets were widened for pavements. Certain occupants were too wealthy or influential to be shifted and you can find their houses still standing out of line along Hang Bac, Ma May and Hang Buom, three of the Old Quarter's most interesting and attractive streets. Ma May also retains its own **dinh**, or communal house (at no. 64), which traditionally served as both meeting hall and

---

TUBE-HOUSES

Hanoi's aptly named **tube-houses** evolved from market stalls into narrow single-storey shops, windows no higher than a passing royal palanquin, under gently curving, red-tiled roofs. Some are just two metres wide, the result of **taxes** levied on street frontages and of subdivision for inheritance, while behind stretches a succession of storerooms and living quarters up to 60m in length, interspersed with open courtyards to give them light and air.

WHAT'S IN A NAME

The Old Quarter's **street names** date back five centuries to when the area was divided among 36 artisans' guilds, each gathered around a temple or a *dinh* (communal house) dedicated to the guild's patron spirit. Even today many streets specialize to some degree, and a few are still dedicated to the original craft or its modern equivalent. The most colourful examples are Hang Quat, full of bright-red banners and lacquerware for funerals and festivals, and Hang Ma, where paper products have been made for at least five hundred years. Nowadays gaudy tinsel dances in the breeze above brightly coloured votive objects, which include model TVs, dollars and cars to be offered to the ancestors. A selection of the more interesting streets with an element of specialization is listed below. *Hang* means merchandise.

STREET NAME	MEANING	MODERN SPECIALITY
Ha Trong	Drum skin	Bag menders, upholsterers
Hang Bo	Bamboo baskets	Haberdashers
Hang Buom	Sails	Imported foods and alcohol, confectionery
Hang Chieu	Sedge mats	Mats, ropes, bamboo blinds
Hang Dau	Oil	Shoes
Hang Dieu	Pipes	Cushions, mattresses
Hang Duong	Sugar	Clothes, general goods
Hang Gai	Hemp goods	Silks, tailors, souvenirs
Hang Hom	Wooden chests	Glue, paint, varnish
Hang Ma	Paper votive objects	Paper goods
Hang Quat	Ceremonial fans	Religious accessories
Hang Thiec	Tin goods	Tin goods, mirrors
Hang Vai	Fabrics	Bamboo ladders
Lan Ong	Eighteenth century	Traditional medicines, towels, physician

7

shrine to the neighbourhood's particular patron spirit, in this case a fourteenth-century mandarin and ambassador to the Chinese court.

Bach Ma Temple

Hang Buom • Tues–Sun 7.30–11.30am & 1.30–6pm • Free

Hang Buom is home to the quarter's oldest and most revered place of worship, **Bach Ma Temple**. The temple was founded in the ninth century and later dedicated to the White Horse (*Bach Ma*), the guardian spirit of Thang Long who posed as an ethereal site foreman and helped King Ly Thai To overcome a few problems with his citadel's collapsing walls. The present structure dates largely from the eighteenth century and its most unusual features are a pair of charismatic, pot-bellied guardians in front of the altar who flaunt an impressive array of lacquered gold teeth. In front stands an antique palanquin, used each year to celebrate the temple's foundation on the twelfth day of the second lunar month.

Dong Xuan market

On the northern side of the Old Quarter, the city's largest covered market, **Dong Xuan**, occupies a whole block behind its recently renovated facade. Its three storeys are dedicated to clothes and household goods, while fresh foodstuffs spill out into a bustling street market stacked with multicoloured mounds of vegetables.

Long Bien Bridge

A block east of Dong Xuan market, you'll find two ramps taking bicycles and pedestrians up onto **Long Bien Bridge**, a road and rail bridge completed in 1902 and originally named after the then governor-general of Indochina, Paul Doumer. Until

> **WEEKEND NIGHT MARKET**
>
> From around 7pm every Friday, Saturday and Sunday, the streets running north from Hang Dao, almost as far as Dong Xuan Market, are closed to traffic and vendors set up stalls selling all kinds of trinkets at the **Weekend Night Market**. Though it's a fun place to touch the pulse of modern Hanoi, there's not much on sale that would interest most Western visitors. Indeed most shoppers are Vietnamese youngsters snapping up fashion accessories like mobile phone covers. It can get very crowded at times, but winds down after 11pm.

Chuong Duong Bridge was built in the 1980s, Long Bien was the Red River's only bridge and therefore of immense strategic significance. During the American War this was one of Vietnam's most heavily defended spots, which American bombs never managed to knock out completely. If you have time, take a bicycle ride across the 1700m span of iron lattice-work, but spare a thought for the maintenance staff: when it's time to smarten it up, it takes a hundred workers five years to repaint the bridge.

The Ceramic Wall

Tran Quang Khai, Tran Nhat Duat, Yen Phu, Nghi Tam and Au Co streets

On the eastern fringe of the city, running along the east side of several roads, the Ceramic Wall, built as part of Hanoi's one thousand-year celebrations in 2010, stretches for nearly four kilometres and adds a splash of colour to the traffic-choked streets. A mosaic of tiny, ceramic tiles depicts scenes from Vietnam's history, famous places in the country and the lifestyles of minority groups.

The French Quarter

The first French concession was granted in 1874, an insalubrious plot of land on the banks of the Red River, southeast of where the **Opera House** stands today. Once in full possession of Hanoi, after 1882, the French began to create a city appropriate to their new protectorate, starting with the area between the old concession and the train station, 2km to the west. In the process they destroyed many ancient Vietnamese monuments, which were replaced with Parisian-style buildings and boulevards. Gradually elegant villas filled plots along the grid of tree-lined avenues, then spread south in the 1930s and 1940s towards what is now **Thong Nhat (Reunification) Park**, a peaceful but rather featureless expanse of green marking the French Quarter's southern boundary.

The Opera House

Trang Tien • Open during performances only • ☎ 04 3993 0113, ⓦ hanoioperahouse.org.vn

A grand example of the Parisian-style architecture for which the quarter is famous is the stately **Opera House** (now officially known as the Municipal Theatre) situated near the eastern end of Trang Tien. Based on the neo-Baroque Paris Opéra, complete with Ionic columns and grey slate tiles imported from France, the theatre was erected on reclaimed land and finally opened in 1911 after ten years in the building. It was regarded as the jewel in the crown of French Hanoi, the colonial town's physical and cultural focus, until 1945 when the Viet Minh proclaimed the August Revolution from its balcony. After Independence, audiences were treated to a diet of Socialist Realism and revolutionary theatre, but now the building has been restored to its former glory after a massive face-lift. Crystal chandeliers, Parisian mirrors and sweeping staircases of polished marble have all been beautifully preserved, although, unfortunately, there's no access to the public unless you go to a performance (see p.384). Otherwise, feast your eyes on the exterior – particularly stunning under evening floodlights or, better still, the soft glow of a full moon.

The History Museum

Trang Tien • Tues–Sun 8–11.30am & 1.30–4.30pm • 20,000đ admission, 15,000đ camera

One block east of the Opera House, Hanoi's History Museum is excellent. Buried among trees and facing the river, the museum isn't immediately obvious, but its architecture is unmissable – a fanciful blend of Vietnamese palace and French villa which came to be called "Neo-Vietnamese" style. The museum was founded in the 1930s by the Ecole Française d'Extrême Orient, but after 1954 changed focus to reflect Vietnam's evolution from Paleolithic times to Independence. Exhibits, including many plaster reproductions, are arranged in chronological order on two floors: everything downstairs is pre-1400, while the second floor takes the story up to August 1945.

The ground floor

On the ground floor, the museum's prize exhibits are those from the **Dong Son culture**, a sophisticated Bronze Age civilization that flourished in the Red River Delta from 1200 to 200 BC. The display includes a rich variety of implements, from arrowheads to cooking utensils, and a lamp in the form of a graceful figurine, but the finest examples of Dong Son creativity are several huge, ceremonial bronze drums, used to bury the dead, invoke the monsoon or celebrate fertility rites. The remarkably well-preserved **Ngoc Lu Drum** is the highlight, where advanced casting techniques are evident in the delicate figures of deer, birds and boats ornamenting the surface – you can see the detail more clearly in the rubbing in the display case behind. Other notable exhibits on this floor include recent finds from excavations in Hanoi's citadel, a willowy **Amitabha Buddha** of the eleventh century, pale-green celadon ware from the same era and a group of wooden stakes from the glorious thirteenth-century battle of the Bach Dang River (see p.332).

The second floor

Displays on the museum's **second floor** illustrate the great leap in artistic skill that took place in the fifteenth century following a period of Chinese rule. Pride of place goes to a 3m-tall stele inscribed with the life story of Le Loi, who spearheaded the resistance against the Chinese and founded the dynasty. More interesting are the extensive collection of ceramics and exhibits relating to the nineteenth-century **Nguyen Dynasty** and the period of French rule. A series of ink-washes depicting Hué's imperial court in the 1890s are particularly eye-catching, as are the embroidered silks and inlaid ivory furniture once used by the emperors cloistered in the citadel.

The Museum of Vietnamese Revolution

216 Tran Quang Khai • Tues–Sun 8–11.45am & 1.30–4.15pm • 10,000đ

The **Museum of Vietnamese Revolution** is housed in a classic colonial building that started life as a customs house. The museum catalogues the "Vietnamese people's patriotic and revolutionary struggle", from the first anti-French movements of the late nineteenth century to post-1975 reconstruction. Much of the tale is told through

---

COLONIAL ARCHITECTURE

After the hectic streets of the Old Quarter, the grand boulevards and wide pavements of Hanoi's **French Quarter** to the south and east of Hoan Kiem Lake are a welcome relief. Again it's the architecture here that's the highlight, with a few specific attractions spread over a couple of kilometres. The houses you see today, which like those of the Old Quarter survived largely due to lack of money for redevelopment, run the gamut of early twentieth-century European architecture from elegant Neoclassical through to 1930s Modernism and Art Deco, with an occasional Oriental flourish.

documents, including the first clandestine newspapers and revolutionary tracts penned by Ho Chi Minh, and illustrated with portraits of Vietnam's most famous revolutionaries. Among them are many photos you won't see elsewhere. There's good coverage of Dien Bien Phu and the War of Independence, and a small but well-presented exhibition on the American War, a subject that is treated in greater depth at the Military History Museum (see p.366).

Residence of the Governor of Tonkin

Two blocks north of the Opera House on Ly Thai To at the junction with Ngo Quyen, diagonally opposite an imposing Art Deco structure with a circular portico, once the French Bank of Indochina and now the **State Bank**, stands one of Hanoi's most attractive colonial edifices, the immaculately restored **Residence of the Governor of Tonkin**. Built in 1918, it's now known as the State Guest House and used for visiting VIPs. Unfortunately you can't get inside, but as you peer in take a close look at the elegant, wrought iron railings, pitted with bullet-mark souvenirs of the 1945 Revolution. More recently the building's terraces appeared in the film *Indochine*.

Trang Tien

Trang Tien, the main artery of the French Quarter, is still a busy shopping street where you'll find bookshops and art galleries, as well as the recently renovated **Trang Tien Plaza** with its flash boutiques and somewhat incongruous supermarket. South of Trang Tien you enter French Hanoi's principal **residential quarter**, consisting of a grid of shaded boulevards whose distinguished villas are much sought after for restoration as embassies and offices or as desirable, expatriate residences. To take a swing through the area, drop down **Hang Bai** onto Ly Thuong Kiet and start heading west.

Museum of Vietnamese Women

36 Ly Thuong Kiet • Tues–Sun 8am–4.30pm • 30,000đ • ☎ 04 3825 9936, ⓦ womenmuseum.org.vn

This museum has undergone a complete overhaul in recent years and is now one of Hanoi's most interesting attractions, with detailed video presentations on different aspects of the lives of Vietnamese women on each floor. It starts off with a look at street vendors, whose presence on the streets of the city with their baskets of goods suspended from bamboo poles is one of the country's most indelible icons. Women's role in the country's wars is the focus of the second floor, while the third floor focuses on family life and the top-floor features an eye-catching display of ethnic minority costumes.

THE METROPOLE LEGEND

The bright, white Neoclassical facade of the *Metropole* – nowadays *Sofitel Legend Metropole* hotel – verges on the austere. The then *Grand Metropole Palace* opened in 1901, and soon became one of Southeast Asia's great hotels. Even during the French War, Bernard Fall, a journalist killed by a landmine near Hué in 1967, described the hotel as the "last really fashionable place left in Hanoi", where the barman "could produce a reasonable facsimile of almost any civilized drink except water". After Independence it re-emerged as the *Thong Nhat* or *Reunification Hotel*, but otherwise stayed much the same, including en-suite rats and lethal wiring, until 1990 when *Sofitel* transformed it into Hanoi's first international-class hotel (see p.378). The *Metropole's* illustrious visitors' book includes Charlie Chaplin and Paulette Goddard on honeymoon in 1936 and Graham Greene, who first came here in 1952. Twenty years later Jane Fonda stayed for two weeks while making her famous broadcast to American troops.

Cho 19–12

Between Hai Ba Trung and Ly Thuong Kiet

Two blocks west of the Museum of Vietnamese Women, **Cho 19–12** (19 Dec Market) is a short covered street of stalls selling mainly fresh fruit, vegetables and meat, including the twisted carcasses of roast dog at the southern end, a repulsive sight for many Westerners. More appealing stalls sell Vietnamese desserts and local dishes such as *pho*.

Hoa Lo Prison

1 Hoa Lo •Daily 8am–5pm • 10,000đ

The Hanoi Towers complex looms over the sanitized remnants of French-built **Hoa Lo Prison**, nicknamed the "Hanoi Hilton" by American prisoners of war as a wry comment on its harsh conditions and often brutal treatment. The jail became famous in the 1960s when the PoWs, mostly pilots and crewmembers, were shown worldwide in televised broadcasts. There's a heavy dose of propaganda in the two rooms dedicated to the PoWs, peddling the message that they were well treated, clothed and fed.

The museum mostly concentrates on the pre-1954 colonial period when the French incarcerated many nationalist leaders at Hoa Lo, including no fewer than five future general secretaries of the Vietnamese Communist Party. Some of the cells – which were still in use up to 1994 – have been preserved, along with rusty shackles and instruments of torture. Other rooms display photos and information on the more famous political prisoners, though only the captions are in English.

Chua Quan Su

73 Quan Su • Daily 8–11am and 1–4pm

Near the junction with Tran Hung Dao, on Quan Su, you'll find the arched entrance of **Chua Quan Su**, the Ambassadors' Pagoda, founded in the fifteenth century as part of a guesthouse for ambassadors from neighbouring Buddhist countries, though the current building dates only from 1942. Nowadays Quan Su is one of Hanoi's most active pagodas: on the first and fifteenth days of the lunar month, worshippers and mendicants throng its forecourt, while inside an iron lamp, ornamented with sinuous dragons, hangs over the crowded prayer-floor and ranks of crimson-lacquered Buddhas glow through a pungent haze of burning incense. The compound, shaded by ancient trees, is headquarters of the officially recognized Central Buddhist Congregation of Vietnam and is a centre of Buddhist learning, hence the well-stocked library and classrooms at the rear. Shops round about specialize in Buddhist paraphernalia.

Ba Dinh District

Hanoi's most important cultural and historical monuments are found in the Ba Dinh district, immediately west of the Old Quarter, where the Ly kings established their Imperial City in the eleventh century. The venerable **Temple of Literature** and the picturesque **One Pillar Pagoda** both date from this time, but nothing else remains of the Ly kings' vermilion palaces, whose last vestiges were cleared in the late nineteenth century to accommodate an expanding French administration. Most impressive of the district's colonial buildings is the dignified Residence of the Governor-General of Indochina, now known as the **Presidential Palace**. After 1954 some of the surrounding gardens gave way in their turn to Ba Dinh parade ground, the National Assembly Hall and two great centres of pilgrimage: **Ho Chi Minh's Mausoleum and Museum**. The nearby Botanical Gardens, however, survived to provide a welcome haven from modern Hanoi's hustle and bustle. East of Ba Dinh Square the **citadel** encloses a restricted military area. Its most famous feature is the **Cot Co Flag Tower** that dominates the extreme southwest corner, next to one of Hanoi's most rewarding museums, the **Military History Museum**. Although there's a lot to see in this area, it's possible to cover everything described below in a single day, with an early start at the mausoleum and surrounding sites, leaving the **Fine Arts Museum** along with the Military History Museum and Temple of Literature until later in the day.

Ba Dinh Square

Two kilometres west of Hoan Kiem Lake, the wide, open spaces of **Ba Dinh Square** are the nation's ceremonial centre. It was here that Ho Chi Minh read out the Declaration of Independence to half a million people on September 2, 1945, and here that Independence is commemorated each National Day with military parades. You'll see the National Assembly Hall, venue for Party congresses, standing on the square's east side.

Ho Chi Minh's Mausoleum

Ba Dinh Square • April–Oct Tues–Thurs 7.30–10.30am, Sat & Sun 7.30–11am; Nov–March Tues–Thurs 8–11am, Sat & Sun 8–11.30am • Free

In the tradition of great Communist leaders, when Ho Chi Minh died in 1969 his body was embalmed, though not put on public view until after 1975. The mausoleum is probably Hanoi's most popular sight, attracting hordes of visitors at weekends and on national holidays; from school parties to ageing confederates, all come to pay their respects to "Uncle Ho".

Visitors to the mausoleum (note the very limited opening hours) must leave bags and cameras at one of the reception centres, the most convenient being that at 8 Hung Vuong, from where you'll be escorted by soldiers in immaculate uniforms. Respectful behaviour is requested, which means **appropriate dress** (no shorts or sleeveless vests) and removing hats and keeping silence within the sanctum. Note that each autumn the mausoleum usually closes for a few weeks while Ho undergoes maintenance.

Inside the building's marble entrance hall Ho Chi Minh's most quoted maxim greets you: "nothing is more important than independence and freedom." Then it's up the stairs and into a cold, dark room where this charismatic hero lies under glass, a small, pale figure glowing in the dim light, his thin hands resting on black covers. Despite the rather macabre overtones, it's hard not to be affected by the solemn atmosphere, though in actual fact Ho's last wish was to be cremated and his ashes divided between the north, centre and south of the country, with each site marked only by a simple shelter. The grandiose building where he now lies seems sadly at odds with this unassuming, egalitarian man.

The Presidential Palace

Follow the crowd on leaving Ho's mausoleum and you pass the grounds of the **Presidential Palace**. The palace was built in 1901 as the home of the governor-general of Indochina – all sweeping stairways, louvred shutters and ornate wrought-iron gates of the Belle Époque – and these days is used to receive visiting heads of state. It's closed to the public but you can admire the outside as you walk through the palace gardens to **Ho Chi Minh's house**.

Ho Chi Minh's house

Daily • April–Oct 7.30–11am & 1.30–4pm; Nov–March 8–11am & 2–4pm • 15,000đ

After Independence in 1954 President Ho Chi Minh built a modest house for himself behind the Presidential Palace, modelling it on an ethnic minority stilthouse, a simple structure with open sides and split-bamboo screens. Ho and his Politburo used to gather in the ground-level meeting area, while his study and bedroom upstairs are said to be as he left them, sparsely furnished, unostentatious and very highly polished. Ho lived here for the last eleven years of his life, even during the American War, tending his garden and fishpond; tradition has it that he died in the small hut next door.

The One Pillar Pagoda

Ong Ich Khiem • Dien Huu Pagoda daily 6–11am & 2–6pm

Just south of the Ho Chi Minh Mausoleum, the **One Pillar Pagoda** rivals the Tortoise Tower as a symbol of Hanoi. It is the most unusual of the hundreds of pagodas sponsored by devoutly Buddhist Ly Dynasty kings in the eleventh century, and represents a flowering of Vietnamese art. The tiny wooden sanctuary, dedicated to **Quan Am** whose statue nestles inside, is only three square metres in size and is supported on a single column rising from the middle of an artificial lake, the whole structure designed to resemble a lotus blossom, the Buddhist symbol of enlightenment. In fact this is by no means the original building – the concrete pillar is a real giveaway – and the last reconstruction took place after departing French troops blew up the pagoda in 1954.

Behind the pagoda grows a **bo tree**, said to be an offshoot of the one under which the Buddha gained enlightenment, which was presented to Ho Chi Minh on a visit to India in 1958. Finally, take a peek in the adjacent **Dien Huu Pagoda**: inside is a delightfully intimate courtyard filled with potted plants and bonsai trees.

7

Ho Chi Minh's Museum

Ong Ich Khiem • Tues–Thurs, Sat & Sun 8–11.30am & 2–4pm; Mon & Fri 8–11.30am • 15,000đ • ☎ 04 3846 3757

The angular, white building housing **Ho Chi Minh's Museum** was built with Soviet aid and inaugurated on May 19, 1990, the hundredth anniversary of Ho's birth. The museum celebrates Ho Chi Minh's life and the pivotal role he played in the nation's history; not surprisingly, this is also a favourite for school outings. Exhibits around the hall's outer wall focus on Ho's life and the "Vietnamese Revolution" in the context of socialism's international development, including documents, photographs and a smattering of personal possessions, among them a suspiciously new-looking disguise Ho supposedly adopted when escaping from Hong Kong. Running parallel on the inner ring are a series of heavily metaphoric "spatial images", six tableaux portraying significant places and events, from Ho's birthplace in Nghe An to Pac Bo cave and ending with a symbolic rendering of Vietnam's reunification. Go in for the surreal nature of the whole experience, but don't expect to come away having learnt much more about the man.

HISTORY OF THE ONE PILLAR PAGODA

The pagoda's origins are uncertain, but a popular legend recounts that it was founded in 1049 by King Ly Thai Tong, an ardent Buddhist with no male offspring. The goddess **Quan Am** appeared before the king in a dream, sitting on her lotus throne and holding out to him an infant boy. Soon after, the king married a village girl who bore him a son and heir, and he erected a pagoda shaped like a **lotus blossom** in thanks. The fact that King Ly Thai Tong already had a son born in 1022, six years before he came to the throne, gives greater credence to a less romantic version. According to this story, King Ly Thai Tong dreamt that Quan Am invited him to join her on the lotus throne. The king's advisers, deeming this an ill omen, advised him to found a pagoda where they could pray for their sovereign's longevity.

Whatever the truth, most people find the pagoda an anticlimax – partly because of its size and the concrete restoration work, and partly because of the overpowering presence of Ho Chi Minh's Museum (see above).

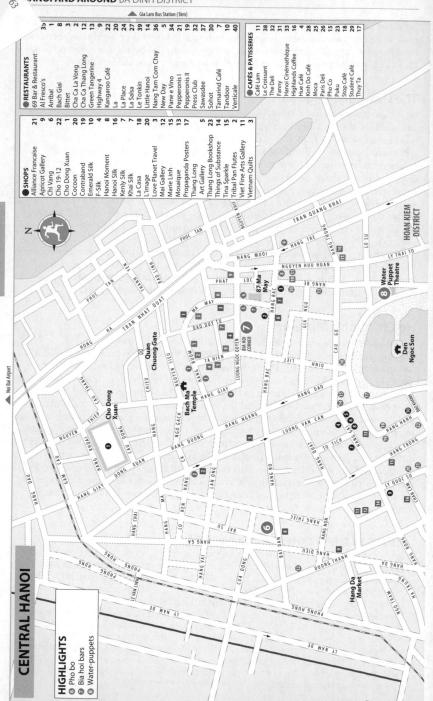

Gia Lam Bus Station (1km)

CENTRAL HANOI

HIGHLIGHTS
- **1** Pho bo
- **7** Bia hoi bars
- **8** Water-puppets

N

Noi Bai Airport

● SHOPS
Alliance Francaise	21
Apricot Gallery	9
Chi Vang	6
Cho 19-12	22
Cho Dong Xuan	1
Cocoon	20
Cha Ca La Vong	19
Cha Ca Thang Long	10
Contraband	4
Emerald Silk	8
F-Silk	16
Hanoi Moment	7
Hanoi Silk	7
Khai Silk	18
Kenly Silk	20
La Casa	3
L'image	12
Love Planet Travel	15
Mai Gallery	13
Marie Linh	17
Mosaique	5
Propaganda Posters	23
Thang Long Bookshop	14
Things of Substance	15
Tina Sparkle	2
Tribal Pan Flutes	11
Viet Fine Arts Gallery	
Vietnam Quilts	

● RESTAURANTS
69 Bar & Restaurant	35
Al Fresco's	1
Arribal	8
Bach Giai	3
Bittet	2
Cha Ca La Vong	12
Cha Ca Thang Long	13
Green Tangerine	9
Highway 4	22
Kangaroo Café	24
La	20
La Place	27
La Salsa	39
Le Tonkin	14
Little Hanoi	36
Nang Tam Com Chay	5
New Day	34
Pane e Vino	21
Pepperonis I	19
Pepperonis II	32
Press Club	37
Sawasdee	30
Sohot	7
Tamarind Café	10
Tandoor	40
Verticale	

● CAFÉS & PATISSERIES
Café Lam	11
Le Croissant	38
The Deli	32
Fanny	31
Hanoi Cinémathèque	33
Highlands Coffee	16
Hue Café	4
Kinh Do Café	28
Moca	25
Paris Deli	26
Pho Co	15
Puku	23
Stop Café	18
Student Café	29
Thuy Ta	17

7

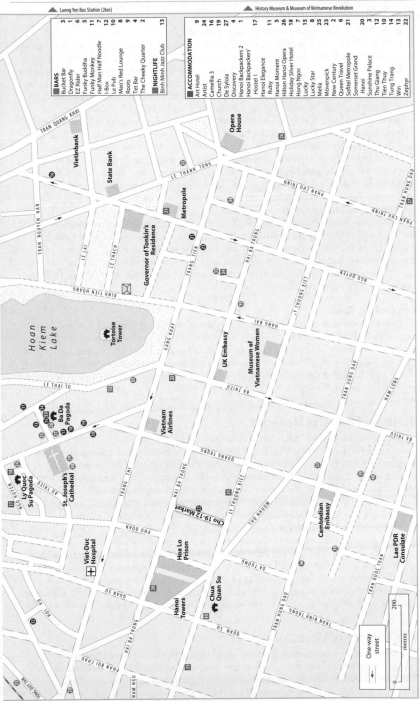

■ BARS	
Bucket Bar	3
Dragonfly	1
EZ Rider	6
Funky Buddha	5
Funky Monkey	11
Half Man Half Noodle	7
I-Box	12
Le Pub	10
Mao's Red Lounge	8
Roots	9
Tet Bar	4
The Cheeky Quarter	2
■ NIGHTLIFE	
Binh Minh Jazz Club	13

■ ACCOMMODATION	
Art Hotel	9
Artist	24
Camellia 3	16
Church	19
De Syloia	27
Discovery	4
Hanoi Backpackers 2	1
Hanoi Backpackers'	17
Hostel 1	11
Hanoi Elegance	5
Ruby	26
Hanoi Moment	18
Hilton Hanoi Opera	7
Holiday Silver Hotel	15
Hong Ngoc	25
Lucky	8
Lucky Star	23
Melia	2
Mövenpick	6
New Century	21
Queen Travel	20
Sofitel Metropole	3
Somerset Grand	12
Hanoi	10
Sunshine Palace	14
Thu Giang	13
Tien Thuy	22
Tung Trang	
Win	
Zephyr	

7

The Military History Museum

28 Dien Bien Phu • Tues–Thurs, Sat & Sun 8–11.30am & 1–4.30pm • 20,000đ

Dien Bien Phu, a road lined with gnarled trees and former colonial offices, interspersed with gingerbread villas, is home to the white, arcaded building of the **Military History Museum**, opposite a statue of Lenin. While ostensibly tracing the story of the People's Army from its foundation in 1944, in reality the museum chronicles national history from the 1930s to the present day, a period dominated by the French and American wars, though it's noticeably quiet on China and Cambodia.

The museum forecourt is full of weaponry: pride of place goes to a Russian MiG 21 fighter, alongside artillery from the battle of Dien Bien Phu (see box, p.412) and a tank from the American War, while the second courtyard is dominated by the mangled wreckage of assorted American planes piled against a tree. The exhibition proper starts on the arcaded building's second floor and runs chronologically from the 1930 Nghe Tinh Uprising, through the August Revolution to the "People's War" against the French, culminating in the decisive **battle of Dien Bien Phu**. If there's sufficient demand, they'll show an English-language video to accompany the battle's diorama; despite the heavy propaganda overlay, the archive footage is fascinating, including Viet Minh hauling artillery up mountain slopes and clouds of French parachutists. Naturally, General Giap and Ho Chi Minh make star appearances – after the ubiquitous still images, it's a shock to see Ho animated. The American War, covered in a separate hall at the rear, receives similar treatment with film of the relentless drive south to "liberate" Saigon in 1975.

Cot Co Flag Tower

Within the museum compound stands the 30m **Cot Co Flag Tower**, one of the few remnants of Emperor Gia Long's early nineteenth-century citadel, where the national flag now billows in place of the emperor's yellow banner. In 1812, Vietnamese architects added several towers to the otherwise European-designed citadel, and when the French flattened the ramparts in the 1890s they kept Cot Co as a handy lookout post and signalling tower.

Vietnam Fine Arts Museum

66 Nguyen Thai Hoc • Tues, Thurs, Fri & Sun 8am–5pm; Wed & Sat 8.30am–9pm • 20,000đ

From the Military History Museum, Hoang Dieu Avenue stretches south past the wonderfully flamboyant Chinese embassy. A right turn on Cau Ba Quat brings you to a three-storey colonial block with chocolate-brown shutters. The **Vietnam Fine Arts Museum** not only boasts the country's most comprehensive collection of fine art, but it is also unusually well presented, with plenty of information in English. Arranged chronologically, the museum illustrates the main themes of Vietnam's artistic development, kicking off with a collection of Dong Son drums and graceful Cham dancers. Though many items in the collection are reproductions, there are some fine pieces, notably among the seventeenth- and eighteenth-century Buddhist art, which spawned such masterpieces as Tay Phuong's superbly lifelike statues. Other highlights include extensive collections of folk art and ethnic minority art, and an interesting exhibition of twentieth-century artists charting the evolution from a solidly European style through Socialist Realism to the emergence of a distinct Vietnamese school of art.

The Temple of Literature

Nguyen Thai Hoc, entrance on Quoc Tu Giam • Daily mid-April–mid-Oct 7.30am–5.30pm; late Oct–late April 8am–5pm • 10,000đ

Hanoi's most revered temple complex, the **Temple of Literature**, or **Van Mieu**, is both Vietnam's principal Confucian sanctuary and its historical centre of learning. The temple is also one of the few remnants of the Ly kings' original city and retains a strong sense of harmony despite reconstruction and embellishment over the nine hundred years since its dedication in 1070.

Entry is through the two-tiered Van Mieu Gate. The temple's ground plan, modelled on that of Confucius's birthplace in Qufu, China, consists of a succession of five walled courtyards. The first two are havens of trim lawns and noble trees separated by a simple pavilion.

The third courtyard

Enter via the imposing Khue Van Cac, a double-roofed gateway built in 1805, its wooden upper storey ornamented with four radiating suns. Central to the third courtyard is the Well of Heavenly Clarity – a rectangular pond – to either side of which stand the temple's most valuable relics, 82 stone **stelae** mounted on tortoises. Each stele records the results of a state examination held at the National Academy between 1442 and 1779, though the practice only started in 1484, and gives brief biographical details of successful candidates. It's estimated that up to thirty stelae have gone missing or disintegrated over the years, but the two oldest, dating from 1442 and 1448, occupy centre spot on opposite sides of the pond.

The fourth courtyard

Passing through the Gate of Great Success brings you to the fourth courtyard and the main temple buildings. Two pavilions on either side once contained altars dedicated to the 72 disciples of Confucius, but now house administrative offices and souvenir shops. During Tet (Vietnamese New Year) this courtyard is the scene of calligraphy competitions and "human chess games", with people instead of wooden pieces on the square paving stones.

The ceremonial hall

The hall, a long, low building whose sweeping tiled roof is crowned by two lithe dragons bracketing a full moon, stands on the courtyard's north side. Here the king and his mandarins would make sacrifices before the altar of Confucius, accompanied by booming drums and bronze bells echoing among the magnificent ironwood pillars. Within the ceremonial hall lies the **temple sanctuary**, at one time prohibited even to

---

BECOMING A MANDARIN

Examinations for admission to the **Imperial bureaucracy** were introduced by the Ly kings in the eleventh century as part of a range of reforms that served to underpin the nation's stability for several centuries. Vietnam's exams were based on the Chinese system, though included Buddhist and Taoist texts along with the Confucian classics. It took until the fifteenth century, however, for academic success, rather than noble birth or patronage, to become the primary means of entry to the civil service. By this time the system was open to **all males**, excluding "traitors, rebels, immoral people and actors", but in practice very few candidates outside the scholar-gentry class progressed beyond the lowest rung.

First came **regional exams**, *thi huong*, after which successful students (who could be any age from 16 to 61) would head for Hanoi, equipped with their sleeping mat, ink-stone and writing brush, to take part in the second-level *thi hoi*. These **national exams** might last up to six weeks and were as much an evaluation of poetic style and knowledge of the classic texts as they were of administrative ability; it was even felt necessary to ban the sale of strong liquor to candidates in the 1870s. Those who passed all stages were granted a doctorate, *tien si*, and were eligible for the third and final test, the *thi dinh*, or **palace exam**, set by the king himself. Some years as few as three *tien si* would be awarded whereas the total number of candidates could be as high as six thousand, and during nearly three hundred exams held between 1076 and 1779, only 2313 *tien si* were recorded. Afterwards the king would give his new mandarins a cap, gown, parasol and a horse on which to return to their home village in triumphal procession.

the king, where a large and striking statue of Confucius sits with his four principal disciples, resplendent in vivid reds and golds. Between the altar and sanctuary is a Music Room, where musicians playing traditional instruments provide a great opportunity for photos.

The fifth courtyard

The fifth and final courtyard housed the **National Academy**, regarded as Vietnam's first university, which was founded in 1076 to educate princes and high officials in Confucian doctrine. Later, the academy held triennial examinations to select the country's senior mandarins (see box, p.367), a practice that continued almost uninterrupted until 1802 when Emperor Gia Long moved the nation's capital to Hué. In 1947 French bombs destroyed the academy buildings but they have now been painstakingly reconstructed, including an elegant two-storey pavilion housing a small museum and an altar dedicated to a noted director of the university in the fourteenth century, Chu Van An. Upstairs, three more statues honour King Ly Thanh Tong, the founder of Van Mieu; Ly Than Tong, who added the university; and Le Thanh Tong, instigator of the stelae. The exhibits are mostly post-eighteenth century, including 1920s photos of the temple, and students' textbooks, ink-stones and other accoutrements, such as a wine gourd for the fashion-conscious nineteenth-century scholar. Recitals of traditional music are held in the side-pavilion according to demand.

West Lake

As in the days of Vietnam's emperors, during the last decade or so, West Lake has once again become Hanoi's most fashionable address, complete with exclusive residential developments, lakeside clubs, spas and a clutch of luxury hotels. A lakeside walk makes a pleasant excursion with one or two sights to aim for. In the seventeenth century, villagers built a causeway across the lake's southeast corner, creating a small fishing lake now called **Truc Bach** and ringed with little cafés.

The causeway and Truc Bach Lake

The name **Truc Bach** derives from an eighteenth-century summer palace built by the ruling Trinh lords which later became a place of detention for disagreeable concubines and other "errant women", who were put to work weaving fine white silk, *truc bach*. The causeway, or Thanh Nien, is an avenue of flame trees and a popular picnic spot in summer when a cooling breeze comes off the water and hawkers set up shop along the grass verges.

Quan Thanh Temple

Quan Thanh · Daily 8am–4.30pm · 2000đ

Although the summer palace no longer exists, the eleventh-century **Quan Thanh Temple** still stands on the lake's southeast bank, erected by King Ly Thai To and dedicated to the Guardian of the North, Tran Vo, who protects the city from malevolent spirits. Quan Thanh has been rebuilt several times, most recently in 1893, along the way losing nearly all its original features.

Tran Vo statue

It's well worth wandering into the shady courtyard to see the 334-year-old black bronze **statue of Tran Vo**, seated on the main altar. The statue, nearly 4m high and weighing four tonnes, portrays the Taoist god accompanied by his two animal emblems, a serpent and turtle; it was the creation of a craftsman called Trum Trong whose own statue, fashioned in stone and sporting a grey headscarf, sits off to one side.

THE LEGEND OF WEST LAKE

Back in the mists of time, a gifted monk returned from China, bearing quantities of bronze as a reward for curing the emperor's illness. The monk gave most of the metal to the state but from a small lump he fashioned a bell, whose ring was so pure it resonated throughout the land and beyond the mountains. The sound reached the ears of a golden buffalo calf inside the Chinese Imperial treasury; the creature followed the bell, mistaking it for the call of its mother. Then the bell fell silent and the calf spun round and round, not knowing which way to go. Eventually, it trampled a vast hollow, which filled with water and became **West Lake**, *Ho Tay*. Some say that the golden buffalo is still there, at the bottom of the lake, but can only be retrieved by a man assisted by his ten natural sons.

More prosaically, West Lake is a shallow lagoon left behind as the Red River shifted course eastward to leave a narrow strip of land, reinforced over the centuries with massive embankments, separating the lake and river. The lake was traditionally an area for royal recreation or spiritual pursuits, where monarchs erected summer palaces and sponsored religious foundations, among them Hanoi's most ancient pagoda, **Tran Quoc**.

7

The Shrine Room

The shrine room also boasts a valuable collection of seventeenth- and eighteenth-century poems and parallel sentences (boards inscribed with wise maxims and hung in pairs on adjacent columns), most with intricate, mother-of-pearl inlay work.

US Anti-Aircraft Gunners Memorial

Passing through the gate of Quan Thanh to where the road bears gently right, keep your eyes peeled for a small memorial in the pavement on the Truc Bach side just a few paces south of the causeway, which is dedicated to teams of **anti-aircraft gunners** stationed here during the American War. In particular the memorial commemorates the downing of Navy Lieutenant Commander John McCain, who parachuted into Truc Bach Lake in October 1967 and survived more than five years in the "Hanoi Hilton". He went on to run for US president in 2008, only to be beaten by Barack Obama.

Tran Quoc Pagoda

Thanh Nien • Daily 7–11.30am & 1.30–6pm • Free • Visitors are requested not to wear shorts

Tran Quoc Pagoda, Hanoi's oldest religious foundation, occupies a tiny spur of land off Thanh Nien, which separates West Lake from Truc Bach. The pagoda's exact origins are uncertain but it's usually attributed to the sixth-century early Ly Dynasty during a brief interlude in ten centuries of Chinese domination. In the early seventeenth century, when Buddhism was enjoying a revival, the pagoda was moved from beside the Red River to its present, less vulnerable location.

Entry is along a narrow, brick causeway lying just above the water, past a collection of imposing brick stupas, the latest of which – towering over its more modest neighbours – was erected in 2003 on the death of the then master of the pagoda. The sanctuary's restrained interior and general configuration are typical of northern Vietnamese pagodas though there's nothing inside of particular importance.

Around West Lake

The east side of West Lake is now largely built up, but it does have a sprinkling of mildly interesting sights. On Yen Phu, halfway up the Red River embankment from the causeway, an arch on the left – inscribed "Lang Yen Phu" – marks the entrance to a narrow lane, down which **Yen Phu Temple** merits a quick detour for its massive entrance hall and a jolly group of statuettes making offerings before the altar. Continuing north, past ostentatious villas – fantasy houses combining a touch of Spanish hacienda with a slice of French château – you get an idea of the pace of development in this district, which for a while outstripped any attempt at planning or design controls. The most notorious example was illegal construction work just east of here, which caused cracks up to 200m long in the city's one thousand-year-old flood defences. After a much-publicized enquiry, in which a few heads rolled, some offending structures were torn down. Ever since, there have been persistent rumours that all buildings between the embankment and the river will have to go.

Nghi Tam District

The district, on the east bank of West Lake, was traditionally a flower-producing area and you'll still find one or two pockets of chrysanthemum, peach or kumquat – depending on the time of year – between the encroaching buildings. It's worth venturing this way at sunrise when Hanoi's flower-sellers gather on a dusty patch of ground to select their choice of blooms at the wholesale **flower market** (see p.385).

Kim Lien Pagoda

About a kilometre north of the causeway, the red-tiled roofs of **Kim Lien Pagoda** huddle in the shadow of the *Sheraton Hotel*. The pagoda's best attributes are its elaborate carvings and unplastered brick walls dating from an eighteenth-century rebuild. Even if pagodas aren't your thing, you could always come out here to indulge yourself at the nearby Zen Spa (see box opposite).

Phu Tay Ho

Sunrise to sunset • Free

Turning left onto Xuan Dieu, and then left again on Dang Thai Mai, takes you along the Ho Tay Peninsula through upmarket housing estates to a row of popular lakeside restaurants and **Phu Tay Ho**. This temple is dedicated to Thanh Mau, the Mother Goddess, who in the seventeenth century appeared as a beautiful girl to a famous scholar out boating on the lake. She refused to reveal her name, just smiled enigmatically, recited some poetry and disappeared. But when the scholar worked out her identity from the poem, local villagers erected a temple where they still occasionally worship the goddess in trances – as at Hon Chen Temple in Hué (see p.294). Phu Tay Ho attracts few tourists and the petitioners here are mostly women and young people asking for favours by burning their fake dollars under the banyan trees; according to Chinese belief, the bats depicted on the facades are symbolic of five wishes – for longevity, security, success, happiness and health.

Museum of Ethnology

6km out of town, signposted left off Hoang Quoc Viet • Tues–Sun 8.30am–5.30pm • 25,000đ; guide 50,000đ; camera use 50,000đ • ⓦ vme.org.vn • You can take the city bus #14 from Dinh Tieng Hoang just north of Hoan Kiem Lake to Nghia Tan on the main road 500m from the museum; a taxi from the Old Quarter costs around 60,000đ

Out in the suburbs of Hanoi on Nguyen Van Huyen, a couple of kilometres west of West Lake, the **Museum of Ethnology** is a bit of a way out, and best visited with a rented vehicle, although it more than repays the effort, particularly if you'll be visiting any of the minority areas. Spread across two floors, the displays are well presented and there's a fair amount of information in English on all the major ethnic groups. Musical instruments, games, traditional dress and other domestic items that fill the displays are brought to life through musical recordings, photos and plenty of life-size models, as well as captivating videos of festivals and shamanistic rites. This wealth of creativity amply illustrates some of the difficulties ethnologists are up against – the museum also acts as a research institute charged with producing ethnologies for Vietnam's 54 main groups plus their confusion of sub-groups. The grounds contain a collection of minority houses relocated from all over Vietnam, dominated by a beautiful example of a Bahnar communal house.

ACTIVITIES

If you start to tire of sightseeing in Hanoi, there are plenty of other activities to keep you occupied, ranging from learning how to cook Vietnamese cuisine to pampering yourself in the city's luxurious spas.

COOKING CLASSES

Given the current popularity of Vietnamese food worldwide, you may want to take some cooking classes. Following are a few of the best places to learn Vietnamese culinary secrets.

Hanoi Cooking Centre 44 Chau Long ⓦ hanoicookingcentre.com. This school offers a range of classes, from Vietnamese Street Food to Vegan Tofu Cookery, at $50 per person.

Hidden Hanoi 147 Nghi Tam, near the *Sheraton Hotel* ⓦ hiddenhanoi.com.vn. Classes are held on Mon to Sat from 11am–2pm and cost $40 per person with a minimum of three people.

Highway 4 31 Xuan Dieu ⓦ highway4.com. After a trip to the market, students are shown their own cooking station at the school and then spend two hours learning how to make three dishes. Prices range from 550,000–1,200,000đ, depending on number in the group (maximum ten).

Old Hanoi 4 Ton That Thiep ⓦ oldhanoi.com. This newish restaurant in Hanoi also offers morning and afternoon cookery classes at $40 in a group or $60 for a private class.

LANGUAGE COURSES

The Vietnamese Language Centre of Hanoi Foreign Language College (1 Pham Ngu Lao, ☏ 04 3826 2468), offers individual instruction from $8 per hour. The centre also arranges student exchanges and student visas.

Hidden Hanoi (☏ 0912 2540454, ⓦ hiddenhanoi .com.vn). Hidden Hanoi runs a range of language classes, from the survival basic course to the advanced course (twenty classes for $200–240). They also offer private tuition.

SPAS AND SALONS

Qi Shiseido Salon and Spa 27 Ly Thoung Kiet ☏ 04 3824 4703, ⓦ qispa.com.vn. Located in the city centre, Qi Spa has a reputation for providing some of the best spa services available.

Salon 15 Ma May ☏ 04 3926 2036. A handy beauty salon in the Old Quarter where you'll pay from around $8 for a foot massage and $12 for a body massage.

Zen Spa 100 Xuan Dieu ☏ 04 3719 1266, ⓦ zenspa .com.vn. For pure pampering at unbeatable prices, indulge yourself at Zen Spa near West Lake. The treatments, which include facials, flower baths and foot and body massages, are derived from traditional minority therapies and come complete with wooden tubs, bamboo showers and mood music. Prices start at $25 for a 1hr foot rejuvenation, up to $180 for a 4hr 30min session.

SWIMMING

All the five-star hotels have swimming pools and fitness centres that are sometimes open to non-residents for a daily fee (expect to pay around $5–10). The *Army Hotel*'s large, open-air saltwater pool at 33C Pham Ngu Lao is popular in summer.

GOLF

Dao Sen Driving Range 125 Nguyen Son, Gia Thuy, Long Bien ☏ 04 3872 7336. This sixty-lane driving range is located about 3km from the city centre.

Hanoi Club 76 Yen Phu ☏ 04 3823 8115, ⓦ hanoi -club.com. One part of the club is the Arena Golf Driving Range, where you can drive floating balls out over West Lake.

The Kings' Island Golf Course 36km west of Hanoi at Dong Mo in Ha Tay Province ☏ 04 3368 6555, ⓦ kingsislandgolf.com. Kings' Island has two eighteen-hole courses open to non-members, though members get priority at weekends. The weekday walk-in fee for eighteen holes is 1,760,000đ.

RUNNING

Information regarding runs organized by Hanoi Hash House Harriers is available on their website (ⓦ hanoih3.com).

7

Downed B-52 Bomber

On the way from the Museum of Ethnology back into central Hanoi, you might want to make a brief detour to Ngoc Ha Village, where the mangled undercarriage of an American **B-52 bomber** lies half-submerged in a small lake. The plane was one of 23 shot down in December 1972 and now serves as a memorial to those who died during intensive raids known as the "Christmas Bombing".

ARRIVAL AND DEPARTURE   HANOI

BY PLANE

Hanoi's airport, **Noi Bai** (☎ 04 33826 8522 or 04 3827 1513, ⓦ hanoiairportonline.com) is 35km north of the city, boasts exchange bureaux, ATMs and a tourist information desk (8am–midnight).

City buses #7 and #17 (roughly every 20min from 5.30am to 10.30pm; 2hr; 5000đ) depart from outside the arrivals hall; #7 takes you to Kim Ma bus station, to the west of centre, and #17 to Long Bien station on the northern edge of the Old Quarter. There may be a charge for bulky luggage.

Shuttle buses run by Noi Bai Minibus and Airport Minibus (45min–1hr; $2, be prepared to haggle) also leave from outside the terminal and drop you near the Vietnam Airlines office just south of Hoan Kiem Lake.

Taxis cost a fixed-rate (45min; $15) but beware of scams (see box, p.375). The safest option is to get your hotel to send a taxi to meet you.

Airlines The following airlines run from here: Aeroflot, ☎ 04 3771 8542; Asiana Airlines, ☎ 04 3822 2671; British Airways, ☎ 04 3934 7239; China Airlines, ☎ 04 3936 6364; China Southern Airlines, ☎ 04 3771 6611; Japan Air Lines, ☎ 04 3826 4 36693; Lao Airlines, ☎ 04 3942 5362; SAS, ☎ 04 3934 2626; and Vietnam Airlines, 25 Trang Thi ☎ 04 3832 0320.

Destinations: Buon Ma Thuot (Daily; 1hr 40min); Da Lat (Daily; 1hr 40min); Da Nang (8 daily; 1hr 15min); Dien Bien Phu (1–2 daily; 1hr); Dong Hoi (3 weekly; 1hr 30min); Ho Chi Minh City (10 daily; 2hr); Thée (3 daily; 1hr 10min); Nha Trang (1–2 daily; 1hr 40min).

BY TRAIN

Hanoi train station The station is roughly 1km west of centre, at 120 Le Duan. Note there are two station exits: arriving from and departing for Ho Chi Minh City and all points south, or from China, you'll use the main station platforms on Le Duan. However, trains arriving and departing from the east and north (Hai Phong, Lang Son and Lao Cai) pull into platforms at the rear of the main station, bringing you out among market stalls on a narrow street called Tran Quy Cap.

Tickets are available in the main station building (daily 7.30am–12.30pm & 1–7.30pm). It's best to make onward travel arrangements well in advance, especially for sleeper berths to Lao Cai, Hué and Ho Chi Minh City. If the station has sold out of tickets for Lao Cai or Hué, try the tour agents as they get their tickets from intermediaries who buy them in bulk. Current timetables and prices can be found on the Vietnam Railways website (ⓦ vr.com.vn/english).

Destinations: Da Nang (6 daily; 14–20hr); Dong Dang (2 daily; 6hr); Dong Ha (4 daily; 12–16hr); Dong Hoi (6 daily; 9–13hr); Hai Phong (2 daily; 2–3hr); Ho Chi Minh City (6 daily; 30–40hr); Hué (6 daily; 11–16hr); Lao Cai (4 daily; 7–9hr); Ninh Binh (3 daily; 2hr 20min); Thanh Hoa (6 daily; 3–5hr); Vinh (8 daily; 5–9hr).

BY BUS

Hanoi's four main long-distance bus stations are all located several kilometres from the centre, and you'll need to catch a city bus (see p.374) or hop on a xe om to get to or from the city centre.

From the south Buses from the south generally terminate at Giap Bat station, 6km south of town on Giai Phong.

From the northeast Buses from Lang Son, Cao Bang, Ha Long and Hai Phong usually arrive at Gia Lam station, 4km away on the east bank of the Red River. However, some Ha Long and Hai Phong services, including the through bus from Cat Ba operated by Hoang Long company, drop you at the more central Luong Yen bus station on the eastern edge of the French Quarter.

ECO TRANSPORT – HANOI STYLE

A recent addition to the streets of the Old Quarter are electric cars that are designed to run tourists along the narrow streets and round neighbouring Hoan Kiem Lake. You can hop on board in front of Dong Xuan Market (see p.357) or hire one for a group opposite the Water Puppet theatre on the northeast corner of Hoan Kiem Lake. While these vehicles themselves are quiet and eco-friendly, and the thirty-minute ride is a fascinating introduction to the Old Quarter, their drivers still hit the horn in a typically relentless Hanoi way.

TOUR AGENTS

Over the years, Hanoi's tourist-service industry has become increasingly sophisticated and now comprises a dizzying array of dedicated **tour agents**. The situation is further complicated by the tendency for newcomers to adopt the same name as a successful rival (as with hotels), or something that sounds similar; there are dozens of outfits claiming to be affiliated to Ho Chi Minh City *Sinh Café*, for example. To be on the safe side, it's best to go to one of the longer-established and more reliable agents such as those listed below.

Buffalo Tours 94 Ma May 04 3828 0702, buffalotours.com. Long-established experts in organizing tailor-made private tours throughout Indochina, with a particular focus on adventure and special interest holidays; prices are a little high but the service is extremely professional.

Ethnic Travel 35 Hang Giay 04 3926 1951, ethnictravel.com.vn. Popular operation with a genuine passion for low-impact, environmentally conscious travel; a maximum group size of six also makes for a more personal adventure.

Exotissimo 26 Tran Nhat Duat 04 3828 2150, exotissimo.com. One-stop travel shop offering all travel-related services from visas and ticketing to tours aimed at the middle market and above. It's a highly professional operation, with a strong focus on adventure tours and responsible tourism.

Explore Indochina 2 Tran Thanh Tong 0913 093159, exploreindochina.com. Reliable tours on "old-school Soviet motorbikes", with a few interesting alternatives to the usual northern mountain routes; tours vary in length from three days to two weeks.

Explorer Tours 85 Hang Bo 04 3923 1430, explorer.com.vn. Specializes in private group tours of Ha Long Bay, but also offers Hanoi day-trips and tours of the northern mountains.

Handspan Adventure Travel 78 Ma May 04 3926 2828, handspan.com. Environmentally conscious adventure-tour specialist. Options range from sea-kayaking in Ha Long Bay to exploring the north on foot or by mountain bike, staying in minority villages.

The tours are well organized, with good equipment and back-up, and are restricted to small groups.

Hanoi Toserco 8 To Hien Thanh 04 3976 0066, tosercohanoi.com. The Hanoi home to *Sinh Café's* open-tour buses offers cheap tours aimed squarely at the backpacker market, from day-trips in and around Hanoi to full-blown Sa Pa and Ha Long Bay excursions.

Hidden Hanoi 147 Nghi Tam 0912 254045, hiddenhanoi.com.vn. This company offers a range of small-group walking tours, including the Old Quarter, French Quarter and a Temple Tour (90min–2hr; $15–20 per person; reservations required). They also run cookery and language classes.

Kangaroo Café 18 Bao Khanh 04 3828 9931, kangaroocafe.com. This Australian-run café is recommended for its innovative, well-organized small-group and adventure tours. Helpful staff and a simple restaurant serving wholesome local, Western and vegetarian food round out the picture.

Queen Travel 65 Hang Bac 04 3826 0860, azqueentravel.com. Aims at the middle market and above with tailor-made and small-group tours.

Sunshine Travel 42 Ma May 04 3926 2641, vietnamsunshinetravel.com. A reliable low-to-middle market agency offering tours throughout Vietnam. It also has a good reputation for its visa services (visavietnam.com).

Vietnam Indochina 71 Bo De 04 3872 2319, vietnamholidays.biz. A small but enthusiastic and efficient company offering customized tours countrywide.

7

From the northwest Services from Son La, Mai Chau and Lao Cai arrive at either Giap Bat or My Dinh, about 10km west of centre. Note that some buses from Mai Chau and Hoa Binh terminate in Ha Dong, a suburb of Hanoi also roughly 10km west on Highway 6; jump on one of the waiting city buses for the 40min ride into town.

Open-tour buses The ubiquitous open-tour buses leave from the offices of their respective tour companies every night (see box above) to make the trek down to Hué and

Hoi An, but it's a long, uncomfortable and noisy journey: many wish they'd shelled out on a train or plane ticket instead.

Destinations from Gia Lam: Bai Chay (Ha Long City; 4hr); Cao Bang (8hr); Hai Phong (2hr 30min); Lang Son (3hr); Thai Nguyen (3hr). From Giap Bat: Hoa Binh (1hr 30min); Hué (12hr); Mai Chau (3hr); Ninh Binh (2hr); Thanh Hoa (3hr); Son La (6–7hr).

TRAVEL TO CHINA AND LAOS

The **China** border is currently open to foreigners at Lao Cai (see p.403), Dong Dang near Lang Son (see p.430) and Mong Cai (see p.417). Direct **train services** between Hanoi and Beijing (42hr) leave Hanoi on Tuesdays and Fridays at 6.30pm; note that only soft-sleeper tickets are available and that in Vietnam you can board the train only in Hanoi. You'll need your passport with a valid Chinese visa when you buy the ticket. The train from Lao Cai to Kunming in Yunnan Province was not running the time of writing, although a bus service covers the same route.

There are currently six land crossings into **Laos** (see p.30), and visas are in theory available at all of them except Na Meo – check locally for the latest situation – though to be on the safe side, it's advisable to get them in advance at the Lao consulate in Hanoi (see p.388). Several companies offer direct overnight bus services from Hanoi to Vientiane (18–24hr). For those flying into Laos, fifteen-day visas are also available on arrival at **Vientiane airport**.

7

GETTING AROUND

Despite the chaotic traffic, getting around **on foot** remains the best way to do justice to Hanoi's central district, taking an occasional motorbike ride to scoot between more distant places. Alternatively, take a leisurely **tour by cyclo**. Cycling is not recommended, since traffic discipline is an unfamiliar concept in Hanoi: teenagers on their Hondas ride without fear, and everyone drives without signalling or even looking. If you prefer something solid between you and the maelstrom, there are numerous **taxi companies** operating in Hanoi and tariffs aren't exorbitant. Finally, the much improved city buses are mainly useful for getting out to the long-distance bus stations.

Motorbike taxis (xe om) These hover at every intersection and provide the main form of cheap, inner-city transport. An average journey within the city centre should cost around 10,000đ and a trip out to Ho's Mausoleum or West Lake in the region of 25,000đ. Always establish terms before setting off. It's wise to write down the figures, making it clear whether you're negotiating in dollars or dong, and for a one-way or return journey; having the exact change ready at the end of the journey can also save argument. Drivers are obliged to carry spare helmets for passengers, but it still can be a fairly hair-raising ride.

Metered taxis Taxis are reasonably priced, and wait outside the big hotels and at the north end of Hoan Kiem Lake. Alternatively you can ask your hotel to call one for you. Hanoi Taxi (☎04 3853 5353), CP Taxi (☎04 3826 2626), Mai Linh Taxi (☎04 3822 2666) and Van Xuan Taxi (☎04 3822 2888) all have a decent reputation. With a short ride across the city centre averaging 20,000đ, and 50,000đ to the suburbs, taxis are definitely worth considering for hopping around the city. Note that prices are metered in dong, though it looks like dollars – for example, 20.00 on the meter means 20,000đ, not $20.

Cyclo Cyclos have been replaced by xe om as the most popular form of public transport, and they now mainly cater to tour groups taking a leisurely amble round the Old Quarter. If you fancy doing the same, the simplest option is to get your hotel to arrange it for you. Otherwise, be prepared to bargain hard, aiming at around $3–5 per hour. Cyclo are banned from certain roads in central Hanoi, so don't be surprised if you seem to be taking a circuitous route or are dropped off round the corner from your destination.

Electric cars Like big golf carts these cars are a new addition to the Old Quarter and provide an alternative way of exploring the congested streets. Hop on in front of Dong Xuan market and click away with your camera for about 30min as it zigzags through the Old Quarter, then round Hoan Kiem Lake and back to the market, all for 15,000đ.

Motorbike rental Bikes are only for the brave in the inner city but are definitely worth considering for exploring sights further afield. Again, most rental outlets are located in the Old Quarter – especially along Ta Hien and Hang Bac – offering a standard 110cc Honda Wave for around $5 per day, with the helmet thrown in. Cuong's Motorbike Adventure, 1 Luong Ngoc Quyen (🖰 cuongs-motorbike -adventure.com), buys, sells, rents and repairs bikes, while Rentabike (21 Yen Thai) is recommended for newer machines and reasonable rates (a Honda Wave for $45 a month). The Minsk Club (🖰 minskclubvietnam.com) is an invaluable source of information and occasionally arranges one-off motorbiking excursions and other events. Always use the designated parking areas (*gui xe may*); the rate for motorbikes should be 5000đ or under.

Car rental This is possible through virtually every tour agency (see box, p.373), and though the traffic congestion makes this a cumbersome method of sightseeing in the central districts, for day-trips out of Hanoi it offers greater flexibility than tours. Prices start at around $50 per day for an a/c car with driver; as few drivers speak English, you may also want to hire a guide for another $20–30 a day.

City buses These are mostly only used by travellers as a means to get to or from Noi Bai Airport (see p.372) but other useful routes connect the far-flung long-distance bus stations. Buses on most routes run approximately every fifteen to twenty minutes between 5am and 9pm, and are fairly empty except during rush hour (7–9am and after 4pm) when some routes can be hideously overcrowded. The fares are heavily subsidized, with a flat rate of 3000đ within the city centre and 5000đ to the airport and the outer suburbs; pay the ticket collector on board.

Routes #3 runs between Gia Lam and Giap Bat (30min) with stops on Hang Tre (or Tran Quang Khai, heading south), Tran Hung Dao and outside the train station; #34 covers Gia Lam and My Dinh (40min) via Hai Ba Trung and the Opera House.

INFORMATION

Tourist information and tours The big state-run tour agencies, such as Vietnamtourism at 30a Ly Thuong Kiet (☎04 3825 9942, ⓦvn-tourism.com), are more interested in signing you up for a tour than dishing out information. A far better option is to try one of the well-established and reliable private tour agencies (see box, p.373), which can provide information on visas, tours, transport and so forth. Most also arrange day city tours, starting at around $20 a person for a full-day tour up to $150 for a luxury option, including meals. If you'd rather go it alone, you can buy leaflets outlining self-guided architectural tours of the Old Quarter, French Quarter and Old Citadel from the museum

at 87 Ma May (see p.356).

Maps of the city are available from a wide variety of outlets, including bookshops and stalls on Trang Tien: those with a street index and large-scale inset of the Old Quarter are the most useful, such as the one published by Ban Do for 20,000đ.

Listings are carried in several publications, but the most useful are *The Word: Hanoi*, *AsiaLife* and *The Guide*, published as a supplement to the monthly *Vietnam Economic Times* (100,000đ). Tourist-oriented cafés, restaurants, bars and so forth usually provide copies of these magazines for customers to read.

ACCOMMODATION

The best place to find **budget accommodation** is in the Old Quarter, and to the west of Hoan Kiem Lake, where you'll find dozens of private hotels ranging from the most basic dormitories to increasingly ritzy places with air-conditioning, broadband internet access and satellite TV. For the cheapest of the cheap, look around Ly Quoc Su and Ngo Quyen, just north of the cathedral, where dorm rooms go for $5 a night. The city's most sought-after addresses are in the French Quarter, headed by the venerable *Sofitel Legend Metropole* and its newer neighbour, the *Hilton Hanoi Opera*. Here, among the quieter streets and more open spaces, you'll also find a rash of modern **business hotels**, but very little in the bargain stakes. North of the centre, there are also a few **high-end hotels** on the eastern shores of West Lake.

THE OLD QUARTER AND WEST OF HOAN KIEM LAKE

Art Hotel 65 Hang Dieu ☎04 33923 3868, ⓦhanoiarthotel.com; map pp.364–365. New places always seem to try harder, which is definitely the case here: the twenty rooms in this minihotel are kitted out with the latest gadgetry, such as two-way a/c units (hot and cold), and staff all over each other to help guests. **$40**

Camellia 3 12c Chan Cam ☎04 3828 5936, ⓦcamelliahanoihotel.com; map pp.364–365. Friendly staff and spruced-up rooms make this little hotel near the cathedral a decent option; deluxe rooms with balconies are bright and roomy. Rates include free internet access and buffet breakfast. **$25**

Church 9 Nha Tho ☎04 3928 8118, ⓔchurchhotel @vnn.vn; map pp.364–365. Prices are surprisingly affordable at this classy boutique hotel on one of Hanoi's trendiest streets. The standard rooms aren't large, but all are furnished to a high standard, featuring tasteful creams, natural wood and original artworks. **$50**

Discovery 22 Luong Ngoc Quyen ☎04 3926 2462, ⓦdiscoveryhotel.com.vn; map pp.364–365. This friendly, family-run hotel tucked up an alley off Luong Ngoc Quyen is one of the best budget deals in the Old Quarter. Its six rooms come with fridges, phones, TVs, a/c and minuscule en-suite bathrooms. **$15**

★ **Hanoi Backpackers' Hostel** 31 & 48 Ngo Huyen ☎04 3828 5372; 9 Ma May ☎04 3935 1890,

---

BEWARE THE COPYCAT SCAM

Be aware that several hotels adopt the same **name**, for example there are multiple *Queen*, *Prince* and *Camellia* hotels, but they are not all under the same management, so you'll need the exact address if arriving by xe om or taxi. Insist on being taken to the hotel you've specified: some drivers will try to persuade you it has closed, moved or changed name, and take you somewhere which pays them commission. If this happens, make a note of the vehicle registration number and report it to the hotel you were aiming for so that they can make a complaint.

7

ⓦhanoibackpackershostel.com; map pp.364–365. Now with three locations, including Ma May in the Old Quarter, this hostel is usually packed to the gills with fun-seeking backpackers. With super-friendly staff, free internet access and breakfast, long happy hours, comfort food and quiet dorm rooms, budget travellers have all they need under one roof. There are also regular barbeque nights and they organize hugely popular – some might say debauched – tours of Ha Long Bay (see p.334). Dorm $6, double $25

★ **Hanoi Elegance Ruby** 3 Yen Thai ⓣ04 3938 0963, ⓦhanoielegancehotel.com; map pp.364–365. This is the most reasonably priced of this swish chain's five branches in Hanoi (see website for details). It gets the basics spot on, and is full of nice touches such as a daily basket of fresh fruit that make the price-tag reasonable when it would otherwise be a little high for the room size. $45

Hanoi Moment 15 Hang Can ⓣ04 3923 3988, ⓦhanoimomenthotel.com; map pp.364–365. One of the newest boutique hotels in the Old Quarter, this place makes good use of limited space, with sixteen tiny but tastefully equipped rooms. All have double glazing (a definite plus), and some even have glassed-in balconies that look like conservatories. $55

Holiday Silver Hotel 9a/10 Ngo Huyen ⓣ04 3938 0565, ⓦhanoiholidayhotel.com; map pp.364–365. On a relatively quiet sidestreet just north of the cathedral, this small hotel has amiable staff, and large, well-furnished rooms at reasonable prices. There's a concierge at the disposal of guests, a babysitting service, plus free breakfast and free wi-fi too. $24

Hong Ngoc 39 Hang Bac ⓣ04 3926 0322, ⓦhongngochotel.com; map pp.364–365. Prices a little above the norm reflect the high standard of fixtures and fittings, which include safety boxes in every room, generous bathrooms and solid, traditional furnishings. It's also spotlessly clean. $30

Lucky 12 Hang Trong ⓣ04 3825 1029, ⓦluckyhotel .com.vn; map pp.364–365. With spacious rooms that are well-equipped, including tubs in all bathrooms, this is the best of the bunch along Hang Trong for comfortable accommodation at a range of prices; all the rooms have safety boxes, fridges, phones, a/c and satellite TV, plus balconies at the higher rates. $38

Lucky Star 11 Bat Dan ⓣ04 3923 1781, ⓦluckystarhotel .com; map pp.364–365. Welcoming hotel on the west side of the Old Quarter, with cheerful floor tiles and satellite TVs, amongst other things. The cheapest rooms have no window, but all rooms include a buffet breakfast. $28

★ **New Century** 12 Cha Ca ⓣ04 3824 4005, ⓦhanoinewcenturyhotel.com; map pp.364–365. This place has just eight rooms, but they constitute some of the best value in the Old Quarter. Some aspects of the rooms like vinyl floors may fail to impress, but others like

computers in all rooms, flatscreen TVs and tubs in the bathroom more than make up for this. $25

★ **Queen Travel** 65 Hang Bac ⓣ04 3826 0860, ⓦazqueentravel.com; map pp.364–365. In the heart of the Old Quarter, this homely hotel (only nine rooms) stands out for its eye-catching Vietnamese-style entrance hall and for the attention to detail in the guestrooms, not to mention a friendly, family atmosphere. The rooms are decked out in restful creams and beiges offset by the dark wooden floorboards and bamboo furniture, and are equipped with DVD players and free wi-fi. $65

Sunshine Palace 42 Ma May ⓣ04 3926 1559, ⓦhanoisunshinehotel.com; map pp.364–365. Re-launched in 2010, this is currently the best deal of several Sunshine hotels, with a choice location in the heart of the Old Quarter. With a well-justified reputation for helpful staff and good standards of service, booking ahead is a must at this welcoming hotel on Ma May. Guestrooms are clean and spacious and come with all the usual mod cons. Tour and travel services and free internet access round out the picture. $30

Thu Giang 5a Tam Thuong alley ⓣ04 3828 5734, ⓔthugiangn@hotmail.com; map pp.364–365. A family-run hotel with incredibly cheap dorm beds and tiny, no-frills rooms. For a few dollars more you can have extra space, a/c and TV. Not much in the way of facilities but an interesting location away from the throngs of tourists and the hosts make you very welcome. Dorm $4, double $10

Tien Thuy 9 Hang Thung ⓣ04 3934 3608, ⓔtienthuyhotelhanoi@gmail.com; map pp.364–365. Well-managed hotel close to Hoan Kiem Lake offering twenty recently renovated and fully equipped rooms at very reasonable rates; bathrooms are unusually generous and all fitted with bathtubs. $30

Tung Trang 13 Tam Thuong alley ⓣ04 3828 6267, ⓔtungtranghotel@yahoo.com; map pp.364–365. A step above the rest along this alley, the *Tung Trang* offers more spacious rooms, all with TVs, a/c and en-suite bathrooms. It's worth paying a couple of dollars extra for a bigger room with a window. $13

Win 34 Hang Hanh ⓣ04 3828 7371, ⓔwinhotel @yahoo.com; map pp.364–365. Perennially popular and friendly hotel on the ultra-cool Hang Hanh café strip. The ten rooms are kitted out with all the usual amenities (a/c, satellite TV, fridges, phones and so forth) and are well maintained. $25

THE FRENCH QUARTER

Artist 22a Hai Ba Trung ⓣ04 3825 3044, ⓔartist _hotel@yahoo.com; map pp.364–365. One of the few cheap options in the French Quarter, this old hotel is recommended for its lovely location around a tree-filled courtyard at the end of a long alley: the rooms, however, aren't super clean. $24

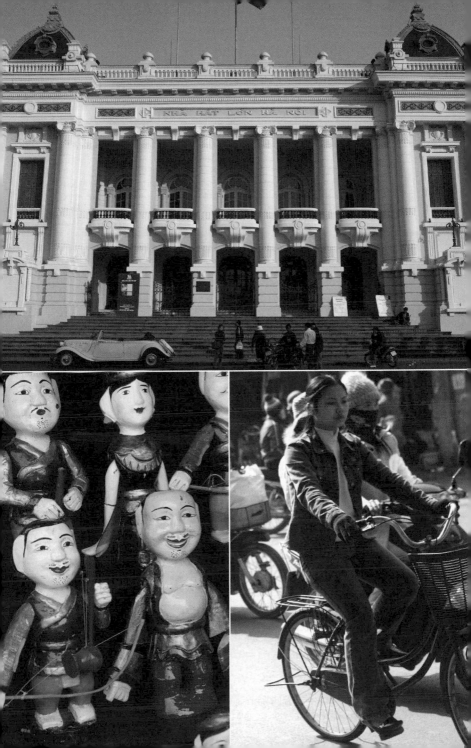

De Syloia 17a Tran Hung Dao ☎04 3824 5346, ⓦdesyloia.com; map pp.364–365. A stylish, boutique business hotel with just 33 impeccably furnished rooms, some a touch on the small side, behind its mock-colonial facade. Service is good and it also boasts a decent restaurant. $70

★ **Hilton Hanoi Opera** 1 Le Thanh Tong ☎04 3933 0500, ⓦhilton.com; map pp.364–365. Arguably Hanoi's top city-centre address for all-round value, this five-star hotel is carefully designed to blend in with the neighbouring Opera House. Facilities include 269 cheerful and well-proportioned rooms with excellent bathrooms and some local touches in the ceramics, contemporary paintings and chunky furniture. In-house services include three restaurants, a business centre and a fitness room with outdoor swimming pool and spa services. $175

Melia 44b Ly Thuong Kiet ☎04 3934 3343, ⓦsolmelia.com; map pp.364–365. While this high-rise hotel is pitched at the executive traveller, it's worth checking out the online deals. Luxurious rooms have a crisp, clean design, but bathrooms at the cheaper end are small considering the price tag. There's an elevated open-air swimming pool, as well as a gym and a choice of restaurants. $140

Mövenpick 83a Ly Thuong Kiet ☎04 3822 2800, ⓦmoevenpick-hotels.com; map pp.364–365. Standard-setting business hotel housed in a colonial-style building near the train station. Rooms are tastefully decorated and equipped with flatscreen TVs, but the hotel's most distinctive feature is a female-only floor, which has slightly different rooms with features like a make-up mirror at the work desk for those who like to apply make-up in natural light, padded hangers for silk blouses and ultra-high-powered hairdryers, as well as direct access to the excellent fitness centre. $150

Nikko 84 Tran Nhan Tong ☎04 3822 3535, ⓦhotelnikkohanoi.com.vn; map pp.352–353. A luxurious hotel on the French Quarter's southern fringes, where well-appointed rooms feature comprehensive five-star facilities. Its Japanese ownership is apparent in its distinct, minimalist feel, and it is home to the excellent *Benkay* restaurant. Other facilities include a business centre, health club and outdoor swimming pool. $150

★ **Sofitel Legend Metropole** 15 Ngo Quyen ☎04 3826 6919, ⓦsofitel.com; map pp.364–365. Opened in 1901 since when it has hosted numerous illustrious guests, the *Metropole* remains one of the most sought-after hotels in Hanoi despite increasingly fierce competition. Though rooms in the modern Opera Wing exude international-class luxury, they lack the old-world charm of the original building, with its wooden floorboards and louvred shutters. In-house services include a business centre, a small open-air swimming pool, fitness centre and a choice of bars and restaurants, notably *Spices Garden*, serving upmarket Vietnamese fare. $280

Somerset Grand Hanoi 49 Hai Ba Trung ☎04 3934 2342, ⓦsomerset.com; map pp.364–365. These serviced apartments, with up to three bedrooms and fully equipped kitchens, can be rented by the night and make a more homely alternative to an upmarket hotel. They also represent surprisingly good value, including access to facilities such as an open-air pool, a gym and a creche. Make sure you book well in advance. $117

Sunway 19 Pham Dinh Ho ☎04 3971 3888, ⓦsunwayhotels.com; map pp.352–353. An award-winning, four-star boutique hotel where consistently high standards of service and comfortable rooms make up for a slightly inconvenient location to the south of the French Quarter, from where it's quite a trek to the city's major sights. There's an in-house restaurant and a fitness centre. $90

★ **Zephyr** 4–6 Ba Trieu ☎04 3934 1256, ⓦzephyrhotel.com.vn; map pp.364–365. This three-star place offers value for money with its 44 tastefully decorated and fully equipped rooms in a prime location just a stone's throw from Hoan Kiem Lake. $123

EATING

The choice of **eating options** in Hanoi now rivals Ho Chi Minh City in terms of quality, range and sophistication. You'll find everything from humble food stalls and street kitchens, the best dishing out top-quality food for next to nothing, to an increasing number of stylish international restaurants: check English-language listings magazines such as *The Word: Hanoi* (ⓦwordhanoi.com) or the New Hanoian website (ⓦwww.newhanoian.xemzi.com) for the latest newcomers. There's no shortage, either, of **cafés**, whether one-room coffee houses serving thick, strong cups of the local brew, or fancy Western-style places serving cappuccinos and café lattes. For a more traditional fix, try **chè**, halfway between a drink and a dessert; there's a clutch of outlets on the ground floor of Hom market. For a few thousand dong you'll get a mug of thick, sweet soup, packed with beans, jelly, coconut and all kinds of seasonal fruits; in winter they also serve it hot, which brings out the sweetness more. **Juice bars** are also becoming increasingly popular: there are several along To Tich, on the Old Quarter's southern edge, which whisk up the fruit while you wait.

RESTAURANTS

THE OLD QUARTER AND WEST OF HOAN KIEM LAKE

When it comes to number and variety of budget and mid-price restaurants, the Old Quarter and the streets to the west of Hoan Kiem Lake take some beating.

69 Bar & Restaurant 69 Ma May; map pp.364–365. Exposed beams and brickwork give a rustic feel to this traditional house now converted into a lively bar-cum-restaurant. The menu includes several innovative dishes

---

EATING ESSENTIALS

Restaurants tend to be small: in the listings we've given phone numbers for those where it's advisable to make **reservations**. Note also that even though this is the capital city, if you're planning to eat in a non-touristy place, you'll need to **eat early**: many local places stop serving before 9pm and peak time is 6–7pm, while Western-style restaurants and hotels tend to stay open later.

---

such as caramelized pork claypot with coconut cream, with most main courses priced at around $3–5. Daily 10.30am–11pm.

Arriba! 48 Hang Buom ☎04 7300 0206; map pp.364–365. Conveniently located in the heart of the Old Quarter, this new Mexican restaurant serves up tasty burritos and enchiladas from around $3, plus a decent drop of sangria to wash it down. Tues–Sun 6pm–midnight.

Bach Giai 23 Hang Mam; map pp.364–365. This unpretentious and inexpensive place offers traditional foods, from breakfast pho and rice soups to full meals costing $2–4. The spring rolls and beef with pepper come highly recommended. Daily 7am–10pm.

Bittet 51 Hang Buom; map pp.364–365. Hidden down a long, dark passage at the back of a tube-house (see p.356), this small and bustling restaurant, with limited opening hours, serves platters of *bittet* – a Vietnamese corruption of French *biftek* – with lashings of garlic and chips for $1.50. Or you can opt for roast chicken, roast pigeon, crab or prawn. Daily 5–9pm.

Cha Ca La Vong 14 Cha Ca ☎04 3825 3929; map pp.364–365. Although it's definitely seen better days, this place – founded in 1871 – is a local institution. It serves just one dish: *cha ca*, fried fish with fresh dill cooked at your table on a brazier, then eaten with cold rice noodles, chilli and peanuts. At $7, it's moderately expensive for what you get. Daily 11am–2pm & 4.30–10pm.

Cha Ca Thang Long 31 Duong Thanh; map pp.364–365. Patronized by locals, this is a newer, cheaper and less touristy version of *Cha Ca La Vong* (see above). Again, there's only one dish – do-it-yourself fried fish with lashings of fresh dill – for $5 a head, but portions are generous. Daily 10am–3pm & 5–10pm.

★ Green Tangerine 48 Hang Be ☎04 3825 1286; map pp.364–365. The setting is a 1920s Art Deco villa and its lovely, plant-filled courtyard. It's worth reserving a table to sample the Vietnamese–French fusion cuisine: rich and unusual flavour combinations such as smoked duck breast with goat's cheese and red tuna carpaccio with frozen yoghurt and lime. The two-course set lunch ($10) is excellent value. Otherwise, this is definitely one for a splurge – a meal for two will set you back $40 or more. Daily 11am–11pm.

★ Highway 4 3 Hang Tre ☎04 3926 4200; map pp.364–365. Midway between a restaurant and a bar, *Highway 4* offers moderately priced mainly north Vietnamese

dishes – steamboat and earthen-pot dishes, as well as more innovative fare such as their famous catfish spring rolls – to accompany traditional rice wine liquors. These come in more than thirty varieties, the medicinal benefits of which are explained in the English-language menu. There are three other branches scattered around town, but this one is most convenient for the Old Quarter (reservations recommended). Daily 10am–1am; food served to 11pm.

Kangaroo Café 18 Bao Khanh; map pp.364–365. Popular Australian-run tour agent-cum-café (see p.373) serving fresh, wholesome food – including a good selection of vegetarian fare – using organic produce as far as possible. The all-day breakfasts and bangers-and-mash are recommended. Daily 7.30am–9pm.

La 25 Ly Quoc Su; map pp.364–365. Standing out among a clutch of restaurants near the cathedral, this mellow dining room is a good place to collect your thoughts and enjoy either a hearty Western dish like an imported steak ($20) or a Vietnamese mild chicken curry ($7). Good range of drinks too. Daily 11.30am–9.30pm.

La Place 6 Au Trieu; map pp.364–365. Sweet little place with views of the cathedral square from its picture windows. The dishes are small but well prepared, and although the coconut chicken curry is a deservedly popular choice ($4.50), the spring rolls are even better. Daily 8am–10.30pm.

La Salsa 25 Nha Tho; map pp.364–365. Decently priced tapas (from $1.50), *gazpacho* and the like in a knockout location opposite the cathedral. Of an evening, the ground-floor bar is also a popular drinking hole for local expats. Daily 10am–11pm.

Little Hanoi 21 Hang Gai; map pp.364–365. This intimate café-restaurant on a busy junction just off Hoan Kiem Lake is perennially popular for its good-value salads, soups, filled baguettes (to eat in or take away) and other light meals, plus an extensive range of bar drinks. Daily 7.30am–11pm.

★ New Day 72 Ma May; map pp.364–365. It may lack the ambience of the popular 69 Restaurant just opposite, but if you're more concerned with content than form, opt for this no-frills diner that turns out consistently delicious Vietnamese staples. If it's full out front, muscle your way in and they'll find a spot for you somewhere. Daily 8am–10.30pm.

Pepperonis I & **Pepperonis II** 29 Ly Quoc Su & 31 Bao Khanh ⊚alfrescosgroup.com; map pp.364–365. With two outlets in the cathedral area alone (and several others around town), this cheap-and-cheerful pizza chain has found a winning formula in its all-you-can-eat buffets: check out their latest promotion online, and get there early to grab a table. Daily 8am–midnight.

★ **Sohot So** 2 Nha Tho (on the left in the cathedral square); map pp.364–365. This place has it all – a wide selection of excellent food, swish decor, views of the cathedral and prices around half what they should be. As such it has become hugely popular with affluent Hanoian youths; come for an insight into where the city is heading. Daily 9am–11pm.

Tamarind Café 80 Ma May; map pp.364–365. A little pricey but worth it for the well-presented contemporary vegetarian food (organic where possible), fresh fruit juices and herbal teas, with a laidback vibe and decor to match: plump sofas, Japanese calligraphy prints and arty Asian-style seating platforms at the rear. Daily 5.30am–11pm.

Tandoor 24 Hang Be; map pp.364–365. A perennially popular Indian restaurant with simple decor but cracking curries: fish tikka, mutton vindaloo and an extensive range of mouthwatering vegetarian dishes. The *thali* set meals offer reasonable value at $5–6. Daily 11am–10.30pm.

THE FRENCH QUARTER

Hanoi's glitziest dining rooms tend to be located in the French Quarter. Here several moderately priced restaurants are charmingly housed in renovated colonial villas; there's also a smattering of less formal, local spots to suit more modest budgets.

Al Fresco's 23 Hai Ba Trung ☎04 3826 7782, ⓦalfrescosgroup.com; map pp.364–365. The sister restaurant to *Pepperonis* (see p.379) is a relaxed place with a pleasant balcony on the first floor. Café, bar and grill in one, the menu includes good-quality Aussie and international fare, including great ribs, salads, steaks and a choice of thin- or thick-crust pizzas from 100,000đ upwards, all served in hefty portions. There are several other locations around town, including on Nha Tho near the cathedral; see the website for details. Daily 9am–11pm.

Highway 4 54 Mai Hac De ☎04 3976 2647; map pp.364–365. The sister outlet to *Highway 4* (see p.371) is very much a restaurant – bigger, less rustic and more spacious – but otherwise follows the same successful formula: varied seating areas, a well-priced menu of classic Vietnamese flavours and, of course, the lip-smacking liquors and herbal teas. Phone ahead if you want a seat on the roof terrace. Daily 10am–1am; food served until 11pm.

Indochine 14 Nam Ngu ☎04 3942 4097; map pp.352–353. Food of consistently high quality keeps this well-established restaurant up there with its younger rivals, though prices are a bit expensive (set meals from $20–25). Beautifully presented, original Vietnamese specialities, from seafood spring rolls to steamboat or the famous prawn on sugar cane, is served either in the colonial villa or its patio-courtyard. Evenings are popular with tour groups, so reservations are recommended. Traditional Vietnamese music performed on Tues & Thurs (7.30–9.30pm). Daily 11am–2pm & 5.30–10pm.

Le Tonkin 14 Ngo Van So ☎04 3943 3457; map pp.364–365. The garden lends more atmosphere to this sister restaurant of *Indochine* (see above), but otherwise follows the same formula: elegant but not exorbitant dining (mains starting at around $20), which makes a great introduction to Vietnamese cuisine. Traditional

STREET FOOD

For sheer value for money and atmosphere your best option is to eat either at the rock-bottom, stove-and-stools **food stalls** or at the slightly more upmarket **street kitchens**, most of which specialize in just one or two types of food. You'll find food stalls and street kitchens scattered across the city, often with no recognizable name and little to choose between individual establishments, but there are a few that stand out from the crowd: we've listed below some of the best places to sample typical Hanoi street dishes.

14 Hang Ga The place to try *banh cuon*, a Hanoi snack consisting of almost transparent rice-flour pancakes usually stuffed with minced pork and black mushrooms and sprinkled with fried shallots.

52 Ly Quoc Su Come here for *banh goi*, fried pastries filled with vermicelli, minced pork and mushrooms, and eaten with a thin sweet sauce, parsley and chilli.

67 Hang Dieu The speciality dish is *bun bo nam bo*, generous bowlfuls of lean beef and noodles, topped with a mound of roasted nuts, garlic and basil.

1 Hang Manh and **1 Pho Hué** Both serve *bun cha*, a Hanoian favourite consisting of barbequed pork chunks

in fish sauce, served up with a plate of cold rice noodles.

34 Cau Go and **48b Phan Boi Chau** These two places specialize in *bun rieu cua*, crab noodle soup laced with tomatoes, spring onions and fried shallots, and usually eaten for breakfast.

45 Ly Quoc Su Come here for delicious *nem chua nuong*, grilled spring rolls, usually served up with cucumber and/or green mango.

49 Bat Dan and **10 Ly Quoc Su** Hanoians come here to eat the city's most famous dish, *pho bo*, a beef noodle soup with chopped spring onion, usually eaten for breakfast.

music performed on Mon and Fri (7.30–9.30pm). Daily 11am–2pm & 5.30–10pm.

Nang Tam Com Chay 79a Tran Hung Dao; map pp.364–365. Small, vegetarian restaurant down a quiet alley off Tran Hung Dao and named after Vietnamese Cinderella character. *Goi bo*, a main-course salad of banana flower, star fruit and pineapple, is recommended, or try one of the well-priced set menus all around $2–3 a head. The food's all tasty and MSG-free, though purists might not like the way some dishes (mostly made of tofu) emulate meat. Daily 11am–2pm & 5–10pm.

Pane e Vino 3 Nguyen Khac Can; map pp.364–365. Popular with the local Italian community for its authentic cuisine and relaxed atmosphere. The menu ranges from *pecorino* salad and minestrone soup through *osso bucco*, roast lamb and veal *saltimbocca* to zabaglione and the obligatory tiramisu – not to mention the gourmet pasta and pizza dishes; count on around $20 per head for three courses, $5–7 for a pizza. There's a daily set lunch ($10) and a popular Fri night buffet with traditional music (7pm; $12). Daily 8am–11pm.

Press Club 59a Ly Thai To ✆04 3934 0888, ⓦhanoi -pressclub.com; map pp.364–365. If you're looking to splurge on a meal in Hanoi, you could do worse than the Press Club, which has an exclusive feel about it with plush leather chairs and starched tablecloths. The menu, featuring mostly fusion and international dishes (mains $25–30), is constantly changing, though you'll always find steaks and other exotics like lobster available. This is also the home of the *Deli* (see p.383). The first Fri of every month is party night, when a live band lets rip on the terrace. Daily 6.30am–10.30pm.

★**Quan An Ngon** 18 Phan Boi Chau; map pp.352–353. A southern import, this open-air food court is a good place to sample upmarket street food in pleasant surroundings. Choose from the menu or see what takes your fancy at stalls cooking up Hanoi and Hué specialities around the garden seating area – there are more tables in the colonial villa behind. Avoid peak hours if you want to sit outside. Daily 6.30am–10pm.

Sawasdee 52a Ly Thuong Kiet; map pp.364–365. Give your taste buds a work out with a fiery *tom yam* soup followed by a green, yellow or red Thai curry, washed down with a Singha beer. Despite the fancy exterior, it's not too pricey – main dishes start at around $2.50. Daily 10am–2pm & 5–10pm.

★**Verticale** 19 Ngo Van So; map pp.364–365. Spice is the word at this converted colonial house – the laboratory-like ground floor is pungent with French chef Didier's cooking. These are possibly the most carefully constructed dishes in the country, such as ocean *escabeche* and swordfish with avocado, and the location is great – the open top level is perfect for an evening drink. Set lunch $12, a la carte $17–36. Daily 11am–2pm, 6pm–midnight.

WEST AND NORTH OF THE CENTRE

There are a few places scattered in the outer districts that come in useful for a respite from sightseeing around Ho Chi Minh's Mausoleum and West Lake.

Bobby Chinn 77 Xuan Dieu ✆04 3934 8577, ⓦbobbychinn.com; map pp.352–353. Hanoi's standard-setting dining experience features Asian-Californian fusion food, mood music, contemporary Vietnamese art and a laidback chill-out zone screened by silk-gauze partitions – indulge yourself with an Egyptian water-pipe (*shisha*). The set lunch menu is priced at $15, while in the evening a starter and main course will set you back around $30. The menu is seasonal but usually contains signature dishes such as filet mignon, blackened barramundi and, as a side dish, grapes wrapped in goat's cheese with a pistachio crust. Daily 9.30am–11pm.

Cafe Goethe 56 Nguyen Thai Hoc; map pp.352–353. Portions can be small for a restaurant with German pretensions, though prices are reasonable (from $4 for mains) and the outdoor courtyard is a pleasant place to eat. Part of the Goethe Institute, and handy for those touring the Temple of Literature and Fine Arts Museum. Daily 8am–10pm.

Foodshop 45 59 Truc Bach ✆04 3716 2959; map pp.352–353. It's worth going out of your way to eat at this welcoming Indian restaurant in an interesting residential district overlooking Truc Bach Lake. The Indian-trained chef magics up a knockout range of curries and accompaniments, such as toothsome tandoor dishes and a cracking Kadhai chicken with big chunks of meat. Excellent value for money, and if you're too lazy to go there they'll deliver to your hotel room. Daily 10am–10.30pm.

★**Hoa Sua** 34 Chau Long ✆04 3942 4448; map pp.352–353. You'll find well-presented Vietnamese and European food with a heavy French influence at *Hoa Sua*, now in a new location near the eastern end of West Lake. *Hoa Sua* is part of a non-profit-making vocational training school giving disadvantaged children a start in the restaurant trade. Try a Vietnamese combo platter (around $2.50), or one of the daily specials, but save room for a wicked dessert. Mon–Fri 11am–10pm, Sat & Sun 7.30am–10pm.

Khai's Brothers 26 Nguyen Thai Hoc; map pp.352–353. Through a traditional entranceway on this busy main road, you'll find a peaceful courtyard restaurant with tables set out under the trees. They only serve buffets, which are well priced at $12.50 for lunch and $18 in the evening (weekends $23, with wine thrown in). Daily 11.30am–2pm & 6.30–10pm.

★**Koto** 59 Van Mieu ✆04 3747 0337; map pp.352–353. Deservedly popular restaurant staffed by erstwhile street kids under a charity programme to train them in hospitality skills. Start the day with muesli and fresh fruits or a full buffet breakfast, then stop by later for a gourmet sandwich or a barbecued duck salad (most main courses are around $3–4), but make sure you leave room for dessert. All

7

7

HANOI'S UNUSUAL EATS

In addition to the traditional favourite street food such as *bun cha* and pho, it's not uncommon to find dishes featuring goat, dog, rat, snake and porcupine. Ethically some readers may find this disturbing but the eating of animals is deeply entrenched in Vietnamese culture, and an invitation to share in the feast is to be considered an honour.

If you want to sample **dog meat** (*thit cho*), a northern speciality eaten mostly in winter and never during days one to ten of the lunar calendar month, then head out of Hanoi along the Red River dyke to **Nghi Tam Avenue**. There are dozens of stilthouse restaurants to choose from, though *Tran Muc* is consistently regarded as the best; alternatively, just head for the busiest. The dog meat comes boiled (*luoc*) or grilled (*cha nuong*) and served with green banana and tofu (*rua man*), and is washed down with rice wine.

Le Mat snake village – 4km over Chuong Duong Bridge in the Gia Lam District – is home to a slew of **snake-meat** restaurants, some of which play to the crowd with elaborate theatrics, including killing the snake in front of you. It's then served up in every possible form, from soup and crispy-fried skin accompanied by rice wine liquors laced with blood and bile. The guest of honour gets to eat the still pumping heart – beware, it's alleged to have amphetamine properties. Though not the cheapest of Le Mat's restaurants, *Quoc Trieu* (☎04 3827 2988; 10am–1pm) has a reliable reputation and leaves out the gory bits.

proceeds are ploughed back into the charity, and you can also visit the training school by prior arrangement. Tues–Sun 7am–10pm; Mon 7am–3.30pm.

CAFÉS

Hanoi's French legacy is particularly apparent in the city's adoption of café culture. The city boasts hundreds of local cafés, offering minimum comfort but great coffee – usually small, strong shots of the local brew. The centre of Hanoi's café-bar scene is Bao Khanh /Hang Hanh, a bustling street near Hoan Kiem Lake, where young Vietnamese hang out.

Café Lam 60 Nguyen Huu Huan; map pp.364–365. This shabby but atmospheric one-room café made its name as a place for artists and young intellectuals to hang out and subsequently has a bohemian vibe. A few paid their bills with paintings, some of which still adorn the walls. If you're not an artist, a coffee will cost you around $1.

Hanoi Cinémathèque 22a Hai Ba Trung; map pp.364–365. Duck down the alley of the *Artist* hotel to find this delightful courtyard café-bar belonging to a cinema club (see p.384). It serves a great range of ready-made Vietnamese dishes at lunchtime, and there are several Western items like steak and chips for around $10. A good people-watching spot at showtime.

Highlands Coffee map pp.364–365. A Vietnamese Starbucks clone with an increasing number of outlets; the best location is on the third floor of the building overlooking the north end of Hoan Kiem Lake, followed by the one outside the Hanoi Opera House. Prices are higher than elsewhere but the quality coffee and comfy seating make it worth it.

Hue Café 26 Hang Giay; map pp.364–365. This tiny store sells strong coffee from the Central Highlands; though quality is high and every cup is freshly ground, prices are very low ($1.50). Also available is "weasel coffee", made

from beans passed through said mammal's digestive system and far more delicious than it sounds; 250g bags make quite the souvenir for unsuspecting friends.

Kinh Do Café 252 Hang Bong; map pp.364–365. "*Café 252*", as this place is also known, became famous after Cathérine Deneuve complimented the patron on his yoghurts, which still merit praise, as do the home-baked pastries. The decor's changed little over the years, though they now offer a wider range of foods, including well-prepared Vietnamese dishes, making it popular with locals, tourists and Francophile movie buffs.

★ **Love Chocolate** 26 To Ngoc Van; map pp.352–353. Located some distance from the centre near the northern side of West Lake, but it's well worth the hike to this faux English living room; think mint paint, pot plants and flowery curtains, with batches of delicious home-made cookies rustled up daily. A bit pricey but worth it for the unique atmosphere.

Moca 14–16 Nha Tho; map pp.364–365. Located in the hip cathedral area, *Moca*'s huge picture windows are ideal for people-watching over a mug of the creamiest, frothiest café latte in town, and prices aren't steep either. In winter hunker down by the open fire.

Paris Deli 13 Nha Tho & 6 Phan Chu Trinh; map pp.364–365. Excellent coffee, tea and cakes at this French-style bakery and café with outlets in prime spots near the cathedral and the Opera House. They also serve reasonably priced sandwiches, savoury snacks and main meals.

Pho Co 11 Hang Gai; map pp.364–365. Finding this fascinating place is half the fun: go through the souvenir shops at number 11, then along a narrow passage and into a hushed courtyard, where you place your order. Head up the stairs, past the family altar, up a spiral staircase and one more flight of regular steps, and you'll finally reach a roof terrace high above Hoan Kiem Lake, where you can sample coffee with added egg white, if you dare. Prices are very reasonable for such a central location.

★ **Puku** 16–18 Tong Duy Tan; map pp.364–365. This popular café has relocated and now offers 24-hr service. It's one of the main hangout venues for Hanoi expats, and deservedly so: good food and coffee, comfy sofas and wi-fi access all around. Not cheap but worth it for the ambience.

Stop Café 11b Bao Khanh; map pp.364–365. An ideal spot for refreshment while slogging round the lake and the Old Quarter. A cheaper alternative to its sister restaurant upstairs (the *Café des Arts*), this place serves good juices and coffees and a decent range of Western and Vietnamese dishes.

Student Café So 2b Nha Tho; map pp.364–365. An amazingly cheap place considering its location just to the left of the cathedral (no English sign but just look for the students squatting on stools): strong coffee and tasty fruit shakes are available for under a dollar, and tiny meat toasties for even less. You get a small plastic chair to sit on – like being back in primary school – and another for your food or drink.

Thuy Ta 1 Le Thai To; map pp.364–365. A breezy lakeside café that's great for breakfast, afternoon tea or an evening beer. It also serves pastries, ice creams and a variety of light meals. Very popular among tourists (there's another branch across the street) and a bit pricey, but you pay for the location here.

PATISSERIES AND BAKERIES AND ICE-CREAM PARLOURS

Le Croissant 21 Ha Hoi; map pp.364–365. The bakery of the *Hoa Sua Training School* (see p.381) turns out excellent breads, cakes, pastries and snacks. Croissants are the real deal – flaky and buttery – and the cakes and pastries counter presents a tough choice if you want to pick just one. Everything is good value and profits go back into the training school.

The Deli 59a Ly Thai To; map pp.364–365. On the third floor of the *Press Club* (see p.381) this deli produces a mouthwatering array of home-made breads, quiches, cold cuts, cakes and suchlike to eat in or take away. It also has an extensive wine selection.

Fanny 48 Le Thai To; map pp.364–365. Hanoi's top ice-cream parlour serves up a bewildering array of flavours, such as chocolate chilli and cinnamon, just opposite Hoan Kiem Lake. The glaring pink decor is unadulterated kitsch – bring your sunglasses.

7

DRINKING AND NIGHTLIFE

For a capital city, Hanoi is pretty sleepy: most **bars** outside the big hotels sweep up around midnight and **nightclubs** don't stay open much later. The authorities blow hot and cold over enforcing a midnight **curfew** on bars and clubs, but one or two places always seem to keep pouring until the last customer leaves: check the English-language listings magazines (see p.375) for the current situation. Hanoi's bar and club scene can't be described as wild, but the choice of **nightspots** is improving. You're no longer restricted to characterless hotel bars or psuedo-pubs, as the number of dedicated drinking holes, some of them packing a bit of designer flair, gradually increases, particularly on Ta Hien, a street packed with lively, dim-lit bars. Nevertheless, the busiest venues are without doubt the **bia hoi** outlets selling pitchers of the local brew (see box below). Note that the Vietnamese tend to drink early, and by midnight few bars remain open.

★ **Binh Minh Jazz Club** 65 Quan Su ☎04 3942 0400; map pp.364–365. Enter the *Hot Life Café* at this address, then go up two floors to find the new den of Hanoi's living jazz legend – the charismatic and highly accomplished saxophonist Quyen Van Minh. Sit back and enjoy a 2hr set of mainstream classics every night between 9–11pm. No cover fee but pricey drinks. Daily 8pm–midnight.

Bucket Bar 32 Ma May; map pp.364–365. Why bother buying drinks by the glass when you can buy them by the bucket? It doesn't seem to bother most punters that the buckets contain cheap spirits and mixers when they only pay $4 a time, but watch out for the hangover the next day. Get chatting to the crowd from the backpackers' hostel (opposite), challenge them to a game of pool, foosball or beerpong, and then try to shuffle to the DJ's tunes. Daily 6pm–late.

The Cheeky Quarter 1 Ta Hien; map pp.364–365. Good music, great food and table football are on the cards here, though given the size and layout things can feel decidedly dead on a midweek night.

Dragonfly 15 Hang Buom; map pp.364–365. Part stylish bar, part lively club, part comfy lounge, this venue has something for everyone; one of the better places to be

BIA HOI CORNER

During the day it's just like any other corner in the Old Quarter, but if you go to the junction of Luong Ngoc Quyen and Ta Hien any time after 5pm, you'll find the crossroads full of Westerners squatting on tiny stools set out by one of a few bia hoi (draught beer) bars around here, drinking their brew. Poured straight from the barrel, bia hoi needs to be drunk quickly before it loses its fizz, but there are usually plenty of takers as it's tasty, refreshing and only 5000đ a glass. If you'd rather sup your suds in a less frenetic environment, head for Bia Tuoi Hoang Dat, at 124a Hai Ba Trung, which is an upmarket joint covering four floors.

locked in when the police are out on prohibition patrol. Daily 6pm–late.

EZ Rider 55 Ma May; map pp.364–365. Close to the *Hanoi Backpackers Hostel*, this new music bar is guaranteed a clutch of customers every night to puff on shisha pipes and groove to the latest international sounds. Daily 3pm–late.

Funky Buddha 2 Ta Hien; map pp.364–365. A focus on fixtures, fittings and lighting has made this one of Hanoi's best-looking lounge bars, and the drink prices remain reasonable too. It has an excellent sound system and attracts a mixed crowd of tourists, expats and locals. Daily 6pm–1am.

Funky Monkey 31 Hang Thung; map pp.364–365. This place is all you'd expect of a music bar – dim lights, loud dance music, powerful cocktails and a crowd of party people. Daily 6pm–1am.

Half Man Half Noodle 62 Dao Duy Tu; map pp.364–365. Friendly little bar hidden away in the Old Quarter and a haunt of Hanoi's English-language teachers, though don't expect much action before 11pm. Daily 6pm–late.

I–Box 32 Le Thai To; map pp.364–365. Indulgent sofas, mock leopard-skin lampshades and vampish red velour set the tone in this café-bar. It's great for a quiet drink during the day, and in the evenings they often crank up the atmosphere with live music. Happy hour 5–8pm. Daily 10am–1am.

Le Pub 25 Hang Be; map pp.364–365. A good range of drinks at reasonable prices – including genuinely *cold* beers – plus above-average food, decent music and friendly bar staff ensures a real pub atmosphere in an Old Quarter tube-house. There are different drink promotions most days. Daily 8am–1am.

★ **Mao's Red Lounge** 7 Ta Hien; map pp.364–365. Cheap prices and strong cocktails make this two-level bar one of the most popular places on Hanoi's nighttime strip; at weekends, it can achieve rowdiness quite at odds with its loungey setting and mood music. Daily 6pm–late.

Roots 2 Luong Ngoc Quyen; map pp.364–365. The reggae and Latin music pumping out of the sound system make this a weekend favourite for those who want to dance, and its slightly out-of-the-way location makes this one of the best bets for late-night drinking. Daily 6pm–late.

Tet Bar 2a Ta Hien; map pp.364–365. Hot, smoky and packed. The service is pleasingly prompt – even when you're desperate for a toasted sandwich at 2am – and you get a fair whack of grog for your dong. Daily 6pm–late.

ENTERTAINMENT

Hanoi is a centre for highbrow entertainment, from traditional Vietnamese **water puppetry** to Western opera and ballet (see box opposite). If your interests stretch to the silver screen, there are several venues that regularly show English-language films, both mainstream and art house. The **Alliance Française** (see p.387) and the **Goethe Institute** (see p.387) both show films in their native language.

Ca Tru Singing House 28 Hang Buom in the Old Quarter ☎ 012 2326 6897, ⓦ catruthanglong.com. Due to UNESCO funding for this vanishing art form, it's possible to watch a one-hour performance of *Ca Tru* singing on Sat nights at 8pm here at this beautifully preserved ancient house.

Cinema National Cinema Centre, 87 Lang Ha, and Megastar, at the top of Vincom Towers. These two main venues show regular English-language films. If you're in Hanoi a while, it's well worth joining the members-only Hanoi Cinémathèque (22a Hai Ba Trung ☎ 04 3936 2648) for its range of international non-mainstream movies (200,000đ per year).

Hong Ha Theatre 51 Duong Thanh ☎ 04 3828 7268. ⓦ vietnamtuongtheatre.com. Hosts performances of *Hat Tuong* (Vietnamese classical opera), usually on Wed and Thurs from 5pm to 6pm, but check the website for details. Admission 100,000đ.

Kim Dong Theatre 57 Dinh Tien Hoang ☎ 04 3824 9494, ⓦ thanglongwaterpuppet.org. By far the most popular, and most polished, of Hanoi's troupes of water-puppeteers is the Thang Long Water Puppet Troupe, which presents an updated repertoire and uses modern stage effects to create an engaging spectacle. They give several performances daily at this small, a/c theatre (front rows 60,000đ, behind 40,000đ). Though these shows are largely put on for tourists, you can't help but admire the artistry and be charmed by the puppets' antics.

Labour Theatre (Rap Cong Nhan) 42 Trang Tien ☎ 04 3824 5707. Renovated for the millennium celebrations in 2010, this theatre offers shows of traditional and contemporary music, dance and theatre that appeal mostly to a local audience.

Opera House Trang Tien ☎ 04 3933 0113, ⓦ hanoioperahouse.org.vn. Occasional performances of classical music and opera take place in this historic building with truly sumptuous interior surroundings of plush red fabrics, mirrors and chandeliers. Tickets (from 150,000đ) are available from the Opera House (daily 8am–5pm) or can be booked by phone or online.

SHOPPING AND MARKETS

When it comes to shopping for crafts, silk, accessories and souvenirs, Hanoi now offers the best overall choice, quality and value for money in the country. **Specialities** of the region are embroideries, wood- and stone- carvings, inlay work and lacquer, and the best areas to browse are the south end of the Old Quarter like Hang Gai and the streets around St Joseph's

TRADITIONAL ENTERTAINMENT

As for traditional entertainment, a performance of **the water-puppets**, Vietnam's charming contribution to the world of marionettes, should be high on everyone's itinerary. When visiting Hanoi most people devote an hour to the water-puppets (*mua roi nuoc*) – literally, puppets that dance on the water – a uniquely Vietnamese art form that originated in the Red River Delta (see p.396). Traditional performances consist of short scenes depicting rural life or historic events accompanied by mood-setting musical narration. While water-puppets provide a light-hearted introduction to Vietnamese performance art, a presentation of **ca tru music** is quite the opposite (see p.482). Consisting of just three musicians, one of whom is a female singer, a *ca tru* ensemble creates an esoteric and haunting sound that is very moving. Apart from the folk music groups playing at the Temple of Literature (see p.366) and one or two other tourist venues, at present these are the only easily accessible venues regularly showcasing Vietnamese traditional culture in Hanoi. However, the situation is evolving rapidly, so keep an eye on the English-language press, or ask around. Otherwise, apart from the odd group playing traditional music at some of Hanoi's main tourist sights, there's little on offer in the cultural sphere that's easily accessible just yet. Very occasionally, events are listed in the English-language press, but are more likely to be announced on street banners or outside the venues themselves, so it's worth asking the concierge at your hotel to see if there's anything interesting happening. Each November, the Minsk Club puts on a popular **music festival**, featuring a wide range of acts from home and abroad; check ⓦminskclubvietnam.com for details. On the traditional side, even if you're not particularly into Western **classical music**, it's well worth catching a concert or ballet at the Opera House.

7

Cathedral. Though smarter establishments increasingly have fixed prices, at many shops you'll be expected to **bargain** (see p.53), and the same goes, naturally, for market stalls. Hanoi has over fifty **markets**, selling predominantly foodstuffs (see below); for the greatest variety of wares, head for Dong Xuan – the mother of Hanoi markets.

FOOD AND FLOWER MARKETS

Hanoi's most numerous – and pungent – markets are those concentrating on **foodstuffs**. You'll rarely be too far from one, but among the most interesting are:

Cho 19–12 Located in a narrow alley that runs between Hai Ba Trung and Ly Thuong Kiet; map pp.364–365. This is a traditional fresh-food market that is a riot of bustle and colour in the early morning but runs out of steam by midday.

Cho Dong Xuan Dong Xuan; map pp.364–365. Also worth exploring is Hanoi's largest covered market, covering two enormous floors with numerous sections to explore. It's the most convenient market for the Old Quarter and also the starting point of electric car tours of the area.

Cho Hom Pho Hué; map pp.352–353. Though it's quite a trek from the Old Quarter, this market is one of the best places to buy fabrics in the city, and it functions as a fresh market as well.

Flower market Beside Nghi Tam Avenue at its most northerly junction with Yen Phu; map pp.364–365. This is one of Hanoi's more unusual and colourful markets, though you'll have to be up early to catch it; action starts around 4am (5am in winter), and lasts around two hours. It is primarily a wholesale market catering to the city's army of itinerant flower-sellers, and prices are that bit cheaper than in town and you'll find people peddling wicker baskets, ferns and ribbons besides bundles of fresh-cut blooms.

ANTIQUES AND INTERIORS

It's illegal to export **antiques** from Vietnam, but you'll find plenty of fake "antique" jewellery or watches on sale, and beautifully crafted copies of ancient religious statues. The following outlets supply elegant if pricey home accessories and gifts.

Dome 10 Yen The & 9 Au Co ⓦdome.com.vn; map pp.352–353. The tempting displays here show off items of home decor such as lacquerware boxes, candle holders and vases at their best.

Hanoi Moment 101 Hang Gai ⓦanoimoment.vn; map pp.364–365. Classy souvenirs are laid out in an uncluttered manner here, unlike most souvenir shops, making it easy to view products like tea sets, original jewellery and bags.

La Casa 15 Nha Chung ⓦlacasavietnam.com; map pp.364–365. Another upmarket souvenir and home decor store along 'big church street', this place sells eye-catching items from an Italian designer and made by Vietnamese craftsmen.

L'Image 34 Nha Chung; map pp.364–365. Located in the trendy shopping area near the cathedral, this place has a good range of souvenirs such as bronze teapots, Buddha images, lacquered picture frames and bead jewellery.

Mosaïque 22 Nha Tho; map pp.364–365. The vaulted windows of this shop reflect the design of the nearby cathedral and *Church Hotel*, while inside are silk hangings, lamps, ready-to-wear items and silver jewellery.

Nguyen Frères 3 Phan Chu Trinh; map pp.364–365. This shop specializes in high-end antique and reproduction furniture, and also sells more portable souvenirs.

BOOKS AND NEWSPAPERS

There's not a great choice of English-language reading material in Hanoi, though wandering vendors in the Old Quarter and near the lake sell pirated English-language publications, including guides, phrasebooks and novels.

Bookworm 44 Chau Long Ⓦbookwormhanoi.com; map pp.352–353. Recently relocated to a spot north of the Old Quarter (in the Hanoi Cooking Centre Complex), this is probably Hanoi's best bookshop with a great selection of new and secondhand English-language books for sale or exchange.

Love Planet Travel 25 Hang Bac; map pp.364–365. This place buys and sells used books, and they also stock a few guidebooks. There are also several state-run bookshops on Trang Tien.

Thang Long Bookshop 53–55 Trang Tien; map pp.364–365. A decent selection of foreign-language papers and magazines is on sale here, as well as some books on Vietnam in English.

CLOTHES AND ACCESSORIES

Although the selection is limited, you'll find no shortage of places to buy embroidered and printed T-shirts, notably along Hang Gai and Hang Dao. To complete your look, head for Hang Dau, near the northeast corner of the lake, and pick up a pair of sneakers or high heels. There's another shoe shop at the junction of Ta Hien and Hang Buom that attracts crowds.

Contraband 23 Nha Chung; map pp.364–365. A new outlet by the owners of Things of Substance, this place also sells versatile fabrics that are comfortable to wear.

Marie-Linh 11 Nha Tho Ⓦmarie-linh.com; map pp.364–365. Beautiful handmade silk clothes are available here, with the emphasis on modernity, glamour and simplicity.

Things of Substance 5 Nha Tho; map pp.364–365. This Aussie-run store features designs for Western sizes, mostly in soft cotton jersey and linens, that look good for both work and leisure.

Tina Sparkle 17 Nha Tho Ⓦipa-nima.com; map pp.364–365. If you're looking for bags and accessories that make heads turn, here's your place. They make outrageous bags – and the decadent decor is worth a look.

EMBROIDERY

Embroideries and drawn threadwork also make eminently packable souvenirs. Standard designs range from traditional Vietnamese to Santa Claus and robins, but you can also take along your own artwork for something different. Many of the silk and accessories shops also sell embroidered items.

Chi Vang 63 Hang Gai; map pp.364–365. This is the place to go for the very finest, albeit expensive, embroidered bedlinen, tablecloths, cushion covers and so forth.

Vietnam Quilts 13 Hang Bac Ⓦmekong-quilts.org; map pp.364–365. Vietnam Quilts is a non-profit organization that raises funds for a variety of causes through the sale of bright, patterned quilts; all are made by women in rural provinces.

HANDICRAFTS

Silk lanterns, **water-puppets** and **silver items** – both plated and solid silver – make manageable souvenirs, as do hand-painted **greetings cards**, usually scenes of rural life or famous beauty spots on paper or silk; the best are unbelievably delicate and sell for next to nothing. Most ordinary souvenir shops also stock **ethnic minority crafts**, particularly the Hmong and Dao bags, coats and jewellery that are so popular in Sa Pa. Though it's virtually impossible to tell, in fact the majority of these are now made by factories in and around Hanoi, partly to meet the huge demand and partly to get a slice of the action. Of course, everyone will insist their goods are genuine, and they are very well made, but it's something to be aware of.

Craft Link 43–51 Van Mieu Ⓦcraftlink.com.vn; map pp.352–353. One of the more interesting craft outlets, Craft Link is a not-for-profit organization working with small-scale producers of traditional crafts, particularly among the ethnic minorities, helping develop increasingly high-quality designs.

Tribal Pan Flutes 42 Hang Bac; map pp.364–365. This place is a real Aladdin's cave of minority crafts, including shoulder bags from the hilltribes around Sa Pa.

LACQUERWARE

Lacquerware is a pretty portable souvenir – chopsticks, boxes, bowls, vases – the variety of items coated in lacquer is endless. Natural lacquer gives a muted finish, usually in black or rusty reds. However, lacquerware in a rainbow array of colours – made from imported synthetic rather than natural lacquer – is now very popular in Old Quarter souvenir shops. You'll find lacquerware items everywhere, especially on Hang Be and Ma May; they are light to carry so make ideal presents. Some designs incorporate eggshell to give a crazed finish, and gold leaf on black lacquer for a more dramatic effect.

MUSICAL INSTRUMENTS

For more unusual mementoes, have a look at the traditional Vietnamese **musical instruments** on sale at a clutch of little workshops on Hang Manh and round the corner on Hang Non. Browse the shops on Hang Manh, where Thai Khue Music Shop, at 1a, and Ta Tham, at 16a, sell a range of unusual instruments from packable pipes and flutes to lithophones and bronze gongs from the central highlands.

PROPAGANDA

Several small shops on Hang Bong supply Communist Party **banners and badges** as well as Vietnamese flags. **Posters** are another popular souvenir from the Communist days, and you'll find these in shops throughout the Old Quarter.

SILK

Hanoi has so many silk shops concentrated on Hang Gai, at the southern edge of the Old Quarter, that it's now referred to as **"Silk Street"**; competition is fierce, but take care since you'll find a fair amount of tat among the more reputable outlets. Classy designer boutiques offering excellent quality at premium prices now also concentrate around the cathedral. Most bigger places have multilingual staff, accept credit cards and offer less expensive souvenirs, such as ties, purses, mobile-phone holders and sensuous, silk sleeping bags.

Cocoon 30 Nha Chung; map pp.364–365. Ready-made silk garments for women are on sale at this cute little shop in the cathedral area.

Emerald Silk 9 Bao Khanh; map pp.364–365. This place is filled with a rainbow array of silk items at reasonable prices.

F-Silk 82 Hang Gai; map pp.364–365. Located on Hanoi's 'Silk Street', this shop stocks a wide range of ready-made clothes at competitive prices.

Hanoi Silk in the Sheraton 11 Xuan Dieu, and Thang Long Opera Hotel at 1 Tong Dan ⓦ hanoisilkvn .com; map pp.352–353. Hanoi Silk specializes in design and tailoring of exclusive silk items; prices are high but the quality is top-notch.

Kenly Silk 108 Hang Gai ⓦ kenlysilk.com; map pp.364–365. Kenly sells expensive but high-quality Vietnamese silks (raw, taffeta, satin and even knitted) as well as other fabrics. They also sell ready-made clothes and have a reputation for reliable tailoring.

Khai Silk 96 Hang Gai (with a branch in the Sofitel Legend Metropole hotel) ⓦ khaisilkcorp.com; map pp.364–365. Exclusive and expensive silk creations from Vietnam's leading fashion designer.

SUPERMARKETS

If you are **self-catering**, there are two well-stocked and easily accessible supermarkets: Citimart, on the ground floor of Hanoi Towers, and Intimex, over the road from Hoan Kiem Lake's western edge.

7

GALLERIES AND EXHIBITIONS

As Vietnamese art continues to attract international recognition, so ever more **art galleries** appear on the streets of Hanoi. Many of these are merely souvenir shops selling reproduction paintings of variable quality but usually at affordable prices, while many of the big galleries, such as Apricot Gallery, 40b Hang Bong (ⓦ apricotgallery.com.vn), and Viet Fine Arts Gallery, 96 Hang Trong (ⓦ vietfinearts.com), deal exclusively with the country's top artists. However, a number of the galleries listed below showcase more **experimental work** and promote promising newcomers; ⓦ hanoigrapevine.com is one of the best sources of up-to-date information. At the cheap end of the spectrum, you can watch artists running up bootleg "masterpieces" at a number of shops at the north end of Hang Trong. A few photographers have also set up shops which double as exhibition space.

Alliance Française l'Espace, 24 Trang Tien ☎ 04 3936 2164, ⓦ ambafrance-vn.org; map pp.364–365. Extensive programme of films (subtitled in English), concerts and exhibitions, plus a members-only media centre (600,000đ per annum). Mon–Fri 8am–8.30pm.

Art Vietnam Gallery 7 Nguyen Khac Nhu ⓦ artvietnamgallery.com; map pp.364–365. Stunning exhibition space on three floors featuring varied works from leading contemporary artists. Gallery owner Suzanne Lecht also organizes cultural events and arranges studio tours on request.

Centre for Exhibition & Art Exchange 2f/43 Trang Tien ⓦ ceae-artgallery.com; map pp.364–365. This government-run gallery combines a small rental space, which changes every month or so with a regular, commercial gallery at the rear.

Dien Dam Gallery 4b Dinh Liet ⓦ diendam-gallery .com; map pp.364–365. Shop-cum-gallery of award-winning photographer Lai Dien Dam.

Goethe Institute 56–58 Nguyen Thai Hoc ☎ 04 3734 2251, ⓦ goethe.de/hanoi; map pp.352–353. Puts on an interesting programme of films, concerts and exhibitions.

Green Palm Gallery 39 Hang Gai & 15 Trang Tien ⓦ greenpalmgallery.com; map pp.364–365. Big, well-established gallery showcasing the big names alongside lesser-known artists.

Hanoi Studio 13 Trang Tien; map pp.364–365. Commercial gallery hosting three or four interesting and well-displayed exhibitions a year promoting young local artists.

Life Photo Gallery 39 Trang Tien; map pp.364–365. Showcases the work of Le Quang Chau and Do Anh Tuan, two of Vietnam's leading photographers.

Mai Gallery 183 Hang Bong ⓦ maigallery-vietnam .com; map pp.364–365. This commercial contemporary art gallery, which also fosters new talent, was actually the first private art gallery to be established in Hanoi in 1993.

Suffusive Art Gallery 35a Ly Thuong Kiet ⓦ suffusiveart .com; map pp.364–365. One-room gallery hosting exhibitions by young artists.

Thang Long Art Gallery 41 Hang Gai. Exhibits leading contemporary artists and hosts the occasional avant-garde exhibition.

DIRECTORY

Banks and exchange Most travellers use 24hr ATMs which are widespread throughout the city; those operated by Vietcombank and HSBC accept the most overseas cards. The Vietcombank head office, 198 Tran Quang Khai (foreign exchange services Mon–Fri 8–11.30am & 1–3.30pm; all other services Mon–Fri 7.30–11.30am & 1–5pm), handles all services including cash withdrawals on credit cards and telegraphic transfers. It has branches at 108 Cau Go, 120 Hang Trong and 2 Hang Bai, amongst other locations.

Dentists The Family Medical Practice Dental Clinic in the Van Phuc Diplomatic Compound, 298 Kim Ma (Mon–Fri 8.30am–4.30pm; ☎ 04 33843 0748, ⓦ vietnammedical practice.com), has a 24hr emergency service. The Hanoi French Hospital and International SOS (see opposite) also provide dental care.

Embassies and consulates Australia, 8 Dao Tan, Van Phuc ☎ 04 33774 0100, ⓦ vietnam.embassy.gov.au; Cambodia, 71a Tran Hung Dao ☎ 04 33942 4789, ⓔ arch @fpt.vn; Canada, 31 Hung Vuong ☎ 04 3734 5000, ⓔ hanoi@international.gc.ca; China, 46 Hoang Dieu ☎ 04 3845 3736, ⓦ vn.china-embassy.org; Lao PDR, 22 Tran Binh Trong ☎ 04 33942 4576, ⓦ embalaohanoi.gov.la; Malaysia, 43–45 Dien Bien Phu ☎ 04 3734 3836, ⓦ kin .gov.my/perwakilan/hanoi; Myanmar, A3 Van Phuc Compound, Kim Ma ☎ 04 3845 3369, ⓔ mevhan@fpt.vn; New Zealand, 63 Ly Thai To ☎ 04 3824 1481, ⓦ nzembassy .com/viet-nam; Singapore, 41–43 Tran Phu ☎ 04 33848 9168, ⓦ mfa.gov.sg/hanoi; Thailand, 63–65 Hoang Dieu ☎ 04 3823 5092 ⓦ thailand.visahq.com; UK, 31 Hai Ba Trung ☎ 04 3936 0500, ⓦ ukinvietnam.fco.gov.uk; US, Rose Garden Tower, 170 Ngoc Khanh ☎ 04 3850 5000, ⓦ vietnam.usembassy.gov. For information on visas to China and Laos, see p.30.

Emergencies Dial ☎ 113 to call the police, ☎ 114 in case of fire and ☎ 115 for an ambulance; better still, get a Vietnamese-speaker to call on your behalf.

Hospitals and clinics The Hanoi French Hospital, 1 Phuong Mai, offers facilities of an international standard including a 24hr emergency service (☎ 04 3574 1111), an outpatients clinic (Mon–Fri 8.30am–noon & 1.30–5.30pm, Sat 8.30am–noon; ☎ 04 3577 1100, ⓦ hfh.com.vn), dental and optical care, and surgery. Alternatively, the Family Medical Practice, Van Phuc Compound, 298 I Kim Ma, is well known for its reasonable pricing (Mon–Fri 8.30am–5.30pm, Sat 8.30am–12.30pm; ☎ 04 3843 0748, ⓦ vietnammedicalpractice.com). It has an outpatient clinic and a 24hr emergency service. International SOS, at 51 Xuan Dieu, provides routine care (Mon–Fri 8am–7pm, Sat 8am–2pm; ☎ 04 33826 4545, ⓦ internationalsos.com) in addition to its 24hr emergency service (☎ 04 3934 0666).

Laundry Most hotels have a laundry service, while top hotels also offer dry cleaning, but prices can be steep. Alternatively, try one of the low-priced laundries (*giat la*) in the Old Quarter. Look out for laundry signs along Hang Be, Ma May or Ta Hien; the standard rate is 15,000–20,000₫ per kilo for a one-day service.

Maps Hanoi city maps of varying quality are available free from hotels and guesthouses. For something more detailed, look out for one published by Ban Don publishers that has a 1:6000 scale map of the Old Quarter, on sale for around $1 in most tour operators and travel agents.

Pharmacies The Hanoi French Hospital, Family Medical Practice and International SOS (see above) all have pharmacies. Of the local retail outlets, those at 2 Hang Bai and 3 Trang Thi stock a wide selection of imported medicines. Traditional medicines can be bought on Lan Ong.

Post offices The GPO occupies a whole block at 75 Dinh Tien Hoang (daily 6.30am–9pm). The main entrance leads to general mail and telephone services, while international postal services, including parcel dispatch (Mon–Fri 7.30–11.30am & 1–4.30pm), are located in the southernmost hall, with poste restante next door. Useful sub-post offices are at 66 Trang Tien, 66 Luong Van Can, 20 Bat Dan and on the ground floor of Hanoi Towers at 49 Hai Ba Trung.

Around Hanoi

When you've taken in Hanoi's main sights, there are plenty more places waiting to be explored in the surrounding area, including the cave-shrine of the **Perfume Pagoda**, which is one of the country's most sacred locations. There are the dozens of other historic buildings, of which the most strongly atmospheric are the **Thay Pagoda** and **Tay Phuong Pagoda**, buried deep in the delta, both of which are fine examples of traditional Vietnamese architecture. You could also spend months exploring the delta's villages – in particular the **craft villages**, which retain their traditions despite a constant stream of tourists passing though. The **Ho Chi Minh Trail Museum**, southwest of the centre, is also well worth a visit, especially if you're heading out of town on Highway 6, for example to Mai Chau. Finally, the ancient citadel of **Co Loa**, just north of the Red River, merits a stop in passing, mostly on account of its historical significance since there's little to recall its former grandeur.

The Perfume Pagoda

Sixty kilometres southwest of Hanoi the Red River Delta ends abruptly where steep-sided limestone hills rise from the paddy fields. The most easterly of these forested spurs shelters north Vietnam's most famous pilgrimage site, the **Perfume Pagoda**, Chua Huong, hidden in the folds of Ha Tay Province's Mountain of the Perfumed Traces, and said to be named after spring blossoms that scent the air.

The Perfume Pagoda, one of more than thirty peppering these hills, occupies a spectacular **grotto** over 50m high. The start of the journey is an hour's ride by row-boat up a silent, flooded valley among karst hills where fishermen and farmers work their inundated fields. From where the boat drops you (memorize your boat's number as there are hundreds of identical craft here), a stone-flagged path shaded by gnarled frangipani trees brings you to the seventeenth-century Chua Thien Chu.

Note that **respectful attire** – meaning long trousers, skirts below the knee and no sleeveless tops – should be worn for this trip; nobody will berate you for not doing so, but you might be the subject of unflattering comments. A hat or umbrella is also a help, as the boats have no shelter.

7

Chua Thien Chu

A magnificent, triple-roofed bell pavilion stands in front of the Chua Thien Chu, ("Pagoda Leading to Heaven"). Quan Am, Goddess of Mercy, takes pride of place on the pagoda's main altar; the original bronze effigy was stolen by Tay Son rebels in the 1770s and some say they melted it down for cannonballs.

Path to the Perfume Pagoda

Cable car 60,000đ one way, 100,000đ return

To the right of the Chua Thien Chu as you face it, a **path** leads steeply uphill for two kilometres (about 1hr) to the Perfume Pagoda, also dedicated to Quan Am. It is a hot and not particularly interesting walk up the mountain or a quick but expensive ride on the cable car.

Note that the hike is hard going and can be highly treacherous on the descent during wet weather; you'll need good walking shoes and remember to drink plenty of water, especially in the hot summer months. It's a good idea to bring your own, or be prepared to pay above the odds at drinks stalls along the route. During festival time, the path is lined all the way with stalls selling tacky souvenirs and refreshments, giving the place more of a commercial than spiritual atmosphere.

The Grotto

The grotto reveals itself as a gaping cavern on the side of a deep depression filled with vines and trees reaching for light beneath the inscription "supreme cave under the southern sky". A flight of 120 steps descends into the dragon's-mouth-like entrance where gilded Buddhas emerge from dark recesses wreathed in clouds of incense that is lit as an offering by Vietnamese visitors.

ARRIVAL AND DEPARTURE   THE PERFUME PAGODA

By car or tour The easiest and most popular way to visit the pagoda is on an organized tour out of Hanoi (from $35, including the boat ride, lunch and entry fee), or with a hired car and driver. One advantage of this is that your guide will shield you from the persistent hawkers who want to sell you postcards and other souvenirs.

By bike and boat To go it alone, it's a two- to three-hour motorbike ride: follow Highway 6 through Ha Dong, from where a sign points you left down the QL21B heading due south through Thanh Oai and Van Dinh, to find My Duc Village and the Ben Yen (Yen River boat station). A six-person boat costs 210,000đ (though the rower will expect a tip too), and the entrance ticket is 30,000đ per person.

Thay Pagoda (the Master's Pagoda)

Admission 5,000đ

Thay Pagoda, or the Master's Pagoda – also known as Thien Phuc Tu ("Pagoda of the Heavenly Blessing") – was founded in the reign of King Ly Nhan Ton (1072–1127) and is an unusually large complex fronting onto a picturesque lake in the lee of a limestone crag.

Despite many restorations over the centuries, the pagoda's dark, subdued interior retains a powerful atmosphere. Nearly a hundred **statues** fill the prayer halls: the oldest dates back to the pagoda's foundation, but the most eyecatching are two seventeenth-century giant **guardians** made of clay and papiermâché, which weigh a thousand kilos apiece and are said to be the biggest in Vietnam. Beyond, the highest altar holds a Buddha trinity, dating from the 1500s, and a thirteenth-century wooden statue of the Master (see box below).

The grounds of the pagoda

In front of the pagoda are two attractive covered bridges with arched roofs built in 1602 (though recently renovated) and dedicated to the sun and moon: one leads to an islet where spirits of the earth, water and sky are worshipped in a diminutive Taoist temple; the second takes you to a well-worn flight of steps up the limestone hill. When Tu Dao Hanh was near death he followed the same route up to Thanh Hoa cave (Dong Thanh Hoa), now a sacred place hidden behind a screen of aerial banyan roots which lies between a mini-pagoda and a temple dedicated to the monk's parents. Though the sanctuaries themselves are well tended, there's nothing special to see beyond expansive views of a typical delta landscape over the pagoda roofs.

ARRIVAL   **THAY PAGODA**

By car or bike The pagoda lies 30km from Hanoi in Sai Son Village. As this isn't a popular tour destination, you'll probably need to hire a car and driver for the excursion, or rent a motorbike. The easiest route is via the new Thang Long Highway, heading west of Hanoi; after about 25km look out for a right turn to Chua Tay and Sunny Garden City, a new satellite development. Note that this is a popular weekend jaunt out of Hanoi, at its busiest on Sun.

THE MASTER

The Master was the ascetic monk and healer **Tu Dao Hanh** (sometimes also known as Minh Khong) who "burned his finger to bring about rain and cured diseases with holy water", in addition to countless other miracles. He was head monk of the pagoda and an accomplished water-puppeteer – hence the lake's dainty theatre-pavilion in the lake – and, according to legend, he was reincarnated first as a Buddha and then as the future King Ly Than Ton in answer to King Ly Nhan Tong's prayers for an heir. To complicate matters further, Ly Than Ton's life was then saved by the monk Tu Dao Hanh. Anyway, the Thay Pagoda is dedicated to the cult of Tu Dao Hanh in his three incarnations as monk (the Master), Buddha and king.

The highest **altar** in the pagoda holds a thirteenth-century wooden statue of the Master as a bodhisattva, dressed in yellow garb and perched on a lotus throne. On a separate altar to the left he appears again as King Ly Than Ton, also in yellow, accompanied by two dark-skinned, kneeling figures which are said to be Cambodian slaves, while to the right sits a mysterious, lavishly decorated wooden chamber. The monk's mortal remains and a statue with articulated legs repose in this final, securely locked sanctuary – though a **photo** on the altar shows the statue's beady eyes staring out of a gaunt, unhappy face – to be revealed only once a year: at 1pm on the fifth day of the third lunar month the village's oldest male bathes Tu Dao Hanh with fragrant water and helps him to his feet.

Traditionally, this event was for the monks' eyes only, but nowadays anyone can see, as long as they're prepared to put up with the scrum. The celebrations, attended by thousands, continue for three days and include daily processions as well as a famous **water-puppet festival** held on the lake (fifth to seventh days of the third lunar month).

Tay Phuong Pagoda

5,000đ • Though Tay Phuong Pagoda is only about 6km west of the Thay Pagoda, a complex network of lanes between them makes it difficult to find alone. It's best to arrange a customized tour of this pagoda, the Thay Pagoda and Tram Gian Pagoda through one of Hanoi's recommended tour operators (see p.373)

The much smaller "Pagoda of the West", **Tay Phuong Pagoda**, perches atop a 50m-high limestone hillock supposedly shaped like a buffalo, 6km west of the Thay Pagoda. Among the first pagodas built in Vietnam, Tay Phuong's overriding attraction is its invaluable collection of jackfruit-wood **statues**, some of which are on view at Hanoi's Fine Arts Museum (see p.366). The highlights are eighteen *arhats*, disturbingly lifelike representations of Buddhist ascetics as imagined by eighteenth-century sculptors, grouped around the main altar; a torch would help pick out the finer details. As Tay Phuong is also an important Confucian sanctuary, disciples of the sage are included on the altar, each carrying a gift to their master, some precious object, a book or a symbol of longevity, alongside the expected Buddha effigies. Tay Phuong's most notable **architectural features** are its heavy double roofs, whose graceful curves are decorated with phoenixes and dragons, and an inviting approach via 237 time-worn, red-brick steps.

7

Tram Gian Pagoda

Coming from Hanoi, the pagoda's signed to the right of Highway 6 at the 21km marker

With time to spare, you could combine a day's outing to the Thay and Tay Phuong pagodas with a quick detour to the **Tram Gian Pagoda**. Again, the large, peaceful temple sitting on a wooded hill is best known for its rich array of statues. Though not as fine as those of Tay Phuong, they are numerous, including more *arhats* in the side corridors, alongside some toe-curling depictions of the underworld, and an impressive group on the main altar. Among them sits the unmistakable, pot-bellied laughing Maitreya, the carefree Buddha, in stark contrast to the black emaciated figure behind him. According to legend, this is the mummified and lacquered body of Duc Thanh Boi (St Boi), who was born nearby in the thirteenth century. He is credited with numerous miracles, including the ability to fly, and with saving the country from a catastrophic drought by summoning rain, though he had to wait for sainthood until a century after his death when devotees disinterred his body to find it in a perfect state of preservation.

Ho Chi Minh Trail Museum

Mon–Sat 7.30–11.30am & 1.30–4.30pm • Admission 20,000đ, camera 10,000đ • The museum is set back to the right of Highway 6, just beyond the 14km marker as you leave Hanoi

While this museum is not really worth making a special trip to see, with a bit of forethought it can be combined with visits to the Perfume Pagoda, the Tram Gian or Tay Phuong Pagodas, or on the way to Mai Chau. Once you're here, there's much to learn, including the fact that the **Ho Chi Minh Trail** was never a single trail but a complex network of muddy tracks that crisscrossed the border with Laos and Cambodia. Visitors are first shown an informative, twenty-minute video about the construction of the trail, which eventually became one of the key factors in the outcome of the American War. Exhibits include some of the equipment used in the trail's construction, along with some of the shrapnel-, nail- and cigarette-bombs that were employed to slow down the trail's progress. Outside are a few vehicles that once used the trail, and behind the museum is a forgettable mock-up of an underground operations centre along the trail.

The craft villages

For centuries **villages** around Vietnam's major towns have specialized in single-commodity production, initially to supply the local market, and sometimes going on to win national fame for the skill of their artisans. A few communities continue to prosper, of which the best known near Hanoi are **Bat Trang** pottery village and **Van Phuc** for silk. These are well-run, commercial operations where family units turn out fine, hand-crafted products, and they are used to foreigners coming to watch them at work. Most other villages are far less touristy, and the more isolated may treat visitors with suspicion. Nevertheless, it's worth taking a guide for the day to gain a rare glimpse into a gruelling way of life that continues to follow the ancient rhythms, using craft techniques handed down the generations virtually unchanged. Hanoi tour agents (see box, p.373) offer organized day-trips to a selection of craft villages for around $20 to $30, or they would mix and match a trip to craft villages with a visit to the pagodas.

Bat Trang

BAT TRANG, across the Red River in Hanoi's Gia Lam District, is an easy jaunt by road over Chuong Duong Bridge, then immediately right along the levy. The village has been producing **bricks** and **earthenware** since the fifteenth century, and the oldest part of the village beside the river has a medieval aura, with its narrow, high-walled alleys spattered with handmade coal-pats (used as fuel in the kilns) drying in the sun; to reach this area, continue straight ahead at the end of the main street (Duong Giang Cao) and keep going generally west. Through tiny doorways, you catch glimpses of courtyards stacked with moulds and hand-painted pots, while all around rise the squat brick chimneys of the traditional coal-fired kilns. Around two thousand families live in Bat Trang, producing time-honoured blue-and-white **ceramics** alongside more contemporary designs as well as mass-produced floor tiles and balustrades to feed Hanoi's building boom. The village has expanded rapidly in recent years, thanks largely to a healthy export market, and now boasts some 2500 kilns. Most are now gas-fired, but air pollution and respiratory infections remain a problem. Showrooms along the main drag offer a bewildering choice. Prices are not necessarily any cheaper than in Hanoi itself, though the range is superior and it's easier to bargain. In some of the bigger workshops (such as Hoa Lan Ceramics, 81 Duong Giang Cao) you can paint your own design and have the piece delivered to your hotel once it's fired.

ARRIVAL AND DEPARTURE THE CRAFT VILLAGES

By bicycle Note that pedal cyclists have to use Long Bien Bridge, a short distance further north. After 10km heading generally south, following signs to Xuan Quan, a right turn indicates the village entrance.

By xe om A half-day xe om excursion is expensive when waiting time is included – around 200,000đ.

By bus The bus is better value than travelling by xe om. Number 47 buses (5000đ) depart from Long Bien bus station every fifteen minutes or so.

Van Phuc

The silk village of **VAN PHUC** is often included as a quick stop on trips to the **Perfume Pagoda**, to the Ho Chi Minh Trail Museum (see p.391), or the Thay, Tay Phuong and Tram Gian pagodas (see p.391). In the village, the clatter of electric looms from the thirty-odd workshops fills the air. You're welcome to wander into any of them, and will be given a brief explanation, but there's nothing much to detain you unless you're shopping for silk. Material is a shade cheaper than in Hanoi, while finished items such as scarves and clothes can be as little as half the price.

ARRIVAL AND DEPARTURE VAN PHUC

By bicycle or motorbike Van Phuc lies 11km west of Hanoi on Highway 6, about a kilometre north of Ha Dong

post office on the Quoac Hai Road.

By bus Take a #1 bus from Long Bien Station.

Chuong

Conical hats are the staple product of **CHUONG** village (also known as Phuong Trung), which is best visited on market days (held six times each lunar month), when hats are piled high in golden pyramids. At other times it's possible to see artisans deftly

HISTORY OF THE CITADEL

The earliest independent Vietnamese states grew up in the Red River flood plain, atop low hills or crouched behind sturdy embankments. First to emerge from the mists of legend was **Van Lang**, presided over by the Hung kings from a knob of high ground marked today by a few dynastic temples north of Viet Tri (Vinh Phu Province). Then the action moved closer to Hanoi when King An Duong ruled Au Lac (258–207 BC) from an immense citadel at Co Loa (Old Snail City). These days the once massive **earthworks** are barely visible and it's really only worth stopping off here in passing, to take a look at a couple of quiet temples with an interesting history.

King An Duong built his citadel inside three concentric ramparts, spiralling like a snail shell, separated by moats large enough for ships to navigate; the outer wall was 8km long, 6–8m wide and at least 4m high, topped off with bamboo fencing. After the Chinese invaded in the late second century BC, Co Loa was abandoned until 939 AD, when **Ngo Quyen** established the next period of independent rule from the same heavily symbolic site. Archeologists have found rich pickings at Co Loa, including thousands of iron arrowheads, displayed here and in Hanoi's History Museum (see p.359), which lend credence to at least one of the Au Lac legends. The story goes that the sacred **Golden Turtle** gave King An Duong a magic crossbow made from a claw that fired thousands of arrows at a time. A deceitful Chinese prince married An Duong's daughter, Princess My Chau, persuaded her to show him the crossbow and then stole the claw before mounting an invasion. King An Duong and his daughter were forced to flee, whereupon My Chau understood her act of betrayal and nobly told her father to kill her. When the king beheaded his daughter and threw her body in a well, she turned into lustrous, pink pearls.

7

assembling the dried leaves on a bamboo frame. Traditionally the designs varied according to the different needs: thick and robust for working in the fields, more delicate for outings to the temple and other special occasions, and flat, ornamented hats for fashion-conscious aristocrats.

ARRIVAL	CHUONG

By bicycle or motorbike Chuong lies just off Highway 21b a couple of kilometres south of Thanh Oai on the road to the Perfume Pagoda (see p.389).

Co Loa Temple Complex

Daily 6am–6pm • 5000đ

The first thing you come to after a couple of kilometres off the highway is an archer's statue standing in a small pond; continue straight on here (west) to find the principal temple. The Co Loa Temple Complex forms part of the Citadel of the same name (see box above). The principal temple, **Den An Duong Vuong**, faces a refurbished lake, with a graceful stele-house to one side. Inside the rebuilt temple, a sixteenth-century black-bronze statue of the king resides on the main altar, resplendent in his double crown, while a subsidiary altar is dedicated to Kim Quy, the Golden Turtle. More interesting, however, is the second group of buildings, 100m north of the archer, where a large, walled courtyard contains a beautifully simple open-sided hall, furnished with huge, ironwood pillars, and containing some of the archeological finds. Next door is the princess's small temple, **Den My Chau**. Sadly, it's all new concrete, but inside she is still honoured in the surprising form of a dumpy, armchair-shaped stone clothed in embroidered finery and covered in jewels but lacking a head.

ARRIVAL	CO LOA TEMPLE COMPLEX

By motorbike Co Loas 16km due north of Hanoi; signposted to the right of busy Highway 3.

By bus Take bus #46 from My Dinh bus station.

The far north

FLOWER MARKET, BAC HA REGION

The far north

As Vietnam fans out above Hanoi towards the Chinese and Laos borders, it attains its maximum width of 600km, the majority of it a mountainous buffer zone wrapped around the Red River Delta. Much of the region is wild and inaccessible, yet it contains some of Vietnam's most awe-inspiring scenery, sparsely populated by a fascinating mosaic of ethnic minorities. Most popular for visitors is the northwest region where the country's highest mountain range and its tallest peak, Fan Si Pan, rise abruptly from the Red River Valley. Within the shadow of Fan Si Pan lies Sa Pa, an easily accessible former French hill station, famous for its minority peoples and for its superb scenery with opportunities for trekking out to isolated hamlets. On the other side of the Red River, a couple of hours' drive away, Bac Ha has one of the most colourful of all minority groups in the form of the Flower Hmong, whose markets are great fun. The attractions of these two towns and the historic battlefield of Dien Bien Phu, site of the Viet Minh's decisive victory over French forces in 1954, draw most tourists, while those with enough time are well rewarded if they follow the scenic route back to Hanoi, passing through Son La, Moc Chau and Mai Chau.

The little-travelled provinces east of the Red River Valley also deserve attention, especially the stunning scenery and mountain people in the border area of **Ha Giang** and **Cao Bang** provinces. The northeast region also features **Ba Be National Park**, where Vietnam's largest natural lake hides among forested limestone crags and impenetrable jungle. Not surprisingly, infrastructure throughout the northern mountains is poor: facilities tend to be thin on the ground, and some roads are in terrible condition. However, this area is becoming increasingly popular with tourists as Hanoi's tour agents organize new tours and independent travellers venture into uncharted terrain by jeep or motorbike.

Whether you travel by public transport or with your own vehicle, you need to allow around six days' actual **travelling time** to cover the northwestern region. Touring the entire northeast also requires at least six days including Ha Giang Province, but more if you want to spend time on Ba Be Lake, or visit Pac Bo Cave or Ban Gioc Waterfall near Cao Bang. Combining the northwest and northeast loops gives you an unforgettable two weeks of exploration, but bear in mind that travelling these roads is unpredictable, becoming downright hazardous during the rains (see box, p.399), and it's advisable to allow some **flexibility** in your programme. If you've got only limited time, Sa Pa, Mai Chau and Ba Be National Park make rewarding two- or three-day **excursions out of Hanoi**, either by public transport or hired vehicle. The other alternative is to join an organized tour with one of Hanoi's tour agencies.

GETTING AROUND
THE NORTH

By bus Travelling through the northern provinces using local buses is possible, though it's an uncomfortable experience and it's only the hardiest adventurers who take them. Most visitors hire a car and driver or join a motorbike tour to go all the way round the loop to Hanoi.

Renting a car or bike This gives you more freedom to stop at villages or jaunt off along side tracks. Either a four-wheel-drive vehicle or a motorbike is recommended; the cost of hiring a jeep and driver (for three to four passengers) in Hanoi averages around $60 per day, while scooters and motorbikes go for between $5 and $8 per day. When planning your route, base your itinerary on an average speed of about 40km per hour.

TREKKING AROUND SA PA

Highlights

❶ **Trekking around Sa Pa** Exploring the mountainous north is all about stretching your legs, taking in great views of the landscape and spending time with the colourfully dressed montagnards. **See p.401**

❷ **Weekend markets** Bac Ha Sunday market is full of Flower Hmong, perhaps the most dazzling dressers in the country. **See p.408**

❸ **Thai minority villages** Around Mai Chau visitors can stay in Thai stilthouses and

see shows of traditional dancing. **See p.418**

❹ **Ha Giang** Gateway to the country's northernmost and wildest province, where the scenery is simply stunning. **See p.421**

❺ **Ba Be Lake** A laidback spot, where you can either glide around in a boat on its glassy waters, or trek to minority villages near its shore **See p.426**

HIGHLIGHTS ARE MARKED ON THE MAP ON P.398

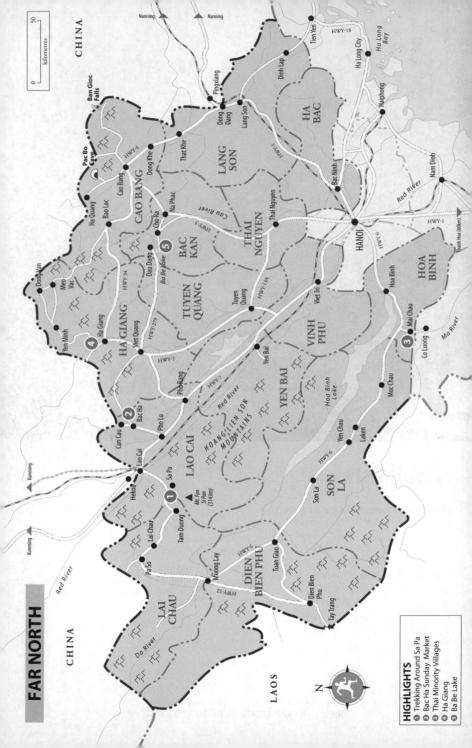

WHEN TO GO

The **best time** to visit the northern mountains is from September to November or from March to May, when the weather is fairly settled with dry sunny days and clear cold nights. **Winters** can be decidedly chilly, especially in the northeast where night frosts are not uncommon from December to February, but the compensation is daybreak mists and breathtaking sunrise views high above valleys filled with early-morning lakes of cloud. The **rainy season** lasts from May to September, peaking in July and August, when heavy downpours wash out bridges, turn unsealed roads into quagmires and throw in the occasional landslide for good measure. Peak season for foreign tourists is from September to November, while the rainy summer months of July and August are when Hanoians head up to the mountains to escape the stifling heat of the delta.

Brief history

There is little recorded history of this region of the country prior to the French establishing a hill station at Sa Pa in the 1920s, and even then their tenure was brief. Remote uplands, dense vegetation and rugged terrain suited to guerrilla activities, plus a safe haven across the border, made this region the perfect place from which to orchestrate Vietnam's independence movement. For a short while in 1941, **Ho Chi Minh** hid in the Pac Bo Cave on the Chinese frontier, later moving south to Tuyen Quang Province, from where the Viet Minh launched their August Revolution in 1945. These northern provinces were the first to be **liberated** from French rule, but over in the northwest some minority groups, notably from among the Thai, Hmong and Muong, supported the colonial authorities and it took the Viet Minh until 1952 to gain control of the area. Two years later, they staged their great victory over the French at Dien Bien Phu, close to the Laos border.

During the late 1970s **Sino-Vietnamese** relations became increasingly sour for various reasons, not least Vietnam's invasion of Cambodia. Things came to a head on February 17, 1979 when the Chinese sent two hundred thousand troops into northern Vietnam, destroying most of the border towns: seventeen days later, however, the invasion force was on its way home, some twenty thousand short. Though much of the infrastructural and political damage from the war has been repaired, unmarked minefields along 1000km of frontier pose a more intractable problem: most areas – including all which regularly receive tourists – have been cleared and declared safe, but in the more remote areas it's sensible to stick to well-worn paths.

The northwest

Vietnam's most mountainous provinces lie immediately west of the Red River Valley, dominated by the country's highest range, Hoang Lien Son. Right on the border where the Red River enters Vietnam sits **Lao Cai** Town, a major crossing point into China and gateway to the former hill station of **Sa Pa** and nearby **Bac Ha**, both now firmly on the tourist map for their colourful minority groups and weekly markets. From Sa Pa a road loops west across the immense flank of **Fan Si Pan**, the country's tallest peak, to join the Song Da (Black River) Valley running south, through the old French garrison towns of **Muong Lay** (formerly Lai Chau) and **Son La**, via a series of dramatic passes to the industrial town of Hoa Binh on the edge of the northern delta. The only sight as such is the historic battlefield of **Dien Bien Phu**, close to the Laos border, but it's the scenery that makes the diversion worthwhile. Throughout the region, sweeping views and mountain grandeur contrast with ribbons of intensively cultivated valleys, and here more than anywhere else in Vietnam the **ethnic minorities** have retained their traditional dress, architecture and languages. After Sa Pa, the most popular tourist destination in these mountains is **Mai Chau**, an attractive area inhabited by the White Thai minority, within easy reach of Hanoi.

THE NORTHERN MINORITIES

Around six million **minority people** (nearly two-thirds of Vietnam's total) live in the northern uplands, mostly in isolated villages. The largest ethnic groups are Thai and Muong in the northwest, Tay and Nung in the northeast and Hmong and Dao dispersed throughout the region. Historically, all these peoples migrated from southern China at various times throughout history: those who arrived first, notably the Tay and Thai, settled in the fertile valleys where they now lead a relatively prosperous existence, whereas late arrivals, such as the Hmong and Dao, were left to eke out a living on the inhospitable higher slopes (see p.467). Despite government efforts to integrate them into the Vietnamese community, most continue to follow a way of life little changed over the centuries. For an insight into the minorities' traditional cultures and highly varied styles of dress, visit Hanoi's informative **Museum of Ethnology** (see p.370) before setting off into the mountains.

VISITING MINORITY VILLAGES

The remoteness of Vietnam's minority villages provides much of their appeal, though many are easily accessible from hub towns such as Sa Pa, Bac Ha, Son La, Mai Chau, Ba Be and Cao Bang. A popular, hassle-free way to visit is to join one of the **organized trips** offered by Hanoi tour agencies (see p.373). The usual destinations are Sa Pa and Bac Ha, coinciding with the Sunday market, or Mai Chau, with the standard package including guided visits to at least two different minorities plus, in the case of Mai Chau, a night in a stilthouse. The four-day Sa Pa tour costs around $200 per person depending on transport and accommodation arrangements, while two days with one night in Mai Chau costs around $50. In Sa Pa and Bac Ha, most **guesthouses** offer trekking and home-stay trips with their own guides, though note that not all the guides can speak English.

VILLAGE ETIQUETTE

Behaviour that we take for granted may cause offence to some ethnic minority people; remember you're a guest. Apart from being sensitive to the situation and keeping an open mind, the following simple rules should be observed when visiting the ethnic minority areas.

- **Dress modestly**, in long trousers or skirt and T-shirt or shirt.
- Be sensitive to people's wishes when taking **photographs**, particularly of older people who are suspicious of the camera; always ask permission first.
- Only go **inside a house** when invited and remove your shoes before entering.
- Small **gifts**, such as fresh fruit from the local market, are always welcome. However, there is a view that even this can foster begging, and that you should only ever give in return for some service or as a sign of appreciation for hospitality. A compromise is to **buy craft work** produced by the villagers – most communities should have some embroidery, textiles or basketry for sale.
- As a mark of respect, learn the local **terms of address**, either in dialect or at least in Vietnamese, such as *chao ong*, *chao ba* (see p.498).
- Try to **minimize your impact** on the often fragile local environment; take litter back to the towns and be sensitive to the use of wood and other scarce resources.
- Growing and using **opium** is illegal in Vietnam and is punished with a fine or prison sentence; do not encourage its production by buying or smoking.

Sa Pa

The tourist capital of Vietnam's mountainous north, **SA PA** is perched dramatically on the western edge of a high plateau, facing the hazy blue peak of **Fan Si Pan**, and is surrounded by villages of ethnic minorities, particularly the Red Dao and Black Hmong. Its refreshing climate and almost alpine landscape struck a nostalgic chord with European visitors, who travelled up from Lao Cai by sedan chair in the early twentieth century, and by 1930 a flourishing hill station had developed, complete with tennis court, church and over two hundred villas. Nowadays only a handful of the old buildings remain, the rest lost to time and the 1979 Chinese invasion, as well as those involved in the current hotel development spree. Although height restrictions are finally being enforced on new buildings, the damage has already been done and Sa Pa's days as an idyllic haven in the hills have been concreted over. However, what the modern town lacks in character is more than compensated for by its magnificent scenery, and it makes an ideal base for tours of the area's varied collection of **minority villages**.

Sa Pa itself is ethnically Vietnamese, but its shops and market serve the minority villages for miles around. Every day is bright and lively in Sa Pa, with the women coming dressed in their finery – the most striking are the Red Dao, who wear scarlet headdresses festooned with woollen tassels and silver trinkets. Black Hmong are the most numerous group – over a third of the district's population – and the most commercially minded, peddling their embroidered indigo-blue waistcoats, bags, hats and heavy, silver jewellery at all hours. In fact, young Hmong girls can often be seen walking hand in hand with Westerners they have befriended prior to making their sales pitch. By contrast, the Red Dao, another common group here, are generally shy about being photographed, despite their eye-catching dress.

Sa Pa's invigorating air is a real tonic after the dusty plains, but **cold nights** make warm clothes essential throughout the year: the sun sets early behind Fan Si Pan, and temperatures fall rapidly after dark. During the coldest months (Dec–Feb), night temperatures often drop below freezing and most winters bring some snow, so it's worth finding a hotel room with heating. Often a thick fog straight out of a Sherlock Holmes novel can creep over the whole town, lending a spooky feel to the market. You'll find the best **weather** from September to November and March to May, though even during these months cold, damp cloud can descend, blotting out the views for several days.

8

The market

Daily sunrise to sunset

What initially attracted visitors to Sa Pa was the **weekend market**, which is when it's at its busiest, though it's now a bustling place on weekdays too. These days it's housed in a concrete eyesore, a far cry from the original Saturday "love market" where the local ethnic minorities would come to court their sweethearts. Plenty of minority people still turn up to peddle ethnic-style bags and shirts to trekkers, though more authentic market fairs can be found on the other side of the Red River on Saturdays at **Can Cau** (see p.409) and on Sundays in **Bac Ha** (see p.408).

Sa Pa Ethnomuseum

2 Fansipan (behind tourist office) • ☎ 020 387 1975 • Daily 7.30–11.30am & 1.30–5pm • Free

This new museum features video presentations and wall displays informing visitors about Sa Pa's history and the lifestyles of the local hilltribes, so it's worth dropping in here when you first arrive to fill in the background. Other exhibits include a Hmong shaman's altar and the social architecture of ethnic minority groups.

TREKKING PRACTICALITIES

It's important to wear the right **clothing** when walking in these mountains: strong boots with ankle support are the best footwear, though you can get away with training shoes in the dry season. Choose thin, loose clothing – long trousers offer some protection from thorns and leeches; wear a hat and sunblock; take plenty of water; and carry a basic medical kit. If you plan on spending the night in a village you'll need warm clothing as temperatures can drop to around freezing, and you might want to take a **sleeping bag**, mosquito net and food, though these are usually provided on organized tours. Finally, **dogs** can be a problem when entering villages, so it's a good idea to carry a strong stick when trekking, and always be watchful for the venomous snakes that are common in this area.

8

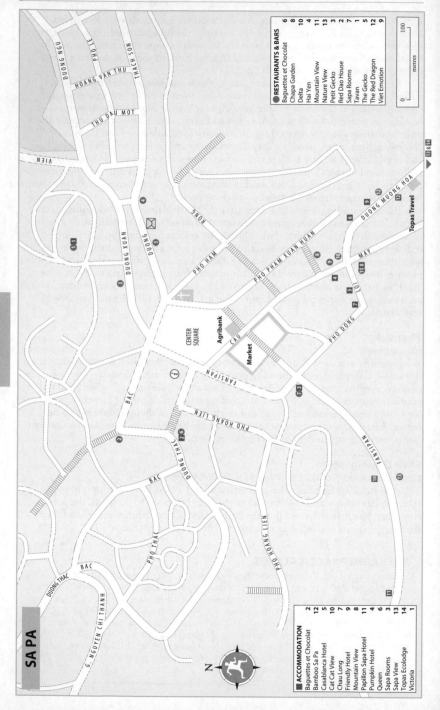

SA PA

■ ACCOMMODATION

Baguettes et Chocolat	2
Bamboo Sa Pa	12
Casablanca Hotel	5
Cat Cat View	10
Chau Long	7
Friendly Hotel	9
Mountain View	8
Papillon Sapa Hotel	11
Pumpkin Hotel	4
Queen	6
Sapa Rooms	3
Sapa View	13
Topas Ecolodge	14
Victoria	1

● RESTAURANTS & BARS

Baguettes et Chocolat	6
Chapa Garden	8
Delta	10
Hai Yen	4
Mountain View	11
Nature View	13
Petit Gecko	3
Red Dao House	2
Sapa Rooms	7
Tavan	1
The Gecko	5
The Red Dragon	12
Viet Emotion	9

0 ——— 100
metres

| ARRIVAL AND DEPARTURE | SA PA |

VIA LAO CAI

The best and easiest way to get to Sa Pa is from Hanoi via the border town of Lao Cai. Most people arriving from Hanoi will pitch up at Lao Cai **train station**, located on the east bank of the Red River, nearly 3km due south of the Chinese border. The journey takes about eight hours and there are five trains a day – one in the morning (6.10am) and four in the evening (between 8.30 and 10pm). The last train, at 9.55pm, includes a luxury carriage reserved for guests of the *Victoria Hotel* in Sa Pa. Many travellers prefer to leave Hanoi on a **night train** so that they arrive in Lao Cai in the early morning, but while the night train saves on both time and accommodation, a daylight journey gives great views along the Red River Valley. The day train arrives at 4.35pm, allowing plenty of time to get to Sa Pa before dark. Also note that there have been several **thefts** on the night train

between Hanoi and Lao Cai and reports of pickpocketing on Hanoi's station platform. It's possible to take a **motorbike** onto the train with you for around $10: if you can, get help from a Vietnamese speaker to fill in the necessary form. The **bus station** is 400m along Phan Dinh Phung, which runs directly opposite the train station, although few people arrive by bus from Hanoi despite the decent roads.

ON TO SA PA

A slew of tourist buses (50,000đ) meet the Hanoi train for the ninety minute journey to **Sa Pa Town**, dropping off on Cau May, Sa Pa's main street. Local buses (30.000đ) also run from here and the nearby bus station, though times are highly irregular. Xe om are always on the prowl, though this is not the best way to tackle the switchback climb, especially with luggage; avoid them at all costs.

GETTING AROUND

By bike or jeep Xe om can be arranged through your guesthouse; self-drive is available (from $7 per day) but you need to be an experienced biker to tackle the stony, mountain tracks; make sure you test the bike for faults before leaving town. It's also possible to hire your own jeep and driver (around $50–60 per day) via guesthouses, depending on availability, but if you want to tackle the whole northwestern circuit you'll find cheaper long-term prices in Hanoi.

INFORMATION

Tourist information There's a dedicated and helpful tourist information office (daily 7.30am–6.30pm; ☏0203 871 975, ⓦ sapa-tourism.com) at 2 Fansipan, facing across the square to the church, though their tour prices tend to be inflated. As such, Sa Pa's guesthouses remain the best source of advice on visiting minority villages.

ACCOMMODATION

Despite the glut of guesthouses and hotels in Sa Pa, **rooms** can still be in short supply in the summer months, pushing up prices by as much as fifty percent. Hotels bump up prices over weekends too, when the town is crawling with tourists, so it's worth considering a midweek visit. Most places offer some kind of **heating**, such as electric blankets, but it's best to check rather than shiver all night. Foreigners can also now stay in many of Sa Pa's surrounding **minority villages**, though you'll need to arrange this through guesthouses and travel agencies, as independent trekking and just turning up in a village is frowned upon.

Baguettes et Chocolat Thac Bac ☏020 387 1766, ⓦ hoasuaschool.com. Run by the Hoa Sua School for disadvantaged youth, this is a quiet and comfy place that looks over the town. It has only two twins and two doubles, but the delightful decor and friendly service make it popular. The price includes breakfast in the fantastic ground-floor café. $25

Bamboo Sa Pa 18 Muong Hoa ☏020 387 1075, ⓦ bamboosapahotel.com.vn. Some of the smartest rooms in town, though somehow rather soulless, with excellent views, bathtubs and fake fireplaces. Minority shows in the large restaurant on request. $75

ONWARD TRAVEL TO CHINA FROM LAO CAI

The border crossing from Lao Cai into China is popular with travellers heading to Kunming. The queues at the Hekou Bridge **border gate** (daily 7am–10pm), on the east bank of the Red River, are longest in the early morning, when local traders get their day pass over to Hekou. There are no Chinese trains to Kunming, as the line has been out of service for many years due to flooding and landslides. However, it is possible to make your own way to Lao Cai (see above), cross the border on foot, then carry on in China by bus (taking twelve hours for the 520km journey to Kunming); you'll need to have arranged your Chinese visa beforehand.

8

8

Casablanca Hotel 26 Dong Loi ☎020 387 2667,⊛ sapacasablanca.com. One of Sa Pa's earliest boutique hotels, this place is certainly quirky and all rooms have character, but it's getting a bit grubby and uncared for, despite the friendly, on-the-ball owner. **$25**

★ **Cat Cat View** 46 Fansipan ☎020 387 1946, ⊛ catcathotel.com. One of the town's longest-standing mini-hotels, *Cat Cat* has a building on each side of the road and a huge variety of rooms, some with private terraces and fantastic panoramic views across to Mount Fan Si Pan. Popular with budget travellers who socialize on the communal balconies. **$30**

Chau Long 24 Dong Loi ☎020 387 1245, ⊛ chaulonghotel.com.vn. Small but smart rooms, all with bathtubs, in this attractive building. Other appealing features are a waiting room for early check-in, a kids' room and swimming pool. Opposite, the pricier four-star wing has excellent facilities and better views. **$45**

Friendly Hotel 11 Muong Hoa ☎020 387 3689. This reliable budget choice has amiable service, fantastic views from some upper-floor rooms, and bedding that puts many of the big boys to shame. Breakfast, however, is poor value for money – head elsewhere. **$15**

Mountain View 54A Cau May ☎020 387 1334, ⊛ sapamountainview.com. A popular choice, with bright, clean, comfy rooms and good vistas. Its outdoor restaurant (see opposite) is a great place to watch the sun go down. Slightly cheaper and shabbier is the *Royal*, their sister hotel across the road. **$15**

Papillon Sapa Hotel 58 Fansipan ☎020 387 2180, ⊛ papillonsapahotel.com.vn. Formerly the *Sa Pa Goldsea*, this hotel has benefited from a thorough renovation; its comfortable, carpeted rooms are equipped with traditional furnishings and all the latest mod-cons such as wi-fi. Ask to see the room first as the view from some is blocked by stands of bamboo. Despite its location just a short walk down the road towards Cat Cat village, there's a pleasant sense of remoteness at this hotel. **$35**

Pumpkin Hotel 42 Cau May ☎020 387 2350, ✉ pumpkin sapa@gmail.com. The owners at this cheapie have aimed

for a fresh look with their peach-and-lemon paint scheme, and views are good from the communal balconies; just watch out for the trinket-selling Hmong girls that often take up residence on the front steps. **$18**

Queen 9 Muong Hoa ☎020 387 1301, ⊛ sapaqueen hotel.com. It's getting on in years, but this budget choice in the centre is well kept and friendly and has some of the cheapest rooms in town. The pricier ones have decent views, but the street below can be noisy. **$10**

Sapa Rooms 18 Fansipan ☎020 650 5228, ⊛ saparooms.com. There are just half a dozen rooms at this welcoming place, though word has got around so they're often booked out weeks ahead. All rooms are a decent size, with traditional furnishings and stylish bathrooms. If you really want to get away from it all, book into their *Hmong Mountain Retreat*, 6km out of town, where the bamboo and thatch bungalows look out over a dream vista of terraced paddies. **$55**

Sapa View 41 Muong Hoa ☎020 387 2388, ⊛ sapaview-hotel.com. This is one of Sa Pa's newest hotels, located to the south of town; most rooms enjoy great views across the valley and the area is fairly quiet. Smallish rooms come with pine furnishings and heaters, and staff are always eager to please. **$70**

Topas Eco–lodge ☎020 387 1331, ⊛ topas-eco-lodge .com. Situated a 45min drive from Sa Pa, the *Topas Eco-lodge* is made up of luxurious yet rustic alpine lodge-style cottages, set on a clifftop with spectacular views looking down over a glorious valley and the ethnic minority village of Ban Ho. The older buildings are eco-friendly, meaning no a/c, TV or wi-fi in rooms, while the refurbished rooms are less so, featuring a/c and even hairdryers. Their office in Sa Pa at 24 Muong Hoa (☎020 387 1331) offers transport to the lodge and a number of tours. **$99**

Victoria Hoang Dieu ☎020 387 1522, ⊛ victoriahotels -asia.com. The *Victoria's* 77 rooms bring a touch of luxury to Sa Pa and find a regular clientele among expat residents of Hanoi looking for an accessible weekend break. Tennis courts, sauna and jacuzzi on site, as well as an excellent restaurant and a spa with heated pool on a hilltop. **$195**

EATING AND DRINKING

Sa Pa has the widest range of **food** in the north outside Hanoi; one benefit of the building boom is that there is plenty of choice, many serving a mixture of local cuisine and foreign dishes. To go where the locals are, try the street **stalls** along Pham Xuan Huan, parallel to Cau May, that serve pho and rice; some stay open late into the night, when the focus shifts to barbecued meat and rice wine. Though there's not much by way of **nightlife**, the *Red Dragon* serves beer and cocktails, or you can shoot some pool at the *Three Sisters Bar* on Muong Hoa opposite the *Bamboo Sa Pa Hotel*.

★ **Baguettes et Chocolat** Thac Bac. Part of a chain that trains disadvantaged children in hospitality, this place offers excellent pastries and, as the name suggests, filling baguettes and chocolate sweets, in a comfortable colonial setting. It also sells custom-made hampers to take on your trekking journey. Mains $3–6. Daily 7.30am–9.30pm.

Chapa Garden 23b Cau May. This secluded restaurant with delectable cuisine (mains $6.50–12), fine wine and a crackling fireplace has something of an Alpine atmosphere. The friendly staff are all Black Hmong, and there's always a local choice among the Western items on the short menu. Daily 7am–10pm.

Delta 33 Cau May. With a prime location and a good wine list, the *Delta* is better known for its pizzas than its pasta ($6–14), and the soft lighting creates an intimate atmosphere. Daily 7am–10pm.

The Gecko Ham Rong. Well-designed, French-run venue serving dishes like clay pot with caramelized fish, which makes a welcome relief from Sa Pa's usual Viet-Western fare. Opposite, its sister restaurant, the tiny *Petit Gecko*, is slightly cheaper and styled like a Black Hmong house, but serves similar fare for around $3–6. Daily 7.30am–10pm.

Hai Yen 14 Pho Thach Son. When the fog comes down and the chill sets in, it's time to head for a steaming hotpot and there's nowhere better to order it than *Hai Yen*. Pick out a good-looking fish from the tank, then sit surrounded by a cloud of aromatic steam and slurp on a nutritious soup ($1–5). Daily 8am–midnight.

Mountain View 54a Cau May. One of the most scenic spots in Sa Pa, the outdoor area is the perfect place to sample traditional north Vietnamese fare (mains $2–5) and look out over the valley. The huge Lao Cai beers they sell also make it a jovial choice for when the sun has set. Daily 7am–10pm.

Nature View 51 Fansipan. You could pay for the views alone and still feel that you'd got value for money; throw in a selection of reasonably priced Vietnamese and Western dishes and it's a really good deal. Mains $2–5. Daily 7.30am–10.30pm.

Red Dao House 4b Thac Bac. Too twee for some but there's a certain kitsch appeal to this large and slightly pricey restaurant; the menu has a good range of Vietnamese and Western dishes, including pastas and pizzas (mains $5–11) staff are all Red Dao. Daily 8am–10pm.

The Red Dragon 23 Muong Hoa. A slice of England in Sa Pa. Run by English expat John and his wife, the effort that goes into the food (think home-made sausages and shepherds' pie) make this a great option. They also have a good range of beers in the bar upstairs, where travellers swap stories till the midnight closing time. Mains $3–7. Daily 8am–midnight.

★ **Sapa Rooms** 18 Fansipan. You could spend the whole day here, grazing on home-made muffins and carrot juice for breakfast, delicious fries for lunch and fish fried with coriander and chilli for dinner. Prices are very reasonable ($2–5), and many customers return again and again. They also run cookery classes at their out-of-town *Hmong Mountain Retreat*. Daily 7am–10pm.

Tavan Victoria Hotel, Hoang Dieu ☎020 387 1522, ⓦ victoriahotels-asia.com. The service and quality is what you'd expect from a hotel like the *Victoria*. Specializing in French cuisine with locally grown produce, the meals are sumptuous but with a price to match. Also offers an excellent breakfast buffet that is perfect fuel for early morning treks. Mains $10–28. Daily 6.30am–10pm.

★ **Viet Emotion** 27 Cau May. Spanish tapas, tempting main courses and a healthy range of cocktails are on the menu at this two-floor gem; try the salmon with sticky rice ($11) or the pork grilled with cardamom, or start the day with a filling set breakfast. Daily 7am–10pm.

DIRECTORY

Banks and money There are several ATMs dotted around Sa Pa, and the Agribank (Mon–Fri 7.30–11am & 1.30–5pm) on Cau May can exchange cash and travellers' cheques.

Internet Most guesthouses and hotels provide free wi-fi or cable internet.

Post office Ham Rong (Mon–Fri 8–11.30am & 1–4pm). Service is poor and mail delivery times are exceptionally long. Hanoi is a better option.

Villages around Sa Pa

There are several Hmong villages within easy walking distance of town, though if you are heading to places like **Sin Chai**, **Tai Giang Phin** or **Bang Khoang**, it's necessary to go accompanied by a local guide. Alternatively, you can take a xe om from Sa Pa for the round-trip, but negotiate an acceptable price first.

Cat Cat

Since it's just 3km from Sa Pa, most people walk independently to the Black Hmong village of **CAT CAT** – follow the track west from the market square, and continue past the steeple-shaped forestry department building. The village hides among fruit trees and bamboo, where chickens and pot-bellied pigs scavenge through trailing pumpkin vines, though the sheer number of visitors makes the experience feel less authentic than it really is. Look out for tubs of indigo dye, used to colour the hemp cloth typical of Hmong dress, and for interlocking bamboo pipes that supply the village with both water and power for de-husking rice. Cat Cat waterfall is just below the village, the site of an old hydroelectric station and now a pleasant place to rest before tackling the homeward journey.

Sin Chai

For a longer walk instead of cutting down to Cat Cat Village from Sa Pa, hire the services of a guide and continue on the main track turning right at the last bend before a river to follow a footpath up the valley towards Fan Si Pan. After 4km you'll reach **SIN CHAI** Village, a large Hmong settlement (nearly a hundred houses) spread out along the path. Some trekking tours include an overnight stop here in a tribal house, and you will also have the chance to watch weavers at work and listen to performances of traditional music.

Ta Van and Lao Chai

You have to venture further afield to reach villages of minorities other than Hmong. One of the most enjoyable treks is to follow the main track 9km down the Muong Hoa Valley to a wooden suspension bridge and **TA VAN** Village, on the opposite side of the river. Ta Van actually consists of two villages: immediately across the bridge is a Giay community, while further uphill to the left is a Dao village. It's possible to get there and back in a day, but if you'd like to stay in a village **overnight**, arrange it through a Sa Pa tour operator.

From Ta Van, it's possible to walk back towards Sa Pa on the west side of the river, as far as another Hmong village, **LAO CHAI**, before rejoining the main track. The complete trek covers about 25km, but if you don't want to walk all the way back up to Sa Pa, you can pick up a **motorbike taxi** at one of the huts you'll find every two to three kilometres along the track.

Giang Ta Chai

Following the main road another 3km south from the turn-off to Ta Van, a track leads to the Dao settlement of **GIANG TA CHAI**. The path branches off to the right, just after a stream crosses the road and before a small shop. After crossing a suspension bridge, take the left fork, directly across a stream, after which it's a kilometre to the village. Giang Ta Chai can also be reached by footpath from Ta Van, but you'll need a guide.

Ban Ho

About 6km south of Giang Ta Chai, the trail passes through Su Pan, an unprepossessing collection of huts home to a number of different minorities (mostly Red Dao). From here, heading 4km straight down into the valley, bear right at each fork and you'll arrive at the Tay village of **BAN HO**, which straddles the river at a suspension bridge; the settlement comes into view at the bottom of the valley soon after you leave Su Pan. Ban Ho is the staging point for two-, three- and four-day treks in the next valley, best tackled in the company of a guide. Organize this through a tour operator in Sa Pa.

TO THE TOP OF VIETNAM – MOUNT FAN SI PAN

Vietnam's highest mountain, **Fan Si Pan** (3143m) lies less than 5km as the crow flies from Sa Pa, but it's an arduous three- to five-day round trip on foot. The usual route starts by descending 300m to cross the Muong Hoa River, and then climbs almost 2000m on overgrown paths through pine forest and bamboo thickets, before emerging on the southern ridge. The reward is a panorama encompassing the mountain ranges of northwest Vietnam, south to Son La Province and north to the peaks of Yunnan in China. Although it's a hard climb, the most difficult aspect of Fan Si Pan is its climate: even in the most favourable months of November and December it's difficult to predict a stretch of settled clear weather and many people are forced back by cloud, rain and cold.

A **guide** is essential to trace indistinct paths, hack through bamboo and locate water sources if climbing Mount Fan Si Pan; Hmong guides are said to know the mountain best. Sa Pa hotels and tour agents (see p.403) can arrange guides and porters as required.

Ta Phin
Xe om from Sa Pa around 80,000đ each way

An excursion to **TA PHIN** Village takes you northeast of Sa Pa, along the main Lao Chai road for 6km and then left on a dirt track for the same distance again, past the blackened shell of an old French seminary. Finally, a scenic footpath across the paddy leads to a community of Red Dao scattered among a group of low hills. The village is known for its handicrafts, though it's now rather commercial and the locals can sometimes be quite aggressive when it comes to selling their beer.

The easiest way to find Ta Phin is to take a xe om from Sa Pa and get dropped off at the start of the footpath; as the leg between Sa Pa and the start of this path isn't so attractive, you might want to do the same on the return journey.

Bang Khoang and Ta Giang Phinh
New villages are being explored all the time as more tourists arrive seeking out ever more remote spots. **BANG KHOANG** is a Dao settlement with over a hundred families located 16km north of Sa Pa; look for a right turn after about 10km along the Lao Chai road and follow the road to the village. From here, the road continues to the Hmong settlement **TA GIANG PHINH**, home to 150 families. Both of these villages require a guide and are best explored by jeep or motorbike in a day-trip from Sa Pa.

GETTING AROUND   **SA PA'S VILLAGES**

On a trek All hotels and tour agents in Sa Pa can organize treks to all the villages above, with prices starting at around $20 per day: for around an extra $10 a day, you can include home-stay accommodation in a village. Trips offered by Topas Travel at 24 Muong Hoa (☎020 387 1331, ⓦtopas -adventure-vietnam.com) and Handspan Adventure Travel in Hanoi (☎04 3926 2828, ⓦhandspan.com) are safe and popular, though fierce competition means that you'll find far lower prices if you shop around.

With a guide When booking a guide locally, make sure you get one from Sa Pa and not from Hanoi, as only a local will speak the dialects necessary to communicate within the villages.

Practicalities There's an admission fee of 20,000đ for each village if you are not with a tour group, payable at a booth at the entrance to each village. Always wear strong shoes, carry water, waterproofs and a basic medical kit. The tourist office sells a decent map of the town and surrounding area for $1, while most hotels provide guests with a simple sketch map of the town centre.

8

Bac Ha
The small town of **BAC HA**, nestling in a high valley 40km northeast of Highway 7, makes a popular day-excursion from Sa Pa. There's little to see in the town itself except on Sunday, when villagers of the Tay, Dao, Nung, Giay and above all Flower Hmong ethnic minorities trek in for the lively **market**. At 1200m above sea level compared to Sa Pa's 1600m, Bac Ha is less spectacularly beautiful, although it's still scenic, with cone-shaped mountains bobbing up out of the mist, and it's also much less touristy, giving out a workaday sense of a bustling agricultural community rather than an alpine resort.

Bac Ha provides a stark contrast to Sa Pa, with little in the way of tourist facilities beyond a few guesthouses. As Sa Pa becomes saturated with tourists seeking out a more authentic experience, so Bac Ha has attempted to emulate Sa Pa's success by developing its own trekking business focused around the nearby rural markets. For the moment, however, it lacks sufficient infrastructure – which, in many ways, is the key to its charm.

If you're travelling independently it's worth spending a whole weekend in Bac Ha, in order to take in the rustic and colourful market at **Can Cau** on Saturday. Bac Ha also makes a good base for trips out to the surrounding Flower Hmong villages of **Ban Pho** and **Coc Ly**.

The Sunday market

Sundays 8am–5pm

The Sunday **market**, the town's one big attraction, gradually fills up from 8 to 10am, and from then till lunchtime it's a jostling mass of colour, mostly provided by the stunningly dressed Flower Hmong women looking for additional adornments to their costume. The scene is filled out with a sizeable livestock market, meat and vegetable sellers, wine sellers and vendors of farming implements. The town returns to a dusty shadow of its former self by 5pm when the ethnic tribes return to their outlying villages.

Hoang A Tuong Palace

Daily 7.30–11.30am & 1.30–5pm

At the northern end of town, on the left along the main road, you'll find the remarkable folly of Hoang A Tuong, formerly known as **Vua Meo**, or Cat King House. Two storeys of pure wedding cake surround a courtyard built in 1924 by the French as a palace for a Hmong leader, Vuong Chiz Sinh, whom they had installed as the local "king" (Meo, or "Cat" in Vietnamese, is a disparaging term formerly applied by Vietnamese and French to the Hmong). The building is now a tourist information office, with a few displays of local ethnic dress and a shop selling hilltribe gear.

ARRIVAL AND DEPARTURE   BAC HA

From Hanoi Coming from Hanoi, get off the bus or train at Pho Lu, from where there are several buses a day to Bac Ha from the bus station (90min; 40,000đ), which lies on the highway just across from the railway station.

From Lao Cai There are four daily buses to Bac Ha from Lao Cai (2hr; 60,000đ), though times are irregular. If you miss the last bus, which theoretically leaves at 3pm, hop on a bus to Pho Lu and change there.

From Sa Pa If you're coming from Sa Pa on a Sunday, your best bet is to take a tour from one of Sa Pa's guesthouses for around $20, which includes spending the morning at the market, a trek in the afternoon and a ride back to Sa Pa, with the option of being dropped off at Lao Cai station. Alternatively, rent a motorbike from your guesthouse in Sa Pa to make the spectacular three-hour journey through the mountains, or take a local bus to Lao Cai and another on to Bac Ha.

INFORMATION

There's no **tourist information** office in town, but you can find helpful tips about the area at ⦿ bachatourist.com.

ACCOMMODATION

The **range of accommodation** available in Bac Ha is limited, with few people spending more than one night in town: all the places listed below are within a minute's walk of the main four-way junction in the town centre.

Cong Fu ⦿ 020 388 0254, ⦿ congfuhotel.com. On the road heading to Can Cau, the *Cong Fu* has bright rooms, with big windows, some of which directly overlook the market. They are equipped with spartan furnishings and clean tiled floors, plus smart bathrooms, some with bathtubs as well as showers. They also arrange local tours to places like Can Cau and Coc Ly markets. $15

Ngan Nga ⦿ 020 388 0231. Tucked back from the main street near the corner, this place is worth hunting down for its good-sized, good-value rooms, and also for its restaurant, which turns out the best food in town (see below). $20

Sao Mai ⦿ 020 388 0288, ⦿ saomai@hn.vnn.vn. One of the more popular places, the *Sao Mai*, just west of the junction, has big, comfortable rooms with satellite TV and a restaurant, and offers many tours of the local area. $30

EATING

Bac Ha's **restaurants** are bursting with tourists on Sundays and practically deserted at all other times, but don't expect the same quality that you'd find in Sa Pa. Most restaurants in town open at around 7am and close at around 8pm. You'll find that you can eat for between $2 and $5.

Cong Fu There are two restaurants in town called *Cong Fu*, one in the *Cong Fu* hotel and another on the market road: both serve excellent food, though the latter is cheaper.

Ngan Nga The tour buses tend to head for the *Ngan Nga*, on the north side of the main drag, thanks to its cheap, no-nonsense menu that features an astounding range of dishes. These include seasonal specialities such as local mushrooms prepared in a tasty sauce, as well as unusual meat dishes like venison.

DIRECTORY

Bank Bac Ha has a couple of ATMs on the main street.
Internet Internet access is available at all hotels including
the *Cong Fu* (see opposite).

Villages around Bac Ha

The game of one-upmanship among travellers in North Vietnam is all about which of the dwindling **ethnic minorities** you have spotted that others haven't. In the vicinity of Bac Ha, there's a great opportunity to go a few points ahead on this score. Tours to these villages can be organized through local hotels or the tourist information centre in Sa Pa (see p.403).

Ban Pho

It's only a 3km stroll from Bac Ha to the picturesque Flower Hmong hamlet of **BAN PHO**. To get there head west out of town past the *Sao Mai Hotel*, turning left at the first major road, which continues up the hill for a couple of kilometres after the village, and affords good views of the valley. Around halfway along this vaguely clockwise loop, you can climb down on some rather dodgy trails to the idyllic Nung village of **NA THA**, from where there is a clearer path directly back to Bac Ha.

Can Cau

Follow the main road north out of Bac Ha for 18km • Tours $15 per person in a group of four • A xe om will charge around $10 for the round-trip

The village of **CAN CAU**, 18km north of Bac Ha, hosts a market each Saturday, which is every bit as colourful as that in Bac Ha, albeit smaller, and is located in a fairy-tale setting among rolling hills. It consists of a disparate mix of livestock on sale – including horses, ponies, buffalo and cattle – with traders trekking in from as far afield as China in search of bargains, plus many vendors selling bright panels of cloth, which attract the Flower Hmong women, already resplendent in their bright outfits. As with Bac Ha, the busy hours are around 10am to lunchtime, and there are some beautiful items of clothing on sale that make great souvenirs. Relatively few visitors get there so the market retains much of its authenticity, a situation that is likely to change now that there is a reasonably good road. Other than the market there's nothing at all to see in Can Cau, but the ride, across a high, empty range with panoramic views on either side, is glorious.

Coc Ly

Another spot rarely visited by foreigners is the Tuesday flower market at **COC LY**, where Tay, Flower Hmong and Dao women stand side by side selling carefully selected flowers

8

TO HA GIANG FROM BAC HA

From Bac Ha, it's possible to go directly to **Ha Giang** (see p.421) and continue exploring the little-known northeast, though for this you will need your own transport. Head back down out of the hills towards Lao Cai, but after crossing the bridge over the Chay River, turn left on Highway 70 and follow it about 40km to Pho Rang. This is a good place for a break as there are reasonable food stalls just beyond the bridge on the left and a lively market off to the right a little further down the main street. Turn left just before the bridge and follow Highway 279 to Viet Quang, then left again on Highway 2, which takes you into Ha Giang. The trip takes about six hours, depending on road conditions. Another option, though only possible in good weather and with good wheels, is to head directly east to **Viet Quang** via Xin Man and Huong Su Phi: the road is awful (though it is being upgraded) but the views are nothing short of spectacular.

to neighbouring minority groups. A visit here is usually combined with a boatride downriver to Nam Mon, a Tay village where it's possible to overnight in a home-stay.

Only **Ban Pho** is within hiking distance of Bac Ha; for the others you'll need to join a tour or hire a xe om to take you around (about $10 for half a day). The *Sao Mai* and *Cong Fu* hotels organize trips to all the villages, as well as to the Tuesday flower market at **Coc Ly**. The latter trip includes transport by jeep and a boat trip down the Blue River Valley and costs $30 per person. There are also possibilities of two- and three-day **trips** costing $15–20 per person per day, which include **overnight home-stays**.

The Hoang Lien Son range

West of Sa Pa the road climbs up the **Hoang Lien Son range** to the 2100m-high **Tram Ton Pass** ("Heaven's Gate"), which marks the boundary with Lai Chau province, and once over the top the views are incredibly scenic. The road hugs the wall of an immense valley into the most sparsely populated region of Vietnam's far north: look out for tumbling waterfalls in the upper reaches, while on lower ground there's a colourful mosaic of **ethnic groups**. The most interesting of these are the Lu, whose members are scattered across Lai Chau Province, Laos, Northern Thailand and the Chinese province of Yunnan. It's possible to stay at a Lu village, where the Lu women often wear distinctive triangular hair clasps, and Lu society runs on extremely traditional lines, so if you do visit, stick to your most unobtrusive behaviour.

Local buses and tours Infrequent local buses connect all towns from Sa Pa to Dien Bien Phu, but it's only hardy adventurers who take them. Most visitors hire a car and driver or join a motorbike tour to travel this stretch of terrain.

INFORMATION

Permits You'll need a permit to stay at a Lu village: this can be organized by travel agencies in Sa Pa (see p.403), or at the security bureau in Lai Chau (look for a lemon-coloured building in the centre of town).

Lai Chau

About two hours' drive from Sa Pa, the new town of **LAI CHAU** – formerly Tam Duong, not to be confused with the former Lai Chau now called Muong Lay (see box opposite) – is getting uglier by the minute despite being surrounded by immaculate mountain scenery. Huge boulevards without any traffic and characterless office blocks are beginning to give the provincial capital an air of importance, though it is of little interest to travellers except for its lively market in the old town, where various ethnic groups turn up to trade each morning.

Muong Thanh 023 379 0888. One of the few good deals in Lai Chau, the *Muong Thanh* is situated between the old and new towns, but is quite self-contained, with an ATM machine, a good restaurant and even tennis courts. Rooms are big, bright and well-equipped, making them good value. It's surrounded by tea fields and affords fantastic views from the upper floors. $30

Nam Na Valley

From Lai Chau the route veers north to Pa So (formerly Phong Tho), after which it swings south, following the gently attractive **Nam Na Valley**: the higher slopes are farmed by groups of Black Hmong and Dao, though the valley floor is predominantly peopled with Thai villages of impressively solid stilthouses. Some of the White Thai communities in this region are surprisingly modern and orderly, as they are recent creations housing those whose original villages were affected by damming.

| ACCOMMODATION | NAM NA VALLEY |

Lan Anh II 023 1389 6337, lananhhotel.com. Easily the best accommodation option around Pa So is the impressive *Lan Anh II* situated 3km east of the village on the riverbank. It has comfortable rooms with quirky, mismatched furniture and a good restaurant. $20

Muong Lay

Road and river track a wooded gorge before emerging at the confluence with the Da River near the town of **MUONG LAY**, some 200km (5–6hr) from Sa Pa. The landscape to the north and south of town is some of the most rugged in the northwest, and thus prone to occasional landslides that can delay progress for long periods.

Some years ago Muong Lay lost its status as provincial capital to Dien Bien Phu, and then in 2011 it disappeared altogether beneath the rising waters of the Da River Reservoir. The town's buildings were either demolished or taken apart to be rebuilt at a higher level, with a massive new bridge spanning the reservoir. Before its demise, the town was a staging point for travellers on their way to Sa Pa, and no doubt it will re-assume that role after re-construction, particularly of the *Lan Anh Hotel*, a long-term favourite that can provide information about exploring the area.

| ARRIVAL AND DEPARTURE | MUONG LAY |

The road from Pa So follows the east bank of the Da River until it reaches Muong Lay, which is mostly on the west bank, across the new bridge. Local buses tackle the route between Sa Pa (6hr) and Den Bien Phu (4hr) during daylight hours, but only the most hardened visitors will appreciate the experience. It is more likely that you will arrive here as part of a tour.

ACCOMMODATION

Lan Anh 9 Song Da 023 385 2370, lananhhotel .com. Muong Lay's only hotel was in the process of re-locating up the hill at the time of this update but will probably continue to be a traveller's favourite, providing comfortable rooms at reasonable rates as well as free use of bicycles, useful information about exploring the local area and tasty dishes in its restaurant. Check their website for details. No doubt boat rides on the reservoir will be possible as well as trekking to local villages. $20

EATING

Lan Anh 9 Song Da 023 385 2370, lananhhotel .com. For food, the best place in town – in fact, one of the best places in the northwest, outside of Sa Pa – is the restaurant at the *Lan Anh* hotel, which serves excellent northern cuisine such as *bun cha* at reasonable prices. Daily 7am–9pm.

Dien Bien Phu

South of Muong Lay the road splits: Highway 6 takes off southeast to Tuan Giao and is the shortest route to Son La; Highway 12 ploughs on south for more than 100km

---

WHAT'S IN A NAME?

Only in Vietnam can things become so confusing. A few years ago, the government decided to change the names of certain towns in the northwest region, which is not that uncommon. However, when places began adopting the old names of nearby towns that already had changed their names, travelling became much harder than it needed to be. While some signs have been slow to change, we use the **new names**.

In Lai Chau Province, Binh Lu has changed to Tam Doung, and Tam Doung to Lai Chau. In Dien Bien Province, Lai Chau Town has changed to Muong Lay Town, and Moung Lay to Muong Tra.

8

(about 3–4hr), making slow progress at first but then zipping through the second 50km, to the heart-shaped valley of **DIEN BIEN PHU**, scene of General Giap's triumph in a battle that signalled the end of French Indochina (see box below). Though the town's trickle of tourists tend to be French history buffs, it's starting to become more popular as a base for trips to local minority villages: the valley's population is predominantly

THE BATTLE OF DIEN BIEN PHU

In November 1953 General Navarre, Commander-in-Chief in Indochina, ordered the French Expeditionary Force's parachute battalions to establish a base in Dien Bien Phu. Taunted by Viet Minh incursions into Laos, with which France had a mutual defence treaty, Navarre asserted that this would block enemy lines through the mountains, force the Viet Minh into open battle and end the war in Indochina within eighteen months – which it did, but not quite as Navarre intended. His deputy in Dien Bien Phu was **Colonel de Castries**, an aristocratic cavalry officer and dashing hero of World War II, supposedly irresistible to women, although Graham Greene, visiting the base in January 1954, described him as having the "nervy histrionic features of an old-time actor".

Using bulldozers dropped in beneath seven parachutes apiece, the French cleared two airstrips and then set up nine heavily fortified positions on low hills in the valley floor, reputedly named after de Castries' mistresses – Gabrielle, Eliane, Béatrice and so on. Less than a quarter of the garrison in Dien Bien Phu were mainland French: the rest were either from France's African colonies or the Foreign Legion (a mix of European nationalities), plus local Vietnamese troops including three battalions drawn from the Thai minority. There were also nineteen women in the thick of things (a stranded French nurse, plus eighteen Vietnamese and Algerian women from the Expeditionary Force's mobile brothel).

Meanwhile, **General Giap**, Commander of the People's Army, quietly moved his own forces into the steep hills around the valley, mobilizing an estimated three hundred thousand porters, road gangs and auxiliary soldiers in support of up to fifty thousand battle troops. Not only did they carry in all food and equipment, often on foot or bicycle over vast distances, but they then hauled even the heaviest guns up the slopes, hacking paths through the dense steamy forest as they went. Ho Chi Minh described the scene to journalist Wilfred Burchett by turning his helmet upside down: "Down here is the valley of Dien Bien Phu. There are the French. They can't get out. It may take a long time, but they can't get out." In early 1954 Giap was ready to edge his troops even closer, using a network of tunnels dug under cover of darkness. By this time the international stakes had been raised: the war in Indochina would be discussed at the Geneva Conference in May, so now both sides needed a major victory to take to the negotiating table.

French commanders continued to believe their position was impregnable until the first shells rained down on March 10. Within five days Béatrice and Gabrielle had fallen, both airstrips were out of action and the siege had begun in earnest; the French artillery commander, declaring himself "completely dishonoured", lay down and took the pin out of a grenade. All French supplies and reinforcements now had to be parachuted in, frequently dropping behind enemy lines, and when de Castries was promoted to general even his stars were delivered by parachute; at the end of the battle, 83,000 parachutes were strewn across the valley floor. The **final assault** began on May 1, by which time the rains had arrived, hindering air support, filling the trenches and spreading disease. Waves of Viet Minh fought for every inch of ground, until their flag flew above de Castries' command bunker on the afternoon of May 7. The following morning, the day talks started in Geneva, the last position **surrendered** and the valley at last fell silent after 59 days. A ceasefire was signed in Geneva on July 21, and ten months later the last French troops left Indochina.

The Vietnamese paid a high price for their victory, with an estimated twenty thousand dead and many thousands more wounded. On the French side, out of a total force of 16,500, some ten thousand were captured and marched hundreds of kilometres to camps in Vietnam's northeastern mountains; less than half survived the rigours of the journey, diseases and horrendous prison conditions.

More than fifty years on, the Battle of Dien Bien Phu remains one of the most significant military conflicts of the twentieth century, with its importance in Vietnam's struggle for independence commemorated in nearly every town by a street named in honour of that famous victory.

Thai (53 percent), while the Viet are concentrated in the urban area. With the recent opening of the border to foreigners, it's also being used as an alternative gateway to Laos.

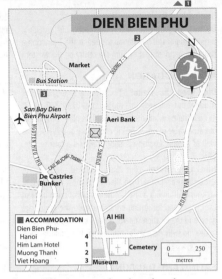

The town museum

Daily 7.30–11am & 1.30–5pm • 5000₫

On the right-hand side as you head south out of town, the **museum** is set back slightly from the road. The displays of weaponry include American-made guns of World War II vintage captured from French troops. Alongside them languish Viet Minh guns, also American-made but newer: these were booty from the Korean War which came via China into Vietnam, to be dragged up the battlefield's encircling hills. Familiar photos of the war-torn valley become more interesting in context, as does the scale model where a video describes the unfolding catastrophe – the message is perfectly clear, even in Vietnamese. To the left of the main museum is a small room displaying outfits of the ethnic minorities that live in the region.

Viet Minh Cemetery

Sunrise to sunset

Directly opposite the museum, some of the fallen heroes are buried under grey marble headstones marked only with a red and gold star. In 1993 an imposing imperial gateway and white-marble wall of names was added in time for the fortieth anniversary of the battle. The outside of this wall features bas-reliefs in concrete of battle scenes.

Hill A1

Daily 7.30–11am &1.30–5pm • 5000₫

A small hill overlooking the cemetery, known as **Hill A1** to the Vietnamese and as Eliane 2 to French defenders, was the scene of particularly bitter fighting before it was eventually overrun towards the end of the battle. You can inspect a reconstructed bunker on the summit and various memorials, including the grave of a Viet Minh hero who gave his life while disabling the French tank standing next to him, and you also get a panorama over the now peaceful, agricultural valley.

De Castries' bunker

Daily 7.30–11am & 1.30–5pm • 5000₫ • It's best to get to the bunker by bike (that can be rented from most guesthouses for 20,000₫ a day), crossing the river on the fantastically rickety Muong Thanh bridge before turning left

There's little to see at the last battle site, a reconstruction of **de Castries' bunker**, located on a dusty country road across the river a couple of kilometres from central Dien Bien Phu; Captured tanks, anti-aircraft guns and other weaponry rust away in the surrounding fields. Carry on past the bunker and you'll come to a concrete enclosure with a memorial to "Those who died here for France".

ARRIVAL AND DEPARTURE   **DIEN BIEN PHU**

By plane Daily flights from Hanoi arrive at the airfield, 1.5km north out of town, with the Vietnam Airlines office next door: it's a ten-minute walk into town from here, though a xe om only costs 10,000₫.

Destinations: Hanoi (2 daily; 1hr).
By bus The journey by bus is interesting but gruelling, terminating at the bus station located at the T-junction a couple of hundred metres from the centre on the western edge of town. This is also where you catch the numerous minibuses for Son La and beyond (first one leaves at 6am).
Destinations: Muong Lay (4hr); Son La (5hr); Sa Pa (10hr); Hanoi (12hr).

ACCOMMODATION

Dien Bien Phu–Hanoi 849, 7 Thang 5, south of the roundabout towards the museum ☎0230 382 5103, ⓔ dienbienphu-hnhotel@vnn.vn. This place has simple but acceptable rooms – the VIP choices are good value – as well as helpful, English-speaking staff and a tour service. **\$25**

Him Lam Hotel Him Lam ☎0230 381 1999, ⓦ himlamhotel.com. Dien Bien Phu's most extravagant accommodation lies a few kilometres out of town on Him Lam, in a peaceful setting on a riverbank. The rooms are good and the location superb, though staff are more used to dealing with Vietnamese tour groups than independent foreigners. **\$25**

Muong Thanh 514, 7 Thang 5, turn left at the town's main roundabout if coming from the bus station and continue for another 800m ☎0230 381 2556, ⓦ muongthanhdienbienhotel.com. This long-running favourite has been razed and rebuilt as the town's top lodgings, with 150 spacious and comfortable rooms, a decent restaurant and a small swimming pool. **\$60**

Viet Hoang 67 Tran Dang Ninh ☎0230 373 5046. This and the neighbouring *May Hong* (under same management) are the best of a poor bunch of mini-hotels near the bus station; rooms range from tiny to a reasonable size and some have balconies. Amenities are basic but there's wi-fi and cable TV. **\$7.50**

EATING AND DRINKING

Locals tend to patronize the **com pho stalls** around the roundabout and along the main roads – it's worth wandering around and choosing the one with the biggest crowd. Look out for the region's speciality dish, which is the Thai minority's black rice (*com gao cam*).

Muong Thanh Turn left at the town's main roundabout if coming from the bus station and continue for another 800m ☎0230 381 2556, ⓦ muongthanhdienbienhotel .com. This hotel's restaurant gets the nod simply for its English menu and English-speaking staff, which are difficult to find in this town. There's a reasonable choice of stir-fries and soups, priced from \$2 to \$5, though it's not exactly gourmet standard. Daily 6.30am–10pm.

DIRECTORY

Bank Head right from the busy roundabout and market if coming from the bus station to find an Agribank (Mon–Fri 7.30–11am & 1.30–5pm), which has an ATM and can change US dollars.

Post office Located next to the Agribank.

Highway 6

East of Dien Bien Phu Highway 279 climbs into steep mountains to the Pha Din ("Heaven and Earth") Pass, one of the highest in the north. If you're lucky there are great views from the top, but more often than not it's enveloped in clouds. The road then drops down to **TUAN GIAO**, where Highway 6 takes off north to Muong Lay or south to Son La. A while later, the road passes through the small town of **THUAN CHAU**, where there's a lively market of predominantly Black Thai people each morning until 9 or 10am. The last stretch passes through a valley bordered by massive karst pillars

---

ONWARD TRAVEL TO LAOS

Dien Bien Phu is only 35km by road from the **border with Laos at Tay Trang**. It's possible to get a visa at the border (prices dependent on nationality), though to be sure, this is best done in advance in Hanoi (see p.386). Buses to **Muang Khoa**, a further 70km over the border in Laos (103,000đ) leave Dien Bien Phu at 5.30am on Monday, Wednesday, Friday and Sunday; at other times you can get a xe om to the border (about 140,000đ), though it's a 3km checkpoint-to-checkpoint walk and you may find it hard to get onward transport.

before reaching a softer landscape of paddy and banana plantations, where water wheels feed sculpted terraces, to the industrious town of **SON LA**.

EATING	HIGHWAY 6

The village of **Tuan Giao** is a convenient lunch stop on a day of tough travel. The obvious place to eat is *Hoang Quat*, about 200m before the T-junction, where it comes as a surprise to see tablecloths and an English menu; the owner can also help travellers find accommodation if necessary.

Son La

Son La's welcoming, low-key charm is enhanced by its valley-edge setting, and it merits more than the usual overnight stop. If time allows, there's enough of interest to occupy a few days, taking in the old French prison and a nearby cave, as well as making forays to nearby **minority villages** on foot or by motorbike.

Certain minority villages stage events for tour groups, such as **traditional Thai dancing** or supping the local home brew, a sweet wine made of glutinous rice; it's drunk from a communal earthenware container using bamboo straws, and hence named *ruou can*, or stem alcohol. The major part of Son La lies off the highway, straggling for little more than a kilometre along the west bank of the Nam La River.

The French prison

Bao Tang Son La • Daily 7.30–11am & 1.30–5pm • 10,000đ

Son La's principal tourist sight is the **French prison**, which occupies a wooded promontory above To Hieu and offers good views over town. The two turn-offs from the highway are both marked with chunky stylized signs suggesting incarceration; walk uphill to find the prison gates and an arched entrance, still announcing "Pénitencier", leading into the main compound. This region was a hotbed of anti-French resistance, and a list of political prisoners interred here reads like a roll call of famous revolutionaries – among them Le Duan and Truong Chinh, veteran Party members who both went on to become general secretary. Local hero To Hieu was also imprisoned for seditionary crimes but he died from malaria while in captivity in 1944. Most of the buildings lie in ruins, destroyed by a French bombing raid in 1952, but a few have been reconstructed, including the two-storey kitchen block (*bep*), beneath which are seven punishment cells. Political prisoners were often incarcerated in brutal conditions: the two larger cells (then windowless) held up to five people shackled by the ankles. Behind the kitchens, don't miss the well-presented collection of prison memorabilia. Enter the second arched gate and upstairs in the building on your right you'll find an informative display about the dozen or so minorities who inhabit the area, including costumes, handicrafts, jewellery and photos.

ARRIVAL AND DEPARTURE

SON LA

By bus Son La's bus station is located 5km southwest of town, so it's necessary to take a xe om into the centre (about 20,000đ).

Destinations: Dien Bien Phu (4hr); Hanoi (7hr); Hoa Binh (5hr), via the Mai Chau junction (3hr).

INFORMATION

Tourist information The best place for information is the helpful *Trade Union Hotel* (see below), where you can also hire transport and English-speaking guides, or arrange to see Thai dancing and sample rice wine. There's just one main street, To Hieu, where you'll find all the important municipal buildings.

ACCOMMODATION

Hanoi Hotel ☎022 375 3288 ⓦhanoihotel299.com .vn. Son La's newest and most appealing hotel has spacious, comfortable doubles and affordable suites offering panoramic views of the countryside around. $30
Sunrise ☎022 385 8799, ⓔsunrisetwostarshotel @yahoo.com.vn. The *Sunrise* is a decent mini-hotel with bright, clean rooms that have wi-fi, and friendly staff who try their best to make their guests' stay a smooth one. $18

Trade Union Hotel ☎022 385 2804, ⓦsonlatradeunion.com.vn. Though this old stand-by is in need of a make-over, its rooms are passable and it's the best place in town to find local information. The restaurant is one of the few in town with an English menu. $25

EATING AND DRINKING

For **food**, the *Trade Union Hotel* has a passable restaurant, but is open to residents only (closes 10.30pm). If you are yet to try Thai speciality black rice (*com gao cam*) then look for it here in one of the com pho stalls near the big junction at the south end of town.

Hai Phi Highway 6. The *Hai Phi* is also a good option, especially if you like goat dishes, and is a popular venue for large gatherings of locals. If you're adventurous, order the *tiet canh*, which is a bowl of goat's blood curd garnished with peanuts. Mains $2–4. Daily 11am–9pm.

DIRECTORY

Banks There are several banks in town, including the Agribank at 8 Chu Van Thinh.
Motorbikes Bikes are available for rent for around $7 a day. Hotel staff can help to arrange this.
Post office On the main drag, To Hieu.

Que Lam Ngu Che Cave

Daily 7.30–11am & 1.30–5.30pm • Free

The cave most convenient to Son La is **Que Lam Ngu Che Cave**, which is situated just north of the town centre and has a small shrine inside surrounded by strange formations in the rock. A five hundred-year-old poem written by King Le Thai Tong carved into the stone remains visible today on the outside of the cave. You can go there alone – just look for the sign 150m as you head north out of town, or a guide from the *Trade Union Hotel* will take you for a small fee.

Ban Mong

An interesting destination for a day's trek or visit by motorbike is **BAN MONG**, a Black Thai village six scenic kilometres along a luxuriant valley south of Son La. The houses of this village are solid, wooden structures surrounded by gardens of fruit trees rather than vegetables. The women of the village usually wear their hair piled up high on their head and secured with a head-dress, on top of which they often wear a precariously-perched crash helmet. The dress of the Black Thai women is particularly striking – especially the brightly embroidered headscarves that they drape over their long hair piled up in huge buns. Their tight-fitting blouses with rows of silver buttons, often in the shape of butterflies, are also distinctive. In colder weather, many wear a green, sleeveless sweater over the blouse, or a modern jacket in pink, blue, green or maroon.

The hike out to Ban Mong is about six hours' walking in all, so you'll need a whole day. **Hire a guide** and take food and plenty of water, as there are **no shops** until you get to the village. It's also possible to take in Ban Mong as part of a longer trek that heads northwest out of Son La before wheeling south through the villages of several minorities; this is best arranged with the folks at the *Trade Union Hotel*.

On to Mai Chau

From Son La Highway 6 climbs east, passing **YEN CHAU** – a town famed for its fruit – and some very pretty Black Thai villages on the right after about 80km, particularly **LA KEN**, which can be visited by crossing swaying suspension bridges over the river. With your own transport, you could make a detour about 20km west over rolling hills to the **Chi Day Cave**, a popular pilgrimage site for Vietnamese; look for a right turn about 36km south of Son La. The main road from Son La climbs onto a thousand-metre-high plateau where the cool climate favours tea and coffee cultivation, mulberry to feed the voracious worms of Vietnam's silk industry and herds of dairy cattle, initially imported from Holland, to quench Hanoi's thirst for milk, yoghurt and ice cream. Just less than 120km out of Son La, the sprawling market town of **MOC CHAU** provides a convenient place for a break. For the next 4km heading towards Hanoi, the road is dotted with stalls selling local **milk products** such as three kinds of flavoured milk, thick home-made yoghurt and blocks of condensed milk (which they advertise as chocolate when cocoa is added), as well as green tea. The rigid lines of tea bushes that border the road round Moc Chau create curious patterns, and though there are few side roads, this is a region in which some might want to linger. Most, however, head on down Highway 6, through valleys where the Hmong live in distinctive houses built on the ground under long, low roofs, and surrounded by fruit orchards, to **MAI CHAU**, which lies up a side valley south of Highway 6.

Mai Chau

The **minority villages** of the Mai Chau Valley, inhabited mainly by White Thai, are close enough to Hanoi (135km) to make this a popular destination, particularly at weekends when it's often swamped with large groups of students. The valley itself, however, is still largely unspoilt, a peaceful scene of pancake-flat rice fields trimmed with jagged mountains.

MAI CHAU is the valley's main settlement – a friendly, quiet place that has a bustling morning **market** frequented by minority people who trek in to haggle over buffalo meat, star fruit, sacks of tea or groundnuts.

By bus Three buses a day leave from My Dinh bus station in Hanoi to Mai Chau (50,000đ) and take about three and a half hours to cover the journey.

On a tour Most people visit Mai Chau on an organized tour out of Hanoi, which usually includes overnighting in a minority village, or as part of a longer trip into the northwest mountains by jeep or motorbike. Tour groups tend to stay in the villages of Ban Lac and Pom Coong to the west of Mai Chau and go on organized walks around the valley.

ACCOMMODATION

Mai Chau Lodge On the main road just south of the town centre ☎0218 386 8959, ⊛maichaulodge.com. By far the most salubrious accommodation in Mai Chau itself is at the *Mai Chau Lodge*, which sits somewhat incongruously amid bucolic scenery: though a little overpriced, its rooms are tastefully decorated with wooden fixtures, and the staff are extremely helpful. $130

Number 1 Ban Van Guesthouse ☎0218 386 7182. The *Number 1 Ban Van Guesthouse*, the first guesthouse on the right as you enter the village of Ban Van, just 1km east of Mai Chau, has a nice setting next to the rice fields. The views may not be as impressive as at Ban Lac and Pom Coong, but the village is much less touristy. $15

EATING

Most people eat a simple set dinner with their hosts in their stilthouse accommodation, with the cost included as part of the tour. If you're peckish, there are many **food stalls** clustered around the market in town, some serving lip-smacking **kebabs**. In the mornings you'll find hawkers here selling piping-hot **banana fritters** and coffee.

Mai Chau Lodge The excellent restaurant at the *Mai Chau Lodge* serves a slap-up set lunch for $9, or set dinner for $20. The setting is quite romantic, with views over lotus ponds and rice paddies stretching across the valley. Daily 7am–10pm.

Toan Thang Some of the best food in town is dished up at the *Toan Thang*, 500m before the *Mai Chau Lodge*, which serves freshly caught fish but has no English menu. Mains $2–4. Daily 7am–9pm.

Ban Lac

Just south of the *Mai Chau Lodge*, a road to the right (west) leads across a few paddy fields to **BAN LAC**, home to a prosperous community of White Thai, though these days their wealth is derived more from tourist dollars than from farming. This is where most people stay on a two-day tour from Hanoi – it's a settlement of some seventy houses (about four hundred people) where you can buy handwoven textiles, watch performances of traditional dancing and sleep overnight.

During the day the lanes between houses are draped with scarves, bags and dresses, with villagers urging passersby to stop for a quick look. Though it seems a bit commercial, the vendors are not as pushy as their Black Hmong counterparts in Sa Pa, and if it does get tiring then a few minutes' walk in any direction from the centre leads out to paddies and a view of the ring of purple mountains which make for some of north Vietnam's most classic scenery.

ACCOMMODATION

BAN LAC

Nowadays just about every house in the village doubles as a guesthouse, and many have sit-down toilets fitted below the houses. Some house owners have even changed their roofs from tile back to the original thatch, perhaps to fulfil visitors' expectations. If you turn up without a tour group, just ask around and someone will put you up for about $5–7 per person for the night, plus $1–2 for a meal depending largely on how much you eat.

Hoa Binh

There's one final pass to go over before Highway 6 leaves the northwest mountains. It's a steady climb along precipitous hillsides up to a col at 1200m, and then an ear-popping descent through sugar-cane plantations to **HOA BINH**, on the edge of the Red River plain. The town's proximity to Hanoi, 76km on a fast road, plus its hotels and easy access to a variety of minority villages mean that Hoa Binh soaks up a lot of tourist traffic. However, the town itself has little character, so unless you need the bus connections, it's preferable to stop over in Mai Chau or push on all the way to Hanoi.

> ### TOURS TO BAN LAC
>
> Most **overnight tours** include a guided trek around the valley, which for many is the highlight of their visit. In the evenings, the traditional dance **performances** staged for tour groups after dinner are also interesting, with coy, long-haired girls acting out agricultural chores in a graceful manner. After the show, the audience is invited to join them in a dance, as well as a sup of local wine from a big bowl through a bamboo straw.
>
> While too touristy for some, Ban Lac does offer the chance to stay in a genuine **stilthouse** – an edifying experience, particularly at dawn if your sleeping quarters happen to be above the henhouse. Avoid a weekend visit if possible, when the village is overrun with students from Hanoi.

FURTHER IN TO THE MAI CHAU VALLEY

Many houses in Ban Lac rent out **bicycles**, which are an ideal way to explore the Mai Chau Valley (20,000đ per day) and one interesting route is to **cycle** 12km south on Highway 15 to **Co Luong**, passing timeless rural scenes and reflections of mountains in the flooded paddy fields. At Co Luong, the Ma River joins the road, and huge limestone walls and dense bamboo growth adorn the riverbank. An active **market** on Saturday mornings is worth the trip, to see the array of handicrafts and fish.

The main highway thunders straight through the centre of modern Hoa Binh (though a by-pass is under construction) but a hint of quieter days lingers in its shaded main boulevard, Cu Chin Lan.

Hoa Binh Dam

Less than 2km above the city to the northwest, the 620m-wide **Hoa Binh Dam** chokes the Da River to create a lake over 200km long, stretching all the way to Son La. The reservoir is earmarked for tourist development, but its main purpose is to feed Vietnam's largest hydroelectric plant which came on stream in 1994 and has gone some way to solving Vietnam's chronic power shortage.

You get a worm's-eye view of the dam from the pontoon bridge that links Hoa Binh's main street with industrial suburbs across the Da River, but Hoa Binh Tourism (see below) can arrange a tour of it, and of the Muong, Thai, Hmong and Dao villages in the vicinity that are impossible to visit without a guide and transport.

ARRIVAL AND DEPARTURE
HOA BINH

By bus Hoa Binh's main bus station lies on its eastern edge, where you'll find the usual gaggle of xe om waiting to take you the kilometre into town (15,000đ). Buses for Hanoi leave regularly, but note that some terminate at Ha Dong where you have to pick up a Hanoi city bus. Keep an eye on your bags as thefts have been reported on this route.

By boat A very scenic way to travel from Hoa Binh to Mai Chau is by boat down the Ma River. A boat holding ten people takes two hours and offers a glimpse of life on the riverbank ($125 per boat). Note: it docks in Bai Sang, 12km north of Mai Chau (50,000đ by motorbike). Bookings can be made through Hoa Binh Tourism (see below)

INFORMATION AND TOURS

Tourist information Hoa Binh Tourism (ⓦhoabinhtourism.com) at the *Hoa Binh Hotel 1* offers guided tours of the dam and hydroelectric plant and of the Muong, Thai, Hmong and Dao minority villages on the shores of the reservoir, although they are geared primarily to tour groups.

Boat trips Hoa Binh Tourism's most popular outing is a day's boat trip on the Da River, visiting Muong and Dao villages ($50 per boat for fifteen people), and they can also arrange a night's accommodation in a showpiece Muong village ($10 per person plus food).

ACCOMMODATION

Hoa Binh 1 and 2 ☏0218 385 2051 & ☏385 2001. The most popular place to stay for foreigners is the *Hoa Binh 2*, although rooms and facilities are almost identical to the

Hoa Binh 1. The hotels are located almost opposite each other on a hillside 2km west of the town centre along Highway 6. Both have about thirty wood-panelled rooms

HOA BINH DURING THE FRENCH WAR

During the French War Hoa Binh was the scene of a disastrous French raid into Viet Minh-held territory, which reads like a dress rehearsal for the epic rout of Dien Bien Phu. In November 1951, French paratroop battalions seized Hoa Binh in a daring attempt to hamper enemy supply routes. They met with little resistance and dug in, only to find themselves marooned as Giap's forces cut both road and river access. In February the following year the French fought their way out towards Hanoi in a battle that came to be known as the "hell of Hoa Binh".

in long, thatched stilthouses, and restaurants. The *Hoa Binh 2* also features folk dancing and music displays and sampling of Thai rice wine from the communal pot. $25 **V Resort** ☎0218 387 1954, ⓦvresort.com.vn. More luxurious is the *V Resort*, situated 20km from Hoa Binh, with a variety of attractions such as a natural hot spring swimming pool, bicycles and a spa. It attracts mostly Vietnamese guests. A xe om will take you there from Hoa Binh, or if travelling from Mai Chau, get off at the Pho Cun junction 10km before Hoa Binh and head right a further 10km to Bai Chao. $35

EATING

As well as the restaurants at the *Hoa Binh 1* and *2* hotels, there's also a group of local **restaurants**, cafés and ice-cream parlours at the west end of Cu Chin Lan, about 50m before the T-junction.

The northeast

The provinces of northeast Vietnam, looping eastwards from **Ha Giang** to Lang Son, lack the grandeur of their counterparts west of the Red River Valley, with the notable exception of the area round **Dong Van** and Meo Vac. In general the peaks here are lower and the views smaller-scale and of an altogether softer quality; there are also less minority folk wearing traditional dress. Getting to see everything is not as straightforward as in the northwest either, though the upgrading of the road between Meo Vac and Cao Bang means it's now possible to visit the fabulous landscapes of Ha Giang Province, as well as Ba Be Lake and the region around Cao Bang, without backtracking.

Highlights of the northeast are its **rural landscapes**, from traditional scenes of villages engulfed in forest to dramatic limestone country, typified by pockets of cultivation squeezed among rugged outcrops whose lower slopes are wrinkled with terraces. However, population densities are still low, leaving huge forest reserves and high areas of wild, open land inhabited by **ethnic minorities** practising swidden farming (see p.464). While many have adopted a Vietnamese way of life, in remoter parts the minorities remain culturally distinct – particularly evident when local markets, their dates traditionally set by the lunar calendar, are in full swing.

8

Ha Giang

HA GIANG is the capital of the north's most remote and least-visited province, where Vietnam's border juts into China and almost reaches the Tropic of Cancer. Until the early 1990s, this region was the scene of fierce fighting between Vietnam and China, and it is still considered a "sensitive area", though its inhabitants nowadays are peaceful and welcoming. It is a sizeable town, and though its buildings are of no great architectural merit, its setting is very impressive, hemmed in by the imposing Mo Neo and Cam mountains. The ochre waters of the Lo River carve southward through the centre of town, and traffic is thick on the bridges that connect the west and east districts.

The town itself has a few attractions, but the main reason for coming is to head on to Meo Vac and Dong Van, both set in valleys surrounded by forbidding peaks and connected by a hair-raising road with spectacular views. The trip from Ha Giang to Dong Van, then on to Cao Bang via Bao Loc, is about 300km and takes at least two (more often three) full days of driving along narrow, bumpy roads, which may become impassable during the rainy season. This border area is home to several **minority groups**, including the White Hmong and the Lo Lo, the latter having only a few thousand members; most towns along the route, including Dong Van and Meo Vac, have a **Sunday market** attended by villagers from the surrounding valleys, where you might just be the only foreigner.

The town of Ha Giang straddles the Lo River, with two bridges connecting the older part on the east bank and the newer part on the west bank.

The market

Located in a purpose-built hall just northeast of the northern bridge, Ha Giang's **market** is a frenzy of activity in the early morning when members of **minority groups** can often be seen. If you plan to go to Dong Van, however, you're likely to see more authentic markets along the way.

The town museum

Tues, Thurs & Sun 8–11am & 2–4pm, with late opening Thurs, Sat & Sun 7.30–9.30pm • Free

The Ha Giang **museum**, located just west of the northern bridge, is well worth a visit to get a preview of the outfits of the many different minority groups who inhabit the region, as well as to see artefacts such as bronze drums and ancient axe-heads that have been unearthed by digs in the region. Archeological evidence shows that there has been a settlement here for tens of thousands of years, and the region seemingly flourished during the Bronze Age judging by the number of beautifully designed drums that have been found.

ARRIVAL AND DEPARTURE

HA GIANG

By bus Ha Giang lies 318km from Hanoi; buses leave from the My Dinh Bus Station (near My Dinh Stadium, 20km southwest of Hanoi) and Gia Lam Bus Station about ten times a day and take six hours to reach Ha Giang via Highway 2, passing through Viet Tri on the banks of the Lo River, and Viet Quang just 60km before Ha Giang. The bus station is just off Nguyen Trai which runs along the west side of the Lo River. Xe om are on hand to run passengers a kilometre or two into the centre.

By car or motorbike With a rented car or motorbike, it's also possible to approach from Bac Ha (see p.407) by heading south on Highway 70 to Pho Rang, then taking Highway 279, which winds its way eastward to Viet Quang, and finally north to Ha Giang; the journey takes the best part of a day.

INFORMATION

Tourist information The town's main tour agent (Ha Giang Tourist Company) is located on Tran Hung Dao, just west of the northern bridge. They can supply permits for travel in the surrounding area (see box opposite) and can also arrange guides if necessary.

DIRECTORY

Bank next to the Ha Giang Tourist Company.

Post office Located along Nguyen Trai.

ACCOMMODATION

There are plenty of **places to stay** in town, though since few foreigners visit, staff speak very little English. This shouldn't be a problem, as rates are usually displayed on the counter, but facilities in all places are rather basic.

Duc Giang ☎0219 387 5648. The *Duc Giang* is typical of most lodgings in town, providing a choice of fan or a/c, tea-making facilities and spartan furnishings. $\overline{\$9}$

Ha Duong ☎0219 386 2555. Arriving from the south along Nguyen Trai, one of the first places you come to is the *Ha Duong*, which has some bland rooms at the front, and some massive rooms that once functioned as karaoke lounges towards the back. $\overline{\$10}$

Huy Hoan ☎0219 386 1288. Close to town, the *Huy Hoan* tries to sell itself as the best hotel in town, and it does have wi-fi, but the rooms are cramped and the service indifferent. $\overline{\$10}$

Sao Mai ☎0219 386 3019. Also located on Nguyen Trai is the *Sao Mai*, which, despite its outside appearance, has good rooms with bathtubs. $\overline{\$7.50}$

Truong Xuan Resort ☎0219 381 1102, ⓦhagiangresort.com. Given the lack of decent hotels in town, it's worth heading out to this budding resort located by the river about 5km north of town. The water may not run in the bathroom and the electricity may constantly go off, but at least the staff understand enough English when you complain, and there's a nice rural view. $\overline{\$13}$

EATING

There are several **restaurants** along Nguyen Van Linh, which runs beside the west bank of the river just north of the museum, and you can find the usual soup and rice places around the market on the east side of town.

GETTING A PERMIT

One of the reasons that few people visit this region is that foreigners currently must obtain a **permit** ($10 per person; discounts for groups) from the immigration office or a tour agent to travel anywhere outside Ha Giang town, including up to the **Chinese border**. Since there are usually no queues at **the immigration office** (5 Tran Quoc Toan; 7.30–11am & 1.30–5pm: ☎ 0219 387 5210) the process can be completed in a few minutes. As the permit costs the same price for any length of time, you should apply for as many days as possible as you won't be able to extend it and, given the beauty of the area, you may well want to. Previously foreigners were required to **hire a guide**, too, though this is no longer the case: however, as the situation is subject to change, it's essential to make enquiries in Hanoi before heading to the area.

North to Dong Van and Meo Vac

The main reason for a trip to Ha Giang Province is to gaze on the stunning scenery around **DONG VAN** and **MEO VAC**, for which it's best to hire a car and driver or, if you're an experienced rider, on a rented motorbike (something strong to deal with the rugged terrain). If you're really brave you could take local buses, but they're infrequent, cramped and do not stop at the viewpoints.

Until recently, it was necessary for visitors to Dong Van and Meo Vac to backtrack to Ha Giang, but the completion of a **new bridge** and upgrading of the road between Meo Vac and Bao Loc mean that it's now possible to do a loop of the northeast (indeed, of the entire north) without retracing your steps.

It's important to note that at the time of writing it was not possible to do this route in reverse, as permits, which need to be shown regularly in Ha Giang Province, can only be issued in Ha Giang. Hopefully as the route becomes more popular, permits will be issued in Cao Bang also.

Highway 4C heads north out of Ha Giang, at first following the Lo River Valley to Yen Minh, then heading east along the Mien River. As the road climbs into the hills, you'll notice a huge, Hollywood-type sign announcing that you are entering the Dong Van Karst Plateau Geopark. This new designation for the region is entirely appropriate as the whole area east of here contains unique geological features. New, informative signboards throughout the region explain the bizarre formation of the landscape.

Tam Son

Roughly 40km northeast from Ha Giang, the long and winding road crosses Quan Ba Pass ("Heaven's Gate"). Just beyond the pass is a pull-off where roadside steps lead up to a delightful view – when the weather is clear – over the town of **TAM SON** and the patchwork fields and dramatic hills around it. Two perfectly rounded karst hills that stand out are dubbed 'Fairy bosom', a typical example of the fanciful terms that Vietnamese, like the Chinese, like to apply to natural phenomena. There's a **market** in Tam Son on Sundays where, apart from the White Hmong, who are the biggest group in this region, you might see Red Dao, Tay, Giay, Co Lao, Pu Peo and Lo Lo people. The valley would be great fun to trek or cycle around and there's a surprisingly decent hotel, the *567* (see p.425).

Yen Minh

Some 97km from Ha Giang and beyond Tam Son, the road follows a pretty stream for some distance, with steep mountain flanks rising on both sides. After climbing over treeless, terraced hills, which serve to increase the feeling of remoteness, it then descends into **Yen Minh**. This makes a good lunch stop, especially since there is a reasonable restaurant here (see p.425) and a couple of passable hotels (see p.425) located on a side street to the left in the centre of town.

8

The route to Dong Van

Just 4km east of Yen Minh, the road splits. The northern fork goes to Dong Van and the southern one to Meo Vac, and this is where the fun really begins. You can follow either road as they join up to form a loop; described below is the route via **Dong Van**, which has slightly more accommodation options than Meo Vac. There's virtually no traffic on the road, which passes through rugged limestone landscapes, the scenery gradually getting wilder and more dramatic, and there is little evidence of settlements at the roadside. For much of the way, the terrain is pocked with blackened knuckles of rock that must make for difficult farming, though small fields of corn are planted here and there, and cone-shaped bundles of corn stalks, used for fodder and fuel, are scattered among the rock-strewn landscape. The locals, for the most part White Hmong, stoop low under heavy burdens of wood, and it's all too evident that life here is tough.

At **Sa Phin**, about 15km before Dong Van, look out on the right for the sturdy building of the People's Committee. A right turn here leads just 400m down to Vuong Palace.

Vuong Palace, Sa Phin

Daily 7am–5pm • 5,000₫

The **Vuong Palace** is a large, two-storey residence with three courtyards that was built by the French for the local Hmong king. In 2006 it was subject to sensitive renovation that replaced many collapsing beams but has retained the integrity of the original building. The thick walls show intricate craftsmanship, and have slits set into them that were used to defend the place with rifles in bygone days. In the shade of pine trees beside the gateway to the palace are several impressive tombs of members of the Vuong family.

Dong Van

Dong Van is the northernmost town in Vietnam, so arriving here is something of an achievement itself. From Sa Phin to Dong Van, the scenery is superb – a constant string of cone-shaped peaks standing above fields in the valley below. There's not much to the place apart from a cacophonous and colourful Sunday market, when hilltribe people dressed in their best come here to buy and sell pigs, farming implements and rice wine. The town is also the jumping-off point to the flag tower at Lung Cu, the northernmost point in the country.

Lung Cu

Daily 7am–5pm • 5,000₫

If you have time, head north out of Dong Van along another narrow road with mind-boggling views and continue 22km to **LUNG CU**. There's nothing here except a new flag tower, built in 2010, that marks the northernmost point of the country. Set on top of a hill, the flag tower is reached by a long flight of steps, and the views from the top, of thatched huts and fields being ploughed by buffalo, has probably remained unchanged for centuries. A plaque at the top records the latitude (23°N) and longitude (105°E). Considering its remoteness, this spot is very popular for Vietnamese visitors.

Dong Van to Meo Vac

The next stage of the journey, covering just 22km on the way to **Meo Vac**, is perhaps the most spectacular part of the whole trip. The road clings to the side of a massive canyon and crosses the Ma Phi Leng Pass at around 1500m. The views down to the Nho Que River, a ribbon of turquoise far below, are simply dizzying. There's little to see in Meo Vac apart from a small statue of Uncle Ho and the town's market that overflows on Sundays, but it's the setting, with a ring of barren mountains forming a bowl around it, which is impressive.

8

ACCOMMODATION

TAM SON

Hotel 567 ☎ 0219 384 6444, **✉** congtytnhh567@gmail .com. Considering the meagre hotels in Ha Giang, it's a pleasant surprise to find this well-maintained place, in the middle of the high street. Some rooms are a bit dingy, but they're all clean and a good size. Terrific views from the back. **$10**

YEN MINH

Minh Hai ☎ 016 6650 1688. This simple hotel/restaurant has reasonably clean, cheap rooms that are OK at a pinch, though the *Hai Son* just down the road is marginally better. **$6.50**

Hai Son ☎ 0219 385 2091. Tucked down a sidestreet near the *Minh Hai Hotel*, the rooms in this place are a bit bigger, brighter and more cared for, so worth the extra few dong. **$8**

DONG VAN

Hoang Ngoc ☎ 0219 385 6020. This friendly and clean

ROUTE TO DONG VAN AND MEO VAC

guesthouse, situated in the middle of Dong Van's main street, is familiar with foreign visitors and offers cable TV and wi-fi. **$10**

Rocky Plateau (Cau Nguyen Da) ☎ 0219 385 6868 **✉** rockyplateau@gmail.com. Conveniently located just near the market, this is the most popular place in town for small groups of foreigners passing through, with clean, if uninspiring, rooms and a restaurant too. **$13**

MEO VAC

Hoa Cuong ☎ 0219 387 1888. Meo Vac's best hotel by a long shot looks over the central market. Rooms are a good size and there are plenty of facilities like cable TV and minibar, but be prepared for frequent electricity cuts. **$17.50**

Nho Que ☎ 0219 387 1322. A bit cheaper than the rest, and rooms are a bit grubby. Its best feature is the large rooftop where you can get a nice view of the surrounding mountains. **$6.50**

EATING

YEN MINH

The **Phuc Cai** serves a good range of soups and stir-fries. It is located directly opposite the *Minh Hai* Hotel.

DONG VAN

Au Viet Directly opposite the Hoang Ngoc Hotel. Apart from the so-so restaurant at the *Rocky Plateau Hotel*, there's just one place in town that caters to foreign travellers.

8

Meo Vac to Ba Be Lake via Bao Loc

The route east from Meo Vac descends from the karst plateau, passing Tay villages and the small town of **Khau Vai**, where the annual love market – actually more like a wife-swapping ceremony – attracts busloads of domestic tourists. Snaking its way south, the route passes through the large but drab market town of Bao Loc, where there's a solitary hotel (see below) if you should be delayed by landslides or floods. Continuing south, the scenery continues to be impressive, particularly near the mining town of **Tinh Tuc**. Shortly after Tinh Tuc, look for a right turn on to Highway 253, which carries you up and over yet another spectacular ridge before dropping down to the valley floor. At the junction with Highway 279, turn right for the last few kilometres to **Ba Be Lake**. For Cao Bang, keep on the main road after Tinh Tuc, passing though Nguyen Binh.

ACCOMMODATION   BAO LOC

Song Gam About 1km north of the bridge near the centre of town **☎** 026 387 0269. There is nothing particularly to write home about, but the rooms are clean and bright, the owners are friendly and there are good views across the river from the back. **$7.50**

Ba Be National Park

Designated as Vietnam's eighth national park in 1992 and covering an area of about one hundred square kilometres, **Ba Be** is a region of astounding beauty, from the lush vegetation mirrored in the lake's still waters to towering limestone pinnacles that reach over 1500m. The main attractions for visitors are **boat trips** to visit caves, waterfalls and minority villages, with the added bonus of seeing at least a few of the 220 animal, 417 plant and 49 fish species recorded here. Bears, tigers and one of Vietnam's rarest and most endangered primates, the Tonkin snub-nosed langur (*Rhinopithecus avunculus*), live in a few isolated communities on the fringes of the park, but nearer the lake there's a good chance of spotting the more common macaque monkeys, herons

ITINERARIES

The Ba Be itinerary usually begins with a boat trip along the Nang River to **Hang Puong**, where the waters have tunnelled a three-hundred-metre-long, bat-filled cave through a mountain. From here they go on to the **Dau Dang Waterfall**, a stretch of beautiful but treacherous rapids. Take care if you walk on the slippery rocks around the falls as there has been at least one tourist fatality here. Next up is a visit to a **Tay** village on the lakeside, and on longer trips an overnight stay in a stilthouse. A road around the south end of the lake has made **Pac Ngoi** less of an isolated Tay community than it used to be, but several other villages in the area, such as **Buoc Luom**, **Ban Vang** and **Bo Lu**, can accommodate visitors too. Few Tay wear traditional dress these days, and you're most likely to see it at a **minority show** at the *National Park Guest House* (see opposite).

and garrulous, colourful flocks of parrots. Few people are around to disturb the wildlife and outside the months of July and August, when Hanoians take their holidays, you'll usually find only a handful of tourists. What puts some people off Ba Be is difficulty of access by **public transport**, but if you join a tour or hire your own transport in Hanoi it becomes easier to justify, especially when combined with a visit to a minority market. Even then, though, a two-night stay is sufficient for most people.

Ba Be Lake

Vietnam's largest natural lake, Ho Ba Be forms the core of the delightful **Ba Be National Park**, a feast of limestone and tropical forest. Enclosed by steep, densely wooded slopes breaking out here and there into white limestone cliffs, the lake is 7km long, up to 30m deep and a kilometre wide in parts. A few islands decorate the surface.

ARRIVAL   BA BE NATIONAL PARK

On a tour Hanoi tour agencies (see p.373) can help with vehicle hire or line up a full programme, either as a three-day excursion or as part of the Cao Bang–Lang Son circuit (4–5 days): total travelling time from Hanoi to Ba Be is around five to six hours.

By rented transport The least-travelled, but most spectacular, way to approach Ba Be is from Meo Vac in Ha Giang Province (see p.425), but for that you'll need your own transport (motorbike or car with driver) and plenty of time – at least a week for the complete circuit. Approaching from Cao Bang, Highway 3 threads west across country to

Nha Phac, then Ba Be (47km later) via Chora, another small town that comes to life on market days (every Sun). If you've got your own vehicle, you can take an interesting alternative route on a back road through stunning rural landscapes: just north of Phu Thong on Highway 3 (near the 174km marker), turn left and after 30km you'll arrive in Cho Ra.

By public transport This is just about possible – infrequent buses leave from Gia Lam bus station in Hanoi and pull up in Cho Ra, from where a xe om to Ba Be Lake will cost around 40,000đ.

INFORMATION

Park information On arrival, first stop for independent travellers should be the park headquarters (entrance fee 20,000đ), which is located a couple of kilometres from the boat jetty on the east side of the lake. Here you can get information about two- to five-day tours, the most popular of which are boat trips to the caves and waterfalls.

Boat trips Most trips are in narrow, covered motorboats, but it's also possible to row (or be rowed) around parts of the lake in a narrow dug-out canoe – a more appropriate way to move about in such a tranquil environment; daily rental for both motorboats and canoes is from $40 a day.

ACCOMMODATION

Aside from the *National Park Guest House*, you can spend a night in a stilthouse in Pac Ngoi, a lakeside Tay village 7km from the park headquarters; home-stays here or in other nearby villages can be arranged through the national park (ⓦ babenationalpark.org).

Thuy Dung 17km away in Cho Ra ☎ 0281 387 6354. The Thuy Dung has large, clean rooms and expansive views from the back, plus friendly staff who can help arrange tours on Ba Be Lake. $17.50

National Park Guest House/Vuon Quoc Gia Ba Be ☎ 0281 389 4136. The most convenient and comfortable place to stay is the National Park Guest House or Vuon Quoc Gia Ba Be, located next to park headquarters, which offers smart but pricey rooms, a restaurant, a swimming pool and occasional minority shows. In the summer months (June–Aug) it is often booked out by party cadres, who find it a good location for meetings, so it's best to reserve ahead. $35

EATING

If your accommodation is a **home-stay**, your hosts will generally provide well-prepared, though not very exciting, set meals, and the guesthouses in Cho Ra serve food, though the kitchens close early, and there are a few com pho stalls around the only road junction in town. **Snacks and drinks** are available at the boat jetty by Ba Be Lake and the speciality in many local restaurants is fish from the lake. The best place to try it is at the National Park Guest House, where they serve whatever's caught that day.

Cao Bang

CAO BANG lies approximately halfway along the route from Ha Giang to Lang Son, and has enough appeal to merit a stopover. The journey from Ha Giang along Highway 34, via Bao Lac, takes the better part of a day, passing through small villages and excellent scenery. Few travellers venture this far north, but those who do usually make the pilgrimage out to **Pac Bo Cave**, where Ho Chi Minh lived on his return to Vietnam in 1941, and to **Ban Gioc Falls**, Vietnam's highest waterfall, right on the border with China. The province is home to several ethnic minorities, notably the Dao, Nung and Tay who still maintain their traditional way of life in the more remote uplands.

8

The town itself is a likeable place: its centre may be dusty and noisy, but its riverside setting, with dense clumps of bamboo backed by sugar-loaf mountains helps to blur the edges. The town is built on the southwestern bank of the **Bang Giang River**, on a spur of land formed by the confluence with the Hien River. Highway 3 drops steeply down from the hills and enters town from the west, crossing a bridge onto a tree-lined avenue of self-important edifices, including the People's Committee, theatre, bank and post office, before turning right along the river. The narrow, shady park on top of the low hill in the centre of town is worth a wander, and the **statue of Uncle Ho** is a reminder of the fact that this region was vital to the thrust for independence that he led.

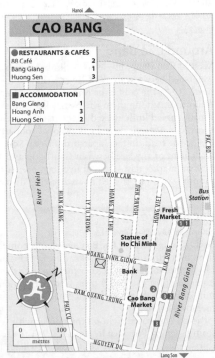

The markets

Held daily, the enormous **markets** form the town's focal points. If possible, try to visit the fresh produce market around sunrise when minority women trek into town and bamboo rafts laden with produce dock beside the bridge. The only thing to do once you've had your fill here is head for the hills north of town.

ARRIVAL

By bus Cao Bang's bus station is on Pac Bo, on the east side of the river, near the Bang Giang Bridge.

Destinations Hanoi (7hr); Lang Son (4hr).

ACCOMMODATION

Bang Giang Kim Dong ☎ 026 385 3431, ✉ nongbatu @yahoo.com. *The Bang Giang* hotel, right next to the bridge, is the largest hotel in town, with restaurants and shops on site, though the uninspiring rooms are rather overpriced. Ask for a room with a river view to make up for the drab decor. $20

★ **Hoang Anh** 131 Kim Dong ☎ 026 385 8969. Compared to other options in Cao Bang, the *Hoang Anh* is a stand-out. Its tastefully furnished rooms are spacious, some with picture postcard views, and all amenities are clean and in working order. Considering the reasonable rates, it's your best choice in town. $17.50

Huong Sen 100 Kim Dong ☎ 026 385 4654. The *Huong Sen* is good value, with river views from most rooms, cable TV, friendly staff and an excellent restaurant in the lobby: the rooms vary in style and size, so ask to see at least a couple. $9

EATING

First stop on cold mornings should be for a **breakfast soup** ladled from the huge steaming cauldrons in the market, while the wallside **snack-shacks** south of the market on Kim Dong have a rustic late-night appeal. Most places are open from around 7am till 9pm, and main dishes cost around $2–5.

88 Café Kim Dong. For a cup of coffee and a bit of people watching, try *88 Café*, just west of the *Huong Sen*.
Bang Giang Kim Dong ✉ nongbatu@yahoo.com. The *Bang Giang* has a tiny English menu and serves reasonable food but in a very depressing dining room.
Huong Sen 100 Kim Dong The *Huong Sen* has no English menu, but since most of the meals are on display it's easy to point.

DIRECTORY

ATMs There are a couple dotted around town – the easiest to find is outside the *Bang Giang* hotel.

Post office On a hill in the centre of town, the post office is recognizable from its radio mast.

Around Cao Bang

West of Cao Bang, Highway 3 climbs up to a high pass (800m), which marks the watershed between the Red River Valley to the south and China's Pearl River in the north. Over the col lie the **Ngan Son Mountains**, which are the domain of several ethnic minorities, among them the Nung, Dao and San Chay (whose women typically carry a broad, curved knife tucked in the back of their belts). There are few villages in sight on these wild uplands, just the occasional split-bamboo hut selling wild honey (*mat ong*) beside the road. In fact, apart from **Ngan Son**, lost in a vast, treeless valley, there's no settlement of any size between Cao Bang and **Na Phac**, 80km down the road. If you're here on market day – held at five-day intervals, starting on the first day of the lunar month – you'll be treated to an arresting display of minority dress.

Pac Bo Cave

Museum open daily 7.30–11.30am & 1.30–4.30pm • Free

Such a lot is made of **Pac Bo Cave** that it comes as a surprise to learn that Ho Chi Minh lived in it for only seven weeks, during February and March 1941. If you're not a fan of Ho memorabilia then neither the cave nor the small museum justifies the 50km excursion (2hr each way) from Cao Bang, though the first part of the journey, passing minority villages moored in rice-paddy seas against craggy blue horizons, is a memorable ride.

Pac Bo is situated right on the border with China. When Ho Chi Minh walked over from Guangxi Province in January 1941, he took his first steps on Vietnamese soil for thirty years. At first he lived in a Nung village but soon left for the nearby cave where he set about co-ordinating the independence movement, and translating the history of the Soviet Communist Party into Vietnamese. The French soon discovered his hideaway and Ho had to move again, this time to a jungle hut not far away where the Viet Minh was founded in May 1941. Later that same year he left for China, to drum up support for his nascent army, and when he next returned to Pac Bo it was after Independence, as a tourist, in 1961. The **cave** today is a strange mixture of shrine and picnic spot, while exhibits in the small **museum** include Ho's Hermes Baby typewriter, bamboo suitcase and Mauser pistol.

ARRIVAL PAC BO CAVE

On a tour or with hired transport Some tours from Hanoi include a visit to the cave on their itineraries, though it's possible to go it alone. To get to Pac Bo from Cao Bang, head northwest across the Bang Giang River on the Ha Quang road until you see a signpost directing you off to the right. From this junction it's another 4km to the entrance (currently no charge).

By public transport Getting to the cave by public transport is not easy, as few buses ply the route between Cao Bang and Ha Quang; if you do take a bus, ask to be dropped off at the turning for Pac Bo, two hours from Cao Bang, where you can pick up a xe om for the last few kilometres.

Over the Ma Phuc Pass

If the revolutionary relics at Pac Bo aren't your thing, take the road northeast towards Tra Linh and Quang Uyen and lose yourself among sugar-loaf scenery beyond the **Ma Phuc Pass**. The road from Cao Bang shoots straight up the valleyside and after a disappointing start you're suddenly looking down on a tortured landscape of scarred limestone peaks and streamless valleys typical of karst scenery. The region is inhabited by Nung people who cultivate the valley floors and terraced lower slopes, living in distinctive wooden houses that are built partly on ground level and partly raised on stilts. Even if you don't have time to explore further, views from the top of the pass – a mere 20km out of Cao Bang – more than repay the effort.

Ban Gioc Falls

Permits are required ($10 per group, irrespective of number of people) to visit the Ban Gioc Falls. This is easily arranged through your hotel in Cao Bang

The only specific sight in the area is the **Ban Gioc Falls**, whose location exactly on the frontier with China made them a bone of contention during the border war. Several tour groups now include the falls on their itinerary. Over 90km and two hours' driving each way, Ban Gioc is really a full day's outing; note that the falls are less than spectacular in the dry season.

Southeast to Lang Son

At Cao Bang you join **Highway 4**, an ambitious road that was originally part of a French military network linking the isolated garrisons right across northern Vietnam's empty mountain country. This road is more subject than many others in the north to falling into disrepair, and the 140km journey to Lang Son takes about four hours, depending on conditions. Beyond **Dong Khe**, a nondescript town roughly 40km out of Cao Bang, the virtually traffic-free road climbs through a gorge of sheer limestone cliffs before cresting the dramatic **Dong Khe Pass**. In 1950 this pass was the scene of a daring ambush in which the Viet Minh gained their first major victory over the French Expeditionary Force. In the ensuing panic, forts all along the border were abandoned, an estimated six thousand French troops were killed or captured, and the Viet Minh netted 950 machine guns, eight thousand rifles and a few hundred trucks.

8

That Khe lies exactly halfway between Cao Bang and Lang Son, and beyond here the road winds through **Na Sam**, an attractive town snuggled beneath a dramatic setting of outcrops. The villages in this area are inhabited by Nung and Tay; their bamboo rafts and huge wooden waterwheels, which form part of sophisticated irrigation works, grace the river that weaves along beside the road. Unfortunately this rural idyll comes to an abrupt end, as the speedy Highway 1 from Dong Dang brings you hurtling into Lang Son.

Lang Son

For most people, **LANG SON** is just a meal stop or overnight rest on the journey through the northeast or en route to China, only 18km away to the north. With a fast highway now linking Lang Son to Hanoi, reasons to linger are even fewer, though the surrounding countryside does have an endearing quality in the form of endless karst outcrops studding the plain. Having acquired the status of a city, Lang Son has a self-important feel, and its booming economy is evident in new construction sites all over town. The Ky Cung River splits Long Son in two, leaving the main bulk on the north side of the Ky Lua Bridge and the provincial offices to the south.

The area round **Mau Son Mountain**, just east of town, is good hiking country. For the intrepid, Lang Son is the start of a little-travelled back road (Highway 4B) cutting across 100km of empty country to Tien Yen on the east coast, offering a route to (or from) Ha Long Bay.

Ky Lua Market

It's along Tran Dang Ninh that you'll find the town's main attraction, bustling **Ky Lua Market**. Just east of the highway, this is well worth investigating, especially in the early morning when Tay, Nung and Dao women come to trade.

Den Ky Cung

Daily 6am–6.30pm • Free

From Ky Lua market, walk a kilometre south to the river and take a quick look at the small temple, **Den Ky Cung**, tucked under the bridge on the north bank. Founded over five hundred years ago, this temple is dedicated to Quan Tuan Tranh, an army officer of the border guard who is reputed to have slain hundreds of Chinese in battle before he himself fell. There's nothing much to see inside apart from a photo of Uncle Ho visiting Lang Son in 1960.

ACROSS THE BORDER TO CHINA

The majority of people taking this route into China travel **by train**, using one of the two weekly services direct from Hanoi to Beijing (see p.30). Note also that you can only board this train in Hanoi (and not at Dong Dang), though on the Chinese side it's possible to disembark up the line; pleasant Nanning is the first major city.

Alternatively, you can use the **road crossing** known as the **Huu Nghi** (Friendship) **border gate**, which lies 18km north of Lang Son and 4km from Dong Dang at the end of Highway 1. If you're travelling by **local bus**, your best bet is to overnight in Lang Son (see above) and then take a motorbike to the border gate. Otherwise, frequent **minibuses** shuttle between Lang Son's Le Loi Street and Dong Dang (look for those marked "Tam Thanh" at the front), but you'll then have to hop on a motorbike for the last leg.

The tiny Huu Nghi border gate is open between 7am and 6pm; there's a walk of less than a kilometre between the two checkpoints. On the Chinese side, infrequent minibuses head to Pingxiang (15km) for the nearest accommodation: it's also the nearest money exchange, so you'll need to have got some yuan in Lang Son for the minibus fare. Note that China is **one hour ahead** of Vietnam.

However you cross the border, you must have a Chinese **visa**, available from the embassy in Hanoi (see p.388).

Dong Kinh Market and around

Following the road that branches off the highway at Den Ky Cung for about 500m will bring you round a bend in the river to the market

The three-storey edifice of **Dong Kinh Market** is a temple to Chinese kitsch, where illuminated Buddhas sit in front of posters of Huangguoshu Falls, China's highest waterfall. The broad boulevards south of the bridge are also worth exploring. The atmosphere is less frenetic than in the centre, and there are some interesting colonial buildings in the tree-lined backstreets. If the weather is good and you have time to spare, take a walk along **Da Tuong** in the southwest of town, which passes remnants of an ancient wall and heads on into a nearby labyrinth of karst hills.

The nearby caves

Daily 7am–5pm • 5000đ each • To get to the caves, walk 100m past the *Hoang Son Hai Hotel*, where you will come to a junction. Turn left and continue for 200m to see the Nhi Thanh Cave. For the Tam Tanh Cave, go straight over the junction and follow for 200m

Also worth exploring are the caves. **Nhi Thanh Cave**, located just near the *Hoang Son Hai Hotel*, follows the Ngoc Tuyen River underground and is worth a look. The **Tam Thanh Cave**, a little further from the town centre, features a series of rockpools and multi-coloured lighting displays. Past the ticket office, 150m further down the road, is a staircase that leads high above to the top of a rocky hill and to a cheesy garden equipped with fake bulls and deer, but has great views over the town.

ARRIVAL AND INFORMATION

LANG SON

By bus The bus from Cao Bang takes about four hours, and from Hanoi three hours. There's also a railway station here, but the train to Hanoi takes almost six hours. Ngo Quyen branches off to the right from Le Loi, where about 100m along you'll find the bus station, though most long-distance buses will drop you on Le Loi or Tran Dang Ninh (Highway 1), the town's main north–south artery.

Information Most of Lang Son's facilities are found on the north bank of the river. There is no official tourist office, but hotel staff at the *Van Xuan* are helpful.

DIRECTORY

Bank Next door to the post office, at 51 Le Loi, the Incombank changes US dollars and has an ATM. Most hotels also exchange dollars and yuan.

Internet There are a couple of internet cafés along Le Loi towards the train station.

Post office Le Loi, next to the Incombank.

ACCOMMODATION

Hoang Son Hai 57 Duong Tam Thanh ☎025 371 0479, ✉hoangsonhails1@gmail.com. The grandest-looking hotel in town, though the rooms are overpriced for what you get. Head along Le Loi from the train station, and keep going straight after it hits Tran Dang Dinh. __$22__

★ **Van Xuan** 147 Tran Dang Ninh ☎025 371 0440, ✉thanh_loan_hotel@hn.vnn.vn. The city's best choice by far – just north of the market, overlooking Phai Loan Lake – has attentive staff and a modern feel; the back rooms have good lake views and all rooms have wi-fi. __$16__

EATING

★ **New Century** Phai Loan Lake opposite the Ky Lua Market. The *New Century* has an English menu that is a welcome sight, especially if you've been living on noodle soup and sticky rice in the mountains. There's a huge range of standard Vietnamese fare such as spring rolls, and clay pot dishes, but there are also unusual items such as rabbit and turtle. It's extremely popular with the locals and Chinese visitors and there's a bit of a beer-hall feel to the place. Mains $2–8. Daily 7am–10pm.

8

STATUE AT THE TAY PHUONG PAGODA

Contexts

History

Vietnam as a unified state within its present geographical boundaries has only existed the early nineteenth century. The national history, however, stretches back thousands of years to a legendary kingdom in the Red River Delta. From there the Viet people pushed relentlessly down the peninsula of Indochina on the "March to the South", Nam Tien. The other compelling force, and a constant theme throughout its history, is Vietnam's ultimately successful resistance to all foreign aggressors.

The beginnings

The earliest evidence of human activity in Vietnam can be traced back to a Palaeolithic culture that existed some five hundred thousand years ago. These hunter-gatherers slowly developed agricultural techniques, but the most important step came about four thousand years ago when farmers began to cultivate irrigated rice in the Red River Delta. The communal effort required to build and maintain the system of dykes and canals spawned a stable, highly organized society, held to be the original Vietnamese nation. This embryonic kingdom, **Van Lang**, emerged sometime around 2000 BC and was ruled over by the semi-mythological Hung kings from their capital near today's Viet Tri, northwest of Hanoi. Archeological finds indicate that by the first millennium BC these people, the Lac Viet, had evolved into a sophisticated Bronze Age culture whose influence spread as far as Indonesia. Undoubtedly their greatest creations were the ritualistic **bronze drums**, discovered in the 1920s near Dong Son, and revered by the Vietnamese as the first hard evidence of an indigenous, independent culture.

Early kingdoms

In the mid-third century BC a Chinese warlord conquered Van Lang to create a new kingdom, **Au Lac**, with its capital at Co Loa, near present-day Hanoi. For the first time the lowland Lac Viet and the hill peoples were united. After only fifty years, around 207 BC, Au Lac was itself invaded by a Chinese potentate and became part of **Nam Viet** (Southern Viet), an independent kingdom occupying much of southern China. For a while the Lac Viet were able to maintain their local traditions and an indigenous aristocracy. Then, in 111 BC the Han emperors annexed the whole Red River Delta and so began a thousand years of Chinese domination.

Chinese rule

A millennium under Chinese rule had a profound effect on all aspects of Vietnamese life, notably the social and political spheres. With the introduction of **Confucianism** came the growth of a rigid, feudalistic hierarchy dominated by a mandarin class. This innately conservative elite ensured the long-term stability of an administrative system

c. 3000 BC	c. 2000 BC	257 BC	111 BC
First evidence of cultivation in Red River Delta.	Birth of Van Lang, first Vietnamese kingdom.	Beginning of Au Lac kingdom.	Chinese invade; would rule Vietnam for nearly one thousand years.

which continued to dominate Vietnamese society until well into the nineteenth century. The Chinese also introduced technological advances, such as writing, silk production and large-scale hydraulic works, while Mahayana Buddhism first entered Vietnam from China during the second century AD.

At the same time, however, the Viet people were forging their national identity in the continuous struggle to break free from their powerful northern neighbour; on at least three occasions the Vietnamese ousted their masters. The first and most celebrated of

FUNAN AND CHAMPA

While China has always exerted a strong influence over north Vietnam, in the south it was initially the Indian civilization that dominated, though as a cultural influence rather than as a ruling power. From the first century AD Indian traders sailing east towards China established **Hindu enclaves** along the southern coast of Indochina. The largest and most important of these city-states was **Funan**, based on a port city called Oc Eo, near present-day Rach Gia in the Mekong Delta (see box, p.150). By the early third century, Funan had developed into a powerful trading nation with links extending as far as Persia and even Rome. But technological developments in the fifth century enabled larger ships to sail round Indochina without calling at any port, and Funan gradually declined.

At around the same time, another Indianized kingdom was developing on the central Vietnamese coast. Little is known about the origins of **Champa**, but in 192 AD, Chinese annals reported that a man named Khu Lien (later to be titled King Sri Mara) had gathered a chain of coastal chiefdoms in the region around Quang Tri in defiance of the expansionism of the Han Chinese to the north, and established an independent state. For most of its existence, Champa was a Hindu kingdom, its economy based on agriculture, wet-rice cultivation, fishing and maritime trade, which it carried out with Indians, Chinese, Japanese and Arabs through **ports** at Hoi An and Quy Nhon. Champa was ruled over by divine kings who worshipped first Shiva and later embraced Buddhism - a fact made apparent in the deities manifest in the extravagant religious edifices that they sponsored, many of which still pepper the Vietnamese coast today (see box, p.226).

Concertinaed between the Khmer to the south and the clans of the Vietnamese (initially under Chinese rule) to the north, Champa's history was characterized by consistent **feuding with the neighbours**. Between the third and fifth centuries, relations with the **Chinese** followed a cyclical pattern of antagonism and tribute, culminating in the 446 AD sacking of Simhapura (near present-day Hoi An) when the Chinese made off with a 50-tonne, solid gold Buddha statue. By the end of the eleventh century Champa had lost its territory north of Hué; wars raged with the **Khmer** in the twelfth and thirteenth centuries, one fateful retaliatory Cham offensive culminating in the **destruction of Angkor**. With the installation on Champa's throne of warmongering Binasuor in 1361, three decades of Cham expansionism ensued; upon his death in 1390, though, the Viets regained all lost ground, and soon secured the region around Indrapura (near today's Da Nang). In a decisive push south, the Viets, led by **Le Thanh Tong**, overran Vijaya in 1471. Champa shifted its capital south again, but by now it was becoming profoundly marginalized.

For a few centuries more, the Cham kings still claimed nominal rule of the area around Phan Rang and Phan Thiet, but in 1697 the last independent Cham king died, and what little remained of the kingdom became a Vietnamese vassal state. **Minh Mang** dissolved even this in the 1820s, finally absorbing Champa into Vietnam, and the last Cham king fled to Cambodia. Most of the estimated one hundred thousand **descendants** of the Cham kingdom reside around Phan Rang and Phan Thiet, though there are also tiny pockets in Tay Ninh and Chau Doc.

40 AD	166	544–602	907
The Trung sisters (Hai Ba Trung) overthrow the Chinese.	First envoys arrive from Roman Empire.	Early Ly Dynasty; brief respite from Chinese rule.	Chinese Tang Dynasty collapses.

these short-lived independent kingdoms was established by the **Trung sisters** (Hai Ba Trung) in 40 AD. After the Chinese murdered Trung Trac's husband, she and her sister rallied the local lords and peasant farmers in the first popular insurrection against foreign domination. The Chinese fled, leaving Trung Trac ruler of the territory from Hué to southern China until the Han emperor dispatched twenty thousand troops and a fleet of two thousand junks to quell the rebellion three years later. The sisters threw themselves into a river to escape capture, and the Chinese quickly set about removing the local lords. Though subsequent uprisings also failed, the sisters had demonstrated the fallibility of the Chinese and earned their place in Vietnam's pantheon of heroes.

Over the following centuries Vietnam was drawn closer into the political and cultural realm of China. The seventh and eighth centuries were particularly bleak as the powerful Tang Dynasty tightened its grip on the province it called **Annam**, or the "Pacified South". As soon as the dynasty collapsed in the early tenth century a series of major rebellions broke out, culminating in the battle of the **Bach Dang River** in 938 AD (see box, p.332). Ngo Quyen declared himself ruler of **Nam Viet** and set up court at the historic citadel of Co Loa, heralding what was to be nearly ten centuries of Vietnamese independence.

Dynastic rule

The period immediately following **independence from Chinese rule** in 939 AD was marked by factional infighting. Ngo Quyen died after only five years on the throne and Nam Viet dissolved in anarchy while twelve warlords disputed the succession. In 968 one of the rivals, Dinh Bo Linh, finally united the country and secured its future by paying tribute to the Chinese emperor, a system that continued until the nineteenth century. Dinh Bo Linh took the additional precaution of moving his capital south to the well-defended valley of Hoa Lu, where it remained during the two short-lived Dinh and Early Le dynasties.

These early monarchs laid the framework for a centralized state. They reformed the administration and the army, and instigated a programme of road building. But it was the following **Ly Dynasty**, founded by **Ly Thai To** in 1009, that consolidated the independence of **Dai Viet** (Great Viet) and guaranteed the nation's stability for the next four hundred years. One of the first actions of the new dynasty was to move the capital back into the northern rice-lands, founding the city of Thang Long, the precursor of modern Hanoi.

Ly Thai To's successor, **Ly Thai Tong** (1028–54), carried out a major reorganization of the national army, turning it into a professional fighting force, able to secure the northern borders and expand southwards. So confident was this new power that in 1076 the army of Dai Viet, under the revered General Ly Thuong Kiet, launched a pre-emptive strike against the Sung Chinese and then held off their counter-attack.

Mongol and Ming invasions

Having ousted the declining Ly clan in 1225, the following **Tran Dynasty** won spectacular military victories against the **Mongol invasions** of 1257, 1284 and 1288. On the first two occasions, Mongol forces briefly occupied the capital before having to withdraw, while the last battle is remembered for a rerun of Ngo Quyen's ploy in the Bach Dang River. This time it was General Tran Hung Dao, a prince in the royal family, who led Viet forces against the far superior armies of Kublai Khan. While the Mongol navy foundered in the

938	968	1009	1076
State of "Nam Viet" declares independence.	Nam Viet unified by Dinh Dynasty.	Ly Thai To inaugurates Ly Dynasty; Vietnam now "Dai Viet".	Major battle with Chinese Sung Dynasty.

Bach Dang River, its army was also being trounced and the remnants driven back into China; soon after, the khan died, and with him the Mongol threat.

In the confusion that marked the end of the Tran Dynasty, an ambitious court minister, Ho Qui Ly, usurped the throne in 1400. Though the **Ho Dynasty** lasted only seven years, its two progressive monarchs launched a number of important reforms. They tackled the problem of land shortages by restricting the size of holdings and then rented out the excess to landless peasants; the tax system was revised and paper money replaced coinage; ports were opened to foreign trade; and public health care introduced. Even the education system was broadened to include practical subjects along with the classic Confucian texts. Just as the Ho were getting into their stride, so the new **Ming Dynasty** in China were beginning to look south across the border. Under the pretext of restoring the Tran, Ming armies invaded in 1407 and imposed **direct Chinese rule** of Vietnam a few years later. The Chinese tried to undermine Viet culture by outlawing local customs and destroying Vietnamese literature, works of art and historical texts.

Le Loi

This time, however, the Chinese occupation faced a much tougher problem as the Viet people were now a relatively cohesive force. Vietnamese resistance gravitated towards the mountains of Thanh Hoa, south of Hanoi, where a local landlord and mandarin, **Le Loi**, was preparing for a war of national liberation. For ten years Le Loi's well-disciplined guerrilla force harassed the enemy until he was finally able to defeat the Chinese army in open battle in 1427.

Le Loi, as King Le Thai To, founded the third of the great ruling families, the **Later Le Dynasty**, and set in train the reconstruction of Dai Viet, though he died after only five years on the throne. Initially the Le Dynasty reaped the economic rewards of its expanding empire, but eventually their new provinces spawned wealthy semi-autonomous rulers strong enough to challenge the throne. As the Le declined in the sixteenth century, two such powerful clans, the **Nguyen and Trinh**, at first supported the dynasty against rival contenders. Towards the end of the century, however, they became the effective rulers of Vietnam, splitting the country in two. The Trinh lords held sway in Hanoi and the north, while the Nguyen set up court at Hué; the Le, meanwhile, remained monarchs in name only.

The arrival of the West

The first Western visitors to the Vietnamese peninsula were probably **traders** from ancient Rome who sailed into the ports of Champa in the second century AD. Marco Polo sailed up the coast in the thirteenth century on his way to China, but more

THE VIETNAMESE DYNASTIES

Ngo	939–65	Ho	1400–07
Dinh	968–80	Ming (Chinese)	1407–28
Early Ly	980–1009	Later Le	1428–1788
Ly	1009–1225	Tay Son	1788–1802
Tran	1225–1400	Nguyen	1802–1945

1225	1257	1288	1400–07
Tran dynasty pushes the Ly out of power; Vietnam now "Dai Ngu".	First Mongol invasion.	Third Mongol invasion.	Short-lived Ho Dynasty.

significant was the arrival of a Portuguese merchant, Antonio Da Faria, at the port of Fai Fo (Hoi An) in 1535. The Portuguese established their own trading post at Fai Fo, then one of Southeast Asia's greatest ports, crammed with vessels from China and Japan, and were soon followed by other European maritime powers.

With the traders came **missionaries**, who found a ready audience, especially among peasant farmers and others near the bottom of the established Confucian hierarchy. It didn't take long before the ruling elite felt threatened by subversive Christian ideas; missionary work was banned after the 1630s and many priests were expelled, or even executed. But enforcement was erratic, and by the end of the seventeenth century the Catholic Church claimed several hundred thousand converts. At this time Vietnam was breaking up into regional factions and the Europeans were quick to exploit growing tensions between the Nguyen and Trinh lords, providing weapons in exchange for trading concessions. However, when the civil war ended in 1674 the merchants lost their advantage. Gradually the English, Dutch and French closed down their trading posts until only the Portuguese remained in Fai Fo.

Towards the end of the eighteenth century, the remaining Catholic missions provided an opening for French merchants wishing to challenge Britain's presence in the Far East. When a large-scale rebellion broke out in Vietnam in the early 1770s, these entrepreneurs saw their chance to establish a firmer footing on the Indochinese peninsula.

The Tay Son rebellion

As the eighteenth century progressed, insurrections flared up throughout the countryside. Most were easily stamped out, but in 1771 three brothers raised their standard in Tay Son village, west of Quy Nhon, and ended up ruling the whole country. The **Tay Son rebellion** gained broad support among dispossessed peasants, ethnic minorities, small merchants and townspeople attracted by the brothers' message of equal rights, justice and liberty. As rebellion spread through the south, the Tay Son army rallied even more converts when they seized land from the wealthy and redistributed it to the poor. By the middle of 1786 the rebels had overthrown both the Trinh and Nguyen lords, again leaving the Le Dynasty intact. When the Le monarch called on the Chinese in 1788 to help remove the Tay Son usurpers, the Chinese

---

ALEXANDRE DE RHODES

European missionaries began to arrive in Vietnam in the early sixteenth century. Portuguese Dominicans had been the first to arrive in the early sixteenth century, but it wasn't until 1615, when Jesuits set up a small mission in Fai Fo, that the Catholic Church gained an established presence in Vietnam. The mission's initial success in the Nguyen territory encouraged the Jesuits to look north. The man they chose for the job was a 28-year-old Frenchman, **Alexandre de Rhodes**, a gifted linguist who, only six months after arriving in Fai Fo, in 1627, was preaching in Vietnamese. His talents soon won over the Trinh lords in Hanoi, where de Rhodes gave six sermons a day and converted nearly seven thousand Vietnamese in just two years. During this time he was also working on a simple **romanized script** for the Vietnamese language, which otherwise used a formidable system based on Chinese characters. De Rhodes merely wanted to make evangelizing easier, but his phonetic system eventually came to be adopted as Vietnam's national language, *quoc ngu*.

1407–27	1427	1535	1627
Short period under rule of Chinese Ming Dynasty.	Le Loi defeats Chinese, inaugurates Later Le Dynasty.	Portuguese create trading post at Fai Fo (now Hoi An).	French missionary Alexandre de Rhodes arrives in Vietnam – his romanized version of Vietnamese script is in use today.

happily obliged by occupying Hanoi. At this the middle brother (Nguyen Hué) declared himself **Emperor Quang Trung** and quick-marched his army 600km from Hué to defeat the Chinese at Dong Da, on the outskirts of Hanoi. With Hué as his capital, Quang Trung set about implementing his promised reforms, but when he died prematurely in 1792, aged 39, his 10-year-old son was unable to hold onto power.

One of the few Nguyen lords to have survived the Tay Son rebellion in the south was Prince Nguyen Anh. The prince made several unsuccessful attempts to regain the throne in the mid-1780s. After one such failure he fled to Phu Quoc Island where he met a French bishop, Pigneau de Béhaine. With an eye on future religious and commercial concessions, the bishop offered to make approaches to the French on behalf of the Nguyen. A treaty was eventually signed in 1787, promising military aid in exchange for territorial and trading concessions, though France failed to deliver the assistance due to a financial crisis preceding the French Revolution. The bishop went ahead anyway, raising a motley force of four thousand armed mercenaries and a handful of ships. The expedition was launched in 1789 and Nguyen Anh entered Hanoi in 1802 to claim the throne as **Emperor Gia Long**. Bishop de Béhaine didn't live to see the victory or to enforce the treaty: he died in 1799 and received a stately funeral.

The Nguyen Dynasty

For the first time, **Vietnam**, as the country was now called, fell under a single authority from the northern border all the way down to the point of Ca Mau. In the hope of promoting unity, Gia Long established his capital in the centre, at Hué, where he built a magnificent citadel in imitation of the Chinese emperor's Forbidden City. The choice of architecture was appropriate: Gia Long and the **Nguyen Dynasty** he founded were resolutely Confucian. The new emperor immediately abolished the Tay Son reforms, reimposing the old feudal order; land confiscated from the rebels was redistributed to loyal mandarins, the bureaucracy was reinstated and the majority of peasants found themselves worse off than before. Gradually the country was closed to the outside world and to modernizing influences that might have helped it withstand the onslaught of French military intervention in the mid-nineteenth century. On the other hand, Gia Long and his successors did much to improve the infrastructure of Vietnam, developing a road network, extending the irrigation systems and rationalizing the provincial administration. Under the Nguyen, the arts, particularly literature and court music, also flourished.

By refusing to grant any trading concessions, Gia Long disappointed the French adventurers who had helped him to the throne. He did, however, permit a certain amount of religious freedom, though his successors were far more suspicious of the missionaries' intentions. After 1825 several edicts were issued forbidding missionary work, accompanied by sporadic, occasionally brutal, persecutions of Christians, both Vietnamese converts and foreign priests. Ultimately, this provided the French with the excuse they needed to annex the country.

French conquest and rule

French governments grew increasingly imperialistic as the nineteenth century wore on. In the Far East, as Britain threatened to dominate trade with China, France began to see Vietnam as a potential route into the resource-rich provinces of Yunnan and

1771	1802	1858
Beginning of Tay Son rebellion, in a village near Quy Nhon.	Proclamation of Nguyen Dynasty, with Hué chosen as the national capital.	Napoleon dispatches an armada to Vietnam.

southern China. Not that France had any formal policy to colonize Indochina; rather it came about in a piecemeal fashion, driven as often as not by private adventurers or the unilateral actions of French officials. In 1847, two French naval vessels began the process when they bombarded Da Nang on the pretext of rescuing a French priest. Reports of Catholic persecutions were deliberately exaggerated until Napoleon III was finally persuaded to launch an armada of fourteen ships and 2500 men in 1858. After capturing Da Nang in September, the force moved south to take Saigon, against considerable opposition, and the whole Mekong Delta over the next three years. Faced with serious unrest in the north, Emperor Tu Duc signed a treaty in 1862 granting France the three eastern provinces of the delta plus trading rights in selected ports, and allowing missionaries the freedom to proselytize. Five years later, French forces annexed the remaining southern provinces to create the colony of **Cochinchina**.

France became embroiled in domestic troubles and the French government was divided on whether to continue the enterprise, but their administrators in Cochinchina had their eyes on the north. The first attempt to take Hanoi and open up the Red River into China failed in 1873; a larger force was dispatched in 1882 and within a few months, France was in control of Hanoi and the lower reaches of the Red River Delta. Spurred on by this success, the French parliament financed the first contingents of the **French Expeditionary Force** just as the Nguyen were floundering in a succession crisis following the death of Tu Duc. In August 1883, when the French fleet sailed into the mouth of the Perfume River, near Hué, the new emperor was compelled to meet their demands. **Annam** (central Vietnam) and **Tonkin** (the north) became protectorates of France, to be combined with Cochinchina, Cambodia and, later, Laos to form the **Union of Indochina** after 1887.

The anti-colonial struggle and Ho Chi Minh

For a population brought up on legends of heroic victories over superior forces, the ease with which France had occupied Vietnam was a deep psychological blow. The earliest resistance movements focused on the restoration of the monarchy, such as the "Save the King" (*Can Vuong*) movement of the 1890s, but any emperor showing signs of patriotism was swiftly removed by the French administration. Up until the mid-1920s, Vietnam's fragmented anti-colonial movements were easily controlled by the *Sûreté*, the formidable French secret police. On the whole, the nationalists' aims were political rather than social or economic, and most failed to appeal to the majority of Vietnamese. Gradually, however, the nationalists saw that a more radical approach was called for, and an influential leader named **Phan Boi Chau** finally called for the violent overthrow of the colonial regime.

Meanwhile, over the border in southern China, the **Revolutionary Youth League** was founded in 1925. Vietnam's first Marxist-Leninist organization, its founding father was a certain **Ho Chi Minh**. Born in 1890, the son of a patriotic minor official, Ho was already in trouble with the French authorities in his teens. He left Vietnam in 1911, then turned up in Paris after World War I under one of his many pseudonyms, Nguyen Ai Quoc ("Nguyen the Patriot"). In France, Ho became increasingly active among other exiled dissidents exploring ways to bring an end to colonial rule. At this time one of the few political groups actively supporting anti-colonial movements were the Communists; in 1920 Ho became a founding member of the French Communist Party and by 1923 he was in Moscow, training as a Communist agent. His task was to unite

1867

1887

Outright French annexation of Cochinchina.

Cochinchina becomes part of wider French Union of Indochina.

LIFE UNDER FRENCH RULE

Despite much talk of the "civilizing mission" of imperial rule, the French were more interested in the economic potential of their new possession. Governor-general Paul Doumer launched a massive programme of **infrastructural development**, constructing railways, bridges and roads and draining vast areas of the Mekong Delta swamp, all funded by raising punitive taxes, with state monopolies on opium, alcohol and salt accounting for seventy percent of government revenues. During the Great Depression of the 1930s markets collapsed; peasants were forced off the land to work as indentured labour in the new rubber, tea and coffee estates or in the mines, often under brutal conditions. Heavy taxes exacerbated **rural poverty** and any commercial or industrial enterprises were kept firmly in French hands, or were controlled by the small minority of Vietnamese and Chinese who actually benefited under the new regime.

On the positive side, mass vaccination and health programmes did bring the frequent epidemics of cholera, smallpox and plague under control. **Education** was a thornier issue: overall, education levels deteriorated during French rule, particularly among unskilled labourers, but a small elite from the emerging urban middle class received a broader, French-based education and a few went to universities in Europe. Not that it got them very far: Vietnamese were barred from all but the most menial jobs in the colonial administration. Ironically, it was this frustrated and alienated group, imbued with the ideas of Western liberals and Chinese reformers, who began to challenge French rule.

the nascent Vietnamese anti-colonial movements under one organization, the Revolutionary Youth League. Among his many talents, Ho Chi Minh (see box, p.320) was an intelligent strategist and a great motivator; though he was now committed to Marxist-Leninist ideology, he understood the need to appeal to all nationalists, playing down the controversial goal of social revolution.

Although many other subsequently famous revolutionaries worked with Ho, it was largely his fierce dedication, single-mindedness and tremendous charisma that held the nationalist movement together and finally propelled the country to independence. The first real test of Ho's leadership came in 1929 when, in his absence, the League split into three separate Communist parties. In Hong Kong a year later, Ho persuaded the rival groups to unite into one **Indochinese Communist Party** whose main goal was an independent Vietnam governed by workers, peasants and soldiers. In preparation for the revolution, cadres were sent into rural areas and among urban workers to set up party cells. The timing couldn't have been better: unemployment and poverty were on the increase as the Great Depression took hold, while France became less willing to commit resources to its colonies.

Throughout the 1930s Vietnam was plagued with strikes and labour unrest, of which the most important was the **Nghe Tinh uprising** in the summer of 1930. French planes bombed a crowd of twenty thousand demonstrators marching on Vinh; within days, villagers had seized control of much of the surrounding countryside, some setting up revolutionary councils to evict wealthy landlords and redistribute land to the peasants. The uprising demonstrated the power of socialist organization, but proved disastrous in the short term – thousands of peasants were killed or imprisoned, the leaders were executed and the Communist Party structure was badly mauled. Most of the ringleaders ended up in the notorious penal colony of Poulo Condore (see p.209),

1890	1925	1940
Birth of Ho Chi Minh.	Ho founds anti-colonial Revolutionary Youth League in southern China.	Japanese occupy Indochina during World War II.

which came to be known as the "University of the Revolution". It's estimated that the French held some ten thousand activists in prison by the late 1930s.

World War II

The German occupation of France in 1940 suddenly changed the whole political landscape. Not only did it demonstrate to the Vietnamese the vulnerability of their colonial masters, but it also overturned the established order in Vietnam and ultimately provided Ho Chi Minh with the opportunity he had been waiting for. The immediate repercussion was the **Japanese occupation** of Indochina after Vichy France signed a treaty allowing Japan to station troops in the colony, while leaving the French administration in place. By mid-1941 the region's coalmines, rice fields and military installations were all under Japanese control. Some Vietnamese nationalist groups welcomed this turn of events as the Japanese made encouraging noises about autonomy and "Asia for the Asians". Others, mostly Communist groups, declared their opposition to all foreign intervention and continued to operate from secret bases in the mountainous region that flanks the border between China and Vietnam.

By this time, Ho Chi Minh had reappeared in southern China, from where he walked over the border into Vietnam, carrying his rattan trunk and trusty Hermes typewriter. The date was February 1941; Ho had been in exile for thirty years. In **Pac Bo Cave**, near Cao Bang, Ho met up with other resistance leaders, including Vo Nguyen Giap, to start the next phase in the fight for national liberation; the League for the Independence of Vietnam, better known as the **Viet Minh**, was founded in May 1941.

Over the next few years Viet Minh recruits received military training in southern China; the first regular armed units formed the nucleus of the **Vietnamese Liberation Army** in 1945. Gradually the Viet Minh established liberated zones in the northern mountains to provide bases for future guerrilla operations. With Japanese defeat looking ever more likely, Ho Chi Minh set off once again into China to seek military and financial support from the Chinese and from the Allied forces operating out of Kunming. Ho also made contact with the American Office of Strategic Services (forerunner of the CIA), which promised him limited arms, much to the anger of the Free French who were already planning their return to Indochina. In return for **American aid** the Viet Minh provided information about Japanese forces and rescued Allied pilots shot down over Vietnam. Later, in 1945, an American team arrived in Ho's Cao Bang base where they found him suffering from malaria, dysentery and dengue fever; it's said they saved his life.

Meanwhile, suspecting a belated French counter-attack, Japanese forces seized full control of the country in March 1945. They declared a nominally independent state under the leadership of Bao Dai, the last Nguyen emperor, and imprisoned most of the French army. The Viet Minh quickly moved onto the offensive, helped to some extent by a massive famine that ravaged northern Vietnam that summer. Then, in early August, US forces dropped the first atom bomb on Hiroshima, precipitating the **Japanese surrender** on August 14.

Independence and division

The Japanese surrender left a power vacuum which Ho Chi Minh was quick to exploit. On August 15, Ho called for a national uprising, which later came to be known as the

1941	1945
Ho re-enters Vietnam; founds the Viet Minh.	Ho proclaims establishment of Democratic Republic of Vietnam.

August Revolution. Within four days Hanoi was seething with pro-Viet Minh demonstrations, and in two weeks most of Vietnam came under their control. Emperor Bao Dai handed over his imperial sword to Ho's provisional government at the end of August and on September 2, 1945 Ho Chi Minh proclaimed the establishment of the **Democratic Republic of Vietnam**, cheered by a massive crowd in Hanoi's Ba Dinh Square. For the first time in eighty years Vietnam was an independent country. Famously, Ho's Declaration of Independence quoted from the American Declaration: "All men are created equal. They are endowed by their Creator with certain inalienable rights, among these are life, liberty and the pursuit of happiness." But this, and subsequent appeals for American help against the looming threat of recolonization, fell on deaf ears as America became increasingly concerned at Communist expansion.

The **Potsdam Agreement**, which marked the end of World War II, failed to recognize the new Republic of Vietnam. Instead, Japanese troops south of the Sixteenth Parallel were to surrender to British authority, while those in the north would defer to the Chinese Kuomintang. Nevertheless, by the time these forces arrived, the Viet Minh were already in control, having relieved the Japanese of most of their weapons. In the **south**, rival nationalist groups were battling it out in Saigon, where French troops had also joined in the fray. The situation was so chaotic that the British commander proclaimed martial law and, amazingly, even deployed Japanese soldiers to help restore calm. Against orders, he also rearmed the six thousand liberated French troops and Saigon was soon back in French hands. A few days later, General Leclerc arrived with the first units of the French Expeditionary Force, charged with reimposing colonial rule in Indochina.

Things were going more smoothly in the north, though the two hundred thousand Chinese soldiers stationed there acted increasingly like an army of occupation. The Viet Minh could muster a mere five thousand ill-equipped troops in reply; forced to choose between the two in order to survive, Ho Chi Minh finally rated French rule the lesser of the two evils, reputedly commenting, "I prefer to smell French shit for five years, rather than Chinese shit for the rest of my life." In March 1946, Ho's government signed a treaty allowing a limited French force to replace Kuomintang soldiers in the north. In return, France recognized the Democratic Republic as a "free state" within the proposed French Union; the terms were left deliberately vague. The treaty also provided for a referendum to determine whether Cochinchina would join the new state or remain separate.

While further negotiations dragged on during the summer of 1946, both sides were busily rearming as it became apparent that the French were not going to abide by the treaty. By late April the Expeditionary Force had already exceeded agreed levels, and there was no sign of the promised referendum; in September 1946 the talks effectively broke down. Skirmishes between Vietnamese and French troops in the northern delta boiled over in a dispute over customs control in Hai Phong; to quell the rioting, the French navy bombed the town on November 23, killing thousands of civilians. This was followed by the announcement that French troops would assume responsibility for law and order in the north. By way of reply, Viet Minh units attacked French installations in Hanoi on December 19, and then, while resistance forces held the capital for a few days, Ho Chi Minh and the regular army slipped away into the northern mountains.

1946	**1949**	**1951**
Beginning of the French War.	Bao Dai becomes head of Associated State of Vietnam.	Viet Minh launches attack on Hanoi.

The French War

For the first years of the **war against the French** (also known as the First Indochina War, or Franco-Viet Minh War) the Viet Minh kept largely to their mountain bases in northern and central Vietnam. While the Viet Minh were building up and training an army, the Expeditionary Force was consolidating its control over the Red River Delta and establishing a string of highly vulnerable outposts around guerrilla-held territory. In October 1947 the French attempted an ambitious all-out attack against enemy headquarters, but it soon became obvious that this was an unconventional "war without fronts" where Viet Minh troops could simply melt away into the jungle when threatened. In addition, the French suffered from hit-and-run attacks deep within the delta, unprotected by a local population who either actively supported or at least tolerated the Viet Minh. Although the French persuaded Bao Dai to return as head of the Associated State of Vietnam in March 1949, most Vietnamese regarded him as a mere puppet and his government won little support.

The war entered a new phase after the Communist victory in China in 1949. With military aid flowing across the border, Bao Dai's shaky government was seen as the last bastion of the free world; America was drawn in and funded the French military to the tune of at least $3 billion by 1954. The Viet Minh, under the command of General Giap, recorded their first major victory, forcing the French to abandon their outposts along the Chinese border and gaining unhindered access to sanctuary in China. Early in 1951, equipped with Chinese weapons and confident of success, the Viet Minh launched an assault on Hanoi itself, but in this first pitched battle of the war, suffered a massive defeat, losing over six thousand troops in a battle that saw napalm deployed for the first time in Vietnam. But Giap (known as "the snow-covered volcano" for his ice-cold exterior concealing a fiery temper) had learnt his lesson, and for the next two years the French sought in vain to repeat their success.

By now France was tiring of the war and in 1953 made contact with Ho Chi Minh to find some way of resolving the conflict. The Americans were growing increasingly impatient with French progress, and at one stage threatened to deploy tactical nuclear weapons against the Viet Minh; the Russians and Chinese were also applying pressure to end the fighting. Eventually, the two sides agreed to discussions at the Geneva Conference, due to take place in May the next year to discuss Korean peace. Meanwhile in Vietnam, a crucial battle was unfolding in an isolated valley on the Lao border, near the town of **Dien Bien Phu**. Early in 1954 French battalions established a massive camp here, deliberately trying to tempt the enemy into the open. Instead the Viet Minh surrounded the valley, cut off reinforcements and slowly closed in. After 59 days of bitter fighting the French were forced to surrender on May 7, 1954, the eve of the Geneva Conference. The eight years of war proved costly to both sides: total losses on the French side stood at 93,000, while an estimated two hundred thousand Viet Minh soldiers had been killed.

The Geneva Conference

On May 8, a day after the French capitulation at Dien Bien Phu, the nine delegations attending the **Geneva Conference** trained their focus upon Indochina. Armed with the knowledge that they now controlled around 65 percent of the country, the Viet Minh delegation arrived in buoyant mood. But the lasting peace they sought wasn't

1953	1954
French approach Ho Chi Minh for ceasefire.	End of French War – almost three hundred thousand lives had been lost, the majority Vietnamese.

forthcoming: hampered by distrust, the conference succeeded only in reaching a stopgap solution, a necessarily ambiguous compromise which, however, allowed the French to withdraw with some honour and recognized Vietnamese sovereignty at least in part. Keen to have a weak and fractured nation on their southern border, the Chinese delegation spurred the Viet Minh into agreeing to a division of the country; reliant upon Chinese arms, the Viet Minh were forced to comply.

Under the terms of July 1954's **Geneva Accords** Vietnam was divided at the Seventeenth Parallel, along the Ben Hai River, pending nationwide free elections to be held by July 1956; a demilitarized buffer zone was established on either side of this military front. France and the Viet Minh, who were still fighting in the central highlands even as delegates machinated, agreed to an immediate ceasefire, and consented to a withdrawal of all troops to their respective territories – Communists to the north, non-Communists plus supporters of the French to the south. China, the USSR, Britain, France and the Viet Minh agreed on the accords, but crucially neither the United States nor Bao Dai's government endorsed them, fearing that they heralded a reunited, Communist-ruled Vietnam.

In the long term, the Geneva Accords served to cause a deep polarization within the country and to widen the conflict into an ideological battle between the superpowers, fought out on Vietnamese soil. The immediate consequence, however, was a massive exodus from the north during the stipulated three hundred-day period of "**free movement**". Almost a million (mostly Catholic) refugees headed south, their flight aided by the US Navy, and to some extent engineered by the CIA, whose distribution of scaremongering, anti-Communist leaflets was designed to create a base of support for the puppet government it was concocting in Saigon. Approaching a hundred thousand **anti-French guerrillas** and sympathizers moved in the opposite direction to regroup, though, as a precautionary measure, between five and ten thousand Viet Minh cadres remained in the south, awaiting orders from Hanoi. These dormant operatives, known to the CIA as "**stay-behinds**" and to the Communists as "winter cadres", were joined by spies who infiltrated the Catholic move south. In line with the terms of the ceasefire, Ho Chi Minh's army marched into Hanoi on October 9, 1954, even as the last French forces were still trooping out.

The Geneva Accords were still being thrashed out as Emperor Bao Dai named himself president and **Ngo Dinh Diem** ("Zee-em") prime minister of South Vietnam, on July 7. A Catholic, and vehemently anti-Communist, Diem knew that Ho Chi Minh would win the lion's share of votes in the proposed elections, and therefore steadfastly refused to countenance them. His mandate "strengthened" by an October 1955 **referendum** (the prime minister's garnering of 98.2 percent of votes cast was more indicative of the blatancy of his vote-rigging than of any popular support), Diem promptly ousted Bao Dai from the chain of command, and declared himself president of the Republic of Vietnam.

Diem's heavy-handed approach to Viet Minh dissidents still in the South was hopelessly misguided: although the subsequent **witch-hunt** decimated Viet Minh numbers, the brutal and indiscriminate nature of the operation caused widespread discontent – all dissenters were targeted, Viet Minh, Communist or otherwise. As the supposed "free world democracy" of the South mutated into a police state, over fifty thousand citizens died in Diem's pogrom.

1954	**1956**
Geneva Accords divide Vietnam at the Seventeenth Parallel.	Rectification of Errors Campaign begins.

Back in Hanoi…
In Hanoi, meanwhile, Ho Chi Minh's government was finding it had problems of its own as, aided by droves of Chinese advisers, it set about constructing a socialist society. Years of warring with France had profoundly damaged the country's infrastructure, and now it found itself deprived of the South's plentiful rice stocks. Worse still, the **land reforms** of the mid-1950s, vaunted as a Robin Hood-style redistribution of land, saw thousands of innocents "tried" as landlords by ad hoc **People's Agricultural Reform Tribunals**, tortured and then executed or set to work in labour camps. "Reactionaries" were also denounced and punished, often for such imperialist "crimes" as possessing works of the great French poets and novelists. The **Rectification of Errors Campaign** of 1956 at least released many victims of the reforms from imprisonment, but as Ho Chi Minh himself said, "one cannot wake the dead".

With Hanoi so preoccupied with getting its own house in order, Viet Minh guerrillas south of the Seventeenth Parallel were for several years left to fend for themselves. For the most part, they sat tight in the face of Diem's reprisals, although guerrilla strikes became increasingly common towards the end of the 1950s, often taking the form of assassinations of government officials. Only in 1959 did the erosion of their ranks prompt Hanoi to shift up a gear and endorse a more overtly military stance. Conscription was introduced in April 1960, cadres and hardware began to creep down the **Ho Chi Minh Trail** (see p.316), and at the end of the year Hanoi orchestrated the creation of the **National Liberation Front** (NLF), which drew together all opposition forces in the South. Diem dubbed its guerrilla fighters **Viet Cong**, or VC (Vietnamese Communists) – a name which stuck, though in reality the NLF represented a united front of Catholic, Buddhist, Communist and non-Communist nationalists.

The American War
American dollars had been supporting the French war effort in Indochina since 1950. In early 1955 the White House began to bankroll Diem's government and the training of his army, the **ARVN** (Army of the Republic of Vietnam). Behind these policies lay the fear of the chain reaction that could follow in Southeast Asia, were South Vietnam to be overrun by Communism – the so-called **Domino Effect** – and, more cynically, what this would mean for US access to raw materials, trade routes and markets. Though President John F. Kennedy baulked at the prospect of large-scale American intervention, by the summer of 1962 there were twelve thousand American advisers in South Vietnam.

Despite all these injections of money, Diem's incompetent and unpopular government was losing ground to the Viet Cong in the battle for the hearts and minds of the population. Particularly damaging to the government was its **Strategic Hamlets Programme**. Formulated in 1962 and based on British methods used during the Malayan Emergency, the programme forcibly relocated entire villages into fortified stockades, with the aim of keeping the Viet Cong at bay. Ill-conceived, insensitive and open to exploitation by corrupt officials, the programme had the opposite effect, driving many disgruntled villagers into the arms of the resistance. In fact, the majority of strategic hamlets were empty within two years, as villagers drifted back to their ancestral lands.

Militarily, things were little better. If America needed proof that Diem's government was struggling to subdue the guerrillas, it came in January 1963, at the **Battle of Ap Bac**,

1959	1960	1962
Hanoi adopts tougher military stance against guerrillas.	Conscription introduced.	Twelve thousand American advisers in Vietnam.

where incompetent ARVN troops suffered heavy losses against a greatly outnumbered Viet Cong force. Four months later, Buddhists celebrating Buddha's birthday were fired upon by ARVN soldiers in Hué, sparking off riots and demonstrations against religious repression, and provoking **Thich Quang Duc**'s infamous self-immolation in Saigon (see box, p.80). Fearing that the Communists would gain further by Diem's unpopularity, America tacitly sanctioned his ousting in a **coup** on November 1; Diem escaped with his brother to Cho Lon, only to be shot the following day.

The capital staggered from coup to coup, but corruption, nepotism and dependence upon American support remained constant. In the countryside, meanwhile, the Viet Cong were forging a solid base of popular support. Observing Southern instability, Hanoi in early 1964 proceeded to send battalions of **NVA** (North Vietnamese Army) infantrymen down the Ho Chi Minh Trail, with ten thousand Northern troops hitting the trail in the first year. For America, unwilling to see the Communists granted a say in the running of the South, yet unable to envisage Saigon's generals fending them off, the only option seemed to be to "**Americanize**" the conflict.

In August 1964, a chance came to do just that, when the American destroyer the USS *Maddox* allegedly suffered an unprovoked attack from North Vietnamese craft; two days afterwards, the *Maddox* and another ship, the *C Turner Joy*, reported a second attack. Years later it emerged that the *Maddox* had been taking part in a covert mission to monitor coastal installations, and that the second incident almost certainly never happened. Nevertheless, reprisals followed in the form of 64 **bombing** sorties against Northern coastal bases. And back in Washington, senators voted through the **Tonkin Gulf Resolution**, empowering Johnson to deploy regular American troops in Vietnam, "to prevent further aggression".

Operation Rolling Thunder

An NVA attack upon the highland town of Pleiku in February 1965 curtailed several months of US procrastination about how best to prosecute the war in Vietnam, and elicited **Operation Flaming Dart**, a concerted bombing raid on NVA camps above the Seventeenth Parallel. **Operation Rolling Thunder**, a sustained carpet-bombing campaign, kicked in a month later; by the time of its suspension three and a half years later its 350,000 sorties had seen twice the tonnage of bombs dropped (around eight hundred daily) as had fallen on all World War II's theatres of war. Despite such impressive statistics, Rolling Thunder failed either to break the North's sources and lines of supply, or to coerce Hanoi into a suspension of activities in the South. Bombing served only to strengthen the resilience of the North, whose population was mobilized to rebuild bridges, roads and railways as quickly as they were damaged. Moreover, NVA troops continued to infiltrate the South in increasing numbers.

As far back as 1954, the American politician William F. Knowland had warned that "using United States ground forces in the Indochina jungle would be like trying to cover an elephant with a handkerchief – you just can't do it". His words fell on deaf ears. The first regular **American troops** from the 3rd US Marine Division landed at Da Nang in March 1965; by the end of the year, two hundred thousand GIs were in Vietnam, and approaching half a million by the winter of 1967. In addition, there were large numbers of Australians and South Koreans, plus smaller units of New Zealanders, Thais and Filipinos. The war these troops fought was a dirty, dispiriting and frustrating

1963

Buddhists killed in Hué; Thich Quang
Duc sets fire to himself in protest.

THE HUMAN COST OF THE WAR IN VIETNAM

The **toll** of the American War in human terms is staggering. Of the 3.3 million Americans who served in Vietnam between 1965 and 1973, some 58,000 died and more than 150,000 received wounds that required hospital treatment. The ARVN lost 250,000 troops, while perhaps two million **civilians** were killed in the South. Hanoi declared that over two million North Vietnamese civilians and one million troops died during the war. Many more on both sides are still listed as "missing in action" (MIA). Since 1975, an estimated 35,000 people – a third of them children – have been killed by leftover ordnance, while **contamination** from Agent Orange and other chemicals continues to cause health problems (see p.474). In the US, some half a million veterans suffer from post-traumatic stress disorder, while **veteran suicides** have now exceeded the total number of US fatalities during the conflict.

one: for the most part, it was a guerrilla conflict against an invisible enemy able to disappear into the nearest village, leaving them unable to trust even civilians.

In the **North**, outrage at the merciless bombing campaign meted out by a remote foreign aggressor engendered a sense of anti-colonial purpose; in the **South**, there was only disorientation. To some, the immensity of the US presence seemed to preclude the possibility of a protracted conflict, and was therefore welcome; to others, it felt so much like an invasion, especially when GIs began to uproot them and destroy their land, that they supported or joined the NLF. The Viet Cong themselves were no angels, though, often imposing a reign of terror, augmented by summary executions of alleged traitors. What's more, successive Saigon governments were corrupt and unpopular, but the alternative was the Northern Communists so gruesomely depicted by American propaganda.

To survive, villagers quickly learned to react, and to say the right thing to the right person. Trying to appease the two sets of soldiers they encountered in the space of a day was like treading a tightrope for villagers, creating a climate of hatred and distrust that turned neighbours into informants. Since children were conscripted by whichever side reached them first, brothers and sisters often found themselves fighting on opposing sides.

The Tet Offensive

On January 21, 1968, around forty thousand NVA troops laid siege to a remote American military base at **Khe Sanh**, near the Lao border northwest of Hué. Wary that the confrontation might become an American Dien Bien Phu – an analogy that in reality held no water, given the US's superior air power – America responded, to borrow the military jargon of the day, "with extreme prejudice", notching up a Communist body count of over ten thousand in a carpet-bombing campaign graphically labelled "Niagara". However, such losses were seen as a necessary evil by the Communists, for whom Khe Sanh was primarily a decoy to steer US troops and attention away from the **Tet Offensive** that exploded a week later. In the early hours of January 31, a combined force of seventy thousand Communists (most of them Viet Cong) violated a New Year truce to launch offensives on over a hundred urban centres across the South. The campaign failed to achieve its objective of imposing Viet Cong representation in the Southern government; only in Hué did Viet Cong forces manage to hold out for more than a few days.

1965	1968
US Army launches massive carpet-bombing campaign known as Operation Rolling Thunder.	New Year's truce violated by Communist forces on the South, nicknamed the Tet Offensive. One hundred urban centres across the south attacked.

WAR TERMINOLOGY

A wholly unconventional conflict at the time, the American War gave birth to a whole raft of new terms, many of which have been reinforced through movies and other wars. Missions to flush active Viet Cong soldiers out of villages, which were initiated towards the end of 1965, became known as **Search and Destroy** operations; the most infamous of these resulted in the **My Lai massacre** (see p.245). In the highlands, **fire bases** were established, from where howitzers could rain fire upon NVA troop movements; elsewhere, **free fire zones** – areas cleared of villagers to enable bombing of their supposed guerrilla occupants – were declared. In addition, **scorched earth**, the policy of denuding and razing vast swathes of land in order to rob the Viet Cong of cover, was introduced. One such way of doing this was with the use of **Agent Orange**, another term that has gone down in infamy, as have specific missions such as **Operation Rolling Thunder**. And all the while, generals in the field were quick to establish that most symbolic arbiter in this bitter war, the **body count**, according to which missions succeeded or failed.

But success did register across the Pacific, where the offensive caused a sea change in popular perceptions of the war. Thus far, Washington's propaganda machine had largely convinced the public that the war in Vietnam was under control; events in 1968 flew in the face of this charade. Around two thousand American GIs had died during the Tet Offensive; but symbolically more damaging was the audacious assault mounted, on the first day of the offensive, by a crack Viet Cong commando team on the compound of the **US Embassy in Saigon**. The Communists had pierced the underbelly of the American presence in Vietnam: by the time the compound had been secured over six hours later, five Americans had died – and with them the popular conviction that the war was being won.

This shift in attitude was soon reflected in President Johnson's **vetoing** of requests for a massive troop expansion. On March 31, he announced a virtual cessation of bombing; a month later, the first bout of diplomatic sparring that was to grind on for five years was held in Paris; and, before the year was out, a full end to bombing had been declared.

Nixon's presidency

Richard Nixon's ill-fated term of office commenced in January 1969, on the back of a campaign in which he promised to "end the war and win the peace". His quest for a solution that would facilitate an American pull-out without tarnishing its image led Nixon to pursue the strategy of "**Vietnamization**", a gradual US withdrawal coupled with a stiffening of ARVN forces and hardware. Though the number of US troops in Vietnam reached an all-time peak of 540,000 early on in 1969, sixty thousand of these were home for Christmas, and by the end of 1970 only 280,000 remained. Over the same time period, ARVN numbers almost doubled, from 640,000 to well over a million.

However, the NVA had for several years been stockpiling both men and supplies in **Cambodia**, and in March 1969 US covert bombing of these targets commenced. Code-named **Operation Menu**, it lasted for fourteen months, yet elicited no outcry from Hanoi since they had no right to be in neutral Cambodia in the first place. The following spring, an American-backed coup replaced Prince Sihanouk of Cambodia

1969	**1973**
Death of Ho Chi Minh.	Peace treaty ends American War; millions died in the conflict, the vast majority of them Vietnamese.

with Lon Nol and thus eased access for US troops, and a **task force** of twenty thousand soldiers advanced on Communist installations there. The American public was outraged: dismayed that Nixon, far from closing down the war, was in fact widening the conflict, they rallied at mass anti-war demonstrations.

After **Ho Chi Minh's death** on September 2, 1969, the stop-start **peace talks** in Paris dragged along with Le Duc Tho representing the North, and Nixon's national security adviser Henry Kissinger at the American helm. Two stumbling blocks hindered any advancement: the North's insistence on a coalition government in the South with no place for then-president, Thieu, and the US insistence that all NVA troops should move north after a ceasefire. Tit-for-tat military offensives launched early in 1972 saw both sides attempting to strengthen their hand at the bargaining table: Hanoi launched its **Easter Offensive** on the upper provinces of the South; while Nixon countered by resuming the **bombing of the North**. Towards the year's end, negotiations recommenced, this time with Hanoi in a mood to compromise – not least because Nixon let rumours spread of his **Madman Theory**, which involved the use of nuclear weaponry – but the draft agreement produced in October (Nixon was keen to see a resolution before the US elections in Nov) was delayed by President Thieu in Saigon. By the time it was finalized in January 1973 Nixon had flexed his military muscles one last time, sanctioning the eleven-day **Christmas Bombing** of Hanoi and Hai Phong in which twenty thousand tonnes of ordnance was dropped and 1600 civilians perished.

Under the terms of the **Paris Accords**, signed on January 27 by the United States, the North, the South and the Viet Cong, a ceasefire was established, all remaining American troops were repatriated by April, and Hanoi and Saigon released their PoWs. The Paris talks failed to yield a long-term political settlement, instead providing for the creation of a **Council of National Conciliation**, comprising Saigon's government and the Communists, to sort matters out at some future date. The agreements allowed the NVA and ARVN troops to retain whatever positions they held. For this fudged deal, Kissinger and Le Duc Tho were awarded the Nobel Prize for peace, though only Kissinger accepted.

The fall of the South

The Paris Accords accomplished little beyond smoothing the US withdrawal from Vietnam: with the NVA allowed to remain in the South, it was only a matter of time before **renewed aggression** erupted. Thieu's ARVN, now numbering a million troops and in robust shape thanks to its new US-financed equipment, soon set about retaking territory lost to the North during the Easter Offensive. The Communists, on the other hand, were still reeling from losses accrued during that campaign. By 1974, things were beginning to sour for the South. An economy already weakened by heavy **inflation** was further drained by the **unemployment** caused by America's withdrawal; corruption in the military was rife, and unpaid wages led to a burgeoning desertion rate. By the end of the year, the South was ripe for the taking.

Received wisdom in Hanoi was that a slow build-up of arms in the South, in preparation for a conventional push in 1976, would be the wisest course of action. Then, over the Christmas period of 1974, an **NVA drive** led by General Tran overran the area north of Saigon now called Song Be Province. Duly encouraged, Hanoi went into action,

1976

Declaration of the unified Socialist
Republic of Vietnam.

and towns in the South fell like ninepins under the irresistible momentum of the **Ho Chi Minh Campaign**. Within two months, Communist troops had occupied Buon Ma Thuot, taking a mere 24 hours to finish a job they'd anticipated would require a week. Hué and Da Nang duly followed, and by April 21 Xuan Loc, the last real line of defence before Saigon, had also fallen. ARVN defiance disintegrated in the face of the North's unerring progress: a famous image from these last days shows a highway scattered with the discarded boots of fleeing Southern soldiers. President Thieu fled by helicopter to Taiwan, and leadership of Saigon's government was assumed by **General Duong Van Minh** ("Big Minh"). Minh held the post for just two days before NVA tanks crashed through the gates of the Presidential Palace and Saigon fell to the North on April 30. Only hours before, the last Americans and other Westerners in the city had been **airlifted out** in the frantic helicopter operation known as "Frequent Wind" (see p.82).

Socialist Vietnam

By July 1976, Vietnam was once again a **unified nation** for the first time since the French colonization in the 1850s. At first the new leaders trod softly, softly in order to impress the international community, but Southerners eyed the future with profound apprehension. Their fears were well founded, as Hanoi was in no mood to grant Saigon autonomy: the Council of National Reconciliation, provided for by the Paris Accords, was never established, and the NLF's **Provisional Revolutionary Government** worked beneath the shadow of the Military Management Committee, and therefore Hanoi, until the **Socialist Republic of Vietnam** was officially born, in July 1976. The impression of a conquering army was exacerbated when Northern cadres – the *can bo* – swarmed south to take up all official posts.

Monumental **problems** faced the nascent republic. For many years, the two halves of Vietnam had lived according to wildly variant political and economic systems. The North had no industry, its agriculture based on cooperative farms, and much of its land had been ravaged during the war. In stark contrast, American involvement in the South had underwritten what John Pilger describes as "an 'economy' based upon the services of maids, pimps, whores, beggars and black-marketeers", buttressed by American cash that dried up when the last helicopter left the embassy in Saigon.

The changes that swept the country weren't limited to economics. Bitterness on Hanoi's part towards its former enemies was inevitable, yet instead of making moves towards national conciliation – and despite the fact that many families had connections in both camps – recriminations drove further wedges between the peoples of North and South. Anyone with remote connections to America was interned in a **re-education camp**, along with Buddhist monks, priests, intellectuals and anyone else the government wanted to be rid of. Hundreds of thousands of Southerners were sent to these camps, without trial. Some were to remain encarcerated for over a decade. The quagmire Vietnam found itself in after reunification prompted many of its citizens to flee the country in unseaworthy vessels, an exodus of humanity known as the **boat people** (see box opposite).

While all this was going on, just three weeks before the fall of Saigon in 1975 **Pol Pot**'s genocidal regime seized power in Cambodia: within a year his troops were making **cross-border forays** into regions of Vietnam that had once fallen under Khmer sway,

1979

The "boat people" start to flee Vietnam in large numbers, and would continue to do so until the 1990s.

1979

Chinese launch invasion of northern Vietnam, but retreat after only sixteen days.

THE "BOAT PEOPLE"

In 1979 the attention of the world was caught by images of rickety fishing boats packed with Vietnamese **refugees** seeking sanctuary in Hong Kong and other Southeast Asian harbours. An untold number – some say a third – fell victim to typhoons, starvation and disease or pirates, who often sank the boats after raping the women and seizing the refugees' meagre possessions. Others somehow fetched up on the coast of Australia or were picked up by passing freighters. The prime destination, however, was Hong Kong, where 68,000 asylum-seekers arrived in 1979 alone. The exodus was at its peak in 1979, but it had been going on, largely unnoticed, since reunification four years earlier, and continued up to the early 1990s. Over this period an estimated 840,000 boat people arrived safely in "ports of first asylum", of whom more than 750,000 were eventually resettled overseas.

The first refugees were mostly **Southerners**, people who felt themselves too closely associated with the old regime or their American allies, and feared Communist reprisals. Some were former nationalists and a few were even ex-Viet Cong, disillusioned with the new government's extremism. Then, in early 1978, nationalization of private commerce was instituted in the South, hitting hard at the **Chinese** community, which controlled much Southern business and the all-important rice trade. As anti-Chinese sentiment took hold, thousands made their escape in fishing boats followed in the late 1970s by more **Vietnamese**, driven by a series of bad harvests, severe hardship and the prospect of prolonged military service in Cambodia.

By 1979 the situation had become so critical that the international community was forced to act, offering asylum to the more than two hundred thousand refugees crowding temporary camps around Southeast Asia. Under the auspices of the UN, the **Orderly Departure Programme** (ODP) also enabled legal emigration of political refugees to the West, resettling over half a million in more than forty Western countries.

In 1987, the South China Sea was once again full of Vietnamese people in overcrowded boats. This **second wave** were mostly Northerners fleeing desperate poverty rather than fear of persecution, with Hong Kong again bearing the brunt of new arrivals. Governments were less sympathetic this time round and, in an attempt to halt the flow, from early 1989 boat people were denied automatic refugee status. Instead, a screening process was introduced to identify "genuine" refugees; the rest, designated "economic migrants", were encouraged to return under the **Voluntary Repatriation Scheme**, which offered concrete assistance with resettlement.

Then, in early 1996, all parties finally agreed that the only "viable solution" was to send the remaining forty thousand failed asylum-seekers still in Southeast Asian camps back home. In theory deportations were to take place "without threat or use of force", though clashes with security forces became more violent as the programme gained momentum. The situation was worst in Hong Kong, where there was pressure to clear the camps before the handover to China in 1997. The rate of repatriation – both voluntary and, increasingly, forced – was stepped up throughout the region and by mid-1997 nearly all the boat people had been either resettled or returned to Vietnam.

The UN High Commission for Refugees (UNHCR), which monitored returnees in Vietnam up until 2000, said there was little evidence of persecution or discrimination. Others, however, claimed that the monitoring was inadequate and ineffective, and cited examples of returnees being imprisoned. At the same time, various international bodies, such as the European Union, helped returnees reintegrate into the community through job creation schemes, vocational training programmes and low-interest loans. In 1998, a scheme known as ROVR got under way, resettling mostly Southerners who were able to prove some sort of relationship with the Americans during the war.

As the Vietnamese economy improved and as relations between America and Vietnam started to thaw around the turn of the millennium, so the ODP and ROVR programmes were gradually wound up. Their completion marked the end – at least as far as officialdom was concerned – of the whole sorry saga of the boat people.

around the Mekong Delta and north of Ho Chi Minh City (as Saigon had been renamed). One such venture led to the massacre at **Ba Chuc** (see p.157), in which almost two thousand people died. Reprisals were slow in coming, but by 1978 Vietnam could stand back no longer; on Christmas Day of that year 120,000 **Vietnamese troops invaded Cambodia** and ousted Pol Pot. Whatever the motives for the invasion, and even though it brought an end to Pol Pot's reign of terror, Vietnam was further ostracized by the international community. In February 1979, Beijing's response came in the form of a punitive **Chinese invasion** of Vietnam's northeastern provinces; Chinese losses were heavy, and after sixteen days they retreated. Meanwhile, Pol Pot had withdrawn across the Thai border, from where he commanded his army in their continued attack on the occupying Vietnamese forces. The Vietnamese remained in Cambodia until September 1989, by which time they had defeated the Khmer Rouge at the expense of fifty thousand soldiers, the majority of them Southern conscripts.

Doi Moi

A severe famine in 1985 and the 775 percent inflation that crippled the country in 1986 were just two of the many symptoms of the **economic malaise** threatening to tear Vietnam apart during the late 1970s and early 1980s. An experimental hybrid of planned and market economies tried out in 1979 came to nothing, and by the early 1980s the only thing keeping Vietnam afloat was Soviet aid. Treaties made it illegal for Americans to do business with the Vietnamese, who, largely due to American pressure, were unable to look to the IMF or World Bank for development loans.

The party's conservative old guard resisted change for as long as it could, but the death of General Secretary Le Duan in 1986 finally cleared the way for more reformist politicians to attempt to reverse the country's fortunes: **Nguyen Van Linh** took over as general secretary, and a raft of market-based economic reforms, known as **doi moi** or "renovation", followed. This encompassed limited moves towards decentralization and privatization; collectivized agriculture was abandoned in favour of individual land-holdings and attempts were made to attract foreign capital by liberalizing foreign investment regulations. Political reforms came a poor second, although the congress did instigate purges on corrupt officialdom and gave the press freer rein to criticize. With the **collapse of Communism** across Europe in 1989, though, the press was again silenced, and in a keynote speech Nguyen Van Linh rejected the concept of a multi-party state; all economic reforms, however, remained in place, and the government set in motion efforts to end Vietnam's isolation.

International rehabilitation, which had already begun with the withdrawal of troops from Cambodia in 1989, gathered momentum in the 1990s, as efforts to aid the US search teams looking for remains of the two thousand-plus American soldiers still unaccounted for (MIAs, or Missing in Action) were stepped up. In 1993, a year after the reformist **Vo Van Kiet** became prime minister, the Americans duly lifted their veto on aid, and Western cash began to flow. By the year's end, inflation was down to five percent. The rapprochement with the US continued into 1994, as the US trade embargo was lifted by President Clinton, and in February 1995 the two countries opened liaison offices in each other's capitals. Vietnam was admitted into **ASEAN** (the Association of Southeast Asian Nations) in July 1995, and the same month saw full **diplomatic relations restored** with the US.

1986	**1995**
Nguyen Van Linh becomes General Secretary of Socialist Party; inaugurates doi moi policy.	Full diplomatic relations restored with the US.

During the next two years foreign investment continued to flood in, pushing economic growth rates close to ten percent per annum. Revenues from oil, manufacturing and tourism took off and everyone was forecasting Vietnam as the next **Asian tiger**. For all the optimism, however, cracks were beginning to appear: the economic upturn was benefiting city-dwellers (particularly in Ho Chi Minh City) far more than the rural population; top bureaucrats were openly criticized in **corruption** scandals; and an alarmed government launched a campaign against "**social evils**" – videos, advertising, pornography and other Western imports which were seen to be undermining traditional society.

By 1997 the honeymoon period was definitely over. Economic growth flagged as foreign companies scaled back, or pulled out altogether, frustrated by an overblown bureaucracy, miles of red tape and regulations in a constant state of flux. As the economic crisis in Southeast Asia took hold, Vietnam's mostly inefficient, state-run industries became increasingly uncompetitive, and smuggling grew at an alarming rate. In May 1997, widespread corruption, growing agricultural unemployment and the ever-widening gulf between urban and rural Vietnam sparked off **demonstrations** by thousands of dissatisfied farmers in Thai Binh Province, part of the traditionally Communist north.

The twenty–first century

National **elections** in July 1997 brought a long-awaited change of government, ushering in a band of younger, more worldly wise ministers under Prime Minister **Phan Van Khai**, who was re-elected in 2002. In 2006 his chosen successor **Nguyen Tan Dung** took over, continuing Khai's economic reforms – no simple task given the inherent constraints of a "state capitalism" system – and the battle against corruption, resulting in a number of high-profile **anti-corruption trials**. Meanwhile, the progress of **international reconciliation** and **trade liberalization** included the ratification in 2001 of a bilateral trade agreement between Vietnam and America, and membership of the World Trade Organization (WTO) in late 2006.

Healthy increases in GDP per head disguise the fact that Vietnam is still finding its feet economically; in 2010 there were genuine fears of a full market collapse. In addition, progress on **human rights** has been erratic to say the least. In 2009, Le Cong Dinh, a local lawyer who had been involved with a number of high-profile human rights cases was arrested; his detention was roundly criticized by Amnesty International and other international organisations. Despite these problems, some Quality of Life indicators seem to be heading the right way, albeit from very low bases: according to World Bank figures, the number of Vietnamese living in poverty has dropped from seventy percent in the 1980s to under fifteen percent today, child mortality has fallen, literacy levels are well over ninety percent, and the average life expectancy is now around 75 years, compared to 65 in 1990.

2006

Vietnam joins the WTO.

Religion and beliefs

The moral and religious life of most Vietnamese people is governed by a complex mixture of Confucian, Buddhist and Taoist philosophical teachings interwoven with ancestor worship and ancient, animistic practices. Incompatibilities are reconciled on a practical level into a single, functioning belief system whereby a family may maintain an ancestral altar in their home, consult the village guardian spirit, propitiate the God of the Hearth and take offerings to the Buddhist pagoda.

The primary influence on Vietnam's religious life has been Chinese. However, in southern Vietnam, which historically fell within the Indian sphere, small communities of Khmer and Cham still adhere to Hinduism, Islam and Theravada Buddhism brought direct from India. From the fifteenth century on, **Christianity** has also been a feature, represented largely by Roman Catholicism but with a small Protestant following in the south. Vietnam also claims a couple of home-grown religious **sects**, both products of political and social turmoil in the early twentieth century: Cao Dai and Hoa Hao.

The **political dimension** has never been far removed from religious affairs in Vietnam, as the world was made vividly aware by Buddhist opposition to the oppressive regime of President Diem in the 1960s. After 1975, the Marxist–Leninist government of

VIETNAMESE DEITIES

BUDDHIST DEITIES

A Di Da or **Amitabha** The Historical Buddha, the most revered member of the Buddhist pantheon in Vietnamese pagodas.

Avalokitesvara A bodhisattva often represented with many arms and eyes, being all-powerful, or as Quan Am (see below).

Di Lac or **Maitreya** The Future Buddha, usually depicted as chubby, with a bare chest and a huge grin, sitting on a lotus throne.

Ong Ac or **Trung Ac** One of the two guardians of the Buddhist religion, popularly known as Mister Wicked, who judges all people. He has a fierce red face and a reputation for severity – of which badly behaved children are frequently reminded.

Ong Thien or **Khuyen Thien** The second guardian of Buddhism is Mister Charitable, a white-faced kindly soul who encourages good behaviour.

Quan Am The Goddess of Mercy, adopted from the Chinese goddess, Kuan Yin. Quan Am is a popular incarnation of Avalokitesvara. She is usually represented as a graceful white statue, with her hand raised in blessing.

Thich Ca Mau Ni or **Sakyamuni** The Present Buddha, born Siddhartha Gautama, who founded Buddhism.

OTHER CHARACTERS

Ngoc Hoang The Jade Emperor, ruler of the Taoist pantheon who presides over heaven.

Ong Tau God of the Hearth, who keeps watch over every family and reports on the household to the Jade Emperor every New Year.

Quan Cong A Chinese general of the Han Dynasty revered for his loyalty, honesty and exemplary behaviour. Usually flanked by his two assistants.

Thanh Mau The Mother Goddess.

Thien Hau Protectress of Sailors.

Tran Vo Properly known as Tran Vo Bac De, Taoist Emperor of the North, who governs storms and generally harmful events.

reunified Vietnam declared the state atheist, while theoretically allowing people the right to practise their religion under the constitution. In reality, churches and pagodas were closed down, religious leaders sent for re-education, and followers discriminated against if not actively persecuted.

In 1992 the situation changed, with the right to **religious freedom** being reaffirmed in a new constitution. A number of high-profile prisoners held on religious grounds were released, while party leaders publicly demonstrated the new freedoms by visiting pagodas and churches. Consequently, an increasing number of Vietnamese are now openly practising their faith again. Indeed, as Vietnam faces the onslaught of new ideas and the "social evils" spawned by the breakdown of its moral codes, people are looking to religion both for personal guidance and as a stabilizing force in society. Despite such moves toward greater freedom of worship, however, the government continues to exercise close control on religious groups through such practices as monitoring appointments, training institutions and publications. It is regularly accused of failing to make real progress on **human rights** issues and came in for particularly severe criticism for its crackdown on ethnic minority Christians following widespread unrest in the central highlands in 2001 and 2004. Later in 2004 the US designated Vietnam a "Country of Particular Concern" because of its violations of religious freedom. The Vietnamese government subsequently released a number of prisoners and passed legislation outlawing forced recantations, amongst other measures. However, the European Parliament echoed the same concerns as recently as 2009, and international human rights organizations continue to criticize the Vietnamese government for its record on religious freedom and other human rights.

Ancestor worship

One of the oldest cults practised in Vietnam is that of ancestor worship, based on the fundamental principles of filial piety and of obligation to the past, present and future generations. No matter what their religion, virtually every Vietnamese household, even hardline Communist, will maintain an **ancestral altar** in the belief that the dead continue to live in another realm. Ancestors can intercede on behalf of their descendants and bring the family good fortune, but in return the living must pay respect, perform prescribed ceremonies and provide for their ancestors' wellbeing. At funerals and subsequent anniversaries, quantities of paper money and other **votive offerings** (these days including television sets and cars) are burnt, and choice morsels of food are regularly placed on the altar. Traditionally this is financed by the income from a designated plot of land, and it is the responsibility of the oldest, usually male, member of the family to organize the rituals, tend the altar and keep the ancestors abreast of all important family events; failure in any of these duties carries the risk of inciting peeved ancestors to make mischief.

The ancestral altar occupies a central position in the home. On it are placed several wooden tablets, one for each ancestor going back five generations. One hundred days after the funeral, the deceased's spirit returns to reside in the tablet. People without children to honour them by burning incense at the altar are condemned to wander the world in search of a home. Some childless people make provision by paying a temple or pagoda to observe the rituals, while the spirits of others may eventually take up residence in one of the small shrine houses (*cuong*) you see in fields and at roadsides. Important times for remembering the dead are **Tet**, the lunar new year, and **Thanh Minh** ("Festival of Pure Light"), which falls on the fifth day of the third lunar month.

Spirit worship

Residual animism plus a whole host of spirits borrowed from other religions have given Vietnam a complicated mystical world. The universe is divided into **three realms**: the

...arth and man, under the overall guardianship of Ong Troi, Lord of Heaven, ...d by spirits of the earth, mountains and water. Within the hierarchy are four ...d **animals** who appear everywhere in Vietnamese architecture: the dragon, representing the king, power and intelligence; the phoenix, embodying the queen, beauty and peace; the turtle, symbol of longevity and protector of the kingdom; and the mythical *kylin*, usually translated as unicorn, which represents wisdom.

In addition each village or urban quarter will venerate a **guardian spirit** in either a temple (*den*) or communal house (*dinh*). The deity may be legendary, for example the benevolent horse-spirit Bach Ma of Thang Long (modern Hanoi), and will often come from the Taoist pantheon. Or the guardian may be a historical figure such as a local or national hero, or a man of great virtue. In either case people will propitiate these tutelary spirits – represented on the altar by a gilded throne – with offerings, and will consult them in times of need. The *dinh* also serves as meeting house and school for the community.

Buddhism

The Buddha was born **Siddhartha Gautama** to a wealthy family sometime during the sixth century BC in present-day Nepal. At an early age he renounced his life of luxury to seek the ultimate deliverance from worldly suffering and strive to reach **nirvana**, an indefinable, blissful state. After several years Siddhartha attained enlightenment while sitting under a bodhi tree, and then devoted the rest of his life to teaching the **Middle Way** that leads to nirvana. The Buddha preached that existence is a cycle of perpetual reincarnation in which actions in one life determine one's position in the next, but that it is possible to break free by following certain precepts, central to which are non-violence and compassion. The Buddha's doctrine was based on the **Four Noble Truths**: existence is suffering; suffering is caused by desire; suffering ends with the extinction of desire; the way to end suffering is to follow the eightfold path of right understanding, thought, speech, action, livelihood, effort, mindfulness and concentration.

The history of Buddhism in Vietnam

It's estimated that up to two-thirds of the Vietnamese population consider themselves Buddhist. The vast majority are followers of the Mahayana school which was introduced to northern Vietnam via China in the second century AD. Within this, most Vietnamese Buddhists claim allegiance to the Pure Land sect (*Tinh Do*), which venerates A Di Da or Amitabha Buddha above all others, while the meditational Zen sect (*Thien*) has a moderate following, predominantly in northern Vietnam.

In fact Buddhism first arrived in southern Vietnam nearly one hundred years earlier as **Theravada**, or the "Lesser Vehicle", introduced via the Indian trade routes through Burma and Thailand. Theravada is an ascetical form of the faith based on the individual pursuit of perfection and enlightenment, which failed to find favour beyond the Khmer communities of the Mekong, where it still counts roughly one million followers. One of the salient features of **Mahayana** Buddhism, in contrast, is the belief that intermediaries – **bodhisattvas** – have chosen to forgo nirvana to work for the salvation of all humanity, and it was this that enabled Mahayana to adapt to a Vietnamese context by incorporating local gods and spirits into its array of bodhisattvas. The best-known bodhisattva is Avalokitesvara, usually worshipped in Vietnam as **Quan Am**, the Goddess of Mercy. Mahayana Buddhism spread through northern Vietnam until it became the **official state religion** after the country regained its independence from China in the tenth century. The Ly kings (1009–1225), in particular, were devout Buddhists who sponsored hundreds of pagodas, prompting a flowering of the arts, and established a hierarchy of monk–scholars as advisers to the court. Great landowning monasteries came into being and Buddhist doctrine was incorporated into the civil service

THE BUDDHIST PAGODA

The Vietnamese word *chua*, translated as "pagoda", is an exclusively Buddhist term, whereas a temple (*den*) may be Taoist, Confucian or house a guardian spirit. **Pagoda architecture** reached a pinnacle during the Ly and Tran dynasties, but thanks to Chinese invasions and local, anti-Buddhist movements few examples remain. A majority of those still in existence are eighteenth- or nineteenth-century constructions, though many retain features of earlier designs. Generally, pagoda **layout** is either an inverse T or three parallel lines of single-storeyed pavilions. The first hall is reserved for public worship, while those beyond, on slightly raised platforms, contain the prayer table and principal altar. Other typical elements are a **bell tower**, either integral to the building or standing apart, and a **walled courtyard** containing ponds, stone stelae and, particularly in Mahayana pagodas, the white figure of Quan Am symbolizing charity and compassion.

The most interesting feature inside the pagoda is often the **statuary**. Rows of Buddhas sit or stand on the main altar, where the Buddhist trinity occupies the highest level: A Di Da or Amitabha, the Historical Buddha; Thich Ca Mau Ni or Sakyamuni, born Siddhartha Gautama, the Present Buddha; and Di Lac, or Maitreya, the Future Buddha. Lower ranks comprise the same characters in a variety of forms accompanied by bodhisattvas: look out for pot-bellied Maitreya as the laughing carefree Buddha who grants wishes; the omnipotent Avalokitesvara of a "thousand" arms and eyes; and the Nine Dragon Buddha (Tuong Cuu Long). This latter is a small statue, found more often in northern Vietnam, of Sakyamuni encircled by dragons, standing with one hand pointing to the sky and the other to the earth. According to legend, nine dragons descended from the sky to bathe the newborn Buddha, after which he took seven steps forward and proclaimed, "on earth and in the sky, I alone am the highest".

Two unmistakable figures residing in all pagodas are the giant **guardians of Buddhist law**: white-faced "Mister Charitable" (Ong Thien), holding a pearl, and red-faced "Mister Wicked" (Ong Ac). Ong Thien sees everything, both the good and the bad, while Ong Ac dispenses justice. From an artistic point of view, some of the most fascinating statues are the lifelike representations of *arhats*, ascetic Buddhist saints; the best examples are found in northern pagodas, where each figure is portrayed in a disturbingly realistic style. Finally, Mahayana pagodas will undoubtedly welcome in a few **Taoist spirits**, the favourites being Thien Hau, the Protectress of Sailors, and Thanh Mau, the Mother Goddess. Somewhere in the pagoda halls will be an altar dedicated to deceased monks or nuns, while larger pagodas usually maintain a garden for their burial stupas. Traditionally Buddhists would bury their dead, but increasingly they practise cremation.

The **best times to visit** a pagoda are the first and fifteenth days of the lunar month (new moon and full moon), when they are at their busiest. Note that it's customary to remove your shoes when stepping on the floor mats and sometimes when entering the main sanctuary – watch what the locals do, or ask, to be on the safe side.

examinations along with Confucian and Taoist texts as part of the "triple world-view", *Tam Giao*. At the same time it became apparent that Buddhism was unable to provide the unifying ideology required by a highly centralized state constantly fighting for its survival. Consequently, by the mid-fourteenth century Buddhism had lost its political and economic influence and, when the Later Le Dynasty came to power in 1427, Confucianism finally eclipsed it as the dominant national philosophy.

But by then Buddhism was too deeply rooted, particularly in the folk religion of the countryside, to lose its influence completely. It enjoyed further brief periods of **royal patronage**, notably during the seventeenth and eighteenth centuries when new pagodas were built and old ones repaired. To many people it still offered a spiritual element lacking in Confucian doctrine, and during the colonial era Vietnamese intellectuals turned to Buddhism in search of a national identity. Since then the Buddhist community has been a focus of **dissent**, not least in the 1960s when images of self-immolating Buddhist monks focused world attention on the excesses of South Vietnam's Catholic President Diem. At the time, protesting Buddhists were accused of being pro-Communist, although their standpoint was essentially neutral. In the event they experienced even greater repression after reunification when pagodas were closed, and monks and nuns were sent to re-education camps.

The situation has eased considerably in recent years, and pagodas affiliated to the officially recognized Vietnam Buddhist Sangha (VBS) have been allowed to resume their social and educational programmes to a certain extent. Many pagodas, now bustling with life again, have been renovated after years of neglect. Nevertheless, the government continues to exert control over the VBS and Buddhist leaders have persisted in their denunciations of the regime. At a time when the country's leaders are seeking international approval, the monks' campaign for **human rights** is causing them acute embarrassment. In particular, the authorities refuse to recognize the Unified Buddhist Church of Vietnam (UBCV), the main pre-1975 Buddhist organization. According to international human rights bodies, its leaders are regularly placed under "house arrest" without any official charges being made against them.

Confucianism

The teachings of Confucius provide a guiding set of moral and ethical principles, an **ideology** for the state's rulers and subjects onto which ritualistic practices have been grafted.

Confucius is the Latinized name of K'ung-Fu-Tzu (Khong Tu in Vietnamese), who was born into a minor aristocratic family in China in 551 BC. At this time China was in turmoil as the Zhou Dynasty dissolved into rival feudal states battling for supremacy. Confucius worked for many years as a court official, where he observed the nature of power and the function of government at close quarters. At the age of 50, he packed it all in and for the next twenty years wandered the country spreading his ideas on social and political reform in an effort to persuade states and individuals to live peacefully together for their mutual benefit. His central tenet was the importance of **correct behaviour** and **loyal service**, reinforced by ceremonial rites whereby the ruler maintains authority through good example rather than force. Important qualities to strive for are selflessness, respectfulness, sincerity and non-violence; the ideal person should be neither heroic nor extrovert, but instead follow a "golden mean". Confucius remained silent on spiritual matters, though he placed great emphasis on observing ancient rituals such as making offerings to heaven and to ancestors.

Confucian **teachings** were handed down in the *Analects*, but he is also credited with editing the Six Classics, among them the *Book of Changes* (*I Ching*) and the *Book of Ritual* (*Li Chi*). Later these became the basic texts for civil service examinations, ensuring that all state officials had a deeply ingrained respect for tradition and social order. Though Confucianism ultimately led to national inflexibility and the undermining of personal initiative, its positive legacy has been an emphasis on the value of education and a belief that individual merit is of greater consequence than high birth.

After the death of Confucius in 478 BC the doctrine was developed further by his **disciples**, the most famous of whom was Mencius (Meng-tzu). By the first century AD, Confucianism, which slowly absorbed elements of Taoism, had evolved into a cult and also become the state ideology whereby kings ruled under the Mandate of Heaven. Social stability was maintained through a fixed hierarchy of interdependent relationships encapsulated in the notion of filial piety. Thus children must obey their parents without question, wives their husbands, students their teacher and subjects their ruler. For their part, the recipient, particularly the king, must earn this obedience; if the rules are broken, the harmony of society and nature is disturbed and authority loses its legitimacy. Therefore, by implication, revolution was justified when the king lost his divine right to rule.

The history of Confucianism in Vietnam

Confucian thinking has pervaded Vietnamese society ever since Chinese administrators introduced the concepts during the second century BC. Reinforced by a thousand years of Chinese rule, Confucianism (*Nho Giao*) came to play an essential role in

Vietnam's political, social and educational systems. The philosophy was largely one of an intellectual elite, but Confucian teaching eventually filtered down to the village level where it had a profound influence on the Vietnamese family organization.

The ceremonial **cult of Confucius** was formalized in 1070 when King Ly Thanh Tong founded the Temple of Literature in Hanoi. But it wasn't until the foundation of the Later Le Dynasty in 1427 that Confucian doctrine gained supremacy over Buddhism in the Vietnamese court. The Le kings viewed Confucian ideology, with its emphasis on social order, duty and respect, as an effective means of consolidating their new regime. In 1442, they overhauled the education system and based it on a curriculum of Confucian texts. They also began recruiting top-level mandarins through doctoral examinations, which eventually gave rise to a scholar-gentry class at the expense of the old landed aristocracy. Confucian influence reached its peak during the reign of King Le Thanh Tong (1460–97), which heralded a golden age of bureaucratic reform when public service on behalf of both community and state became a noble ideal. At the same time, however, a strongly centralized administration, presided over by a divine ruler and a mandarin elite, eventually bred corruption, despotism and an increasingly rigid society. The arrival of Western ideas and French rule in the late nineteenth century finally undermined the political dominance of Confucianism, though it managed to survive as the court ideology until well into the twentieth century. The cult of Confucius continues in a few temples (*Van Mieu*) dedicated to the sage, and he also appears on other altars as an honoured ancestor, an exemplary figure remembered for services to the nation.

Many **Confucian ideals** have been completely assimilated into Vietnamese society. After Independence, the Communist Party struggled against inherent conservatism and the supremacy of the family as a political unit; indeed, leaders can still be heard railing against the entrenched "feudal" nature of rural Vietnam. But the party was also able to tap into those elements of the Confucian tradition that suited their new classless, socialist society: conformity, duty and the denial of personal interest for the common good. Today, however, Confucian ideals are being seriously undermined by the invasion of materialism and individual ambition.

Taoism

Taoism is based on the **Tao-te-Ching**, the "Book of the Way", traditionally attributed to **Lao-tzu** (meaning "Old Master"), who is thought to have lived in China in the sixth century BC. The Tao, the Way, emphasizes effortless action, intuition and spontaneity; the Tao is invisible and impartial; it cannot be taught, nor can it be expressed in words. It is the one reality from which everything is born, universal and eternal. However, by virtuous, compassionate and non-violent behaviour, it is possible to achieve ultimate stillness, through a mystical and personal quest. Taoism thus preached non-intervention, passivity and the futility of academic scholarship; Confucians viewed it as suspiciously subversive.

Chinese immigrants brought Taoism (*Dao Giao*) to Vietnam during the long period of Chinese rule (111 BC–939 AD). Between the eleventh and fourteenth centuries the philosophy enjoyed equal status with Buddhism and Confucianism as one of Vietnam's three "religions", but Taoism gradually declined until it eventually became a strand of folk religion. A few Taoist temples (*quan*) exist in Vietnam but on the whole its deities have been absorbed into other cults. The Jade Emperor, for example, frequently finds himself part of the Buddhist pantheon in Vietnamese pagodas.

Central to the Tao is the **duality** inherent in nature; the whole universe is in temporary balance, a tension of complementary opposites defined as **yin** and **yang**, the male and female principles. Yang is male, the sun, active and orthodox; yin is female, the earth, flexible, passive and instinctive. Harmony is the balance between the two, and experiencing that harmony is the Tao. Accordingly all natural things can be categorized by their property of yin or yang, and human activity should strive not to disrupt that

> ### GEOMANCY
>
> The **practice of geomancy** is a pseudo-scientific study, much like astrology or reading horoscopes, which was introduced to Vietnam from China. The underlying idea is that every location has harmful or beneficial properties governed by its physical attributes, planetary influences and the flow of magnetic energy through the earth. Geomancy is used mainly in **siting buildings**, particularly tombs, palaces, temples and the like, but also ordinary dwellings.
>
> Geomancers analyse the general **topography** of the site, looking at the location of surrounding hills, as well as rivers, streams and other bodies of water, to find the most auspicious situation and orientation. They may suggest improving the area by adding small hills or lakes and, if a family suffers bad fortune, a geomancer may be called in to divine the cause of the imbalance and restore the natural harmony.

balance. In its pure form Taoism has no gods, only emanations of the Tao, but in the first century AD it corrupted into an organized religion venerating a deified Lao-tzu. The new cult had popular appeal since it offered the goal of immortality through yogic meditation and good deeds. Eventually the practice of Taoism developed highly complex **rituals**, incorporating magic, mysticism, superstition and the use of geomancy (see box above) to ensure harmony between man and nature, while astrology might be used to determine auspicious dates for weddings, funerals, starting a journey or even launching a new business. Ancient spirit worship, the cult of ancestors and the veneration of legendary or historic figures all fused happily with the Taoist idea of a universal essence.

The vast, eclectic pantheon of Taoist **gods and immortals** is presided over by Ngoc Hoang, the Jade Emperor. He is assisted by three ministers: Nam Tao, the southern star who records all births; Bac Dau, the north star who registers deaths; and Ong Tao, God of the Hearth who reports all happenings in the family household to Ngoc Hoang at the end of the year. Then there is a collection of immortals, genies and guardian deities, including legendary and historic figures. In Vietnam among the best known are Tran Vo, God of the North, Bach Ho, the White Tiger of the West and Tran Hung Dao, who protects the newborn and cures the sick. Confucius is also honoured as a Taoist saint. A distinctive aspect of Taoism is its use of **mediums** to communicate with the gods; the divine message is often in the form of a poem, transmitted by a writing brush onto sand or a bed of rice.

Christianity

Vietnam's **Catholic community** is the second largest in Southeast Asia after the Philippines. Exact figures are hard to come by but estimates vary between six and eight million (seven to ten percent of the population), of which perhaps two-thirds live in the south. The south is also home to the majority of the one million or so adherents to the **Protestant** faith, known as *Tin Lanh*, or the Good News, which was introduced by Canadian and American missionaries in the early twentieth century. Perhaps two-thirds of Protestants belong to ethnic-minority groups in the central highlands and northwest mountains. There's evidence that the number of adherents has been growing rapidly, despite government restrictions on proselytizing.

The first Christian **missionaries** to reach Vietnam were Portuguese and Spanish Dominicans who landed briefly on the north coast in the sixteenth century. They were followed in 1615 by French and Portuguese Jesuits, dispatched by the pope to establish the first permanent missions. Among the early arrivals was the Frenchman Alexandre de Rhodes, a Jesuit who impressed the northern Trinh lords and won, by his reckoning, nearly seven thousand converts. The inevitable **backlash** against Christianity, which opposed ancestor worship and espoused subversive ideas such as equality, was not long in coming. In 1630 the Trinh lords expelled all Christians, including de Rhodes, who returned to France where he helped create the Society of Foreign Missions (*Société des Missions Etrangères*). This society soon became the most active proselytizing body in

Indochina; by the end of the eighteenth century it had claimed thousands of converts, particularly in the coastal provinces.

Official attitudes towards Christianity fluctuated over the centuries, though the Vietnamese kings were generally suspicious of the Church's increasingly political role. The most violent **persecutions** occurred during the reign of Minh Mang (1820–41), an ardent Confucian, and reached a peak after 1832. Churches were destroyed, the faces of converts were branded with the words *ta dao*, meaning "false religion", and many of those refusing to renounce their faith were killed; 117 martyrs, both European and Asian, were later canonized. Such repression, much exaggerated at the time, provided the French with a pretext for greater involvement in Indochina, culminating in full colonial rule at the end of the nineteenth century.

European Influence

Not surprisingly, Catholicism **prospered** under the French regime. Missions re-opened and hundreds of churches, schools and hospitals were built. Vietnamese Catholics formed an educated elite among a population that counted some two million faithful by the 1950s. When partition came in 1954 many Catholics chose to move south, partly because of their opposition to Communism and partly because the new leader of South Vietnam, President Ngo Dinh Diem, was a Catholic. Of the estimated nine hundred thousand Vietnamese who left the North in 1954, it's said that around two-thirds were Catholic; many of these became refugees a second time in the 1970s.

Diem actively discriminated in favour of the Catholic community, which he viewed as a bulwark against Communism. As a result he alienated large sections of the population, most importantly Buddhists whose protests eventually contributed to his downfall. Meanwhile in North Vietnam the authorities trod fairly carefully with those Catholics who had chosen to stay, allowing them freedom to practise their religion, but the Church was severely restricted and reports of persecution persisted.

After reunification, churches were permitted to function but still came under strict **surveillance**, with all appointments controlled by the government, and members of the Church hierarchy frequently received heavy jail sentences for opposition to the regime. Since 1986 the party has been working to reduce the tension by re-opening seminaries, allowing the Church to resume religious educational work and releasing some clergy from prison. Catholics throughout Vietnam now regularly attend Mass, and, when the previous Cardinal of Hanoi died in 1990, thousands attended the funeral in the largest postwar demonstration of Catholic faith. Since the government still insists on vetting all appointments, it took more than seven years to find a new cardinal acceptable to both Vietnam and the Vatican. However, relations between the two continue to improve. All the bishoprics are now filled and there's even talk of re-establishing diplomatic relations in the not too distant future. A senior Vatican emissary visited Hanoi in 2005, though it will undoubtedly be several years before the much hoped-for papal visit occurs.

Protestant problems

The situation is not quite so rosy as regards Vietnam's **Protestant** communities. While the government now officially recognizes the Southern Evangelical Church of Vietnam (SECV) and the smaller Evangelical Church of Vietnam (ECVN), based in the north, it remains deeply suspicious of another evangelical branch known as "Dega Protestantism" practised mainly by the ethnic minorities of the **central highlands**. It's not so much the belief system itself that the authorities are concerned about, but the movement's potential as a political force and, specifically, its alleged association with demands from certain minority groups for greater autonomy. There have been (sometimes violent) clashes between ethnic minorities in the central highlands and the authorities in recent years (see p.455). While the protests were generally sparked by disputes over land and continued poverty, some demonstrators also cited **religious persecution** amongst their grievances. As a result, the government imposed significant restrictions on all Protestant churches in the region. The government continues to keep a close eye on all Christian activity in the central highlands – as recently as 2010 propaganda campaigns were launched against Catholic sects, and forced renunciation ceremonies took place in Gia Lai province.

Cao Dai

Social upheaval coupled with an injection of Western thinking in the early twentieth century gave birth to Vietnam's two indigenous religious sects, **Cao Dai** and Hoa Hao. Of the two, Cao Dai claims more adherents, with an estimated following of around two million in south Vietnam, plus a few thousand among overseas Vietnamese in America, Canada and Britain. The sect's headquarters, the **Holy See**, resides in a flamboyant cathedral at Tay Ninh (see p.112), where they also maintain a school, agricultural cooperative and hospital. Vietnam's most northerly Cao Dai congregation worships in Hué.

The religion of Cao Dai (meaning "high place") was revealed by the "Supreme Being" to a middle-aged civil servant working in Phu Quoc, called **Ngo Van Chieu**, during several trances over a period of years from 1919 to 1925. What Chieu preached to his followers was essentially a distillation of Vietnam's religious heritage: elements of Confucian, Taoist and Buddhist thought, intermixed with ancestor worship, Christianity and Islam. According to Cao Dai beliefs, all religions are different manifestations of one **meta-religion**, Cao Dai; in the past, this took on whatever form most suited the prevailing human need, but during the twentieth century could finally be presented in its unity. Thus the **Supreme Being**, who revealed himself in 1925, has had two earlier manifestations, always in human guise: the first in the sixth century BC, appearing as various figures from Buddhism, Taoism and Christianity among many other saints and sages; the second as Sakyamuni, Confucius, Jesus Christ, Mohammed and Lao-tzu. In the third manifestation the Supreme Being has revealed himself through his divine light, symbolized as an all-seeing Eye on a sky-blue, star-spangled globe.

Cao Dai **doctrine** preaches respect for all its constituent religions and holds that individual desires should be subordinate to the common interest. Adherents seek to escape from the cycle of reincarnation by following the five prohibitions: no violence, theft or lying – nor indulgence in alcohol or sexual activity; priests are expected to be completely vegetarian though others need only eschew meat on certain days of the lunar month. The Cao Dai **hierarchy** is modelled on that of the Catholic Church, and divides into nine ranks, of which the pope is the highest. Officials are grouped into three branches, identifiable by the colour of their ceremonial robes: the Confucian branch dresses in red, Buddhist in saffron and Taoist in blue. Otherwise practitioners wear white as a symbol of purity, and because it contains every colour.

Practising Cao Dai

The **rituals** of Cao Dai are a complex mixture of Buddhist and Taoist rites, including meditation and seances. Prayers take place four times a day in the temples (6am, noon, 6pm and midnight) though ordinary members are only required to attend on four days per month and otherwise can pray at home. Note that shoes should always be removed when entering a Cao Dai temple or mansion. At the start of the thirty-minute-long ceremony, worshippers file into the temple in three columns, women on the left, men in the middle and on the right; they then kneel and bow three times – to the Supreme Being, to the earth and to mankind. Cao Dai's most important **ceremony**, a sort of feast day for the Supreme Being, takes place on the ninth day of the first lunar month; other special observances are the day of Taoism (fifteenth day of the second month), Buddha's birthday (fifteenth of the fourth lunar month), the day of Confucius (28th of the eighth lunar month) and Christmas Day.

The religion of Cao Dai is further enlivened with a panoply of **saints**, encompassing the great and the good of many countries and cultures: Victor Hugo, Joan of Arc,

William Shakespeare, Napoleon Bonaparte, Lenin, Winston Churchill, Louis Pasteur and Sun Yat Sen, alongside home-grown heroes such as Tran Hung Dao and Le Loi. These characters fulfil a variety of roles from prophet to bodhisattva and even spirit medium, through which followers communicate with the Supreme Being. Contact can occur by means of a ouija board, messages left in sealed envelopes or through human mediums – who enter a trance and write using a planchette (a pencil secured to a wooden board on castors, on which the medium rests his hand, sometimes known as a *corbeille à bec*). Apparently, adherents of Cao Dai once appointed an official to take down the further works of Victor Hugo by dictation from his spirit.

The ideology, which had widespread appeal, attracted **converts** in their hundreds of thousands in the Mekong Delta, but only gained official recognition from the French colonial authorities in 1926. Over the next decade the Holy See developed into a **semi-autonomous state** wielding considerable political power and backed by a paramilitary wing which mustered around fifty thousand men in the mid-1950s. Although originally nationalist, Cao Dai followers clashed with Communist troops in a local power struggle, and the sect ended up opposing both the North Vietnamese and President Diem's pro-Catholic regime. Diem moved quickly to dismantle the army when he came to power and exiled its leaders; then after 1975 the Communists purged the religious body, closing down Cao Dai temples and schools, and sending priests for re-education. However, Cao Dai survived as a religion and has gained some **new adherents** since 1990 when its temples and mansions, approximately four hundred in all, were allowed to re-open, albeit under strict control.

Hoa Hao

The second of Vietnam's local sects, **Hoa Hao**, meaning "peace and kindness", emerged in the late 1930s near Chau Doc in the Mekong Delta (see p.151). The movement was founded by a young mystic, **Huynh Phu So**, who disliked mechanical ritual and preached a very pure, simple form of Buddhism that required no clergy or other intermediaries, and could be practised at home by means of meditation, fasting and prayer. Gambling, alcohol and opium were prohibited, while filial piety was once more invoked to promote social order.

As a young man Huynh Phu So was cured of a mysterious illness by the monks of Tra Son Pagoda near his home town of Chau Doc. He continued to live at the pagoda, studying under the monk Xom, but returned to his home village after Xom died. During a storm in 1939, So entered a trance from which he emerged to develop his own Buddhist way. The sect quickly gained followers and, like Cao Dai, was soon caught up in **nationalist politics**. To the French, So was a mad but dangerous subversive; they committed him to a psychiatric hospital (where he promptly converted his doctor to Hoa Hao), and then placed him under house arrest. During **World War II** Hoa Hao followers were armed by the Japanese and later continued to fight against the French while also opposing the Communists. At the end of the war Hoa Hao members formed an anti-Marxist political party, prompting the Viet Minh to assassinate So in 1947.

However, the movement continued to grow, its **private army** equalling the Cao Dai's in size, until Diem came to power and effectively crushed the sect's political and military arm. The sect then splintered, with some members turning to the National Liberation Front, while most sided with the Americans. As a result, when the Communists took over in 1975 many Hoa Hao leaders were arrested and its priesthood was disbanded. Nevertheless some claim that there are now over 1.5 million Hoa Hao practising in the Mekong Delta. The government recognized the principal Hoa Hao sect in 1999, although its more radical offshoots, which are accused of anti-government activities, remain outlawed.

Vietnam's ethnic minorities

The population of Vietnam currently numbers just over ninety million people, of whom around 86 percent are ethnic Vietnamese (known as Viet or Kinh), while almost nine hundred thousand are Chinese, or Hoa, in origin. The remaining eleven million people comprise 53 ethnic minority groups divided into dozens of subgroups, some with a mere hundred or so members, giving Vietnam the richest and most complex ethnic make-up in the whole of Southeast Asia. The vast majority of Vietnam's minorities live in the hilly regions of the north and central highlands – all areas that saw heavy fighting in recent wars – and several groups straddle today's international boundaries.

Little is known about the origins of many of these people, some of whom already inhabited the area before the ancestors of the **Viet** arrived from southern China around four to five thousand years ago. At some point the Viet emerged as a distinct group from among the various indigenous peoples living around the Red River Delta and then gradually absorbed smaller communities until they became the dominant culture. Other groups continued to interact with the Viet people, but either chose to maintain their independence in the highlands or were forced up into the hills, off the ever-more-crowded coastal plains.

Vietnamese legend accounts for this fundamental split between **lowlanders** and **highlanders** as follows: the Dragon King of the south married Au Co, a beautiful northern princess, and at first they lived in the mountains where she gave birth to a hundred strong, handsome boys. After a while, however, the Dragon King missed his watery, lowland home and decamped with half his sons, leaving fifty behind in the mountains – the ancestors of the ethnic minorities.

Vietnam's ethnic groups are normally differentiated according to three main **linguistic families** – Austronesian, Austro-Asian and Sino-Tibetan – which are further subdivided into smaller groups, such as the Viet–Muong and Tay–Thai language groups. Austronesians, related to Indonesians and Pacific Islanders, were probably the earliest inhabitants of the area but are now restricted to the central highlands. Peoples of the two other linguistic families originated in southern China and at different times migrated southwards to settle throughout the Vietnamese uplands.

Despite their different origins, languages, dialects and hugely varied traditional dress, there are a number of similarities among the highland groups that distinguish them from Viet people. Most immediately obvious is the **stilthouse**, which protects against snakes, vermin and larger beasts as well as floods, while also providing safe stabling for domestic animals. The communal imbibing of **rice wine** is popular with most highland groups, as are certain **rituals** such as protecting a child from evil spirits by not naming it until after a certain age. Most highlanders traditionally practise **swidden farming**, clearing patches of forest land, farming the burnt-over fields for a few years and then leaving it fallow for a

VIETNAM'S MOST COLOURFUL MINORITY PEOPLE

White Thai	Mai Chau (p.418)	Red Zao	Sa Pa (p.400)
Black Thai	Son La (p.415)	Jarai	Pleiku (p.198)
Flower Hmong	Bac Ha (p.407)	Bahnar	Kon Tum (p.200)
Black Hmong	Sa Pa (p.400)	Cham	Phan Rang (p.225)

specified period while it recovers its fertility. Where the soils are particularly poor, a semi-nomadic lifestyle is adopted, shifting the village location at intervals as necessary.

Recent history

Traditionally, Viet kings demanded tribute from the often fiercely independent ethnic minorities but otherwise left them to govern their own affairs. This relationship changed with the arrival of Catholic missionaries, who won many converts to Christianity among the peoples of the central highlands – called **montagnards** by the French. Under colonial rule the minorities gained a certain degree of local autonomy in the late nineteenth century, but at the same time the French expropriated their land, exacted forced labour and imposed heavy taxes. As elsewhere in Vietnam, such behaviour sparked off rebellions, notably among the Hmong in the early twentieth century.

The northern mountains

The French were quick to capitalize on ancient antipathies between the highland and lowland peoples. In the northwest mountains, for example, they set up a semi-autonomous Thai federation, complete with armed militias and border guards. When war broke out in 1946, groups of Thai, Hmong and Muong in the northwest sided with the French and against the Vietnamese, even to the extent of providing battalions to fight alongside French troops. But the situation was not clear-cut: some Thai actively supported the Viet Minh, while Ho Chi Minh found a safe base for his guerrilla armies among the Tay and Nung people of the northeast. Recognizing the need to secure the minorities' allegiance, after North Vietnam won independence in 1954 Ho Chi Minh created two **autonomous regions**, allowing limited self-government within a "unified multinational state".

The central highlands

The minorities of the **central highlands** had also been split between supporting the French and Viet Minh after 1946. In the interests of preserving their independence, the ethnic peoples were often simply anti-Vietnamese, of whatever political persuasion. After partition in 1954, anti-Vietnamese sentiment was exacerbated when President Diem started moving Viet settlers into the region, totally ignoring local land rights. Diem wanted to tie the minorities more closely into the South Vietnamese state; the immediate result, however, was that the Bahnar, Jarai and E De joined forces in an organized opposition movement and called a general strike in 1958.

Over the next few years this well-armed coalition developed into the United Front for the Liberation of Oppressed Races, popularly known by its French acronym, **FULRO**. They demanded greater autonomy for the minorities, including elected representation at the National Assembly, more local self-government, school instruction in their own language and access to higher education. While FULRO met with some initial success, the movement was weakened after a number split off to join the Viet Cong. An estimated ten thousand or more remained, fighting first of all against the South Vietnamese and the Americans, and then against the North Vietnamese Army until 1975. After this, FULRO rebels and other anti-Communist minority groups, mainly E De, operated out of bases in Cambodia. The few who survived Pol Pot's killing fields later fled to Thailand and were eventually resettled in America.

During the **American War**, those minorities living around the Seventeenth Parallel soon found themselves on the front line. The worst fighting occurred during the late 1960s and early 1970s, when North Vietnamese troops were based in these remote uplands and American forces sought to rout them. Massive bombing raids were augmented by the use of defoliants and herbicides which, as well as denuding protective forest cover, destroyed crops and animals; this chemical warfare also killed an unknown number of people and caused severe long-term illnesses. In addition, villages were often subject to night raids by Viet Cong and North Vietnamese soldiers keen to "encourage" local support and replenish their food supplies.

It's estimated that over two hundred thousand minority people in the central highlands, both civilian and military, were killed as a result of the American War, out of a population of around one million. By 1975, 85 percent of villages in the highlands had been either destroyed or abandoned, while nothing was left standing in the region closest to the Demilitarized Zone. At the end of the war thousands of minority people were living in temporary camps, along with Viet refugees, unable to practise their traditional way of life.

Post–reunification

After reunification things didn't really get much better. Promises of greater autonomy came to nothing; even the little self-government the minorities had been granted was removed. Those groups who had opposed the North Vietnamese were kept under close observation and their leaders sent for re-education. The new government pursued a policy of **forced assimilation** of the minorities into the Vietnamese culture and glossed over their previous anti-Viet activities: all education was conducted in the Vietnamese language, traditional customs were discouraged or outlawed and minority people were moved from their dispersed villages into permanent settlements. At the same time the government created **New Economic Zones** in the central highlands and along the Chinese border, often commandeering the best land to resettle thousands of people from the overcrowded lowlands. According to official records, 250,000 settlers were moved into the New Economic Zones each year during the 1980s. The policy resulted in food shortages among minorities unable to support themselves on the marginal lands, and the widespread degradation of over-farmed upland soils.

Doi moi brought a shift in policy in the early 1990s, marked by the establishment of a central office responsible for the ethnic minorities. Minority languages are now officially recognized and can be taught in schools, scholarships enable minority people to attend institutes of higher education, television programmes are broadcast in a number of minority languages, and there is now greater representation of minorities at all levels of government. Indeed, in 2001 Nong Duc Manh, a member of the Tay ethnic group, became the first non-Viet secretary general of the Communist Party (though some rumours, which refuse to go away, suggest that his father was a certain Ho Chi Minh). Cash crops such as timber and fruit are being introduced as an alternative to illegal hunting, logging and opium cultivation. Other income-generating schemes are also being promoted and healthcare programmes upgraded.

All this has been accompanied by moves to preserve Vietnam's **cultural diversity**, driven in part by the realization that ethnic differences have greater appeal to tourists. However, in many areas the minorities' traditional lifestyles are fast being eroded and extreme **poverty** is widespread; while minorities constitute around fourteen percent of Vietnam's population, they account for one-third of those living under the poverty line. This, along with grievances over ancestral land rights and religious freedoms, was one of the issues that sparked widespread **demonstrations** by minority people in the central highlands in 2001 and 2004. While the prime minister ordered more favourable land distribution and promised greater socio-economic development for the region, human rights organizations have criticized the authorities for their harsh treatment of demonstrators, some of whom have received jail sentences of up to twelve years. In 2010, more than seventy Montagnards were arrested in Gia Lai province alone. Human Rights Watch estimates that, from 2001 to 2011, more than 350 Montagnards from the central highlands were given long prison sentences for reasons that remain dubious; at least 65 of them were arrested trying to seek asylum in Cambodia.

Minorities in the northern highlands

The mountains of northern Vietnam are home to a large number of ethnic groups, all of them originating from southern China. The dominant minorities are the Tay and Thai, both feudal societies who once held sway over their weaker neighbours. These powerful, well-established groups farm the fertile, valley-bottom land, while Hmong and Dao people, who only arrived in Vietnam at the end of the eighteenth century, occupy the least hospitable land at the highest altitudes. These isolated groups have been better able to lead an independent life and to preserve their traditional customs, though most exist at near-subsistence levels. Local **markets**, usually held at weekly intervals, fulfil an important role in social and economic life in the highlands; the best known are at Sa Pa and Bac Ha, though there are others throughout the area (see Chapter 8 for details). Most groups maintain a tradition of **call-and-response singing**, which is performed at ceremonies and festivals.

Dao

Population: 500,000 • Based in: Lao Cai, Ha Giang

The **Dao** (pronounced "Zao") ethnic minority is incredibly diverse in all aspects of life: social and religious practices, architecture, agriculture and dress. For several centuries, small, localized groups have settled in the northern border region after crossing over from China; there are related groups in Laos, Thailand and China.

Long ago the Dao adopted the Chinese writing system and have a substantial literary tradition. One popular legend records the origin of the twelve Dao clans: Ban Ho, a powerful dog of five colours, killed an enemy general and was granted the hand of a princess in marriage, who gave birth to twelve children. Ban Ho is worshipped by the Dao and the five colours of Dao embroidery represent their ancestor. The Dao boast a particularly striking traditional dress, the most eye-catching element of which is a bulky red turban. Dao people live at all altitudes, their house style and agricultural techniques varying accordingly. While groups living at lower levels are relatively prosperous, growing rice and raising livestock, those in the high, rocky mountains live in considerable poverty.

Giay

Population: 50,000 • Based in: Lao Cai, Lai Chau, Ha Giang

The **Giay** (pronounced "Zay") are a relatively small minority group. Traditional society is feudal, with a strict demarcation between the local aristocracy and the peasant classes. All villagers work the communal lands, living in closely knit villages of stilthouses. A few Giay women still wear the traditional style of dress, distinguished by the highly coloured, circular panel sewn around the collar and a shirt-fastening on the right shoulder; the shirt itself is often of bright green, pink or blue. On formal occasions, women may also wear a chequered turban.

Hmong

Population: 800,000 • Based in: the north, villages at high altitude

Since the end of the eighteenth century, groups of Miao people have been fleeing southern China, heading for Laos, Burma, Thailand and Vietnam. Miao meant "barbarian", whereas their adopted name, **Hmong**, means "free people". Poor farming land, geographical isolation and their traditional seclusion from other people have left the Hmong one of the most impoverished groups in Vietnam; standards of health and education are low, while infant mortality is exceptionally high. Hmong farmers grow maize, rice and vegetables on burnt-over land, irrigated fields and terraced hillsides. Traditionally they also grow poppies, though this is now discouraged by the government. Hmong people raise cattle, buffaloes and horses, and have recently started growing fruit trees, such as peach, plum and apple. They are also skilled hunters and gather forest products, including honey, medicinal herbs, roots and bark, either for their own consumption or to trade at weekly markets. Hmong houses are built flat on the ground, rather than raised on stilts.

Until recently there was no written Hmong language, but a strong oral tradition of folk songs, riddles and proverbs. Perhaps the Hmong are best known, however, for their handicrafts, particularly weaving hemp and cotton cloth which is then coloured with indigo dyes. Many Hmong women, and some men, still wear traditional indigo apparel and chunky silver jewellery. The main subgroups are **White**, **Red**, **Green**, **Black** and **Flower Hmong**; though the origin of the names is unknown, there are marked differences in dialect and social customs as well as dress and hairstyle, especially among the women.

Muong

Population: 1.2 million • Based in: Yen Bai, Son La, Thanh Hoa

The lower hills from the Red River Valley are the domain of the **Muong** ethnic minority, with the majority now living in Hoa Binh Province. The Muong are believed to share common ancestors with the Viet. It's thought that the two groups split around two thousand years ago, after which the Muong developed relatively independently in the highlands. Society is traditionally dominated by aristocratic families, who distribute communal land to the villagers in return for labour and tax contributions; the symbols of their authority are drums and bronze gongs.

Muong stilthouses are similar to those built by the Thai, and the main staple is rice, though fishing, hunting and gathering are all still fairly important. Muong people have a varied cultural tradition, including call-and-response singing and epic tales, and they are famed for their embroidery, typically creating bold geometric designs in black and white. Older Muong women continue to wear the traditional long black skirt and close-fitting shirt; a broad, heavily embroidered belt is the main accessory, and many women also wear a simple white headscarf.

Nung

Population: 750,000 • Based in: Cao Bang, Lang Son

Nung people are closely related to the Tay, sharing the same language and often living in the same villages. Nung farmers terrace the lower slopes to provide extra land, and are noted for the wide variety of crops they grow, including maize, groundnuts and a whole host of vegetables. In fact, the Nung are reckoned to be the best horticulturalists in Vietnam, while their blacksmiths are almost as renowned. Unusually, the traditional Nung house has clay walls and a tiled roof, and is built either flat on the ground or with only one section raised on stilts.

Most Nung are Buddhist, worshipping Quan Am, though they also honour the spirits and their ancestors. They are particularly adept at call-and-response singing, relishing the improvised double entendre. Not surprisingly, Nung traditional dress is similar to that of the Tay, though hemmed with coloured bands. Women often sport a neck scarf with brightly coloured fringes and a shoulder bag embroidered with the sun, stars and flowers, or woven in black and white interspersed with delicately coloured threads.

Tay

Population: 1.5 million • Based in: Cao Bang, Lang Son, Bac Kan

The **Tay** are Vietnam's largest minority group living in the highlands, and are concentrated in the northeast, from the Red River Valley east to the coastal plain, where they settled over two thousand years ago. Through centuries of close contact with lowlanders, Tay society has been strongly influenced by Viet culture, sharing many common rituals and Confucian practices.

Many Tay have now adopted Viet architecture and dress, but it's still possible to find villages of thatched stilthouses, characterized by a railed balcony around the building.

Nowadays it's largely the women who still wear the Tay's traditional long, belted dress of indigo-dyed cloth, with a similarly plain, knotted headscarf peaked at the front and set off with lots of silver jewellery. Tay farmers are famous for their animal husbandry, and they also specialize in fish-farming and growing high-value crops, such as anise, tobacco, soya and cinnamon.

The Tay have developed advanced irrigation systems for wet-rice cultivation, including the huge waterwheels found beside rivers in the northeast. They have had a written language – based on Chinese ideograms – since the fifteenth century, fostering a strong literary tradition; call-and-response singing is also popular, as are theatrical performances, kite-flying and a whole variety of other games. Some Tay groups in the more remote regions occasionally erect a funeral house, decorated with fluttering slips of white paper, over a new grave.

Thai
Population: 1.3 million • Based in: Dien Bien Phu, Son La, Mai Chau

The **Thai** minority is the dominant group in the northwest mountains from the Red River south to Nghe An, though most live in Lai Chau and Son La provinces. They are distantly related to the Thai of Thailand and to groups in southern China, their ancestral homeland. However, Thai people have been living in Vietnam for at least two thousand years and show similarities with both Viet and Tay cultures. Traditional Thai society was strongly hierarchical, ruled over by feudal lords who controlled vast land-holdings worked by the villagers. Their written language, which is based on Sanskrit, has furnished a literary legacy dating back five centuries, including epic poems, histories and a wealth of folklore. The Thai are also famous for their unique dance repertoire and finely woven brocades decorated with flowers, birds and dragons, which are on sale in local markets. From their early teens women learn how to weave and embroider, eventually preparing a set of blankets for their dowry. Thai houses are often still constructed on stilts, with wood or bamboo frames, though the architecture varies between regions.

There are two main subgroups: **Black Thai** (around Dien Bien Phu, Tuan Giao and Son La) and **White Thai** (Mai Chau, Muang Lay), whose names are often attributed to the traditional colour of the women's shirts, though this is open to dispute. Both groups wear long, narrow skirts and fitted shirts, topped with an intricately embroidered headdress.

Minorities in the central highlands

Nearly all minority groups living in the central highlands are indigenous peoples; most are matrilineal societies with a strong emphasis on community life and with some particularly complex burial rites. Catholic **missionaries** enjoyed considerable success in the central highlands, establishing a mission at Kon Tum in the mid-nineteenth century; then early in the twentieth century Protestantism was also introduced to the region. Most converts came from among the E De and Bahnar, though other groups have also incorporated Christian practices into their traditional belief systems and the number of converts has been increasing in recent years. Likewise, **Vietnamese influence** has been stronger here than in northern Vietnam, while the **American War** caused severe disruption. Nevertheless, their cultures have been sufficiently strong to resist complete assimilation. For how much longer is a matter of debate, as thousands of lowland Viets, plus significant numbers of northern minorities, are moving into the region, clearing huge swathes of land for coffee plantations on the back of a booming export market.

Bahnar (Ba Na)

Population: 170,000 • Found in: Kon Tum

Now a highland people, the **Bahnar** trace their ancestry back many centuries to communities coexisting on the coastal plains with the Cham and Jarai. The most distinctive aspect of a Bahnar village is its *rong*, or communal house, the roof of which may be up to 20m high. This is the centre of village cultural and ceremonial life, and also the home of adolescent boys, who are taught Bahnar history, the skills of hunting and other manly matters. Village houses grouped around the *rong* are typically stilthouses with a thatched or tiled roof, and are often decorated with geometric motifs.

The Bahnar people are skilled horticulturalists, growing maize, sweet potato or millet, together with indigo, hemp or tobacco as cash crops. Bahnar groups also erect funeral houses decorated with elaborate carvings, although they are less imposing than those of the Jarai. Sometime after the burial, wooden statues, gongs, wine jars and other items of family property are placed in the funeral house.

E De

Population: 270,000 • Found in: Dak Lak

People of the **E De** minority live in stilthouses grouped together in a village, or *buon*. These longhouses, which can be up to 100m in length, are boat-shaped with hardwood frames, bamboo floors and walls, and topped with a high thatched roof. As many as a hundred family members may live in a single house, under the authority of the oldest or most respected woman, who owns all family property, including the house and domestic animals; wealth is indicated by the number of ceremonial gongs. Other much prized heirlooms are the large earthenware jars used for making the rice wine drunk at festivals. Like the Jarai, E De people worship the kings of Fire and Water among a whole host of animist spirits, and also erect a funeral house on their graves. Both the original longhouse and its grave-site replica are often decorated with fine carvings.

The E De homeland lies in a region of red soils on the rolling western plateaux. In the nineteenth and twentieth centuries French settlers introduced coffee and rubber estates to the area, often seizing land from the local people they called Rhadé. Traditional swidden farming has gradually been disappearing, a process accelerated by the American War and the forced relocation of E De into permanent settlements.

Jarai (Gia Rai)

Population: 300,000 • Based in: Gia Lai

The **Jarai** are the largest minority group in the central highlands. It's thought that they left the coastal plains around two thousand years ago, settling on the fertile plateau around Pleiku. Some ethnologists hold that Cham people are in fact a branch of the Jarai, and they certainly share common linguistic traits and a matrilineal social order. Young Jarai women initiate the marriage proposal and afterwards the couple live in the wife's family home, with children taking their mother's name. Houses are traditionally built on stilts, facing north. The focus of village life is the communal house, or *rong*, where the council of elders and their elected chief meet.

Animist beliefs are still strong, and the Jarai world is peopled with spirits, the most famous of which are the kings of Water, Fire and Wind, represented by shamans who are involved in rain-making ceremonies and other rituals. Funeral rites are particularly complex and expensive: each family maintains a funeral house which they ornament with evocative sculptures of people, birds and objects from everyday life. The Jarai also have an extensive musical repertoire, the principal instruments being gongs and the unique *k'long put*, made of bamboo tubes into which the players force air by clapping their hands. During the American War the majority of Jarai villagers moved out of their war-torn homeland, many being resettled in Pleiku; only in recent years are some slowly returning.

Koho (Co Ho) and Lat

Population: 130,000 • Based in: Da Lat

The **Koho** minority is subdivided into six highly varied subgroups, including the **Lat**. The typical Koho house is built on stilts with a thatched roof and bamboo walls and flooring. Despite the fact that many Koho were converted to Christianity in the early twentieth century, spirit worship is widely practised and each family adopts a guardian spirit from the natural world. Catholic missionaries developed a phonetic script for the Koho language but the oral tradition remains strong. Unlike many minorities in this region, the Koho incorporate dance into their religious rites, and it is an important element of them; a variety of musical instruments, such as gongs, bamboo flutes and buffalo horns, are also involved. Subgroups of the Koho minority are famed for their pottery and ironwork, whereas Lat farmers have a reputation for constructing sophisticated irrigation systems.

Mnong

Population: 90,000 • Based in: Dak Lak, Da Lat

The **Mnong** ethnic minority is probably best known for its skill in hunting elephants and domesticating them for use in war, for transport and for their ivory. Mnong people are also the creators of the lithophone, a kind of stone xylophone thought to be among the world's most ancient musical instruments; an example is on show at the Ethnographic Museum in Buon Ma Thuot (see p.192). Mnong houses are usually built flat on the ground and, though the society is generally matrilineal, village affairs are organized by a male chief. Mnong craftsmen are skilled at basketry and printing textiles, while they also make the copper, tin and silver jewellery worn by both sexes. In traditional burial rituals a buffalo-shaped coffin is placed under a funeral house which is peopled with wooden statues and painted with black, red or white designs.

Sedang (Xo Dang)

Population: 130,000 • Based in: Kon Tum

The **Sedang** were traditionally a warlike people whose villages were surrounded with defensive hedges, barbed with spears and stakes, and with only one entrance. Inter-village wars were frequent, and the Sedang also carried out raids on the peaceable Bahnar, mainly to seize prisoners rather than territory. In the past, Sedang religious ritual involved human sacrifices to propitiate the spirits – a practice that was later modified into a profitable business, selling slaves to traders from Laos and Thailand.

In the 1880s, an eccentric French military adventurer called Marie-David de Mayréna, established a kingdom in Sedang territory by making treaties with the local chiefs (see box above). A few decades later, the French authorities conscripted Sedang labour to build Highway 14 from Kon Tum to Da Nang; conditions were so harsh that many died, provoking a rebellion in the 1930s. Soon after, the Viet Minh won many recruits among the Sedang in their war against the French. In the American War some Sedang groups fought for the Viet Cong while others were formed into militia units by the American Special Services. But when fighting intensified after 1965, Sedang villagers were forced to flee, and many now live in almost destitute conditions, having lost their ancestral lands.

Each Sedang extended family occupies a longhouse, built on stilts and usually facing east; central to village life is the communal house where young men and boys sleep, and where all the major ceremonies take place. Because villages historically had relatively little contact with each other, there are marked variations between the social customs of the subgroups, and so far seventeen Sedang dialects have been identified. Agricultural techniques are more consistent, mainly swidden farming supplemented by horticulture and hunting. Some Sedang farmers employ a "water harp", a combined bird-scarer, musical instrument and appeaser of the spirits. The harp consists of bamboo tubes linked together and placed in a flowing stream to produce an irregular, haunting sound.

VIETNAM'S REAL-LIFE KURTZ

The Sedang played their part in one of colonial Vietnam's oddest interludes and one which finds echoes in Joseph Conrad's novella, *Heart of Darkness*, in which a mysterious voyager named Kurtz proclaims himself king, deep in the Belgian Congo – a story later borrowed by Francis Ford Coppola for his film *Apocalypse Now* (see p.494).

The career of French rogue **Marie-David de Mayréna** was a chequered one to say the least. After a stint with the French army in Cochinchina in the mid-1860s, he made his way back to Paris, only to return to the East after having failed as a banker. Back in Vietnam by the 1880s, he established himself as a planter around Ba Ria, until 1888 when the governor sent him to explore the highlands. Of the hundred or so porters and soldiers who accompanied him, only one, a Frenchman named Alphonse Mercurol, remained by the time he reached Kon Tum. Through the contacts of the French missionaries based there, Mayréna was able to arrange meetings with local tribal chiefs; soon the leaders fell under the spell of his "blue eyes" and "bold, confident stare", and he conspired to proclaim himself **King Marie I of Sedang**, while Mercurol adopted the title "Marquis of Hanoi". For three months, Mayréna ruled from a straw hut flying the national flag (a white cross on a blue background, with a red star in the centre), legislating, creating an army and even declaring war on the neighbouring Jarai people.

But Mayréna was more interested in money than sovereignty, and within months he had decamped, setting off in the hope of getting some mileage from his "title". In his book, *Dragon Ascending*, Henry Kamm quotes an erstwhile manager of Saigon's *Continental*, where Mayréna boarded on credit with assorted courtiers: "Alas, when, several days later, Mayréna moved out of the hotel, nothing was left to Laval [the then hotel manager] as payment for his services, except for a decoration, that of the National Order of the Kingdom of the Sedangs, which the king gave him before departure." Returning to Europe, Mayréna took to selling fictitious titles and mining concessions to raise cash but, inevitably, cracks began to appear in his story, and he fled back to Southeast Asia in 1890 where he died in penury on Malaya's Tioman Island, supposedly of a snake bite.

Minorities in the southern lowlands

As the Viet people pushed down the coastal plain and into the Mekong Delta they displaced two main ethnic groups, the Cham and Khmer, whose descendants remain today.

Cham

Population: 130,000 • Based in: Ninh Thuan, Binh Thuan, Cambodian border area

Up until the tenth century powerful **Cham** kings had ruled over most of southern Vietnam (see p.434). Today's surviving coastal communities are still largely Hindu worshippers of Shiva and follow the matrilineal practices of their Cham ancestors; they earn a living from farming, silk-weaving and crafting jewellery of gold or silver. Groups along the Cambodian border are Islamic and, in general, patrilineal. They engage in riverfishing, weaving and cross-border trade, with little agricultural activity. On the whole, Cham people have adopted the Vietnamese way of life and dress, though their traditional arts, principally dance and music, have experienced a revival in recent years.

Hoa

Population: 800,000 • Based in: Mekong Delta

Ethnic Chinese people, known in Vietnamese as **Hoa**, form one of Vietnam's largest minority groups. Throughout the country's history, Chinese people, mostly from China's southern provinces, have been emigrating to Vietnam as administrators and merchants or as refugees from persecution. In the mid-seventeenth century the collapse of the Ming Dynasty sent a human deluge southwards, and there were other large-scale migrations in the nineteenth century and then the 1940s. Until the early nineteenth century all Hoa, even those of mixed blood, were considered by the Viets to be Chinese. After that date, however, they were admitted to public office and

THE VIET KIEU

Overseas Vietnamese are known in their homeland as **Viet Kieu**. There are over two million worldwide, the figure rocketing up in the 1980s as 750,000 fled Vietnam by boat (see box, p.451). Many settled in America, Australia and France, but in recent years the Vietnamese government has gradually made it easier for Viet Kieu to return; procedures for sending money back to family members from overseas were also simplified, providing an important source of extra income for individuals and becoming increasingly valuable in the wider economy, especially in the south. Not surprisingly, however, the attitudes of those who stuck it out in Vietnam towards Viet Kieu are ambivalent, and the government itself is unsure about how to handle relations with the Viet Kieu; in general their money and expertise are welcomed but not necessarily their politics, nor their Western ways.

gradually became integrated into Vietnamese society. Nevertheless, the Hoa remain slightly apart, living in close communities according to their ancestral province in China and preserving elements of their own culture, notably their language and traditional lion dances.

The Hoa have tended to settle in urban areas, typically becoming successful merchants, artisans and business people, and playing an important role in the economy. Viet people have tended to distrust the Hoa, mainly because of their dominant commercial position and their close links with China. After 1975 the Hoa were badly hit when socialist policies were enforced, in what amounted to an anti-Chinese persecution. Tensions rose even further when China invaded Vietnam in 1979 and thousands of Hoa left the country to escape reprisals, forming a large majority of the "boat people" (see box, p.451). It's estimated that up to one third of the Hoa population eventually left Vietnam.

Khmer

Population: 1,000,000 • Based in: Mekong Delta

Ethnic **Khmer** (known in Vietnam as *Kho Me Khrom*) are the indigenous people of the Mekong Delta, including Cambodia; some arrived in Vietnam in the late 1970s as refugees from Pol Pot's brutal regime in Cambodia. Khmer farmers are noted for their skill at irrigation and wet-rice cultivation; it's said that they farm nearly 150 varieties of rice, each suited to specific local conditions. Traditionally, the Khmer live in villages of stilthouses erected on raised mounds above the flood waters, but these days are more likely to build flat on the earth, along canals and roadways. The pagoda, however, is still a distinctive feature of Khmer villages, its brightly patterned roofs decorated with images of the sacred ancestral dragon, the *neak*. Although ancient beliefs persist, since the late thirteenth century the Khmer have been devout followers of Theravada Buddhism, as practised in Cambodia, Laos and Thailand. They produce fine silk and basketry and wear distinctive red-and-white scarves.

Environmental issues

Vietnam is endowed with a wide variety of fauna and flora, including an unusually high number of bird species and a rich diversity of primates. Current estimates suggest there are over 12,000 plant species, around three hundred mammals and 850 birds, though remote areas are still being explored. Over recent years, particularly in the forest reserves bordering Laos, the identification of several species of plants, butterflies, snakes, birds and even mammals that were previously unknown to scientists has caused a sensation in the scientific community.

Such diversity is largely attributable to Vietnam's range of habitats, from the subalpine mountains of the north to the Mekong Delta's mangrove swamps, in a country that is 75 percent mountainous, has over 3400km of coastline and extends over sixteen degrees of latitude. However, the list of endangered and critically endangered species is also long – over 120 types of animals and plants – as their domains are threatened by population pressure, widespread logging and pollution, particularly of the coastal zone. One of the biggest environmental challenges facing Vietnam is to preserve its rapidly diminishing forest areas by establishing methods of sustainable use.

Happily, the government does at least seem to recognize the value of Vietnam's biodiversity and the need to act quickly. It has now put in place a number of **laws** dealing with environmental issues, the most important being the Environmental Protection Law, revised in 2005, which sets out national policy covering the prevention and control of pollution, the protection, conservation and sustainable use of natural resources and improving environmental quality. The promulgation of a new Law on Tourism also came about in 2005, which for the first time contains provisions on sustainable tourism from an environmental and social perspective, aiming to encourage greater community participation and spreading the benefits more widely. The law also includes tougher regulations on tourism-related pollution, though ensuring these laws are effectively implemented is a problem.

Ecological warfare

The word "**ecocide**" was coined during the American War, in reference to the quantity of herbicides dropped from the air to deprive the Viet Cong of their safe areas, deep under the triple-canopy forest, and their food crops. The most notorious defoliant used was **Agent Orange**, along with agents Blue and White, all named after the colour of the respective storage containers. Their active ingredient was **dioxin**, a slowly dissolving poison that has a half-life of eight to ten years in the environment – but remains much longer in human tissue. It's estimated that over eighty million litres of chemical defoliants were sprayed from American planes crisscrossing the forests and mangrove swamps of South Vietnam and the Demilitarized Zone between 1961 and 1971. Figures vary, but somewhere between twenty and forty percent of the South's land area was sprayed at least once and in some cases more frequently, destroying up to a quarter of the forest cover.

The environmental impact was perhaps greatest on the **mangrove forests**, which are particularly susceptible to defoliants. Spraying destroyed about a half of all Vietnam's mangrove swamps and forests, and since they don't regenerate naturally, they have to be replanted by hand, a slow operation with a low success rate. The herbicides also had a severe impact on **soldiers**, both Vietnamese and American, and **villagers** who were caught in the spraying or absorbed dioxins from the food chain and from drinking water. Children and the elderly were the worst affected: some died immediately from the poisons, while others suffered respiratory diseases, skin rashes and other ailments. Soon it became apparent that the dioxins were also causing abnormally high levels of miscarriage, birth defects, neurological disease and cancers. Surveys suggest that over three million Vietnamese may be affected, many of whom now receive a tiny monthly allowance from the government.

For years, doctors in Ho Chi Minh City's Tu Do Hospital, supported by international experts, have been trying to convince the American government of the link between the use of defoliants and these medical conditions, in the hope of claiming **compensation** for the victims. In 2004, a group of Vietnamese took their case to a New York court, claiming compensation from 37 American chemical companies on behalf of all victims. The case was dismissed in March 2005 on the grounds that the use of defoliants was not prohibited under international law at the time.

For their part, American war veterans who were exposed to dioxins, many of whom have children with serious birth defects, have also been seeking reparations. In 1984, a group of ex-servicemen won a landmark out-of-court settlement from the manufacturers; though the government refused to accept culpability, they were later forced to reimburse the chemical company following legal proceedings.

Apart from using herbicides, American and South Vietnamese troops cut down swathes of forest land with specially adapted bulldozers, called **Rome Ploughs**. These vehicles were capable of slicing through a three-metre-thick tree trunk, and were used to clear roadsides and riverbanks against ambushes, or to remove vestiges of undergrowth and trees left after the spraying. Finally, there were the **bombs** themselves: an estimated thirteen million tonnes of explosives were dropped during the course of the war, leaving a staggering 25 million bomb craters, the vast majority in the South. In addition to their general destructive power, explosions compact the soil to the point where nothing will grow, and napalm bombs sparked off forest fires. The worst single incident occurred in 1968 when U Minh forest, at the southern tip of Vietnam, burned for seven weeks; 85 percent of its trees were destroyed.

Since the war, Vietnamese environmentalists led by Professor Vo Quy, founder of the Center for Natural Resources and Environmental Studies at Hanoi University, have instigated **reforestation programmes**, slowly coaxing life back into even the worst-affected regions. This has involved pioneering work in regenerating tropical forest, planting native species under a protective umbrella of acacia and eucalyptus.

A symbolically significant success of local environmentalists has been the **return of the Sarus crane** to the Mekong Delta (see p.141), near the Cambodian border. The crane, a stately bird with an elaborate courtship dance, abandoned its nesting grounds when the Americans drained the wetlands and dropped herbicides and then napalm in their attempts to rout Viet Cong soldiers from the marshes. After the war thousands of landless farmers were settled in the area, but the acid soils proved difficult to farm so the provincial governor re-established a portion of the wetlands, thus restoring the cranes' natural habitat. The first Sarus cranes reappeared in 1986, after which Tam Nong Bird Sanctuary, now the Tram Chim National Park (see p.141), was set up to protect the crane and other returning species. Though the population remains highly vulnerable, as many as four hundred Sarus cranes now spend the dry season in the delta's wetlands.

Postwar deforestation

It's estimated that more than two million hectares of Vietnam's forest reserves were destroyed during the American War as a result of defoliation, napalm fires and bombing. Since 1975, however, at least three million hectares have been lost to commercial **logging**, agricultural **clearance**, forest **fires**, firewood collection and **population pressure**. Originally, perhaps 75 percent of Vietnam's land area would have been covered by forest. By 1945 it had dwindled to 43 percent and was down to just 24 percent (roughly eight

CONSERVATION AND THE NATIONAL PARKS

Vietnam recognized the need for conservation relatively early, establishing its first national park (Cuc Phuong) in 1962 and adopting a **National Conservation Strategy** in 1985. The more accessible or interesting of Vietnam's thirty **national parks** are listed below, but unless you're prepared to spend a lot of time there, it's unlikely that you'll see many animals. Birds, insects and butterflies, however, are more readily visible and often the dense tropical vegetation or mountain scenery are in themselves worth the journey. To learn more about Vietnam's protected areas, and how to access them, get hold of Fauna and Flora International's excellent *Ecotourism Map of Vietnam*, available in local bookshops and through select tour operators; all proceeds go to support Vietnamese primate conservation. For further information about biodiversity in Vietnam, search the World Conservation Monitoring Centre's comprehensive website, ⓦ unep-wcmc.org.

Ba Be (see p.425). A park of 8000 hectares, containing Vietnam's largest natural lake, over 350 butterfly species and a few extremely rare Tonkin snub-nosed langur. The park has limited tourist facilities, but boat trips, jungle walks and overnight stays in a minority village are possible.

Bach Ma (see p.277). This park of 22,000 hectares sits on the climatological divide between the tropical forests of the south and the northern subtropical zone, and contains Vietnam's lushest tropical rainforests. It is also home to a wide variety of bird species, including several rare pheasants, and over 1400 recorded flora species. Bach Ma is well set up for tourism, with a network of marked trails, campsites and guesthouses.

Cat Ba (see p.341). The park covers only 15,200 hectares, but 5400 of these are important marine reserves, including areas of coral reef. The limestone island supports a broad range of habitats, a wealth of medicinal plants and a critically endangered population of Golden-headed langurs. The park is accessible to tourists either on foot or by boat from Cat Ba Town.

Cat Tien (see p.178). This 74,000-hectare park is most famous for its tiny population of Java rhino, the only ones known in mainland Asia. Otherwise the park's wetlands are a haven for water birds, including the critically endangered White-winged duck and White-shouldered ibis, as well as the equally rare Siamese crocodile. Although it's relatively close to Ho Chi Minh City, Cat Tien is not easy to reach by public transport and tourist facilities are fairly limited.

Cuc Phuong (see p.327). Vietnam's first national park, Cuc Phuong was established in 1962 in an area of limestone hills relatively close to Hanoi. The park covers 22,000 hectares and contains a number of unique, ancient trees and provides excellent birdwatching, as well as an opportunity to see some of the world's rarest monkeys in its Endangered Primate Rescue Center. Cuc Phuong is one of the most accessible parks, where it's possible to hike and stay overnight.

Phong Nha-Ke Bang (see p.315). Established in 2002, this 86,000-hectare park along the mountain chain bordering Laos is best known for its extensive underground river system. The park itself is home to more than sixty endangered animal species, including several types of langur. At present access is limited to visiting Phong Nha Cave.

Tram Chim (see p.127). One of Vietnam's most important wetlands ecosystems, comprising 7500 hectares in the Mekong Delta and providing haven to thousands of overwintering water birds. Its most famous visitors are the critically endangered Sarus crane.

Yok Don (see p.196). Lying on the border with Cambodia, Yok Don constitutes 115,000 hectares carved out of Vietnam's most extensive forests. The area is also one of the most biologically diverse in the whole of Indochina, supporting rare Indochinese tigers and Asian elephants. Visitors can overnight in minority villages and camp; elephant-back rides are also on offer.

To support environmental programmes already taking place in Vietnam, contact the following organizations.

BirdLife International Wellbrook Court, Girton Rd, Cambridge CB3 0NA, UK (☎01223 277318, ⓦ birdlife.org); trip reports are welcomed by their Hanoi office (ⓦ birdlifeindochina.org) via email (ⓔ birdlife@birdlife.netnam.vn).

Fauna and Flora International 4th Floor, Jupiter House, Station Rd., Cambridge CB1 2JD, UK (☎01223 571000, ⓦ fauna-flora.org).

International Crane Foundation E-11376 Shady Lane Rd, PO Box 447, Baraboo, Wisconsin, 53913 0447 US (☎608 356 9462, ⓦ savingcranes.org).

WWF International Ave du Mont-Blanc 27, 1196 Gland, Switzerland (☎22 364 9111, ⓦ wwf .panda.org).

million hectares) in 1980. It's now edged back up to 36 percent, thanks to one of the world's most ambitious reforestation programmes, launched in 1998, to replant five million hectares, and the government plans to raise it to 42 percent by 2015. Although an impressive 130,000 hectares are planted each year, this only just exceeds the area being lost to clearance, and the new growth is largely acacia and eucalyptus rather than native species. The area under "high-quality" native forest continues to shrink.

The **worst-affected areas** are Vietnam's northern mountains, the central province of Nghe An and around Pleiku in the central highlands. In these areas soil erosion is a major problem, and countrywide floods are getting worse as a result of deforestation along the watersheds. Many rare hardwoods are fast disappearing and the fragile ecosystems are no longer able to support a wildlife population forced into ever-smaller pockets of undisturbed jungle. Much of the blame for this rapid reduction in the forest cover is often laid on the **ethnic minorities** who traditionally clear land for farming and rely on the forests for building timber and firewood. However, lowland Vietnamese settling in the mountains have also put pressure on scant resources.

Both lowland Vietnamese and minority people have cleared huge swathes of the central highlands for **coffee plantations**, while the carefully replanted coastal mangrove forest is threatened by uncontrolled development of intensive **prawn farming**. Another significant threat to the forests is the highly lucrative **timber trade**, both legal and illegal. By **replanting**, it's hoped to create sustainable forests for commercial logging and to protect the tiny remaining areas of primary forests, but **enforcement** is hampered by lack of resources. The authorities have devolved the management and protection of the forest reserves to local communities, with some success.

Wildlife

Forest clearance, warfare, pollution and economic necessity have all contributed to the loss of natural habitat and reduced Vietnam's broad species base. In 1994, when Vietnam signed the **Convention on International Trade in Endangered Species** (CITES), which bans the traffic in animals or plants facing extinction, the species list identified 365 animal species in need of urgent protection. Among these, the Java rhino, the world's rarest large mammal, is reduced to a mere five to eight animals, while no fewer than five of the world's most endangered primate species, including the Golden-headed (or Cat Ba) langur and the Tonkin snub-nosed langur, survive in small isolated communities in the northern forests. Other severely endangered species include the Indochina tiger and Asian elephant. Vietnam is also home to around 850 species of **birds**, with the highest number of endemic species in mainland Southeast Asia. Again, many of these are under threat of extinction, including the Vietnamese pheasant, small numbers of which have been recorded in Ha Tinh and Quang Binh provinces.

Hunting continues to be a vital source of local income, as a walk round Vietnamese markets soon reveals. Wild animals and birds are sought after for their meat or to satisfy the demand for **medicinal products** and live specimens, an often illegal (but extremely lucrative) business. Since the border with China was re-opened in the early 1990s, smuggling of rare species has increased, among them the Asiatic black bear, whose gall bladder is prized as a cure for fevers and liver problems; relentless hunting has decimated the population to small numbers in the north. Similarly, Vietnam's population of wild Asian elephants is now reduced to fewer than one hundred individuals, down from two thousand in the 1970s. Not only has their habitat along the Cambodian border declined, but since 1975 poachers have been hunting elephants for their tusks. At least ten elephants were killed in Dak Lak and Dong Nai provinces during 2010 and 2011, and wildlife experts are warning that the Asian elephant could be extinct in Vietnam within a decade.

Fortunately, quite large areas of the Vietnamese interior remain amazingly untouched, especially the Truong Son Mountains north of the Hai Van Pass, the southern central highlands and lowland forests of the Mekong Delta. These isolated areas are rich in

biodiversity and have yielded spectacular discoveries in recent years, with much still to be explored. In 1992, Dr John MacKinnon and a team of Vietnamese biologists working in the Vu Quang Nature Reserve, an area of steamy, impenetrable jungle on the Lao border, identified a species of ox new to science, now known as the saola. Two years later the giant muntjac, a previously unknown species of deer, and a new carp were found in the same region, followed in 1997 by a smaller type of muntjac deer and the Grey-shanked douc langur, and in 1999 by a striped rabbit thought to be related to the now extinct Sumatran striped rabbit. Three new bird species were also discovered in the late 1990s in the mountains of Kon Tum province: two types of laughing thrush and the black-crowned barwing.

An all-out effort is being made to protect this "biological gold mine" and other similar areas both within Vietnam and over the border in Laos. After the saola was discovered, the reserve was put strictly off limits and the total **protected area** enlarged to almost 160,000 hectares, with buffer zones and corridors linking the reserve to conservation areas in Laos. The task is fraught with difficulties, such as achieving cross-border cooperation and establishing effective policing of the reserve – especially against poaching and illegal logging – with inadequate personnel and financial resources. At the same time, the authorities have been working to find alternative sources of income and food for people living in or near the reserve, and carrying out educational work on the importance of conservation and its relevance to their daily lives.

In a related scheme, special protection areas have also been established around Yok Don and Ba Be national parks as part of a project to establish models of stable biodiversity conservation. The government has also been adding to the number of national parks and nature reserves over recent years. Among the more recent are U Minh Ha National Park, near the southernmost tip of the Mekong Delta, and Xuan Nha Nature Reserve, in Son La Province in the country's northwest. As a further boost to conservation efforts, in 2000 UNESCO recognized an area of mangrove forest at Can Gio in the Mekong Delta and Cat Tien National Park as Vietnam's first "Man and Biosphere" reserves. Since then another half dozen sites have been added.

Sustainable tourism

There's a growing awareness among tourists and travel companies of the negative impact tourism can have on the environment and local culture – the very things most people come to see. All too often the terms **eco-tourism** and **sustainable tourism** are reduced to mere marketing gimmicks, but behind them lies a serious desire, albeit ambitious, to find a new model of small-scale tourism that contributes to the long-term development of the local community without destroying its traditional social and economic structures or the often fragile environment.

Mass tourism didn't really get going in Vietnam until the mid-1990s. From just ten thousand in 1993, the number of foreign visitors (including business trips) is projected to top six million in 2011, while the number of domestic holidaymakers currently stands at around 25 million, and is growing even faster. Not surprisingly, the Vietnamese government is eager to promote tourism as a **key revenue-earner** and is gradually easing visa regulations, among other things, in the hope of attracting more foreign visitors. This sudden influx of sightseers, coupled with a lack of effective planning or control, is putting pressure on some of the country's most famous beauty spots.

In response, the government has gradually introduced a number of laws and initiatives placing greater emphasis on the conservation of the nation's natural – and cultural – heritage. Local authorities in **Hoi An** have banned cars from the centre and put a block on further hotel construction in addition to introducing restrictive pricing to control the flow of tourists. Some of this revenue is being ploughed back into improving the townscape – for example, renovating the old houses, hiding television aerials and burying cables. In **Ha Long Bay**, the problems of notoriously haphazard hotel

RESPONSIBLE TOURISM

Though domestic tourism has the greatest impact through sheer weight of numbers, international travellers can play a positive role by setting examples of **responsible behaviour**. Various NGOs and groups involved in the travel industry (see below) have developed **guidelines** for tourists and travel companies. Some of the most important points are: to avoid buying souvenirs made from endangered species or which damage the environment – notably tortoiseshell, ivory and coral in Vietnam; as far as possible, to eat in local restaurants, buy local produce, employ local guides and stay in home-stays or locally owned hotels – not only is it usually a lot more fun, but also your money is more likely to benefit smaller communities; to be sensitive to the local culture, including appropriate standards of dress, as well as adopting a responsible attitude towards drugs, alcohol and prostitution. Finally, when booking tours, ask how much – if anything – the tour company contributes to conservation and community development at its chosen destinations. Tour agents in Vietnam with a reputation for their conscientious approach include Handspan, Buffalo Tours, Sinhbalo, Footprint and Ethnic Travel. Intrepid also has a long track record of engaging in sustainable tourism.

development are exacerbated by **pollution** from tourist boats (plastic bags and bottles floating on the water tend to spoil otherwise idyllic views), fish farms and nearby coalfields, and by the presence of a major port. Concern over the future of this World Heritage Site, however, means that the issues are at least being discussed, and various measures, such as more effective management of the caves, have been put in place. One or two more remote islands are also being developed as eco-tourism destinations.

Perhaps the key areas, however, are the **uplands** of north and central Vietnam. These are increasingly popular destinations, both for their outstanding natural beauty and their communities of **ethnic minority people**. In the honey-pot market town of **Sa Pa**, for example, the number of hotels and guesthouses has mushroomed over the last decade – from none before 1991 to 150 in 2009 – and the famous weekend market attracts more tourists than minority people. Some of these people, disturbed by the unwanted attention and intrusive cameras, now shy away from Sa Pa completely, in favour of more inaccessible markets. Most of the "minority crafts" on sale are actually shipped up from Hanoi and, though they are the major attraction, the minority people themselves receive very little economic benefit from tourism; most goes to Kinh Vietnamese or foreign travel companies. There are even signs of an emerging sex industry in Sa Pa and the beginnings of both child prostitution and drug-related crime.

Sa Pa's superb setting and trekking opportunities will continue to make it a popular destination, and it's likely that the surrounding area will be developed further. The challenge is how to achieve this in a way that contributes to the **long-term development** of the local community while also preserving cultural and biological diversity. Among other initiatives, the Netherlands Development Organization (SNV; ⍟snvworld.org), an NGO active in developing **community-based tourism** in many countries, including Vietnam, is working with local authorities to draw up tourism development plans and to raise awareness of sustainable development issues. It recently established a tourism information centre in Sa Pa and is involved in providing training for local guides and hotel and restaurant owners. In Sa Pa and Son La, SNV has also helped devise trekking routes and supported local communities in managing visitor numbers, ensuring revenue is equitably distributed and establishing a code of conduct expected of tourists and tour agents.

The international conservation body Flora and Fauna International (FFI; ⍟fauna -flora.org) is also active in Vietnam, helping develop **community-based eco-tourism**. In Pu Luong Nature Reserve, for example, FFI helped install toilets and washing facilities and supplied bedding and mosquito nets in minority villages wishing to set up home-stays. At the same time, it also provided training in home-stay management and service provision and helped promote the reserve as an eco-tourism destination.

Music and theatre

The binding element in all Vietnam's traditional performing arts is **music**, and particularly singing (*hat*), which is a natural extension to an already musical language. The origins of Vietnamese music can be traced back as far as the bronze drums and flutes of Dong Son (see p.364), and further again to the lithophone (stone xylophone) called the *dan da*, the world's oldest known instrument. The Chinese influence is evident in operatic theatre and stringed instruments, while India bestowed rhythms, modal improvisations and several types of drum. Much later, especially during the nineteenth century, elements of European **theatre** and music were coopted, while during the twentieth century most Vietnamese musicians received a classical, Western training based on the works of Eastern bloc composers such as Prokofiev and Tchaikovsky.

From this multicultural melting pot Vietnamese artists have generated a variety of musical and theatrical forms over the centuries, though, surprisingly, dance is less developed than in neighbouring Thailand, Cambodia and Laos. One of the most famous home-grown performance arts is water-puppetry, Vietnam's unique contribution to the world of marionettes, where puppeteers work their magic on a stage of water. The folk tradition is particularly rich, with its improvised courtship songs and the strident, sacred music of trance dances, to which the more than fifty ethnic minorities add their own repertoire of songs and instruments.

Traditionally, the professions of artists or performers were hereditary, but the wars and political upheavals of the twentieth century have contributed to the loss of much of this largely oral tradition. While certain art forms continue to attract new talent, the younger generation is, on the whole, more interested in higher-paid professions and Vietnamese pop. As revolutionary ("red") music has waned since 1986, so pre-1975 music from the South, previously outlawed as "decadent and reactionary", is back with a vengeance, mixed with a sprinkling of artists from other Asian countries and the West.

The traditional strand

Vietnam's traditional theatre, with its strong Chinese influence, is more akin to opera than pure spoken drama. A musical accompaniment and well-known repertoire of songs form an integral part of the performance, where the plots and characters are equally familiar to the audience. Nowadays, however, the two oldest forms, **Cheo** and **Tuong**, are struggling to survive, while even the more contemporary **Cai Luong** is losing out to television and video. However, other traditional arts have seen something of a revival, most notably **water-puppetry** and folk-song performances. The stimulus for this came largely from tourism, but renewed interest in the trance music of **Chau Van** and the complexities of **Tai Tu** chamber music has been very much home-grown.

Theatre

Vietnam's oldest surviving stage art, **Hat Cheo**, or "Popular Opera", has its roots in the Red River Delta where it's believed to have existed since at least the eleventh century. Performances consist of popular legends and everyday events, often with a biting satirical edge, accompanied by a selection of tunes drawn as appropriate from a common fund. Though the movements have become highly stylized over the centuries, Cheo's free form allows the actors considerable room for interpretation; the audience demonstrates its approval, or otherwise, by beating a drum.

Cheo has the reputation of being anti-establishment, with its buffoon character who comments freely on the action, the audience and current events. So incensed were the kings of the fifteenth-century Le Dynasty that Cheo was banned from the court, while artists and their descendants were excluded from public office. Nevertheless, Cheo survived and received official recognition in 1964 with the establishment of the

Vietnam Cheo Theatre, charged with reviving the ancient art form. It is now promoted as the country's national theatre, although its local popularity continues to decline despite a body of new work dealing with contemporary issues.

Hat Tuong (also known as *Hat Boi* or *Hat Bo*), probably introduced from China around the thirteenth century, evolved from classical Chinese opera, and was originally for royal entertainment before being adopted by travelling troupes. Its story lines are mostly historic events and epic tales dealing with such Confucian principles as filial piety and relations between the monarch and his subjects. Tuong, like Cheo, is governed by rigorous rules in which the characters are rendered instantly recognizable by their make-up and costume. Setting and atmosphere are conjured not by props and scenery but through nuances of gesture and musical conventions with which the audience is completely familiar – and which they won't hesitate to criticize if badly executed. Of the clutch of Tuong troupes still in existence, Hanoi's Vietnam Tuong Theatre is one of the most active.

While performances of Tuong are comparatively rare events these days, if you see a large building with peanut- and candy-sellers outside, the chances are that there's a performance of **Hat Cai Luong**, or "Reformed Theatre", going on inside. Cai Luong originated in southern Vietnam in the early twentieth century, showing a French theatrical influence in its spoken parts, with short scenes and relatively elaborate sets. The action is a tangle of historical drama (such as *The Tale of Kieu*) and racy themes from the street (murder, drug deals, incest, theft and revenge). Its music is a similar hodgepodge: eighteenth-century chamber music played on amplified traditional instruments for the set pieces; electric guitar, keyboards and drums during the scene changes. Cai Luong's constant borrowing from contemporary culture – from language and plots to the incorporation of hit songs – has enabled it to keep pace with Vietnam's social changes. Around thirty professional Cai Luong troupes are currently performing, of which the best known are the National Cai Luong Theatre in Hanoi and Ho Chi Minh City's Tran Huu Trang Cai Luong Theatre.

The origin of **water-puppetry** (*mua roi nuoc*) is obscure, beyond that it developed in the flooded rice paddies of the Red River Delta and usually took place in spring when there was less farm work to be done. The earliest record is a stele in Ha Nam Province dated 1121 AD, suggesting that by this date water-puppetry was already a regular feature at the royal court.

The art of water-puppetry was traditionally a jealously guarded secret handed down from father to son; women were not permitted to learn the techniques in case they revealed them to their husbands' families. This contributed to its decline until the art seemed in danger of dying out altogether. Happily, a French organization, the *Maison des Cultures du Monde*, intervened and, since 1984, with newly carved puppets, a revamped programme and more elaborate staging, Vietnam's water-puppet troupes have played various international capitals to great acclaim – and can be seen daily in Hanoi (see p.385) and Ho Chi Minh City (see p.102). Where before gongs and drums alone were used for scene-setting and building atmosphere, today's national troupes often maintain a larger ensemble, similar to Hat Cheo, including zithers and flutes. The songs are also borrowed from the Cheo repertoire, particularly declamatory styles and popular folk tunes, and the show often includes a short recital of traditional music before the puppets emerge to create their own unique illusion.

Music, dance and song

One of Vietnam's oldest song traditions is that of **Quan Ho**, or "call-and-response singing", a form which thrives in the Red River Delta, particularly Ha Bac Province, and has parallels among the north's ethnic minorities. These unaccompanied songs are usually heard in spring, performed by young men and women bandying improvised lyrics back and forth. Quan Ho traditionally played a part in the courtship ritual and performers are applauded for their skill in complimenting or teasing their partner, earning delighted approval as the exchange becomes increasingly bawdy.

Found in north and central Vietnam, **Hat Chau Van** is a form of ancient, sacred ritual music used to invoke the spirits during trance possession ceremonies. Statues of a pantheon of goddesses are placed in shrines to the Mother Goddess, Thanh Mau, found in both Buddhist pagodas and village temples. Throughout the performance of hypnotically rhythmic music (the performers may be one or many, male or female) a medium enters a trance state and is possessed by a chosen deity. Because of the anti-religious stance of the Vietnamese government until 1986, the style was practised in secret, though some pieces were adapted for inclusion in state-sponsored Cheo theatre. Chau Van is currently being revived by older practitioners in its original religious setting, promoted by a class of nouveaux riches keen for the goddesses to intercede and protect their business interests.

Although the song tradition known as **Ca Tru**, or *Hat A Dao*, dates back centuries, it became all the rage in the fifteenth century when the Vietnamese regained their independence from China. According to legend, a beautiful young songstress, A Dao, charmed the enemy with her songs of the verdant countryside and the way of life in the villages. Fascinated by her voice, the soldiers were encouraged to drink until they became incapacitated and could be pushed into the river and drowned. The lyrics of Ca Tru are often taken from famous poems and are traditionally sung by a woman. The singer also plays a bamboo percussion instrument, and is accompanied by a three-string lute (*dan day*) and drum. She has to master a whole range of singing styles, each differentiated by its particular rhythm, such as *Hat noi* (similar to speech) and *Gui thu* (a more formal style, akin to a written letter). This beguiling genre has undergone something of a revival in Hanoi in recent years, and it's well worth catching the weekly Saturday performance at the Ca Tru Singing House in Hanoi (see p.384). In Hué excerpts from the closely related **Ca Hué** song tradition are performed for tourists on sampans on the Perfume River (see p.292).

The traditional music accompanying Cai Luong theatre originated in eighteenth-century Hué. Played as pure chamber music, without the voice, it is known as **Nhac Tai Tu**, or "skilled chamber music of amateurs". This is one of the most delightful and challenging of all Vietnamese genres. The players have a great degree of improvisational latitude over a fundamental melodic skeleton; they must think and respond quickly, as in a game, and the resulting independently funky rhythms can be wild. Although modern conservatory training fails to prepare students for this most satisfying of all styles, there is now a resurgence of interest among young players in learning the demands of Tai Tu.

It was also in Hué under the Nguyen emperors that the specialized body of **royal music and dance** reached its peak of sophistication. These solemn ceremonial dances again owed their origins to the Chinese courtly tradition and were categorized into a highly complex system according to the occasion on which they would be performed: ritual dances to be held in temples or pagodas, during feasts or at various civil and military functions, and dances to mark particular anniversaries were just some of the distinctions. As the Imperial court fell under European sway in the twentieth century, so the taste – and opportunity – for such music waned, until the late 1980s when it was revived by the provincial authorities with assistance from UNESCO. Hué's former Royal Theatre has now been renovated and is the venue for occasional performances of courtly music and dance by students of Hué University of Fine Arts. In 2003 UNESCO recognized Nha Nhac ("refined music") as a Masterpiece of Oral and Intangible Heritage.

Traditional instruments

A visiting US general once stepped off a plane with the intention of smoothing relations by attempting a little Vietnamese. This being a tonal language, instead of "I am honoured to be here", listeners heard "the sunburnt duck lies sleeping". The voice and its inherent melodic information are behind all Vietnamese music, and most instruments are, to some extent, made to do what voices do: delicate pitch bends, ornaments and subtle slides. According to classical Confucian theory, instruments fall into eight

categories of sound: silk, stone, skin, clay, metal, air, wood and bamboo. Although few people play by the rules these days, classical theory also relates five occasions when it is forbidden to perform: at sunset, during a storm, when the preparations have not been made seriously, with improper costumes and when the audience is not paying attention.

Many instruments whose strings are now made of steel, gut or nylon originally had **silk** strings; silk is now out of fashion, more for acoustic than ecological reasons. The most famous of these, and unique to Vietnam, is the monochord **dan bau** (or *dan doc huyen*), an ingenious invention perfectly suited to its job of mimicking vocal inflections. It is made from one string (originally silk obtained by yanking apart the live worm), stretched over a long amplified sounding box, fixed at one end. The other end is attached to a buffalo-horn "whammy bar" stalk which can be flexed to stretch or relax the string's tension. Meanwhile the string is plucked with a plectrum at its harmonic nodes to produce overtones that swoop and glide and quiver over a range of three octaves. Other "silk-stringed" instruments include the *dan nguyet* (moon-shaped lute), the *dan tranh* (sixteen-string zither), *dan nhi* (two-string fiddle with the bow running between the strings), *dan day* (a three-stringed lute with a long fingerboard used in Ca Tru and also unique to Vietnam) and *dan luc huyen cam* (a regular guitar with a fingerboard scalloped to allow for wider pitch bends).

The *dan da* **stone** lithophone is the world's oldest instrument, consisting of six or more rocks (most commonly eleven) struck with heavy wooden mallets. Several sets have been found originating from one slate quarry in the central highlands where the stones sing like nowhere else. The oldest *dan da* is now in Paris, but other sets exist in museums throughout Vietnam, such as the Ethnographic Museum in Buon Ma Thuot (see p.192).

Various kinds of **drums** (*trong*) are used, played with acrobatic use of the sticks in the air and on the sides. Some originated in China, while others were introduced from India via the Cham people, such as the double-headed "rice drum" (*trong com*), which was developed from the Indian *mridangam*; the name derives from thin patches of cooked rice paste stuck on each membrane.

Representing **clay**, four thimble-size teacups are held in the fingers and often played as percussion instruments for Hué chamber music. Representing **metal**, the *sinh tien*, **coin clappers**, are another invention unique to Vietnam, combining in one unit a rasping scraper, wooden clapper and a sistrum rattle made from old coins. Bronze **gongs** are occasionally found in minority music, but Vietnam is the only country in Southeast Asia where tuned gamelan-type gong-chimes are not used.

Air, **wood** and **bamboo** furnish a whole range of wind instruments, such as the many side- and end-blown flutes used for folk songs and to accompany poetry recitals; or the *ken*, a double-reed oboe common across Asia and played, appropriately, in funeral processions and other outdoor ceremonies. Five thin bones often dangle from the *ken* player's mouthpiece to suggest the delicate fingers of a young woman, while disguising the hideous grin necessary to play the instrument. The *song lang* is a slit drum, played by the foot, used to count the measures in Tai Tu skilled chamber music, while the *k'long put*, consisting of racks of bamboo pipes, is the only percussion instrument you don't actually touch but clap in front of. Another instrument from the same folk tradition is the *t'rung*, a type of xylophone made of ladders of tuned bamboo. Some of these instruments can be seen and heard in musical recitals at the Temple of Literature in Hanoi (see p.366).

New folk

Turn on the TV during the Tet Lunar New Year festivities and you can't miss the public face of Vietnamese traditional music: ethnic-costumed dancers, musicians and singers smilingly portraying the happy life of the worker. Fancy arrangements of well-known tunes from all over the country, including some token minorities' music, are spiced up with fancy hats and bamboo pianos. This choreographed entertainment known as **Modernized Folk Music** (*Nhac Dan Toc Cai Bien*) has only been "traditional" since

1956, when the Hanoi Conservatory of Music was founded and the teaching of folk music was deliberately "improved".

For the first time, music was learned from written Western notation (leading to the neglect of improvisational skills while opening the way for huge orchestras), and conductors were employed. Tunings of the traditional eight modes were tempered to accommodate Western-style harmonies, while bizarre new instruments were invented to play bass and to fill out chords in the enlarged bands. Schools, with the mandate of preserving traditional music through "inheritance development", took over from the families and professional apprenticeships, which had formerly been passed on via the oral tradition.

Not surprisingly, a new creature was born out of all this. Trained conservatoire graduates have spread throughout the country and been promoted through competitions and state-sponsored ensembles on TV, radio and even in the lobbies of classier hotels. The new corpus of music and song arrangements has become an emblem of national pride and scientific improvement. Folk songs, melodies from the ethnic minorities, Mozart and Chinese tunes are all ripe fodder for the arranger's pen. Much to the chagrin of the few remaining traditional musicians outside this system, this is now the predominant folk-based music generally heard in public. A visitor to the central highlands asked the local tribal musicians how they felt about their music being "improved". At first they replied what an honour it was for their music to be considered by city people, but after the official interview they privately confessed their horror.

Music for new folk is entertaining and accessible, albeit risking tawdriness; at its best, though, it can be an astonishing display of a lively new art form. One family of six brothers (and one sister-in-law), led by Duc Loi, formed a percussion group in Ho Chi Minh City under the name **Phu Dong**, whose members spent time in the highlands learning the instruments of several minorities. Since 1981 they have played together and developed an infectious musical personality. Circular breathing and lightning-speed virtuosity are just some of the dazzling features of a performance, and their collection of instruments is like a zoo of mutant bamboo. Most striking, though, is their use of the lithophone (*dan da*), a replica of the original, six thousand-year-old stone *marimba*. The effect of awakening this ancient voice, whatever changes in performance practice there may have been over the last six millennia, is shattering.

Vietnamese pop

There is no shortage of pop-star wannabes in Vietnam and the fine line between karaoke hacks on CD and major commercial pop releases can be tough to pinpoint. The vast majority of pop music would be filed under **light pop-rock**, but it is also referred to as "misery pop" or "yellow music". Most composers in the country have tried their hand at writing a pop hit but only about three are acknowledged masters: Van Cao (who also wrote the national anthem), Pham Duy (now in his nineties and back in Vietnam, having spent many years writing pointed political songs from the safe distance of California) and Trinh Cong Son (whose life of wine, women and song ended in 2001). Joan Baez was not far off when she dubbed him "the Vietnamese Bob Dylan": the tunes are catchy and the lyrics right-on. His first songs were written while in hiding from the military draft, and in 1969, when his album *Lullaby* sold over two million copies in Japan, Son's works were banned by the South Vietnamese government, which considered the lyrics too demoralizing. Even the new government sent him to work as a peasant in the fields, but after 1979 he lived in Ho Chi Minh City, painting, writing apolitical-but-catchy love songs and celebrating Vietnam's natural wonders, with over six hundred songs to his credit.

There are two main centres for Vietnamese pop-music production: **Ho Chi Minh City** and Southern California. Those in the country have the advantage of being close to the source of folk inspiration (arrangements of traditional Ca Tru and Chau Van songs are currently in vogue), and the young generation has taken singing lessons at the Conservatory (leading to a vast technical improvement of late). Singers of note include: Tran Thu Ha, My Linh, Phuong Thanh, Bang Kieu, Hong Nhung Lam Truong, Thanh Lam and Quang Dung. Albums are bootlegged under different titles so just keep an eye out for these names and you'll be fine.

Meanwhile in Orange County, **California**, the scene is busy but somewhat stagnant. The stars of yesterday and today are: Khanh Ha, Don Ho, Lam Nhat Tien, Nhu Quynh, Y Lan, Khanh Ly and Tuan Ngoc. Look out, too, for Jimmi Nguyen, Trizzie Phuong Trinh and Thanh Ha, all of whom perform regularly in Vietnam. Some of these are the performing children of former superstars, so in many cases the entertainment genes have been passed on despite relocation and social upheaval.

The ubiquitous **pop-rock band** comprises a singer, bass guitar and one or two electronic keyboards, hailed throughout the country as the greatest labour-saving device, despite their cheesy sound. Indeed, in rural areas where there is no electricity, these portable keyboards run happily on batteries, and all the rhythm buttons that are so rarely used elsewhere – rumba, tango, bossa nova and surf-rock – are here employed liberally. The slap-echo on the singer's microphone is intentional; without it, they say, it sounds "unprofessional". Each evening, when the traffic noise dies down, you can hear the mournful laments of neighbouring karaoke bars mingling together, the ghostly echoes of lonely pop singers reverberating from another dimension.

Discography

There are more recordings of traditional music available outside the country than in. But if you find yourself in Hanoi, stop by the Vietnamese Institute of Musicology at CC2, My Dinh urban area, Tu Liem (Ⓦvnmusicology-inst.vnn.vn) and check out their display of over 150 instruments and their extensive database of field recordings.

TRADITIONAL

SAMPLERS

Hò! Roady Music from Vietnam Trikont, Germany. Crass, crazy, funky street music taken from pop cassettes and recorded in situ with mopeds and car horns in the soundscape. It opens in cracking style with a plucked *dan bau* doing "*Riders in the Sky*" with what sounds like fireworks as well. There's a wild funeral brass band and all sorts of surprises. Highly recommended.

Music from Vietnam Vol 1 Caprice, Sweden. An introduction (in conservatoire style) featuring songs, instrumental tracks and theatrical forms. Featured instruments include the *dan bau, dan nguyet* and *k'long put*. Music includes Quan Ho folk songs, Cai Luong and Hat Cheo theatre, Hat Chau Van possession ritual and Nhac Dan Toc Cai Bien new folk.

Stilling Time: Traditional Musics of Vietnam Innova, US. A sampler of field recordings from all over Vietnam, including songs and gong music of the ethnic minorities. An introduction to the many surprises in store for the musical traveller. Recorded and compiled by Philip Blackburn.

THEATRE

The Art of Kim Sinh King, Japan. Blind singer/guitarist Kim Sinh has something of a cult following and knows how to wrench the emotions from those old Cai Luong opera songs. His venerable musical personality is more affecting than many of the commercial Cai Luong releases available, and one struggles not to make comparisons to the blues. This recording has influenced a whole generation of California guitarists.

Vietnam: Traditions of the South Audivis/UNESCO, France. Southern ritual music from the eclectic Cao Dai, Buddhist and indigenous spirit-possession religions, as well as a good helping of Cai Luong theatre music (the traditional, not the cheesy Western-style band!). The liner notes and recording quality are on the dry side but the music is very lively.

Vietnamese Folk Theatre: Hat Cheo King, Japan. Cheo theatre, expertly played by the Quy Bon family and recorded in Hanoi. Features a Chau Van possession ritual and the famous story of the cross-dressing Thi Mau going to a temple.

SONG AND CLASSICAL MUSIC

Anthology of World Music: The Music of Viet Nam Rounder, US. This is the Vietnamese equivalent of the Rosetta Stone, the earliest published recordings of some of the standards of the repertoire, performed by the masters of their day. Music and Theatre of the Court, Ritual Music and Entertainment Music and the Music of South Vietnam. The presentation may seem a little dusty by modern flashy conservatoire standards, but it's still revelatory.

Ca Tru: The Music of North Viet Nam Inedit, France and Ca Tru Singing House Ho Guom Audio, Hanoi. Performed by the Hanoi Ca Tru Thai Ha Ensemble and Ca Tru Thang Long respectively. Tenacious vestiges of Vietnam's five hundred-year tradition of women's "songs for bamboo tokens", Ca Tru (or Hat A Dao) is a private entertainment forced underground until recently. Solo voice (with "bouncing seeds" vibrato), lute and chopsticks titillate male visitors for hours on end.

Music from Vietnam Vol 2: The City of Hué Caprice, Sweden. Ceremonial music with *shawms*, drums and a big gong, a military ensemble and a great court orchestra, as well as more intimate chamber groups of singers with *dan bau*, *dan nguyet*, *dan nhi* and *dan tranh*. Three local instrumental and vocal groups give the enticing flavour of this city, and the disc features the sprightly aged Nguyen Manh Cam, former drummer to the emperor. Good notes.

Vietnam: Buddhist Music from Hué Inedit, France. An atmospheric recording, full of ceremonial presence. It begins with sonorous drums and bells before two oboes enter for music marking the ascent to the "Esplanade of Heaven". The complete ceremony of *Khai Kinh*, "Opening the Sacred Texts", is recorded in one of Hué's best pagodas, the Kim Thien. Not easy listening, but the music is nevertheless impressive. Good notes.

Vietnam: Poésies et Chants Ocora, France. Master musician Tran Van Khe and friends chant poetry (*ngam tho*) and ravish the *dan tranh* and *dan nguyet* (in the Nhac Tai Tu skilled chamber music repertory). Specialized and intimate performances with excellent notes and translations.

ETHNIC MINORITY MUSIC

Gongs: Vietnam, Laos Playasound, France. Before there were skipping records or Steve Reich patterns there were these delicious mellifluously clangorous loops filling the jungle nights.

Music from Vietnam Vol 3: Ethnic Minorities Caprice, Sweden. The mosaic of cultures residing in the central and northern mountains has some astonishing musical traditions. This excellent and accessible selection kicks off with a piece from the E De: a beautiful "free-reed" cow-horn solo followed up by clattering poly-rhythmic gong patterns. There's also music from the Nung, Muong and Hmong. Wonderful pipes, flutes, mouth organs and songs. Good notes.

Musiques des Montagnards Chant du Monde, France. Two CDs of extraordinary archival and recent recordings (1958–97) from the central and northern highlands. Fourteen ethnic groups are covered and excellently described in the copious 119-page booklet.

Northern Vietnam: Music and Songs of the Minorities Buda Musique/Musique du Monde, France. A selection of recordings from the Giay, Nung, Tay, Dao, Thai and Hmong ethnic groups. A love song, courting melodies, wedding music, funeral music and the extraordinary Hmong *khen*.

NEW FOLK

Echoes of Ancestral Voices: Traditional Music of Vietnam Move, Australia. Music performed by husband and wife duo Dang Kim Hien and Le Tuan Hung. No fireworks, just a fragile, uncompromising intensity.

Moonlight in Vietnam Henry Street/Rounder, US. New music expertly played on Vietnam's most extraordinary musical instruments, including the *dan bau*, *k'long put* and a stick-fiddle with a resonating disc held in the player's mouth. The players are a Vancouver-based ensemble led by *dan bau* virtuoso Ho Khac Chi.

The Music of Vietnam Vols 1.1 & 1.2 Celestial Harmonies, US. Accessible, virtuoso and expertly recorded, these discs document an array of Vietnam's best conservatoire-mediated styles. Through a compelling series of pieces, this is an entertaining overview of the full range of Vietnamese instruments. Full documentation.

POP

Don Ho *Ru Em/Lullaby* Thuy Nga, US. Heart-throb lullabies from one of California's hottest singers.

Khanh Ha *Doi Da Vang/Vacant Rock-strewn Hill* Khanh Ha Productions, US. Bilingual singing legend compared (favourably) to Barbra Streisand and Celine Dion.

My Linh *Toc Ngan/Short Hair* My Linh Productions, Vietnam. Hot arrangements of pieces all written for her sultry, crackly voice.

Nguyen Thanh Van *Ho Khoan Le Thuy/River Song* Van Nguyen Productions, US. Passion, pathos and folk references from this San Francisco-based artist.

Pham Duy *Voyage Through the Motherland* Co Loa, US. The first Vietnamese CD-ROM, featuring patriotic songs, karaoke options, video and fine photos. A real "coffee table" disc.

Y Lan *Muon Hoi Tai Sao/I Want to Ask Why* Y Lan Productions, US. From a well-known artistic family, she became a café owner before becoming a regular at the *Ritz* and *Paris By Night* circuit.

With contributions by Philip Blackburn (from *The Rough Guide to World Music*).

Books

Of the vast canon of books written on the subject of Vietnam, the overwhelming majority concern themselves, inevitably, with the American War. Indigenous attempts to come to terms with the conflicts that have caused Vietnam such pain are only now beginning to filter through the country's overcautious censorship. Some of the few novels that have reached the West in recent years are also reviewed below.

For a decent copy of a book on Vietnam, your best bet is to scour bookshops before you set off from home – only Hanoi and Ho Chi Minh City have ranges of literature of any breadth, and then often only in photocopied offprint form. The exceptions to this are books produced by local publishers, notably The Gioi Publishers, which you'll have difficulty finding outside Vietnam.

TRAVEL WRITING

Maria Coffey *Three Moons in Vietnam*. Delightfully jolly jaunt around Vietnam by boat, bus and bicycle. Coffey conspires to meet more locals in one day than most travellers do in a month, making this a valuable snapshot of modern Vietnam.

Sue Downie *Down Highway One*. In 1988 Sue Downie was one of the first Westerners since the American War to travel the length of Highway 1. Returning in the early 1990s, she witnesses the changes – not all good – transforming the country and people's daily lives.

Graham Greene *Ways of Escape*. Greene's global travels in the 1950s took him to Vietnam for four consecutive winters; the coverage of Vietnam in this slim autobiographical volume is intriguing, but tantalizingly short, its memories of dice-playing with French agents over vermouths and opium-smoking in Cho Lon are evidently templates for scenes in *The Quiet American*.

Christopher Hunt *Sparring with Charlie*. Hunt can be a maddening travelling companion, but this account of his jaunt down the Ho Chi Minh Trail on a Russian-made motorbike is undeniably a page-turner.

★ **Norman Lewis** *A Dragon Apparent*. When in 1950 Lewis made the journey that would inspire his seminal Indochina travelogue, the Vietnam he saw was still a land of longhouses and Imperial hunts, though poised for renewed conflict; the erudite prose of this doyen of travel writers reveals a Vietnam now long gone.

W. Somerset Maugham *The Gentleman in the Parlour*. The fruit of Maugham's grand tour from Rangoon to Hai Phong to recharge his creative batteries, *The Gentleman in the Parlour*, finds him less than enamoured of Vietnam, his last stop. Nevertheless, his accounts of the Hué court teetering on the brink of extinction, and of a run-in with an old acquaintance in a Hai Phong café, are vintage Maugham.

Karin Muller *Hitchhiking Vietnam*. A feisty American, Karin Muller went searching for the "real Vietnam", a Vietnam untouched by commercialism and Western culture. On the way she gets deported, is arrested on numerous occasions and meets some motley characters, but eventually finds what she's looking for among the minorities of the northwest mountains. Beautifully told, with great compassion and a never-failing sense of humour.

Andrew X. Pham *Catfish and Mandala*. After twenty years in America, Pham takes a gruelling bike ride through Vietnam to rediscover the country, his family and – in the process – himself. A compelling insight into the frustrations and fascinations of Vietnam.

Gontran de Poncins *From a Chinese City*. Believing that "the ancient customs of a national culture endure longer in remote colonies than in the motherland", de Poncins opted for a sojourn in Cho Lon as a means to a better understanding of the foibles of the Chinese; the resulting document of life in 1955 Cho Lon is a lively period piece, backed up by fluid illustrations.

Pam Scott *Hanoi Stories* and *Life in Hanoi*. Hanoi and its inhabitants – both local and expat, from its celebrities to its cyclo drivers – viewed through the lens of an Australian who came on business and stayed ten years.

James Sullivan *Over the Moat*. Cultures collide as Sullivan courts a Hué shop-girl he met while cycling through Vietnam in 1992. Part love story, part travelogue.

Paul Theroux *The Great Railway Bazaar*. His elaborate circumnavigation of Europe and Asia by train took Theroux, in 1973, to a South Vietnam still bewildered by the recent American withdrawal. In bleak sound-bite accounts of rides from Saigon to Bien Hoa and Hué to Da Nang, he describes the war's awful legacy of poverty, suffering and infrastructural breakdown, but marvels at the country's unbowed, and unexpected, beauty.

Gabrielle M. Vassal *On and Off Duty in Annam*. An enchanting wander through early twentieth century southern Vietnam, penned by the intrepid wife of a French army doctor. A stint in Saigon is followed by a boat trip to Nha Trang (where she was carried ashore "on the backs of natives through the breakers") and a gutsy foray into the central highlands; amazing prints of the Vietnamese and *montagnards* she encountered further enhance the account.

Justin Wintle *Romancing Vietnam*. Wintle's genial but lightweight yomp upcountry was one of the first of its kind, post-*doi moi*, and remains a pleasing aperitif to travels in Vietnam.

VIETNAMESE ABROAD

Donald Anderson (ed) *Aftermath: An Anthology of Post-Vietnam Fiction*. As the war's tendrils crept across the Pacific to America, they touched not only the people who fought, but also those who stayed at home. In their depictions of Americans, Amerasians and Asians regathering the strands of their lives, these short stories run the gamut of emotions provoked by war.

★ **Robert Olen Butler** *A Good Scent from a Strange Mountain*. Pulitzer Prize-winning collection of short stories that ponder the struggles of Vietnamese in America to maintain the cultural ley lines linking them with their mother country, and the gulf between them and their Americanized offspring. War veteran Olen Butler's assured prose ensures the voices of his Vietnamese characters find perfect pitch.

★ **Le Ly Hayslip** *Child of War, Woman of Peace*. In this follow-up to *When Heaven and Earth Changed Places* (see p.490), Hayslip's narrative shifts to America, where the cultural disorientation of a new arrival is examined.

VIETNAMESE LITERATURE

John Balaban and Nguyen Qui Duc (eds) *Vietnam: A Traveller's Literary Companion*. The editors of this entertaining volume of short stories, written by Vietnamese writers based both at home and abroad, chose to avoid tales of war and politics during their selection process, though both themes inevitably make their presence felt.

★ **Bao Ninh** *The Sorrow of War*. This is a ground-breaking novel, largely due to its portrayal of Communist soldiers suffering the same traumas, fear and lost innocence as their American counterparts.

Steven Bradbury *Poems from the Prison Diary of Ho Chi Minh Tinfish*. This beautifully rendered selection of the poems Ho penned while behind bars in 1942, in which he looks to birdsong and moonlight to ease the loneliness of prison life, provide a touching glimpse of the man behind the myth.

Alastair Dingwall (ed) *Traveller's Literary Companion to South-East Asia*. Among the bite-sized essays inside this gem of a book is an enlightening thirty-page segment on Vietnam, into which are crammed biopics, a recommended reading list, historical, linguistic and literary backgrounds.

Excerpts range from classical literature to the writings of foreign journalists in the 1960s.

★ **Duong Thu Huong** *Novel Without a Name*. A tale of young Vietnamese men seeking glory but finding only loneliness, disillusionment and death, as war abridges youth and curtails loves. A depiction of dwindling idealism, and a radical questioning of the political motives behind the war. Other highly acclaimed works by the same author include *Paradise of the Blind* and *Memories of a Pure Spring*.

★ **Duong Van Mai Elliot** *The Sacred Willow*. Mai Elliot brings Vietnamese history to life in this compelling account of her family through four generations.

Wayne Karlin, Le Minh Khue and Truong Vu (eds) *The Other Side of Heaven*. A unique anthology of postwar fiction by Vietnamese and American authors. Though written by former enemies from all sides of the conflict, these stories echo back and forth the unifying themes of sorrow, pain and survival.

Le Minh Khue *The Stars, The Earth, The River*. Fourteen short stories by one of Vietnam's leading contemporary writers, an ex-sapper who gently details the seesaw of "tragedy and hope" which defines her war-torn generation.

Nguyen Du *The Tale of Kieu*. Vietnamese literature reached its zenith with this tale of the ill-starred love between Kieu and Kim.

★ **Nguyen Huy Thiep** *The General Retires and Other Stories*. Perhaps Vietnam's pre-eminent writer, Nguyen Huy Thiep articulates the lives of ordinary Vietnamese in these short stories – instead of following the prevailing trend of re-imagining the lives of past heroes.

NOVELS SET IN VIETNAM

Marguerite Duras *The Lover*. Young French girl meets wealthy Chinese man on a Mekong Delta ferry; the ensuing affair initiates her into adulthood, with all its joys and responsibilities. The novel's depiction of a dysfunctional, hard-up French family in Vietnam provides an interesting slant on colonial life, showing it wasn't all vermouths and tennis.

★ **Camilla Gibb** *The Beauty of Humanity Movement*. Gibb's deft characterization creates an endearing and poignant, contemporary tale that revolves around Hung, an old man whose life is dedicated to making pho even when there are no ingredients to be had in post-reunification Hanoi.

★ **Graham Greene** *The Quiet American*. Greene's prescient and cautionary tale of the dangers of innocence in uncertain times, which anticipated America's boorish manhandling of Vietnam's political situation by several years, is still the best single account of wartime Vietnam. Its regular name-drops of familiar locales – Tay Ninh, the *Continental*, Dong Khoi – make it doubly enjoyable.

★ **Anthony Grey** *Saigon*. Vietnamese history given a blockbuster makeover: a rip-roaring narrative, whose Vietnamese, French and American protagonists conspire to be present at all defining moments in recent Vietnamese history, from French plantation riots to the fall of Saigon.

Nguyen Kien *Tapestries*. This rich and beautifully woven novel is based on the extraordinary real-life story of the author's grandfather, who eventually became an embroiderer in the royal court of Hué. The context is a country on the cusp of change as French influence gains the upper hand.

★ **Tim O'Brien** *Going After Cacciato*. A highly acclaimed, lyrical tale of an American soldier who simply walks out of the war and sets off for Paris, pursued by his company on a fantastical mission that takes them across Asia. The savage reality of war stands out vividly against a dream-world of peace and freedom.

HISTORY

William J. Duiker *The Communist Road to Power in Vietnam*. One of America's leading analysts of the political context in Vietnam takes a long close look at why Communist Vietnam won its wars – as opposed to why France and America lost.

William J. Duiker *Ho Chi Minh: A Life*. Duiker turns his spotlight on the patriot and revolutionary who led Vietnam to independence. It's a thoroughly researched and exhaustive tome, particularly good on Ho's political evolution, though fails to get under the skin of this enigmatic man.

Bernard Fall *Hell in a Very Small Place*. The classic account of the siege of Dien Bien Phu, capturing the claustrophobia and the fear, written by a French-born American journalist.

★ **Bernard Fall** *Street Without Joy*. Another masterpiece by Fall, charting the French debacle in Indochina, which became required reading for American generals and GIs – though it didn't prevent them committing exactly the same mistakes just a few years later.

David Halberstam *Ho*. Diminutive, sympathetic and highly readable biography of Vietnam's foremost icon, though no attempt is made to apportion blame for the disastrous land reforms of the 1950s.

★ **Stanley Karnow** *Vietnam: A History*. Weighty, august tome that elucidates the entire span of Vietnamese history.

Michael Maclear *Vietnam: The Ten Thousand Day War*. A solid introductory account of the French and American wars, from Ho's alliance with Archimedes Patti, to the fall of Saigon.

Nguyen Khac Vien *Vietnam: A Long History*. Published by Hanoi's The Gioi Publishers, and therefore heavily weighted in favour of the Communists, but easier to get hold of in Vietnam than most histories.

Keith Weller Taylor *The Birth of Vietnam* University of California Press. As a GI, Taylor was struck by the "intelligence and resolve" of his enemy. This meticulous account of the dawn of Vietnamese history, trawling the past from the nation's first recorded history up to the tenth century, is the result of his attempt to uncover their roots.

★ **Martin Windrow** *The Last Valley: Dien Bien Phu and the French Defeat in Vietnam*. This meticulously researched and detailed account of the battle of Dien Bien Phu gives a brutally realistic picture of what it was like for the French soldiers (many actually Vietnamese, Thai and North African) trapped in what came to be known as the "toilet bowl". Windrow's sympathy and admiration for the soldiers – on both sides – comes across loud and clear.

THE AMERICAN WAR

Mark Baker *Nam*. Unflinching firsthand accounts of the GI's descent from boot camp into the morass of death, paranoia, exhaustion and tedium. Gut-wrenchingly frank at times, the book depicts war as a rite of passage, and moral deterioration as a prerequisite to survival.

Tad Bartimus (ed) *War Torn: Stories of War from the Women Reporters Who Covered Vietnam*. Nine pioneering women journalists who covered the American War tell their tales, from the struggle to get there in the first place and be recognized in what was then an almost exclusively male profession to their reactions to the war itself and coming to terms with the aftermath.

★ **Michael Bilton and Kevin Sim** *Four Hours in My Lai*. Brutally candid and immaculately researched reconstruction of the events surrounding the My Lai massacre of 1968; as harrowing a portrayal of the depths plumbed in war as you'll ever read.

★ **Philip Caputo** *A Rumour of War*. One of the classics of the American War, Caputo's straightforward narrative is a powerful account of the numbing daily routine of the ordinary US soldier's life, the strange exhilaration of combat and the brutalization that accompanies war.

★ **Denise Chong** *The Girl in the Picture*. Kim Phuc was the little girl running naked away from her napalm-bombed village in what is arguably the most famous – and most harrowing – photo taken during the American War. Not only did she survive the burns, just, but her resilience and capacity for forgiveness are quite remarkable. Denise Chong tells Kim's story simply, letting the horrific events speak for themselves.

Michael Clodfelter *Mad Minutes and Vietnam Months*. Combat reminiscences from a man who found war's false promise of "courage, sacrifice, glory and adventure" displaced by monotony and, occasionally, atrocity.

W.D. Ehrhart *Going Back: An Ex-Marine Returns to Vietnam*. A veteran of the battle for Hué, Ehrhart returned to Vietnam in 1985. *Going Back*, a record of that trip, mixes diary, memory and Ehrhart's own poetry to very readable effect.

★ **Horst Faas and Tim Page** (eds) *Requiem*. Turning through this compendium of shots by photographers who subsequently lost their lives in Vietnam, Laos or Cambodia will haunt you for weeks. Never was a book more aptly named.

James Fenton *All the Wrong Places*. In Vietnam at the moment of Saigon's liberation, Fenton somehow managed to hitch a lift on the tank that rammed through the palace gates; his easy prose and poet's eye for detail make his account an engrossing one.

⭐ **Frances Fitzgerald** *Fire in the Lake*. Pulitzer Prize-winning analysis of the historical, political and cultural context of the war, this time told from the Vietnamese perspective.

Albert French *Patches of Fire*. Examining his experiences of the infantryman's life in Vietnam and his attempts to exorcise his war-conjured demons back in the States, French's autobiography is at once moving and engrossing.

⭐ **Le Ly Hayslip** *When Heaven and Earth Changed Places*. For giving a human face to the slopes, dinks and gooks of American writing on Vietnam, this heart-rending tale of villagers trying to survive in a climate of hatred and distrust is perhaps more valuable than any history book.

⭐ **Michael Herr** *Dispatches*. Infuriatingly narcissistic at times, Herr's spaced-out narrative still conveys the mud, blood and guts of the American war effort in Vietnam. Herr's distinctive tone is also evident in the classic war movie, *Apocalypse Now* (see p.494), for which he wrote the screenplay.

John Laurence *The Cat from Hué*. Highly acclaimed for his coverage of the Vietnam conflict for CBS News from 1965 to 1970, Laurence has written not only an evocative memoir but also a moving testimony to the courage of the American troops who, like him, came of age in the battlefields of Vietnam.

Tom Mangold and John Penycate *The Tunnels of Cu Chi*. The most thorough, and the most captivating, account yet written of the guerrilla resistance mounted in the tunnels around Cu Chi.

⭐ **Robert Mason** *Chickenhawk*. Few people can be better qualified than Mason to deliver an account of the American War: a helicopter pilot with over a thousand missions under his belt, his blood-and-guts, bird's-eye account of the war is harrowing but compelling.

Harold G. Moore and Joseph Galloway *We Were Soldiers Once...and Young*. This blow-by-blow account of the ferocious battle of the Ia Drang valley, among the earliest encounters of the American War, makes compelling reading as the authors recapture the chaos and fear alongside moments of incredible courage and the sheer determination to survive.

⭐ **Tim O'Brien** *The Things They Carried and If I Die in a Combat Zone*. Through a mix of autobiography and fiction O'Brien lays to rest the ghosts of the past in a brutally honest reappraisal of the war, his own actions and the events he witnessed (see also O'Brien's novel *Going After Cacciato*, reviewed on p.525).

⭐ **John Pilger** *Heroes*. Journalist Pilger's systematic dismantling of the myth that America's role was in any way a justifiable "crusade" makes his Vietnam reportage required reading.

William Prochnau *Once Upon a Distant War*. Now that all the journos ever to set foot in Vietnam have published memoirs, Prochnau presents a new twist – the intriguing story of the people (amongst them Neil Sheehan, David Halberstam and Peter Arnett) who wrote the stories of Vietnam.

⭐ **Neil Sheehan** *A Bright Shining Lie*. This monumental and fluently rendered account of the war, hung around the life of the soldier John Paul Vann, won the Pulitzer Prize for Sheehan; one of the true classics of Vietnam-inspired literature.

Justin Wintle *The Vietnam War*. Written in reaction to the shelves of long-winded texts available on the subject, Wintle's succinct overview manages to condense this mad war into fewer than two hundred pages.

⭐ **Tobias Wolff** *In Pharaoh's Army*. A former adviser based in My Tho, Wolff's honest, gentle autobiographical tale takes a wry look at life away from the "front line".

POSTWAR VIETNAM

Bui Tin *Following Ho Chi Minh*. An erstwhile colonel in the North Vietnamese Army, Bui Tin effectively defected to the West in 1990, since when he has been an outspoken critic of Vietnam's state apparatus. These memoirs don't flinch from addressing the underside – corruption, prejudice, naivety and insensitivity – of the party.

Adam Fforde and Stefan de Vylder *From Plan to Market*. Highbrow, laudably researched book plotting the route Vietnam has taken from Stalinist central planning to market economy. Fforde and de Vylder hold the fabric of *doi moi* up to the light for examination in the mid-1990s.

David Lamb *Vietnam, Now: A Reporter Returns*. War journalist David Lamb returned to Vietnam for a four-year stint in 1997. While the war is a constant presence, this is primarily a commentary on contemporary Vietnam and its prospects for the future. Lamb is ultimately optimistic, though his criticisms of the government – notably its failure to reconcile the still-deep divisions between north and south – were sufficient to get the book banned.

Tim Page *Derailed in Uncle Ho's Victory Garden*. The war photographer with a legendary ability to defy death, returns to Vietnam in the 1980s. Buried among the flashbacks and meandering discourse, Page's eye for detail and his delight in the bizarre give a flavour of postwar Vietnam.

Neil Sheehan *Two Cities: Hanoi and Saigon*. Sheehan returned to Vietnam in 1989 to witness first-hand the legacy of the war. Down south, the memories really begin to flow as encounters and travels trigger wartime flashbacks, interspersed with commentary on re-education camps and other deprivations of the dark, pre-*doi moi* years.

⭐ **Robert Templer** *Shadows and Wind*. This hard-hitting book casts a critical eye over Vietnam's decades of reform, from corruption and censorship to the emergence of a consumer-oriented youth culture. Though written in the late 1980s, the informative and balanced analysis still holds true today.

CULTURE AND SOCIETY

James Goodman *Uniquely Vietnamese*. Asia-based author Goodman has produced an informative catalogue of Vietnamese ingenuity, ranging from conical hats to Cheo theatre, from local festivals to water-puppets and the haunting, one-stringed *dan bau*.

Gerald Cannon Hickey *Shattered World*. Detailed but readable account of ethnic minorities living in Vietnam's central highlands by one of the region's leading ethnologists. A fascinating analysis of the minorities' tragic struggle to survive both war and peace.

Henry Kamm *Dragon Ascending*. Pulitzer Prize-winning correspondent Kamm lets the Vietnamese – art dealers, ex-colonels, academics, doctors, authors – speak for themselves. This they do eloquently, resulting in a convincing portrait of contemporary Vietnam.

Norma J. Livo and Dia Cha *Folk Stories of the Hmong*. The Hmong's fading oral tradition is captured in this unique collection, gleaned from US immigrants, while its scene-setting introduction offers a valuable overview of Hmong culture, accompanied by illustrations of traditional costume and embroidered "storycloths".

William S. Logan *Hanoi: Biography of a City*. A heritage adviser, Logan peels back the layers of history revealed in Hanoi's architecture and streetscapes to provide an academic but engaging account of the city. In doing so, he also examines the challenges facing Hanoi at the start of the new millennium as it strives to preserve its unique heritage while also meeting the needs of its citizens.

Robert S. McKelvey *The Dust of Life*. Moving oral histories by Vietnamese Amerasians abandoned by their American fathers and discriminated against by the Vietnamese.

Mai Pham *Pleasures of the Vietnamese Table*. Saigon-born chef and restaurateur rediscovers her Vietnamese culinary roots and puts together one of the best Vietnamese cookbooks.

Nguyen Van Huy and Laurel Kendall (eds) *Vietnam: Journeys of Mind, Body and Spirit*. A broad range of contemporary commentators present an evocative snapshot of Vietnamese society and culture at the start of the new millennium.

★ **Christina Noble** *Bridge Across My Sorrows*. Life-affirming autobiography by a Dublin woman spurred by a dream to channel her considerable strengths into helping Ho Chi Minh City's *bui doi*, or street children. In her sequel, *Mama Tina*, Noble continues the story of her work in Vietnam, and describes her more recent campaign for children's rights in Mongolia.

VIETNAM ON FILM

Gilbert Adair *Hollywood's Vietnam: From the Green Berets to Full Metal Jacket*. Adair's excitable prose guides you past the fire-fights, f-words and R&R hijinks, to a real appreciation of how Hollywood reflected shifting American attitudes to the war.

Jeremy Devine *Vietnam at 24 Frames a Second*. The most wide-ranging analysis of Vietnam movies, covering more than four hundred films.

Linda Dittmar and Gene Michaud (eds) *From Hanoi to Hollywood*. Collected essays on the way the American War encroached on Hollywood.

Vietnam in the movies

The embroilment of France and the US in Vietnam and its conflicts has spawned hundreds of movies, ranging from fond soft-focused colonial reminiscences to blood-and-guts depictions of the horrors of war. As a means of brushing up on your Indochinese history, their value is questionable: for the most part, they're hardly objective. Yet, through the reflections they cast of the climates in which they were created, these films amplify the West's efforts to come to terms with what went on there, and for this reason they demand attention.

Early depictions

Hollywood was setting movies in Indochina long before the first American troops splashed ashore at Da Nang. As early as 1932, Jean Harlow played a sassy Saigon prostitute to smouldering Clark Gable's rubber-plantation manager, in the steamy pot-boiler, **Red Dust**. At this early stage, however, Vietnam was no more than an exotic backdrop.

Even by the mid-1950s, as the modest beginnings of American involvement elicited from Hollywood its first real moves to acquaint itself with Vietnam, the country was often treated less as a nation with its own discernible identity and unique set of political issues, and more as a generic Asian theatre of war, in which the righteous **battle against Communism** could be played out. In its portrayal of noble and libertarian French forces, aided by American military specialists, confronting the evil of Communism, **China Gate** (1957) is an early example of this trend. Dedicated to the French *colons* who "advanced this backward society to its place as the rice bowl of Asia", its laboured plot, concerning an attempt to destroy a Viet Minh arms cache, is of much less interest than its heavy-handed politics.

Vietnam provided Hollywood with a golden opportunity to project its militaristic fantasies, and a chance to tap into the prejudices brought to the surface by more than a decade of anti-Japanese World War II movies – prejudices that painted American involvement as a reprise of past battles with the inscrutable **Asian hordes**. Rather more depth of thought went into the making of **The Quiet American** (1958), in which Michael Redgrave played the British journalist and cynic, Fowler, while Audie Murphy (America's most decorated soldier in World War II) played Pyle, the eponymous "hero" of Graham Greene's novel. To Greene's chagrin, Pyle was depicted not as a representative of the American government, but of a private aid organization – something which the author felt blunted his anti-American message; nevertheless, the movie retained its source's sense of the futility of attempting to rationalize of Vietnam's political quagmire.

Gung ho!

The military mandarins who led America into war failed to get the message, though: with American troops duly deployed in a far-flung corner of the globe by 1965, it was only a matter of time before **John Wayne** produced a patriotic movie to match. This came in the form of the monumentally bad **The Green Berets** (1968), in which a paunchy Wayne starred as "Big" Bill Kirby, a loveable colonel leading an adoring team of American soldiers into the central highlands. That Wayne, while on a promotional trip out to Vietnam, handed out cigarette cases inscribed with his signature and the message "Fuck Communism", speaks volumes about the film's subtlety. Kicking off with a stirring marching song ("Fighting soldiers from the sky, Fearless men who jump and die..."), the movie depicts American soldiers in spotless uniforms and perma-grins fighting against no less a threat than total "Communist domination of the world", yet still abiding, as the critic Gilbert Adair has it, "by Queensberry rules". In stark contrast to the squeaky-clean GIs are the barbaric Viet Cong, depicted as child-abusing rapists who whoop and holler like madmen as they overrun a US camp, all to the strains of suitably eerie Oriental music.

Sweeping Vietnam under the carpet

The war in Vietnam was a much dirtier affair than *The Green Berets* made it seem, its politics far less cut and dried. As the struggle turned into tragedy and popular support for it soured, movie moguls sensed that the war had become **taboo**. "Vietnam is awkward," said the journalist Michael Herr, "...and if people don't even want to hear about it, you know they're not going to pay money to sit there in the dark and have it brought up." It was to be a full decade before another major combat movie was released. Instead, film-makers trained their gaze upon returning Vietnam veterans' doomed attempts to ease back into society. The resulting pictures were low in compassion: America's national pride had been collectively compromised by the failure to bring home a victory, and sympathy and forgiveness were at a premium.

A raft of **exploitation movies** was churned out, boasting names such as *Born Losers* (1967), *Angels from Hell* (1968) and *The Ravager* (1970), in which the mental scars of Vietnam provided topical window-dressing to improbable tales of martial arts, motorbikes and mayhem. At best, vets were treated as dysfunctional vigilantes acting beyond the pale of society – most famously in **Taxi Driver** (1976), which has Robert De Niro's disturbed insomniac returnee, Travis Bickle, embarking on a one-man moral crusade to purge the streets of a hellish New York. At worst, they were wacko misfits posing a threat to small-town America. With veterans being portrayed as anything but heroes, it was left to the stars of the **campus riot movies**, and films lionizing **draft-dodgers**, to provide role models.

Coming to terms with the war

Only in 1978 did Hollywood finally pluck up enough courage to confront the war head-on, and so aid the nation's healing process – **movies-as-therapy**. In the years since John Wayne's *Green Berets* had battened down the hatches against Communism, America had first lost sight of justification for the war, and then effectively lost the war itself. Movies no longer sought to make sense of past events, but to highlight their futility; for the generation of young Americans unfortunate enough to live through Vietnam, mere survival was seen as triumph enough. As audiences were exposed to their first dramatized glimpses of the war's unpalatable realities, they were confronted by disaffected troops seeking comfort in prostitution and drug abuse, along with far more shocking examples of soldiers' fraying moral fibre.

Such themes were woven through the first of the four movies of note released in 1978, **The Boys in Company C**, which follows a band of young draftees through their basic training stateside, and then into action. In one particularly telling scene, American lives are lost transporting what turns out to be whisky and cigarettes to the front. A similar futility underpins **Go Tell the Spartans**, in which Burt Lancaster's drug- and alcohol-hazed troops take, and then abandon, a camp – an idea reused nine years later in *Hamburger Hill*.

Coming Home (1978), which cast Jane Fonda as a military career-man's wife who falls in love with a wheelchair-bound veteran (Jon Voight), was significant for its sensitive consideration of the emotional and physical tolls exacted by the war, and initiated the trend for more measured and intelligent vet movies.

Similarly concerned with the ramifications of the war, both home and away, was **The Deer Hunter** (1978), in which the conscription of three friends fractures their Russian Orthodox community in Pennsylvania. The friends' "one-shot" code of honour, espoused on a last pre-Vietnam hunting trip, contrasts wildly with the moral vacuum of the war, whose random brutality is embodied in the movie's central scenes of Russian roulette. The picture's ending, with its melancholy rendition of *God Bless America* by the central characters, is only semi-ironic, and alludes to the country's regenerative process. For all its power, *The Deer Hunter* is marred by overt racist stereotyping of the Vietnamese who, according to John Pilger, are dismissed as "sub-human Oriental barbarians and idiots". The Vietnamese we see are grotesque caricatures interested only in getting their kicks from gambling and death, and there's a strong sense that American youths ought never to have been exposed to such primordial evil as existed across the Pacific.

Francis Ford Coppola's hugely indulgent but visually magnificent **Apocalypse Now** (1979) rounded off the vanguard of postwar Vietnam combat movies. Described by one critic as "Film as opera…it turns Vietnam into a vast trip, into a War of the Imagination", the picture's Dantean snapshots of the war rob Vietnam of all identity other than as a "heart of darkness". Fuelled by his desire to convey the "horror, the madness, the sensuousness, and the moral dilemma of the Vietnam war", Coppola totally mythologizes the conflict, rendering it not so much futile as insane. The usual elements of needless death, casual atrocity, moral decline and spaced-out soldiers leaning heavily on substance abuse are all here, played out against a raunchy soundtrack. However, with its stylized representation of montagnards as generic savages deifying Westerners, and its depiction of the Viet Cong as butchers who happily lop the arms off children who have had "American" inoculations, *Apocalypse Now* is little more enlightened than *The Deer Hunter*. Coppola subsequently compared the creation of the film itself to a war: "We were in the jungle, there were too many of us. We had access to too much money and too much equipment and little by little we went insane" – a process graphically depicted in **Hearts of Darkness: A Filmmaker's Apocalypse** (1991).

Returning home

The precedent set by *Coming Home* of sympathetic consideration for **returning veterans**' mindsets spurred many movies along similar lines in subsequent years. These focused on the disillusionment and disorientation felt by soldiers coming back, not to heroes' welcomes, but to indifference and even disdain.

One of the first of these movies was **First Blood** (1982), which introduced audiences to Sly Stallone's muscle-bound super-vet, John Rambo. As we witness Rambo's torment in small-town America, the picture is more "shoot 'em up" than cerebral. Yet its climax, in which Rambo's former colonel becomes a surrogate father figure to him, underscores the tender ages of the troops who fought the war. Other movies of the genre – among them Alan Parker's **Birdy** (1984) and Oliver Stone's **Born on the 4th of July** (1989) – reiterated the message of stolen youth and innocence by screening idyllic, elegiac scenes of childhood. Stone has his hero (played by Tom Cruise) swallowing the anti-Communist line, and returning to an indifference symbolized by the squalor of the army hospital in which he recuperates and by the breakdown of his relationship with his mother. In *Birdy*, doctors at a loss as to how to treat a catatonic patient turn to a fellow vet for help – this sense of America's inability to relate to returnees subsequently resurfaces in **Jacknife** (1989).

Rewriting history

Not content with squaring up to the war in Vietnam, Hollywood during the 1980s attempted, bizarrely, to rewrite its script in a series of **revisionist movies**. Richard Gere had made the armed forces hip again in 1982's weepie **An Officer and a Gentleman**; a year later the first of an intriguing sub-genre of films hit cinemas, in which Americans returned to Vietnam, invariably to rescue MIAs, and "won". Given a righteous cause (and what could be more righteous than rescuing fellow soldiers), and freed from the chains of moral degradation that had shackled him in previous movies, the US soldier could now show his true mettle. In stark contrast to the comic-book superhuman Americans of these pictures, are the brainless **Vietnamese**, who appear only as cannon fodder.

Uncommon Valor (1983), a rather silly piece about an MIA rescue starring Gene Hackman, kicked things off, closely followed by **Missing in Action** (1983), in which Chuck Norris, the poor man's Stallone, karate-kicks his way towards the same resolution with sufficient panache to justify a speedy follow-up. The mother of them all, though, was **Rambo: First Blood, Part II** (1985), in which the hero of *First Blood* gets to settle some old scores. "Do we get to win this time?" asks Rambo, at the top of the movie. As he riots through the Vietnamese countryside in order to extricate a band of American PoWs, he answers his own question by slaying Vietnamese foes at an approximate rate of one every two minutes.

"It don't mean nothing"

The backlash to the patent nonsense of the revisionist films came in the form of a series of shockingly realistic movies which attempted, in the words of the director Oliver Stone, to "peel the onion" and reveal the **real Vietnam**, routine atrocities, indiscipline and all. There are no heroes in these GI's-view movies, only fragile, confused-looking young men in fatigues, emphasizing that this was a war that affected a whole generation – not just its most photogenic individuals.

In **Platoon** (1986), Oliver Stone, himself a foot soldier in Vietnam, created the most realistic cinematographic interpretation of the American involvement yet. Filmed on location in the Philippines, this movie reminded audiences that killing gooks wasn't as straightforward as Rambo made it seem. As well as portraying the depths to which humankind can sink, Stone shows the circumstances under which it was feasible for young American boys to become murderers of civilians. Its oppressive sensory overload powerfully conjures the paranoiac near-hysteria spawned by fear, confusion, loss of motivation and inability to discriminate between friend and foe. Inherent in its shadowy, half-seen portrayal of the enemy is a grudging respect for their expertise in jungle warfare.

If *Platoon* portrays a dirty war, in **Hamburger Hill** (1987), which dramatizes the taking of Ap Bia hill during May 1969's battle for the A Shau valley, it has degenerated into a positive mud bath. As troops slither and slide on the flanks of the hill in the highland mists, they become indistinguishable, and the image of an entire generation stumbling towards the maws of death is strengthened by the fact that the cast includes no big-name actors – the men who fall on the hill are neighbours, sons or brothers, not film stars. American losses are taken in order to secure a useless hill, a potent symbol of the futility of America's involvement in the war; as one soldier says, time after time, in a weary mantra, "it don't mean nothing, not a thing." Stanley Kubrick's **Full Metal Jacket** (1987) picks up *Hamburger Hill's* theme of the war's theft of American youth in its opening scene, as the camp barber strips conscripts of their hair and, by implication, their individuality. A brutal drill-sergeant completes the alienation process by replacing the soldiers' names with nicknames of his choosing, and then sets about expunging their humanity – on the grounds that it will only hamper them when they experience first-hand the insanity of the war. However, as US troops plod wearily through a smouldering Hué in the movie's final scene, the usual macho marching tunes are replaced with a plaintive echo of youth: "Who's the leader of the club that's made for you and me, M-I-C, K-E-Y, M-O-U-S-E".

A different perspective

French cinema only began to tackle the subject of Vietnam in the 1990s. If in **Dien Bien Phu** (1992) it confronted its own ghosts, on the whole its output has been limited to visually captivating colonial whimsies, to which the Vietnamese setting merely adds an exotic tang. For example, **The Lover** (1992) works not because it does justice to Marguerite Duras' poignant rites-of-passage novella, but because its extended interludes of heaving flesh are cloaked with a veneer of Oriental mystique created by location filming in Ho Chi Minh City, Sa Dec and Can Tho.

Even **The Scent of Green Papaya** (1993), filmed entirely in Paris by French-Vietnamese director Tran Anh Hung, is a fondly nostalgic period piece in which the East's languorous elegance and beauty are shown, minus its squalor, and nothing of import is said about the war experience. Tran Anh Hung's second film, *Cyclo* (1996), is an altogether different matter, a grimy tale of murder and prostitution set in a bleak rendition of Ho Chi Minh City – so bleak that the film is banned in Vietnam. Nevertheless, Tran Anh Hung obtained permission to shoot **At the Height of Summer** (aka *The Vertical Ray of the Sun*, 2000), on location in Hanoi. It's a gentler film with the same languid, dream-like quality of *Cyclo*, in which three sisters prepare to commemorate their parents' deaths. Hung's latest offering is *Norwegian Wood*, based on the novel by Haruki Murakami.

The censors lightened up a little more in allowing Vietnamese director Dang Nhat Minh to make his ground-breaking **The Season of Guavas** (2001), which deals with the extremely sensitive issue of 1950s Communist land reforms – the film, however, has yet to be released in Vietnam. Other **Vietnamese directors** beginning to attract an international audience include Tran Van Thuy (*Sand Life*, 2000), Bui Thac Chuyen (*Course de Nuit*, 2000) and **Le Hoang**, whose stark portrayal of prostitutes in **Bar Girls** (2003) caused a major stir. That the film was made at all is thanks to a radical change of policy at Vietnam's Ministry of Culture, which in 2002 stopped vetting scripts and allowed private film studios to start making films.

In Hollywood's output, Vietnamese people have mostly been noticeable by their absence, or through the filter of blatant stereotyping. **Heaven and Earth** (1993), the final part of Oliver Stone's Vietnam trilogy, went some way towards rectifying this imbalance. Its depiction of a Vietnamese girl's odyssey (based on the life of Le Ly Hayslip), from idyllic early childhood to the traumas of life as a wife in San Diego, symbolizes the trials and tribulations of the country as a whole, and acts as a timely reminder that not only Americans suffered during the struggle. Almost a decade later, Randall Wallace brought a certain impartiality to **We Were Soldiers** (2002), his adaptation of Lt Col Hall Moore and Joe Galloway's blow-by-blow account of the catastrophic battle of Ia Drang, with Mel Gibson as the caring commander. Not that it met with Vietnamese approval: the government banned the film, saying it distorted Vietnamese history, and branded actor Don Duong a "traitor" for his portrayal of the NVA leader pitting his wits – and his men – against the Americans.

Only in the late 1990s were American movie-makers allowed to shoot on location in Vietnam again. Filmed in Ho Chi Minh City, **Three Seasons** (1999) was directed by Vietnamese-Californian Tony Bui, and features Harvey Keitel at the head of a predominantly local cast. It provides a lyrical and graceful portrayal of a city trying to come to terms with the return of the West – personified by an ex-marine (Keitel) looking for the Amerasian daughter he abandoned decades before. The film doesn't dwell upon the war – the state censors on set during filming made sure of that. Nevertheless, by focusing upon the disenfranchised prostitutes, cyclo drivers and street children of the city, it ensures that the conflict's ravages are implicit.

Into the new millenium, Philip Noyce's atmospheric remake of **The Quiet American** (2002) sticks much closer to Graham Greene's novel in its indictment of American involvement in Vietnam. This, coupled with its portrayal of the Vietnamese struggle as a patriotic fight against colonial oppression, earned the film official approval, allowing it to be screened widely within Vietnam – a first for a major Hollywood production.

Vietnamese

Linguists are uncertain as to the exact roots of Vietnamese, though the language betrays Thai, Khmer and Chinese influences. A tonal language, it's extremely tricky for Westerners to master, though the phrases below should help you get by. English superseded Russian as *the* language to learn following the sweeping changes of *doi moi*, and you'll generally find that Vietnamese isn't called for. Then again, nothing will endear you to locals as much as showing conversational willingness.

Vietnamese was set down using Chinese characters until the fourteenth century, when an indigenous **script** called *chu nom* was created. This, in turn, was dropped in favour of *quoc ngu*, a Romanized script developed by a French missionary in the seventeenth century, and it's this form that's universally used today – though you'll still occasionally spot lavish *chu nom* characters daubed on the walls of more venerable pagodas and temples.

Three main **dialects** – northern, central and southern – are used in Vietnam today, and although for the most part they are pretty similar, pronunciation can be so wildly variant that some locals have trouble understanding each other; in the words and phrases listed below, we indicate important differences between variants used in the north and south. Bear in mind, too, that Vietnam's minority peoples have their own languages, and may look blankly at you as you gamely try out your Vietnamese on them.

If you want more scope than the expressions below allow, invest in a **phrasebook**. *Vietnamese: A Rough Guide Phrasebook* is the last word in user friendly phrasebooks, combining everyday phrases and expressions with a dictionary section and menu reader, all with phonetic transliterations. If you're determined to master the basics of spoken Vietnamese, there are a number of **self-teaching packs** on the market, such as *Language '30* produced by Audio-Forum (ⓦaudioforum.com).

Pronunciation

The Vietnamese language is a **tonal** one, that is, one in which a word's meaning is determined by the pitch at which you deliver it. Six tones are used – the mid-level tone (syllables with no marker), the low falling tone (syllables marked à), the low rising tone (syllables marked ả), the high broken tone (syllables maed â), the high rising tone (syllables marked á) and the low broken tone (syllables marked ạ) – though you'll probably remain in the dark until you ask a Vietnamese person to give you spoken examples of each of them. Depending upon its tone, the word *ba*, for instance, can mean three, grandmother, poisoned food, waste, aunt or any – leaving ample scope for misunderstandings and diplomatic faux pas.

With tones accomplished, or at least comprehended, there are the many vowel and consonant sounds to take on board. These we've listed below, along with phonetic renderings of how they should be pronounced.

VOWELS

a	'a' as in f**a**ther	o	'o' as in h**o**t
ă	'u' as in h**u**t (slight 'u' as in unstressed English 'a')	ô	'aw' as in **a**we
â	'uh' sound as above only longer	ơ	'ur' as in f**ur**
e	'e' as in b**e**d	u	'oo' as in b**oo**
ê	'ay' as in p**a**y	ư	'oo' closest to French 'u'
i	'i' as in -**i**ng	y	'i' as in -**i**ng

VOWEL COMBINATIONS

ai	'ai' as in Th**ai**	oe	'weh'
ao	'ao' as in M**ao**	ôi	'oy'
au	'a-oo'	ơi	'uh-i'
âu	'oh' as in **oh**!	ua	'waw'
ay	'ay' as in h**ay**	uê	'weh'
ây	'ay-i' (as in 'ay' above but longer)	uô	'waw'
eo	'eh-ao'	uy	'wee'
êu	'ay-oo'	ưa	'oo-a'
iu	'ew' as in f**ew**	ưu	'er-oo'
iêu	'i-yoh'	ươi	'oo-uh-i'
oa	'wa'		

CONSONANTS

c	'g'	ng/ngh	'ng' as in si**ng**
ch	'j' as in **j**ar	nh	'n-y' as in ca**ny**on
d	'y' as in **y**oung	ph	'f'
đ	'd' as in **d**ay	q	'g' as in **g**oat
g	'g' as in **g**oat	t	'd' as in **d**ay
gh	'g' as in **g**oat	th	't'
gi	'y' as in **y**oung	tr	'j' as in **j**ar
k	'g' as in **g**oat	x	's'
kh	'k' as in **k**eep		

Useful words and phrases

How you greet and then speak to somebody in Vietnam depends very much on their sex, and on their age and social standing, relative to your own. As a general rule of thumb, if you address a man as *ông*, and a woman as *bà*, you can be sure you aren't being impolite. If you find yourself in conversation, either formally or informally, with someone of your approximate age, you can use *anh* (for a man) and *chi* (for a woman). You can also use the same formula to address someone when you know their name. Vietnamese names are traditionally written with the family name first (Nguyen, Tran, Le and Pham are among the most common) and the given name last and between them a qualifying name, which often indicates a person's sex or the particular branch of the family to which they belong. People are usually referred to by their given name so, for example, you would address an older man called Nguyen Van Hai as Ong Hai.

GREETINGS AND SMALL TALK

Hello	chào ông/bà	Where do you come from?	ông/bà ở đâu đến?
How are you?	ông/bà có khỏe không?		
Fine, thanks	toè, cảm ơn.	I come from...	tôi ở ...
Pleased to meet you	hân hạnh gặp bạn ông/bà	...England	...nước Anh
Goodbye	chào, tạm biệt	...America	...nước Mỹ
Good night	chúc ngủ ngon	...Australia	...nước Úc
Excuse me (to say sorry)	xin lỗi	What do you do?	ông/bà làm gì?
Excuse me (to get past)	xin ông/bà thứ'lỗi	Do you speak English?	ông/bà biết nói tiếng Anh không?
Please	làm ơn		
Thank you	cảm ơn ông/bà	I don't understand	tôi không hiểu
Thank you very much	cảm ơn bạn rất nhiều	Could you repeat that?	xin ông/bà lặp lại?
Don't mention it	không có chi	Yes	vâng (north); dạ (south)
What's your name?	ông/bà tên gì?	No	không
My name is...	tên tôi là...		

EMERGENCIES

Can you help me?	ông/bà có thể giúp tôi không?	Please call a doctor	làm ơn gợi bác sĩ
There's been an accident	có một vụ tai nạn	hospital	bệnh viện
		police station	đồn cong an

GETTING AROUND

Where is the...?	ở đâu...?	train station	bến xe lửa
How many kilometres is it to...?	bao nhiêu cây số thì đến...?	taxi	tắc xi
How do I get to...?	tôi phải đi...bà`ng cách nào?	car	xe hơi
We'd like to go to...	chúng tôi muốn đi...	filling station	trạm xăng
To the airport, please	làm ơn đưa tôi đi sân bay	bicycle	xe đạp
Can you take me to the...?	ông/bà có thể đưa tôi đi...?	baggage	hành lý
Where do we catch the bus to...?	ở đâu đón xe đi...?	bank	nhà băng
When does the bus for Hoi An leave?	khi nào xe Hội An chạy?	post office	sở bưu điện
		passport	hộ chiếu
Can I book a seat?	tôi có thể đặt ghế trườc không?	hotel	khách sạn
How long does it take?	phải tốn bao lâu?	restaurant	nhà hàng
ticket	vé	Please stop here	xin dừng lại đây
aeroplane	máy bay	over there	bên kia
airport	sân bay	here	đây
boat	tàu bè	left/right	bên trái/bên phải
bus	xe buýt	north	phía bắc
bus station	bến xe buýt	south	phía nam
		east	phía đông
		west	phía tây

ACCOMMODATION AND SHOPPING

Do you have any rooms?	ông/bà có phòng không?	room with a private bathroom	một phòng tấm riêng
How much is it per night?	mỗi đêm bao nhiêu?		
How much Is It?	bao nhiêu tiền?	cheap/expensive	rẻ/đắt
How much does it cost?	cái này giá bao nhiêu?	single room	phòng một ngươi
Can I have a look?	xem có được không?	double room	phòng hai ngươi
Do you have...?	ông/bà có không...?	single bed	giương một ngươi
I want a...	tôi muốn một...	double bed	giương đôi
I'd like...	cho tôi xin một...	air-conditioner	máy lạnh
How much is this?	cái này bao nhiêu?	fan (electric)	quạt máy
That's too expensive	đắt quá	mosquito net	cái màn
Do you have anything cheaper?	ông/bà còn gì rẻ hơn không?	toilet paper	giấy vệ sinh
		telephone	điện thoại
Could I have the bill please?	làm ơn tính tiền?	laundry	quấn ào dơ
		blanket	chăn (north); mén (south)
room with a balcony	một phòng có ban công	open/closed	mở cửa/đóng cửa

TIME

What's the time?	mấy giờ rời?	tomorrow	mai
noon	buổi trưa	yesterday	hôm qua
midnight	nửa đêm	now	bây giờ
minute	phút	next week	tuần tới
hour	giờ	last week	tuần vừa qua
day	ngày	morning	buổi sáng
week	tuần	afternoon	buổi chiều
month	tháng	evening	buổi tời
year	năm	night	ban đêm
today	hôm nay		

NUMBERS

Note that for numbers ending in 5, from 15 onwards, *nhăm* is used in northern Vietnam and *lăm* in the south, rather than the written form of *năm*. Also, bear in mind that an alternative for numbers that are multiples of ten is *chục* – so, for example ten would be *một chục*, twenty would be *hai chục*, etc.

zero	không	fifteen	mười lăm /nhăm
one	một	sixteen	mười sáu
two	hai	seventeen	mười bảy
three	ba	eighteen	mười tám
four	bốn	nineteen	mười chín
five	năm	twenty	hai mười
six	sáu	twenty–one	hai mười một
seven	bảy	twenty–two	hai mười hai
eight	tám	thirty	ba mười
nine	chín	forty	bốn mười
ten	mười	fifty	năm mười
eleven	mười một	one hundred	một trăm
twelve	mười hai	two hundred	hai trăm
thirteen	mười ba	one thousand	một ngàn
fourteen	mười bốn	ten thousand	mười ngàn

EATING AND DRINKING

USEFUL PHRASES

bát (north); **chén** (south)	bowl
bao nhiêu?	how much is it?
cạn chén (north); **cạn ly** (south)	cheers!
chúc sức khỏe	to your good health
cúp	cup
đá	ice
không có đá cảm ơn	no ice, thanks
đũa	chopsticks
ít đường	a little sugar
lạnh	cold
chay	vegetarian
tôi không ăn thịt	I don't eat meat
nóng	hot
rất ngon	delicious

RICE AND NOODLES

bún	round rice noodles
bún bò	beef with bun noodles
bún chả	vermicelli noodles with pork and vegetables
bún gà	chicken with bun noodles
cơm	cooked rice
cơm rang (north); **cơm chiên** (south)	fried rice
cơm trắng	boiled rice
cháo	rice porridge
mì xào	fried noodles
phở	flat rice noodle soup
phở bò	noodle soup with beef
phở với trứng	noodle soup with eggs

FISH, MEAT AND VEGETABLES

cá	fish
cá rán (north); **cá chiên** (south)	fried fish
cua	crab
con lươn	eel
mực	squid
tôm	shrimp or prawn
tôm hùm	lobster
thịt	meat
bít tết	beefsteak
bò	beef
gà	chicken
lợn (north); **heo** (south)	pork
vịt	duck
rau cỏ or rau các loại	vegetables
bắp cải	cabbage
cà chua	tomato
cà tím	aubergine
đậu	beans
giá	beansprouts
khoai tây	potato
khoai lang	sweet potato
măng	bamboo shoots
ngô (north); **bắp** (south)	sweet corn
rau xào các loại	stir-fried vegetables
xà lách	salad
xà lách cà chua	tomato salad
xà lách rau xanh các loại	green salad

DESSERTS AND FRUIT

bánh ngọt	cakes and pastries

đường	sugar	muối	salt
kem	ice cream or cream	mứt	jam
mật ong	honey	ớt	chilli
sữa chua	yoghurt	tàu hũ (north); đậu phụ (south)	tofu
trái cây	fruit	tiêu	pepper
bưởi	pomelo/grapefruit	trứng	egg
cam	orange	trứng tráng or trứng ốp lếp	omelette
chanh	lemon/lime	trứng rán (north)	fried eggs
chôm chôm	rambutan	or trứng chiên (south)	
chuối	banana		
dâu tây	strawberry	**DRINKS**	
dừa	coconut	bia	beer
dứa (north);	pineapple	cà phê	coffee
thơm (south)		cà phê đá	iced coffee
dưa hấu	watermelon	cà phê đen	black coffee
đu đủ	papaya	cà phê đen không đường	black coffee without sugar
khế	star fruit	cà phê nóng	hot coffee
măng cầu (north);	custard apple	cà phê sữa	coffee with milk
quả na (south)		cà phê sữa nóng	hot milk coffee
măng cụt	mangosteen	trà	tea
mít	jackfruit	trà với chanh	tea with lemon
nhãn	longan	trà với sữa	tea with milk
quả bơ	avocado	không đá	no ice
sầu riêng	durian	nước	water
xoài	mango	nước khoáng	mineral water
táo tây	apple	nước xô-đa	soda water
thanh long	dragon fruit	nước cam	orange juice
vải	lychee	nước chanh	lime juice
		nước dừa	coconut milk
MISCELLANEOUS		rượu rắn	snake wine
bánh	cake (sweet or savoury)	rượu cơm	rice alcohol
bánh mì	bread	xô-đa cam	orange soda
bơ	butter	xô-đa chanh	lime soda
pho mát	cheese	sữa	condensed milk
lạc (north); đậu phộng (south)	peanuts (groundnuts)	sữa tươi	fresh milk

Glossaries

WORDS AND ABBREVIATIONS

Agent Orange Defoliant herbicide used by the Americans during the American War to deprive guerrillas of forest cover.

Annam ("Pacified South") A term coined by the Chinese to refer to their protectorate in northern Vietnam before 939 AD; the French later applied the name to the middle reaches of their protectorate, from the southern central highlands to the edge of the Red River Delta.

ao dai Traditional Vietnamese dress for women, comprising baggy pants and a long, slit tunic.

arhat Ascetic Buddhist saint, whose statues are found in northern pagodas.

ARVN (Army of the Republic of Vietnam) The army of South Vietnam.

ben xe Bus station.

bo doi Northern soldiers.

boat people Ethnic Chinese who fled Vietnam by boat in the late 1970s to escape persecution at the hands of the Communists and, later, Vietnamese escaping poverty (see p.451).

bodhisattva An intermediary who has chosen to forgo Buddhist nirvana to work for the salvation of all humanity.

body count Term coined by the Americans to measure

the success of a military operation, determined by the number of dead bodies after a battle.

bonze Buddhist monk.

buu dien Post office.

Cao Dai Indigenous religion, essentially a hybrid of Buddhism, Taoism and Confucianism, but hinged around an attempt at unification of all earthly codes of belief (see box, p.111).

Champa Indianized Hindu empire that held sway in much of the southern half of Vietnam until the late seventeenth century (see box, p.434).

Charlie Nickname for the VC ("Vietnamese Communists") used by American soldiers.

Cheo Form of classical theatre (see p.480).

cho Market.

chu nom Classic Vietnamese script, based upon Chinese.

chua Pagoda Buddhist place of worship.

Cochinchina A Portuguese term adopted by the French colonial government for their southern administrative region.

colon French colonial expatriate.

com pho Literally, "rice noodles", often used to indicate restaurant serving basic dishes.

cyclo Three-wheeled bicycle with a carriage on the front.

dao Island.

den Temple (Taoist or other non-Buddhist place of worship).

dinh Communal meeting hall.

DMZ ("dee-em-zee") The Demilitarized Zone along the Seventeenth Parallel, marking the border between North and South Vietnam from 1954 to 1975.

doi moi Vietnam's economic restructuring.

DRV (Democratic Republic of Vietnam) The North Vietnamese state established by Ho Chi Minh following the August Revolution in 1945.

duong Avenue.

FULRO (United Front for the Liberation of Oppressed Races) An opposition movement formed by the ethnic minorities of the central highlands, demanding greater autonomy.

Funan Indianized empire, a forerunner of the great Khmer empires.

GI (General Infantryman) Soldier in the US Army.

gopuram Bank of sculpted deities over the entrance to a Hindu temple.

"grunt" American infantryman.

gui xe Bicycle compound.

hang Cave.

ho Lake.

Ho Chi Minh Trail Trail used first by the Viet Minh and later by the North Vietnamese Army to transport supplies to the South, via Laos and Cambodia.

Hoa Ethnic Chinese people living in Vietnam.

Honda om Literally "Honda embrace" – a motorbike taxi.

"Huey" Nickname given to American helicopter, the HU-1.

Indochina The region of Asia comprising Vietnam, Laos and Cambodia.

kalan Sanctuary in a Cham tower.

khach san Hotel.

Khmer Ethnic Cambodian.

kylin Mythical, dew-drinking animal (often translated as unicorn); a harbinger of peace.

Lien Xo Translating as "Soviet Union", this is also used as a term of abuse – and may very occasionally be hurled at foreigners in more remote regions.

lingam A phallic statue representing Shiva, often seen in Cham towers.

mandapa Meditation hall in Cham temple complex.

MIAs (Missing in Action) Soldiers who fought – on both sides – in the American War, but have still not been accounted for.

montagnards French term for Vietnam's ethnic minority peoples.

mua roi nuoc Water-puppet show.

mui Cape.

mukha lingam Lingam fashioned into the likeness of a deity.

napalm Jellied fuel dropped by US forces during the American War, and capable of causing terrible burns.

ngo Alley.

NGO Non-governmental organization.

nha hang Restaurant.

nha khach Hotel or guesthouse.

nha nghi Guesthouse.

nha tro Basic dormitory accommodation, usually found near stations.

NLF (National Liberation Front) Popular movement formed in South Vietnam in 1960 by opponents of the American-backed Southern regime.

nui Mountain.

nuoc mam Fish sauce.

NVA (North Vietnamese Army) The army of the Democratic Republic of Vietnam.

Oc Eo Ancient seaport of the Funan empire, east of modern-day Rach Gia in the Mekong Delta.

ODP (Orderly Departure Programme) A United Nations-backed scheme enabling legal emigration of Vietnamese refugees.

paddy Unharvested rice.

PoW Prisoner of war.

quan District.

R&R ("Rest and Recreation") Term coined during the American War to describe a soldier's temporary leave of duty.

roi nuoc see mua roi nuoc.

rong Communal house of ethnic minorities in the central highlands.

RVN (Republic of Vietnam) The official name for South Vietnam from 1954 to 1976.

sampan Small, flat-bottomed boat.

song River.

SRVN (Socialist Republic of Vietnam) The post-liberation amalgamation of the DRV and RVN, and the official name of modern Vietnam.

tai chi Chinese martial art, commonly performed as early-morning exercise.

Tet Vietnam's lunar New Year.

thung chai Coracle.

Tonkin One of the three administrative regions of French colonial Vietnam, from Ninh Binh northwards.

tunnel rats American soldiers trained for warfare in tunnels such as those at Cu Chi.

VC (Viet Cong) Literally "Vietnamese Communists"; term used by the Americans to describe the guerrilla forces of the NLF.

Viet Kieu Overseas Vietnamese.

Viet Minh Shortened version of Viet Nam Doc Lap Dong Minh, the League for the Independence of Vietnam, established by Ho Chi Minh in 1941.

VNQDD Abbreviation for Viet Nam Quoc Dan Dang, the Vietnam Nationalist Party, founded in 1927.

xe lam Motorized three-wheeler buggy carrying numerous passengers.

xe om Northern equivalent of the Honda om, a motorbike taxi.

STREET NAMES

In travelling around Vietnam, it doesn't take long before you can recite the **street names**, a litany of the principal characters in Vietnamese history. Just a few from this cast list of famous revolutionaries, Party leaders, legendary kings and peasant heroes are given below. Other favoured names commemorate the glorious victories of Bach Dang and Dien Bien Phu, and the momentous date when Saigon was "liberated" in 1975: 30 Thang 4 (30 April).

Hai Ba Trung The two Trung sisters led a popular uprising against the Chinese occupying army in 40 AD and established a short-lived kingdom (see p.435).

Hoang Hoa Tham (or De Tham) Famous pirate with a Robin Hood reputation and anti-French tendencies, assassinated in 1913.

Hung Vuong The semi-mythological Hung kings ruled an embryonic kingdom, Van Lang, around 2000 BC.

Le Duan General Secretary of the Communist Party, 1960–86.

Le Hong Phong Leading Communist and patriot who died from torture in Poulo Condore prison (Con Son Island) in 1942.

Le Loi One of the most revered Vietnamese heroes, Le Loi defeated the Ming Chinese in 1427, and then ruled as King Le Thai To.

Ngo Quyen First ruler of an independent Vietnam following his defeat of the Chinese armies in 938 AD (see p.435).

Nguyen Hué Middle member of the three Nguyen brothers who led the Tay Son rebellion in the 1770s (see p.438), and then ruled briefly as Emperor Quang Trung.

Nguyen Thai Hoc Founding member of the Vietnam Nationalist Party (VNQDD), executed in 1930 following the disastrous Yen Bai uprising.

Nguyen Thi Minh Khai Prominent anti colonialist revolutionary of the 1930s, the wife of Le Hong Phong (see above) and sister-in-law of General Giap.

Nguyen Trai Brilliant strategist who helped mastermind Le Loi's victories over the Chinese. His ideas on the popular struggle ("It is better to conquer hearts than citadels") were used to good effect by Northern leaders in the French and American wars.

Pham Ngu Lao General in the army of Tran Hung Dao (see below).

Phan Boi Chau Influential leader of the anti-colonial movement in the early twentieth century (see p.439).

Tran Hung Dao Thirteenth-century general who beat the Mongols twice in the space of four years, and reached the ripe old age of 87.

Tran Phu Founding member and first General Secretary of the Indochinese Communist Party (see p.440), he died in prison in 1931 at the age of 27.

Small print and index

Rough Guide credits

Editor: Charlotte Melville
Senior editor: Alice Park
Layout: Jessica Subramanian
Cartography: Jasneet Kaur & Ed Wright
Picture editor: Mark Thomas
Proofreader: Anita Sach
Managing editor: Kathryn Lane
Assistant editor: Dipika Dasgupta
Editorial assistant: Eleanor Aldridge
Production: Rebecca Short
Cover design: Nicole Newman, Jess Carter

Photographer: Tim Draper
Senior pre-press designer: Dan May
Design director: Scott Stickland
Travel publisher: Joanna Kirby
Digital travel publisher: Peter Buckley
Reference director: Andrew Lockett
Operations coordinator: Becky Doyle
Operations assistant: Johanna Wurm
Publishing director (Travel): Clare Currie
Commercial manager: Gino Magnotta
Managing director: John Duhigg

Publishing information

This seventh edition published April 2012 by
Rough Guides Ltd,
80 Strand, London WC2R 0RL
11, Community Centre, Panchsheel Park,
New Delhi 110017, India
Distributed by the Penguin Group
Penguin Books Ltd,
80 Strand, London WC2R 0RL
Penguin Group (USA)
375 Hudson Street, NY 10014, USA
Penguin Group (Australia)
250 Camberwell Road, Camberwell,
Victoria 3124, Australia
Penguin Group (NZ)
67 Apollo Drive, Mairangi Bay, Auckland 1310,
New Zealand
Rough Guides is represented in Canada by Tourmaline
Editions Inc. 662 King Street West, Suite 304, Toronto,
Ontario M5V 1M7
Printed in Singapore
© Jan Dodd, Ron Emmons, Mark Lewis and
Martin Zatko 2012
Maps © Rough Guides

The publishers and authors have done their best to
ensure the accuracy and currency of all the information in
The Rough Guide to Vietnam, however, they can accept
no responsibility for any loss, injury, or inconvenience
sustained by any traveller as a result of information or
advice contained in the guide.
1 3 5 7 9 8 6 4 2

Help us update

We've gone to a lot of effort to ensure that the seventh
edition of **The Rough Guide to Vietnam** is accurate
and up-to-date. However, things change – places get
"discovered", opening hours are notoriously fickle,
restaurants and rooms raise prices or lower standards. If
you feel we've got it wrong or left something out, we'd like
to know, and if you can remember the address, the price,
the hours, the phone number, so much the better.

Please send your comments with the subject
line "**Rough Guide Vietnam Update**" to ❸mail
@uk.roughguides.com. We'll credit all contributions and
send a copy of the next edition (or any other Rough Guide
if you prefer) for the very best emails.

Find more travel information, connect with fellow
travellers and book your trip on ⓦroughguides.com

ABOUT THE AUTHORS

Born in Africa, **Jan Dodd** caught the travel bug early. In the early 1980s she resurfaced in Southeast Asia and spent six happy years exploring the region before settling down in France. Jan has now been visiting Vietnam regularly for over a decade, giving her an unrivalled perspective on one of Asia's fastest changing countries.

After graduating from Bristol University in 1989, **Mark Lewis** taught English in Singapore for a year, and regularly contributed book reviews to the *Singapore Straits Times*. He then spent a year exploring Southeast Asia. Mark is author of the *Rough Guide to Singapore* and co-author of the *Rough Guide to Malaysia, Singapore and Brunei*, and is now Editor of *Caterer and Hotelkeeper* magazine.

Ron Emmons (⊕ronemmons.com) lived and worked in Africa and the Americas before moving to North Thailand, where he is now based. He is the author and photographer of *Portrait of Thailand* and *Walks along the Thames Path* and author of *Top Ten Bangkok*. He has contributed to several other guidebooks and his travel articles and images appear regularly in international publications.

Martin Zatko views Asia as some sort of large and entertaining home, and can think of little better than skinny-dipping in the phosphorescent waters of Ha Long Bay. He has written or contributed to the Rough guides to Korea, China and Europe.

Acknowledgements

Ron Emmons would like to thank Dang Duc Thuc in Hanoi and Le Van Sinh in HCMC for sharing their knowledge of this rapidly changing country, and for taking me to see some of those changes. Others who gave generously of their time and shared valuable local knowledge were: in the far north and Hanoi, Nguyen Duc Tuyen; in Ho Chi Minh City, John Wong; on Phu Quoc Island, Mike Carden; and throughout the Mekong Delta, Ly Quang Hoan.

Martin Zatko would like to thank each and every one of the locals and travellers he had the fortune to run into on his trip, particularly Slo in Hanoi, Max at the Kangaroo Cafe, Ha Phuong in Kon Tum, the *Dreams* staff in Da Lat, the Farmstay crew in Phong Nha, and Buffalo Tours for their assistance in the Central Highlands.

Readers' letters

Thanks to all the readers who have taken the time to write in with comments and suggestions (and apologies if we've inadvertently omitted or misspelt anyone's name):

Philippa and Graham Baws, Tami Gabay, Stuart Gallimore, Hoang Van Truong, Maureen O'Keeffe, Andy Pollack, Samuel Pourias-Cellier, Alex Reid, Daniel Sabbagh, Paul Schmitz, Ian Skelton, Robin Syme, Robyn Szeto, Michael Terrell, Per Thorlacius, Richard Williams

Photo credits

All photos © Rough Guides except the following:
(Key: t-top; b-bottom; c-centre; l-left; r-right;)

Index

Maps are marked in grey

Map symbols

The symbols below are used on maps throughout the book

Post office	Bridge	Cave	Airport
Tourist office	Gate	Viewpoint	Golf course
Hospital	Tower	Swimming area	Steps
Lighthouse	Museum	Snorkelling	Church
Border crossing	Cao dai temple	Spring	Building
Point of interest	Mosque	Wall	Stadium
Internet access	Hindu temple	Mountain range	Park
Gardens	Pagoda	Mountain peak	Beach
Statue	Waterfall	Transport stop	Cemetery

Listings key

Accommodation

Restaurant/café

Bar/pub/club

Shop

Inspirational Travel
Vietnam * Cambodia * Laos * Thailand
www.buffalotours.com

All trips are different.
The trip we tailor for you is exceptional.
We are waiting to see you smile.

VietIndo